Conflict, Catastrophe and Continuity

Conflict, Catastrophe and Continuity

Essays on Modern German History

Edited by

Frank Biess
Mark Roseman
Hanna Schissler

Berghahn Books
New York • Oxford

Published in 2007 by
Berghahn Books
www.berghahnbooks.com

Library of Congress Cataloging-in-Publication Data

Conflict, catastrophe and continuity : essays on modern German history / edited by Frank Biess, Mark Roseman, Hanna Schissler.
    p. cm.
Includes bibliographical references and index.
ISBN 1-84545-200-3 (hardcover : alk. paper)
 1. Germany--History--20th century. I. Biess, Frank, 1966- II. Roseman, Mark. III. Schissler, Hanna.

DD235.C66 2007
943.087--dc22
                          2006100356

British Library Cataloguing in Publication Data

A catalogue record for this book is available from the British Library.

Printed in the United States on acid-free paper.

ISBN 978-1-84545-200-1 hardback

Contents

⁓

Part 4 ∼ Smooth Surfaces, Murky Depths: The Social and Cultural History of the Federal Republic

Preface

The roots of this volume lie in a 2003 conference celebrating the 65th birthday of Professor Volker Berghahn. Bringing together historians from Britain, Canada, Germany, and the United States (many of whom are represented in the present collection), the conference was a fitting occasion to pay tribute to a scholar who has done so much to bridge the academic communities on both sides of the Atlantic. Good scholarship depends, after all, on the productive exchange of research, including the cross-national fertilization of ideas. Such an exchange requires, in turn, scholars who can function as "translators" between the different scholarly communities and national environments. Over the last thirty years, no one in the field of German history has played this role with greater breadth, intellectual generosity, modesty, and humanity than Volker Berghahn.

Born in Berlin on February 15,1938, the son of a high-level Siemens manager and the eldest of three brothers, Volker Berghahn was schooled in Essen, Braunschweig, and Hamburg and began his university education at Göttingen studying law. After taking courses in politics and history at the University of North Carolina at Chapel Hill, Volker definitively opted for history, joining the émigré historian Professor Francis Carsten at the University of London, where he wrote his doctoral thesis on the post–World War I veterans' organization, the *Stahlhelm*. Obtaining his Ph.D. in 1964, Volker took a post-doctorate at St. Antony's College, Oxford, turning the thesis into a highly regarded first book.[1] A stint as *Assistent* with Professor Erich Matthias in Mannheim followed, during which time, and funded by a DFG fellowship, Volker Berghahn wrote his groundbreaking *Habilitation* on Tirpitz, which appeared in 1971.[2]

Having married Marion Koop in 1969, Volker turned his back on what he saw as an over-hierarchical German academic system and took a lectureship at the University of East Anglia in 1970, followed by a chair at the University of Warwick in 1975. Here, as well as maintaining a very active publication record and becoming a father of three, Volker did much to invigorate the field of German history in the U.K., with a highly successful stint as chairman of the German History Society alongside his responsibilities as departmental chair. He also helped advise his wife Marion as she masterminded an explo-

later at Berghahn Books. But in the 1980s even the most effective advocate for German history could not avoid becoming frustrated at the increasingly ramshackle education system of the Thatcher years. In 1988, Volker moved to Brown University, where he was at last able to foster a lively community of graduate students. His preeminence in the field of modern German history was recognized by his appointment in 1998 to replace Fritz Stern (1967–1992) and Istaván Deák (1993–1997) as Seth Low Professor at Columbia University.

It is not possible in a short preface to do justice to Volker Berghahn's contribution to modern German history, a contribution that includes major interventions in at least four different debates, and over twenty books along with innumerable articles and conference papers. After examining the nature and impact of paramilitary politics in the Weimar period in his Ph.D., Volker established himself as one of the clearest, and most social-historically grounded exponents of the idea that the First World War, and Germany's involvement in it, was above all the expression of a deep-seated crisis or set of crises in German society.[3] His study of Tirpitz remained the "most authoritative book on German navalism for three decades."[4] More broadly, at the same time, he opened up the social history of politics—and indeed the social history of militarism—in a way which has cast lasting influence on many of his contemporaries and students.[5]

Building on this work, Volker's early 1980s textbook, *Modern Germany*,[6] showed the enormous strength of his socially and economically informed emphasis on the role of elites. This sophisticated awareness of interlocking networks of power-holders, connecting politics, economy, and society, has continued to be the hallmark of his approach to modern German history, informing a series of outstanding textbooks and survey texts.[7] It has also been reflected in a number of highly regarded and innovative works on German business history, tracing the evolution of both changing management and labor relations styles, and also of international marketing and investment strategies.[8]

Volker's emphasis on the relationships between economic elites and politics has been deployed to greatest effect, perhaps, in his contribution to understanding the process by which American elites sought to influence and reconnect with their German—and European counterparts—after 1945. This gave a much-needed economic dimension to our understanding of the "pax Americana," bringing such dry issues as de-cartelization and de-concentration to the center of debates about U.S. policy.[9] It also offered an interesting generation-based sociology of German industrialists, making clear how uneven and complex was the interaction between U.S. and German businessmen.[10] Above all, it furnished the concept of Americanization with new depth and impetus in the postwar historiography, so that it now competes happily with westernization and modernization as a broad model of social, economic, and cultural change.[11] More recently, Volker has given studies of cultural Americanization a much-needed elite and institutional *Unterbau* with his complex and stylish account of Shepard Stone.[12]

Despite this truly formidable record of scholarship and publication, Volker's impact on the historical profession has derived as much from the quality of the human relationships he has formed with colleagues, students, institutions and donors. His kindness, conscientiousness, and openness are legendary, and his ability to combine his own active research career with enormous commitment to supporting research students, forging institutional links, assisting younger colleagues—let alone maintaining a full and rich family life—has been absolutely daunting. The volume brings together representatives of each of the three generations of scholars who have benefited from Volker Berghahn's intellectual contribution, friendship, and support.

With a chronological range extending from the 1860s to the 1960s, the present volume has attempted to match the temporal terrain of Volker's own research. In posing questions about society, elites, and domestic conflict, about the logics and continuities in German foreign policy, and about the transformation of postwar Germany, the book seeks to address the central themes of Volker's impressive oeuvre. Most of the essayists belong to the younger or middle generation of active scholars, and are either his former doctoral students or historians influenced by his work at important moments in their careers. As a mentor, Volker Berghahn has always sought to facilitate diversity and innovation more than he has tried to lay down a particular orthodoxy, and, reflecting this, the approaches and questions in the present volume vary considerably. Many of Volker's pupils have responded to recent currents in scholarship on areas of gender and sexuality, genocidal violence, memory, discourse, and representation in ways that differ from the approach of their mentor. The collection's diversity is further enhanced by the presence in the volume of a number of senior scholars who have been in spirited and mutually enriching debate with Volker over many years. In that sense, this volume serves as a showcase of key contemporary debates in modern German historiography and, at the same time, as a testament to the continuing openness, generosity, and wide-ranging character of Volker Berghahn's interactions in the field of modern German history.

The editors would like to express their gratitude to the German Academic Exchange Service, New York Office; the Alfred Krupp von Bohlen und Halbach-Stiftung; the History Department of Columbia University; Deutsches Haus at Columbia University; and John P. Birkelund for making the 2003 conference possible, and also to Berghahn Books for assistance in transforming the conference idea into a volume.

Frank Biess, San Diego
Mark Roseman, Bloomington
Hanna Schissler, Berlin

Notes

1. *Der Stahlhelm. Bund der Frontsoldaten 1918–1935* (Düsseldorf, 1966).
2. *Der Tirpitz-Plan. Genesis und Verfall einer innenpolitischen Krisenstrategie* (Düsseldorf, 1971).
3. In addition to the Tirpitz volume, cited above, see *Rüstung und Machtpolitik; zur Anatomie des "Kalten Krieges" vor 1914* (Düsseldorf, 1973); *Germany and the Approach of War in 1914* (London, 1973); and, with Wilhelm Deist, *Rüstung im Zeichen der wilhelminischen Weltpolitik: grundlegende Dokumente 1890–1914* (Düsseldorf, 1988).
4. Dirk Bönker, review of Rolf Hobson, *Maritimer Imperialismus*, http://hsozkult .geschichte.hu-berlin.de/rezensionen/id=4594.
5. *Militarismus: Francis Carsten z. 65. Geburtstag* (Kiepenheuer und Witsch, 1975); *Germany in the Age of Total War*, with Martin Kitchen, (London, 1981); *Militarism: the History of an International Debate, 1861–1979* (Leamington Spa, 1981).
6. *Modern Germany* (Cambridge, 1982).
7. *Imperial Germany 1871–1914: Economy, Society, Culture, and Politics* (New York and Oxford, 1994); *Sarajewo, 28. Juni 1914: der Untergang des alten Europa* (Munich, 1997); *Europa im Zeitalter der Weltkriege* (Frankfurt, 2002).
8. *Industrial Relations in West Germany* (Leamington Spa, 1987); *European Strategies of German Big Business: The Quest for Economic Empire* (Oxford, 1996). And see below.
9. *The Americanization of West German Industry, 1945–1973* (Oxford, 1986).
10. See *Unternehmer und Politik in der Bundesrepublik* (Frankfurt, 1985), and also *Otto A. Friedrich, ein politischer Unternehmer: sein Leben und seine Zeit, 1902–1975* with Paul J. Friedrich (Frankfurt, 1993).
11. For a brief review of the literature and a sense of Volker Berghahn's significance in the field, see Mary Nolan's contribution in this volume.
12. *America and the Intellectual Cold Wars in Europe: Shepard Stone Between Philanthropy, Academy and Diplomacy* (Princeton, 2001).

Introduction

Frank Biess and Mark Roseman

The German "rupture of civilization," as National Socialism and the Holocaust have been dubbed, continues to generate enormous fascination and controversy.[1] The present collection offers new perspectives on Germany's journey into and out of the abyss. Several essays are concerned with the sources of violence and conflict in German society before and during the Nazi era. In particular, they analyze the interaction between the state, elites, and the wider population in generating the often violent and volatile course of German history between national unification and the collapse of Nazism. For the pre-1933 period, these essays emphasize broadly based societal involvement in conflict or resistance to which the state was forced to respond. For the Nazi period, it was above all the regime itself that was responsible for violence, and the contributors here explore society's complex involvements in and responses to that violence. Another set of contributions considers the societal anchoring of foreign policy, and examines whether the abrupt regime changes in 1918, 1933, and 1945 produced similarly abrupt discontinuities in Germany's relationships with the wider world. In recent years the search for National Socialism's roots and rationale has been joined by a new interest in the Third Reich's postwar impact, legacy, and memory.[2] A final cluster of papers thus examines the way post-1945 Germany society emerged from the shadow of fascism and genocide, total war and total defeat.

Taken together, the volume's contributions show the continuing centrality of Nazism and the Holocaust as structuring questions for understanding modern German history. But they also remind us that recent work has left behind both older teleological readings of what Friedrich Meinecke termed the "German catastrophe"[3] and the more simplistic redemptive narratives of (West) Germany's post-1945 development. Indeed, some of the contributions here are explicitly concerned with the broader project of identifying multiple continuities and ruptures across the thresholds of 1933 and 1945, and thus of seeking to understand a German twentieth century that included both unparalleled violence and destruction and also unprecedented stability and prosperity.[4] In a concluding historiographical paper, Hanna Schissler examines the way *Zeitgeschichte* has evolved in recent decades and ponders what new questions might be posed in the future as Nazism and the Holocaust begin to lose some of their claim on the historical imagination.

German Elites and an Unruly Society

The relationship between elites and mass society has been at the heart of some of the central controversies about Germany's fateful development in the late nineteenth and twentieth centuries. Since the *Sonderweg* debates of the 1960s, Germany's elites have been held responsible for steering the nation into disaster, and for responding repressively to the democratic impulses of a modernizing society.[5] From his earliest writings, Volker Berghahn has shown a keen moral sense of the shortcomings of Germany's ruling classes and perhaps more than any other historian of his generation has illuminated the thinking and behavior of Germany's political, economic, and military leaders from the Kaiserreich through to the post-1945 period.[6] The essays in this volume show failures of leadership in many respects. But they also remind us that Germany's elites were not making history under conditions of their own choosing; nor were they simply manipulating a passive and quiescent society. Instead, nineteenth century liberal politicians embroiled in the *Kulturkampf,* or the statesmen, civil servants, and businessmen responding to the Ruhr crisis, or Weimar's judges trying the latest episode of political street violence, found themselves confronting an "unruly" society to which they responded sometimes with fear, sometimes with acquiescence, sometimes with sympathy.

Michael Gross's chapter proceeds from the assumption that the *Kulturkampf,* the fledgling German empire's attack on the Catholic church, was not a peripheral episode but an event of central importance for understanding the history of German liberalism and indeed that of nineteenth-century Germany more generally. He joins scholars such as David Blackbourn, Jonathan Sperber, and Helmut Walser Smith who have revived our sensitivity to the significance of Germany's distinctive confessional divide as a central complicating element of its political framework to 1945 and beyond.[7] More particularly, Gross is part of a small group of historians, represented also by Dagmar Herzog and Mark Ruff in this volume, who have shown that religious and confessional conflicts were often played out on the terrain of gender and sexuality. Gross argues that the *Kulturkampf* should be understood as a *Geschlechterkampf,* a battle between the sexes. When liberals worried about the Catholic threat, they saw a movement in which women played a major role, challenging received ideas about women's proper sphere. Beyond these concerns about a "feminized" Catholic church, liberals gendered the struggle against the church also on a more symbolic level. They believed women's alleged deficiencies—the weak purchase of rationality, the penchant for emotional display and superstition, and the insidious arts of manipulation—mirrored those of the Catholic church. By contrast, liberalism and the new German state were understood as virile male entities, trumpeting the call of reason against the alleged emotionality and superstition of the Catholic mission.

By introducing gender into his analysis, Michael Gross not only opens up an innovative new perspective on the *Kulturkampf* but also introduces the theme of a fractious society unsettling and challenging Germany's elites. Here is a German society that is not the quiescent subject of elite manipulation. Yet this is not a return to the false heroics of some older social history–writing "from below"; Gross's Catholic women are not the heroic agents of emancipatory politics. This is a story of female activism and of emancipation from certain conventional roles and constraints, yet under distinctly conservative auspices. Gross's work represents a new kind of social history of politics, in which symbolic and emotional goods play their full part in shaping perceptions and behavior.

Like Michael Gross, Conan Fischer offers some striking new findings on an episode we thought we knew well. The *Ruhrkampf* of 1923, Germany's campaign of passive resistance (and some active sabotage) has often been portrayed as part of the politics of illusion: it merely deferred tasting the bitter medicine of defeat while centrally contributing to the disastrous hyperinflation of 1923.[8] Yet Conan Fischer focuses on another, less well known aspect of this conflict. He shows organized labor's part not only in bearing the cost of passive resistance, but also in providing the momentum. It was not primarily the right-wing radicals, whose violent actions were often decried by the Ruhr population, but rather the republican majority that ensured both government and industry alike would stand up to the French. Fischer, like Gross, thus offers us an image of an "unruly" populace, here not in the sense of the feminized Catholics that so incensed nineteenth-century liberals but as a broad-based movement of feeling that put governments and other elites under pressure. This popular pressure Fischer sees not as illusory revanchism but, like the earlier trade-union campaign against the Kapp Putsch in 1920, as a fight motivated by the desire to defend the Republic. Fischer thus gives the Ruhkampf a rather more democratic, more republican, and more benign face than many conventional interpretations. He leaves no doubt, however, as to its ruinous consequences for the working people of the region and elsewhere. His essay also points to the central significance of memory and mythmaking in the destruction of Germany's first democracy: while the democratic aspect of the struggle on the Ruhr has largely been forgotten, its insignificant activist and terrorist aspect became a central myth of the political Right and was eventually used to destroy the Republic.

Pamela Swett too offers a surprising take on a well-worn trope of Weimar history, and she too tells a complex story of interplay between an unruly *Volk* and the state. One of the commonplaces of the standard account of Weimar's downfall is that the Republic was betrayed by the anti-democratic, right-wing bias of its judiciary, witnessed in grotesque high-profile cases such as the very lenient sentence for treason handed down to Hitler in 1924.[9] By contrast, Swett offers a striking reappraisal of the legal system's handling of political violence. It was, she shows, neither so biased to the right nor so unsympathetic to the left as has often been assumed. Indeed, court verdicts related to political violence were dangerous less for being partisan than for endorsing a culture of violence that would prove disastrous after 1933.

Swett's essay challenges a Foucauldian reading of the Weimar welfare state that has emphasized its disciplinary, rationalizing, and exclusionary elements and thus the continuities between Weimar and the Third Reich.[10] Swett demonstrates that by employing social workers' reports about the young defendants involved in street brawls, Weimar courts often took into consideration as mitigating circumstances the protagonists' difficult living conditions. Judges followed a trend in German jurisprudence that had emerged in the *Kaiserreich* of looking at the defendant's *Gesinnung*—a term conveying character, outlook, and motive—as much as the deed itself. In Swett's reading of the encounter between unruly street fighters and Weimar professionals, welfare workers and the judiciary acted with considerable sensitivity and discretion. At the same time, Swett's essay also points to a different kind of continuity across the threshold of 1933, namely, legitimating and accepting violence. Violence had an accepted role in the moral economy not only of those who came before the bench but also of the judges who were trying their cases. If violence appeared to be motivated by an honorable *Gesinnung*, judges were prepared to treat it leniently. This kind of "ethical" approach to evaluating the use of force facilitated the introduction of Nazi standards of jurisprudence after 1933, when *Gesinnung* became all that mattered. As Swett shows, Germany's elites, or at least its judges, were in effect accepting the norms of the unruly society. During the Weimar years, "honorable violence" became part of established legal discourse with fateful consequences for the rule of law after 1933.

German Society and an "Unruly" State

The kind of migration and dissemination of violent norms described by Swett recurs in Mark Roseman's analysis of the forces and beliefs shaping participation in the Holocaust. But whereas Swett looks at a jurisprudence that absorbs the violent assumptions of the street, Roseman looks at how after 1933, it was the state that, as it were, became unruly. Society then faced the choice of mobilizing its energies along lines tolerated by the regime, accepting quiescence, or risking the most brutal repression. As recent research has become increasingly aware, the regime did indeed manage to motivate hundreds of thousands of individuals to become active perpetrators of racial war and genocide. How do we explain this participation? In different ways, the chapters by Roseman, Mommsen, and Biess all demonstrate how complex were the mechanisms and trajectories that tied regime and society together and that, toward the end of the war, also began to draw them apart.

Echoing the recent work of Nicolas Berg and others, Roseman's historiographically based analysis of Holocaust perpetrators begins by tracing the slow process by which historians after 1945 came to embrace the idea of the ideologically motivated perpetrator.[11] Roseman explores the distancing strategies that led the post-Holocaust world to suppress evidence that a large cohort of participants had been believers in the cause of racial war. In Germany and in much of the West, the perpetrators were initially seen as a small group of madmen or psychologically damaged individuals. Later, as emphasis shifted from a small coterie of sworn Nazis to a larger army of bureaucrats, the monster was replaced by the neutral functionary and the "banality of evil." Both paradigms downplayed the idea of intelligent men openly embracing the cause.

By the 1990s, however, an explosion of research was taking place on the "perpetrators," and a new influential (though never uncontested) model of the perpetrator as ideological warrior *(Weltanschauungskrieger)* was emerging. The shift responded in part to the changing moral climate of memory in the Federal Republic, where a postwar generation of historians no longer felt under the same pressure to deny their parents' and grandparents' active involvement in the regime. The participants' embrace of violence and commitment to the cause now seemed at least as important as their obedience or bureaucratic efficiency.

While recognizing the progress in throwing off old taboos, Roseman is critical of the model of the *Weltanschauungskrieger*. A growing body of recent empirical research has shown, in fact, how complicated and nonlinear was the relationship between the perpetrators' convictions and their actions. Though many key players brought with them values and ideals that helped spur their involvement in a racial war of extermination, most had to travel very far from their earlier selves in order to participate in genocide. To understand these journeys we not only have to recognize the degree of displacement but also have to see that "ideas" as such (for example, strongly held anti-Semitism) may not be the relevant starting point. Recent work has indicated that we often need to think in terms of past experiences of violence as much as a clearly anti-Semitic intellectual pedigree. Moreover, we need to explain not only the unabated participation in racial killing to the last minute but also the abrupt ending of violence with the war's end—a fact that suggests the limits to the recent model of an "unconditional generation" driven by its own ethos.[12] In fact, Roseman argues that earlier interpretations of the perpetrator from Hannah Arendt and Hans Mommsen were by no means "apologetic" but rather were acutely conscious of the problem for understanding motivation posed by the easy adaptation of Nazi perpetrators to the postwar world.[13]

Both Hans Mommsen and Frank Biess take as their starting point that closing phase of the war that marks a pivotal moment in Mark Roseman's argument about Nazi perpetrators as well. Until very recently, the last stages of the Nazi dictatorship did not feature prominently in the historiography of the Third Reich. The violence, disintegration, and improvisation of the 1944–45 period seemed of little interest compared with the grand designs of the earlier years. The endgame's primary significance, for a long time, was reduced to providing evidence in support of functionalist explanations from Hans Mommsen and others of the increasing breakdown of orderly structures of governance. Recently, however, interest has grown in the last year or two of fighting as a discrete phase of the war.[14] The primary reason for this has been historians' move away from questions about Nazi grand strategy to a growing focus on the regime's success at mobilizing the energy and violence of the population. Why, despite increasingly clear evidence that defeat was unavoidable, and despite dramatically increasing German losses, did fighting continue unabated, and violence against domestic opponents and racial enemies escalate?

Building on more than forty years of research, Hans Mommsen, the most eminent German historian of the Nazi period, offers a powerful and insightful account of this phase by linking his earlier work on growing administrative chaos to the new interest in the relentlessness of the fighting. How is it, he asks, that despite the accelerating dissolution of any unity in government, the regime was able to fight effectively even when four-fifths of Reich territory had fallen to the Allies? Unlike much recent work, Mommsen finds the answers less in the popular mentality of ordinary Germans than in the structures of power Hitler had created, and in particular in the constellation of competing interests and views among the leading figures in the Nazi Party who enjoyed Hitler's confidence. Mommsen traces the course of what he dubs the "partification" of the state under the leadership of Goebbels and especially of Bormann. Through its role in welfare and resettlement work, the party insinuated itself into everyday life in a way that made it almost impossible for any organized opposition to emerge. Despite—and in some strange way, because of—the knowledge of impending defeat, the party leadership threw itself into ever greater zealotry, invoking heroic myths from the pre-1933 "time of struggle" to persuade itself that only will was needed to survive. Increasingly, as

Mommsen shows, the propaganda and thinking of party leaders blurred the distinction between achieving victory in the current war and creating the ideological foundations for future revival.

Yet that revival did not take place, even though the recent experience of the U.S. occupation of Iraq has reminded us how even a militarily superior power may have great difficulty controlling an occupied territory if oppositional energies and impulses remain within the subject population. In 1945, however, the disappearance of active support for the Nazi regime, and the cessation of violent acts by its former servants, was almost complete.

The question posed by this rapid turnabout provides the starting point for Frank Biess's analysis, which seeks to understand the closing phase of the war not only as the explosion of violence but also a period in which the population began to disengage from the regime and mentally to prepare for the postwar period. This disengagement was in many respects a passive one, and thus not so much the story of an unruly society as of a society beginning to disengage from a horrifically "unruly" state. Biess shows that even in previously loyal circles, concern for family members lost in action or held in Soviet captivity created networks of communication that subverted official information management. Among groups who had family members in Soviet captivity, Nazi morale surveys noted growing hopes for a rapid end to the war so that families could be reunited with their missing loved ones. While some demanded revenge attacks on Jews and Russians for their losses, others went so far as to call for a change of official conduct of war to avoid military disasters and to ensure German actions did not engender reprisal killing of captured German soldiers. Nevertheless, Biess's analysis complements Mommsen's emphasis on party-state control by emphasizing the ability of the Nazi state's security organs—often with considerable help from denunciations—to intercept informal communications. Private longings for an end to the war thus rarely assumed public force.

As Biess makes clear, the issue of the missing soldiers was caught between two conflicting priorities for the Nazi regime. On the one hand, it concerned a matter of the gravest political significance, namely, the struggle with the archenemy in the East. It undermined some of the regime's most politically sensitive claims, above all that the enemy was completely inhuman in its treatment of German troops, and that the German army continued to show a spirit of unalloyed heroism and sacrifice in its unwillingness to surrender. Communication about the prisoners of war was thus intensely political. At the same time, it also involved a sphere the Nazis had propagandistically celebrated as sacrosanct, feminine, and private (even if that privacy had been disrupted in many ways in practice), namely, family and the home. It was in the private realm of the family that the loss of soldier husbands and sons could begin to be read in ways that involved a distancing from the regime. It was also the emerging self-definition of wives and mothers of themselves as apolitical victims of war that, as Biess argues, represented the body of experience and self-identification that could most easily be carried over into the postwar period. In this way, the communication and reflection on the MIAs began a process of reflection and discourse that would lay the foundation for Germany's postwar memories of war and defeat.

Change and Continuity in German Foreign Policy

It was Fritz Fischer's discovery of the remarkable parallels between the war plans of 1914 and Hitler's territorial aims that helped to launch the cluster of interpretations that became known as the German *Sonderweg*.[15] As well as identifying continuities in foreign policy from the *Kaiserreich* to the Third Reich, the *Sonderweg* model attributed those continuities to enduring structural problems within German society. According to the model's adherents, German elites failed to create the requisite liberal and democratic superstructure necessary to respond to the challenges of industrial society. Instead, those elites papered over social and political problems at home by resorting to social imperialism and aggressive nationalism. Volker Berghahn produced one of the clearest and most incisive analyses of the way the *Kaiserreich*'s domestic crises helped to shape foreign decision making.[16] While some of the assumptions of the early *Sonderweg* model have been called into question, the basic questions about continuity and discontinuity across the changes of regime, and about the degree to which domestic issues and problems helped to provoke or shape Germany's foreign policy remain crucial.

John Röhl is one of the contributors to this volume who has been in critical and constructive dialog with Volker Berghahn for some forty years. In the 1970s, when the Bielefeld school's emphasis on underlying societal structures dominated the historiography, Röhl's biographical approach, foregrounding Wilhelm II's personal quirks and influence, appeared out of step. Since the 1980s, however, Röhl's own oeuvre and a series of other notable studies both on Wilhelm II (some of them from Röhl's former pupils) and on the role of the court and royal symbolism in international relations have made it clear how important were both monarch and court for shaping the *Kaiserreich*'s fate.[17]

In the present piece, Röhl returns to the Kaiser's problematic relationship with England, offering striking evidence of a classic love-hate syndrome that emerged early on in childhood. Wilhelm was the victim of a strange upbringing, in which the future German emperor was continually informed by his "English" mother of the British empire's superiority. Desperate for personal recognition from the British royal family, and seemingly naively unaware of the reasons of state that perforce conditioned their responses to his overtures, the adult Wilhelm grew more and more threatening in his demands for appreciation and honor in ways that merely intensified distrust and alienation. The man whom Count Bismarck once mocked as the "complete anglomaniac" would later in life be second to none in his fulmination against the circles of "Juda" running British affairs.

Of course, Röhl acknowledges the many factors influencing the Anglo-German relationship that lay beyond royal purview. But Wilhelm's overwhelming wish to impress or best Great Britain undoubtedly had huge consequences for German foreign policy. At the very least he limited his governments' scope for maneuver. At most, he may have prevented Germany from pursuing a more emollient policy that would have secured its continental and commercial interests in ways that did not threaten Britain to the point of war. And beyond shedding light on Wilhelm's particular personality, Röhl's chapter illuminates some of the strange contradictions that resulted from the transnational dynastic ties that continued to criss-cross the frontiers of modern rival nation states.

If Röhl's biographical take on Germany's foreign policy stands in productive tension with Berghahn's approach, Hartmut Pogge von Strandmann's intriguing analysis of the Nazi-Soviet Pact is much closer to Berghahn's interest in the economic factors shaping international relations. Historians have tended to analyze the 1939 Nazi-Soviet Pact primarily with reference to the two powers' geopolitical and military strategic interests.[18] The trade and commerce resultant from the accord is treated as a mere sideshow or at most of symbolic significance. Pogge von Strandmann shows by contrast that trade both helped create the impetus for the German-Soviet rapprochement and offered both sides important incentives for its continuance. The German and Russian economies, as he reminds us, had long proved complementary. German capital goods exports were as welcome in Tsarist Russia and the Soviet Union as Russian raw materials were important for the German economy. Partly because of this, as Pogge argues, trade had always also served political and diplomatic purposes, rescuing both Germany and Russia from isolation in the 1920s, and providing a bridge between the Cold War blocs in the 1950s and 1960s.

While Soviet-German trade took a sharp downturn in the first half of the 1930s, the memory of mutually conducive economic relations remained strong among leading actors in both countries in the late 1930s. Industry's hope of gaining access to Russian raw materials provided the chief incentive on the German side, while leading Politburo members drew up wish-lists of German goods. In 1939 a major trade deal preceded the two countries' nonaggression pact and helped to create a climate of trust (albeit ill-founded trust) prior to the political agreements. Negotiations over the precise terms of trade were tough, as Pogge demonstrates, and fulfillment fluctuated according to the degree to which foreign engagements and military circumstances left Germany or Russia feeling dependent on each other. Nevertheless, the volume of goods not just promised but actually delivered was striking, proving the deals to have been far more than the symbolic dowry of a marriage of convenience. To be sure, it is not entirely clear how far actors on both sides were aware that they were—like the international capitalists both regimes loved to decry—equipping each other to fight each other. From autumn 1940 at the latest, the Germans calculated that the risk of supplying weapons to the Soviet Union was smaller than the benefit of lulling the USSR into a false sense of security. Stalin may indeed have fallen for the ruse, and have hoped that the trade's real mutual benefits would prevent a German attack. In that sense, Soviet policies may have been driven by the primacy of economics, whereas the primacy of ideology dominated on the German side. Or to put it another way, neither side had any illusions about their future conflict, but Stalin may well have hoped that economic benefits would be allowed to rule the day for longer.

Whereas John Röhl's and Hartmut Pogge von Strandman's essays foreground particular moments in the making of German foreign policy, Uta Poiger and Mary Nolan take a longer-term perspective, reminding us that Germany's relations with the outside world were subject to longer-term processes bridging particular political caesurae. Aspirations, influences, challenges, and structures, some peculiar to Germany, others not, outlived particular regimes, including the fall of the Third Reich. By taking, respectively, "imperialism" and "Americanization" as conceptual vantage points from which to assess Germany's foreign relations, Poiger and Nolan consciously deploy paradigms that have played an important role in Volker Berghahn's own work.

With imperialism, Uta Poiger introduces a term that has enjoyed only limited purchase in the historiography of modern Germany. Yet quite apart from its recent global revival as an object of discourse,[19] the concept of empire, as Poiger notes, raises intriguing questions not least because of the different international contexts in which it locates Germany, be it as a player in the pre–World War I colonial race, as an agent of domination in European conquest, or as a major power in the European and global economies after all dreams of formal empire had gone. But how far can the concept of imperialism link these very different moments in German policy, and, in particular, what relevance has it for the post-1945 period when Germany neither possessed nor sought any kind of formal empire?

Poiger traces the evolution of the imperialism paradigm from the 1970s onward, when it was primarily seen as a symptom of domestic tensions. While some Marxist scholars followed Hobson's and Lenin's classical view that imperialism was the symptom of a crisis of capitalist over-accumulation, most West German historians emphasized elite "bonapartism" in an undemocratic political system.[20] In recent years, however, it is the issue of race that has come to the fore. The experiences of colonial domination and the celebration of imperial grandeur are now linked by historians to far-reaching changes in the imperial powers' identity, racial thinking, and self-perception—changes that extend well beyond the limited number of people directly involved in the colonial project.[21] This historiographical shift has had profound implications for the kind of continuities historians discern in German foreign policy. Of interest in the 1960s and 1970s was above all the marked similarities between Germany's pre-World War I and wartime foreign-policy ambitions and the territorial scope of Hitler's quest for *Lebensraum.* As historians grew more concerned with colonial practices and race consciousness, however, attention turned from continuities in territorial ambitions to precedents for genocide, especially since the historiography of the Holocaust itself has also seen a renewed interest in race and ideology, as Mark Roseman's contribution makes clear. Yet, as Poiger argues, the link between nineteenth-century colonialism and twentieth-century genocide are complex and by no means straightforward. Since imperialism was a shared European pursuit, the imperialist connection raises important questions about how specifically German are the Holocaust's causes.[22]

It is in the second part of her essay that Poiger makes her most original contribution by extending the imperialism paradigm to the post-1945 period. While Volker Berghahn has already made us aware of continuities in German business's search for informal economic empire that linked the *Kaiserreich* to the Federal Republic, Poiger focuses on advertising and commodity culture as a theater of perceptions and images of the outside world. By the 1920s, she notes a self-conscious shift away from the racist images of colonial domination of the late nineteenth and early twentieth centuries toward a self-fashioning of Germany as a cosmopolitan, postcolonial power. These images found their echoes in the explicitly anticolonial propaganda of the Nazi regime, which, of course, was accompanied by extremely brutal, indeed genocidal, forms of colonial domination in Eastern Europe. After 1945, Poiger argues, both Germanys were able to present themselves as post-imperial, though for different reasons. Using conventional Marxist analysis, the GDR simply denounced the Federal Republic as the successor to the capitalist imperialist tradition. The Federal Republic, by contrast, portrayed itself (and was indeed seen by some African countries) as relatively unencumbered by the legacies of imperialism in an age of decolonization. Yet, as Poiger demonstrates, West German advertisers continued to market their products through images of "nonwhite" populations, even though they did so in divergent ways and for different purposes. Racism thus did not disappear in postwar West Germany, although it became more subtle, more varied, and less overtly pernicious. In this sense, Poiger concludes convincingly, "imperialism" can serve as useful conceptual tool to analyze how different social groups within Germany related and continue to relate to what became known as the "Third World."

Mary Nolan's essay takes Germany's relationship and interaction with "America" as her vantage point for observing twentieth-century German history. From the 1920s on, at the latest, the United States became associated with cultural and economic modernity per se. In the post-1945 era, the U.S. was to be decisive in determining the shape and orientation of the new West German state. As Mary Nolan notes, the concept of "Americanization" is sometimes deployed open-endedly as a question about the degree of influence the U.S. exerted on Germany, but it is used also in a more focused and prescriptive way to denote a particular set of changes. As Nolan makes clear, Volker Berghahn's work has lent the concept credibility and sophistication, not least because Berghahn acknowledges not only the U.S. role as exemplar, proselytizer and school-master, but also the recipients' contribution in welcoming, modifying, and sometimes rejecting American models. As such, Americanization has much to tell us about a set of interactions in the fields of industrial organization, mass culture, consumerism, and gender roles that provides important insights into German history from the 1920s through to the 1950s and 1960s.

The core of Nolan's analysis is nevertheless a critique of the concept, prompted by recognition that the recent upsurge of anti-Americanism in Germany has raised doubts about Germany's successful "Americanization." Above all Nolan believes that analysts of Americanization have brought normative assumptions of their own to bear, and have marginalized or excluded key facets of Germany's development in a way that ultimately distorts our understanding of the nature of German modernity. The Americanization paradigm, for example, has tended to juxtapose a negative non-Americanization (or failed Americanization) before 1945 and a successful Americanization thereafter. Such morally drawn contrasts fail to do justice to the complex ways even Nazis appropriated facets of American practice before 1945, and also ignore those aspects of U.S. influence after 1945 that do not fit the benign model—for example the anti-black racism the U.S. imported via occupation. For all the discontinuities wrought by the end of the war, there has been an overly moralized and simplistic distinction made between good and bad modernities. Secondly, the bipolar focus on "Americanization" or "Sovietization" fails to capture the intra-European exchange of ideas and influences that generated a distinctly European model of modernity. This European alternative manifested itself especially in a more statist welfare capitalism, which even now has not fully converged with (and partly competes with) the neoliberal American model. Yet, while the Americanization of Germany was thus less complete than proponents of the concept like to suggest, the current surge of anti-Americanism in Germany does not primarily derive from traditional resistance to Americanization. The America against which Germany is now reacting—aggressively unilateral, committed to a religious crusade, pessimistically reliant on military might, hostile to international institutions and to anything more than the meanest welfare states—could hardly be more different from the kind of "New Deal" synthesis that characterized U.S. policy in the post-1945 years. In that sense we are entering a new era, to which the familiar twentieth-century story of Americanization offers few clues. Germany, one might well conclude from Nolan's analysis, is in a number of respects now closer to the U.S. model it was offered in 1945 than is George Bush's America today.

Smooth Surfaces, Murky Depths: German Society in the 1950s

The historiography of post-45 Germany has not generated grand theories of the stamp of the German *Sonderweg*. Indeed, the *Sonderweg* theory itself was predicated on the idea that after 1945 Germany (or at least West Germany) lost its peculiarity and became more like a normal, Western state, an idea that Ralf Dahrendorf had already examined with wit and sophistication in the 1960s.[23] In the 1970s, much historical research on the postwar era was in search for the explanations for "restoration," as a generation of left-wing students sought to explain the failure of radical dreams in the immediate postwar period.[24] But even here there was no dominant school, and writing was characterized by a large variety of positions on the question of new beginnings, continuity or restoration.[25] Since the 1980s, a growing number of sophisticated studies has appeared in the English language (and here Volker Berghahn, as well as his growing body of present and former doctoral students, has made a very significant contribution).[26] Attention has shifted increasingly from the immediate postwar years to the 1950s and now to the 1960s and 1970s; and there has also been a move away from questions about institutional change or continuity to broader inquiries about the way West Germany reacted to, remembered, and forgot its recent past. Indeed, the consistent theme in the essays represented in this section is the subtle mixture of remembering and forgetting, on the one hand, and the equally subtle balance between conservatism and innovation, on the other. These two sets of choices—about how to respond to and remember Nazism, war, and Holocaust and about what kinds of social and cultural innovations and outside influences to adopt—stood, as a number of the essays show, in a complex and sometimes paradoxical relationship to one another. Their interrelationship and shifting balance accounted for the intriguing mixture of stability, dynamism, and unease that characterized the Federal Republic in the 1950s.

As do some of the earlier essays in this volume, Ian Connor's contribution addresses a potentially unruly group that threatened to destabilize Germany's political and social equalibrium, in this case, the almost eight million refugees and expellees from the "lost" territories in the East. Connor's essay is part of a more recent trend, which has put into perspective the allegedly "quick" and smooth integration of German expellees.[27] While social-history studies have cast some doubt on this success story, Connor's essay traces the considerable fears and anxieties that West German elites harbored about the expellees' potential radicalization. Against the background of National Socialism, fears of the "political mass" powerfully shaped elite behavior in postwar West Germany and fostered elites' willingness to cooperate with the occupation authorities. Connor's essay thus restores some contingency to the West German success story, which seemed much less self-evident to contemporary elites than it might appear in retrospect.[28]

At the same time, Connor's article also begins to explain why contemporary anxieties ultimately proved groundless. The experience of flight from the Red Army largely immunized expellee populations against any Communist inclination. By contrast, the attraction of right-wing splinter parties was initially much greater. Here, Connor emphasizes the crucial significance of Adenauer's CDU in attracting and eventually integrating expellees and refugees.[29] This "success," to be sure, depended not merely on the economic miracle that, unlike in Weimar, provided the economic leverage to pacify war-damaged groups through an extensive "equalization of burdens" law. It also came at considerable moral and political costs that entailed, for example, open toleration of highly compromised former Nazis in the highest echelons of the West German government. Political stability was indeed created on the basis of "murky depths," which would soon be pushed to the surface.

Connor's story of elite adaptations to the changed political circumstances of the postwar period is also a major theme in Alexander Nützenadel's essay. Nützenadel, like Connor, emphasizes the centrality of economics in postwar Germany. Yet his focus is less on the material basis of economic growth than on the theories that inspired the "miracle." In arguing that Keynesian economics had already substantially infiltrated the language of politics in the 1950s, Nützenadel revises the orthodox reading of the decade as being dominated by the neoliberal Freiburg school. As such, Nützenadel joins a number of historians who have challenged the idea of the 1950s as a conservative decade (though in this case, it should be noted that the "conservativism" of the Freiburg school in international terms was innovative in a Germany context in which old-fashioned liberalism had not shaped economic policy since the nineteenth century). Nützenadel's position here is not merely an echo of Werner Abelshauser's work, questioning whether neoliberal prescription were responsible for Germany's economic miracle.[30] He also questions neoliberalism's intellectual primacy more generally and argues that it lost ground to Keynesianism much earlier than had previously been assumed.

Nützenadel attributes Keynesianism's rapid march through the institutions to a series of factors, of which Germany's integration into international organizations and exposure to Anglo-American economic thinking assumed prime significance. The power and success of the U.S. economy and war effort made the modified U.S. version of Keynesianism very attractive to younger

German economists, an attraction bolstered by the kinds of academic interchange the U.S. did so much to support. Echoing Mary Nolan's plea for recognizing the complexity of transnational exchanges, Nützenadel shows that this was not just "Americanization" but that American ideas were also reformulated and processed through European institutions and individuals before being finally implemented in Germany. In addition, the Federal Republic's integration in a series of international economic institutions contributed to the rise of new forms of economic expertise that then provided the tools for macroeconomic intervention. Finally, shifting memories of Germany's economic experience in the past also facilitated the ascendancy of Keynesianism. By the 1950s, it was no longer the inflation of the 1920s or the overdominance of the Nazi state that served as most important historical reference points, but rather the Great Depression. The belief gained ground among economic experts that the "German catastrophe" could have been averted if the state had adopted Keynesian measures. Whereas Germany's historical experience had formerly seemed to caution less state involvement and less state spending, now the reading of Hitler's rise began to suggest the opposite. As a result, Keynesianism became part of a new consensus among all major parties that centered on the management of growth and demand as a technical, nonpolitical issue essential for democratic stability. This consensus began to unravel only in the 1970s, when a new international economic crisis discredited Keynesianism and led to the rise of neoliberalism and monetarism in West Germany and the Western world at large.

Mark Ruff's essay tells a similar story of "modernization under conservative auspices" as Nützenadel. But his focus is on the Catholic milieu and especially on Catholic youth culture. The Catholic church, as Ruff points out, emerged triumphant from the Nazi dictatorship and appeared to exert enormous political, social, and cultural authority in the early Federal Republic. Yet his essay reveals important tensions below this surface of an apparently stable and restorative Catholic milieu. In fact, his essay alerts us to the complexity of "conservativism" in the 1950s by unearthing important reform impulses within West German Catholicism, which eventually eroded the cohesion of that milieu itself.

Ruff also joins a number of other contributors in highlighting the significance of sex and gender for understanding the larger social and political dynamics of the postwar period. Like postwar society at large, the Catholic church needed to decide how far to absorb the more liberal approach to sex and marriage on offer from the U.S. and other modern influences. Church figures also sought to distance the Catholic church from that traditional association with a "feminized" sphere, which, as Michael Gross has shown, so incensed liberals in the *Kaiserreich*. Instead, post-1945 Catholics defined new forms of civilian male authority, which focused on the family and included, for example, greater engagement of fathers with children. In that sense, the "modern patriarchalism" of the church contributed to the discourse of a more egalitarian family and promoted wider sociocultural changes in society at large. That these internal Catholic reform efforts eventually eroded the basis of the Catholic milieu itself constituted one of the ironic and, as Ruff argues, largely unintended consequences of conservative modernization in West Germany. In this sense, Ruff joins Connor and Nützenadel in demonstrating that the 1950s were not simply a period of restoration but a decade in which sub-milieus such as Catholicism and Socialism integrated themselves into larger social and political dynamics even at the price of their self-abrogation.

While Mark Ruff traces shifting Catholic attitudes as indicative of a larger modernization process, Dagmar Herzog's essay leaves no doubt as to the deep conservativism of the 1950s, especially in matters relating to sex and gender. The church appears as a united conservative force, even if some of its adherents were more liberal or progressive on other matters. Yet her principal interest is the significance of sexual conservativism for managing the memory of Nazism. She argues that in the conservative reaction against Nazism in the early postwar period, Nazi licentiousness was foregrounded in ways that allowed the conventional morality of the church to appear unscathed by the recent encounter. The church thus became a symbol of the true, moral Germany that lost its way in modern times. Whereas the sexual conservativism of the 1950s can be understood only in relation to a particular memory of Nazism, the later progressive assault on sexual conservativism was directed against both the 1950s and the Nazi period. The Nazis now came to be seen as puritanical and sexually repressed. This, as Herzog argues, was a distortion of the real experience of Nazi Germany, which for heterosexuals had been a time of relative openness, if tightly controlled abortions. Yet it facilitated the making of certain kinds of progressive argument that linked antifascism to sexual liberation. Herzog's essay thus challenges not only our understanding of the 1950s but also of the sexual revolution of the 1960s, which, as she argues in her recent book, was not just antifascist but "anti-postfascist" (i.e., directed against the sexual conservativism of the 1950s rather than the Nazi period itself.)[31] As such, the 1960s did not engender a more comprehensive memory of the Nazi past but rather a different and, one might argue, equally fictitious repackaging of it.

Jonathan Wiesen's essay further complicates our picture of the 1950s. Like Ruff and Herzog, he too shows bourgeois Germany worrying about social mores, ethics, and family life, in this case via the activities and discussions of Rotary clubs. Yet while Ruff and others argue that even the early 1950s were not as restorative and conservative as they once seemed, Wiesen demonstrates the continued resonance well into the later 1950s of many of the conservative, cultural-critical tropes of the early postwar years, notably the juxtaposition between *Vermassung* and personality. He is concerned with the reconstruction of a distinctly bourgeois ethics of individuality and civic-mindedness in the context of Rotary clubs in West Germany. By tracing the pre- and post-1945 history of American forms of bourgeois sociability, Wiesen offers an example of the kinds of nuanced analysis of "Americanization" that Nolan called for in her more theoretically oriented essay.

What stood in the way of a simple adoption of the American style and attitudes in German Rotary was, as Wiesen shows, not just traditional anxieties about mass culture and mass consumption but the central experience of National Socialism. Rotary clubs became an important site for managing a bourgeois memory of National Socialism. The organization's outspoken commitment to "internationalism" compelled its members to emphasize their anti-Nazi convictions and thus to distance themselves, at least in public, from the Nazi past. At the same time, Wiesen also reveals the difficulties of the organization in coming to terms with more critical accounts of its history during the Nazi period. Yet, however mendacious and self-serving individual Rotarians' accounts of their life in Nazi Germany may have been, Wiesen makes clear that any effort to reinvent a *collective* identity for the West German *Bürgertum* after 1945 could not evade the central legacy of National Socialism and of German elites' complicity with it.

The essays by Robert Moeller and Heide Fehrenbach echo many of the themes discussed by the authors above, but they draw on a source that is particularly revealing for analyzing the history of the 1950s: movies. Before the onset of television, the 1950s were a decade of movie-going. Popular films spoke to a large part of the population. Their popularity was a sign of hitting a nerve, and they helped to set the tone of debates. Robert Moeller's piece focuses on the highly successful film trilogy *08/15*, which looked at the experience of ordinary German soldiers during the Second World War. His reading shows how the film both manifested and helped shape the way in which the war was remembered in postwar Germany, not least via its exclusions, distinctions, and treatment of Germany's former enemies. Produced in the context of West Germany's rearmament and entry into NATO, the film was also in effect a comment on the nature of the future German army, and it offered prescriptive guidelines for the new "citizen in uniform." At the same time, the film also showed how the (re)construction of the new German army and of German masculinity was intrinsically linked with memories of a catastrophic past. Moeller's reading thus reveals a fascinating double-distancing from the past. Through its critique of the military, the film challenged the senseless militarism of the Wehrmacht and thus took a clear anti-Nazi stance. At the same time, *08/15* also invented a new phony past that was sanitized not just of German violence but of violence against Germans. In *08/15*, the real scars of the war and its aftermath were no longer visible. As such, the film offered a past that many Germans indeed wanted "to see and hear" in 1955. Yet, as Moeller also makes clear, it was precisely the symbolic reconstitution of the nation through such critical but sanitized representations that then also paved the way for more realistic cinematic confrontations with the Second World War in later movies. To this day, film thus remains a central site for understanding the renegotiation and reinvention of the German past.

Heide Fehrenbach's essay, like Moeller's, uses cinematic representation as a way to unearth the social and cultural history of the 1950s. Her essay also joins Herzog's and Wiesen's contributions by examining how West Germans defined social and ethical behavior in the postwar period. All three contributions analyze the reconstruction of an ethical Germany in which the Nazi era provides an ever-present backdrop. This is notably true for Fehrenbach's essay, which in examining race, considers an issue particularly burdened by the legacy of the Holocaust. Fehrenbach focuses on the small number of mixed-race children fathered by African-American occupation soldiers in postwar Germany. These children enjoyed a persistent symbolic power, which, however, evolved in meaning as the Federal Republic's relationship to its past, to race, and to the outside world changed in the course of the postwar period.

Initially, mixed-race sex was a symbol of Germany's violation. Women who were pregnant by African-American GIs were particularly likely to be given abortions. Yet postwar Germans soon eschewed open racism and prided themselves for the equal treatment of mixed-race children. At the same time, welfarist arguments still highlighted nonwhite children's difference. Their removal through international adoption to the United States or to other countries perceived to be less racist was still advocated, though now ostensibly for the children's own welfare. Fehrenbach cites the film "Toxie" as a particularly telling example of racism's changing nature and function in postwar Germany. As in Ruff's and Moeller's accounts, here too we encounter postwar concern with the reconstruction of masculinity and new definitions of fatherhood. In the film, the intrusion into a white middle-class family of Toxi, a mixed-race foundling, eventually cures the German paterfamilias of his inherited prejudice and forces him to take on family responsibilities. Yet the real, African-American father's appearance as deus ex machina at the conclusion of the film, ready to whisk the mixed-race child off to an affluent middle-class life in the U.S., offered the audience the payoff of restored "whiteness" in the German family. In this sense, Fehrenbach's essay offers another perspective on the subtle interplay of both change and continuity in postwar West Germany.

As the essays in this section show, the historiography of the 1950s now constitutes one of the richest and most innovative subfields in the discipline. Long dominated by political and diplomatic approaches, the history of the postwar period has increasingly been written from the perspective of social and cultural history.[32] The 1950s now appear as an extremely dynamic period in which West German society underwent crucial transformations. In retrospect, the 1950s were an "unruly" decade, marked by deep fissures and tensions that juxtaposed enormous pressures for change and modernization (often resulting from foreign, especially American influences) with more indigenous, conservative traditions. As the contributions to this volume make clear, the legacy of the Second World War and of the Holocaust permeated all facets of society, cutting across the traditional fault lines of class and gender, though it often remained below the surface in the murky depths of private lives and frequently traumatic memories. While the contributions to this volume thus subscribe to a critical historiography of West Germany, they also begin to suggest the reasons for the (always tenuous) stabilization of the Federal Republic. Most importantly, West German society managed to resolve its considerable internal tensions and conflicts without resorting to the internal or external violence that appeared so appealing in earlier periods of German history discussed in this book.

What distinguishes the current historiography of the 1950s (and, increasingly, of the 1960s and 1970s) from the literature on earlier periods is that it is often still being written by contemporaries who themselves lived through the times they are now consigning to history. This double frame of reference, which marks the particular epistemological problem of writing contemporary history or *Zeitgeschichte,* is addressed in Hanna Schissler's concluding historiographical chapter. Schissler focuses on the links between historians' subjectivities and historical writing, or, in other words, between history and memory. By introducing the concepts of pattern recognition and self-referentiality, Schissler shows how ways of doing history reflect researchers' own experiences, be it the particular trajectories of their own biography, their academic socialization, or the national context in which they are writing. Schissler thus takes issue with the long-lasting objectivist stance that has informed German *Zeitgeschichte* in particular and shows how postmodernism has rendered boundaries, determinants of meaning, and worldviews more visible and has opened up new questions about agency and structure. In particular, historians have become aware of the ways in which memory shapes our understanding of history.[33] That recognition in turn implies that different groups and individuals bring differing memories to the fore. It boycotts any authoritative interpretation along the nation-state paradigm or along some dominant narrative, and brings into focus the uniqueness of individual as much as of group experiences. Those need to be negotiated, and from those experiences new narratives will be formed. The time of one dominant narrative has given way to the multiplicity of stories. History has transformed into histories.

In this context, Schissler explores differences in national approaches to contemporary history in Germany, Austria, and in the United States. Appropriately enough for a volume celebrating Volker Berghahn's contribution to modern German history, she highlights the evolving conversation between German and U.S. historians, noting the distinctive approaches that the latter have brought to German history, not least in the awareness of gender and racial difference. Such differences in national historiographies have resulted in a rich transatlantic cross-fertilization of historical research on Germany.

To be sure, German *Zeitgeschichte,* as indeed this present volume shows, remains centrally concerned with the origins and impact of Germany's catastrophe. Although both the *Sonderweg* paradigm and its rejection were based at least implicitly on cross-national comparisons, German history continues to be written, for perfectly legitimate reasons, as a distinct national history. At the same time, however, the global, post-territorial perspective found in recent work by Charles Maier, among others, poses a challenge to historical approaches that take the nation-state as their starting point or are writing within its confines.[34] Schissler argues that in coming years the Holocaust and Gulag narratives will begin to lose some of their power to control what still functions as a distinctly national narrative. As they do, emphasis on the "uniqueness" of German history will recede, while postcolonial and global questions and developments may well come to dominate our enquiry. Yet both approaches— the national and the global—do not need to be mutually exclusive, as Volker Berghahn's own oeuvre has so impressively documented. While his work has always been centrally concerned with the German catastrophe, he has continually reminded us of the larger international dimensions of German history. As such, a transnational and global perspective allows us to see how European and, indeed, world history both framed and were themselves altered by the conflicts, continuities, and catastrophes of modern German history.

Notes

1. Dan Diner, *Zivilisationsbruch. Denken nach Auschwitz* (Frankfurt, 1988); a search on World Cat using the keyword "Holocaust" yields 23,790 publications since 1990 (27,243 for the keyword "World War II").

2. For a review of recent publications, see Robert Moeller, "What Has Coming to Terms with the Past Meant in the Federal Republic of Germany," *Central European History* 35 (2002): 223–56, and Alon Confino, "Telling about Germany: Narratives of Memory and Culture," *Journal of Modern History* 76 (2004): 389–416. See also Richard Bessel and Dirk Schumann, eds., *Life after Death: Approaches to the Social and Cultural History of Europe during the 1940s and 1950s* (Cambridge, 2003); for Germany, see Klaus Naumann, ed., *Nachkrieg in Deutschland* (Hamburg, 2001).

3. Friedrich Meinecke, *The German Catastrophe: Reflections and Recollections,* trans. Sidney B. Fay (Boston, 1963).

4. Michael Geyer and Konrad Jarausch, *Shattered Past: Reconstructing German Histories* (Princeton, 2003).

5. The classic statement is Hans Ulrich Wehler, *The German Empire 1871–1918*, trans. Kim Traynor (Leamington Spa, 1985); for an updated and revised version referring to "peculiar conditions" of German history, see idem., *Deutsche Gesellschaftsgeschichte*, vol. 3. *Von der "Deutschen Doppelrevolution" bis zum Beginn des Ersten Weltkrieges, 1849–1914* (Munich, 1995).

6. Volker Berghahn, *Der Tirpitz Plan. Genesis und Verfall einer innenpolitischen Machtstrategie* (Düsseldorf, 1971).

7. Notable titles include David Blackbourn, *Class, Religion, and Local Politics in Wilhelmine Germany* (Oxford, 1980); Jonathan Sperber, *Popular Catholicism in Nineteenth Century Germany* (Princeton, 1984); Thomas Mergel, *Zwischen Klasse und Konfession. Katholisches Bürgertum im Rheinland 1794–1914* (Göttingen, 1994); Helmut Walser Smith, *German Nationalism and Religious Conflict: Culture, Ideology, Politics, 1870–1914* (Princeton, 1995); Jonathan Sperber, "Kirchengeschichte or the Social and Cultural History of Religion?" *Neue Politische Literatur* 43 (1998): 13–35.

8. For older accounts of the Ruhr crisis, see Klaus Schwabe, ed., *Die Ruhrkrise. Wendepunkt der internationalen Beziehungen nach dem Ersten Weltkrieg* (Paderborn, 1984); Stephen A Schuker, *The End of French Predominance in Europe: The Financial Crisis of 1924 and the Adoption of the Dawes Plan* (Chapel Hill, 1976); see also Hans Mommsen, *Die verspielte Freiheit. Der Weg der Republik von Weimar in den Untergang 1918 bis 1933* (Frankfurt am Main, 1990), 142.

9. Heinrich Hannover and Elisabeth Hannover-Drück, *Politische Justiz, 1918–1933*, (Frankfurt am Main, 1966); Kenneth F. Ledford, *From General Estate to a Special Interest: Germany Lawyers, 1878–1933*, (Cambridge, 1996).

10. For classic statements of this approach, see Detlev Peukert, *Grenzen der Sozialdisziplinierung. Aufstieg und Krise der deutschen Jugendfürsorge von 1878 bis 1932* (Cologne, 1986); Christoph Sachße and FlorianTennstedt, eds., *Soziale Sicherheit und soziale Disziplinierung. Beiträge zu einer historischen Theorie der Sozialpolitik*, (Frankfurt, 1986); Detlev J.K. Peukert, *The Weimar Republic: The Crisis of Classical Modernity* (New York, 1989). For more recent critiques, see Young-Sun Hong, *Welfare, Modernity, and the Weimar State, 1919–1933* (Princeton, 1998), and David Crew, *Germans on Welfare from Weimar to Hitler* (Oxford, 2001).

11. Nicolas Berg, in *Der Holocaust und die westdeutschen Historiker. Erforschung und Erinnerung* (Göttingen, 2003).

12. Michael Wildt, *Generation of the Unbound: The Leadership Corps of the Reich Security Main Office* (Jerusalem, 2002).

13. Hannah Arendt, *Eichmann in Jerusalem: A Report on the Banality of Evil* (New York, 1964). Hans Mommsen, "Die Realisierung des Utopischen. Die 'Endlösung der Judenfrage' im Dritten Reich," *Geschichte und Gesellschaft* 9 (1983): 381–420.

14. Andreas Kunz, *Wehrmacht und Niederlage. Die bewaffnete Macht in der Endphase der nationalsozialistischen Herrschaft 1944 bis 1945* (Munich, 2005). Michael Geyer, "'There is a Land Where Everything is Pure: Its Name is the Land of Death'," in *Sacrifice and National Belonging in Twentieth Century Germany*, ed. Greg Eghigian and Matthew Paul Berg (College Station, 2002), 118–47; Wolfram Wette, Ricarda Brenner, and Detlef Volgel, eds., *Das letzte halbe Jahr. Stimmungsberichte der Wehrmachtpropaganda 1944/45* (Essen, 2001).

15. Fritz Fischer, *Germany's Aims in the First World War* (New York, 1967); Fritz Fischer, *War of illusions: German Policies from 1911 to 1914* (New York, 1975).

16. Volker R. Berghahn, *Germany and the Approach of War in 1914*, 2nd ed. (New York, 1993).

17. Isabel Hull, *The Entourage of Kaiser Wilhelm II, 1888–1918*, (Cambridge, 1982); Thomas A. Kohut, *Wilhelm II and the Germans: A Study in Leadership* (Oxford, 1991); Johannes Paulmann, *Pomp und Politik: Monarchenbegegnungen in Europa zwischen Ancien Régime und Erstem Weltkrieg* (Paderborn, 2000); Giles MacDonogh, *The last Kaiser: Wilhelm the Impetuous* (London, 2000).

18. On the latter point see Gabriel Gorodestky, *Grand Delusion: Stalin and the German Invasion of Russia* (New Haven and London, 1999). For other recent works, see Albert L. Weeks, *Stalin's Other War: Soviet Grand Strategy, 1939–1941* (Lanham, Md., 2002); Lev Besymenski, *Stalin und Hitler. Das Pokerspiel der Diktatoren* (Berlin, 2002); Richard Overy, *The Dictators: Hitler's Germany and Stalin's Russia* (London, 2004).

19. Michael Hardt and Antonio Negri, *Empire* (Cambridge, Mass., 2000).

20. Eckart Kehr, *Schlachtflottenbau und Parteipolitik 1894–1901: Versuch eines Querschnitts durch die innenpolitischen, sozialen und ideologischen Voraussetzungen des deutschen Imperialismus* (Berlin, 1930); Hans Ulrich Wehler, *Bismarck und der Imperialismus* (Cologne, 1984). Wolfgang Mommsen, *Theories of Imperialism*, trans. P. S. Falla (New York, 1980).

21. Frederick Cooper and Ann Laura Stoler, eds., *Tensions of Empire: Colonial Cultures in a Bourgeois World* (Berkeley, 1996); Lora Wildenthal, *German Women for Empire, 1884–1945* (Durham, N.C., 2002).

22. In this way historians have revived interest in a connection first explicitly mooted by Hannah Arendt in the second part of her pathbreaking work *The Origins of Totalitarianism* (San Diego and New York, New Edition 1966). For the most recent intervention, see especially Isabel Hull, *Absolute Destruction: Military Culture and the Practices of War in Imperial Germany* (Ithaca, 2005).

23. Ralf Dahrendorf, *Society and Democracy in Germany* (Garden City, N.Y., 1967).

24. Classic statements included Eberhardt Schmidt, *Die verhinderte Neuordnung* (Frankfurt am Main, 1970); Ernst-Ulrich Huster, Gerhard Kraiker et al., *Determinanten der westdeutschen Restauration 1945–1949* (Frankfurt am Main, 1972).

25. See the essay on restoration, continuity, or new beginnings in Carola Stern and Heinrich August Winkler, *Wendepunkte Deutscher Geschichte* (Frankfurt am Main, 1979)

26. The emerging body of research on East Germany has also claimed growing attention, though this has not been a primary area of interest for Berghahn and is thus not reflected in the current volume.

27. Paul Lüttinger, "Der Mythos der schnellen Integration. Eine empirische Analyse zur Integration der Vertriebenen," *Zeitschrift für Soziologie* 15 (1987): 20–36.

28. On this context, see Hans Peter Schwarz, "Die ausgebliebene Katastrophe. Eine Problemskizze zur Geschichte der Bundesrepublik," in *Den Staat denken. Theodor Eschenburg zum Fünfundachtzigsten*, ed. Hermann Rudolph (Berlin, 1993), 151–74.

29. On the CDU more generally, see also Frank Bösch, *Die Adenauer-CDU. Gründung, Aufstieg und Krise einer Erfolgspartei (1945–1969)* (Munich, 2001).

30. Werner Abelshauser, *Wirtschaftsgeschichte der Bundesrepublik Deutschland (1945–1980)*, 1. Aufl. ed., Neue historische Bibliothek (Frankfurt am Main, 1983).

31. Dagmar Herzog, *Sex after Fascism: Memory and Morality in 20th Century Germany* (Princeton, 2005).

32. See, for example, Axel Schildt and Arnold Sywotteck, ed., *Modernisierung im Wiederaufbau. Die westdeutsche Gesellschaft der 50er Jahre* (Bonn, 1993); Robert G. Moeller, ed., *West Germany under Construction: Politics, Society, and Culture in the Adenauer Era* (Ann Arbor, 1997); Hanna Schissler, ed., *The Miracle Years: A Cultural History of West Germany* (Princeton, 2001).

33. Dan Diner, *Gedächtniszeiten. Über jüdische und andere Geschichten* (Munich, 2003), esp. "Von 'Gesellschaft' zu 'Gedächtnis'—Über historische Paradigmenwechsel," 7–15.

34. See Charles S. Maier, "Consigning the Twentieth Century to History: Alternative Narratives for the Modern Era," *American Historical Review* 105 (June 2000): 807–31; Michael Geyer and Charles Bright, "World History in a Global Age," *American Historical Review* 100 (1995): 1034–60.

PART ONE

❦

GERMAN ELITES AND AN UNRULY SOCIETY

❦

CHAPTER 1

Kulturkampf and Geschlechterkampf
Anti-Catholicism, Catholic Women, and the Public

Michael B. Gross

By the time of the founding of the German empire in 1871, new and large movements alarmed the liberal middle-class and challenged its prescription for political, social, and sexual order. One of them was the dramatic revival of popular Catholicism underway since the Revolution of 1848. With a well-orchestrated and sweeping missionary campaign led by the Jesuit, Dominican, and Franciscan religious orders, the Catholic church had successfully re-pietized the Catholic population of Germany.[1] For middle-class liberals dedicated to modern progress—capitalist industrialization, rationalization, and secularization—the resurgence of the power of Catholicism and the influence of the Roman Church seemed to be a throwback to the superstition and fanaticism of the Middle Ages. Another challenge to the liberal vision for Germany was the reemergence of the women's movement for social and political emancipation in the mid-1860s. The women's movement, which had been suppressed after the Revolution in the subsequent decade of reaction, now insisted on access to education and professional life and, in its most radical version, political rights, including the right to vote. The *Frauenfrage*, as the question of women's roles in society and their access to the public spheres of social and political citizenship became known, was hotly debated the length and breadth of Germany. Men who participated in the organized and political liberal movement of the third quarter of the nineteenth century worried that the revival of the Catholic church and the reawakening of the women's movement might derail their cherished plans for a modern, united Germany.[2]

For German liberals during the founding period of the new empire, these two problems, the women's movement for access to the public and the presence of popular Catholicism in public, were inextricably intertwined. Recognizing this link is one important key to understanding the meaning of the anti-Catholicism and the Kulturkampf of the 1870s, that is, the "cultural struggle" between, on the one hand, the state and liberals and, on the other hand, the Roman Catholic Church and Catholics, a conflict that contemporaries believed was the decisive turning point in German, and indeed, world history. Though the Kulturkampf and anti-Catholicism in the nineteenth century were once relegated to the margins of historiography, historians have come to appreciate that these are seminal themes that must be fully integrated into the history of modern Germany. In contrast to older historical studies, historians have realized over the last few years that the Kulturkampf was not simply an attempt to preserve the secular state from the reach of the Roman Catholic Church. Influential recent studies of German politics, society, and religion, for example, have viewed the church-state conflict variously as a campaign to break the threat of political Catholicism, an attempt to rebuild the German nation after unification according to the precepts of high-cultural Protestantism, or a battle between the "modern" outlook of liberal nationalists and "backward" Catholics.[3] The Kulturkampf was undoubtedly a broad enough campaign against the church to include all of these dimensions. Yet even these perspectives fall short of identifying all the fundamental issues that were at stake in liberal anti-Catholicism in general and the Kulturkampf in particular.

In this essay I would like to suggest that the Kulturkampf was a *Geschlechterkampf,* a more complex (and perhaps more interesting) contest between men and women for the public sphere than has been recognized in other views. Examining the Kulturkampf as a confrontation not simply between the state and the church but between men and women for access to the public permits a dramatically different appraisal of the meaning of anti-Catholicism in the period following the 1848 Revolution and of the origins of the state-sponsored anti-Catholic campaign in the 1870s. It makes clear why liberals during a period of sweeping social, economic, and political transformation (e.g., Catholic revival, the women's movement, industrial expansion, a measure of democratization with the manhood suffrage introduced with the North German Confederation in 1867, and national unification), banded together with such dedication and fury, with the incessant invocation of masculine bravura, against the Catholic church as a threat to middle-class social, political, and sexual order.

The Gender of Catholicism

In the late 1860s and through the 1870s, leaders of the Kulturkampf were as much infuriated by the topic of women in public as they were about the Catholic church. Leading *Kulturkämpfer* ("cultural warriors") were out-spoken opponents of women's emancipation, and they relentlessly attacked the feminist movement. For the sake of specificity and brevity, two leading and representative Kulturkämpfer, one on the progressive left and the other on the nationalist right of the liberal political spectrum, serve to demonstrate that, whatever else might have divided them, German liberals of every hue were as much antifeminist as they were anti-Catholic. Rudolf Virchow, the secular scientist, leader of the Progressive Party in the Prussian Landtag and the one who later coined the phrase Kulturkampf, immediately attacked the reemergence of the women's movement.[4] He believed it was a self-evident axiom of nature that men belonged in public life while women belonged at home. He argued that it was a mistake to think that women should "enter the market of public life and actively participate in the disputes of the day."[5] Only at home as wives and mothers could women serve the fatherland and humanity.

On the liberal right, the Protestant nationalist Heinrich von Sybel, editor of the prestigious *Historische Zeitschrift* and cofounder in Bonn of the anticlerical and anti-Catholic *Deutscher Verein*, argued that, however popular, the campaign for equal rights for women was merely throwing sand against the wind: the separation of male and female "spheres of life" *(Lebenssphäre)* outside and inside the family was an immutable law of nature and arguing otherwise was simply futile. The raising of children had to be left to the wife for the obvious reason that the "the crude hand" of the father was useless. A career for the mother outside the home would lead to the demise of her health, the destruction of the household, the ruin of her children, and the betrayal of the entire purpose of her existence.[6]

The idea that bourgeois ideology prescribed gendered separate spheres is, of course, a commonplace. It has been thoroughly examined by a generation of scholars of nineteenth-century Western society and is now so basic to understanding the period that historians take it for granted. Historians recognize too that this prescription should not be confused with the reality of social organization that included (and had always included) women outside the home. What is interesting, rather, is the coupling of the liberal middle-class ideology of separate spheres with anti-Catholicism and the anti-Catholic campaign in Germany. As Kulturkämpfer defended the public against the intrusion of the women's movement, they made sense of the relationship between liberalism and the Catholic church in terms of gender and the relationship between genders. Again for purposes of brevity, one prominent Kulturkämpfer, Johann Caspar Bluntschli, National Liberal in Baden, publicist of the *Staatswörterbuch*, and a rabid anti-Catholic, provides an illuminating example. In a series of essays in the liberal literary journal *Gegenwart*, Bluntschli argued that the Roman Church, just like a woman, was inclined toward irrationalism and sentiment rather than knowledge and thinking.[7] In the war with the Catholic church, the enemy of all modern culture, liberalism, and progress, Bluntschli warned that liberals had to remember that the church would use her feminine

wiles to exploit men to her advantage.[8] The church was like a woman who appeared innocent yet knew very well how to manipulate men now one way with
her charms, now another way with her tears to attain her desires.

At the same time, if the Catholic church was a woman in liberal social-
sexual ideology, then liberalism was a man, young and assertive. The model is
again offered by Bluntschli, who argued in his highly influential *Charakter und
Geist der politischen Parteien* that liberalism was "a young man who has his
formal education behind him and steps forward into life fully aware of his
strength and self-confidence."[9] He has abandoned irrational fantasies for logical discourse: he tests the ground on which he plans to build with scientific
criticism and precision. Above all, liberalism as a young man was distinguished
by his strength of character and his desire for independence and freedom
properly understood. Liberalism, according to Bluntschli, loathed the notion
that "a mindless mass of humanity ruled by superstitions" (read Catholics)
could ever be as free as "a manly *Volk* exercising thought and will."[10] At the
center of liberal anti-Catholicism was not simply the problem of religion but
also that of women. For Kulturkämpfer the sweeping Catholic revival taking
place at the missions, on pilgrimages, in religious associations, and in philanthropic work all over Germany was, therefore, always the issue of women in
public.

Catholic Women in Public

This liberal notion that Catholicism was feminine reflected the shifting de-
mography of faith taking place within the church. Since the late eighteenth
century women had been playing an increasingly prominent role in the
Catholic church and in the lay practice of Catholicism.[11] Social historians of
religion have argued that this constituted a feminization of the church, a
transformation occurring not just in the German states but also in England,
France, and the United States throughout the nineteenth century.[12] To contemporary observers and liberal critics of the Catholic revival in the two
decades after the 1848 Revolution, however, the role of women in Catholicism
seemed especially dramatic in the German states. Nowhere was this more evident than in the growth of female religious orders and congregations devoted
to public philanthropy.[13] This too was part of the feminization of the church.

But the point here is that the new female religious congregations responded
to revived demands by women for independence, emancipation, and larger
social relevance. As nuns and sisters in the new religious congregations, Catholic women found that they could combine a religious life with a professional
life. In Catholic schools, hospitals, orphanages, asylums, women's shelters, and
reformatories they found rewarding public roles as teachers, nurses, welfare

workers, and administrative personnel.[14] Contemporary critics warned that the dramatic rise in the number of Catholic sisters devoted to work in philan-thropic congregatons indicated a shift in the role of the church in society. As one argued, "In the old [closed monastic] orders women are completely dead to the outside world. But in the new congregations they often have a far-reaching influence. The new congregations pursue mostly social work including educa-tion and instruction, caring for the poor and sick."[15]

Catholic women not only joined the new religious congregations in num-bers that were revolutionary in the church. They also participated more prom-inently in Catholic communities and in the lay practice of Catholicism. Lay Catholic women were motivated to assume new roles in the church in unprec-edented numbers by the thousands of dramatic missions taking place across Germany. The missionaries revived popular Catholicism, driving the laity back into church with terrifying sermons that invoked fire and brimstone and promised damnation for unrepentant sinners. The liberal press and state au-thorities believed the missionaries concentrated their efforts on women. Crit-ics castigated the missions as disgusting displays of women in public at their worst: women swooning or prostrate before the missionaries, kissing their robes, weeping, and apparently mentally and emotionally unhinged.[16]

Social observers also complained that the missions disrupted family life. When mothers, they argued, surrendered themselves to religious fanaticism and flocked to the sermons at the missions, it was their children who suffered most: they were simply abandoned. "You very often see children hungry and freezing in the streets. They wander about uncared for, crying in front of the doorways and calling for their mothers. 'The mother? And where is the mother?'—'At the mission! At the mission!' sob the poor orphans."[17] The mis-sions were extraordinary events in the otherwise quiet, even boring routines of rural, village life, so there was considerable truth to the accusations that they disrupted normal family routines. When the Franciscan mission came to the town of Dahl in 1857, for example, even the parish priest admitted in a report to his Bishop in Paderborn that "all the grownups streamed to the church, and many houses were just left to the children."[18] Women who flocked to the missions, joined religious associations, participated in the pilgrimages, and attended church events were, therefore, not simply an embarrassment in public, that sphere reserved for male-dominance and rational discourse. They betrayed their responsibilities as mothers and caretakers of the home.

In the decades following mid-century, lay women were drawn to the Catholic church because it offered one of the few social and public spaces available to them outside the workplace. Following a visit by missionaries to their communities, women established their own religious organizations. For wives and mothers the religious associations offered opportunities to share and discuss their problems, and they offered the rare chance to flee from the responsibilities of the home and the family. Female religious organizations also attracted women because they offered some independence from male supervision, even if the priest remained.[19] More important, joining the new religious associations set up by the missionaries was one of the new opportunities for Catholic women to assume organizational and leadership positions previously denied them by men, and to do so with the assurance that it was a religious duty.

The new female religious organizations became so popular that among the laity women often dominated the religious life of the parish. One liberal critic complained that lay religious organizations and communities in many Catholic regions had become, in the absence of men, "mere ladies' societies."[20] Meanwhile, liberal newspapers like the *Vossische Zeitung* did not fail to notice the large attendance of women at the public assembly of the Catholic Association in Düsseldorf in 1869.[21] Despite the legal ban on female participation in political clubs and gatherings, in predominantly Catholic cities hundreds of women continued to participate in "lecture evenings" dedicated to clear political questions like state supervision of schools.[22] At the same time, Catholic women also helped organize mass pilgrimages to religious shrines like the one at *Marpingen* so vividly described and analyzed by David Blackbourn. The participants, critics remarked, were mostly female.[23]

Women's new roles in the church reflected a shift in patterns of Catholic popular piety as well. The promulgation of the Immaculate Conception of the Virgin by the Vatican in 1854 and introduction of new forms of Marian devotion were part of the rebirth of Roman Catholicism after mid-century. Hymns, prayers, and liturgical practices devoted to the Mother of Christ were encouraged by the Vatican and inculcated by missionaries all over Germany. These changes not only helped establish papal authority; they also promoted the more prominent role of women.[24] For Catholic women the new veneration of the Virgin sanctified motherhood, including the "female virtues" of humility and forbearance. Just as important, however, the Mother of Christ also offered an image of feminine grace and authority. In the world of Catholic women, the presence of Mary was everywhere and with her the model for feminine behavior. She was invoked in the recitation of the rosary, in the omnipresent pins, pictures, and statuettes that bore her image, and by the millions of Catholic women who were her namesake through the ages. All these things—the new Marian devotion, the religious philanthropic congregations, participation in religious associations, assemblies, pilgrimages, and missions—were dramatically changing the lives of Catholic women. As they inculcated piety in women and bolstered their status within the church, they also brought Catholic women into public life.

Of course, the church fathers were no more proponents of feminism than they were of democracy. Indeed, they continued to see women as large children requiring supervision, morally weak vessels prone to sin, sexually dangerous and untrustworthy. The church's teachings continued to confine women in the home and upheld matrimony, procreation, and motherhood as the responsibilities of women. The new opportunities for women within the church were also qualified. Even so, the Catholic revival opened up opportunities that had been limited for young women and mothers in Germany. At the very time that critics complained that the Roman Church was "antimodern" and "backward," exploiting "naive" women to enhance the power of the church, Catholic women within the church organized together, entered public life, expanded their roles within their communities, and exercised authority and leadership. By comparison, it was only much later and then only rarely that the German labor movement would be able to mobilize and employ so many women. It would not be the case, therefore, that Catholic women were lagging behind middle-class secular and Protestant women in their demand for access to public space. Already in the 1850s and early 1860s, while the bourgeois women's movement had disappeared with the decade of conservative reaction following the Revolution and well before the founding of the *Allgemeine Deutscher Frauenverein* in 1865, Catholic women were coupling religious life with public life in religious congregations, associations, and assemblies.

To be sure, Protestant middle-class women had engaged in public philanthropic work, charitable activities, and poor relief initiatives since the early decades of the century. National organizations like the Patriotic Women's Associations, the nursing sisterhood established in 1866 after the Austro-Prussian war, and the various local and municipal societies all provided ample opportunities for such service. The participation of Catholic women in public was, however, both quantitatively and qualitatively different from that of their Protestant counterparts. The flood of Catholic women in the years after 1848 entering the public through congregations, church organizations, parish life, and religious devotion was faster and more dramatic and therefore more conspicuous than the engagement of Protestant women. To contemporaries the influx of Catholic women into the public looked like a sudden expansion, a veritable explosion relative to the number of Protestant women who remained committed to philanthropic work and church affairs.

The new engagement of Catholic women was more dramatic and alarming because it happened relatively quickly but also more importantly because it was coupled to the power of the missions and the revival of popular Catholicism. Women of the Protestant middle class joined in public work primarily through secular organizations like the Patriotic Women's Associations in the nationalist spirit of service and through municipal charities in the civic spirit of volunteerism characteristic of their class. But Catholic women joined in public work as an act of Catholic piety. Their work in hospitals, asylums, schools, orphanages, shelters for women, and correctional homes for wayward women was, like their religious worship, suffused with and empowered by female forms of devotion including the Marianism specific to Roman Catholicism and by the new religious zeal unleashed by the popular missionary crusade. All this meant that Catholic middle-class women were entering the public in ways that were quite different to those of Protestant women and that drew greater attention and controversy. It was therefore Catholic women in their religious life, whether in congregations, in church associations, or in the missions, not Protestant women, who seemed to critics to be doing the demonstrable damage to the traditional separation of public and private.

Meanwhile, most Catholic men did not challenge the participation and relative autonomy of Catholic women in the religious associations and activities. Instead middle-class Catholic men preferred their own separate and secular associational life, joining the numerous political and social organizations closed to women. This was only consistent with the gendered attitude that middle-class men held toward religious practice. They were in general not particularly devout themselves and often resented the priests' challenge to their own authority within the family and in the community. But middle-class Catholic men also valued the religious inculcation of moral discipline among people and believed a certain piety in their wives and daughters and their presence at church and in religious associations was respectable and entirely appropriate to their sex. At the same time and in large numbers, Catholic workers retreated to the tavern, that refuge of male fellowship. Here they developed together anticlerical and secular attitudes.[25] Many Catholic workers felt betrayed by their priests, who in response to their complaints about starvation wages and oppressive working conditions, advised only useless prayer, forbearance, and obedience.

One example was Nikolaus Osterroth, a clay miner in the Bavarian Palatinate who has left testimony not only of his physically crippling work but also of the indifference of his parish priests. In the taverns after church in the company of his coworkers he learned to despise the parish priests: "How did the priest use his influence? Instead of defending the rights of the oppressed, whose leadership he regarded as his monopoly, he preached submission and patience to the workers. He sat at the table of the rich and accepted their gifts that they had wrung from the poor, instead of reminding them that their actions were hardhearted and unchristian."[26] Osterroth's disillusionment led him to abandon his faith and convert from the Catholic Center Party to the Social Democratic Party, an indication that in politics confession did not always trump class identity. One historian of religion in the nineteenth century has concluded that Catholicism (not just in Germany but also in England, France, and the United States) became increasingly feminized both because more women joined the church and because men fled from it, a process that only accelerated as the size of the industrial working class increased during the century.[27]

Liberal men hoped Catholic men would sooner or later turn their backs on the church not because their priests were too often blind to the reality of their lives but because Catholicism itself, with its emphasis on irrationalism, superstition, and subservience to the clergy, was, they claimed, unworthy of men. Catholic women were irretrievably lost to Catholicism, liberals concluded, but Catholic men by virtue of their sex were, after all, endowed with the faculty of reason and might finally use it. By 1868 even Johann Bluntschli thought there was some reason for hope. He believed that the majority of educated Catholic men no longer accepted the teachings of the church. Men had left it, he thought, to women and the ignorant.[28]

Kulturkampf and Geschlechterkampf

Their larger measure of piety and participation in the associational life of Catholicism helped prepare Catholic women for another role, as public protesters during the Kulturkampf. The antichurch campaign of the 1870s, led by the liberal political leadership and sponsored by the state, generated in the Catholic population an unexpected and determined resistance movement. Initially, liberals and state authorities underestimated both the loyalty of the Catholic laity to its political and religious leadership and the capacity of the Catholic population for open rebellion. Liberals and state officials assumed that any resistance to the Kulturkampf would be staged by a relatively small number of readily identifiable elements within the Catholic population: the clergy, the Catholic Center Party, the Catholic press, and a few Catholic associations like the *Mainzverein.*[29] They were confident that these isolated pockets of resistance would bend to the authority and power of the modern state.

But the reaction of the Catholic population was instead broad-based, defiant, and often violent. In 1872, for example, when the hotly contested Jesuit Law banned the Society of Jesus from the soil of the new empire, Catholic reaction was dramatic. After police authorities in the predominantly Catholic city of Essen had cleared out the Jesuits and locked up their residence, the Catholic population poured into the streets in open revolt. Police forces and Catholics fought in the streets in scenes not witnessed since the Revolution of 1848. Catholic rioters tried to reclaim the Jesuit chapel by force and demolished the home of a local Freemason, targeted because of the prevalent belief among Catholics that Freemasonry, liberalism, and hatred of Jesuits were synonymous.[30] On the front page of the *Essener Blätter,* the *Oberbürgermeister* pleaded with the city's Catholics to return to order and resume work. When it became clear that Essen authorities themselves would not be able to restore peace, two full battalions of fusiliers from the VII Army, 14th Division moved in to suppress the rebellion.[31] Here was the clear indication of things to come.

The Catholic *Duisburger Zeitung* told its readers that the riots proved that "you can't always answer deeds with mere words."[32] The liberal *Spener'sche Zeitung* said that the "Essen rebellion" was just the beginning.[33] The Catholic population in Essen forced state authorities across the empire to retreat. Momentarily stunned and afraid of inciting more Catholic rebellions, they slowed the closure of Jesuit missions and houses.[34] At the same time, the Jesuit law and the explosion of the Catholic population moved the Kulturkampf into more dangerous and contested terrain, one in which the new empire found itself in a "Kriegszustand," a condition of war. Not until the Revolution of 1918 would Imperial Germany experience such levels of collective action and spontaneous resistance.

What especially surprised both liberals and state authorities about the passive and active defiance of the Kulturkampf, however, was the predominant role of women. In the cities, towns, and villages of Prussia, Catholic women of all classes organized themselves, attended rallies, demonstrated in cathedral squares and churchyards, circulated petitions of solidarity, wrote newspaper editorials, and marched in support of their church leadership. One good example was the over one thousand Catholic aristocratic women in Cologne, including the wives of local *Landräte* and judicial officials, who publicly expressed their support for the bishop.[35] Again during the summer of 1874, thirty-five women of the Westphalian aristocracy created a major scandal when they were arrested and put on trial for lending their support to the Bishop of Münster. Authorities claimed their address included an affront to the majesty of the law.[36] Such scenes were repeated across Prussia, in almost all episcopal centers where long processions of women paid tribute to their church leaders as an act of piety.

Women also took more obstinate action against the state and its authorities. When in Freiburg im Breisgau, state authorities auctioned off the furniture of the bishop, Catholic ladies came armed with umbrellas. They threatened to thrash anyone who might try to bid against the buyer designated by the Catholic community to purchase the furniture and return it to the bishop.[37] At a town school in Upper Silesia, military intervention was required to break apart women who had assembled to guard religion classes conducted by priests not authorized by the state. At another town close by, the army was again ordered in to put down women rioting against a school where classes were conducted by an Old Catholic (a dissident, liberal Catholic, often a Kulturkämpfer who refused to recognized the ultimate authority of the pope) and a supporter of state legislation designed to terminate the church's supervision of schools.[38] Women also provided the leadership for passive forms of resistance to the state. In their local parishes, they coordinated the social ostracizing of so-called state pastors, clerics who had agreed to the state's demand that they take an oath of allegiance in accordance with new Kulturkampf legislation. Women of the parish organized the boycotts of shops and businesses of Kulturkampf sympathizers and informers. Catholic women openly defied state prohibitions against demonstrations and other scenes of public support for the church leadership and proved themselves quite willing to pay the penalty. They were arrested, sent to jail, and charged fines.

Girls too had a special role to play in the orchestration of Catholic public protest against the Kulturkampf. When in 1874, for example, a young priest who had been jailed in Koblenz for refusing to abide by Kulturkampf legislation returned to his congregation, a jubilant crowd of cheering parishioners greeted him on the banks of the Moselle River. Young girls dressed in white then stepped forward, formed a circle around the priest, and offered him flowers.[39] Here was a poignant gesture that conveyed both youthful innocence and feminine defiance. This scene was repeated in Catholic communities in villages, towns, and cities all over Prussia whenever interned priests were released by the authorities and came back to their parishes. It understandably infuriated supporters of the Kulturkampf, who realized that the ritual mocked the state, exposing its ultimate incapacity despite all its force to impose its will on the Catholic population.

Of course, Catholic men also participated in counter-Kulturkampf protests. But Kulturkämpfer accounted for the presence of Catholic men in demonstrations by simply taking for granted that they had been ordered to participate by their wives. They routinely branded mass protests that had to be contained with policemen as "feminine" even if those joining in the agitation were men.[40] This was the case with the huge crowds that greeted bishops released from imprisonment. The crowds were so ecstatic that they had to be subdued by the gendarmes. Liberal men and state authorities believed this and other demonstrations were "female" even though they had been clearly organized by prominent Catholic men and led by priests. Their opinions were typical of a nineteenth-century bourgeois culture, not just in Germany but throughout Europe, that considered the masses feminine (authentic culture belonged alone to men).[41] They were grounded in theories of mass behavior such as those expounded by the French social psychologists Hippolyte Taine, Gabriel Tarde, and particularly Gustave Le Bon in his enormously popular *The Crowd*. Social psychologists argued that mobs—impulsive, irrational, and prone to violence— were characteristically "feminine" (as well as mentally ill, alcoholic, and savage).[42] "The simplicity and exaggeration of the sentiments of crowds," according to Le Bon, "have the result that a throng knows neither doubt nor uncertainty. Like a women, it goes at once to extremes.... A commencement of antipathy or disapprobation, which in the case of an isolated individual would not gain strength, becomes at once furious hatred in the case of an individual in a crowd."[43] Le Bon believed that crowds exhibited a peculiar religious sentiment (namely Catholic), accompanied therefore with intolerance and fanaticism.

Policemen and gendarmes, soldiers, mayors, municipal officers and school supervisors, civil servants, deputies, and other men in positions of authority who tried to implement and enforce Kulturkampf legislation repeatedly faced Catholic women protesters who heckled, jeered, and beat them with umbrellas. When they did so, they often coupled the scandal of Catholic women demonstrators with that of other disreputable women in public. In a typical incident, a representative of the state squared off against women protesters. Exasperated, he finally declared them "all a bunch of prostitutes." This was, of course, the standard rhetorical slander directed at "impudent" women present in public without the supervision of men.[44] But it also revealed in a flash of frustration and anger the sexed dynamics of power at work in the church-state conflict. The feminine character of Catholic agitation against the Kulturkampf became so prominent that it colored the attitude of those at even the highest level of state power. At the beginning of 1875, with the Kulturkampf at its height, Otto von Bismarck found himself locked in rhetorical combat with Ludwig Windthorst, the most important leader of the Catholic Center Party. During a dinner party Bismarck expressed worries about those "feminine influences" that were thwarting the campaign against the Catholic church.[45] By the end of the evening he confessed that his hatred of Windthorst was matched only by his love for his wife—a twisted association that suggested how thinking about the Kulturkampf and Catholic recalcitrance could lace together politics and gender, misogyny and intimacy in ways that are not immediately obvious.

Not just the opponents of Catholicism and the Catholic church were inclined to imagine the Catholic counter-Kulturkampf in these gendered terms. The Catholic ecclesiastical and political leadership not only did not challenge but in fact embraced and co-opted the image of the church as feminine, turning what was intended as an insult into a virtue. They propagated the image of a Catholic community at its very best in a time of crisis, inspired by the feminine qualities of endurance and down-to-earth good sense. As Margaret Lavinia Anderson has shown, the Center Party deputies on the floor of the Prussian Parliament and in the Reichstag and journal and newspaper editors in Catholic press organs invented the "Catholic woman." She gave a level-headed voice to Catholics collectively in the face of the state's and liberals' outlandish attacks against the church.[46] In the Catholic counter-Kulturkampf, innocent girls and common-sense women were symbols of moral superiority in the face of the physical force of soldiers and gendarmes and the slander of liberal and state leaders.

If for Kulturkämpfer Catholic resistance was an act of feminine defiance, they believed that the success of their campaign required more concerted exertions of masculinity and public character. For example, in 1869 the liberal *National Zeitung* urged its readers to practice "independence, manliness, and freedom" against Catholic oppression.[47] In 1873 a liberal political manifesto in the *Crefelder Zeitung* demanded the election of a "man" who, in the face of the ultramontane opposition, wanted "political freedom and independence."[48] The National Liberal president of the Reichstag, Max von Forckenbeck, himself a Catholic, called upon his colleagues to offer a "manly defense" of their parliamentary achievements. As David Blackbourn has pointed out, Heinrich Kruse of the liberal *Kölnische Zeitung* was congratulated for the paper's "firm, manly role" in the campaign against clericalism, and the National Liberal Heinrich von Sybel as president of the Rhenish, anticlerical *Deutscher Verein* was praised by its executive committee for his "manly demeanor."[49] In terms of intra-group dynamics, such displays of masculine bravura rallied Kulturkämpfer together in the homosocial fight against Catholicism. At the level of social-sexual ideology, the incessant invocation of masculinity in the face of Catholicism defined the public space as masculine.

The Kulturkampf campaign and Catholic resistance, therefore, increasingly took on the aspect of a battle between men and women for access to the public, between men of authority charged with the maintenance of public order on the one side and wives and mothers and even girls on the other. This was the element of the ordeal, distorted and exaggerated, that repeatedly focused the attention of Kulturkämpfer. For liberals, Catholic women on the loose attending the missions, joining assemblies and associations, and organizing in anti-Kulturkampf protests were women who literally did not know their place. Their public recalcitrance was a formidable challenge to the state at the same time that the state's reliance on physical force against the "weaker sex" was a public embarrassment of authority. It was, therefore, not only the practice of Catholicism itself gendered as a woman but also Catholic women themselves in acts of religious faith and with resistance to the state that defied the proscription against women in public.

What has emerged in this exploration of liberal gender ideology and anti-Catholicism is a reorientation of our perspective on the campaign against the Catholic Church in the 1870s. The Kulturkampf can be understood as a dimension of the Frauenfrage: Roman Catholics, because they seemed irrational, superstitious, and excessively emotional were as unacceptable in the liberal vision of the modern nation as women, for the same reasons, were in the public sphere. At the center of liberal anti-Catholicism was the sexism typical of the middle-class. During the founding of the new empire, the problem with Catholics was, as liberals understood them, not simply their religion but more fundamentally their sex. In the last analysis Kulturkämpfer are, therefore, better understood not as self-evident anti-Catholics but as sexists. In this light, the Kulturkampf was a complex attempt during a period of dramatic pressures for change to preserve the distinction between gender-specific public and private spaces. Exploring the Kulturkampf as a *Geschlechterkampf,* as a contest between men and women for access to the public sphere, allows for a different evaluation of the origins and meaning of liberal anti-Catholicism in the nineteenth-century.

Notes

A version of this chapter in different form appeared in Michael B. Gross, *The War against Catholicism: Liberalism and the Anti-Catholic Imagination in Nineteenth Century Germany* (Ann Arbor: University of Michigan Press, 2004).

1. At the time of the founding of the German empire, approximately one-third of the population of the empire was Roman Catholic. For the Catholic missionary campaign, which lasted from 1848 to the closing of religious orders in 1872, see Erwin Gatz, *Rheinische Volksmission im 19. Jahrhundert: Dargestellt am Beispiel des Erzbistums Köln* (Düsseldorf, 1963); Michael B. Gross, *The War against Catholicism: Liberalism and the Anti-Catholic Imagination in Nineteenth-Century Germany* (Ann Arbor, 2004); P. Klemens Jockwig, "Die Volksmission der Redemptoristen in Bayern von 1848 bis 1873. Dargestellt am Erzbistum München und Freising und an den Bistümern Passau und Regensburg. Ein Beitrag zur Pastoralgeschichte des 19 Jahrhunderts." In *Beiträge zur Geschichte des Bistums Regensburg,* ed. Georg Schwaiger and Josef Staber, 41–407 (Regensburg, 1967); Thomas Klosterkamp, *Katholische Volksmission in Deutschland* (Leipzig, 2002); Otto Weiss, *Die Redemptoristen in Bayern (1790–1909): Ein Beitrag zur Geschichte des Ultramontanismus* (St. Ottilien, 1983); Bernhard Scholten, *Die Volksmission der Redemptoristen vor dem Kulturkampf im Raum der Niederdeutschen Ordensprovinz* (Bonn, 1976); Jonathan Sperber, *Popular Catholicism in Nineteenth-Century Germany* (Princeton, 1984); and for a rebuttal to Sperber, Simon Hyde, "Roman Catholicism and the Prussian State in the Early 1850s," *Central European History* 24 (1991): 95–121.

2. According to liberals, women were not among those in the population who could become, either now or in the future, emancipated and independent members of bourgeois society, and their thinking on this did not change until late in the century. Dieter Langewiesche, *Liberalismus in Deutschland* (Frankfurt am Main, 1988), 101.

3. See respectively for these arguments, Margaret Lavinia Anderson, "The Kulturkampf and the Course of German History," *Central European History* 19 (1986): 82–115; idem, *Practicing Democracy: Elections and Political Culture in Imperial Germany* (Princeton, 2000); idem, *Windthorst: A Political Biography* (Oxford, 1981); and Helmut Walser Smith, *German Nationalism and Religious Conflict in Germany: Culture, Ideology, Politics, 1870–1914* (Princeton, 1995); and David Blackbourn, *Marpingen: Apparitions of the Virgin Mary in Nineteenth-Century Germany* (New York, 1994); idem, "Progress and Piety: Liberals, Catholics, and the State in Bismarck's Germany," in *Society and Politics in Wilhelmine Germany,* ed. Richard J. Evans (London, 1978), 160–85.

4. Rudolf Virchow, *Über die Erziehung des Weibes für seinen Beruf* (Berlin, 1865).

5. Ibid., 19–20.

6. Heinrich von Sybel, "Über die Emancipation der Frauen," in *Vorträge und Aufsätze,* (Berlin, 1874), 59–79.

7. Johann Caspar Bluntschli, "Deutsche Briefe über das Verhältnis von Staat und Kirche: Der Dualismus von Staat und Kirche," *Gegenwart* (2 March 1872); idem, "Deutsche Briefe über das Verhältnis von Staat und Kirche: Der Staat als Geisteswesen," *Gegenwart* (19 March 1872); See also idem, "Über den Unterschied der mittelalterlichen und der modernen Staatsidee" (Munich, 1855), 15–16.

8. Johann Caspar Bluntschli, *Charakter und Geist der politischen Parteien* (Nördlingen, 1869), 50.

9. Ibid., 119.

10. Ibid., 128.

11. For a discussion of the more prominent role of women both in Catholicism and Protestantism in the nineteenth-century see Hugh McLeod, "Weibliche Frömmigkeit–männlicher Unglaube? Religion und Kirche im bürgerlichen 19. Jahrhundert," in *Bürgerinnen und Bürger: Geschlechterverhältnisses im 19. Jahrhundert*, ed. Ute Frevert (Göttingen, 1988), 134–56; Rebekka Habermas, "Weibliche Religiosität–oder Von der Fragilität bürgerlicher Identitäten," in *Wege zur Geschichte des Bürgertums. Vierzehn Beiträge,* ed. Klaus Tenfelde und Hans-Ulrich Wehler (Göttingen, 1994), 125–48; Norbert Bush, "Die Feminisierung der ultramontanen Frömmigkeit," in *Wunderbare Erscheinungen. Frauen und katholische Frömmigkeit in 19. und 20. Jahrhundert,* ed. Irmtraud Götz von Olenhusen (Paderborn, 1995), 203–20. For indications that the church was becoming more feminine see also Lucian Hoelscher, "Moglichkeiten und Grenzen der statistischen Erfaßung kirchlicher Bindungen," in *Seelsorge und Diakonie in Berlin: Beiträge zum Verhältnis von Kirche und Grossstadt im 19. Jahrhundert,* ed. Kaspar Elm and Hans-Dietrich Loock (Berlin, 1990), 39–62. For a critical appraisal of the feminization of religion see Caroline Ford, "Religion and Popular Culture in Modern Europe," *Journal of Modern History* 65 (1993): 152–75, and for the German case see the comments by Margaret Lavinia Anderson, "The Limits of Secularization: On the Problem of the Catholic Revival in Nineteenth-Century Germany," *The Historical Journal* 38 (1995): 654.

12. For France see Ralph Gibson, *A Social History of French Catholicism, 1789–1914* (London, 1989) and Claude Langlois, *La Catholicisme au féminin: les congrégations français à supérieure générale au XIX siècle* (Paris, 1984). For the United States see Richard D. Shiels, "The Feminisation of American Congregationalism 1730–1835," *American Quarterly* 33 (1983): 46–62, and Barbara Welter, "The Feminization of American Religion 1800–1860," in *Clio's Consciousness Raised: New Perspectives in the History of Women,* ed. Mary Hartmann and Lois Banner (New York, 1976): 136–57. See also Mary Ewens, *The Role of the Nun in Nineteenth-Century America* (New York, 1978). To make a comparison to the Roman Catholic female religious orders and congregations in England, see Susan O'Brien, "*Terra Incognita:* The Nun in Nineteenth-Century England" *Past & Present* 121 (1988): 110–40; and idem, "French Nuns in Nineteenth-Century England," *Past & Present* 161 (1997): 142–80.

13. Johann Friedrich von Schulte, *Die neueren katholischen Orden und Congregationen besonders in Deutschland* (Berlin, 1872); Paul Hinschius, *Die Orden und Kongregationen der katholischen Kirche in Preußen. Ihre Verbreitung, ihre Organisation und ihre Zwecke* (Berlin, 1874).

14. This is the refreshing argument offered by Relinde Meiwes, "Religiosität und Arbeit als Lebensform für katholische Frauen. Kongregationen im 19. Jahrhundert," in *Frauen unter dem Patriarchat der Kirchen. Katholikinnen und Protestantinnen im 19.*

und 20. Jahrhundert, ed. Irmtraud Götz von Olenhusen (Stuttgart, Berlin, Köln, 1995), 69–88, and *"Arbeiterinnen des Herrn."* *Katholische Frauenkongregationen im 19 Jahrhundert* (Frankfurt, 2000).

15. Schulte, *Die neueren Katholischen Orden und Congregationen,* 8.

16. See for example, *Aktenstücke zur Geschichte der Jesuiten-Missionen in Deutschland, 1874–1872,* ed. Duhr Bernhard (Freiburg im Breisgau, 1903); *Allgemeine Zeitung,* no. 316, 1852, 174.

17. A. L. Stachelstock, *Licht und Finsterniß oder die freien Gemeinden und die Jesuiten* (Altona, 1861), 76–77.

18. Aubert Groeteken, *Die Volksmissionen der norddeutschen Franziskaner vor dem Kulturkampf (1849–1872)* (Münster, 1909), 46–47.

19. See McLeod, "Weibliche Frömmigkeit," 145. See also Jonathan Sperber, "The Transformation of Catholic Associations in the Northern Rheinland and Westphalia 1830–1870," *Journal of Social History* 15 (1981): 253–63. For France see Martine Segalen, *Mari et femme dans la société paysanne* (Paris, 1980), 156–58. For England, see L. Davidoff and C. Hall, "The Architecture of Public and Private Life: English Middle Class Society in a Provincial Town 1780 to 1850," in *The Pursuit of Urban History,* ed. Derek Fraser and Anthony Sutcliffe, (London, 1983), 327–45.

20. Schulte, *Die neueren katholischen Orden und Congregationen,* 41.

21. *Vossische Zeitung,* 11 Sept. 1869.

22. Anderson, *Practicing Democracy,* 127.

23. Blackbourn, *Marpingen.*

24. Michael N. Ebertz, "Maria in der massenreligiosität. Zum Wandel des populären Katholizismus in Deutschland," in *Volksfrömmigkeit in Europa. Beiträge zur Soziologie populärer Religiosität aus 14 Ländern,* ed. Michael N. Ebertz and Franz Schultheiss (Munich, 1986), 65–84. On Marian devotion encouraged by the missions see Gatz, *Rheinische Volksmission,* 126.

25. For the tavern as a bastion of male anticlericalism, see Sperber, *Popular Catholicism,* 62–63.

26. "Nikolaus Osterroth, Clay Miner," in *The German Worker: Working Class Autobiographies from the Age of Industrialization,* ed. Alfred Kelly (Berkeley, 1987), 169.

27. McLeod, "Weibliche Frömmigkeit," 134–56.

28. Bluntschli, "Verhältniss des modernen States zur Religion," 166.

29. Ronald J. Ross, *The Failure of Bismarck's Kulturkampf: Catholicism and State Power in Imperial Germany 1871–1887* (Washington, D.C, 1998), 132.

30. Hauptstaatsarchiv Düsseldorf (hereafter HSTAD), Regierung Düsseldorf (hereafter RD), no. 20111, Bd. 1, report of Bürgermeister Gustav Adolf Waldthausen, Essen, 14 Aug. 1872; report of Abtheilung des Innern, 19 Aug. 1872; report of the Police Inspector, Essen, 24 Aug. 1872; newspaper clip, *Essener Zeitung,* 25 Aug. 1872.

31. *Vossische Zeitung,* 7 Sept. 1872; HSTAD, RD, Bd. 1, no. 20111, newspaper clip, *Essener Blätter,* 25 Aug. 1872; Commander, VII Army Corps, 14th Division, to Regierungspräsident von Ende, Düsseldorf, 26 Aug, 1872.

32. HSTAD, RD, no. 20111, Bd. 1, newspaper clip, *Berliner Börsen Zeitung,* n.d.

33. HSTAD, RD, no. 20112, Bd. 2, newspaper clip, *Spenersche Zeitung,* 6 Sept. 1872.

34. See HSTAD, Regierung Aachen, no. 10699, "Orden der Gesellschaft Jesu bzw. die Ausführung des Gesetzes vom 4 July 1872," Landrat to Regierung, Abtheilung des Innern, Aachen, 4 Dec., 1872, 88–89.

35. Anderson, *Windthorst,* 174.

36. Ross, *Bismarck's Kulturkampf,* 133, n. 45.

37. Anderson, *Windthorst,* 174.

38. For both incidents, see idem, *Practicing Democracy,* 126.

39. Ross, *Bismarck's Kulturkampf,* 142.

40. Blackbourn, "Progress and Piety," 150.

41. Andreas Huyssen, "Mass Culture as Woman: Modernism's Other," in *After the Great Divide: Modernism, Mass Culture, Postmodernism,* ed. Andreas Huyssen (Bloomington and Indianapolis, 1986), 44–62.

42. Susanna Barrows, *Distorting Mirrors: Visions of the Crowd in Late Nineteenth-Century France* (New Haven and London, 1981). This is the point made in Blackbourn, "Progress and Piety," 149–50.

43. Quoted in Huyssen, "Mass Culture as Woman," 53.

44. McLeod, "Weibliche Frömmigkeit," 143.

45. Otto Pflanze, *Bismarck and the Development of Germany,* 3 vols. (Princeton, 1990), 2:241.

46. Anderson, *Practicing Democracy,* 127.

47. *National Zeitung,* 6 Sept. 1869.

48. HSTAD, RD, no. 2619, "Die Anordnung der Schulpfleger bzw. Kreisschulinspektoren (kath.) und Förderung des Schulwesens durch die Geistlichen, Bd. 1 (1872–1873), newspaper clipping, *Crefelder Zeitung,* 23 Oct. 1873.

49. See Blackbourn, *Marpingen,* 261.

CHAPTER 2

The 1923 Ruhr Crisis
The Limits of Active Resistance

Conan Fischer

I

On 12 May 1923, the Prussian police arrested a certain Heinz Hauenstein in the Rhenish town of Barmen, and charged him with membership of an illegal organization and the unlawful possession of firearms.[1] Hauenstein was leader of a shadowy outfit that was involved in intelligence gathering and sabotage in the Ruhr District, in an effort to dislodge the Franco-Belgian forces that had occupied the region in January 1923. Such antics had caused consternation in official Prussian circles, where sabotage was condemned as futile and inflammatory, and its practitioners regarded as dangerous anti-republicans into the bargain.[2] During subsequent interrogations, however, Hauenstein lodged a special defence that claimed, far from being illegal, his operations were known to the national authorities and even enjoyed their support:

> On the basis of this … cooperation with all official bodies and my consultations in Berlin, I am compelled to assume that I acted with the consent of, and in the interests of, the government bodies concerned, and to feel that my actions were fully justified.[3]

These actions included eighteen bombings and the killing of eight French agents,[4] all of which contravened the aforementioned Prussian orders to refrain from provocative acts of any kind in the occupied territories of western Germany.[5]

The chief investigating police officer, Detective Commissioner Weitzel, submitted detailed interrogation reports to Berlin, whereupon the Prussian interior minister, Carl Severing, intervened in the matter. Before discussing the case personally with Chancellor Cuno, Severing wrote to the secretary of state in the National Chancellory, Eduard Hamm, who happened to belong to the pro-Weimar German Democratic Party (DDP). The burden of his protest focused on the apparent undermining of Prussian authority and policy during the Ruhr crisis by members of the national government. The ultimate responsibility for Hauenstein's arrest, Severing asserted, rested with those in the national defence and transport ministries who had covertly sanctioned his illicit operations.[6] To make matters worse for the Social Democratic interior minister, a storm of protest blew up in the right-wing press against Hauenstein's arrest. The hapless adventurer claimed that he had been on the point of rescuing one of his lieutenants, Leo Schlageter, from French custody. Quite how he proposed to achieve this begs a host of questions, but Schlageter was languishing in the death cell on a charge of sabotage and was indeed executed on 26 May. As the man ultimately answerable for Hauenstein's arrest, Severing, so the nationalist press raged, was indirectly responsible for Schlageter's death.[7]

As part of its wider onslaught against the Prussian authorities, the radical right consistently distinguished between the national and Prussian governments, claiming common ground with the former and even suggesting that Severing's anti-terrorist measures amounted to a simultaneous attack on official national interests. So it was with Gerhard Rossbach, a Freikorps adventurer who had also been locked away during 1923, on a charge of treason. In June he wrote from his prison cell directly to Chancellor Cuno, bemoaning his ongoing imprisonment and asserting that his incarceration was a put-up job by no less than Interior Minister Severing.[8] Rossbach went on to claim that the right-radical *völkisch* movement stood alongside the national government, which, in turn, was under attack from the Prussian interior minister. "Now that [Severing] realizes that his theory regarding 'high treason by the *Völkische*' is collapsing, he is quite openly beginning to attack the national government, in particular the Chancellor and also the army."[9]

If Hauenstein's personal history remains obscure,[10] the fate of his hapless subordinate, Leo Schlageter, is far better known. Following his execution, both the Communist International in Moscow and the German radical right praised his allegedly heroic part in Germany's struggle during 1923 against French ambitions in the Ruhr District.[11] After the Nazi takeover in 1933, Schlageter came to be fêted as the very embodiment of the entire 1923 Ruhr struggle, which transformed his campaign of terror against the French invaders into the defining element of anti-French resistance as a whole.[12] Contemporary French diplomacy and propaganda made similarly hyperbolic and patriotic claims on the other side, seeing in Prime Minister Raymond Poincaré the punctilious defender of the 1919 international settlement.[13] French cartoons depicted Marianne, peace treaty in hand, knocking politely at the door to the Ruhr District, behind which a snarling assortment of Wagnerian nightmares sought to bar her passage.[14] Similarly, Poincaré himself insisted that Paris and Brussels had invaded the Ruhr District reluctantly, as a sanction against Germany's repeated and wilful noncompliance with the terms of the Versailles Treaty in general and the reparations settlement in particular. He condemned German resistance against his enterprise as a violent affair that "did not originate with the people, ... the German government itself had organized bloody encounters, attacks on the French garrison, acts of sabotage and common crimes in the Ruhr District."[15]

All of this accords with a highly influential, more recent historiography that posits lines of continuity from the Bismarckian and Wilhelmine eras, through the disappointments and failings of the Weimar period, and so into the Third Reich. The "Battle of the Ruhr" has been widely regarded as a confrontational attempt by the German authorities to evade or even reverse the verdict of Versailles. As Hans Mommsen has observed, German policy during the Ruhr crisis amounted to a "reversion to the politics of national prestige" as had been pursued in 1919 by opponents of the peace treaty,[16] while Stephen Schuker once remarked that: "The ministries in Berlin determined every feature of this resistance ... non-cooperation by the citizenry, railway workers, and factory owners alike."[17]

However, such interpretations conflict irreconcilably with contemporary Social Democratic and trade union perceptions of the 1923 conflict. At the height of the crisis itself, Social Democratic leaders claimed moral and substantive ownership of the passive resistance campaign, with Hermann Müller declaring that: "The resistance is possible only because the workers, particularly the Socialist workers, have risen up to a man."[18] His colleague Rudolf Breitscheid taunted the Conservative parliamentarian, Karl Helfferich, that big business in particular was less enamoured with resistance, concluding that: "Unfortunately [your] friends are not quite so determined as the Social Democrats to reject capitulation."[19] This conviction was not confined to the labor movement's leaders, for ordinary workers in the Ruhr regarded passive resistance as their particular struggle. They were fighting, they believed, to defend their revolutionary gains against a belligerent, right-wing French government that neglected working-class interests in its own country, and now sought unilaterally to overthrow the 1919 international settlement.[20] Even in September, with Germany in chaos and conditions in the Ruhr near intolerable, Stresemann's government feared that the imminent collapse of passive resistance would trigger widespread riots and disorder in the occupied region. Despite their predicament, there were unmistakable signs that many of the Ruhr's workers would regard an official abandonment of the struggle as naked betrayal,[21] and, indeed, these fears were realized.[22]

Bourgeois circles, too, acknowledged at the time that passive resistance was a grassroots phenomenon. As the newspaper, the *Vossische Zeitung,* commented: "The resistance, as every well-informed person knows, has grown from within the people, and its principal champions are the working-class masses."[23] Gustav Stresemann had advocated international mediation almost from the start of the crisis,[24] but writing in *Die Zeit* in May, none the less recognized that passive resistance was a popular movement, which held the government of the day in its thrall. "No German government," he observed, "is conceivable that could embody anything else than the idea of resistance.... Anyone who speaks and writes of a 'more adaptable' Cabinet, that is to say, a Cabinet with a weaker will to resistance, exhibits himself as entirely out of touch with popular feeling at large."[25]

In the end of course, capitulation followed on 26 September under Stresemann's leadership, but even thereafter, the republican left continued to identify with the passive resistance campaign. In 1924 the Free Trade Unions commissioned a history of the Ruhr crisis, which claimed for organized labor a pivotal role in the struggle,[26] while the the SPD celebrated in print the region's unarmed campaign against the Franco-Belgian invasion.[27] The Marxist historian, Arthur Rosenberg, came to comparable conclusions in his classic history of Weimar, claiming that the workers and civil servants of the Ruhr had borne the brunt of the struggle.[28] Civil servants, it should be noted, included the tens of thousands of railwaymen who played a pivotal role in the passive resistance campaign.

In other words, both the radical right and the republicans of interwar Germany laid claim to the conduct and ethos of the passive resistance campaign. For their part, senior French officials, like their Prime Minister, had few doubts that the whole episode formed part of a concerted, official German effort to overthrow the peace settlement.[29] As noted, influential historians have tended toward this contemporary French view, although no one questions that a mass campaign occurred. However, some writers have recently tended to endorse Weimar republican perceptions of passive resistance, including Barbara Müller[30] and, indirectly, the French historian Stanislas Jeannesson, who argues that during 1923 France's leaders attempted unilaterally to revise the Versailles settlement both territorially and with regard to the reparations regime[31]—a situation that could put German resistance in a defensive light. The complexities of the wider passive resistance campaign require, and have received elsewhere,[32] more extensive examination than would be possible within the confines of this particular paper. However, a closer examination of the role, nature and relative importance of the more violent campaign of active resistance, as pursued by Hauenstein, Schlageter, and their ilk, will serve to provide a revealing insight into the ethos and character of the wider struggle in the Ruhr.

II

The German government was curiously ill prepared for the Franco-Belgian invasion of the Ruhr District, leaving the official policy of passive resistance improvized and to a large degree reactive.[33] As often as not, and despite Poincaré's claims to the contrary, Cuno's administration seemed to be swept along by events rather than pursuing any coherent strategy of its own. However, alongside their somewhat laggardly support for the mainstream campaign of nonviolent, passive resistance, members of the government were, from late January, prepared to underwrite a campaign of sabotage in the occupied territories. Soon enough this came to focus on railway communications, for the crux of the Ruhr crisis appeared to rest on whether France would or would not be able to secure and transport supplies of coke and coal from the region. Identifiable government funding of sabotage stood at the equivalent of some 6,000 U.S. dollars in February, but thereafter fell away steadily to some $1,450 by June, and $330 by August.[34] An estimated 78 percent of this expenditure occurred between January and April 1923,[35] and the national authorities more or less washed their hands of the whole business in July.[36]

Money apart, government ministers had mixed feelings about active resistance, and it should be remembered that senior Prussian ministers attended some national Cabinet meetings.[37] The division between national and Prussian interests was less acute than right-wing activists imagined. The chancellor, and his labour minister, Heinrich Brauns of the Center Party, accepted in January that a controlled campaign of sabotage would disrupt Franco-Belgian operations, while serving to rein in any damaging freelance initiatives. To this end a wartime secret agent, Kurt Jahnkes, was put in touch with Colonel von Stülpnagel in the Armed Forces Office, to organize "sabotage as a means of increasing the effectiveness of passive resistance."[38] Cuno and his colleagues, however, were sufficiently embarrassed to maintain an official distance from any such activity, and in March Brauns appeared to wash his hands of any further responsibility.[39]

Matters thereafter were complicated by a particularly serious confrontation between workers and French troops on 31 March at the Krupp casting mills in Essen. Whatever the cause of this confrontation, the standoff at Krupp ended only when the lieutenant commanding the French soldiers ordered his men to fire on the workers, killing thirteen of them and wounding many more.[40] In the emotional aftermath of this so-called Krupp massacre, Cuno declared himself reluctant to leave the nationalist right in the lurch,[41] but this left him caught between two stools. The right-wing terrorists themselves threatened to undermine the moral credibility of the entire, avowedly peaceful, passive resistance campaign and, of course, entertained wider ambitions of destabilizing the Republic itself.[42] The controversy surrounding the Hauenstein affair served, as we have seen, to symbolize the resulting sensitivities of republicans and anti-republicans alike at the high noon of the Ruhr Crisis. Matters came to a head shortly thereafter when saboteurs dynamited a train carrying Belgian soldiers over the Hochfeld Bridge at Duisburg-Friemersheim on 30 June, forcing Cuno publicly to denounce the entire campaign of violence, under domestic and British pressure.[43]

Cuno's subordinates were divided in their opinions, although support tended to be for "semi-active" resistance, which was taken to encompass attacks on the enemy's military installations. Where ministers were associated with active resistance, this could be by virtue of their office, rather than through personal involvement. Wilhelm Groener was a case in point. French interrogation reports identified the Transport Minister as heavily implicated in the political and financial support of terrorism, but the same man was condemned by German hawks at the time for obstructing a significant sabotage campaign until it was "much too late."[44] The historian Michael Ruck agrees that Groener was "opposed to significant sabotage initiatives from the very outset,"[45] and while Severing had doubted the bona fides of the Transport Ministry, his specific accusations focused on the Reichsbahn's Western Directorate, which was located in Elberfeld. It was heavily involved in intelligence gathering in the occupied western territories and, beyond this, undoubtedly developed links with the murky, semi-legal world of sabotage.[46] Indeed, since intelligence gathering and sabotage were frequently carried out by the self-same people,[47] such links were virtually unavoidable, with or without the direct involvement of Berlin.

The role of big business in the active resistance campaign was similarly equivocal, and in this regard the Krupp conglomerate was no exception. The undeniable involvement of certain Krupp officials in intelligence gathering and sabotage activities enraged the French authorities;[48] equally so Krupp's role in the mass breakout of railway freight trains from the Ruhr, pulled by brand new, company-built locomotives and heavily laden with its own products, on the night of 30/31 March.[49] Whether the ensuing confrontation between French soldiers and Krupp workers just hours later was coincidental remains unclear,[50] but the subsequent court martial of Gustav Krupp and several of his senior directors in connection with the killings in Essen made plain French views on the matter. The German industrialists were sentenced to lengthy terms of imprisonment.[51] That said, overall corporate policy at Krupp during 1923 was rather more subtle, being driven by commercial necessities rather than vacuous notions of revanchism.

Such commercial imperatives applied more generally in Ruhr business circles. Immediately after the Franco-Belgian invasion, many of the larger Ruhr conglomerates were minded to sustain reparations deliveries in kind to France and Belgium, and even to find ways of circumventing a decision by Berlin no longer to fund such deliveries. Complex negotiations followed with Allied officials, which envisaged delivery contracts between the French government and individual companies, and also the creation of an *ad hoc* new committee to coordinate these deliveries. This body would consist of mining company representatives and be entirely independent of the erstwhile German regulatory regime. Fritz Thyssen led these discussions on the German side, but Krupp was among the major companies represented at a senior level. It was to take the invocation of wartime legislation by Berlin, including the threat both of fines and the imprisonment of company directors, to put a stop to all this and force Ruhr industry to participate in passive resistance.[52] Thereafter, senior Krupp officials remained pessimistic, with Heinrich Vielhaber predicting gloomily in late January that: "The strength of the French is much greater than ours and they will be able to hold out longer than we can; despite all, we will come to a bad end."[53] And indeed, once passive resistance had collapsed, Krupp was among those companies that agreed terms unilaterally with the French authorities, before a collective settlement on reparations deliveries and taxation was concluded between industry and the Allies in late November.[54]

All in all, therefore, Germany's political and business elites lent the campaign of active resistance qualified and opportunistic support. Paramilitary adventurism initially served to exert additional pressure on the Franco-Belgian forces in the Ruhr, but with the passage of time the moral and political disadvantages inherent in any terrorist campaign became increasingly apparent. As we shall see, by mid 1923 active resistance had few friends beyond the paramilitary adventurers directly involved and as a consequence was in terminal decline.

III

Beyond the issue of who did, or did not, support the active resistance campaign, it would be helpful to gain an impression of its organisation and scale. The most significant and effective espionage and sabotage outfit was the Zentrale Nord, which had been created by Heinz Kölpin at the beginning of the Ruhr crisis. Hauenstein was among the saboteurs connected to the Zentrale. Kölpin had retired in December 1922 as chief intelligence officer for the Sixth Military District, which was headquartered in Münster (Westphalia). As such, he had dedicated most of his energies to the surveillance of far-left organizations, but now, in early 1923, he resolved to deploy his skills "against the *Franzmann*." Kölpin's organization omitted to list itself in the local telephone directory, and even its name may have been no more than a cover for the "Sabotage Section in the Army Command in Münster." The whereabouts of its headquarters remained a closely guarded secret, but is believed to have been in Wesel, where the River Lippe flows into the Rhine, and just beyond the Belgian demarcation line.[55]

The Zentrale Nord defined its primary task as intelligence gathering, warning its volunteer agents "to be reliable, distinguish between rumour and fact, date every observation, and forward it as quickly as possible." Particular attention was paid to Allied troop dispositions and morale, to developments in the mining and railway sectors, left-wing radicalism, and to collaboration of various kinds, including prostitution (!) and genuine love matches.[56] Substantial archival records of this espionage activity survive, but the Zentrale's tally of sabotage (by whichever party) in the occupied territories was more modest. By 16 June it had chronicled a total of thirty-eight incidents in the Rhineland and Ruhr District combined, some of which admittedly were particularly violent and deadly. These included the dynamiting of French-controlled railway tracks (the Régie lines) and the shooting of Allied soldiers, all of which, the Zentrale claimed, was undermining morale in the French and Belgian armies of occupation.[57]

That said, French sources indicated a greater level of sabotage, reporting eighty-six attacks on the railways alone in March, fifty-five in May, and sixty-two in June.[58] However, the French definition of sabotage was eclectic. Spontaneous damage by ordinary railwaymen, looting by civilians, deliberate wrecking by the Allied armies, and a spate of railway disasters of the Régie's own making seem to have been combined with major instances of sabotage to arrive at these higher figures.[59] Accidents were commonplace. Two major collisions occurred on 19 June, for example, as reparations trains, steaming through the night for the German frontier, smashed into stationary trains; a further disaster was precipitated by an incompetent French shunting crew. On 20 June a supplies train was diverted onto a stretch of track from which French soldiers had removed sections of rail, with lamentable results.[60] In addition to this there was a straightforward derailment elsewhere on the railway network, all of which reflected the widespread use by the French authorities either of auxiliary workers ill-versed in the complexities of the railways, or of French railway workers brought in to serve relatively short tours of duty.[61] However, whether Poincaré really wanted to hear about all this is best left to the imagination, and blanket accusations of "sabotage" certainly served to protect the Régie's staff from unpleasant disciplinary consequences. This self-inflicted misery aside, the wrecking of points and signalling equipment by German railwaymen was self-evidently "sabotage" in French eyes. However, these railwaymen were organized within the Free and Catholic trade unions and, alongside the miners, represented the bedrock of the republican, passive resistance campaign. They regarded these same initiatives as a particularly robust example of passive resistance, no doubt distinguishing between republicans rendering the railways unusable in this way, and rightist radicals inflicting death and destruction through bomb attacks and shootings. Active resistance is, indeed, normally taken to encompass the latter, and the Zentrale Nord's tally excluded spontaneous acts by railway workers. All in all, it does appear that the distinction between the two types of resistance could sometimes be relatively subtle, with definition dependent on the eye of the particular beholder.

Whatever problems might arise in defining and quantifying active resistance, it is telling that the Zentrale Nord itself regarded the overall campaign as relatively unsuccessful. The paramilitary activists rapidly discovered that saboteurs were extremely unwelcome in the Ruhr District, and that their operations were stymied both by popular disapproval and official countermeasures. A furious account of the public mood in the city of Bochum, for example, described it as "little Paris, with fraternization in full swing," this including brisk trade between local business interests and the French garrison.[62] In reality, Bochum witnessed a grim struggle between the local population and the French invaders that encompassed almost every dimension of personal, economic, and social life and saw the city's population pay a shocking price for its defiance.[63] Such was typical of the struggle throughout the Ruhr, but the realities of military repression, slow starvation, mass evacuation, and workplace resistance appear to have been too subtle to register on the Zentrale's scale of resistance.

With the exception of a few individual company officials, heavy industry was even more hostile to the activists. On the day after Hauenstein's arrest, the Zentrale complained bitterly that:

> Resistance by the heavy industrialists to our sabotage campaign is assuming increasingly burdensome forms.... All of industry is sick of sabotage activities. They simply lead to repression and restriction of goods traffic and inflict more financial damage on industry than on the French. They would oppose each and every form of sabotage. The Haniel Concern has taken the lead in this regard, Krupp is following suit. At the end of the day we can still carry out sabotage acts in the remotest areas west of the Rhine, where industrial interests are absent, but east of the Rhine they would forbid even one further act. They refuse to be raped by Berlin, still less by wildcat military.
>
> The Gute Hoffnungshütte has strenuously prohibited any participation in sabotage activities by numerous members of staff. All leave has been cancelled. Director Woltmann threatened a former officer with instant dismissal were the slightest suspicion to arise.[64]

The Thyssen conglomerate was singled out by the Zentrale Nord as more helpful, but a month later the saboteurs' overall mood had darkened further. The Zentrale observed that initial support had rapidly evaporated: "Now we are confronting a Franco-German alliance; every 'sensible' German rejects sabotage, everyone seems to be fighting it."[65] And indeed, the sympathetic host population that is required by any successful guerrilla-style operation was patently lacking in the Ruhr District. Activists were isolated and extremely vulnerable to arrest, leaving the Zentrale to complain that: "Saboteurs living near the scene of the crime must quite literally prepare an alibi days in advance."[66] Those terrorists still on the loose felt particularly unloved and unwanted, fearing the Prussian administration and justice system every bit as much as the French. The Prussian authorities alone had arrested twenty-five terrorists, conducted forty-one house searches, offered nine rewards to secure further arrests, and issued an estimated forty to fifty arrest warrants.[67] These warrants had even been passed on to their French counterparts, and right-wing newspapers had indeed accused the Prussian authorities of betraying Schlageter to the French.[68] Even the German Red Cross had been instructed by the Refugee Agency in Münster not to help saboteurs on the run.[69] As for the national government, hopes of forging some kind of anti-Prussian or anti-republican alliance with it seemed to be evaporating. It was accused of contemplating capitulation, while business was yet again condemned for looking to its profits. The labor movement was held in equal disdain, with trade unions and "reds" of every kind vilified for dismissing the activists as: "rogues, nationalist fanatics, swastika types, reactionaries."[70]   ·

This bleak picture was compounded by efficient and sometimes deadly Allied counter-insurgency measures. These were given legal substance through a counter-terrorism decree issued by the Allied commandant, General Jean-Marie Degoutte, on 12 February that made provision for the collective punishment of entire communities.[71] Among other things, it sanctioned draconian curfews, such as that imposed on the towns of Buer and Marl following the killing locally of a Belgian NCO and private soldier. The resulting decree not only forbade traffic movements outside permitted hours, but also 'Going out into the garden, the courtyard etc.; even house windows must remain closed and no one must show themselves, even at a closed window.'[72] Not surprisingly, death and injury to German civilians followed; even lingering on the doorstep chatting to a neighbor after the curfew deadline could prove fatal. When unidentified Germans hurled a rock in revenge at a Belgian motorcar passing through Buer, killing its two occupants, the Belgian commander-in-chief, General de Longueville, reacted to the outrage by extending the curfew for a month, to include the closure of all bars and cafés and a ban on the use of public transport.[73] Furthermore the Allied authorities did not baulk at taking civilians hostage and using them as human shields on troop trains in response to terrorist attacks on the railway system. Each week rotas of such hostages, along with a list of trains on which they were to travel, were drawn up and displayed at town halls.[74] Similarly, local government officials were arrested immediately any explosive device was discovered by the trackside and, as an Allied decree made clear, required to bear a share of the ensuing risk: "The official will remain in the proximity of the explosive device until the arrival of a

specialist, in whose presence he will be ordered to investigate the device himself. Thereafter he is to remain with the specialist during all operations and efforts at removal, until the device is dismantled."[75]

Whatever the Hague Convention might have made of such abuse of civilians' rights, it is small wonder that right-wing terror groups, self-appointed
liberators of the Ruhr and Rhine, were extremely unwelcome visitors in the
occupied territories. Following the bombing of the Hochfeld Bridge and the
draconian reprisals that followed this, the Lord Mayor of Duisburg felt obliged
to apologize for the atrocity in the name of his entire community: "The population sympathizes deeply [with the victims] and condemns without exception such attacks, regardless of the perpetrator. The entire Duisburg press has
repeatedly expressed such feelings in recent days."[76] Whether or not this particular example amounted to special pleading, it appears that Allied countermeasures did indeed succeed in containing the active resistance campaign. But
as the saboteurs themselves, often Freikorps veterans, were forced to observe,
the Allies' task was made very much easier thanks to intense hostility from a
population that did not hold paramilitary adventurers in particularly high es-
teem.[77] Memories of the Ruhr workers' rising of 1920, against which the government had deployed military and paramilitary forces in the region, remained
strong.

As seen, the Prussian authorities were equally hostile, and with the High
Presidencies and Regional Presidencies now firmly in the grip of Social Democrats such as Walther Grützner, or Center Party men (whether trade union-
ists such as Johannes Gronowski or gentry such as Raban von Adelmann), the
outlook for soldiers and adventurers of the old school was always going to be
bleak. The policemen and officials in the occupied territories had no wish
simply to see the French and Belgians replaced by the losers of the 1918 Revolution, and made this very plain in a series of public pronouncements.[78] The
Catholic gentry, it is true, were less delighted with the Revolution and its aftermath,[79] but remained loyal to the Center Party and thus, whether or not by default, to the new Prussian administration.

As for heavy industry, despite a degree of support for active resistance from
particular individuals, commercial survival, as noted, remained the bottom
line for most corporate bosses and their senior staff. The mentality and ethos
of the saboteurs was something apart from that of the polytechnic-trained
works managers of the mining and metallurgical companies, who had often
commenced their careers in the state-owned Prussian fiscal mines.[80] And, contrary to received wisdom, these plant managers (whatever the personal views
of the mine owners themselves) were usually prepared to work with the trade
unions and works councilors within the post-revolutionary legislative framework.[81] Violence and mayhem were far removed from their workplace agendas.

IV

Active resistance, then, amounted to limited sound and fury signifying not very much. However, this is not to deny the enomity of the Battle of the Ruhr. The trauma suffered by western Germany's railwaymen as they refused, almost to a man, to work for the Allied authorities, was indicative of the wider crisis. Over 28,600 railwaymen and 64,000 members of their families were evicted from their homes, and most were subsequently expelled, virtually empty-handed, from the occupied territories. Almost 2,600 railwaymen were arrested, 400 imprisoned, and many more fined. Eight railwaymen were killed and 269 injured.[82] Their status as public servants had complicated the situation, but the industrial working class, and in particular the miners, were equally engaged in a struggle that brought misery, suffering and even death upon themselves and their families. This was part of a complex and exceptionally bleak story which saw the people of the Ruhr go to the wall in order, as they saw it, to defend their Republic against foreign militarism and imperialism. One might quibble over the validity of their beliefs, or over the precise nature of French ambitions at the time, but it appears that the labor movement's retrospective accounts of the crisis were designed, among other things, to pay these workers and blue-collar civil servants due tribute.[83]

The collapse of passive resistance in September 1923 brought further grief in its wake, for during the autumn of 1923 an endgame was played out in western Germany that set the Republic on the road to destruction. In brief, the social and political compacts between industry and labor that had underpinned the post-revolutionary settlement were destroyed in a maelstrom of economic turmoil. Although this complex dimension of the crisis cannot be done justice here, we can conclude that Germany's capitulation in September set in train a crushing if unavoidable blow against the supporters of the German Republic. However, this blow was triggered by remorseless Allied pressure, in the face of which Germany as a whole was unable to sustain and succour the mass campaign of passive resistance in the Ruhr District and thereafter was forced temporarily to abandon the region to its fate. In contrast, the campaign of active sabotage was of marginal significance and the Schlageter myth was exactly that, a myth. Yet despite this, and despite the virtual absence in 1923 of Nazi activity on the Rhine and Ruhr, the Third Reich was later to celebrate Schlageter and the myth of active resistance as the very essence of the struggle. Nazis, after all, had little time for brave, patriotic working-class republicans and, perforce, shoehorned the history of the Ruhr crisis into a bogus teleology from which it has struggled to escape ever since.

Notes

1. *Akten der Reichskanzlei. Weimarer Republik. Das Kabinett Cuno. 22. November 1922 bis 12. August 1923* (Boppard am Rhein, 1968) no. 184, 8 June 1923, 550 n. 2.

2. Staatsarchiv Münster (StAM) Regierung Münster: Besatzung (R Mü Nr Bes) 69, Der Regierungspräsident. Nr 6.I.4. Geheim. Münster, 11 January 1923; Hauptstaatsarchiv Düsseldorf (HStAD) Regierung Düsseldorf. Politische Akten: IV Besatzungsangelegenheiten (R Dü) 16535(5), 17 January 1923; StAM R Mü, VII-Nr 88(93), Münster, 14 March 1923.

3. *Reichskanzlei Cuno,* no. 184, 8 June 1923, 550 n. 2.

4. Ibid.

5. StAM R Mü Nr Bes 69, as in note 2 above.

6. *Reichskanzlei Cuno,* no. 184, 8 June 1923, 550–51.

7. Ibid., 550 note 3.

8. *Reichskanzlei Cuno,* no. 190, 15 June 1923, 570–72.

9. Ibid., 570.

10. For a discussion of the wider context within which Hauenstein operated see: Gerd Krüger, "'Ein Fanal des Widerstandes im Ruhrgebiet'. Das 'Unternehmen Wesel' in der Osternacht des Jahres 1923. Hintergründe eines angeblichen 'Husarenstreiches'," *Mitteilungsblatt des Instituts für soziale Bewegungen* 24 (2000): 95–140.

11. Conan Fischer, *The German Communists and the Rise of Nazism* (Basingstoke, 1991), 54–57.

12. See, for example, Conan Fischer, *The Ruhr Crisis, 1923–1924* (Oxford, 2003), 2–3.

13. See, for example, StAM, Kreis Recklinghausen (Kr Rhn) Nr 269 (71), "Was verlangen wir?" [undated].

14. Thus: StAM Kr Rhn Nr 269(73), "Wollen Sie bitte zuerst umziehen Madame?" [undated]; StAM Kr Rhn Nr 269(70), "Alldeutsche Friedenspolitik" [undated].

15. Quoted in Carl Bergmann, *The History of Reparations* (Boston and New York, 1927), 193.

16. Hans Mommsen, *Die verspielte Freiheit. Der Weg der Republik von Weimar in den Untergang 1918 bis 1933* (Frankfurt am Main, 1990), 142.

17. Stephen A Schuker, *The End of French Predominance in Europe: The Financial Crisis of 1924 and the Adoption of the Dawes Plan* (Chapel Hill, N.C., 1976), 25. More recently, a comparable tone has been adopted by Gerd Krumeich, "Der Ruhrkampf, Krieg im Frieden," *Damals. Das Magazin für Geschichte und Kultur* 35 (December 2003): 36–42.

18. *Reichskanzlei Cuno,* no. 109, 27 March 1923, 342–43.

19. Ibid., 347.

20. Deutsches Bergbau-Museum Bochum, Bergbau Archiv (BBA) Bestand 32: Hibernia Bergwerksgesellschaft, Herne (32)/4371, Abschrift. Protokoll über die Besprechung der Arbeitervertreter der hiesigen 6 Schachtanlagen, mit dem Kommandeur der Besatzungstruppe, Oberst Homgie, vom Infant. Regiment 147 [23. January 1923]; BBA 32/4364, Entschließung, quoted in "So reden Bergarbeiter," *Gelsenkirchener Allgemeine Zeitung,* 26 February 1923; BBA 32/4359, Abschrift. Herrn Direktor Middelmann. 'Heute, den 7. Februar, vormittags …'.

21. HStAD R Dü 16606(97), Abschrift. Ks. Nr. 140 vom 25.9.

22. Cf. *Akten der Reichskanzlei. Weimarer Republik. Die Kabinette Stresemann I u. II, 13. August bis 6.Oktober; 6. Oktober bis 30. November* (Boppard am Rhein, 1978), here *Stresemann I*, no. 91, 29 September 1923, 403–04; BBA 32/4365, "Die Lage im Ruhrgebiet," *Bochumer Zeitung*, 132, 28 September 1923.

23. Quoted in: BBA 32/4364, "Das unmögliche Verlangen. Berliner Stimmen zum passiven Widerstand," *Kölnische Zeitung*, 296, 28. April 1923.

24. Thus: *Reichskanzlei Cuno*, no. 109, 27 March 1923, 346.

25. Eric Sutton, ed. and trans., *Gustav Stresemann: His Diaries, Letters and Papers* (London, 1935), I:66.

26. Lothar Erdmann, *Die Gewerkschaften im Ruhrkampfe. Im Auftrage des Allgemeinen Deutschen Gewerkschaftsbundes* (Berlin, 1924).

27. Vorstand der Vereinigten Sozialdemokratischen Partei Deutschlands (VSPD), ed., *Handbuch für sozialdemokratische Wähler. Der Reichstag 1920 bis 1924* (Berlin, 1924), 30–33, 73–77.

28. Arthur Rosenberg, *Geschichte der Weimarer Republik* (Frankfurt am Main, 1980), 127.

29. For examples of the mood in senior French circles: StAM Findbuch B644 Zentrale Nord, Nachrichtenstelle (ZN) Nr 55, Louis Barthou, *Frankreichs Rechte und Deutschlands Verpflichtungen* (undated), 37; *Akten zur deutschen auswärtigen Politik 1918–1945. Serie A: 1918–1925 Band VI 1 März bis 31. Dezember 1922* (Göttingen, 1988) (Hereafter *AP*, vi) no. 26, 23 May 1923, 55; Stanislas Jeannesson, *Poincaré, la France et la Ruhr (1922–1924). Histoire d'une occupation* (Strasbourg, 1998), 202.

30. Barbara Müller, *Passiver Widerstand im Ruhrkampf. Eine Fallstudie zur gewaltlosen zwischenstaatlichen Konfliktaustragung und ihren Erfolgsbedingungen* (Münster, 1996).

31. Jeannesson, *Poincaré*.

32. As in notes 30 and 31 above. See also: Conan Fischer, *The Ruhr Crisis, 1923–1924* (Oxford, 2003), and Michael Ruck, *Die Freien Gewerkschaften im Ruhrkampf 1923* (Frankfurt am Main, 1986).

33. Fischer, *Ruhr Crisis*, 31–39, 88–93.

34. Krüger, "Fanal," 104, table 1a.

35. Ibid., table 1b.

36. Jeannesson, *Poincaré*, 264–65.

37. Heinrich August Winkler, *Weimar 1918–1933. Die Geschichte der ersten deutschen Demokratie*, 2nd ed. (Munich, 1994), 188–89.

38. Krüger, "Fanal," 101–10. Quote on 110.

39. *Reichskanzlei Cuno*, no. 95, 11 March 1923, 304.

40. Fischer, *Ruhr Crisis*, 145–48.

41. Ruck, *Ruhrkampf*, 397.

42. StAM R Mü Nr Bes 69, Der Regierungspräsident. Nr 6.I.$_4$. Geheim. Münster, 11 January 1923; HStAD R Dü 16535(5), 17 January 1923.

43. Jeannesson, *Poincaré*, 264–65.

44. French reports cited in: Jeannesson, *Poincaré*, 263. Condemnation of Groener by the German right in: Ruck, *Ruhrkampf*, 397.

45. Ruck, *Ruhrkampf*, 397–98.

46. *Reichskanzlei Cuno*, no. 184, 8 June 1923, 550 n. 2.

47. StAM ZN, Findbuch, "Vorbemerkung"; StAM ZN Nr 1(25–26), Undated.

48. Krüger, "Fanal," 99–100, 101–02; Ruck, *Ruhrkampf*, 397.

49. Krüger, "Fanal," esp. 125–27.

50. Fischer, *Ruhr Crisis*, 166–67.

51. BBA 32/4364, "Eine Justizkomödie," *Kölnische Zeitung*, 300, 1 May 1923; Jeannesson, *Poincaré*, 262; Alfred Baedeker, *Jahrbuch für den Oberbergamtsbezirk Dortmund 1922/25* (Essen, 1925), 226, 243; cf. Krüger, "Fanal," 128–31.

52. A full account can be found in: Fischer, *Ruhr Crisis*, 50–56.

53. Gerald D. Feldman, *The Great Disorder: Politics, Economics, and Society in the German Inflation, 1914–1924* (New York, 1997), 636.

54. Hans Spethmann, *Zwölf Jahre Ruhrbergbau. Aus seiner Geschichte von Kriegsanfang bis sum Franzosenabmarsch 1914 bis 1925, iii. Der Ruhrkampf 1923 bis 1925 in seinen Leitlinien* (Berlin, 1929), 234–39, 390–92.

55. StAM ZN, Findbuch, "Vorbemerkung"; StAM ZN Nr 1(25–26), Undated.

56. StAM ZN Nr 1(25–26), Betrifft Militärisches. Richtlinien für Meldungen. Undated; ZN Nr 21(48), P.S.M. Pr. Liste: Mädchen. 17 July [1923]; ZN Nr 21(49), P.S.M. Pr. Liste: Verschiedenes. 17 July 1923; ZN Nr 21, P.S.M. Pr. Liste: Verschiedenes, Mädchen. 7 August 1923.

57. StAM ZN Nr 3, Bericht zu dem Unternehmen "Essen West." Mülheim-Ruhr, 11 August 1923.

58. Jeannesson, *Poincaré*, 262.

59. *Reichskanzlei Cuno*, no. 95, 11 March 1923, 304; no. 165, 23 May 1923, 503; HStAD R Dü 16185(45), 20 February 1923.

60. StAM R Mü Nr Bes 65, Deutsche Reichsbahn. Generalbetriebsleitung West. Lagebericht, Elberfeld, 25 June 1923, 4.

61. *Reichskanzlei Cuno*, no. 165, 23 May 1923, 503.

62. StAM ZN Nr 30(28), Bericht, 15 April 1923.

63. Thus: HStAD R Dü 16606(121), April 1923; HStAD Industrie- und Handelskammer. 2. Ruhrbesetzung. Passiver Widerstand (henceforward RW 49)/60 Band I(48), received 5 March 1923; StAM Provinzialstelle für Landaufenthalt (henceforward PfL) Nr 24, Magistrat der Stadt Bochum, Jugendamt. Tageb. La VIIIb. Bochum, 3 February 1923; StAM PfL Nr 24, Stadt Bochum, Dienststelle VIIIb, Bochum, 6 March 1923; StAM ZN Nr 24(3), 31 May 1923.

64. StAM ZN Nr 1, Z.N., Notiz. "Der Widerstand Grossindustriellen gegen unsere S-Tätigkeit...," 13 May 1923.

65. StAM ZN Nr 1, Zentrale Nord No 152. Bedrängte Lage, 5 June 1923. See also: StAM ZN Nr 1, Zentrale Nord No 171, Nachtrag zu "Bedrängte Lage" no. 152 v. 5.6.23, 23 June 1923.

66. Ibid.

67. Ibid.

68. *Reichskanzlei Cuno*, no. 184, 8 June 1923, 550 n. 3.

69. As note 65 above.

70. Ibid.

71. HStAD R Dü 17062(6V&R), 13 February 1923.

72. StAM R Mü Nr Bes 88, Der Magistrat. Abteilung Vd Nr. 13. Buer i.W., 28 June 1923. See also StAM R Mü Nr Bes 19, Belgische Ruhr-Armee. Generalstab. Im Hauptquartier zu Sterkrade, 21 June 1923.

73. StAM R Mü Nr Bes 19, Der Generalleutnant de Longueville, Kommandant der belg. Ruhrabteilung. Bottrop, 3 July 1923.

74. StAM R Mü Nr Bes 21, Cantonement de Gladbeck. Etat Major III/23. Objet: Trains Voyageurs-Otages. Gladbeck, 7 July 1923; cf. HStAD R Dü 16567(15), 4 August 1923; StAM R Mü Nr Bes 19, Der Oberbürgermeister Besatzungsamt. Betr. Verwendung von Geiseln. Bottrop, 25 September 1923.

75. HStAD R Dü 16170(21), 27 June 1923. See also: HStAD R Dü 16170(23), 14 June 1923.

76. HStAD R Dü 16224(197), 14 July 1923.

77. As note 65 above. See also: Krüger, "Fanal," 131–32.

78. See note 2 above.

79. Larry Eugene Jones, "Catholic Conservatives in the Weimar Republic; The Politics of the Rhenish-Westphalian Aristocracy, 1918–1933," *German History* 18, no. 1 (2000): 60–70.

80. See, inter alia, Michael Fessner, "Rheinisch-Westfälische Hüttenschule zu Bochum" *Beiträge zur Geschichte Dortmunds und der Grafschaft Mark* 80 (1989): 99–125.

81. Thus: Conan Fischer, "Arbeitgeber, Arbeitnehmer und das Scheitern des passiven Widerstands 1923 im Ruhrgebiet," *Mitteilungsblatt des Instituts für soziale Bewegungen* 26 (2001): 89–104; Conan Fischer, "Continuity and Change in Post-Wilhelmine Germany: From the 1918 Revolution to the Ruhr Crisis," in *Wilhelminism and Its Legacies: German Modernities, Imperialism, and the Meanings of Reform, 1890–1930*, ed., Geoff Eley and James Retallack (New York, Oxford, 2003), 202–18.

82. StAM R Mü Nr Bes 65, Deutsche Reichsbahn. Generalbetriebsleitung West. Lagebericht Nr 98. Anlage. Elberfeld, 12 July 1923; Deutsche Reichsbahn. Generalbetriebsleitung West. Lagebericht. Elberfeld, 1 August 1923, 2, Zahlenmässige Übersicht …; Deutsche Reichsbahn. Generalbetriebsleitung West. Lagebericht Nr 145. Elberfeld, 13 September 1923, 2, Zahlenmässige Übersicht …; Deutsche Reichsbahn. Generalbetriebsleitung West. Lagebericht. Elberfeld, 23 October 1923, 2, Zahlenmässige Übersicht …

83. See notes 26 and 27 above.

CHAPTER 3

Political Violence, *Gesinnung,* and the Courts in Late Weimar Berlin

Pamela E. Swett

On October 7, 1931, at around 1 a.m., a number of young people aligned with the radical left approached a Nazi bar on a busy street in the Berlin district of Schöneberg. One of the Communists was hit in the face by a pub patron, and since the young Communists were far outnumbered, they fled. Later a metal worker S. was attacked on the same street by four young Communists—one of whom allegedly yelled "Yeah, you're a Nazi," chased down the metal worker, knocked him to the ground, and continued to beat the man until police arrived. A female witness pointed out the main attacker as H. S., a nineteen-year-old unemployed butcher.[1] H. S. was convicted of inflicting bodily injury with a dangerous weapon (boot heel) and sentenced to a three-month imprisonment.[2]

This story is not a unique one for Berlin in the early 1930s. Political violence, ranging from individual attacks like this one to large-scale brawls and riots, had become such an everyday occurrence on city streets that most in the capital saw in it the sign of a republic in its death throes. But how did the judiciary respond to the violence? Given the Weimar justice system's notorious leniency toward right-wing radicals and harsh sentencing of the radical left, we might well assume that the trials of those involved were clear-cut affairs and that the decisions and sentencing practices provide uniform examples of *Klassenjustiz.*[3] Though the charge of imbalance still stands, this chapter will demonstrate that a whole host of officials were involved in making subtle and complex determinations about the defendants that, far from relying on party affiliation alone, depended on carefully weighed information about the defendants' ethical makeup, behavior, and lifestyle.

This essay will explore the murky terrain of such deliberations, looking first at the social workers assigned to the cases of juvenile defendants, then at the judges who presided in their cases, and finally to the larger body of laws and values that informed their judgments. Social workers, who in some cases had followed the young men and their families for years prior to arrest, made an important contribution to the judicial process because they were asked to submit appraisals of young defendants. The introduction of these reports in the mid-1920s represented a change both to youth welfare policies and to the Weimar justice system, and it appears from judicial documents that case workers' views were indeed taken seriously at the sentencing stage.[4] Through the evaluations of young criminals and their lifestyles, we learn how welfare officials assessed the causes of radicalism. The decisions of the judges in these cases also demonstrate the limits and legitimacy of political violence in this society. These two groups were quite different: the social workers were often women and the majority tended to be Social Democrats.[5] The judicial officials were older men who represented a conservative profession and elite social rank.[6] Nonetheless, members of both groups accepted the violence to some extent as natural, thereby affording it some level of legitimacy as a political strategy. The ramifications of such a claim are, of course, important for understanding the relative ease with which the institutionalization of violence took place in the weeks following the naming of the first Hitler-led cabinet.

Street Fighters and Welfare Workers

The participants in this violence, mostly men in their late teens and twenties, were not simply marionettes controlled by party bosses on the far left (KPD) and far right (NSDAP), nor were they driven chiefly by those parties' long-range ideological goals. Rather, they were taking stock of their own positions within their families and communities, and choosing for themselves the best course of action to address the personal crises they were facing. Each individual identified and prioritized his own set of concerns, which ranged from underemployment and unemployment, to generational and gender conflicts, and the increasing bureaucratization of daily life in a modern metropolis. The solutions they found to these personal and local crises were not always violent, but sometimes they were. For a series of complicated reasons, some young men in this society perceived violence to be a legitimate, logical strategy for laying claim to masculine power and authority in their families and communities.[7]

That such violence was largely homespun and impromptu in nature does not mean, however, that such actions were without structure or significance to a wider audience. Street fighting may not have been driven by systematic ideological reasoning or coordinated by party bosses, but it did have an internal logic that was understood and accepted by the participants. There were common causes for attacks: some fights found their origins in arguments about money, others in personal jealousies. Territorial transgression was one of the most common provocations, and revenge for earlier physical and nonphysical acts of aggression was similarly prevalent. The sites of violent events also conformed to certain patterns. Besides the large campaign rally sites and meeting halls, neighborhood landmarks ranked high as trouble spots. Transportation nodes, neighborhood pubs, and central squares all exhibited social and political significance as central sites in the upheaval.[8] In short, acts of violence were structured around ritualized displays of bravery based on commonly held assumptions about the defense of "turf," comrades, and communities. Participants even expected that rules of "fair play" would be followed.

Though the Weimar *Sozialstaat* was hampered from its infancy by economic upheaval and ideological debates about the role of state intervention in people's personal lives, we can see the tangible consequences of Weimar's welfare legislation when we look at Berlin's young radicals.[9] These men, struggling for independence and control over their own lives, had often been under the long-term care of state or private assistance agencies. Unfortunately, the harder they tried to free themselves from their difficult circumstances through radical behavior, the more embroiled many of them became in economic and legal problems which hindered their escape. When viewed together, the reports sent at the requests of the criminal courts in Berlin during the preparation for trial and during appeal or application for early release illustrate quite dramatically the extent of the devastation wrought by over a decade of upheaval and the particular intensification of economic, generational, and gender crises during the Depression era. These reports also provide one view of how non-participants—in this case state representatives who had at least a modicum of personal contact with the accused—viewed the violence.

Not surprisingly, almost all of these young defendants had faced difficulties finding stable employment. The vast majority of the men were not, however, unskilled. Many had learned a trade, often completing long-term apprenticeships with positive evaluations by their masters, only to have problems finding employment in their chosen fields. The young defendant described at the outset of this chapter had fulfilled a three-year apprenticeship as a butcher, but had been let go from the two positions he found thereafter owing to a shortage of work during the Depression.[10] One nineteen-year-old from Schöneberg had learned from his father how to build decorative moldings, yet lasting employment was elusive. He held twelve different positions in 1929 and the first half of 1930 before joining the ranks of the unemployed, where he had remained for seven months at the time of the report.[11] A twenty-year-old born outside the city had similar problems. At age fifteen he had entered a cabinetmaking apprenticeship. After years of training he received a "very good" assessment on his exams and scored well in an additional training course for cabinetmakers. However, entering the job market in 1929, he never secured employment in his area of expertise. He worked for a time as an unskilled laborer, but was eventually laid off. In the following months he was employed as a household servant, Christmas-tree salesman, and messenger. By May 1930 he was again without a job.[12]

By 1929, of course, unemployment in Berlin was a mass phenomenon with over 600,000 registered jobless in a city of close to four million inhabitants. In assessing the street fighters, welfare workers noted that these young men were not the only ones who were unable to sustain steady employment. Living at home out of financial necessity was the common pattern, as all family members pooled their resources in an attempt to make ends meet. In one family the twenty-year-old son who was in trouble with the law, though trained as a metal grinder, had been unemployed for six months. His father, who had the same occupation, had lost his job at about the same time. Since his firing, however, the father had procured temporary work, which was crucial since his was the only paid employment among the five adults in this family of seven.[13] It is also clear from the reports that this level of poverty and instability was not new to many of these families. Instead the young welfare clients-turned-criminal defendants had been monitored by the youth office throughout their childhoods, and the long-term commitment of Weimar's extensive welfare system becomes evident in their stories. The family of one boy had been assisted since 1924. When he was eleven, he and his sisters were found begging. The oldest boy spent the next three years at a state-run children's facility in the countryside, until he was old enough to go to work. At the time the report was filed in 1931, two younger siblings still lived in a group home in a nearby town, and the family's youngest child lived with foster parents.[14]

The long shadow of World War One is particularly evident in the caseworkers' assessments. Many fathers were missing from these families, and single mothers frequently suffered from work-related diseases or were debilitated by "nerves." H.S., whose crime began this chapter, was an orphan. His father fell on the battlefield in 1914, and his mother had died by war's end. He was only six and was shuttled among relatives in the years that followed.[15] For those fathers still present, alcoholism, possibly linked to war service, was another common problem that limited the chances for childhood stability. One caseworker even began her essay by noting the uniqueness of her subject's father, who "is not a drinker."[16] For a variety of reasons, therefore, the older sons and daughters in a large number of families were expected to take on greater responsibility, and their incomes and participation in family matters were critical. The inability to contribute in these ways owing to unemployment and/or political involvement led to a great sense of failure or resentment among some young people, leading to tension within families, and concern about radical youth among state officials.

The judges expected the welfare workers to use their rather intimate information about past and current conditions within their clients' families to assess whether the young man in question had a criminal character or had been simply "politically misled."[17] While the extent of one's poverty did play a role in this decision, welfare workers also considered the young man's intellectual level and reputation in his family and community. The authors drew their conclusions about this last category from views offered by relatives, friends, and neighbors of the accused. The first questions were directed toward the parents and focused on behavior at home and whether the subject donated any of his income or weekly public assistance to the household budget. Contributing to family expenses was considered an important sign of sociability and respect for elders. It also indicated the man did not spend his money foolishly on alcohol or women. Welfare workers also asked whether the son posed discipline problems for his parents.[18] Maternal devotion may have inspired many positive reviews of defendants, but remaining tight-lipped was likely also a strategy to maintain family dignity, privacy, and to ensure that public assistance would not be withdrawn.

The caseworkers then turned to other apartment house residents. The most convenient interviewees, and perhaps the most willing when the caseworker turned up at the defendant's address, were often the building superintendents—recognized experts on residents' comings and goings. The scope of the investigations makes it clear that the reputations of all family members were important in the assessment of the individual. The parents of one defendant remarked that they were satisfied with his behavior. As the caseworker explained: "They were dissatisfied only with his political engagement, which they could not persuade him to give up. G. donates his public assistance to the house, keeping only two or three marks for himself." When asked about G.'s behavior in the building, the superintendent at 9 Max Street agreed that "he is respectful and polite to his parents and the other residents. [The superintendent]," concluded the caseworker, "also knew his grandparents to be hardworking and honest people."[19]

At first it is surprising that these reviews from the youth bureau did not dwell on party affiliations. But to those writing the reports, all violent activity, whether associated with the far left or the far right, fell under the category of "radicalism." The absence of references to specific organizations in these evaluations is in marked contrast to the reports filed by the police in the same cases. In police reports, a suspect's organizational membership was listed alongside the most basic information, including date of birth, address, and marital and employment status. The difference can be explained by the two separate understandings of the men's behavior. For the police, Communist activities were presumed to be criminal, whereas involvement in the Nazi and Social Democratic parties or paramilitary organizations was presumed to be political.[20] It was crucial, therefore, to make specific reference to the organizational affiliation of the suspect. For the often Social Democratic welfare workers in Berlin, this bifurcation did not apply. In their minds all radicalism was first and foremost antisocial. Therefore arriving at an assessment of the person's overall character (as either criminal or not) meant weighing antisocial political behavior against the client's other social roles, as family member, worker, and neighbor.

Though the individual's political affiliations and ideological positions were not discussed in the welfare reports, in a great number of cases the client's medical history and bodily attributes were noted, including major childhood diseases suffered by the subject, surgeries, and accidental injuries. In addition, other less specific physical qualities of the defendant were also considered: size, level of muscular fitness, and any miscellaneous infirmities such as a limp.[21] Attention to physical characteristics can be seen as illustrative of the trend dating back to the last decades of the nineteenth century of finding biological roots for criminal behavior.[22] Though the theories of Cesare Lombroso and others were certainly discussed, revised, and adapted by many in the German criminal justice system, the language of biological degeneracy does not play a primary role in these reports. Instead radicalism found its roots in the material and moral disadvantages experienced by many of these men, disadvantages that were intensified by physical shortcomings or found their manifestations in certain illnesses. If the accused was a healthy, robust looking young man, the general tenor of the report improved, just as it did for those who lived in an orderly apartment or were well respected by family members and neighbors alike.

Lastly, the mental capacity of the defendant came under scrutiny. Some clients did impress their caseworkers as "mentally well developed," though, more often than not, the young person was seen as intellectually stunted. Codefendants in one case elicited different reactions from the same welfare investigator. Twenty-one-year-old L. made a "good impression" as a consistently employed unskilled worker. Yet he was assessed as lacking strong mental capacity.[23] For L., and many others like him, the fact that he was not believed capable of making his own decisions meant that he would not be held fully responsible for his actions. In other words, he was not thought to possess a "criminal nature." Instead his caseworker concluded that he simply had been misled. In this and other similar cases the report's author held out hope that if the client could extricate himself from the bad influence of friends, who "held him to drinking and loitering about," his radical activism would cease.[24] As in other cases where the caseworker believed the young man had been duped, probation was recommended for L. This decision was undoubtedly welcomed by the defendant. However, it is also easy to see how the assessment of L. and others like him fit the stereotype of radicals, especially Communists, in Berlin. As the judge in L.'s trial concluded: "Due to his age and his severe lack of judgment," the accused was vulnerable to the "misuse" of conspiring local leaders.[25] The individual agency of these men and any political motiva-

tions they may have held—be they revolutionary or focused on local change—
were overlooked because of presumptions about the poor and the "string-
pullers" of the KPD.

His partner in crime, the fifteen-year-old worker Z., also had a job, contributed financially to the household, but "made an intelligent impression."[26]
The actions of those like Z., who made a good impression because they did
"not look demoralized," had employment, and seemed able to reason sufficiently, were much more difficult for the welfare officials to analyze. Usually
their responsibility was simply downplayed, as in the case of another young
defendant V. His caseworker described him as a "calm and orderly youth" who
was to be "viewed as a hanger-on [Mitläufer]." The report concerning V. concluded: "based on his character and in light of his previous good behavior it
can be assumed with confidence that he will behave well in the future and will
prove worthy of probation."[27] For young men like Z. and V., it was not on
grounds of mental naiveté that probation was recommended. Rather, it was
the assessment of their "firm characters" that deflected charges of criminal
"string-puller" and led the welfare authorities to assume that their law-breaking
behavior was simply a fluke.

In general, Berlin's welfare workers were compassionate in their assessments of youthful defendants and characterized very few as willful criminals.
Perhaps their willingness to seek milder punishments was a result of witness-
ing firsthand the poverty and instability under which many of Berlin's workers suffered in these years. These low-level state representatives, who likely
supported the social justice platform of the Weimar Republic, still largely believed that their services could make the difference. Whatever the reason, however, their compassion harbored a specific understanding of radicalism which
failed to identify its true causes. Though they pointed to unemployment and
squalor, they saw only unlucky misfits. Where they found political engagement, they blamed a lack of intelligence and bad friends.

Gesinnung and Radicalism

It is clear that welfare administrators were not asked to judge the violent act
itself. What the defendant had actually done to find himself in such a legal
predicament was never entered into the report. The caseworkers were asked
specifically to evaluate the individual and not the deed. Caseworkers believed
that knowing an individual's background, current standard of living, personal
relationships, physical makeup, and mental ability allowed them to form a
picture of the person's character. This alone, when viewed within the mitigating context of the highly charged political atmosphere of early 1930s Berlin,
led the caseworkers to the recommendations for sentencing that ended the

reports. Turning to the judges serving in these trials, it is clear that the legal decisions handed down also reflected this emphasis on the circumstances surrounding the violent incident, in particular the defendant's character and the political climate, and not the crime itself. By issuing judgments and sentences in this way, judges not only showed tolerance for certain types of violence, they also legitimized those violent acts as acceptable political behavior. Support for this culture of radicalism, therefore, came from circles beyond the relatively small numbers of participants in street violence.

The lack of interest in the illegal act itself is explained not solely by biological understandings of criminal behavior. It also illustrates the importance in German legal tradition attributed to the perpetrator's *Gesinnung*. This concept is not easily translatable and is most frequently used to describe a person's political leanings or beliefs, but in German criminal law it had a more complicated meaning; most simply put it described a person's ethical framework. It was, however, used by some legal scholars interchangeably with the word personality or character. The concept was not new to the Weimar era, but can be traced back in legal discussions predating unification. *Gesinnung's* significance was codified in the 15 May 1871 Criminal Code (*Strafgesetzbuch*, StGB) under §20, which stated that when the law demanded confinement in a penitentiary or fortress, penitentiary could only be chosen when the crime was committed from *"ehrlosen Gesinnung"* (dishononorable character or convictions). Attempts were made to reform the StGB in 1909 and 1913, and the process got underway again shortly after peace was declared in 1918, leading to numerous drafts throughout the 1920s. Though the debate and attempts at reform kept up throughout the republican period, no new version of the criminal code went into effect.[28] Even though *Gesinnung* appears only in this one instance in the 1871 StGB, its significance was far greater, leading to a number of treatises on this elusive concept and reworkings of the statute in each successive draft. As one judicial scholar explained in 1903, "this principle *[Gesinnung]* works like a central nerve throughout all main sections of the criminal law system and into its most outlying periphery."[29]

Writing in 1909, but drawing on sources that date as far back as the 1820s, law professor Philipp Allfeld began his book on *Gesinnung* by explaining that in the future: "The crime as such should not be taken into consideration less than was previously the case, [but] it should no longer be at all decisive in the determination of the degree of punishment. The law and judge should only look at the individual criminal, the punishment should fit this alone."[30] Allfeld and those reform-minded jurists who agreed with him reasoned that punishing a criminal was not about retribution for the act.[31] Rather, the type and length of punishment served as a proactive measure to guard society against future crime. Therefore, to determine a suitable punishment, one needed to assess how much of a threat the criminal posed to his or her community. In

Allfeld's words: "What the criminal has done cannot be decisive, rather what he is capable of doing in the future; the perpetrated act can only be a basis for arriving at this prognosis."[32]

As Nikolaus Wachsmann has pointed out, debate raged about what to do with those individuals judged as continued threats to society, but there were also more fundamental questions at hand: what counted as a "dishonorable character?" Did such judgments even belong in the courtroom?[33] Put most simply, the difference between honorable and dishonorable was that those who were honorable committed their crimes out of deeply held religious or political beliefs, while those who were dishonorable, and thereby deserving of harsher punishment, had acted out of a selfish and contemptible nature.[34] To some extent the existence of a separate "fortress" imprisonment for honorable crimes was a holdover from the age of the duel. Yet the reasoning behind the statute remained. A few judges in the 1920s, including the Social Democrat Gustav Radbruch, questioned the statute, concluding that the "ethical evaluation of the perpetrator's honor" should be replaced by a "criminal-psychological factual assessment" of the individual's actions and motives. Most scholars and judges, however, continued to fine-tune the uses and meaning of *Gesinnung* itself. Hans Lipmann argued in 1930, following directly from previous writers like Allfeld, that reform was needed to end the overreliance on *Gesinnung* that had led to two separate prisons over which one door read "Pressure and Bending of Wills" while the other read "Respect for [political and religious] Convictions."[35] According to Lipmann, *Gesinnung* would still have a place in this unified prison system, but it would be limited to determining the length of a prison stay.[36] By the 1927 draft, which also failed to be ratified, the wording had been made more positive and less specific to religious or political ideals, yet the focus on the perpetrator's character was still present. Instead of penitentiary, prison confinement was the appropriate judgment if the perpetrator had acted purely out of commendable motives and the act was not particularly "reprehensible" in the way it was carried out or in its consequences.[37]

The difficulty came when trying to reconcile such reasoning with the political crimes of the late 1920s and early 1930s. The assembly hall brawls between Communists and Nazis that followed provocative statements by the evening's speaker or taunting from within the audience sometimes had hundreds of participants. The combatants in these altercations often went free or were given minimal sentences. Though scholars are familiar with the conservatism of the courts that contributed to the particular leniency shown right-wing activists, the judges' concern with *Gesinnung* made it difficult to convict violent radicals of any color. In these large melées it was often impossible to determine who was responsible for instigating the fight. *Gesinnung* is a purely individual trait, not one that can be easily applied to crowds. Even when certain individuals could be targeted for investigation, the intent of the accused's actions were very difficult to ascertain.[38] The police witnesses made up a small minority of the audience and were frequently unable to tell who had struck the first blow or who was acting in self-defense. Similarly, it was not always apparent if the intent was to disrupt the meeting alone or cause real bodily harm to one's adversaries.

In January 1932, for example, unemployed workers in Berlin staged demonstrations at various locations around the city to protest cuts in welfare benefits that were to take effect on February 1. About 150 Nazis showed up at one of the rallies in Berlin-Neukölln, claiming later that they had been invited, since the posters for the event described one of the speakers' topics as the "National Socialist Campaign of Terror." Before the rally got underway, a fight broke out between members of both sides. Coal shovels and chair legs were the primary weapons used in the brawl, which erupted on the front lawn of the assembly hall and subsequently spilled into the street as Communists tried to block the growing Nazi crowd from the entrance to the site. Twenty-four people were arrested, only four of whom were Communists. The police doubted the large Nazi presence had been a coincidence and described the incident as a "planned action" to "break up the rally through force...."[39] In the trial that followed, two Nazis, a nineteen- and twenty-two-year-old, were both given six-month sentences for felony disturbance of the peace.

On appeal, however, both were set free. In its judgment the court presented two arguments as to why the original decision could not stand. First, the judge recognized that the provocative statement by a Nazi: "We want to show that the SA [Stormtroopers] still lives in Neukölln" implied the desire "to act violently against the Communists," but noted that one individual's statement did not prove that "the other Nazis had this same intention and that they mutually wanted to assault the Communists." Second, because most of the fighting took place outside the meeting hall, and the demonstration went on regardless of the unrest, it could not be proven that the actions of the Nazis had disrupted the political event.[40] In other words, the specific intentions of the two Nazis on trial were not clear, and the fighting could not even be ruled political, since the political event—the rally by the unemployed—was able to proceed despite the disruption at the outset. Sympathies for the Nazi cause may have made this decision easier to hand down, but similar criteria were applied in other cases.[41]

In a less dramatic trial, a member of the Social Democratic mass organization, the Iron Front, was charged with leading a number of his comrades in the threatening and physical mishandling of three Nazis. It was a typical story in that members of both sides were returning home from their respective party pubs in Berlin when a tussle broke out after midnight. Witnesses identified a thirty-year-old, previously convicted metal fitter as the instigator. Men judged to be leaders or instigators of violence who had "misused" or "misled" their innocent followers were regarded as especially dangerous to society and were charged with the additional crime of "ringleader," which required a lengthier prison sentence. His primary defense was the commonly used excuse that he was too drunk to have been involved in any activity that took physical coordination, like a fight. He claimed to have finished off a bottle of wine (in celebration of a friend's birthday and the republican Constitution Day), twenty to thirty small glasses of beer, and a number of shots of schnapps.[42] He was found innocent of all charges and did not even receive a fine for his behavior. The court decided that though he was at least guilty of threatening the Nazis, medical records showing the defendant suffered from a weak heart, combined with his undisputed drunkenness, "without having had anything to eat," meant either that he had not participated in the violence or that his true noncriminal *Gesinnung* was clouded by his intoxication.

Though drunkenness was not an uncommon defense, the most frequently cited mitigating factor when assessing violent behavior was the age of the defendant. Youngsters, especially if they were first time offenders, were treated with more lenience than those considered old enough to know better. Like their counterparts in the welfare bureaus, officers of the courts saw these young men in part as victims themselves of clever older party leaders and seasoned veterans of neighborhood battles. For a serious riot in which numerous injuries resulted, the sixteen-year-old Communist defendant received three months imprisonment, which was then reduced on appeal to a three-year suspended sentence. This decision was not based entirely on his age. In fact, the trial record reads that there was "no doubt that at the time of the incident he was able, according to his mental and moral development, to see that his was an unlawful act and to voice his will. The court is, however, of the opinion that the defendant W.D. can be improved and committed the crime primarily under the influence of his brother and older like-minded comrades."[43] This judgment offers further proof that *Gesinnung*, rather than biology, was seen as the individual's most basic trait in assessing crime. W.D.'s character was presumed to be mutable. He was thought to have been persuaded by others to act out of character but was deemed capable of learning from this error. Moreover, the judges clearly understood how powerful camaraderie had become to many young males in the capital. Though it is not likely that W. D. would have held the exact same conception of comradeship as the gentlemen on the bench, there was enough in common for the strength of these bonds in this case and others to be recognized as a natural, respectable force, central to a healthy, masculine identity. As such, violent acts committed under this powerful bond were not considered a sign of dishonorable convictions or a criminal character.[44]

Links between violence, comradeship, and *Gesinnung* come up in another case in which two Nazi Stormtroopers beat a young Social Democrat and member of the Reichsbanner republican defense league (RB) on his way to work early one morning. The young RB apprentice had been grabbed on the street, punched in the face, and then dragged by a moving car while being beaten from inside with a table leg. The court had a difficult time weighing two contradictory elements in this case. They accepted the chief defendant G.'s explanation for why he had been so brutal: "In sentencing, the court has allowed for milder punishment, since as a result of [the local shooting death of another Nazi] on the previous night, great excitement existed. G., in particular, is still a young person, who could not remain uninfluenced by the death of his friend Thielsch." It was understandable in the court's opinion for the SA man to seek physical revenge for the death of his comrade. Had he chosen a Communist in this neighborhood where Thielsch had been killed by KPD members, the sentencing may have been lighter. The tumultuous political climate in Berlin, not G.'s character, was to blame for his use of violence. But even for conservative judges there were limits to what would be tolerated. "Nevertheless," argued the judge, "the political incitement must not go so far, that a completely innocent person, unknown to the defendant, can be assaulted on his way to work because the insignia he wears is hated by the accused."[45] In this case, the defendant stepped beyond those bounds by selecting a victim who had played no part in the previous evening's attack. It was this element of the case, which showed the defendant's character to be morally suspect and a danger to others.[46]

There were other limits to what the courts would accept, and these followed the same sort of moral standards which the street fighters used to order their own conduct. The courts and street fighters alike found it especially offensive, for example, to attack a small force with a much larger one, to victimize women, or to attack in the dark without warning. Incidents in which men transgressed these boundaries existed, but we know that in such cases the perpetrators were held accountable in the courts and criticized in local and national newspapers of all political stripes as both cowardly and feminine.[47] It is worth restating, however, that the basic use of violence as a political strategy was not itself routinely questioned within these communities or in the courts.

One final case illustrates these points quite clearly, demonstrating in particular how street fighters and the officers of the court operated under the same standards of behavior—standards that regulated and legitimized male violence. In January 1932, a thirty-nine-year-old married mechanic and the father of three children, who had no related prior convictions was sentenced to nine months in prison for his pivotal role in a riot and physical assault. Though one man was badly beaten, no gunshots were fired, and no deaths occurred, making this sentence a heavy one even under the stricter legislation against political violence introduced in March 1931 by presidential decree. Like many incidents of street violence in Berlin, this one unfolded during the intensity of a political campaign. In August 1931, a statewide referendum was held on the question of whether the Prussian parliament should be dissolved.

The NSDAP made the campaign in favor of dissolution a major priority, and on the day before the vote party sections throughout Berlin were busy circulating propaganda in favor of the measure.

The accused worker P. S. had been a member of the NSDAP from its very beginnings. Early in 1931, however, he severed his ties with the party and declined to join other political organizations. Between ten and eleven o'clock on the evening before the vote, a small scuffle broke out in Berlin-Bohnsdorf between the propaganda troops of the NSDAP and the local Communists who had been meeting in a pub. One of the Nazis involved in the initial incident left to round up more of his comrades. When they first returned to the scene, everything seemed calm. Soon a number of Communists came out of their pub and others appeared from the side streets. The partyless defendant S. was among this growing crowd and after drawing attention by blowing a whistle, he walked over to the encircled Nazis and identified, by name, the leader of the local NSDAP troop. He then pointed out another as the party's treasurer, and fingered a third as "the jerk who … ruined my business." Next he allegedly encouraged the Communists to attack, which they did using canes and fence poles. The accused pleaded not guilty to all charges stemming from the incident, including the weighty charge of instigator.[48]

However, since a number of witnesses identified S. as having led the assault and as having actively participated in the beating of at least one man, he was convicted on all counts. The court recognized that he had not been arrested since 1920 and as usual took into account the high level of "political excitement" due to the impending vote. To this point the court's decision reads like hundreds of others in Berlin during this period. However, the judge then turned to the reason for handing down the harsh sentence of nine months imprisonment at Plötzensee to this family man. S. was guilty, explained the judge, of specific "reprehensible actions" in this conflict. The reference here was not to the fact that S. held down one Nazi, so that a cohort could beat the restrained man with a fence pole. Rather, the convicted P. S. deserved an especially severe punishment, "since he led the members of one party, to which he admittedly did not belong, to assault his former party comrades and used his prior knowledge of the organization to these ends."[49] The lengthy sentence reflected the court's disgust with his failure to participate within acceptable boundaries. It was certainly not illegal to participate politically without officially joining a party or organization, but for this judge it signaled perhaps a disingenuous or cowardly personality—at the very least it was a sign that he had acted out of criminal and not political intentions. Moreover, it was considered particularly disgraceful that S. would then use private, internal organizational knowledge of the NSDAP, "to which he admittedly did not belong," against his former comrades.

Only a few weeks into his prison term, S. wrote a letter to the district attorney in order to bring a mistake to the prosecutor's attention. The error, as he saw it, was that he had been housed at the Plötzensee penal institution with the "criminal prisoners" rather than with the "political prisoners." Within a week, he received a response from the district court, which explained that no error had been made. Because he had "acted reprehensibly," wrote the court administrator, he had been placed with other similarly motivated criminals.[50] This exchange offers a neat conclusion and further evidence that all involved were using the same standards of judgment. The prisoner's complaint shows that those involved in street fighting were equally concerned with reputation and character. He did not want to be seen as a common prisoner, but one who had acted politically. This designation implied courage and support of his family and neighbors. The court clearly upheld this distinction as well. In fact, the distinction was institutionalized by prison procedure and regarded so highly by the court that here a guilty participant in a campaign-triggered incident, who was not viewed worthy of this special designation because he had not played by the rules, was denied this status.

Conclusion

Although we know that the conservative bias of many judicial officials led to frequent injustices in sentencing, we must look beyond ideological affinity as the only cause for the imbalance in sentencing practices. In this brief examination of the reports of caseworkers and the sentences handed down to street fighters by judges, we can see that across the political spectrum those evaluating political violence were more interested in the individual perpetrator's *Gesinnung*—combining an evaluation of character, intent, and motive—than in the crime itself.[51] Even violent crimes that appeared to champion respect for discipline within an organization, the protection of friends or women, or claimed to avenge a personal affront were often treated lightly, as representing a healthy, masculine character.[52]

Weighing a defendant's *Gesinnung* heavily in the determination of punishment, I would argue, legitimized specific uses of political violence and thus helped prepare the way for the relatively smooth transfer to the state-sanctioned violence of the Third Reich. Conservative judges were simply less likely to view a Communist's *Gesinnung* as honorable, thereby weakening the republic by enabling right-wing radicalism and leading others to lose faith in a state that practiced *Klassenjustiz*. In addition, the tradition of emphasizing character and ethics in criminal cases before 1933 made it easier to introduce National Socialist standards of "ethics" after the NSDAP came to power. As has been recently argued, this was a regime that "murder[ed] in the name of morality."[53] The central critique of the practice of considering *Gesinnung* in sentencing in the Weimar era, however, had been the subjectivity involved and resultant lack of uniformity in measuring the relative ethical standards of a "cultural epoch or cultural sphere."[54] A pluralistic society like the republic made the determination of a code of ethics quite difficult, juridical scholars agreed, even when we are talking about a fairly homogenous cadre of judges. This indeterminacy changed after 1933.

One law professor noted in 1935 that what set Nazi criminal law apart from the modern school of criminal law that preceded it was that in the Volksgemeinschaft based on "honor, loyalty, and duty," no illegal act could be "ethically indifferent." Instead every crime should be judged in ethical terms, as an "offense of duty" *(Pflichtverletzung)* to the community.[55] The racial community and its ethical system were to be safeguarded above all by the law.[56] The old problems of agreeing on ethical standards were therefore gone. In 1934, a second Nazi legal scholar explained the difference between the two eras: "Judging *[Gesinnung]* is more difficult still, when one cannot be certain of the worldview, as in democratic states, where we have only majority and minority opinions, but no absolute *[alleinherrschende]* idea." He concluded cheerfully: "These [concerns] lose their basis in today's society, where through the national revolution a fundamental worldview and a valid ethical value judgment *[gültige ethische Wertung]* have come to power, which is National Socialism, measurable not only in political but also in ethical ways."[57] In this legal scholar's opinion, therefore, though significant latitude in sentencing had been available to judges before 1933, the change in power simply took the guesswork out of their task.[58]

Notes

1. Landesarchiv Berlin (LAB), Rep. 58, No. 192, Film 379, Political Police IA report, October 7, 1931.

2. LAB, Rep. 58, No. 192, Film 379, Court proceedings against H. S. at the Schöfengericht Schöneberg.

3. My point is not that class-based injustice did not exist. Rather the argument put forward in this piece works in conjunction with the *Klassenjustiz* critique. A number of classic works have provided clear evidence that members of the political left often received harsher sentences than their right-wing counterparts. See Heinrich Hannover and Elisabeth Hannover-Drück, *Politische Justiz, 1918–1933* (Frankfurt a. M., 1966) and Gotthard Jasper, "Justiz und Politik in der Weimarer Republik," in *Vierteljahrshefte für Zeitgeschichte* (30. Jg, Heft 2, 1982). In addition, see also Manfred Krohn, *Die deutsche Justiz im Urteil der Nationalsozialisten, 1920–1933* (Frankfurt a. M, 1991).

4. The courts defined juvenile defendants as those up to age eighteen, but youth services assisted in the trials of "young adults" as well. This category included those facing charges between the ages of eighteen and twenty-one.

5. For the best analysis of the lives and duties of Germany's welfare workers, see David F. Crew, *Germans on Welfare: From Weimar to Hitler* (New York, 1998).

6. On the precarious position of the judicial caste in the Weimar era, see Ralph Angermund, *Deutsche Richterschaft 1919–1945: Krisenerfahrung, Illusion, politische Rechtsprechung* (Frankfurt a. M, 1990). On lawyers in the republican era, see Kenneth F. Ledford, *From General Estate to a Special Interest. German Lawyers, 1878–1933* (Cambridge, 1996), pp. 275–89. See also Fritz Ostler, *Die Deutschen Rechtsanwälte, 1871–1971* (Essen, 1982), pp. 202–20.

7. There is an obvious paradox here. That men felt the need to resort to violence to demonstrate control over their lives illustrates how threatened and powerless they must have felt. The literature on street fighting and paramilitarism in Weimar Germany is extensive. See among many texts and articles, Richard Bessel, *Political Violence and the Rise of Nazism: The Storm Troopers in Eastern Germany, 1925–1934* (New Haven, 1984); Conan Fischer, *Stormtroopers: A Social, Economic and Ideological Analysis 1929–1935* (London, 1983); Peter Merkl, *The Making of a Stormtrooper* (Princeton, 1980); Eve Rosenhaft, *Beating the Fascists? The German Communists and Political Violence 1929–1933* (New York, 1983); Dirk Schumann, *Politische Gewalt in der Weimarer Republic, 1918–1933: Kampf um die Strasse und Furcht vor dem Bürgerkrieg* (Essen, 2001); and Pamela E. Swett, *Neighbors and Enemies: The Culture of Radicalism in Berlin, 1929–1933* (New York, 2004).

8. See those works cited above as well as Pamela E. Swett, "Political Networks, Rail Networks: Public Transportation and Radicalism in Weimar Germany," in Ralf Roth and Marie-Noelle Polino, eds., *The City and the Railway in Europe* (London, 2003) and Michael Haben, "Die Waren so unter sich': Über Kneipen, Vereine und Politik in Berlin Kreuzberg," in Karl-Heinz Fiebig, et al. eds., *Kreuzberger Mischung: die innerstädtische Verflechtung von Architektur, Kultur und Gewerbe* (Berlin, 1984).

9. On the republic's policies concerning Germany's youth, see Elizabeth Harvey, *Youth and the Welfare State in Weimar Germany* (Oxford, 1993).

10. LAB, Rep. 58, No. 192, Film 379, Welfare report on H. S, no office listed, October 16, 1931.

11. LAB, Rep. 58, No. 131, Film 364, Youth welfare bureau Schöneberg to the District Court Schöneberg, November 10, 1930.

12. LAB, Rep. 58, No. 143, Film 367, Youth welfare bureau Schöneberg to the District Court Berlin-Charlottenburg, May 3, 1930.

13. LAB, Rep. 58, No. 154, Film 370, Youth welfare bureau Neukölln to the District Attorney's office, March 3, 1931.

14. LAB, Rep. 58, No. 161, Film 373, Youth welfare bureau Kreuzberg to the District Attorney's office, February 26, 1931.

15. LAB, Rep. 58, No. 192, Film 379, Welfare report on H. S, no office listed, October 16, 1931.

16. LAB, Rep. 58, No. 183, Film 378, Welfare bureau Neukölln to the District Attorney's office, report on H. M., August 16, 1931. For an example of the problems caused by alcohol, see LAB, Rep. 58, No. 135, Film 364. In this family the alcoholic father had been sent to numerous treatment centers without success. He had been

unemployed for some time, and his wife, who worked as a janitor in their apartment house, was unable to support her six children, some of whom were removed from her care.

17. Common charges included inciting violence, participating in a riot, inflicting bodily harm, and illegal weapons possession.

18. Mothers were consistently reluctant to show their sons in a bad light. And more than one mother conspired to keep the news of the arrest from her potentially abusive husband as long as possible. See LAB, Rep. 58, No. 136, Film 364, Youth welfare bureau Neukölln report on E.F., February 26, 1930. In this family the father was described as "very strict." And it was "out of fear" that the son had not told his father the news. The mother, "who could barely speak through her tears," had also kept the story quiet and had not yet decided how to handle the situation. However, she praised her son as "ambitious and obedient."

19. LAB, Rep. 58, No. 131, Film 364, Youth welfare bureau Schöneberg report on G. S., November 10, 1930.

20. The presumption that the revolutionary intentions of the Communist Party were by definition criminal is discussed in the following analyses of Berlin's police culture: Richard Bessel, "Policing, Professionalisation and Politics in Weimar Germany," in Clive Elmsley and Barbara Weinberger, eds., *Policing Western Europe: Politics, Professionalism, and Public Order, 1850–1940* (New York, 1991); Peter Leßmann, *Die Preußische Schutzpolizei* (Düsseldorf, 1989); and Hsi-Huey Liang, *The Berlin Police Force in the Weimar Republic* (Berkeley, 1970).

21. Cf., LAB, Rep. 58, No. 132, Film 364, Youth welfare bureau Neukölln to the District Attorney's office, report on W.S., November 25, 1929. The first line in this summary of the accused's background and current situation reads: "G.S.: left-side paralysis of the hand and foot—and mentally backward."

22. Recent work shows quite clearly the tension and debate between those who sought reform of the criminal justice system during the 1920s and those who believed that any attempts to provide convicts more rights or chances at rehabilitation were signs of the soft republic's descent into chaos. See further Nikolaus Wachsmann, *Hitler's Prisons: Legal Terror in Nazi Germany* (London, 2004) and Richard Wetzell, *Inventing the Criminal: A History of German Criminology, 1870–1945* (Chapel Hill, 2000). More generally on the language of biology and society, see also Moritz Föllmer, "Der 'kranke Volkskörper': Industrielle, hohe Beamte und der Diskurs der nationalen Regeneration in der Weimarer Republik," *Geschichte und Gesellschaft* 27 (2001), 41–67. For a discussion of how this debate carried into the Third Reich, see George C. Browder, *Hitler's Enforcers: The Gestapo and SS Security Service in the Nazi Revolution* (New York, 1998).

23. LAB, Rep. 58, No. 132, Film 364, Youth welfare bureau Neukölln to the District Attorney's office, report on L.G. and E.Z., November 16, 1929.

24. LAB, Rep. 58, No. 143, Film 367, Youth welfare bureau Schöneberg to the District Attorney's office, report on H.R., July 30, 1930.

25. LAB, Rep. 58, No. 135, Film 364, Youth welfare bureau Steglitz to the Schöffengericht Schöneberg, report on K.D., May 12, 1930.

26. LAB, Rep. 58, No. 132, Film 364, Youth welfare bureau Neukölln to the District Attorney's office, report on L.G. and E.Z., November 16, 1929.

27. LAB, Rep. 58, No. 161, Film 373, District Office Tempelhof to the District Court Tempelhof, report on E.V., July 27, 1931.

28. In fact the 1871 Criminal Code was retained by the Third Reich. Though many amendments were made, Hitler decided not to adopt a new Code, believing that doing so would in effect be more limiting. The debate carried on the cabinet in 1937, but the new administration reasoned that it was politically expedient to keep the old Code around as a straw man—criticizing it as ineffective and "liberalistic" whenever it chose to ignore the legal norms it embodied. See Nikolaus Wachsmann, *Hitler's Prisons*, 83.

29. Kahl from the 26th Deutsche Juristen Tag, 1903, quoted in Hans Lipmann, *Gesinnung und Strafrecht* (Diss.; Universität zu Bonn, 1930), 15.

30. Philipp Allfeld, *Der Einfluß der Gesinnung des Verbrechers auf die Bestrafung* (Leipzig, 1909), 1.

31. See further, M. Liepmann, "Strafen" in Aschrott and Kohlrausch, eds. *Reform des Strafrechts. Kritische Besprechungen des amtlichen Entwurfs eines Allgemeinen Deutschen Strafgesetzbuchs* (Berlin, 1926), in particular 129–30. The notion that retribution is the correct form of punishment for a crime has been termed the classical school of criminal law. The trend at the end of the nineteenth century toward defining punishment as corrections—preventative measures to ward against future crime— is known as the modern school of criminal law.

32. Allfeld, 5.

33. For some examples of the diverse opinions about the meaning of *"ehrlose Gesinnung,"* see Eduard Guckenheimer, *Der Begriff der ehrlosen Gesinnung im Strafrecht. Ein Beitrag zur strafrechtlichen Beurteilung politischer Verbrecher* (Hamburg, 1921), 14–22.

34. The honorable and dishonorable criminals were referred to also as the *"Überzeugungsverbrecher"* and *"gemeinen Verbrecher"* respectively. Radbruch from 1924 quoted in Liepmann, p. 25. The *Zuchthaus* or penitentiary was a harsher punishment than any other type of confinement because of lengthier mandatory sentences and the loss of certain civil rights.

35. Lipmann, 5.

36. In his own suggestion for legal reform, Lipmann calls for penitentiary when a perpetrator acts out of *"unsittlicher Gesinnung* [immoral convictions]." See his conclusion, Lipmann, 32.

37. Lipmann, 13.

38. The Communist Party told its supporters to deny all participation in political events that turned violent. Their denials, noted Tübingen law professor R. Gaupp, made it especially hard to determine whether honorable political ideals were at the heart of the actions. R. Gaupp, "Der Überzeugungsverbrecher" in *Monatsschrift für Kriminalpsychologie und Strafrechtsreform* (Bd. 17, Heft 9/10, 1926), 397.

39. LAB, Rep. 58, No. 224, Film 387, Final Report of the Political Police Ia, February 15, 1932.

40. LAB, Rep. 58, No. 224, Film 387, Decision by the Criminal Division 3a in the District Court II, June 22, 1932.

41. For an example of a case concerning a Communist attack on a Nazi pub, in which the same criteria concerning political motivation and public versus private space were considered, see GSta, Rep. 84a, 2.5.1., No. 10598.

42. LAB, Rep. 58, No. 233, Film 389, Indictment of the fitter S. at the District Court II, November 7, 1932. This case is also of interest because the defense attorney

asked for a list of the lay assessors before the beginning of the trial. Due to the "political nature of the case and the tense atmosphere," he requested information concerning "the personality and outlook" of the assessors. Ibid, Attorney Bergmann to the Presiding Judge at the Criminal Division of the District Court II, November 2, 1932.

43. LAB, Rep. 58, No. 159, Film 372, Decision of the Court of Appeals, August 14, 1931.

44. For more on comradeship, see Thomas Kühne's insightful discussion of the many readings of comradeship among Wehrmacht soldiers "Zwischen Männerbund und Volksgemeinschaft: Hitlers Soldaten und der Mythos der Kameradschaft," *Archiv für Sozialgeschichte* (Vol. 38, 1998) and Donna Harsch's article on the many understandings of comradeship in the diverse SPD of 1920s Munich: "Codes of Comradeship: Class, Leadership, and Tradition in Munich Social Democracy," *Central European History* 13, no. 4 (1986). Richard Bessel also examines the importance of comradeship to this younger generation of German men who felt bereaved by missing out on what they perceived to be the quintessential unifying experience of the age: serving in the trenches of World War I. See Richard Bessel, *Germany after the First World War* (Oxford, 1993).

45. LAB, Rep. 58, No. 186, Film 378, Decision of the Schöffengericht Tempelhof, November 4, 1931.

46. A similar argument was made by the judge in the trial of our first defendant H.S. He too was determined to have committed a "contemptible … act of brutality," because the man he assaulted was not in fact a member of the Nazi Party. His motivations, therefore, could not be seen as political, and hence honorable. See LAB, Rep 58, No. 192, Film 379, Court proceedings against H.S. at the Schöffengericht Schöneberg.

47. Though newspapers certainly used gendered language about feminine cowards who attacked and ran, criminal court proceedings rarely referred to actions in explicitly gendered terms, though it is clear their conceptions of honorable and dishonorable behavior are bound up in masculine norms and ideals. See, for example, Ute Frevert's work on dueling: *Men of Honour* (Cambridge, Mass., 1995). For more on gendered readings of violence in Berlin's newspapers see Pamela E. Swett, *Neighbors and Enemies,* chap. 2.

48. LAB, Rep. 58, No. 188, Film 379, Proceedings from the case against mechanic P.S. at the Schöffengericht Schöneberg, January 4, 1932.

49. Ibid.

50. LAB, Rep. 58, No. 188, Film 379, Letter from P. S. to the District Attorney, October 26, 1932 and Response to P.S. from the Amtsgericht Schöneberg, November 2, 1932. S. was given a leave from prison sometime in November in order to complete urgently needed repairs on his home before winter arrived. On December 27, 1932, he was released under the terms of a nationwide amnesty declared for the Christmas holiday. A large number of the prisoners discussed in this chapter benefited from this amnesty.

51. For a detailed breakdown of the relationship between character, motive, will, and *Gesinnung* in the law, see Guckenheimer, *Der Begriff der ehrlosen Gesinnung,* 79–87.

52. It should not surprise us then that defendants who were also Nazi Party members were sure to mention their party affiliation, while their Communist counterparts often hid their membership from police and others, for fear that any links to the ille-

gal Communist paramilitary organization, the RFB, would tarnish their hopes of a positively assessed *Gesinnung*. There was an element of respect associated with the SA as a legal political organization and an official arm of the NSDAP that those on the left never enjoyed, especially after the banning of the RFB in May 1929.

53. Claudia Koonz, *The Nazi Conscience* (Cambridge, Mass., 2003), 99.

54. For one critique of the diversity of sentences handed down to criminals, see "Strenge und milde Richter" by the jurist Siegert in the liberal newspaper, *Vossische Zeitung,* January 17, 1930.

55. Friedrich Schaffstein, *Das Verbrechen als Pflichtverletzung* (Berlin, 1935), 7 and 19. The previous year Schaffstein made a similar point. He argued that all school of legal thought since the Enlightenment have been characterized by the separation of law and morality; whereas, in the National Socialist era, the law's "most basic principle is the unity of legal and moral judgment." Schaffstein, "Ehrenstrafe und Freiheitsstrafe in ihrer Bedeutung für das neue Strafrecht," *Deutsches Strafrecht,* (Heft 9, Band 1, 1934), 278–79.

56. Michael Burleigh makes this point when discussing the demise of the rule of law after 1933. As he notes: all crimes were understood as betrayal of the racial community. "A burglar in the blackout became a plunderer." See Burleigh, *The Third Reich* (New York, 2000), 165. Ingo Müller provides similar examples in *Hitler's Justice: The Courts of the Third Reich* (Cambridge, Mass., 1991), 49.

57. Alfred Balzer, "Die ehrlose Gesinnung im geltenden und zukünftigen Strafrecht" (Diss. der juristischen Fakultät der Friedrich-Alexanders-Universität zu Erlangen, 1934), 13. Balzer was working with the same definition of *Gesinnung* used during the republican era. He noted that *Gesinnung* was to be measured "by determining the strength and nature of the motives, … comparing the transgressed law with the aimed outcome and the manner in which the act was carried out." (Balzer, 13).

58. The wording of §20 of the StGB was finally altered by the Gesetz zur Änderung strafrechtlicher Vorschriften of May 26, 1933 to read: "Where the law offers a choice between penitentiary or prison confinement, imprisonment can only be chosen when the act is not directed against the welfare of the Volk and the perpetrator acted exclusively out of honorable motives." For further material on how the concept of *Gesinnung* was applied in the sentencing practices of young lawbreakers during the Third Reich, see Jörg Wolff, *Jugendliche vor Gericht im Dritten Reich: Nationalsozialistische Jugendstrafrechtspolitik im Justizalltag* (Munich, 1992).

PART TWO

~

GERMAN SOCIETY AND
A VIOLENT REGIME

~

CHAPTER 4

Beyond Conviction?

Perpetrators, Ideas, and Action in the Holocaust in Historiographical Perspective

Mark Roseman

I

The Holocaust is the most utopian[1] of all the great murders of the twentieth century. Unlike most other ethnic conflicts, it responded to no preexisting competition for control of the state.[2] It was a "final solution" to no security problem and brought in no new territory. At times it allowed the expropriation of considerable wealth, but never sufficient to transform Germany's fortunes,[3] while at other times wasting good productive labor the embattled Reich could ill afford to squander. Given that the Holocaust was more purely ideological than any other mass killing, it is striking how slow postwar historians have been to see its perpetrators as motivated by ideas or convictions. Hitler and perhaps one or two of his henchmen were allowed to have a "Weltanschauung"; in most postwar analyses the beliefs of the rest barely figured. Where the staffers of the killing machine were given attention at all, they figured as neutral functionaries, ticking along with the bureaucratic clockwork. Perhaps they were kept at their desks by fear, perhaps they were mesmerized by loyalty, perhaps they were driven by ambition—but they were not inspired by conviction. That was one reason why in the mid-1990s Daniel Goldhagen's claims about the motivating power of the perpetrators' antisemitism were so shocking.[4] The first part of this essay considers why it took so long for perpetrators to be taken seriously as active, conscious participants, embracing their cause.

Over the last five to ten years, work into the perpetrators has blossomed into its own separate subdiscipline of research into the Third Reich.[5] The ideological pedigree of men across a wide range of institutions and organizations has entered the spotlight; beliefs and convictions, it is clear, mattered. If any paradigm has captured the imagination in recent years, it is that of the "Weltanschauungskrieger" ("warrior with a cause") rather than the banal bureaucrat. Yet while this recent work is transforming our understanding of the human reality of the killing process, it has also underlined the complexity and elusiveness of the relationship between ideas and action. If it is no longer possible casually to dub the participants ordinary men, it is equally clear that they were not all zealots, either, and certainly not all zealots as a *cause* rather than a *consequence* of their participation in the Holocaust. Indeed, as the concluding part of this essay will argue, the choice between ordinary men and zealots (as for example seemed to be offered by the celebrated Browning-Goldhagen debate about Police Batallion 101)[6] turns out to be a false one. This is partly for obvious reasons that there was never just one kind of perpetrator, partly because the truth often lies somewhere in the middle, but more meaningfully and interestingly because it is clear the choice between ordinary men and zealots, or between neutral functionaries and those acting from conviction, significantly narrows and distorts the processes and impulses that guided men—and a few women—along the road to genocide. Seen in this light, the reluctance of earlier classics to embrace the idea of the zealot does not look quite so willful or repressive; it sometimes involved "looking away," but it also reflected profound insight into the essential ambiguity of human involvement in the Holocaust.

II

In an immediate postwar era seeking distance from the recent horror, survivors of Nazi policies wondered if their tormentors had been members of the same species. "You should have seen their faces," was the comment the writer Eva Hoffman remembered from her mother, a Polish-Jewish survivor, "they were not really human."[7] Eugen Kogon, a veteran of the German concentration camps and writer of the first systematic account of the SS state, believed he had observed in the camp personnel the dregs and misfits of humanity, men "who had been failures in civilian life and who generally lacked all professional or character training"—a claim he extended beyond the camp SS to the Gestapo as well.[8] Continuing to deploy the Nazis' own language, though now against them, Hitler's former conversation partner, Hermann Rauschning, would go so far as to argue that the camp personnel represented "a true selection of sub-humans," specially chosen to carry out their monstrous tasks.[9]

True, the definitional forays into the boundaries of humanity by Mrs. Hoffman in Poland and Eugen Kogon in postwar Germany had different implications. Were these monsters national archetypes or social misfits? For many non-German survivors of the Holocaust and, indeed, for much of the postwar world, the Nazis' inhumanity and their "Germanity" lay close together. What was monstrous was shared across the culture, something poisoning the blood. The popular sense of what was wrong with the Germans came at times perilously close to a counter-version of the Nazis' own racism. The German memory (when Nazi crimes were acknowledged at all) was quite different. In the preface to his study, Kogon made clear that his account was intended as "a mirror of humanity" (Ecce Homo-Spiegel) and not as an accusation against Germandom.[10] Germany's misfortune had been to allow a few very singular madmen—Meinecke wrote of a "criminal clique"[11]—into power at the top; they in turn had allowed the dregs of humanity at the bottom to vent their spleen. In the German view, Nazi terror was, as it were, a conversation between psychopaths. The madmen at the top unleashed the beasts at the bottom, with the rest of Germany unhappily sandwiched in between. But wherever the line was being drawn between the "monsters" and the rest, the point was that psychological deformation, rather than intellectual conviction, was seen as the motive force. Particularly in the German context, where the nation as a whole was at pains to forget the degree to which it had identified with the defeated Nazi regime, it was safer to remember the perpetrator as the deviant, rather than as everyman.

Where the perpetrators did not seem overtly to be monsters, the prosecutors at Nuremberg fell back on the gothic idea of doubling. Confronted with the polite and apparently sincere and forthright Dr. Otto Ohlendorf, the judge at his trial reached for his Victorian literature. "The evidence in this case could reveal not one but two Otto Ohlendorfs," he concluded. "There is the Ohlendorf represented as the student, lecturer, administrator, sociologist, scientific analyst, and humanitarian…. On the other hand, we have the description of an SS General Ohlendorf who led Einsatzgruppe D into the Crimea on a race-extermination expedition…. If the humanitarian and the Einsatz leader are merged into one person, it could be assumed that we are here dealing with a character such as that described by Robert Louis Stevenson in his "Dr. Jekyll and Mr. Hyde."[12] Such references, telling though they were, were as much an admission of bewilderment as a coherent model of a personality. Even so, devils in human form remained the predominant note of the 1950s.

III

In the late 1950s and early 1960s, however, we find a different tone emerging. True, hints of doubling remain in Joachim Fest's popular though scholarly account, *The Face of the Third Reich,* which appeared in German in 1963, the same year that Hannah Arendt's *Eichmann in Jerusalem* was published in New

York. "Figures like Rudolf Höß, Otto Ohlendorf or Adolf Eichmann," observed Fest, "represented, each in his own horrifying way, this type of the totally malleable man able to bring utterly incompatible elements into equilibrium without a hint of inner discomfort."[13] But Fest showed that he was moving in a different direction when he concluded that "Rudolf Höß's declaration in his posthumous notes that he also had "a heart" and was "not wicked" is all the more horrifying because in a sense it is the truth."[14] The real story, it now seemed, was not that of a monster at all.

The most important trigger for this "normalization" of the perpetrators was undoubtedly the Eichmann trial, and in particular Hannah Arendt's account of it, serialized in *The New Yorker* from 1961 and published as a separate book in 1963. Eichmann, Arendt wrote:

> was not Iago and not Macbeth, and nothing would have been farther from his mind than to determine with Richard III "to prove a villain." Except for an extraordinary diligence in looking out for his personal advancement, he had no motives at all. And this diligence in itself was in no way criminal; he certainly would never have murdered his superior in order to inherit his post. He *merely*, to put the matter colloquially, *never realized what he was doing*.[15]

For Arendt, this was familiar ground. As early as 1946 she wrote that we had been so accustomed to trust the family man as society's good natured carer that "we hardly registered how [he] ... was transformed by the chaotic economic conditions of our time into an adventurer against his will."[16] Echoing such early postwar insights, Arendt observed in her Eichmann report that half a dozen psychiatrists had certified the defendant as "normal"—"'More normal at any rate than I am after having examined him,' one of them was said to have exclaimed."[17] The only way in which Arendt saw Eichmann and the family men of her earlier article as part of a distinctive (albeit very large) group was that the economic insecurity of the interwar period had uprooted them and made them *Massenmenschen* and thus deprived them of the independent judgment necessary to withstand the blandishments and incentives of the regime. This perpetrator might have the blemish of limited vision but he was no longer demonic; indeed it was the very banality of what was required to unleash such horror that provided the subtitle for Arendt's book and the core of her analysis.

Arendt's portrayal was informed and reinforced by Raul Hilberg's magisterial account of the destruction of European Jewry, published in 1961.[18] More than Arendt, Hilberg emphasized the relentless clockwork of bureaucracy itself. Given a vague target, he wrote, the bureaucrats "displayed a striking pathfinding ability in the absence of directives, a congruity of activities without jurisdictional guidelines, a fundamental comprehension of the task even when there were no explicit communications." Ordinary men thus came to perform extraordinary tasks.[19]

What should we make of the shift from the monster to the mundane, other than reaffirming our sense that the postwar world had great difficulty forming a stable picture of the Nazi perpetrator? The publication of Rudolf Höß's memoirs in 1958 and the Eichmann trial confronted the world with men who were clearly neither psychopaths nor mad. Orderly, at least of average intelligence, possessed of the usual virtues of everyday civility, these were not monsters or sadists but executive civil servants, or as Werner Jochmann noted of Höß, men "well equipped to live amongst us today."[20] A sensitive observer of the Auschwitz camp such as the former Communist and camp inmate, Hermann Langbehn, felt that only 5–10 percent of the guards had been "instinctual criminals in the clinical sense."[21] To some extent, then, what had happened was simply a correction of the inadequate earlier image of the psychopath or monster.

Yet the new approach was scarcely simply a reaction to the encounter with the testimonies of Höß or Eichmann or others. As already noted, Arendt had had similar ideas up her sleeve since the war—indeed Raul Hilberg has wryly observed that her presence at the trial itself was so limited that her conclusions must have been preformed.[22] But why did these ideas find such resonance now—and to what extent were they being imposed upon, rather than merely reflecting, raw experience? Fest's work in particular reveals the power of the discourse of totalitarianism. In the preface to *The Face of the Third Reich*, Fest noted, it was "the purpose of this book to contribute towards an explanation of modern man's vulnerability to totalitarianism."[23] Thinking about Rudolf Höss, Fest concluded that:[24]

> the suppression of personal "spontaneity" and the absolute, reliable automatism of thought and action that are the models of every form of totalitarian training succeeded so completely in this case because Höss had from an early age, through his own character and circumstances, felt at home only in a world of commands and found the consciousness of merit and self-confirmation only within this framework.

Höß's principal shortcoming, according to Fest, was thus the same kind of blindness Arendt had found in Eichmann. In Höß, "the capacity for rational and responsible action had atrophied to an almost unique degree, and the only doubt which ever shadowed his docile face was whether any measure that was ordered was covered by the authority of the moment."[25] "It is impossible to avoid the suspicion," Fest went on, "that even in admitting his guilt he was merely making a final effort to obey, this time the investigating officials and the court, who now condemned organized genocide and whom "always in accordance with orders" he wished to please by repudiating his own actions."[26]

I quote this at some length, because it was a genuinely astonishing reading of a man who from an early stage in his life—freely and at great personal
risk—had pursued a consistent career in violence and in right-wing causes,
from being a volunteer soldier in World War I, through his role as a Freikorps
member at 19, fighting both on Germany's borders and Communists at home
(Höß was convicted of the murder of a member deemed to have been a trai-
tor), to being an active member of the radical-right wing Artamen league and
finally of the Nazi party, for which he became one of the first concentration
guards at Dachau.[27] To stylize such a trajectory as the passive obedience of the
automaton showed how hard it was, particularly for German observers, to
contemplate the idea of intelligent, orderly, recognizable men subscribing to
Nazi ideals.

Nicolas Berg has recently noted the striking willingness in the 1950s and
1960s of even the critical historians at the Institut für Zeitgeschichte (IfZ) to
take the postwar testimonies of men like Höß at face value—and indeed Fest
was clearly strongly influenced by IfZ director Martin Broszat's take on the
Höß memoirs.[28] In the German context, this willingness to take the former
perpetrators at their (postwar) word was almost bound to result in ideology
and conviction being taken out of the story, because of the way the German
legal system treated motive. In German jurisprudence, and particularly in the
case-law that developed on Nazi crimes, defendants were likely to be convicted
of first-degree murder (rather than "Beihilfe" or accessory) only if low motives could be established; low motives included greed, lust, and so on, but also
zealotry and anti-Semitism.[29] The result was to create courtrooms full of men
who had ostensibly never believed in the cause.

Fest's emphasis on totalitarianism also reveals the striking degree to
which the cold war atmosphere shaped perceptions of the pre–Cold War period. The 1950s were, after all, the years in which Daniel Bell wrote influen-
tially about the *End of Ideology* and Helmut Schelsky invoked the image of the
Skeptische Generation.[30] It is perhaps not surprising that during the nuclear
age, in which global stand-off, rather than zealotry and conviction ruled the
day, historians generally assumed that the men who had run the Nazi machine
had been rational, neutral, professionals.[31] At the time of the Eichmann trial,
the *New Statesman* mused explicitly about the links between the bespectacled
ex-Nazi and servants of the Cold War: "Eichmann is no longer a solitary figure.
The commander of a single British V-bomber, for instance, now carries in his
aircraft weapons which can achieve comparable destruction of human life."[32]
These were the quiet men in whose charge lay the execution of our destiny.

Against this Cold War background, the interest was increasingly in the
policy machine, not the men who staffed it. The big debates between the intentionalists (who focused on Hitler's directives) and the structuralists (who

emphasized the imbalances of the Nazi system and the competitive drive of Hitler's subordinates) revolved around the mechanics of high policy, above all whether Hitler figured as policy-maker or merely furnisher of murderous rhetoric. For our purposes it is certainly important that the functionalists emphasized the perpetrators' role, with their argument that Hitler's subordinates transformed what been only loose rhetoric into murderous reality. The outstanding synthesis of this position, Hans Mommsen's essay "Die Realiserung des Utopischen," published in 1983, explored with great intellectual courage and clarity the process by which recognizable men, ambitious, hard, committed to their brief, egged each other on over the brink in a world in which a charismatic leader offered for guidance only the vaguest of precepts.[33] Like Arendt, Mommsen was writing about "officials" (the metaphor of the "satrap" also makes an appearance) rather than the "perpetrators"; but whereas for Arendt the story was about the loyal bureaucrat perfecting commands, for Mommsen, the functionaries themselves wrote the commands that were then retrospectively sanctioned on high.

The interesting thing about the "functionalists," though, was that they shared a similar view of what the perpetrators were like to those "intentionalists" who emphasized Hitler's directive force. The disputes were conducted with such vehemence that one often lost sight of the fact that both sides regarded the functionaries' intentions as rather limited and secondary. The intentionalists tended to see the subordinates as mesmerized or dutiful, the functionalists viewed them as aggressively ambitious and competitive. But neither side believed it possible or plausible that a broad cohort of educated policy-makers should have consciously aspired to the irrational genocidal program of the Holocaust. Both sides were agreed in ascribing the specific murderousness of the vision to Hitler—in the form of a plan, said the intentionalists, in the form of vague, catalytic rhetoric, said the structuralists. Both sides, though particularly the functionalists, thus viewed the murderous language used by the perpetrators as the currency of power, deployed purposely, but not authentically believed. Both sides argued that it took the Third Reich's peculiar power structure (though they disagreed about what this was) to galvanize Hitler's army of helpers into action. Given this consensus, and the focus of interest in policy processes and structures, the years following the publication of *Eichmann in Jerusalem* saw relatively few detailed biographical studies of perpetrators. Nevertheless, Günther Deschner's portrait of Heydrich as a cold technocrat of murder,[34] Albert Speer's carefully calibrated self-descriptions as a star-struck architect who fell in with the wrong sort,[35] and Christopher Browning's meticulous account of the entrepreneurial Martin Luther who inveigled his way into the German Foreign Office, with an eye to the main chance,[36] all reinforced the "de-ideologization" of the perpetrators.

IV

One reason that this "end of ideology" survived so long in histories of the Holocaust was that as the generation of 1968 entered the history profession, it brought with it in the short term a set of intellectual assumptions not conducive to engaging with the Holocaust. Above all, Marxist analyses of fascism offered very little to explain either the centrality of racism or the single-minded murderousness of Nazi rule—an explanatory gap later acknowledged by Tim Mason, perhaps the most sensitive and sophisticated Marxist historian of the Third Reich.[37] True, the rediscovery of the Frankfurt school might have had a more constructive impact, but with the exception of Klaus Theweleit's *Männerfantasien,* there were few attempts to apply the notion of the authoritarian or fascistic personality to perpetrator studies.[38] Beyond these conceptual barriers, as a number of historians have recently argued, the 1970s and early 1980s continued to be characterized by an emotional unwillingness to engage with the reality of perpetrating murder. Ulrich Herbert has written of "a second wave of repression" and, indeed, abstract, rather detached language was no preserve of Marxist-influenced historiography.[39] It could also be found in the wording of such memorial plaques for the victims of the Holocaust as were created in this period; using the passive voice, they customarily spoke of the victims "having to give their lives" with no mention of the killers. The Holocaust continued to be conceptualized as an almost automated process or clean machine, symbolized by the ostensibly smooth functioning of Auschwitz.[40] There were admittedly a limited number of impressive individual accounts in the 1980s that offered a very different view, both of the process, and individual participants.[41] But they made little impact on historical understanding of the Third Reich as a whole because the intellectual models and concerns of the period simply provided no vocabulary and framework for interpreting them.

In the course of the 1980s, however, the picture changed. As Marxist analysis gave way to more Foucauldian approaches and the idea of capitalist exploitation was replaced by a broader and deeper critique of the pathology of the modern, an intellectual framework emerged that allowed for more active engagement with the perpetrators.[42] Götz Aly, Susanne Heim, and others introduced us to a raft of intellectuals and bureaucrats, and particularly a core of around 500 planning staffs, population planners, and agronomists, for example, men not numbed by totalitarianism, men not driven by external bureaucratic dictates, but with a clear eye to the rational virtues of murder—virtues revolving around efficiency, population, settlement, and agriculture.[43] What had always seemed absolutely absurd—why spend all these resources on non-strategic murder in the middle of total war—now seemed suddenly, horribly more logical. To feed the Russian army and send food back to the front, "zig millionen" citizens had to die as Herbert Backe drily concluded. To make

Poland "Germanisable," agrarian experts calculated that the population density had to fall. Planners calculated for the general government a total of 4.5 to 5.83 million "superfluous" people out of a total of 12 million.[44]

The power of this new wave of writing lay above all in the way it rescued the middle and lower ranking officials from the unsatisfactory state of being mesmerized, blinkered, or in other words "never realizing what they were doing," to paraphrase Arendt. The choice in the literature had been between mad visionaries (Hitler and one or two henchmen) and sane but blind executors. Now, here was a phalanx of sturdy, rational players actively embracing genocide.

The shortcoming of this research, particular in its early incarnations, however, was the blinkers imposed by the desire to establish the inherently modern character of the Holocaust—in other words to underscore the continuities and parallels between it and present day societies. (From the German vantagepoint, the political brisance lay above all in continuity with the players and policies of the postwar Federal Republic).[45] Aly et al thus emphasized the recognizable modern logics of economic efficiency, social control and social welfare as the ultimate goals, and downplayed the racial-nationalist and anti-Semitic sentiment that did not fit so easily into a generic critique of the modern. From the start, therefore, the work of Aly and others was criticized for giving too little credence to anti-Semitism and for taking the apparent technical-rational arguments for genocide at face value. The claim of continuity did not answer the question why, if modern planning impulses generically leant themselves to murder, it was only this particular cohort that had mooted such uniquely stark proposals; could it really be just because they were the only ones who had been allowed to? Nor did it address why the Jews were targeted, and targeted so consistently. Striking too in that context were the shifting varied logics that seemed to point to murder. When Jews were initially killed in the Soviet Union in the first weeks after the outbreak of Barbarossa, the selected groups were men of arms-bearing age who were killed because of a vague but deadly notion of a link between Bolshevism and Judaism. At that time, the economic specialists were being killed too, as part of the elimination of leading cadres. Later it was the specialists who were reprieved and the "useless eaters" who were killed, because the logic had become more economic.[46] In Hungary, it was not the useless eaters who provided the logic to killing; it was, as Christian Gerlach and Götz Aly argued in a more recent work, the potential benefits of deploying Jewish capital for a policy of economic redistribution that would provide Hungary with stability without unseating its elites.[47] There was something arbitrary—or at least secondary—about arguments that were so versatile, something more off the page of the memorandum than on it.

It was partly out of frustration with this emphasis on rationality that in the early 1990s historians began to question the paradigm of the neutral-rational perpetrator. Equally important in creating new sensitivity to the racial-nationalism of Hitler's helpers, however, was the end of the cold war. The violence in the Balkans provided daily reminders of the continued ability of nationalist ideas and movements to unleash the most horrific ethnic violence. In this new unsettled age, the Foucauldian emphasis on the rationality of the modern began to give way to renewed respect for the power of ideas and be-liefs, and particularly for the particularity and power of nationalisms and racisms. The new note to emerge in the 1990s was the perpetrator as "Weltan-schauungskrieger," or warrior with a cause.

The most important exponents of this view have been Ulrich Herbert and Michael Wildt, with their respective pathbreaking studies on Werner Best and the Reich Security Main Office (Reichsicherheitshauptamt RSHA).[48] In their accounts, the driving force behind the radicalization of the Final Solution was no longer the quasi-automatic bureaucratic machine, staffed by neutral experts, but rather the momentum and enthusiasm provided by highly qualified, lead-ing cadres who demonstrated remarkable intellectual continuity from their youth in the 1920s to the killings in the 1940s. Both Herbert and Wildt uncov-ered a cohort of young, right-wing activists, born for the most part just too young to participate in the First World War, and socialized by the home-front experiences of war, defeat, and postwar upheaval. Entering university in the early to mid-1920s, Best and many of the later leading cadres in the SD and RSHA encountered nationalist student politics, and embraced the virtues of Völkisch nationalism. In the Völkisch definition of the nation, they saw an ideal that transcended class conflict, just as it transcended the arbitrary and humiliating boundaries imposed by the postwar international treaties. For such student radicals, the Völkisch idea of nationalism opposed modern con-cepts of citizenship, an opposition expressed most openly in the leading stu-dent bodies' decision to deny Jews the right to be a member.

Growing up in disturbed times, the members of this "unconditional" or "no-holds-barred generation" (Michael Wildt) regarded themselves as hard-headed and practical, rejecting the flowery romanticism of their forbears. Yet, as Herbert argues, the claim to pragmatic-realism was in itself an ideology that incorporated a dedication to a ruthless fight for the interests of the Volk. It was the combination of radical nationalism and hard-headedness that was meant to be conveyed by the term Werner Best coined, "heroic realism." As part of this heroic realism, Best, despite his respectable background and up-bringing, rejected much of the commitment to law that is supposed to be the preserve of the bourgeoisie. He eschewed the concept of citizenship, the no-tion of international law, even the validity of domestic law against the state's definition of what was in the interest of the Volk. Well before Best joined the Nazi party, he wrote a striking journal article, distinguishing between irrational resentments and the objective needs of the Volk: "We can respect even those whom we fight and whom we may have to exterminate."[49]

The end of the cold war prompted new work not only because of the savage vistas reopened by the mayhem in the Balkans, but also because of the huge swathe of new documents about Nazi policy in the East now accessible in Soviet and East European archives.[50] This work facilitated and was accompanied by a growing willingness to descend below the level of the elite functionaries and look at lower ranks and officials. Above all, the twin controversies unleashed by the publication of Daniel Goldhagen's *Hitler's Willing Executioners* and the near simultaneous appearance of the exhibition *Crimes of the Wehrmacht,* provided the decisive impetus for the explosion of interest in all levels of participation in the Holocaust. The main trends in this burgeoning literature have been well described elsewhere and do not need repeating here.[51]

V

Only in the last few years has the term "perpetrator" entered the vocabulary of studies of the Holocaust. Its appearance has been in some ways paradoxical. On the one hand, the deployment of the term—rather than the more neutral "functionary," or the less specifically Holocaust-related "Nazi"—is a sign that after fifty years the perpetrators are finally being taken seriously as a phenomenon. The term has justified itself in one sense, too, in identifying the "unsettling" (Alf Lüdtke) scope for individual decisions, initiative and energy evident all the way down the hierarchy.[52] Responsibility, though unevenly shared, was nevertheless shared across the ranks. The claim of "ownership" of the deed, implicit in the term perpetrator, thus has considerable justification. Moreover, recent work has demonstrated that, for all the undoubted division of labor in the system, there were many players who moved between roles—oscillating between desk jobs and being active in the field. This was true above all of the security police. Some of the older assumptions about the tiny piece of the mosaic that was the job of each individual functionary are clearly not true here.[53]

On the other hand, the explosion of new research, and the discovery of the sheer diversity of the groups involved, has opened up to question as never before whether there is such a thing as *the* perpetrator. Hidden in the changing representations of Holocaust perpetrators over the postwar era was already considerable diversity: successive waves of historians shifted the focus of interest to different groups, from Kogon's camp guards, to Arendt's and Hilberg's bureaucrats, to the high level competing state, Party, and SS figures examined by Mommsen, to the planning experts and technocrats looked at by Aly, to the intellectuals who made up the SD and the Reich Security Main

Office, investigated by Herbert and Wildt. But now the variation is wider still. Horizontally, historians have recognized the huge diversity of institutions and organizations involved—the very significant number of civilian bodies (particularly in the Occupied East), the many military units, from the *Feldpolizei* to ordinary military regiments, the large range of different criminal and regular police units, and all this in addition to the more familiar Party and SS organizations. The result is to complicate enormously our sense of who a perpetrator was. The low-grade characters Bogdan Musial has rescued from oblivion in the "gangsterland"[54] civilian administration of the Lublin district,[55] for example, are a world apart from the high-flyers Michael Wildt has uncovered in the headquarters of the SD.[56] There were, as one would expect, far more committed Nazis in core SS units than in auxiliary police forces.[57] Moreover, historians have expended their horizons vertically, too, in looking at individuals right down to the grass roots, instead of the narrow elite cadres to whom attention was previously restricted. The more we descend to ground level, the less distinctive the profile is. In that sense, the intensive search for the perpetrator has demonstrated that there *is* no single phenomenon.

That diversity does not mean there are no hegemonic or defining groups or characteristics among the perpetrators that played a crucial role, even if the overall recruitment was more heterogeneous. Alongside and offsetting the diversity of organizations and staff involved, the single most important discovery of recent literature is the number of key players who reveal some kind of strong prior commitment to the cause before 1933. This was true even in many of the civilian administrations; it is clear we need to wrest ourselves from the stereotype of the neutral educated bureaucrat, assiduously fulfilling the orders of the ignorant, irrational Nazi.[58] The evidence of the degree to which radical nationalist ideas had made substantial inroads into Germany's educated youth before 1933 is even stronger when we turn to the leading corps of the security police and SD. Alongside Herbert and Wildt, Jens Banasch too has demonstrated the ideological cohesion among this body.[59] Himmler's Higher SS and Policemen, though from a slightly older generation, demonstrate a similar track-record of ideological engagement.[60] Most recently, in a series of studies with a very eclectic and broad quantitative base, Michael Mann has shown how many of the leading and a good many of lower level perpetrators in all formations already had a strong activist record in the pre-1933 period.[61] Of those born in his sample before 1900, over half had a Nazi pedigree before 1933, for example, while the activist proportion of the war-youth generation (joining the Nazi party before 1933, or at a young age in the 1930s) was even higher.[62] Moreover, a very significant proportion had engaged in violence before 1933—a point to which we will return in a moment.

The lower we move down in the hierarchy, true enough, the less we have to do with a special selection of ideologically pre-motivated individuals. And yet the Nazis could count on mobilizing a sense of resentful nationalism among many of the lower level cohorts too. As Michael Mann has pointed out, Nazi killers were "disproportionately drawn from lost territories or threatened borders" where national identity seemed doubly beleaguered.[63] This, coupled with background levels of anti-Semitism, anti-Russianism and anti-Communism, certainly helped to mobilize enthusiasm and support on the eastern front. But it is the large numbers of educated and ideologically committed leading cadres that is most important.

Even a cursory glance at the key protagonists, however, reveals the other side of the coin—almost all of even the ideologically most committed had by the time of the Holocaust moved astonishingly far from where even just a few years earlier, they might have imagined they would be. In the late 1930s, for example, Wilhelm Stuckart the high-flying Nazi who represented the Interior Ministry at Wannsee, was still arguing that Jews were not inferior, only different; he may well have assumed in the 1930s, that the Jewish problem would be solved by emigration.[64] By 1942, however, Stuckart asserted that Jews' lower quality justified their extermination.[65] In the 1930s, Heydrich and Eichmann too, had assumed, as revealed in position papers and memoranda since 1935, that the Jewish problem was above all one of emigration. If we can trust the sources, several leading members even of the SS Security Service (SD) were taken aback by the violence of the Kristallnacht pogrom, a pogrom they had not initiated.[66] Striking though the degree is to which educated young men subscribed to Nazi ideas, the fact is that they nevertheless embarked on a journey that left far behind what they could have imagined.

The reasons for this movement are complex, and take us back into older debates about the policy process as well as into newer work on "genocidal careers."[67] At the centre of the process was of course Hitler, setting the tone, prescribing the boundaries, licensing every radical action, and spanning a rhetorical canopy that could shelter the most brutal of actions. More than anything or anyone else, it was he who shaped pace and direction of the journey his men had traveled. It was his signals that had brought anti-Semitism to the centre of the SD's agenda or that had prompted Interior Ministry chipping away at Jewish citizenship rights for the best part of a decade. Under his strident but often vague leadership, different agencies jostled with each other, strove to run with the beacon of anti-Semitism to assert their ideological credentials, came up with new more radical measures when earlier proposals had run aground on their own contradictions. But the important point here is, as Michael Wildt has eloquently argued, that the structures and process, as much as the prior convictions of the individuals, were responsible for the outcome.[68]

Quite apart from this striking radicalization, it would in any case be a naïve understanding of the role of ideology to imagine that in a process like this each actor was guided by clear-eyed enunciation of the final goal. Instead, characteristically in a modern bureaucracy the goals become the framework, or platform that is taken for granted; the discussion then becomes technical. Consider the example of the rationalization that Jews as "useless eaters" needed eliminating. It is clear that the argument would not have occurred outside a system in which Jews were earmarked as undesirable and expendable. It was always an ideological and not a technical choice. (And, indeed, to the extent that there was any logic at all to the claim that Jews looked liked parasites it was because exclusions, restrictions and killings had already removed them from the productive cycle of the economy.) But at the same time, it is easy to imagine that for many participants the discussion of useless eaters did become a technical one once the contours of Nazi policy were clear. The broad framework and the overall goals of the state were such a given, that the details were the logical result of the goals. Teasing out the balance between value-rationality and instrumental rationality among the players is a complex and perhaps ultimately impossible task.

All this is not meant to suggest that individuals had no choice. As early as 1967 Herbert Jäger showed the astonishing variety of responses: he distinguished between excess deeds, by which he meant deeds that went completely beyond orders, and he saw six different forms of these; acts of initiative, in which participation was within the spirit of commands but nevertheless showed a distinctive degree of personal initiative—and here he found seven different forms; and following orders, where he distinguished between a range of kinds of response from enthusiastic acceptance, through automatic obedience, criminal self-interest, opportunistic adaptation and conflict. Individuals *had* choices—but what is clear is that most ended, willy-nilly, somewhere very far from where they began.[69]

Something misleading about the way zealotry is often conceptualized, is the too easy conflation of ideas and action. The intellectual history and the history of violence are separate and it is only recently that we have begun to think about violence as a category in its own right. The intellectual history of German racial anti-Semitism goes back to the nineteenth century, but has little linkage with violence; such limited violence as there was in nineteenth and early twentieth centuries Germany was of a very traditional sort, based on age old blood libels and not racial anti-Semitism.[70] This is one reason why the historian Enzo Traverso in his *The Origins of Nazi Violence* ventured the idea that Auschwitz had in a way "invented" anti-Semitism for the postwar world, by "conferring the appearance of a coherent, cumulative and linear process upon a body of discourse and practices that, before Nazism, had been perceived in the various European countries as discordant, heterogeneous and in many ways decidedly archaic."[71] Nazi persecution of gays and lesbians makes the point about violence more clearly. There was nothing at all distinctive about Nazi homophobia, which drew on the most banal of barroom prejudice, from the feeling that homosexuals deserved kicking, to the idea that queer men could be made straight if they were forced to sleep with women. What was distinctive was Nazi willingness to deploy camps, torture, murder—in other words, not their ideas, but their capacity and propensity for violence.

The history of that violence is far too complex and extended to be told here. In a remarkable essay, Mark Mazower recently pointed out how many of the most vicious crimes of the twentieth century were shaped or forged by war.[72] In the case of Nazi Germany, the Second World War presented challenges, opportunities, and an atmosphere of apocalyptic struggle that helped ratchet up actions against Jews from thoughts of instituting a reservation to the murderous program of the death camps. "War," as Christopher Browning noted, following John Dower, "and especially race war, leads to brutalization, which leads to atrocity."[73] But it was not the Second but the First World War that plays the more important role in forging the Nazi's violent capacities. That war introduced rationalized mass slaughter into the European imagination.[74] It was John Kegan who mused that there was "something about the massacres of the Somme that calls to mind Treblinka."[75] There was, though, no simple transfer of wartime experience to postwar politics. It is better to think of the war as an experiential and cultural shock that was there to be interpreted by the postwar worlds. In some places, that shock produced a pronounced pacifism in the interwar period—England was one, where Oxford University students would later vote not to serve King and country. But in defeated Germany, where rationing failed during wartime, and civil war erupted in the immediate post-war period, the home front was brutalized by war.[76] Nazism introduced a new violent rhetorical style and language, participated in the brawling thuggish paramilitary politics of Weimar Germany, and cultivated a brutal actionism—proposing to clean up with internal enemies. Much of the pedigree that Michael Mann has uncovered lies as much in a history of personal violence—in war, in the Freikorps, in street battles during the Slump and so on—as in a coherent set of ideas.[77] To be sure, antisemitism belonged to the everyday intellectual world of right thing thugs, but it is the socialization in violence, rather than the existence of a clearly defined eliminatory anti-Semitism, that is often the early defining marker of the later perpetrators.

The paramilitary style, the swagger and thuggishness of Nazi storm troopers is not quite the same as the cool, organized approach to Nazi killing. Further evolutions were necessary. Indeed, many of those who were later to be decisive in shaping the killing machinery were alienated in the 1920s precisely by the Nazis' brutal style. Hans Frank, Wilhelm Stuckart, Werner Best, were all deterred from joining the party because of its rowdy plebian style. Eventually, Best's SD outfit would have much more influence than the rowdy SA storm troopers. Even after the SA was emasculated in 1934, the rowdy rank and file continued to push the more elite SS to absorb its violent methods. Heydrich's men may have been shocked by the violence of the Kristallnacht that was un-leashed by Goebbels and the SA; but they recognized its utility and absorbed its lessons. Over time, the cool rational style of intellectuals like Best and the rowdy actionism of the paramilitary arm melded.

Indeed, a whole series of such high-temperature weldings took place. In the Nazi approach to eugenics and euthanasia, for example, scientific racism and vulgar Völkisch anti-Semitism became fused together. Professionally based hopes for new population policy become imbued with the brutal, cor-ner cutting of Nazi never-mind-the-human-cost policy-making. By 1941, the medical staffs involved in eliminating the mentally ill had become free-for-all murder squads being offered for any killing program Hitler and Himmler had in mind. The victims would be Polish Jews, killed in the extermination camps of the Aktion Reinhard by former euthanasia personnel.

In short a particular kind of cool savagery emerges, in which the ration-ality of controlled state policy had been hooked up with the popular power of ethnic nationalism and the brutality of paramilitary politics. This synthetic style drew on and reshaped the propensities of its participants—indeed, drew on national traits, but stretched them and shifted them. Nazi observers could be sincerely shocked by the wild orgy of bestial violence they saw unleashed against Jews by Lithuanian mobs or Rumanian troops in 1941—and then go on coolly to engage in mass shootings of hundreds of thousands of Jews.[78]

A sign of the complexity of the relationship between ideas and action is the astonishing turnaround at the end of the war. On the one hand, as Hans Mommsen explores elsewhere in this volume, the radicalism of the regime survived until almost all German territory had been lost. Nazi leaders—the Higher SS and Police Leaders played a particularly important role here—gave orders that no concentration camp inmates should fall into the hands of the enemy; as the front moved closer to the eastern camps, their hapless inmates were to be marched into the interior, to be used as labor or as hostages.[79] Those who could not make the march were to be shot. Even though the war was clearly about to end, and the Allies were clearly very unsympathetic to such actions, and even after Himmler opportunistically rescinded some of the killing instructions, individuals at all levels could be found who continued the killings to the very last minute.[80] And yet, as Frank Biess notes, also in this vol-ume, as soon as the war was over, the killing stopped. This was no Iraqi occu-pation; the "Wehrwolves" turned out to be largely mythical, there were very limited numbers of suicides (even of the leading SS and Gestapo personnel only 5 percent committed suicide).[81] Indeed, Germany turned into a safe-haven for Jews; soon Jews would be streaming onto German soil to take refuge from Polish pogroms. As Hannah Arendt observed with irony, "when it finally came to the day of judgment it turned out there had been no convinced fol-lowers after all."[82] Within a very short time, many of the former perpetrators would be providing solid service to the new democratic Republic. Even Hannah Arendt's own German editor was, notoriously, none other than Hans Rößner, Otto Ohlendorf's former assistant in the SD-Inland.[83] The hypocrisy and opportunism could not have been greater, but here was ample evidence of the limits of the zealotry or "unconditionality" of the Nazi cadres.

Writers such as Hannah Arendt and Hans Mommsen have been acutely aware of the challenge to understanding posed by this sudden transformation from radicalism to indifference. Arendt, after all, opened the third part of her *The Origins of Totalitarianism*—the part that deals with totalitarianism itself— with the sentence "Nothing is more characteristic of the totalitarian movements in general and of the quality of the fame of their leaders in particular than the startling swiftness with which they are forgotten…" This impermanence she saw as perhaps having something to do with the "fickleness of the masses," but above all it could be "traced to the perpetual-motion mania of totalitarian movements which can remain in power only so long as they keep moving and set everything around them in motion."[84] It is easy to see how the thrust of this kind of analysis came to be narrowed to the misunderstanding that the system was all, and the individuals brought nothing with them beyond a prescriptive human malleability. The image of the neutral perpetrator that arose in this context was entirely wrong, a misrepresentation of the way whole classes of men (and some women) brought agendas to the table that helped to provide the dynamism of Hitler's annihalatory program. Yet Arendt and others had grasped an essential problem that continues to be posed to us by the Nazi regime, and which lies at the core of Mommsen's analysis too— namely, how a body of men could operate with such comprehensiveness and relentlessness right up to the last minute, and then let go of the program, like that, as if it had never been theirs.

Notes

1. Hans Mommsen, "Die Realisierung des Utopischen. Die 'Endlösung der Judenfrage' im Dritten Reich" *Geschichte und Gesellschaft* 9 (1983): 381–420.

2. Cf Michael Mann, *The Dark Side of Democracy: Explaining Ethnic Cleansing* (Cambridge, 2005).

3. Götz Aly's book, *Hitlers Volksstaat. Raub, Rassenkrieg und nationaler Sozialismus* (Frankfurt am Main, 2005), appeared too late to be properly assimilated into this piece. Even in the absolute peak year of Aryanization, German-Jewish assets accounted to no more than 10 percent of national income. Götz Aly, "Wie die Nazis ihr Volk kauften" *Die Zeit*, 6 April 2004, reproduced at http://www.zeit.de/2005/15/Erwiderung_ Wehler.

4. Daniel Goldhagen, *Hitler's Willing Executioners: Ordinary Germans and the Holocaust* (New York, 1996).

5. Gerhard Paul and Klaus-Michael Mallmann, "Sozialisation, Milieu und Gewalt. Fortschritte und Probleme der neueren Täterforschung," in Klaus-Michael Mallmann/ Gerhard Paul, eds., *Karrieren der Gewalt. Nationalsozialistische Täterbiographien* (Darmstadt, 2004), 1–32, 1.

6. Christopher Browning, *Ordinary Men: Reserve Police Batallion 101 and the Final Solution in Poland* (New York, 1992); Goldhagen, *Hitler's Willing Executioners.*

7. Eva Hoffman, *After Such Knowledge: Memory, History and the Legacy of the Holocaust* (New York, 2004), 12.

8. Eugen Kogon, *The Theory and Practice of Hell: The German Concentration Camps and the System behind Them* (New York, 1979), 25.

9. Cited in Hermann Langbein, *People in Auschwitz* (Chapel Hill and London, 2004), 276.

10. A point noted by Nicolas Berg, in *Der Holocaust und die westdeutschen Historiker. Erforschung und Erinnerung* (Göttingen, 2003), 100.

11. Berg, *Der Holocaust und die westdeutschen Historiker,* 76.

12. *Nazi War Crime Trials: International Military Tribunal* ('Blue Series'), IV:510.

13. Joachim Fest, *The Face of the Third Reich* (London, 1970), 302.

14. Ibid.

15. Hannah Arendt, *Eichmann in Jerusalem: A Report on the Banality of Evil* (Harmondsworth, revised and enlarged edition 1994), 287.

16. My translation from Hannah Arendt, "Organisierte Schuld" [1946] reprinted in *In der Gegenwart. Übungen im politischen Denken II* (Munich, Zürich, 2000), 26–37, here 34. Svenja Goltermann kindly alerted me to this text.

17. Arendt, *Eichmann in Jerusalem,* 25–6.

18. Raul Hilberg, *The Destruction of the European Jews* (Chicago, 1961); on Hilberg's chagrin at Arendt's reliance on his work, see Raul Hilberg, *The Politics of Memory: The Journey of a Holocaust Historian* (Chicago, 1996), 148–50.

19. Raul Hilberg, *The Destruction of the European Jews,* 3rd ed. (New Haven, 2003), 1059–60.

20. "Ein Mann, wie er der Anlage nach unter uns leben könnte." My translation of a citation in Berg, *Der Holocaust und die westdeutschen Historiker,* 302.

21. Langbein, *People in Auschwitz,* 277.

22. Hilberg, *The Politics of Memory,* 148.

23. Fest, *Face,* xiii.

24. Fest, *Face,* 278.

25. Ibid.

26. Ibid.

27. See Mann, *The Dark Side,* 213.

28. Berg, *Der Holocaust und die westdeutschen Historiker,* 577–8, 582f.

29. Michael Greve, *Der justitielle und rechtspolitische Umgang mit den NS-Gewaltverbrechen in den sechziger Jahren* (Frankfurt am Main, 2001). On the importance of *Gesinnung* in German jurisprudence earlier in the century, see Pamela Swett's chapter in this volume.

30. Daniel Bell, *The End of Ideology: On the Exhaustion of Political Ideas in the Fifties* (Glencoe, Ill., 1960); Helmut Schelsky, *Die skeptische Generation: eine Soziologie der deutschen Jugend* (Düsseldorf, 1956).

31. See for example the *Life* report on Eichmann cited in David Cesarani, *Eichmann: His Life and Crimes,* (London, 2004), 61.

32. *New Statesman,* 14 April 1961, cited in Ibid.

33. Mommsen, "Realisierung."

34. Günther Deschner, *Reinhard Heydrich. Statthalter der totalen Macht. Biographie,* (Esslingen am Neckar, 1977).

35. Albert Speer, *Erinnerungen* (Frankfurt/M., 1969); *Spandauer Tagebücher* (Frankfurt aM.), Berlin, Wien, 1975).

36. Christopher Browning, *The Final Solution and the German Foreign Office: A Study of Referat DIII of Abteilung Deutschland 1940–1943* (New York, 1978).

37. See Tim Mason, "Epilogue," in idem., *Social Policy and the Third Reich: The Working Class and the 'National Community',"* ed. Jane Caplan (Oxford, 1993).

38. Klaus Theweleit, *Männerphantasien,* 1.–20. Tsd. ed. (Frankfurt am Main, 1977). Translated into English as Klaus Theweleit, *Male Fantasies* (Cambridge, 1987).

39. On the 'Zweite Verdrängung', see Ulrich Herbert, 'Vernichtungspolitik. Neue Antworten und Fragen zur Geschichte des 'Holocaust,' in Herbert, ed., *Nationalsozialistische Vernichtungspolitik,* 9–66; and Paul, "Von Pyschopathen," 31–3.

40. See, in this vein, Yehuda Bauer, "The Place of the Holocaust in Contemporary History," *Studies in Contemporary Jewry,* 1 (1984): 201–24.

41. Ernst Klee, Willi Dressen, *Schöne Zeiten": Judenmord aus der Sicht der Täter und Gaffer* (Frankfurt am Main, 1988); Omer Bartov, *The Eastern Front 1941–1945, German Troops and the Barbarisation of Warfare* (Oxford, 1985); Tom Segev, *Soldiers of Evil: The Commandants of the Nazi Concentration Camps* (New York, 1988).

42. On this shift see Mark Roseman, "National Socialism and Modernisation," in Richard Bessel, ed., *Fascist Italy and Nazi Germany: Comparisons and Contrasts* (Cambridge, 1996), 197–229.

43. Götz Aly, et al, *Sozialpolitik und Judenvernichtung. Gibt es eine Ökonomie der Endlösung?,* (Berlin, 1987); Götz Aly and Susanne Heim, *Vordenker der Vernichtung: Auschwitz und die deutschen Pläne für eine neue europäische Ordnung* (Hamburg, 1991).

44. Susanne Heim and Götz Aly, "The Holocaust and Population Policy: Remarks on the Decision on the 'Final Solution'," *Yad Vashem Studies* XXIV (1994): 45–70, here 51.

45. As noted recently by Michael Wildt "Vertrautes Ressentiment" in Die Zeit, 04.05.2005, reproduced in the website: http://www.zeit.de/2005/19/P-Aly, viewed on May 30 2005.

46. On shifts of policy, see Christian Gerlach, *Kalkulierte Morde. Die deutsche Wirtschafts- und Vernichtungspolitik in Weißrußland 1941 bis 1944* (Hamburg, 1999).

47. Christian Gerlach, Götz Aly, *Das letzte Kapitel. Realpolitik, Ideologie und der Mord an den ungarischen Juden 1944/1945* (Stuttgart, Munich, 2002).

48. Ulrich Herbert, *Best. Biographische Studien über Radikalismus, Weltanschauung und Vernunft 1903–1989* (Bonn, 1996); Michael Wildt, *Generation des Unbedingten. Das Führungskorps des Reichsicherheitshauptamtes* (Hamburg, 2002).

49. Herbert, *Best,* 94.

50. Some of the best of this recent work is summarized in Ulrich Herbert, ed., *National Socialist Extermination Policy* (Oxford and New York, 1999).

51. See Herbert, "Vernichtungspolitik"; Paul, "Von Psychopathen," 37–43; Paul & Mallmann, "Sozialisation," 1–32.

52. See Alf Lüdtke's essay "'Fehlgreifen in der Wahl der Mittel.' Optionen im Alltag militärischen Handelns," *Mittelweg 36*, No. 12 (2003): 61–75, here 75.

53. Jens Banach, *Heydrichs Elite. Das Führerkorps der Sicherheitspolizei und des SD 1936–1945*, (Paderborn, 1998); Holger Berschel, *Bürokratie und Terror. Das Judenreferat der Gestapo Düsseldorf, 1935–1945* (Essen, 2001).

54. Frank Bajohr, *Parvenüs und Profiteure: Korruption in der NS-Zeit* (Frankfurt am Main, 2001), 75–89.

55. Bogdan Musial, *Deutsche Zivilverwaltung und Judenverfolgung im Generalgouvernement. Eine Fallstudie zum Distrikt Lublin 1939–1944* (Wiesbaden, 1999).

56. Wildt, *Generation.*

57. Michael Mann, "Were the Perpetrators of Genocide 'Ordinary Men' or 'Real Nazis'? Results from Fifteen Hundred Biographies," *Holocaust and Genocide Studies* 2000, 329–66, here 335.

58. See, e.g. Mark Roseman, *The Wannsee Conference and the Final Solution: A Reconsideration* (New York, 2002), 126–32.

59. Banasch, *Heydrichs Elite.*

60. Ruth Bettina Birn, *Die Höheren SS- und Polizeiführer. Himmlers Vertreter im Reich und in den besetzten Gebieten* (Düsseldorf, 1986).

61. Mann's sample draws on 1,581 presumed German war criminals, Mann, "Were the Perpetrators of Genocide 'Ordinary Men'"; Mann, *Dark Side.*

62. Mann, "Were the Perpetrators of Genocide 'Ordinary Men,'" 350–55.

63. Mann, *Dark Side*, 239.

64. Roseman, *Wannsee*, 132.

65. Herbert, *Best*, 285–6.

66. See Helmut Großcurth's comments in, *Tagebücher eines Abwehroffiziers 1938–1940* (Stuttgart, 1970), 162. See also the comments of Heinz Höhne, cited in Deschner, *Heydrich*, 174.

67. On perpetrator careers, see Mallmann & Paul "Sozialisation," 4–6; Mann, *Dark Side*, 240–78.

68. Wildt, *Generation.*

69. Herbert Jäger, *Verbrechen unter totalitärer Herrschaft. Studien zur nationalsozialistischen Gewaltkriminalität* (Frankfurt am Main, 1982).

70. See for example Helmut Walser Smith, *The Butcher's Tale: Murder and Anti-Semitism in a German Town* (New York, 2002).

71. Enzo Traverso, *The Origins of Nazi Violence* (New York and London, 2003), 6.

72. Mazower, Mark, "Violence and the State in the Twentieth Century," *The American Historical Review* 107, no.4 (2002): 1158–1178.

73. Browning, *Ordinary Men*, 160.

74. Traverso, *Origins*, 78.

75. Cited in Traverso, *Origins*, 83.

76. James M. Diehl, *Paramilitary Politics in Weimar Germany* (Bloomington and London, 1977), 16.

77. Pamela Swett's essay in this volume illustrates the complex relationship between ideas and violence in the Weimar period.

78. Mark Levene, "The Experience of Armenian and Romanian Genocide 1915–16 and 1941–42," in Hans-Lukas Kieser, ed., *Der Völkermord an den Armeniern und die Shoah* (Zurich, 2002), 423–62, here 442–3.

79. Karin Orth, *Das System der nationalsozialistischen Konzentrationslager. Eine politische Organisationsgeschichte* (Hamburg, 1999), 272ff.

80. Ibid.

81. Mallmann & Paul "Sozialisation," 19. And see the references in Frank Biess's chapter, n. 19.

82. My translation from Hannah Arendt, "Was heißt persönliche Verantwortung unter einer Diktatur" [1964], reproduced in Arendt, *Nach Auschwitz*, 81–97, here 85.

83. Wildt, *Generation*, 797–813.

84. Hannah Arendt, *The Origins of Totalitarianism* (San Diego and New York, new edition 1966), 305–6.

CHAPTER 5

The Dissolution of the Third Reich

Hans Mommsen

The unconditional surrender of the German Reich on the 8th and 9th of May, 1945, marked not only Germany's total military defeat but also the complete internal collapse of its political system. The dissolution of coherent government had been gathering speed ever since the defeat of the German army at Stalingrad in January 1943. Fueled by the increasing efforts of Nazi Party agencies to wrest administrative prerogatives from the state, the internal breakdown was already well underway by the time of the Allied invasion of France in June 1944; it shifted up another gear after the summer, when the Red Army's breakthrough in the middle sector of the Eastern front made it certain that Germany would lose the war.

Against this background the question arises how the regime was able to fight right up to the very last moment. Not until four-fifths of Reich territory had been occupied did the German army surrender to the Allies. Right up to the last minute, the Nazi leadership had not taken any serious steps to enter negotiations either with the West or with Stalin. Only after Hitler's suicide, did Goebbels start his abortive attempt to negotiate with Marshall Tchuikov over separate armistice conditions.[1] Heinrich Himmler's halfhearted efforts to make contact with the Western Allies through representatives of "World Jewry," as well as his diplomatic feelers through Count Folke Bernadotte, not only failed completely but also prompted Hitler to oust him from the party and his office.[2]

As long as Hitler was alive, the regime was unable to stop fighting a war that was clearly already lost. Even in the earlier phase of the war Hitler had prevented any settlement with the defeated countries that might serve as a precedent for postwar peace negotiations. Despite the pressure of Allied pro-European propaganda, Hitler had avoided any regulation of territorial and political issues with regard to Germany's western neighbors. To the minister of the Reich Chancellery, Hans-Heinrich Lammers, Hitler confided that any discussion about a National Socialist concept for reordering postwar Europe was "unimportant for the war effort," and he prohibited even draft planning for the future.[3] Once he had made the decision to wage a war of racial annihilation against the Soviet Union, the notion of peace became meaningless to him. It is clear that he was thinking now in terms of perennial warfare in the East.[4]

At the same time, Hitler's reluctance to make priority decisions extended even to the conduct of the war. When Goebbels urged him to stop the two fronts war either by an arrangement with the *"jüdische Mache"* in Moscow (which he preferred) or the capitalistic *"Börsenjudentum"* in Washington, he avoided either option by stressing his conviction that any negotiation was out of the question as long as the *Wehrmacht* had not achieved any crucial military success.[5] The strategically problematic occupation of Hungary in 1944, which involved a serious weakening of the German defense in the middle sector, as well as Hitler's hopeless attempt to turn the tide with the offensive in the Ardennes in December 1944, were rooted in deliberations of this kind.[6]

Obviously, Hitler's strategic decisions were subject to the same indecisiveness that characterized his approach to domestic politics. Whenever the regime ran into problems, it reacted with short-term improvisation and avoided making difficult long-term choices. In the long run, it paid for that with increasing inefficiency and lack of coordination between divergent policies. The chronic inclination to disregard the limits of human and material resources derived both from an overestimation of what could be achieved with sheer willpower and from the built-in competition of rival agencies. The political system thus gradually lost its internal steering capacities and underwent growing disintegration.

During the period between July 1943, when Mussolini was dismissed with the support of the Fascist Grand Council, and July 1944 the ruling elite in the Nazi regime began to realize how the critical the situation was as a result of the never-ending chain of military set-backs. It was above all the defeat and surrender of the Sixth Army at Stalingrad that provided an ominous warning that could not be overlooked and ultimately destroyed the German army's myth of invincibility. On 18th February 1943, less than three weeks after the Stalingrad catastrophe, Joseph Goebbels proclaimed in his public speech at the Berlin Sport Palace the necessity of "total war." As well as calling for underused manpower resources to be fully exploited and consumer goods' production to be cut back, the Minister for Propaganda demanded that government be concentrated and streamlined.[7]

Despite attempts to regenerate the Reich Defense Council and, after those attempts failed, to install a Three Man Committee in order to enforce overdue rationalization measures, the lack of coordination within the Reich government persisted through the critical year of 1943. The replacement of Wilhelm

Frick as minister of the interior by Heinrich Himmler as reaction to the fall of
Mussolini did not prevent increasing chaos in the administration. Nor did it
reduce the infighting between party and state agencies that absorbed most of
the energies of the Hitler's subordinates. Himmler was less interested in the
agenda of the Ministry and failed to come up with efficient rationalization
measures in the general administration while he transferred some of its com-
petencies to the SS.[8]

Not until the crisis of July 1944 did Goebbels' efforts to regenerate a more
effective central government find Hitler's still-reluctant approval. Yet even
then the dictator timidly avoided any fundamental reform of the leadership
structure. Hitler continued to obstruct the mobilization of economic and
manpower resources that was clearly both essential and long overdue. Thus,
the dictator rejected almost all reform incentives as they were proposed by
Goebbels and Bormann because he feared that measures of this kind might
raise opposition among other Nazi leaders or affect his personal prestige. Goebbels' incessant pressure to dismiss Ribbentrop, the minister of foreign affairs
who was held responsible for the Reich's desperate diplomatic isolation, as
well as the attempts by Bormann and Himmler to bring Hitler to withdraw his
nomination of Göring as his designated successor, proved to be futile.

Given this state of indecision, the crucial impetus to strengthen the German war effort came from the minister of armament and war production,
Albert Speer, who had taken over almost all the prerogatives of the Four Year
Plan while leaving Göring's nominal status untouched.[9] Relying on Hitler's
unalloyed support, Speer was able to subject the *Heereswaffenamt*, the armament office of the army, to his orders and thereby attain control over most parts
of the German armament production. With his direct access to the Führer,
Speer became one of the most influential satraps within the regime. He made
use of the same unorthodox methods as the party chieftains and did not hesitate to circumvent ordinary administrative channels and legal procedures.
Like the Nazi leaders he believed in the principle of *Menschenführung* and preferred to rely on the personal loyalty of individuals rather than on official
chains of command, a strategy that proved to be remarkably successful in the
short run and enabled him to increase armaments output severalfold (although much of it was rather the merit of his predecessor, Fritz Todt, and
sometimes the product of skillfully manipulated production statistics).[10]

Confronted with the crisis at the Eastern Front, Speer sent a detailed memorandum to Hitler, demanding an immediate intensification of armament efforts. Criticizing the "Three-Man-Committee" for its obvious shortcomings
and inefficiency, Speer pleaded for the installment of a responsible leadership,
which should be entrusted to personalities who were not involved in the continuous infighting between party and government agencies and would not
loose their stamina even in critical situations. These demands were tantamount

to nominating a special plenipotentiary for domestic political affairs (similar to the economic dictator who had been appointed in the late Weimar era).[11]

Speer's memorandum coincided with Goebbels' repeated proposals to establish an internal dictatorship and to restore the unity of the Reich government. Goebbels did not hesitate to enter into an alliance with Speer, since earlier efforts to win Göring over for resolute action had foundered on the Reich Marshal's passivity. Goebbels supported Speer's demands in a widely noted article in the weekly *Das Reich*.[12] In a second memorandum, Speer reiterated his arguments for the necessity of achieving a more efficient leadership and came out with the proposal of entrusting Goebbels with this task, being convinced that the propaganda minister would have the energy that was needed to push this program through and to neutralize the protests of antagonistic interests.

Goebbels knew very well that the biggest obstacle to implement the plan lay in Hitler's notorious distrust and concern for keeping up his personal prestige. In his article, he argued that Speer's proposal had met with overwhelming approval in the German public. There was some truth in this, but the argument was designed above all to overcome Hitler's apprehension.[13] In addition, a week later Goebbels presented a comparable memorandum of about fifty pages to Hitler in which he reiterated the arguments of his Sport Palace speech of February 1943 and demanded that the Three Man Committee be replaced by an independent commissioner.[14]

The timing of Goebbels' initiative was perfect and strengthened his position in a top conference convened by Hitler for 22 July in order to discuss the Speer memorandum. At the meeting Goebbels presented himself as the uniquely qualified candidate and gained the endorsement of Borman, Keitel, Speer, Funk, and Lammers, who attended the meeting. Mindful of Hitler's usual hesitancy, he requested a unanimous vote for his nomination. Nobody dared oppose him.[15] Hitler yielded to pressure and installed Joseph Goebbels on 25 July 1944 as "Reich Plenipotenitary for the Total War Effort." This happened only five days after the failed assassination attempt of 20 July.

The new position, however, did not really amount to being "the domestic leader" that Goebbels had optimistically claimed for himself in his diary,[16] because Goebbels did not obtain the prerogative to issue orders either to the NSDAP or to the Wehrmacht, both of which were exempt from his general authority to give directives to the administrative bodies. Furthermore, the minister for propaganda grossly overestimated his capability to override vested interests when it came to mobilizing additional manpower or closing down shops and consumer industries. This overestimation was partly the consequence of his specific perception of politics, which stressed the role of propagandistic indoctrination while ignoring the impact of bureaucratic factors. Goebbels believed his role was to set things in motion and act as a catalyst. He preferred the local and regional party apparatus to the civil administration or the military institutions, believing in the superiority of the principle of "*Menschenführung*" over that of public administration. However, the mixed committees, consisting of representatives of the party, the regional administration and the Labor Front, founded in order to speed up the military mobilization turned out to be rather inefficient and simply added to the red tape.[17]

Thus, Goebbels' total mobilization fell far behind the expected results. For Goebbels, however, the important thing was the propagandistic effect of the whole enterprise, since he was well aware it would at least take a couple of months before any sizable influx of new conscripts and an increase in the overall labor force could be realized. But he was convinced that the campaign was indispensable if the announcement of "Total War" should not loose its credibility, and he saw the main effect of the campaign as lying in a "dramatic improvement of the public mood" and a reactivation of the people through giving them "fresh hope."[18] It was thus primarily propagandistic deliberations that induced Goebbels to come out as advocate of exploiting all available human and material resources for the war effort, including obligatory labor for women. The practical impact on the actual mobilization of the labor force was secondary. The primary consideration was to demonstrate through sweeping action that the *Volksgemeinschaft* (People's Community) possessed a "united will to action."[19]

The palliative that Goebbels had in mind against the threatening German defeat consisted of the establishment of a fanatical will to hold out and not so much in utilizing available resources, which were rather seen as a means to attain this purpose. There was another reason, too, for emphasizing political rather than economic mobilization. Even before this initiative, the rumor that Speer might become Hitler's successor raised the envy of the party chieftains. Above all, Martin Bormann, the chief of the party chancellery, and Goebbels were alarmed by the perspective that Speer might outflank the party and gain decisive influence on Hitler. Hitler himself tended to neglect day-to-day politics, and since he had taken over military command his energies were almost completely absorbed by the conduct of the military operations in the East. Goebbels and Bormann were resolved to react without delay. The Reich propaganda minister, and, along with him, Martin Borman as head of the party chancellery and Robert Ley as Reich organization leader of the NSDAP, responded to the crisis, albeit in an uncoordinated fashion, with an all-embracing ideological mobilization. Crucial in this respect was their common conviction that it was only the party that was able to achieve the turn in German and world history by implementing the revolutionary program that had been but partially fulfilled during the early years of the regime.

In this attempt to offer itself as the true dynamo behind the mobilization "of the ultimate effort," the NSDAP returned to the propaganda methods and the self-perception that had characterized the so-called combat period ("Kampfzeit"), that is, the period before the seizure of power. The experiences of the combat period were incessantly referred to in order to demonstrate that through the heroic exertion of the powers of will, the imminent crisis situation could be overcome—and for this the party appeared to be indispensable. The provisional defeat of the movement on 9 November 1923 was taken as proof that only the party was and would be able to overcome even serious setbacks. A directive of the Party Chancellery declared on September 1943: "The National Socialist movement has mastered every situation! It has never let itself be led astray through occasional set-backs and severe difficulties," and in the instructions for party-speakers published by the Reich Propaganda Office one could read, that "the struggle which we as the German people and nation have to carry on today is fundamentally the same struggle against the same enemy which the movement had to carry on at home in the years of the combat period."[20] By unremitting references to the party's past, the impression was created that if only the party took things into its own hand, the turn to victory would be feasible.

Meanwhile, Bormann had started an internal offensive to increase the unity and active strength of the movement after the mass party had become numerically bloated and politically sterile. In seeking to mold the movement into a political combat instrument, Bormann could rely on the support of Robert Ley, who, besides his function as the leader of the German Labor Front, still held the influential position of Reich organization leader of the NSDAP. Both recognized the party's obligation to support the war effort and its primary task to improve public morale. In order to achieve this and to restore the badly shaken public reputation of the party and its affiliated organizations, Bormann tried to activate the rank and file by arranging ever more obligatory membership assemblies, propaganda marches, and public demonstrations.

By the same token, Bormann tried to improve the party's contact with the population by introducing special office hours, so-called *Sprechabende,* where visitors could report their grievances to the local functionaries.[21] Furthermore, since the summer of 1943 Bormann arranged a wave of public rallies in order to underscore the party's claim for political leadership.[22] The officially voluntary character of the requested activities was accompanied by radical disciplinary measures against those who did not comply with the enforced reactivation of the rank and file. These steps at least held the functionaries in line, though without significantly improving the party's negative public image.

Bormann's efforts to polish the party image were more effective when he took to boosting public functions in the welfare sector. The party took the responsibility to take care for those *Volksgenossen* who had lost their homes in conjunction with the Allied air raids or who had to be evacuated from the combat zones.[23] In conjunction with this, Bormann ordered the NSV, the National

Socialist Welfare organization, to act expressly in the name of the political organization of the NSDAP.[24] By the same token, the party usurped the compe-
tencies of private or public relief institutions. This tactical move helped to
repair the damaged party image to a certain extent, because an increasing percentage of the German population had to rely on the support of the NSV and
the party apparatus for assistance with war damage, air raids, and flight from
the East.

Alongside the continuous efforts to reorganize the party and improve its
public image, Bormann put increasing pressure on the public administration
and usurped additional state functions for the party at local and regional levels. This process of "partification"—a term coined by Dietrich Orlow[25]—was
fueled by the role of the Gauleiter in their function as Reich defense commissioners and culminated in the take-over of the civil administration by a growing number of the Gauleiter.[26] Thus, the role of the party apparatus on local
and regional levels increased to a degree that surpassed the party's boldest
dreams entertained in the period of the seizure of power. The NSDAP became
more and more engaged as an auxiliary of the Security Police and the Gestapo.
It also became responsible for the construction of defense lines and fortifica-
tion measures as well as the sheltering of the evacuated population.[27]

This development coincided with the perception among party leaders
that only the party could secure the final victory and led to the conviction that
only by eliminating still existing non-National Socialist elements could this
target be achieved. The distribution of power that had been established in
1933 between the party and the bourgeois elite had definitively to be overcome. Hence, demands to complete a Nazi revolution that had stalled in 1933
gained new strength and led to the illusion that the crisis could be overcome
by establishing unrestricted party rule in all relevant political realms.

In the view of party leaders, the regime's military and political crisis
showed that the Nazi movement's impetus had been blocked by the interference and halfhearted compromises of conservative bureaucrats lacking in dynamism and will power. Only the party and its spirit could achieve an overall
mobilization of the nation's strength and resources. The precondition for realizing the idolized "unity of the will" consisted not only in the complete elimination of Jews and other racial aliens, but also in the cleansing of society from
clandestine opponents or dissidents, in other words in achieving total racial
and political homogeneity.

This voluntaristic attitude, which was rooted in the Nietzschean cult of
the will and the ultimate rejection of established historical structures,[28] had
been symptomatic of the early stages of the movement in which the vision of
future victory had served to bridge the gap with the party's day-to-day reality.
Now, under the pressure of imminent defeat it emerged again. A milestone on
the road to what I would like to call this terroristic decisionism was Goebbels'

speech in the Berlin Sport Palace where he argued that the promised final victory was dependent less on the availability of material resources than on fanatical will power to hold out to the last man. The all-embracing ideological mobilization of the party promulgated by Bormann fit exactly into this picture.

The party's retreat to the reminiscence of the combat period coincided with Hitler's personal conviction that the "final victory" was the predestined outcome of the internal and external fight against the Jewish arch enemy. In his mind the unity of the will was the guarantee for final success. In his last radio speech on 30 January 1945, Hitler argued that the internal unification of the German people, the realization of which he attributed to himself and the Nazi movement, was a unique world-historical achievement proving his and the Nazi movement's invincibility.[29] Goebbels encouraged him to cling to this view and reminded him of the constellation in December 1932, when Gregor Strasser, opposed to Hitler's "all-or-nothing strategy," had predicted the breakdown of the party after Hitler resolved not to infringe the "purity of the National Socialist idea" by entering a right-wing coalition. Hitler's decision had turned out to be successful.[30] Simultaneously, Goebbels reminded Hitler that November 1918 as well as November 1923 proved that given steadfastness until the very end, defeat would be followed by final victory. The recourse to the "cult of the will" was reflected in Goebbels' move to compare the dictator to Frederick the Great and the latter's endurance in the Seven Years War. In his last proclamation on February 24 1945, the anniversary of the founding of the NSDAP, Hitler evoked again "our unshakable will" that in the end would prevail.[31] According to Hitler's vision, the Allies would necessarily fail, being incapable of fighting a protracted war on German soil against the desperate resistance of a people who would defend every village, every house, and every barn to the last man. Then the Western powers, at least, would have to acknowledge that it was futile to continue an increasingly costly battle between an entire people and an army of paid soldiers.[32]

Hitler's vision of the "final victory" was reflected in the official propaganda and the activities of the party. He thereby returned to his ideological point of departure and took refuge in the rhetoric of the combat period. As an undercurrent of the hold-out propaganda, the idea also surfaced that even if immediate defeat could not be averted, the fight to the last man would secure "the victory of the National Socialist idea" in the future, providing inspiration for the later renewal of Germany's struggle against its oppressors. Symptomatic of such reasoning was Goebbels' attempts in March 1945 to build up the *"Werwolf"* not so much to perform military actions but to guarantee the survival of the Nazi ideology.[33] A series of training camps were set up, in which Hitler youths were systematically indoctrinated to fight for the attachment of future generations to the "National Socialist idea" even under Allied occupation.[34]

The process of "partification" found a significant expression in Bormann's pressure to introduce "National Socialist Leadership Officers" into the armed forces and thereby to copy the model of the "political officer" in the Soviet army, the much denounced commissars. Selected and trained by the party organization, these "National Socialist Leadership Officers" were attached to every military unit and had to monitor the political reliability of the commanders as well as to intensify the ideological indoctrination of the troops.[35] They were directly responsible to the Party Chancellery. Possibly, Bormann calculated that in the not-too-distant future the demobilization would engender the chance to replace the professionals by the party officers and, thereby, achieve the partification of the armed forces that had failed in 1934.

Another facet of Party Chancellery's ideological mobilization campaign was the establishment of the *Deutscher Volkssturm* in October 1944. This move was an attempt not only to mobilize the last levy after the severe casualties of the fighting troops, but also to put the propagandistic pattern of the total mobilization of the German people into practice. Indeed, it was accompanied by attempts to gain control over the army in the long run. Therefore, Bormann put pressure on the Supreme Command of the Army to accept that the new militia should be led by party functionaries and that the authority of Heinrich Himmler as chief of the reserve army be restricted to providing weaponry and to the operational leadership.[36]

As immediately became obvious, the party echelons could not provide the urgently needed militarily trained staff, never mind that the local party chiefs were often militarily incompetent; but in the view of Bormann and Goebbels, who strongly favored the militia project, its military value was of secondary importance. In their view, the *Volkssturm* should be utilized for the envisaged total fanaticization of the population in order to guarantee the "final victory." Goebbels declared that the "unified deployment of the entire people united in the idea of National Socialism" would be the final realization of the Peoples' Community.[37] On the occasion of the pledge of allegiance of the *Volkssturm* he again deployed the last-fight discourse and argued: "We know that an idea lives, even if all its bearers have fallen. The enemy who has nothing more to fight with than the material resources it can deploy will eventually capitulate before the massed strength of a fanatically fighting people."[38]

The ambivalence characterizing these and many similar propagandistic proclamations blurred the distinction between the current situation and a heroic future of self-sacrifice. Recalling Wagnerian death rhetoric, it was accompanied by an increasing self-historization, making frequent recourse to great moments from the German national past. It was not accidental that the founding declaration of the *Volkssturm* was issued by Himmler on October 18, the anniversary of the 1813 Battle of Nations at Leipzig, and that he referred in his speech expressly to the Prussian *Landsturm* which allegedly had carried the main weight of the fight against Napoleon as a "revolutionary people's movement."[39]

The twin themes of total mobilization and heroic historicization were brought together in the UFA film *Kolberg* by Veit Harlan. Harlan's production had been sponsored and heavily subsidized by Joseph Goebbels, who regarded *Kolberg* as the equivalent of at least four military divisions.[40] The film premiere occurred in the fortress of La Rochelle on 30 January 1945 (the film reels were brought to the already beleaguered city by airplanes and submarines), and it was subsequently shown in the Tauentzien Palace and other Berlin cinemas for several weeks. The film portrayed the allegedly heroic defense of the city of Kolberg against the superior forces of Napoleon I, and repeated the myth that it was this struggle that had unleashed the German uprising in 1813.[41]

The extent to which the mobilization campaign by the party took hold in the rank and file as well as in the population in general is difficult to assess, but it probably prolonged the war. Bormann's intention to form a special task force by the party that should organize the defense "to the last man" in the cities and villages under attack failed because of the opposition by the troop commanders in charge who refused to order activities of this kind. But the extreme pressure upon civilians made active resistance extremely dangerous and brought dissenting party functionaries in line. This helps to explain why up to the very last moment public resistance against the irresponsible continuation of the fighting occurred only in exceptional cases.

The almost total partification had destroyed the last institutional backbone for resistance as well as for dissent. After the failed assassination attempt on Hitler on 20 July 1944, the military leadership definitively lost its former institutional autonomy. The army leadership lay exclusively in the hands of fanatic generals who backed the party's last-ditch propaganda. They also supported the terrorist proceedings of the numerous peripatetic field court-martials and the ordinary military judiciary, a system that resulted in the passing and carrying out of more than 30,000 death sentences.[42]

By the same token, the almost omnipotent *Gauleiter*/Reich defense commissioners unleashed an intense wave of terror primarily directed against the civil population and the numerous conscript laborers. In each *Gau*, drumhead courts were formed by the ordinary judiciary that sentenced thousands of people to death. They did not hesitate to assert the liability of clan and kin *(Sippenhaft)* when the defendants escaped their grip. At the same time, the Labor Education Camps that had been established by the local and regional *Gestapo* in order to discipline foreign and German workers, turned into virtual death centers and were used for mass-killings until the last days of the war.[43] It remains to be discovered how many Germans, Soviet prisoners of war, compulsory laborers, and other foreigners fell victim to the death brigades of the SS, the *Gestapo,* and the Security Police and in many cases to self-proclaimed drum-head field martials. The figure will possibly amount to several hundred thousand individuals murdered during the last phase of the war.[44]

The complete partification had thus destroyed all institutional backbones for active resistance or dissent. The atrophy of the political system as such paralyzed all possible initiatives to resist the last-ditch strategy pursued by the party and the SS, even under utterly hopeless conditions. A relatively small minority of fanatics were able to dominate the entire scene. The identification of the external and the internal enemy in the minds of the Nazi elite implied the necessity to eliminate any inimical element or potential dissident. The escalation of terror was, therefore, inseparably bound to the survival myth and the propaganda of fighting to the last man. The fictitious world to which the responsible party leaders had become accustomed was shaped by the re-emerging cult of the combat period, which itself was glossed over with heroism and reflected a strong tendency toward self-historization. As long as they were spellbound by the *Führer-myth,* the majority of the *Gauleiter* were prevented from taking any realistic action and from stopping the process of self-destruction.[45]

The Nazi elite was thus running amok and had lost any touch with reality, immersed as it was in the fictitious world of the early stages of the movement. Yet apart from the self-deceiving party activists and their entourage, there was nobody left who could stop the process. The voluntarist origins of National Socialism came into the foreground. It resulted in an escalation of crime and terror and accelerated the atomization and increasing atrophy of the governmental system. The process of self-destruction that had accompanied the expansionist policy of the regime was a necessary corollary of the military defeat. After Hitler's suicide, the whole system collapsed overnight and the myth of any survival of National Socialism fell asunder.

Notes

1. Ralph Georg Reuth, *Goebbels. Eine Biographie* (Munich, 1990), 608 f.; cf. H. R. Trevor-Roper, *Hitlers letzte Tage* (Frankfurt, 1968), 197; Georgi K. Schukow, *Erinnerungen und Gedanken* (Stuttgart, 1969), 604 f.

2. Felix Kersten, *Totenkopf und Treue. Heinrich Himmler ohne Uniform* (Hamburg, 1952), 343; Folke Bernadotte, *Das Ende. Meine Verhandlungen in Deutschland im Frühjahr 1945 und ihre politischen Folgen* (Zürich, 1945), 66 f.; see Klaus-Dietmar Henke, *Die amerikanische Besetzung Deutschlands* (Munich, 1995), 886 ff.

3. Lammers to Rosenberg on Aug. 10, 1944, in. Hans Werner Neulen, *Europa und das 3. Reich. Einigungsbestrebungen im deutschen Machtbereich 1939–1945* (Munich, 1987), 163 f. Goebbels changed his former position and eventually announced a program for a "socialist reordering of the continent" (Elke Fröhlich, ed., *Die Tagebücher von Joseph Goebbels,* Part II, vol. 15, [Munich, 1995], 467).

4. Cf. Andreas Hillgruber, *Hitlers Strategie, Politik und Kriegsführung* 1940–41 (Frankfurt, 1965), 562 ff.; Rolf-Dieter Müller, *Hitlers Ostkrieg und die deutsche Siedlungspolitik* (Frankfurt, 1991), 23 f.

5. Memorandum Goebbels to Hitler on July 25, 1944, BA Berlin, NL 118/100; cf. Ralph Georg Reuth, Goebbels, 567 and Goebbels diaries of September 10. 20 and 23, 1944 (Tagebücher Part II, vol. 9, 464, 542, 655).

6. See Hitlers speech to the division commanders on Dec. 28, 1944 (Helmut Heiber, ed., *Hitlers Lagebeprechungen. Die Protokollfragmente sener militärischen Konferenzen* (Stuttgart, 1962), 738 ff.)

7. Helmut Heiber, ed., *Goebbels Reden 1932–1945* (Düsseldorf, 1991), no. 17, 172 ff.; cf. Günter Moltmann, *Goebbels Rede zm Totalen Krieg am 18. Februar 1943*, in *VfZ* 12 (1964): 13 ff.

8. See Dieter Rebentisch, *Führerstaat und Verwaltung im Zweiten Weltkrieg* (Stuttgart, 1989), 499 ff.

9. See Alfred Kube, *Pour le Mérite und Hakenkreuz. Hermann Göring im Dritten Reich* (Munich, 1986), 340 f.

10. See Richard J. Overy, *War and Economy in the Third Reich* (Oxford, 1994), 356 f.; Gregor Jansen, *Das Ministerium Speer. Deutschlands Rüstung im Krieg* (Berlin, 1968), 175 f.

11. Memorandum by Speer, July 12 and 20, 1944, printed in: Willy Boelcke, ed., *Deutschlands Rüstung im Zweiten Weltkrieg. Hitlers Konferenzen mit Albert Speer* (Frankfurt, 1969), no. 2; cf. Albert Speer, *Erinnerungen* (Frankfurt, 1969), 405.

12. "Führen wir einen totalen Krieg?" *Das Reich* (July 7, 1944); see Peter Longerich, *Joseph Goebbels und der totale Krieg*, in *VfZ* 35 (1987): 298.

13. See Heinz Boberach, ed., *Meldungen aus dem Reich 1938–1945*, vol. 17 (Herrsching, 1984), 6636 ff.

14. Printed in Longerich, *Joseph Goebbels und der totale Krieg*, 305–14.

15. Chefbesprechung on July 22, 1944 (BA Potsdam R 43II/664a, 87).

16. See Fröhlich, *Goebbels Tagebücher*, series II, vol. 11, Februry 27, 1943.

17. See Horst Matzerath, *Nationalsozialismus und kommunale Selbstverwaltung* (Stuttgart, 1970), p. 240 f.; cf. letter from State Secretary Stuckart to Bormann, Dec. 19, 1944 (BA Potsdam R 18/1263, fol. 19.).

18. Longerich, op. cit. 313; in the chief meeting on July 22 he had ascertained: "Die Reform des öffentlichen Lebens werde zum Teil nur optischen Charakter haben können, doch dürfe die Bedeutung solcher Maßnahmen nicht unterschätzt werden" (see the document quoted in footnote 15, fol. 86).

19. See *Aufklärungs- und Rednermaterial der Reichspropagandaleitung der NSDAP, Lieferung* 9 (Sept. 1943), 2 and 4.

20. See ibidem and Anordnung 55/43 on September 29, 1943, in: *Verfügungen, Anordnungen, Bekanntgaben*, ed. by the Partei-Kanzlei der NSDAP, 7 vls., Munich, 1942–45, here vol. 4 (1993), 9.

21. Verfügungen, Anordnungen, Bekanntgaben, ed. by the Partei-Kanzlei der NSDAP, vol. 4 (1943), p. 24 ff. and vol. 5 (1944), A5/43; cf. Akten der Partei-Kanzlei T. II, No. 06561 ff.

22. Meldungen zur Versammlungswelle der NSDAP on Nov. 8, 1943, in. BA Potsdam NS6/ 408, Fol. 397 and 404.

23. Cf. Martin Rüther, *Köln, 31. Mai 1942: Der 1000-Bomber-Angriff* (Kölner Schriften zur Geschichte und Kultur, 18), (Cologne, 2002), 66 f.

24. See Herwart Vorländer, *Die NSV. Darstellung und Dokumentation einer nationalsozialistischen Organisation* (Boppard, 1988), 514 and 173 f.

25. Dietrich Orlow, *The History of the Nazi Party, vol. II: 1933–1945* (Pittsburgh, 1973), 345 ff.

26. Cf. Karl Teppe, "Der Reichsverteidigungskommissar. Organisation und Praxis in Westfalen," in *Verwaltung contra Menschenführung*, eds. Rebentisch/Teppe, 279 and 299 ff.

27. Cf. Peter Hüttenberger, *Die Gauleiter* (Stuttgart, 1969), 189: RMdI to Himmler, Sept. 9, 1944 concerning preparations for the defense of the Reich, in *Ursachen und Folgen*, vol. 21, 555 f.

28. See Peter J. Stern, *The Fuehrer and the People* (London, 1975).

29. Printed in *Ursachen und Folgen*, vol XXII, 480 ff.

30. See Fröhlich, *Goebbels Tagebücher*, Part II, vol. 15, 232 f and vol. 7, p. 177f.; Udo Kissenkoetter, *Gregor Strasser und die NSDAP* (Stuttgart, 1978), 202 f.

31. Printed in *Ursachen und Folgen*, vol. XXII, 484 ff.

32. See Anlage zum Rundschreiben 255/1944 of Sept. 21, 1944 (Anordnungen der Parteikanzlei etc., 1944, fiche 80180634 f.).

33. Fröhlich, *Goebbels Tagebücher* Part II, vol. 15, ß. 393 f, 457, 498; cf. Charles Whiting, *Werewolf. The Story of the Nazi Resistance 1944–1945* (London, 1972), 145 f. and Arno Rose, *Werwolf 1944–1945* (Stuttgart, 1980), 70 ff.

34. Cf. Fröhlich, *Goebbels Tagebücher* Part II, vol. 15, p. 673.

35. See Volker Berghahn, "NSDAP und "Geistige Führung" der Wehrmacht 1939–1945," *VfZ* 17 (1969): 7–71; Arne W. G. Zoepf, *Wehrmacht zwischen Tradition und Ideologie. Der NS-Führungsoffizier im Zweiten Weltkrieg* (Frankfurt, 1988).

36. See Franz Seidler, *Deutscher Volkssturm. Das letzte Aufgebot, 1944/1945* (Munich, 1989), 383 ff.

37. Goebbels on the Gauleiter meeting on Aug. 8, 1944 (see Wolfgang Bleyer, "Pläne der faschistischen Führung zum totalen Krieg," *ZfG* 17 (1969): 132 f.).

38. Zeitschriftendienst/Deutscher Wochendienst, ed. by the Reichsministerium für Volksaufklärung und Propaganda, 154th ed., Oct. 20, 1944, Berlin, ZD No. 285.

39. See Franz W. Seidler, *Deutscher Volkssturm. Das letzte Aufgebot 1944/45* (Munich, 1989), p. 383.

40. S. Veit Harlan, *Im Schatten meiner Filme. Selbstbiographie* (Gütersloh, 1966).

41. See "Kolberg—Ein Film. Ein Beispiel," *Völkischer Beobachter,* January 31, 1945; cf. Francois Courtage/Pierre Cadars, *Geschichte des Films im Dritten Reich* (Munich, 1975), 217 ff.

42. Cf. Manfred Messerschmitt and Fritz Wüllner, *Die Wehrmachtsjustiz im Dienste des Nationalsozialismus. Zerstörung einer Legende* (Baden-Baden, 1987); Jürgen Thomas, "Die Wehrmachtsjustiz im Zweiten Weltkrieg," in *Die anderen Soldaten*, eds. Norbert Haase/Gerhard Pauls (Frankfurt, 1995), 43.

43. Gabriele Lotfi, *KZ der Gestapo. Arbeitserziehungslager im Dritten Reich* (Stuttgart, 2000), 294 ff.

44. Cf. Klaus-Dietmar Henke, *Die amerikanische Besetzung Deutschlands*, 846.

45. See the last Gauleiter meeting in the Reich Chancellery on February 25, 1945, where they promised "to stand and fall with the final victory" (Rudolf Jordan, *Erlebt und erlitten. Der Weg eines Gauleiters von München nach Moskau* (Freiburg, 1971), 252 ff. and Karl Wahl, "...es ist das deutsche Herz." *Erlebnisse und Erkenntnisse eines ehemaligen Gauleiters* (Augsburg, 1954), 385 f.).

CHAPTER 6

The Search for Missing Soldiers
MIAs, POWs, and Ordinary Germans, 1943–45

Frank Biess[1]

The ferocious ending of the Second World War presents an ongoing puzzle for historians of modern Germany. Nazi Germany's tenacious resistance in the face of all-but-certain defeat turned the last two years of the war into the most destructive period of modern European history. Military and civilian casualties on all sides exploded during this period. According to a recent study, more than 80 percent of German losses occurred during the last two years of the war, and more German soldiers died after the failed assassination attempt on Hitler on 20 July 1944 than during the entire six-year period before.[2] Allied and, to a much greater extent, Soviet forces experienced similarly skyrocketing casualty figures during this period.[3] Moreover, the genocidal quality of the war on the Eastern front also spilled over to the Western front, and German troops committed numerous massacres in their effort to fight indigenous resistance movements in Western Europe.[4] German society's tenacious resistance, finally, made possible the ongoing mass murder of European Jews, which did not cease with the liberation of the killing centers in the East but continued unabated inside Nazi Germany until May 1945.[5]

Historians of this period have tended to focus on the reasons for the continuation of the war effort and genocidal killing right to the end. In direct terms, the violent ending of the war resulted from the National Socialist (NS) regime's ability to hold on to power throughout this period of impending defeat. As Hans Mommsen demonstrates in this volume, Hitler and the Nazi-leadership could not contemplate any alternative to the escalation of violence during the last years of the war. In fact, Hitler might even have deliberately orchestrated Nazi Germany's own self-destruction once it was clear that the war was lost.[6] Beyond the obsessions of Hitler and the party, historians have also extended their focus to analyzing the attitudes and actions of ordinary Germans during this period of extreme (and self-destructive) violence. While for as astute an observer as the late Tim Mason the "behavior of the German population between 1943 and 1945" remained "simply incomprehensible," more recent research has laid particular emphasis on the degree of genuine popular consensus during the last years of the Nazi dictatorship.[7] Peter Fritzsche argued, for example, that the "keynote to popular attitudes during the Third Reich" was not "*Resistenz*" but "collaboration."[8] Along similar lines, Robert Gellately has identified a "social consensus" that extended into the last years of the war.[9]

The same emphasis on the regime's tenacity and ordinary Germans' commitment to the cause characterizes historical treatments of the military history of the last few years of the war. Focusing on the Wehrmacht leadership, pioneering work by Volker Berghahn and Manfred Messerschmitt, for example, stressed ideological indoctrination as a key factor for the military elites' loyalty to Hitler.[10] Omer Bartov and others have extended this argument to rank-and-file soldiers in the Wehrmacht.[11] In this view, the Wehrmacht indeed became "Hitler's army," and its member came to share the ideological assumptions that drove the war of annihilation on the Eastern front. This research was extremely important in undermining the deeply engrained myth of a "clean Wehrmacht." At the same time, this emphasis on ideology also tended to portray ordinary soldiers as "other-directed," as being manipulated and indoctrinated but not really acting out of their own initiative. More recent interpretations tend to assign more agency to ordinary soldiers' own motivations during the final stages of the Second World. For Hans-Ulrich Wehler, Wehrmacht morale depended not so much on "National Socialist indoctrination" but rather on ordinary soldiers unbroken emotional investment in the "myth of the Führer."[12] Similarly, Michael Geyer stresses German soldiers' deep fear of "revenge" and their own feelings of guilt about their previous implication in genocidal warfare as crucial motivating force during the last years of the war. According to Geyer, soldiers were also driven by a desperate effort to hang on to communal bonds, a "catastrophic nationalism" that manifested itself in an unflagging allegiance to a larger collective such as the *Volksgemeinschaft* or the nation.[13]

Invaluable as this recent work has been, it explores the war's end phase primarily as the astonishing last gasp of the murderous Nazi regime. This essay proposes a different perspective for writing the history of the last years of the war. It portrays this period as the onset of the postwar period during which German society was beginning to confront military defeat and its aftermath. It does so from the vantage point of the official and popular responses to German casualties, in particular soldiers missing-in-action on the Eastern front and POWs in Soviet captivity. Their numbers had been steadily rising since the German defeat at Stalingrad in January 1943, when the Red Army succeeded in capturing 110,000 German POWs. During the last two years of the war, MIAs and POWs accounted for an increasing segment of German losses, and popular concerns for missing or captured soldiers extended far into the 1950s. In 1943, MIAs amounted to 40 percent of German losses; in 1944, the figure went up to almost 60 percent.[14] By far the largest share of German POWs on the Eastern front, however, were captured during the last few months of the war. At the end of the war, the total number of soldiers missing-in-action was 1.5 million,[15] while the Soviet Union held about three million POWs, one million of whom are estimated to have died in Soviet captivity. By contrast, the Western allies held eight million German POWs by the end of the war. Captivity in the West, however, was much shorter and resulted in lower and—in the case of American and British captivity—almost insignificant death rates.[16]

By focusing on MIAs and POWs, this essay shifts the perspective from trying to explain the tenacity of German society during the last years of the war to seeking to account for the transition from war to postwar. This transition not only consisted of a social-structural transformation "from Stalingrad to the Currency Reform," as Martin Broszat and his collaborators have argued.[17] It also entailed less tangible transformations in popular attitudes and expectations for the future that have received less attention in the historiography. In particular, official and popular responses to the increasing number of MIAs and POWs point to processes of gradual disengagement from National Socialism among at least a segment of the German population, even if disengagement did not translate into open opposition to the NS regime. Instead, this popular withdrawal from National Socialist consensus anticipated key elements of postwar confrontations with the consequences of total war and total defeat.

Identifying such links between war and postwar seems important also in light of the almost complete absence of opposition to military occupation after 1945 despite Allied and Soviet expectations to the contrary.[18] If all Germans had indeed linked their personal and collective identities so closely to the National Socialist regime as some of the more recent historiography suggests, then what happened to these sentiments after the Wehrmacht's unconditional surrender on 8 May 1945? To be sure, as Richard Bessel has shown, a considerable number of Germans brought the "no-exit" attitude from the last years of the war to its logical conclusion and followed Hitler and other Nazi leaders into collective suicide.[19] Total military defeat, the exposure of Nazi inhumanity, and the presence of Allied occupation authorities also clearly also mitigated against continued identification with National Socialism after 1945.[20] Still, this essay argues that the absence of postwar resistance as well as the specific forms of "coming to terms with the past" after 1945 can be traced back to popular responses to rising casualties during the last years of the war.[21]

～

Official Nazi propaganda found it difficult to incorporate German MIAs and POWs into its political mythology. Whereas the dead Wehrmacht soldier replaced the "old fighter" as the central object of the Nazi cult of the fallen hero, MIAs' and POWs' liminal position between active fighting and heroic death ran counter to the National Socialist "all-or-nothing" logic. The existential uncertainty associated with the increasing number of MIAs did not lend itself to fashioning official tales of heroic sacrifice. Likewise, captivity signaled the individual desire for—as well as the actual possibility of—survival and thus threatened to undermine the National Socialist myth of heroic death. This is why the NS regime initially tried to deny that any German soldiers had fallen into Soviet captivity at Stalingrad. The official Wehrmacht proclamation on Stalingrad on 3 February 1943 asserted that that the members of the Sixth Army had "fought to the last bullet" and had died a heroic death "so that Germany will live."[22] Consequently, Field Marshall Paulus' decision to go into Soviet captivity rather than to commit suicide infuriated the Nazi leadership. Shortly after the surrender at Stalingrad, Goebbels noted in his diary the "depressing news that Paulus and fourteen of his generals had fallen into Bolshevist captivity."[23] Some days later, he worried that "it would be the most severe shock to the army's prestige ... during the entire National Socialist regime" if "several German generals had indeed voluntarily entered Bolshevist captivity."[24]

Popular responses to the increasing number of MIAs and POWs also differed from ordinary Germans' reaction to increasing death tolls. Mass casualties often triggered apathy and depression, and, in some cases even bound ordinary Germans more closely to the regime. In April 1942, for example, a 66-year old widow denounced the soldier Herbert N. to the Gestapo who had told her that the war was lost. For Martha S., this statement was utterly shocking because "it would be inconceivable to experience that all the sacrifices of this would have been in vain."[25] By contrast, the existential uncertainty about the fate of a missing or captured family member produced a massive desire for information that posed a challenge to NS-authorities. Official statements that a "segment of the missing comrades in the Soviet Union has died a heroic death for the fatherland" clearly did not suffice to alleviate nagging concerns about the fate of relatives missing on the Eastern front.[26] Moreover, in contrast to the depressing certainty of an official death notification, captivity—even Soviet captivity—represented "good news." "I wish Kurt were in Russian captivity, it would be better for him than to have died a heroic death for nothing," wrote the brother of a missing soldier in the East to his mother in June 1943, and, in so doing, willingly or unwillingly undermined the Nazi myth of heroic sacrifice.[27] Throughout the last years of the war, family members of MIAs and POWs confronted the political and military authorities with pressing demands to account for the fate of their sons, brothers, or husbands. Sooner or later, this effort brought them in contact with the main agency in charge of recording German losses, the "Wehrmacht Agency for War Losses and POWs" (Wehrmachtsauskunftsstelle für Kriegsverluste und Kriegsgefangene, WAST).

The WAST was in charge of recording all German losses and providing *Wehrmacht* agencies as well as individual family members with information about German losses.[28] The massive losses at Stalingrad prompted the establishment of a separate "working agency" *(Abwicklungsstab)* that was supposed to determine who had been killed at Stalingrad. After additional losses in Northern Africa and on the Eastern front in June 1944, its responsibilities were extended to all German casualties that could no longer be reported by military units themselves.[29] Yet the skyrocketing casualty rates often made it impossible to secure any definitive information regarding the whereabouts of hundreds of thousands of missing soldiers. As a result, family members were left in a state of fundamental uncertainty that often lasted far into the postwar years.[30]

Military and political authorities largely failed in alleviating popular concerns regarding MIAs and POWs. While Goebbels clearly recognized the potential for popular discontent relating to this issue, he was even more concerned about hostile propaganda emanating from enemy sources.[31] The WAST, for example, was instructed to share information about German POWs drawn from Radio Moscow only if family members contacted the agency directly.[32] Moreover, NS authorities undermined the few existing avenues for establishing contact with German POWs. Since August 1942, several German POWs had managed to write letters and postcards to their family members in Germany. But most of this mail from Soviet captivity was intercepted by the censorship office and forwarded to the Reich Security Main Office (RSHA). By October 1943, an RSHA report listed 7,000 such letters from Soviet captivity; the total number for the entire duration of the war is estimated to be 20,000.[33] For NS authorities, the potentially detrimental propagandistic impact of news about the survival in Soviet captivity took precedence over the existential anxieties of family members of MIAs and POWs.

Official failures to provide reliable information regarding MIAs and POWs prompted widespread discontent and suspicion toward military and political authorities. From the defeat at Stalingrad virtually to the end of the war, family members of MIAs and POWs suspected NS authorities (rightly, as it turned out) of withholding information about the number and identity of missing soldiers and POWs.[34] In December 1943, military authorities in Dresden reported that family members of missing Stalingrad soldiers felt "not sufficiently supported, and even abandoned or almost betrayed" by the political and military authorities. The report estimated that the number of affected persons in that army district alone amounted to more than 100,000 people. In light of the "serious general situation," this "loss of confidence in the *Wehrmacht* among wide sections of the population" entailed "serious dangers."[35]

As a result of their frustration with official (dis)information policy, family members began to undertake their own efforts to investigate the fate of missing soldiers and POWs. In so doing, they felt justified in resorting to illegal sources, such as Soviet flyers or Soviet radio broadcasts. In March 1943, Karl R. brought with him a Soviet flyer, which listed the names of German POWs in Soviet captivity and indicated that they "were doing well" *(sind wohlauf)*. His parents subsequently contacted the families of several of these soldiers, who then forwarded this information to more families. When this communication was eventually broken up by the Gestapo, Karl R.'s mother explained that the loss of two brothers in the First World War and her youngest son in 1942 had motivated her actions. "I wanted to help the affected persons, and I felt sorry for them because they did not have any news about their relatives," as she explained to the Gestapo. The "good reputation" that Frau R. had earned through engagement in Nazi welfare organizations and her role as bloc leader of the Nazi Women's League local branch saved her from prosecution. But her case illustrates how private experiences of loss and empathy with uncertainty over missing soldiers led otherwise loyal Germans to transcend the codes of acceptable behavior in Nazi Germany.[36]

Listening to Soviet radio broadcasts represented another, equally illegal, means of gathering information about MIAs and POWs in the East. A report from June 1943 stated that "undoubtedly, a large number of faithful National Socialist Germans are listening to the Russian radio station night after night hoping to receive any news about missing soldiers."[37] The case of Fritz M. illuminates just how widespread this practice had become by the spring of 1943. A former World War I veteran and SPD member who also suffered from multiple sclerosis, Fritz M. began to listen to Soviet radio broadcasts in January 1943 and then sent forty-six letters to relatives of German POWs. When the Gestapo arrested him in May 1943, it also traced the recipients of these letters who were then hard pressed to explain why they had not reported these communications earlier. One woman declared that she had already received thirteen such letters regarding the fate of her husband from different sources.[38] In October 1943, Fritz M. was charged with spreading "Communist propaganda" by countering the "common assumption ... that German soldiers in Russian captivity were treated badly" and by telling family members "that the allegedly missing German soldiers were in captivity and doing well." This, the Gestapo asserted, was tantamount to undermining the "morale of the troops on the front" and constituted an offense that earned Fritz M. two years in prison.[39]

Not only did family members seek information about MIAs and POWs, they also began to contact each other to share the scarce bits of information available to them. The months after Stalingrad saw the emergence of an entire subculture of informal networks among family members of missing or captured soldiers. In a liberal-democratic or even authoritarian system, these networks would have represented the preliminary stages of legitimate interest-group formation.[40] Within the context of the totalitarian Nazi dictatorship, these informal contacts assumed a subversive quality. They promoted a plethora of rumors about the fate of MIAs and POWs in order to compensate for the deficiencies of officially available information.[41] Such rumors represented a less than public but more than private counter-sphere in which it was possible to imagine alternative futures that diverged from the official insistence on holding-out at any price.

The most prominent of these rumors centered on the former commander of the VIII. Army Corps of the Sixth Army, Generaloberst Walter Heitz. At Stalingrad, Heitz had lived up to his reputation as one of the most loyal Nazi generals by threatening to execute everybody who surrendered to the Red Army voluntary.[42] Yet on 31 January, Heitz himself went into Soviet captivity. In April 1943, Heitz managed to write a letter from Soviet captivity, which reached his wife Gisela in June 1943 due to a mistake of the censorship office in Vienna.[43] In his letter, Heitz reported that he was healthy and that he was allowed to write once a month as well as receive letters and packages. The Heitz letter quickly became the stuff of popular rumors and informal communications. Frau Heitz began to pass on the news about her husband to other wives of missing soldiers. Some months later, she reported that she had received "hundreds of inquiries" regarding this matter.[44] Several other wives of officers of the Sixth Army engaged in similar communications and further extended these informal networks among family members of MIAs and POWs.[45]

Rumors and informal discussions about conditions in Soviet captivity flew in the face of the Nazi myth of heroic sacrifice. By stating that "no officer has committed suicide up to the very end," the letters circulating among family members of Stalingrad fighters stressed Wehrmacht officers' refusal to die a "heroic death" for an increasingly elusive "final victory."[46] More importantly, these rumors articulated alternative visions for the future that diverged from the one offered by the NS regime. For one letter writer, stories about contacts with German POWs in Soviet captivity served as an inspiration to "look into the future with much more hope and to expect a good ending."[47] This hope for a "good ending," however, was no longer predicated on the expectation of a "final victory" in the distant and indeterminate future.[48] Instead, family members began to define the notion of a "good ending" in primarily private rather than national terms. They were hoping for a quick ending of the war that then would presumably result in a reunion with their captured or missing husbands, sons, and brothers.[49] "If only this war were finally over, and those poor people were freed," wrote one family member of a German POW.[50] The same popular sentiment was reported from Bensheim a.d. Bergstrasse in March 1943, a military district with a particularly high concentration of relatives of Stalingrad fighters. This report noted an increasingly "defeatist tendency" among the population which manifested itself in frequent expressions of the wish "that the war will be over soon."[51] Within the limited milieu of family members of former Stalingrad fighters, the congruence between private interests and the war effort began to split apart in the spring of 1943. The NS regime's policies increasingly revealed their suicidal character and began to clash with the interests of those Germans who developed an alternative perspective for the conclusion of the war.[52] For those Germans, the private hope for a reunion with their families superseded the regime's scenario of national sacrifice.

At the same time, widespread dissatisfaction over the NS regime's failure to account for missing soldiers and POWs did not necessarily translate into an oppositional attitude toward the regime at large. As Detlev Peukert has argued, popular rumors did not signal a broad based popular opposition but rather represented an extreme "fragmentation of public opinion," which disintegrated into several sub-spheres. The increasing discrepancy between public statements and private communications had a disorienting effect that ran counter to goal-oriented political resistance.[53] In addition, the security organs of the Third Reich were highly successful in breaking up informal communication among family members of missing soldiers. Gestapo and Sipo also benefited from close cooperation with Wehrmacht agencies and vice versa in prosecuting these activities. The *Abwicklungsstab* Stalingrad and the *Abwehr* regularly exchanged information about the activities of family members of missing soldiers with the Gestapo and the SD.[54] Finally, ordinary citizens quite willingly collaborated with the Gestapo by denouncing letter writers and reporting rumors about MIAs and POWs.[55]

The personal nature that gave popular concerns about MIAs and POWs their urgency also simultaneously limited their potential political significance. For the most part, these concerns remained limited to the immediate range of one's own kin. Rather than opening up ordinary Germans' perspective to larger questions of politics and morality, these personal grievances actually fostered a narrowing of one's perspective to the exclusive focus of the survival of the family. This "inward-turn" was far from innocent. It allowed for a far-reaching emotional disengagement from the orgy of destruction that the NS regime orchestrated during the last few years of the war. Precisely at the moment when the regime unleashed its unrestrained genocidal violence, ordinary Germans' increasing self-referentiality took precedence over any residual empathy with Nazi victims. It is in these popular responses to the increasingly personal quality of the war that we can detect the origins of postwar Germans' denial of empathy that so shocked outside observers like Hannah Arendt.[56]

Still, not everyone reacted to the mounting losses during the last years of the war by blocking out of the fate of Germany's victims. The remarkable, albeit highly unusual, case of Dr. Christian Schöne illustrates the range of popular responses, extending from fantasies of revenge all the way to outspoken empathy with Germany's victims.[57] The case also illuminates the limited but real scope remaining for individual choice and volition. Schöne was a medical doctor who headed a small military hospital near Frankfurt/Oder. When his brother Konrad Schöne was reported missing at Stalingrad in January, Christian Schöne began to participate in the informal network of family members of missing soldiers. In March 1943, he started to send out chain letters to other family members of MIAs in which he recounted his activities to research the fate of missing soldiers. While Schöne's activities up to that point did not differ from those of many family members of missing soldiers, he made a most unusual rhetorical move in the third chain letter that he sent out on 3 May 1943 (the birthday of his missing brother): he linked the fate of German MIAs and POWs with the mass murder of Jews on the Eastern front.[58] He decided to address this "serious" and "sensitive" issue in response to suggestions from other family members of missing soldiers who wanted to take revenge on the "6–7 million Jews in our hands" if Moscow's "Jewish rulers were to harm our captured soldiers." By seeking to subject Jewish civilians to reprisal measures for German losses, this proposal itself reflected the success of Nazi propaganda among some family members of missing soldiers. Schöne, however, was strongly opposed to such plans and argued that Soviet Jews "have already been shot by us in numbers for which the pits of Katyn would be insufficient." He related that his missing brother had also told him of the killing of 64,000 Jews, including women and children, from Kiev. Moreover, as he knew from an SS man who had participated in 150 executions per day, these killings were continuing on the Eastern front. Schöne drew clear consequences from his knowledge about mass murder: out of concern that "our prisoners will have to pay the price for this," but also for reasons of "morality" and "honor" he came to the conclusion that these "morally reprehensible" actions have to cease. As a result, he encouraged the recipients of his letter to confront official party, state, and military authorities with two demands: first, "responsible military experts" should lead the military operations, thus preventing another military disaster such as it had occurred at Stalingrad, and secondly, petitioners should demand an end to the killing of the Jews.

This was a remarkable intervention. Schöne's letter bespeaks the extensive knowledge about mass killings of Jews in the East that was available inside Nazi Germany by early 1943.[59] In contrast to many ordinary Germans' self-centeredness, Schöne's personal concern for his brother did not lead him to ignore or deny what was happening at the same time to the victims of Nazi Germany. Instead, his personal loss enabled him to empathize with Jewish victims and to move toward a morally grounded opposition to the NS regime. Secondly, the outcome of the case was just as surprising as the letter itself. In November 1943, a military court tried Schöne for his activities but meted out the relatively mild sentence of one year in prison. Significantly, the verdict never questioned the truth of Schöne's assertions about mass killings on the Eastern front, but simply argued that these utterances threatened to subvert German morale. This ruling might have constituted an exception in the otherwise increasingly military justice system. But the court might also have feared negative propagandistic consequences in punishing more harshly a member of the "national community" for his concern for his missing brother. Schöne survived war and dictatorship but died in March 1947, shortly before his brother was able to send a postcard from a POW camp in Siberia.[60]

⁓

The military and political leadership of the Third Reich was gravely concerned that proliferating rumors among family members of MIAs and POWs might spill over from the home front to the front and undermine the morale of the troops. This was especially true in light of the propaganda of the "National Committee Free Germany" (NKFD) and the "League of German Officers" (BdO), the two Soviet-sponsored, anti-fascist organizations of German POWs in Soviet captivity founded in July and September 1943. Both organization openly encouraged soldiers to desert by portraying Soviet captivity as "the shortest way home."[61] The OKW and the Nazi leadership took NKFD propaganda very seriously.[62] In National Socialist memory, the NKFD and the BdO evoked the specter of 1918 and of defeat not on the battlefield but through a "stab in the back"—this time not by a revolutionary homefront but by "treacherous" generals such as Walter von Seydlitz, one of the BdO's founding members.[63] While the Nazi-regime initially tried to deny the BdO's existence, from early 1944 it denounced both NKFD and BdO as the creation of "Communist emigrants, mostly of the Jewish race."[64]

Despite such counter-propaganda, the military and political leadership exhibited great interest in the attitudes and the experiences of German POWs in Soviet captivity. In the first half of 1944, two confidential reports—one compiled by the Reich Security Main Office, the other one by the Wehrmacht counter-espionage division *Fremde Heere Ost*—summarized official knowledge about Soviet captivity. Both reports cited numerous political selections and executions of German POWs by "NKVD agents, German emigrants, and Jews," and they told of deportations of POWs in "cattle trains that resembled animal cages," which then led to "mass death."[65] While recent research indicates that shootings of German POWs did occur occasionally, German POWs were not subjected to a policy of deliberate annihilation.[66] Instead, the military and political authorities of the Third Reich projected their own practices of genocidal warfare onto their Soviet enemy. Reports of political selections, executions, and mass deportation of German POWs in Soviet captivity legitimized the similar criminal transgressions by German SS and regular army units in the war of annihilation on the Eastern front.[67]

At the same time, both reports needed to concede that Soviet treatment of German POWs had improved considerably, largely due to Soviet efforts to exploit the POWs' labor force.[68] Finally, the reports revealed officials' concerns regarding the susceptibility of German POWs to the activities of the NKFD. While the *Wehrmacht* report came to the conclusion that "only a very small number of German POWs decides to participate in the treacherous activity of these elements," the RSHA evaluated the political loyalty of German soldiers in captivity much more skeptically. "Most prisoners," it stated, "sooner or later succumb to these influences."[69]

These were highly explosive findings. Just as uncertainty about MIAs and POWs threatened to subvert morale on the homefront, information about improved conditions in Soviet captivity raised official anxieties about *Wehrmacht* cohesion. Indeed, impressionistic evidence suggests that after Stalingrad perceptions of Soviet captivity gradually changed, at least among a segment of Wehrmacht soldiers. In May 1943, a soldier writing from the front declared that "for some time, Russian captivity has sounded a bit better than earlier." In January 1944, another soldier reckoned that "the Russians no longer shoot all the injured POWs. They probably need them too."[70] In some cases, soldiers also reported such sentiments to their family members at home. In Margarete K. reported to her thirteen-year-old son that his father was in Soviet captivity because he "would rather be in captivity than having his bones shot to pieces."[71] Official orders, such as the one by Wilhelm Keitel from January 1944, that prohibited any statements regarding the allegedly good treatment of German POWs in Soviet captivity indirectly confirmed the increasing prevalence of such sentiments among *Wehrmacht* soldiers.[72] At least to some Wehrmacht soldiers, Soviet captivity no longer appeared as an utterly horrifying conclusion to the war equal to or even worse than death as it had during the early stages of the war. This assumption is born out by the extremely high number of soldiers who were either reported missing-in-action or captured by enemy forces on the Eastern front during the last stages of the war. It is well known that rumors about the good treatment in British or American captivity contributed to the mass surrender of German forces on the Western front.[73] But voluntary surrender or at least a more passive refusal to fight constituted, as Benjamin Ziemann has argued, "one of the most common, yet least researched forms of nonconformist behavior of ordinary soldiers" on the Eastern front as well.[74]

The ending of the war thus may have been more complex than the prevalent construct of "fighting to the bitter end" suggests.[75] Still, the salient fact about the *Wehrmacht* during the last years of the war was not dissent and disintegration but remarkable cohesion. For most *Wehrmacht* soldiers, rumors about improving conditions in Soviet captivity were not sufficient to overcome long-held assumptions regarding cultural or even racial superiority towards "the Russians."[76] In addition, many soldiers must have witnessed the mass death of Soviet POWs in German captivity during the early stages of the war.[77] Here too, German soldiers' own guilty conscience lay behind their own fears of "revenge" if they should end up in captivity.[78] In the end, official anxieties about collapsing Wehrmacht morale thus ultimately proved unfounded, and most German soldiers followed the Nazi-regime into total defeat.[79]

∼

Popular responses to the increasingly personal quality of the war thus diverged on front and homefront. For civilians, the "privatization" of the war implied an inward turn and an almost exclusive focus on kinship relations. For the vast majority of soldiers, by contrast, the same process often inspired an ethics of ferocious fighting that militated against voluntary surrender as an alternative conclusion to the war. The Nazi regime's most important achievement during the last years of the war resided in its ability to mobilize ordinary soldiers' personal motivations for its own self-destructive logic. In retrospect, this attitude hardly reflected a Weberian "ethics of responsibility," as historian Andreas Hilgruber has argued.[80] Instead, it was precisely this increasingly "personal" quality of the war—combined with an utter dehumanization of the enemy—that accounted for its increasing lethality on all sides.

These diverging responses to increasing losses shaped postwar confrontations with total war and total defeat. The gradual and partial disengagement from National Socialism among family members of MIAs and POWs, as well as their focus on a private future centered on the family, provided emotional and experiential bridges across 1945.[81] Informal communications among family members over the fate of MIAs and POWs also anticipated the postwar discourse on German victimization that completely severed German losses from previous German aggression.[82] Women's prominence in these informal networks on the homefront also points to the gender-specific dimension of this particular transition from war to postwar. Ironically, the National Socialist emphasis on women's significance in the private sphere ultimately turned against the Nazism itself: during the last years of the war, the family (and kinship relations more broadly) constituted a repository of alternative futures that fostered a disengagement from National Socialism.[83] This was true despite women's prominence in the war industry, air-defense battalions, and in the colonization of the East.[84] Postwar memories of women's experiences blocked out their significant participation in *these* wars. Instead, postwar memories drew on predominantly female experiences of personal loss and private resilience, which then were easily transformed into national narratives of German innocence and victimization.[85] By contrast, the parallel male experience was much more difficult to incorporate into postwar memories of war and defeat, not the least because it was a narrative of abysmal failure on both the individual and the collective level. The collapse of the Nazi regime paralleled the failure of German men to protect the homeland and their families against the Red Army. This absence of an adequate male narrative of the war's ending also deprived any potential postwar resistance to the victors of its ideological basis. Instead, the rehabilitation of the male narrative of war and defeat became a central ideological project of postwar reconstruction in both Germanys after 1945.

Notes

1. My thanks to Ulrike Strasser for her extremely helpful comments on an earlier version of this essay. The fact that I continue to rely, in this essay as in the rest of my work, on the advice and intellectual generosity of Pamela Swett and Jonathan Wiesen testifies to Volker Berghahn's success in fostering an intellectual community among his students that extends far beyond graduate school. This essay is an abridged version of Chapter I of my book *Homecomings: Returning POWs and Legacies of Defeat in Postwar Germany* (Princeton, 2006).

2. Rüdiger Overmans, *Deutsche militärische Verluste im Zweiten Weltkrieg* (Munich, 1999), 228, 265–66, 279.

3 Michael Geyer, "'There is a land Where Everything is Pure: Its Name is the Land of Death.' Some Observations on Catastrophic Nationalism," in Greg Eghigian and Matthew Paul Berg, eds., *Sacrifice and National Belonging in Twentieth Century Germany* (College Station, Tex., 2002), 118–47.

4. Mark Mazower, "Militärische Gewalt und nationalsozialistische Werte. Die Wehrmacht in Griechenland," in Hannes Heer and Klaus Naumann, ed., *Vernichtungskrieg. Verbrechen der Wehrmacht* (Hamburg, 1997), 157–90; Michael Geyer, "'Es muß daher mit schnellen und drakonischen Maßnahmen durchgegriffen werden.' Civitella in Val di Chiana am 29. Juni 1944;" in ibid., 208–38; Sarah Farmer, *Martyred Village: Commemorating the 1944 Massacre at Oradour-sur-Glane* (Berkeley, 1999).

5. This was one of the important findings in the otherwise highly problematic book by Daniel J. Goldhagen, *Hitler's Willing Executioners: Ordinary Germans and the Holocaust* (New York, 1996).

6. Bernd Wegner, "Hitler, der Zweite Weltkrieg, und die Choreographie des Untergangs," *Geschichte und Gesellschaft* 26 (2000): 493–518; and in general Ian Kershaw, *Hitler. 1936–1945 Nemesis* (London, 2000).

7. Tim Mason, "Epilogue," in idem., *Social Policy and the Third Reich: The Working Class and the 'National Community',*" edited by Jane Caplan (Oxford, 1993), 276.

8. Peter Fritzsche, "Where Did All the Nazis Go? Reflections on Resistance and Collaboration?," *Tel Aviver Jahrbuch für Geschichte* 23 (1994): 191–214.

9. Robert Gellately, *Backing Hitler: Consent and Coercion in Nazi Germany* (Oxford, 2001), 224.

10. Manfred Messerschmitt, *Die Wehrmacht im NS-Staat. Zeit der Indoktrination* (Hamburg, 1969), Volker Berghahn, "NSDAP und 'Geistige Führung' der Wehrmacht 1939–1945," *Vierteljahrshefte für Zeitgeschichte* 17 (1969): 7–71.

11. Omer Bartov, *Hitler's Army: Soldiers, Nazis, and War in the Third Reich* (New York, 1990.)

12. Hans-Ulrich Wehler, *Deutsche Gesellschaftsgeschichte: Vierter Band 1914–49* (Munich, 2003), 869.

13. Geyer, "'There is a land Where Everything is Pure: Its Name is the Land of Death.'"

14. Overmans, *Deutsche Militärische Verluste,* 300.

15. According to recent estimates, half of them had died on the Eastern front, the other half in Soviet captivity. Ibid., 285–89.

16. Ibid., 286.

17. Martin Broszat, Klaus Dietmar Henke, and Hans Woller, eds., *Von Stalingrad zur Währungsreform. Zur Sozialgeschichte des Umbruchs in Deutschland* (Munich; Oldenbourg, 1988)

18. Klaus-Dietmar Henke, *Die amerikanische Besetzung Deutschlands* (Munich, 1995), 160–69. On this issue see also Mark Roseman's contribution to this volume.

19. Richard Bessel, "Leben nach dem Tod: Vom Zweiten Weltkrieg zur Zweiten Nachkriegszeit in Bernd Wegner, ed., *Wie Kriege Enden* (Paderborn, 2002), 239–58.

20. Popular resistance against Allied denazification efforts and war crimes trials can also be read as the "secondary confirmation of the Nazi *Volksgemeinschaft,*" see Norbert Frei, *Vergangenheitspolitik. Die Anfänge der Bundesrepublik und die NS-Vergangenheit* (Munich, 1996), 304.

21. For a recent study that challenges the dominant picture of "fighting to the bitter end" and points to processes of disintegration also within the Wehrmacht, see Andreas Kunz, *Wehrmacht und Niederlage. Die bewaffnete Macht in der Endphase der nationalsozialistischen Herrschaft 1944 bis 1945* (Munich, 2005).

22. Cited in Behrenbeck, *Kult um die toten Helden,* 556.

23. *Die Tagebücher von Joseph Goebbels, Teil II: Diktate 1941–1945, Band 7: Januar-März 1943,* 239, 255.

24. Ibid., 253.

25. Interrogation of Martha S., 7 April 1943; 20 May 1942, NRWHStA, RW 58/30367, 7, 17.

26. Merkblatt für die Angehörigen der in Sowjetrussland vermissten deutschen Soldaten, BA-M, RH15/291, 21.

27. Letter by "Pepi" to his "liebe schwer geprüfte Mutter," Basel, 10 June 1943, BA-M, RH 15/310, 30.

28. Overmans, *Deutsche militärische Verluste,* 23–43. The agency was founded in 1939 in Berlin and transferred to Thuringia in August 1943.

29. Ibid., 36–37.

30. See the case cited in Dörr, *"Wer die Zeit nicht miterlebt hat.." Bd.2, Kriegsalltag,* 237–38.

31. Propagandaparole Nr.57 an alle Gauleiter, Gaupropagandaleiter und Leiter der Reichspropagandaämter, 26 May 1943, BA, R55/977; Leiter der Partei Kanzlei, Rundschreiben Nr.83/43, 28 May 1943, BA, NS6/341, cited in Absolon, *Wehrmacht im Dritten Reich,* Bd.VI, 543.

32. Oberkommando des Heeres, Betr.Namhaftmachung von deutschen Kriegsgefangenen in sowj. Flublättern, (Abschrift), 29 October 1942; Aktenvermerk über Be-

sprechung AWA am 15.10.1942 betreffen Benachrichtigung der Angehörigen von angeblichen deutschen Kriegsgefangenen in der UdSSR, BA-M, RW 48/10.

33. Boddenberg, *Die Kriegsgefangenenpost deutscher Soldaten*, 44. Rundschreiben des RSHA betr. Deutsche Kriegsgefangene in der Sowjetunion, 18 May 1943, BA-M, RH58/268, 45–47, also cited in *ibid;* see also Behrenbeck, *Kult um die toten Helden*, 556, footnote.97.

34. Notiz 27 March 1943, BA-M, RH 15/310, 134; Stellv Gen.Kdo, III, AK an Kommandeur Abwicklungsstab 6. Armee, Berlin 28 June 1943, BA-M, RH 15/308; RPA Lüneburg, Vermisstenmeldungen, 11 December 1944, BA, R55/604, 215.

35. Stellv. Generalkommando IV Ak (Wehrkreiskommando IV) IC/WVW Nr.63/43 geh.-Aktion Stalingrad, Bericht über die Stimmung bei den Angehörigen der Stalingrad Kämpfer, 8 December 1943, BA-M, RH 15/340, 5.

36. Flyer "Kameradschaftsdienst," Interrogation of August R., Gerard K, and Christine R.; Gestapo Stettin to Gestapo Düsseldorf, 21 May 1943; Schlussbericht, 6 August, 1943, all in NRWHStA, RW 58/26362.

37. Stellv Gen. Kdo III Ak, Arbeitsstab Stalingrad u. Tunis an Kommandeur Abwicklungsstab 6.Armee, 28 June 1943, BA-M, RH 15/308.

38. Interrogation Hildegard Z., 1 June 1943, NRWHStA, RW58/41982, 39; on this case, see also Gellately, *Backing Hitler*, 237–38.

39. Wuppertal, 22 June 1943, 44–45, NRWHStA, RW58/41982; Verdict, 16 October 1943, *ibid.*, 72–73. It is not clear whether Fritz M. survived the war.

40. For Vichy-France, see Sarah Fishman, *We Will Wait: Wives of French Prisoners of War, 1940–1944* (New Haven, 1991).

41. On the function of rumors in the Third Reich, see Franz Dröge, *Der zerredete Widerstand. Soziologie und Publizistik des Gerüchts im Zweiten Weltkrieg* (Stuttgart, 1970).

42. On Heitz, see Bernd Wegner, "Der Krieg gegen die Sowjetunion 1942/43" in *Das Deutsche Reich und der Zweite Weltkrieg, Band 6: Der Globale Krieg: Die Ausweitung zum Weltkrieg und der Wechsel der Initiative, 1941–1943* (Stuttgart, 1990), 1060.

43. Werner Boddenberg, "Der Kriegsgefangenenbrief des Generaloberst Heitz" in *Philatelie und Postgeschichte* 21/94 (1987): 1–9 and idem., *Die Kriegsgefangenenpost deutscher Soldaten in sowjetischem Gewahrsam und die Post von ihren Angehörigen während des II. Weltkrieges* (Selbstverlag, 1985), 94–98.

44. Gisela Heitz to Fräulein G., [no date], probably early 1944, BA-M, RH 15/310, 6.

45. Hedwig Strecker to Frau von P., 25 June 1943, BA-M, RH15/310, 18; Erika Hollunder, no date [probably October 1943], BA-M, RH15/310, 53.

46. Hedwig Strecker to Frau von P., 25 June 1943, BA-M, RH15/310.

47. Letter Erika H., 29 June1943 (Abschrift), BA-M, M, RH15/310, 65.

48. Michael Kumpfmüller, *Die Schlacht von Stalingrad* (München, 1995), 71–7 .

49. This evidence thus runs counter to Susanne zur Nieden's findings in diaries of women, which, according to her, demonstrated the "incapability to imagine a future beyond the National Socialist ideas," zur Nieden, "Chronistinnen des Krieges. Frauentagebüchder im Zweiten Weltkrieg," in Hans-Erich Volkmann, ed., *Ende des Dritten Reiches—Ende des Zweiten Weltkrieges. Eine perspektivische Rückschau* (Munich, 1995), 848.

50. Käte B. to Frau R.; 1 May 1943, NRWHStA, RW58/26362.

51. Notiz, 27 March 1943, BA-M, M, RH-15/310, 134.

52. Wette, "Zwischen Untergangspathos und Überlebenswillen. Die Deutschen im letzten Kriegshalbjahr 1944/45," in idem et al., eds., *Das letzte halbe Jahr. Stimmungsberichte der Wehrmachtpropaganda 1944/45* (Essen, 2001), 13–15.

53. Detlev Peukert, *Volksgenossen und Gemeinschaftsfremde. Apassung, Ausmerze und Aufbegehren unter dem Nationalsozialismus* (Köln, 1982), 55–77.

54. Wehrkreiskommando VIII Arbeitstab Stalingrad to Abw.Stab 6.Armee und Hegru. Afrika, 2 March 1944, BA-M, RH 51/311; Chef der Sicherheitspolizei und des SD an OKW, Abwicklungsstab VI. Armee und Hegru. Afrika, 16 March 1944, BA-M, RH 15/392, 199; Abwicklungsstab 6. Armee und Hegru Afrika to Chef der Sicherheitspolizei und des SD, 19 April 1944, BA-M, RH15/316, 121; Chef der Sicherheitspolizei und des SD to Oberkommando der *Wehrmacht*, Abwicklungsstab der VI. Armee und Hegru. Afrika, 19 February 1944, BA-M, RH 15/311.

55. This was, for example, the reaction of Fieldmarshall Paulus' family after receiving a letter from Soviet captivity'; Hptm. Ernst Paulus to stellvert. Generalkommando XVIII A.K., 10 July 1944, BA-M, RH 15/316.

56. Hannah Arendt, "The Aftermath of Nazi Rule," *Commentary* 10 (1950): 347–53; see also Carolyn Dean, *The Fragility of Empathy after the Holocaust* (Ithaca, 2004), 76–105.

57. Apart from the evidence cited below, see "Kettenbriefe gegen die deutschen Verbrechen im Zweiten Weltkrieg," *Frankfurter Allgemeine Zeitung*, 91, 18 April 1996, 13–14, cited in Wette, *Die Wehrmacht*, 321–22, fn.75.

58. Unless otherwise indicated, all quotations are from the verdict of the military court in Berlin against Schöne, 22 November 1943, reproduced in "Kettenbriefe gegen die deutschen Verbrechen im Zweiten Weltkrieg," *Frankfurter Allgemeine Zeitung*, 91, 18 April 1996, 13–14.

59. See David Bankier, *The Germans and Final Solution: Public Opinion under Nazism* (Oxford, 1992), 101–15.

60. Verdict cited in "Kettenbriefe gegen die deutschen Verbrechen im Zweiten Weltkrieg," *Frankfurter Allgemeine Zeitung*, 91, 18 April 1996, 13–14; Albrecht Schöne, "Lesehilfe für Nachgeborene," in ibid.

61. Gerd Überschär, "Das NKFD und der BdO im Kampf gegen Hitler 1943–1945," in idem., ed., *Nationalkomitee "Freies Deutschland,"* 31–51; "Wie lebt der deutsche Kriegsgefangene in Russland," BA-M, RH15/346, 179 and Front-Illustrierte für den deutschen Soldaten, Nr.15–16, June 1943, BA-M, RH15/340, 231–37.

62. Haider, "Reaktionen der Wehrmacht."

63. OKW counter-propaganda against the NKFD made frequent references to 1918, see Mitteilungen für das Offizierskorpes, Sondernummer 1943, in Überschär, ed., *Nationalkomitee "Freies Deutschland,"* 269–79 and "Stellungnahme des OKW zu einigen Flugblättern des NKFD in "Mitteilungen für die Truppe," Nr.351 vom August 1944," in ibid., 281–83.

64. Abt. Fremde Heere Ost (IIb), Behandlung der deutschen Kriegsgefangenen in der SU, 18 June 1944, BA-M, RH2/2780, 7; Sonderdienst der Reichspropagandaleitung, HA Propaganda, Amt Propagandalenkung, Ausgabe B, Folge 11, 20 January 1944, BA-M, R55/517, 139.

65. M. Bormann, Leiter der Parteikanzlei an Gauleiter, Betr. Deutsche Kriegsgefangene in der Sowjetunion, 8 February 1944, BA-M, NS6/350, 38–41; Abt. Fremde

Heere Ost, "Behandlung der deutschen Kriegsgefangenen in der SU," 18 June 1944, BA-M, RH2/2780, 2.

66. Hilger, *Deutsche Kriegsgefangene,* 103–05.

67. On this argument more generally, see Bartov, *Hitler's Army.*

68. While recent research indicates that shootings of German POWs did occur occasionally, systematic selections as described in this account had most likely not taken place, Andreas Hilger, *Deutsche Kriegsgefangene in der Sowjetunion Kriegsgefangenenpolitik, Lageralltag und Erinnerung* (Essen, 2000), 103–05; on "projections" more generally, see Bartov, *Hitler's Army.*

69. M. Bormann, Leiter der Parteikanzlei an Gauleiter, Betr. Deutsche Kriegsgefangene in der Sowjetunion, 8 February 1944, BA-M, NS6/350, 38–41; Abt. Fremde Heere Ost, "Behandlung der deutschen Kriegsgefangenen in der SU," 18 June 1944, BA-M, RH2/2780, 2.

70. Cited in Latzel, *Deutsche Soldaten-Nationalsozialistischer Krieg. Kriegserlebnis-Kriegserfahrung 1939–1945* (Paderborn, 1998), 199.

71. NRWHStA, RW 58/37037.

72. Keitel, Oberkommando des Heeres (Abschrift), 5 January 1944, BA-M, NS6/350, 43.

73. See Wette, ed., *Das letzte halbe Jahr,* 149, 168, 308; on mass surrender along the Elbe, see Henke, *Die amerikanische Besetzung,* 674–94.

74. Benjamin Ziemann, "Fluchten aus dem Konsens zum Durchhalten. Ergebnisse, Probleme und Perspektiven der Erforschung soldatischer Verweigerungsformen in der *Wehrmacht* 1939–1945" in Rolf-Dieter Müller and Hans-Ulrich Volkmann, eds., *Die Wehrmacht. Mythos und Realität* (Munich, 1999), 589–613. On voluntary surrender on the Eastern front, see also the evidence cited in Hilger, *Deutsche Kriegsgefangene,* 78 and Messerschmit, *"Wehrmacht* in der Endphase," 43, who estimates that "hundreds of thousands" or even "millions" of soldiers surrendered without fighting to the very end; for a report of large scale desertion, see Grünewald, Generalrichter und Abt.Chef, Vortragsvermerk für Herrn Feldmarschall, BA-M, RW4/725, 7; see also Kunz, *Wehrmacht und Niederlage,* 268.

75. Kunz, *Wehrmacht und Niederlage,* 338–43.

76. Latzel, *Deutsche Soldaten-Nationalsozialistischer Krieg,* 138–96. This attitude often persisted throughout captivity into the postwar period, see Hilger, *Deutsche Kriegsgefangene.*

77. Christian Streit, *Keine Kameraden. Die Wehrmacht und die sowjetischen Kriegsgefangenen, 1941–1945* (Stuttgart, 1978).

78. Geyer, "There is a Land Where Everything Is Pure."

79. On the wide variety of individual soldiers' experience of defeat, see Kunz, *Wehrmacht und Niederlage,* 290–327.

80. Andreas Hilgruber, *Zweierlei Untergang. Die Zerschlagung des Deutschen Reiches und das Ende des europäischen Judentums* (Berlin, 1986) and the important critique by Omer Bartov, "Historians on the Eastern front," in idem., *Murder in Our Midst: The Holocaust, Industrial Killing, and Representation* (New York, 1996), 71–89.

81. Both Christian churches shaped this process in highly significant ways, see my forthcoming book *Homecomings,* 38–42.

82. Moeller, *War Stories.*

83. For a discussion of this significance, see Koonz, *Mothers in the Fatherland;* for an excellent discussion of women on the homefront, see Birthe Kundrus, *Krieger-frauen. Familienpolitik und Geschlechterverhältnisse im Ersten und Zweiten Weltkrieg* (Hamburg, 1996).

84. See Karen Hagemann, "'Jede Kraft wird gebraucht.' Militäreinsatz von Frauen im Ersten und Zweiten Weltkrieg," in Bruno Thoss and Hans-Ulrich Volkmann, eds., *Erster Weltkrieg-Zweiter Weltkrieg. Ein Vergleich. Krieg, Kriegserlebnis, Kriegserfahrung in Deutschland* (Paderborn, 2002), 79–106; Kundrus, *Kriegerfrauen;* Elziabeth Harvey, *Women and the Nazi East: Agents and Witnesses of Germanization* (New Haven, 2003).

85. Heineman, "'The Hour of the Woman.' Memories of Germany's 'Crisis Years' and West German National Identity," *AHR* 101 (1996): 29–60.

PART THREE

~

CHANGE AND CONTINUITY IN GERMANY'S FOREIGN RELATIONS

~

CHAPTER 7

The Kaiser and His English Relations Revisited

John C. G. Röhl

> I have tried to get on with him & shall nominally do my best till the end—but trust him—*never*. He is *utterly* false & the bitterest foe that E[ngland] possesses!

King Edward VII on Kaiser Wilhelm II, 15 April 1905

In June 1889, one year after his accession to the Prusso-German throne, Queen Victoria conferred the rank of British Admiral of the Fleet on her grandson Kaiser Wilhelm II.[1] Beside himself with glee,[2] the Kaiser wrote to the British ambassador: "Fancy wearing the same uniform as St. Vincent and Nelson; it is enough to make one quite giddy."[3] According to Count Herbert von Bismarck, the German foreign secretary, this act intensified the Kaiser's "commitment ... to England ... in the extreme."[4] The younger Bismarck listened in disbelief as Germany's Supreme War Lord announced that as Admiral of the Fleet he now had "the right to be consulted on English naval matters and to give the Queen the benefit of his expert advice. I looked up in astonishment, but H.M. was speaking in all earnestness."[5] Arriving at the Isle of Wight in his new uniform, Wilhelm became, as Count Bismarck mocked, "the complete anglomaniac."[6] The Kaiser's behaviour there convinced the Reich Chancellor's son that "in his English family relationships H.M. had not kicked off his children's shoes; he was still completely under the influence of his earlier visits to the Isle of Wight, where as a child and youngster he was treated in accordance with his mother's precepts."[7] On the last day, the German sailors paraded past the royal tent under Wilhelm's command. The German foreign secretary later recalled: "The culmination was the parade of 1200 sailors … led personally by H.M. on the lawn in front of the tent in which the Queen sat in her armchair, waving. H.M. commanded and dressed the ranks like a lieutenant on the barrack square and with drawn sword led the contingent goosestepping past the tent. Our generals turned away grumbling and murmuring the words 'unseemly comedy'."[8] On his cruise to Athens for his sister's wedding later that year, Wilhelm stood on deck, scanning the horizon for the British Mediterranean squadron. When at last the ships were sighted, he commanded the Union Jack, signalling the rank of Admiral of the Fleet, to be hoisted next to the Imperial Standard. "A German battleship with an English admiral's flag!" muttered the Commandant of the *Deutschland* in disbelief, neatly capturing the "two souls" in the Kaiser's breast.[9]

In his letters and speeches at this time, the Kaiser spoke of his conviction that, together, the British Royal Navy and the Prusso-German Army would safeguard world peace, but that if that ever failed, the Pommeranian Grenadier would fight shoulder to shoulder with the Red Coat.[10] Throughout his reign he emphasised the religious and "racial" consanguinity of the British and German peoples, which made them natural allies. As late as 1912, his wife the Kaiserin complained to Grand Admiral Alfred von Tirpitz, Britain's arch foe in Germany, that Wilhelm was "at heart an enthusiast for England and all things English. It's in his blood and his upbringing."[11] Yet two years later the two countries were at war. Why were British politicians not able to exploit the happy chance that Queen Victoria's eldest grandchild had inherited the "mightiest throne on earth,"[12] and why were the Kaiser and German statesmen unable to reach an understanding with the British empire which they declared to be their goal?

Our first answer must be that Wilhelm II was by no means—or by no means only—the "anglomaniac" Herbert Bismarck or the Kaiserin made him out to be. His formative experiences of England and Englishness were not confined to happy holidays at Osborne House with his grandmother, or to exciting visits to the Royal Dockyard at Portsmouth with his uncle the Duke of Edinburgh.[13] From his earliest childhood, Wilhelm was given to understand that the country he was destined to rule was inferior to the British Empire, and his grim determination to achieve recognition as an equal dogged him all his life. With breathtaking insensitivity, his "English" mother informed him that England was "the largest & most powerful Empire in the world, in wh[ich] the sun never sets! As England is the freest, the most progressive advanced, & liberal & the most developed race in the world, also the *richest,* she clearly is more suited than any other to civilize *other* countries!"[14] When the seventeen-year-old heir presumptive protested that the German Reich would one day rise to become the leading power in Europe, his mother put him down. "You can say that you have the most *daring* statesman in Europe & also the largest & most powerful Army, furthermore that your population has a fair share of *good* qualities, of intelligence and many a *good* and useful institution to govern it. But alas I cannot admit that your *form* of *Government is first rate, nor* the development of your trade & agriculture *nor* your *social* condition, even in *Art* you cannot beat the rest—and you are *behind hand* in *many many* things which *civilized modern* nations *have* to be perfect in, if they think themselves the leaders of the rest!"[15] Clearly, such "*urging* of English superiority," as his alarmed tutor Dr. Hinzpeter called it,[16] was to make the work of the military men appointed to influence the future King and Kaiser in a "Prussian" direction that much easier, especially after Hinzpeter's plan to send the young Prince to Oxford for a year—perhaps the last chance to change his attitude—was abandoned.[17]

By the 1880's, Wilhelm's reactionary and anglophobic views were set. In letters to the Tsar he reviled his own parents and his uncle Albert Edward, the Prince of Wales, as liberal English agents seeking to implement Queen Victoria's Anglo-Coburg agenda in Germany. He sent his old grandfather Kaiser Wilhelm I details of the Prince of Wales's sexual excesses in Vienna.[18] In 1885, in the first of many counterproductive attempts to cajole Wilhelm into a friendlier attitude, the Queen instructed the Prince of Wales to inform him that he would not be welcome in England. When his father fell ill in 1887, Wilhelm could barely contain his ambition to exclude him from the succession to become emperor himself, and his hatred for his mother, his grandmother and the English doctors now plumbed new depths. "That our family shield should be besmirched and the Reich brought to the brink of ruin by an English princess who is my mother—that is the most terrible thing of all," he declaimed.[19] He denounced his mother and sisters as the "English colony," his father's doctors as "Jewish louts" obsessed with "racial hatred [and] anti-Germanism," and Queen Victoria as the "empress of Hindustan" whose time had come to die. Not only were the English doctors trying to kill his father; they were, he convinced himself, also responsible for crippling his own left arm. "One cannot have enough hatred for England," he cried.[20] Even General von Waldersee, truly no friend of England, was shocked by the way in which the young Prince and Kaiser spoke in the most disdainful manner of the English "as the most good-for-nothing people, as our enemies, as miserable shopkeepers."[21]

When he succeeded to the throne on 15 June 1888, the British ambassador warned of the immense power that Wilhelm would now wield as Kaiser. "If we were dealing with a country in which the foreign policy was guided by the Government & not by the Sovereign," he wrote, the personal feelings of the monarch would be "a matter of small moment, but that is not the case.... His sentiments will count as a strong factor in the policy which may be adopted towards us.”[22] All too soon it became apparent that dark human emotions—family rivalries, vanity and envy, injured pride and craving for acceptance—would henceforth overshadow Anglo-German relations. Within days of his accession, Wilhelm complained that the Queen was treating him “more as a grandson than as German Kaiser.”[23] He described his uncle the Prince of Wales as an “idiot” for suggesting that Kaiser Friedrich might have sought reconciliation with France by returning Alsace and Lorraine,[24] and then added insult to injury by demanding that the heir to the British throne leave Vienna for the duration of his, Wilhelm’s, own visit. Queen Victoria was as incensed by Wilhelm’s behavior as was her son “Bertie.” She wrote of “the most *outrageous* behaviour of Willie the Gt. (& I fear ‘the bad hearted’) towards Bertie.... To treat the Pce of W.—the oldest son of one of the gtst Sovereigns in ~~the World~~ Europe [sic], & his own kind Uncle in such a manner is one of the greatest insults ever committed!”[25]

The family crisis escalated into a major international incident when the Bismarcks announced that the Kaiser wished to visit England, and both the Queen and the Prince of Wales retorted that they could not contemplate receiving him until he had apologized for his outrageous behavior. As Victoria told the Prime Minister Lord Salisbury, Wilhelm’s complaint that his uncle had not treated “his nephew as Emperor” was “really too *vulgar* and too absurd as well as untrue almost *to be believed*. We have always been very intimate with our grandson and nephew, and to pretend that he is to be treated *in private* as well as in public as ‘His Imperial Majesty’ is *perfect madness!*”[26] The thirst for revenge spread through the extended royal family and poisoned the minds of the next generation. As the Danish-born Princess of Wales (the sister of the Tsarina) wrote to her son, the future King George V, Wilhelm had been “personally most *frightfully rude* & *impertinent* towards Papa” and “actually refused to meet him at Vienna!! He is perfectly infuriated against *England* that beast.... Oh he is mad & a conceited ass—who also says that Papa & Grandmama don’t treat him with proper respect as the *Emperor* of *all & mighty Germany!* But my hope is that *pride* will have a *fall* some day!!—Won’t we rejoice then.”[27]

If we recall how closely juxtaposed in time this episode was with the Kaiser’s delight at receiving the admiral’s uniform, we shall see how difficult it is to disentangle the contradictory strands that comprised his attitude to England. In the face of many indications to the contrary, Wilhelm believed all his life that, though British statesmen and the press might have turned against him, his “Frau Grossmutter” always felt an “extraordinary love” for him, her “favourite” grandson.[28] He was genuinely hurt when, after the Krüger telegram and on several other occasions, the Queen let him know that he would not be welcome in England.[29] He tried to rationalize such hostile signals by drawing a distinction between her attitude toward him as “Sovereign” on the one hand and "Grandmother" on the other.[30] To Philipp Eulenburg the Kaiser confessed: "The [German] people have no idea how much I love the Queen.... How profoundly she is interwoven with all my memories of childhood and youth!";[31] and in 1901, just after she had died with him at her bedside, he wrote: "I have only just learned how much she loved me and how highly she thought of me."[32] As Eulenburg remarked when he sent the Kaiser's telegram on to Reich Chancellor Bernhard Count von Bülow, "what a curious, childish, touching naiveté lies in [these] words."[33]

However, the Kaiser's belief that his grandmother was especially fond of him was the product largely of wishful thinking. In reality, for several years before Victoria's death, the always volatile personal relationship between her and her German grandson had come under increasing strain as a result of the deterioration in the political relationship between the two countries, due in no small part to Wilhelm's own anti-British aims. In 1896, on receiving news of the Jameson Raid, he demanded that German troops be sent to defend the Boer Republic, and when the Chancellor objected that that would mean war with England, he inanely retorted: "Yes, but only on land."[34] As Lothar Reinermann's fine study of British views of the Kaiser has shown, the ensuing Krüger telegram did more to inflame popular hatred of Germany in England than any other event before 1914.[35] It also brought a reprimand from the Queen: "I gave him a piece of my mind as to his dreadful telegram," she wrote in her diary, stressing her "pain and astonishment" at Wilhelm's behavior.[36] The latter replied, pharisaically, that his anger had been directed not against England but against the international "mob of gold diggers" who had rebelled against Her Majesty the Queen. "Rebels against the will of H. Most Gracious Majesty the Queen are to me the most execrable beeings [sic] in the world & I was so incensed at the idea of your orders having been disobeyed ... that I thought it necessary to show that publicly! ... I was standing up for ... obedience to a Sovereign whom I rever[e] & adore & whom to obey I thought paramount for her subjects.... It is simply nonsense that two great nations nearly related in kinsmanship & religion, should ... view each other askance, with the rest of Europe as lookers on, what would the Duke of Wellington & old Blücher say if they saw this?"[37]

If the British had difficulty in seeing in such protestations more than a ploy to lull them into a false sense of security, this was above all because of the battleship-building program that, from early 1895 onward, as Jonathan Steinberg and Volker Berghahn have shown, became the Kaiser's chief obsession.[38] In October 1896, his mother wrote in alarm to Queen Victoria of Wilhelm's plans to usurp Britain's hegemonial position by building a "Navy that shall beat the English." "William admires England very much and is very fond of you—& especially enjoys himself in England," she wrote, "but he is not steady & coolheaded and farsighted enough to see that to strain every nerve for Germany to succeed in outdoing England—& wrest fr[om] her the position of supremacy she has in the world—is simply *nonsense!*"[39] The only hope she now saw of averting disaster lay in an Anglo-German alliance.

When the first Navy Bill was passed in 1898, the Kaiser's mother urged him to accept offers of an alliance that she believed were about to be made by the British government, pointing out "the *immense* importance of an alliance between the 2 great Germanic & Protestant nations." In her view, such an alliance would be "the *most blessed* thing that could happen *not only* for the 2 Countries but for the *world* and civilization!!" "For *yourself,* your *own* position, your *own* future, for Germany, I could conceive no more magnificent opportunity. Misunderstandings would be swept away—and *peace* secured!," for with "the German Army and English Fleet *combined, who* would take up the gauntlet?"[40] Wilhelm's reply shows the extent to which he felt rebuffed in his own efforts to reach precisely such an "Alliance of the Anglo-Saxon race," which in his view conformed to the aims pursued by "dear Papa & Grandpapa (Consort)." "In the first 5 years of my reign I tried to the very utmost of my powers ... to elicit from L[ord] S[alisbury] a word implying the approval of the idea of a Anglo-German cooperation," he wrote. "But it was utterly without any result." Instead of earning England's gratitude, "I for the last 3 years have been abused, illtreated & a butt of any bad joke any musikhall singer or fishmonger or pressman thought fit to let fly at me!" As a result of "the treatment I have gone through at the hands of the British Government & notably of L[ord] S[alisbury], & the result of the experience I had in the 10 years of my reign of British Foreign Politics!," he, Wilhelm, now felt "pushed back, illtreated & riled by Grt Britain & her Prime Minister." He was still interested in an "Alliance of England-Amerika & Germany," but only if the British proposal were made openly and formally, for Salisbury could not expect him, the German Kaiser, "to 'slip in by the back door' like a thief at night whom one does not like to own before ones richer friends."[41]

Not only did Wilhelm throw away whatever slim chance there was of an Anglo-German alliance because of his sense of personal injury; he turned to Tsar Nicholas II and asked him for even more favorable terms in return for rejecting the British offer! Claiming, untruthfully, that the British had approached him "with such enormous offers showing a wide and great opening for the future of my country," the Kaiser asked Nicholas to "make your proposals to me and tell me what you are willed to do with regard to us if we refuse [the offer of an alliance with England], before I make my decision."[42] Only a few months later, in the aftermath of the Fashoda crisis, the Kaiser, in the words of Lord Salisbury, expressed "his outspoken desire that there should be a war between England and France," Russia's ally.[43] The moment was well chosen, Wilhelm now told his mother, for Britain "to settle the accounts with France on the whole globe," and he assured her of Germany's benevolent neutrality if Britain went to war against France alone, and her active military support if Russia became involved. "Should it come to war, I of course in private as Grandmama's grandson will pray for the success of her arms with all my heart—which is to me of no doubt whatever—as France is no equal to England on the Sea. Officially as head of the German Empire I would uphold a strict & benevolent neutrality. Should a second Power think fit to attack England from the rear, whilst it is fighting, I would act according to our arrangements made with [the British ambassador] Sir Frank Lascelles."[44] In consternation, both Queen Victoria and Salisbury asked Lascelles what Wilhelm might be referring to, since no such "arrangement" existed.[45] It is hardly surprising, in view of such sly stratagems, that British statesmen regarded Wilhelm's scheming and irascible personality as a hindrance to better Anglo-German relations. Prince Bismarck, too, must have been turning in his freshly-dug grave.

In May 1899, stung once again by his grandmother's refusal to invite him to England for her birthday,[46] the Kaiser accused the British prime minister of grossly insulting behavior toward Germany. "Public opinion over here has been very much agitated & stirred up to its depths by the most unhappy way in which Lord Salisbury has treated Germany," he complained to the Queen. "This way of treating Germany's feelings & interests has come upon the People like an electric shock & has evoked the impression that Lord Salisbury cares for us no more than for Portugal, Chili [sic], or the Patagonians, & out of this impression the feeling has arisen that Germany was beeing [sic] despised by his government, & this has stung my subjects to the quick." In a remarkable fit of self-pity the Kaiser lamented: "I of course have been silent as to what I have *personally* gone through these last six months, the shame & pain I have suffered, & how my heart has bled when to my despair I had to watch how the arduous work of years was destroyed—to make the two Nations understand each other & respect their aspirations & wishes—by one blow by the highhanded & disdainful treatment of Ministers who have never come over to stay here & to study our institutions, & People, & hardly ever have given themselves the trouble to understand them. Lord Salisbury's Government must learn to respect us as equals."[47] The Queen, shocked by this and other signs of the Kaiser's hostility,[48] retorted: "I doubt whether any Sovereign ever wrote in such terms to another Sovereign—& that Sovereign his own Grand Mother, about their Prime Minister."[49] As Eulenburg noted, "old Victoria's offensive letter really has hurt him more deeply than one can say!"[50]

With the outbreak of the Boer War in 1899, Wilhelm's mother pointed out to him how wounding the anti-British cartoons appearing in Germany were to Queen Victoria in particular. "Her Mother was German, her Husband was German, her Sons in Law & Daughters in Law (nearly all)—her sympathies *always were* German.... You can imagine *my* feelings when I see *her* made the subject of gross and insulting caricatures sent as Post cards through the Imperial Post at Berlin!!"[51] Surprisingly, and risking immense unpopularity at home, the Kaiser remained pro-British throughout the crisis, twice sending plans of campaign drawn up by his general staff to Windsor to facilitate a British victory over the Boers,[52] and conferring the Order of the Black Eagle on Field Marshal Lord Roberts.[53] For a brief moment, as public anglophobia in Germany reached new levels of hysteria, relations between the two dynasties improved. As his uncle Edward wrote in 1900: "You have no idea, my dear William, how all of us in England appreciate the loyal friendship which you manifest towards us on every possible occasion. We hope always to look upon Germany as our best friend as long as you are at the helm."[54]

After Queen Victoria's funeral in January 1901, Wilhelm telegraphed from London that the love that King Edward VII and the British people had shown him had created "an immovable foundation … on the basis of which the relations of our people will become good and friendly, for the benefit of the world, provided they are based on mutual understanding and respect."[55] A year later, Edward stressed how anxious he was, "in spite of jealousies & Anglophobism on the part of Germany," to have a "thorough 'Entente Cordiale' with him [Wilhelm] on all subjects which are of importance to both countries."[56] The Kaiser, looking back on the year which had seen the death of both Edward's mother and his own, responded: "Thank God that I could be in time to see dear Grandmama once more, & to be near you & Aunts to help you in bearing the first effects of the awful blow! What a magnificent realm, she has left you, & what a fine position in the world! In fact the first 'World Empire' since the Roman Empire! … I gladly reciprocate all you say about the relations of our two Countries and our personal ones; they are of the same blood, & they have the same creed, & they belong to the Great T[e]utonic Race, which Heaven has intrusted with the Culture of the World; … that is I think grounds enough, to keep Peace & to foster *mutual* recognition & *reciprocity* in all what draws us together, & to sink everything, which could part us." Edward should ignore the anglophobia of the German newspapers, he urged. "The Press is awful on both sides, but here it has nothing to say, for I am the sole arbiter & master of German Foreign Policy & the Government & Country *must* follow me, even if I have to face the Musik!"[57]

In spite of such a promising beginning, during the reign of Edward VII, relations between the two dynasties deteriorated rapidly. The King's decision to cancel his son's visit to Berlin for the Kaiser's birthday in 1902 on the grounds that George would be "liable to be insulted" by the German public,[58] "deeply wounded" the German monarch, who spoke of "another Fashoda" and considered recalling the German ambassador from London.[59] Only months later, the Kaiser was aghast to learn of Edward's decision to donate Osborne House to the Royal Navy. "This is absolutely shameless and unheard of!" he thundered. "To destroy in this way 2 years after her death the Queen's very own private property and the sacred place where she worked, where we spent our youth, and where she died!!"[60] Wilhelm made no secret of his hurt feelings when he realized that his uncle was avoiding visiting Berlin.[61] He in turn insulted Edward by refusing to allow the German Crown Prince to visit England, accusing the King of inviting his son "behind his back" with the dual Machiavellian purpose, he revealingly claimed, first, "to divide father and son, [and] second, to secure (according to an old English recipe) a member of the family here, who could serve him as a spy and observer and whom he could use in his own interests just as he thought fit."[62] Edward VII then outraged the Kaiser by refusing to permit his son George to attend the wedding of the German Crown Prince.[63] When, at the wedding, the British ambassador asked Wilhelm if he had a message for the King, the Kaiser replied: "No, I have nothing to say to your King, nor to your Minister, nor to anyone else in England. I don't want to have anything to do with any of these gentlemen so long as they don't behave in a better way towards me."[64] It was painfully clear that the personal animosity between uncle and nephew had become a grave factor in the worsening relationship between the two countries. As the German ambassador put it in 1905, the King's attitude was characterised by "a profound ill-feeling … towards German policy and unfortunately towards the person of His Majesty the Kaiser in particular."[65] Edward now talked about the Kaiser "in terms which make one's flesh creep."[66] The deterioration in the family relationship was all the more dangerous as the dynastic link was one of the few things still holding the two countries together.[67]

For of course an issue far more fundamental than royal family squabbles lay at the center of the rising Anglo-German antagonism, namely, the Reich's drive to become a *Weltmacht* both in Europe and in the wider world. An early hint of the Kaiser's ambition came in 1892, when he revealed that the "basic aim" of his policy was to achieve the "leadership" of Europe by establishing "a kind of Napoleonic supremacy" for Germany, albeit, he hoped, by "peaceful means."[68] He returned to this idea after Queen Victoria's funeral in 1901. Addressing the new King, Edward VII, he proposed: "We ought to form an Anglo-German alliance, you to keep the seas while we would be responsible for the land; with such an alliance, not a mouse could stir in Europe without our permission."[69] In practice, the Kaiser's proposal implied the acceptance by Great Britain of German domination of the European continent, and thus ran counter to the most fundamental principle of British foreign policy, the maintenance of the balance of power. As Bülow put it in a letter to the Kaiser in 1900, "How true it is that in Your Majesty's reign the British are playing the same role as the French played under the Great Elector and the Austrians under the Great King. Handling the English is infinitely troublesome, infinitely difficult, and demands infinite patience and skill. But just as the Hohenzollern eagle drove the double-headed Austrian eagle from the field and clipped the wings of the

Gallic cock, so with God's help and Your Majesty's strength and wisdom he will be successful against the English leopard."[70]

Once we grasp the idea that the Kaiser's paramount aim was to establish German hegemony in Europe, we shall hold the key to understanding the many apparently contradictory elements of his policy toward England: the Tirpitz Navy was to act as a "power-political lever" to prize Britain out of her position as guarantor of the balance of power on the Continent; until the battle fleet was ready, the royal family, the government, and public opinion in Britain would have to be lulled into believing that no such challenge was intended; Germany's colonial demands—in Africa, South America, the Middle East and Asia—were best postponed until after the attainment of continental hegemony, when Britain would be powerless to resist them. None other than the future Chancellor Theobald von Bethmann Hollweg revealed the consistent aim behind the Kaiser's seemingly vacillating policy when he said in 1903: "His [Wilhelm's] first and most fundamental idea was to break England's position in the world in Germany's favour; to achieve this he needs a fleet, to have a fleet he needs much money, and, since only a rich country can give him this, Germany must become wealthy."[71]

Both Wilhelm II and Edward VII were naturally fully aware of the irreconcilable conflict between the Pax Britannica that existed and the Pax Germanica that the Kaiser sought to establish. The German monarch complained that Salisbury was "obsessed of the idea that there is a balance of power in Europe. There is no balance of power in Europe except me, me and my twenty-five [Army] corps."[72] He informed the British Foreign Secretary in 1901 that the policy of the balance of power had become obsolete; "the balance of power in Europe is me."[73] And to a diplomat at the German embassy in London he proclaimed: "It was not the British fleet but the twenty-two German Army Corps that were the Balance of Power."[74] Edward VII realized the true purpose behind the Tirpitz navy and saw through his nephew's protestations of friendship when he observed that if Britain gave in to German naval blackmail and remained neutral in a continental war, "Germany would have the power of demolishing her enemies, one by one, with us sitting by with folded arms, & she would then probably proceed to attack us."[75]

As Britain responded to the German challenge by forming first the Anglo-Japanese alliance, then the Anglo-French Entente, and finally the Triple Entente with France and Russia, the Kaiser was seized by panic attacks. In 1903, when the London government, in the person of Joseph Chamberlain, issued its first public warning against the German battlefleet-building program, Eulenburg recorded: "The rejection of the Kaiser, of his attempts to win 'England's love', confronts him for the first time seriously with the fact that through his *battle-fleet* he has become England's enemy. He is now lying to himself in thinking that he can call Mr. Chamberlain 'to order' by means of the support which he *thinks* he has among his relatives and even among the English *people*. He even thinks that in this regard he can depend on his uncle Edward. But in his innermost soul terrible demons have been roused."[76] By 1904, Wilhelm had convinced himself that England was about to launch an attack on Germany. As Edward VII's private secretary, Sir Francis Knollys, commented: "What an extraordinary idea ... the Emperor has got into his head as to our intending to attack Germany. One could understand the German Public, though it is very absurd of them, more or less believing it, but that the Emperor himself should, who ought to know England so well, is inconceivable, & is almost laughable."[77]

Edward, for his part, was no less suspicious of his nephew's intentions. To Prince Louis of Battenberg the King referred to the Kaiser as that "most energetic but tactless not to say dangerous Sovereign!"[78] When Battenberg reported that the Kaiser had told him on the day after his landing in Tangiers that the world would eventually be divided between the Teutons and the Slavs, and that the German army knew "the road to Paris," Edward's patience snapped. "I consider the Tangiers incident was one of the most mischievous & uncalled for events which H.M. G[erman] E[mperor] has ever undertaken. It was a gratuitous insult to 2 Countries.... It was a regular *case* of 'Bombastes Furioso'! I suppose G[erman] E[mperor] will never find out as he will never be told how ridiculous he makes himself.... I have tried to get on with him & shall nominally do my best till the end—but trust him—never. He is *utterly* false & the bitterest foe that E[ngland] possesses!"[79]

Incredibly, Wilhelm II seems to have expected Britain to accept Germany's domination of the Continent and the instrument for achieving it, Tirpitz's battlefleet, without protest. At a disastrous meeting between the Kaiser and Edward VII at Schloss Friedrichshof in the Taunus Mountains above Frankfurt in 1908, Wilhelm refused even to consider a lessening in the pace of German naval armaments and actually threatened war if Britain continued her efforts to slow it down.[80] In his correspondence with British admirals, and in the disastrous "interview" that appeared in the *Daily Telegraph* in October 1908, he stressed the peaceful nature of German intentions; and when these assurances were not believed, his anger and frustration was boundless: "Your people must first learn manners again vis-à-vis to me & my country," he wrote to the daughter of Admiral Victor Montagu. "It is incomprehensible to me how they can behave in such a manner to the eldest grandson of their Queen who was the last of her relatives she recognised & smiled upon before she died & in whose loving arms she drew her last breath!"[81] In exasperation he complained in 1910:

> With regard to your political celebrities & so called great statesmen, their behaviour towards me & my country, seen from here, can only awaken pity, &

mirth, for they really make the impression of people all let loose together from Bedlam! In order to 'rouse' your people they go & invent, & tell the most un-heard of nonsense, fables, & even brazenfaced lies about the intentions, or supposed intentions, of a country they mostly never have seen, certainly not studied & of its ruler whom they dont know & who has never honoured them with any of his views!! … Your politicians seem like actors in a panto-mime, they are a set of screaming clowns or hysterical old women! as far as their utterances about Germany & its plans are concerned! … You … say that it would be well that our two countries should stand together. That is my ideal I am working for since 20 years of my reign. But the violent press & the violent & senseless speeches in England make the task next to impossible."[82]

In 1912, with the Haldane mission, the issue at the heart of the Anglo-German antagonism came fully into view. Brushing aside the conciliatory advice of his civilian statesmen and diplomats, who he hoped had "learned the lesson to pay greater heed to their master and his commands and wishes …, especially when anything is to be accomplished with the British, with whom they do not know how to deal, whereas I understand them well!,"[83] the Kaiser formulated his aim in the negotiations by stating that Germany was demanding from England "an immense reorientation of its entire political stance insofar as it must give up its Entente a[nd] we step more or less into France's shoes." He made this demand despite his clear recognition that in Britain's eyes "the En-tente with France provides her with the best safeguard against an overpower-ful Germany."[84] The British Government naturally found it impossible to accede to the German demand for an "unconditional" guarantee of neutrality in the event of a European war, as this would have allowed Germany to attack France and Russia at will without fear of British intervention.[85] As Tirpitz later recalled, the British Cabinet was prepared, in return for a reduction in the pace of the German naval build-up, "to stay neutral in the event that France attacked Germany; but in the event that Germany attacked France it wanted to retain a free hand."[86]

Nine months later, in December 1912, Wilhelm revealed his innermost thinking when he reacted furiously to a report from Prince Karl Max von Lich-nowsky, the new ambassador in London, according to which Haldane had stated that Britain would feel obliged to stand by France and Russia in any future war. Over and over again, the Kaiser declared the British principle of the "bal-ance of power" to be an "idiocy" which would make England "eternally into our enemy." That principle was nothing more than an attempt by that "nation of shopkeepers" to prevent other powers from defending their interests with the sword. Incredulously, he registered that in the approaching "final struggle be-tween the Slavs and the Teutons," the "Anglo-Saxons will be on the side of the Slavs and Gauls."[87] In the coming "struggle for existence" between the "Teutons" and the "Slavs supported by the Latins (Gauls)," the Kaiser thundered, England—motivated by "envy and hatred of Germany" and by her "fear that we are becoming too strong"—would stand on the side of the Slavs and Gauls.[88] He informed Archduke Franz Ferdinand that Lord Haldane's statement had been "typically English," "full of poison and hatred and envy of the good development of our mutual alliance and our two countries." Britain's "balance of power" policy had been revealed "in all its naked shamelessness" as the "playing off of the Great Powers against each other to England's advantage."[89] In similar vein, he wrote to the Prussian envoy in Karlsruhe that Haldane had declared "in unscrupulous, raw and typically English terms … that if Germany were to become involved in a war with Russia-France—in support of Austria—England would not only not remain neutral, but would immediately come to France's aid"; for, according to Haldane, England could "not tolerate Germany's becoming the predominant Power on the Continent and that the latter should unite under its leadership!!"[90] Wilhelm told the Bavarian envoy that Haldane had explained that England "could not permit Germany to subjugate France, after which there would be only one Power on the Continent which would then exercise an absolute hegemony." The "Germanic English," the outraged Kaiser exclaimed, would therefore "fight with the French and Russians against their own racial comrades."[91] He informed Albert Ballin that Haldane had declared that England could not tolerate "a subjugation of France by ourselves"; it could not allow "us to achieve a predominant position on the Continent under which the Continent could then be united."[92] The Swiss ambassador was told by Wilhelm that Haldane had announced "that England would never tolerate Germany's taking a predominant position over her neighbours in Central Europe. Is this not an impertinent statement which should really have been answered by a breaking off of diplomatic relations?," the Kaiser asked. "Is it not incredible … that these Anglo-Saxons with whom we are related by common ancestry, religion and civilisatory striving, now wish to allow themselves to be used as the tools of the Slavs." The Kaiser declared that Austria and Germany would have to prevent the creation of a strong Serbian state, for the vital interests of both empires required that they must not be "encircled by a Slav ring." Ominously he stated: "If this question … cannot be solved by diplomacy, then it will have to be decided by armed force. The solution can be postponed," declared the Kaiser. "But the question will arise again in 1 or 2 years."[93]

The conclusion seems inescapable that the Kaiser's outrage over Britain's unequivocal support for the balance of power brought Europe a significant step closer to war. On 8 December 1912, he summoned his chief of general staff and the three top admirals and informed them that in a future war of the Triple Alliance against France and Russia, England would stand at the side of her Entente partners. He greeted this news, he said, as a "desirable clarification of the situation" and concluded that Austria should now deal forcefully with the Serbs. Should Russia support the Serbs, "which she evidently does," then "war would be unavoidable for us too." But Germany would be free to "fight the war with full fury against France." The fleet would have to prepare for a war against England, involving "immediate submarine warfare against English troop transports in the Scheldt or by Dunkirk" and "mine warfare in the Thames." Tirpitz, however, pleaded for a "postponement of the great fight for 1½ years"—until the widening of the Kiel Canal had been completed in the summer of 1914![94]

One and a half years later, at the end of the July Crisis that was to plunge the world into war, the Kaiser's emotional turmoil took on an ever more psychopathological form as it became apparent that Britain would indeed not stay neutral. In the savage marginal comments he scrawled on the official diplomatic documents he exclaimed:

> "England, Russia and France have *agreed* among themselves … to take the Austro-Serbian conflict for an *excuse* for waging a *war of extermination* against us.… That is the real naked situation *in nuce,* which, slowly and cleverly set going, certainly by Edward VII, has been carried on, and systematically built up by disowned conferences between England and Paris and St. Petersburg; finally brought to a conclusion by George V and set to work.… The net has been suddenly thrown over our head, and England sneeringly reaps the most brilliant success of her persistently prosecuted purely *anti-German world-policy,* against which we have proved ourselves helpless.… A great achievement, which arouses the admiration even of him who is to be destroyed as its result! Edward VII is stronger after his death than am I who am still alive!"[95]

Again the Kaiser railed against "this hated, lying, conscienceless nation of shop-keepers" with its "pharisaical hypocrisy" of maintaining the balance of power in Europe, which was nothing more than "playing the card of all the European nations in England's favour against us!" He demanded that, "if we are to be bled to death, England shall at least lose India."

As the war dragged on, the Kaiser's hatred of England acquired a quasi-religious intensity. In January 1917, he wrote that the conflict was "a struggle between 2 Weltanschauungen: the Teutonic-German for morality, right, loyalty a[nd] faith, genuine humanity, truth and real freedom, against the Anglo-Saxon [Weltanschauung], the worship of mammon, the power of money, pleasure, land-hunger, lies, betrayal, deceit and … treacherous assassination! These two Weltanschauungen cannot be 'reconciled' or 'tolerate' one another, one must be *victorious,* the other *go under!*" The British and French leaders were, Wilhelm believed, "under the spell of Satan," but they had unwittingly succeeded in turning the war into a German "crusade"—"a crusade against *evil*—Satan—in the world, prosecuted by us as *tools* of the Lord.... We *warriors of God* will fight until the band of robbers in the service of mammon and the *foes of the Kingdom of God* lie in the dust!, whose coming into the world would be rendered completely impossible by the Anglo-Saxon Weltanschauung, but which will be assisted by our victory! God wants this struggle, we are his tools, He will direct it, we need not worry about the outcome, we will suffer, fight and be victorious under His Sign! Then we shall have *the* peace, the *German* peace, *God's* peace, in which the entire liberated world will breathe a sigh of relief; liberated from the Anglo-Saxon Satanic service of mammon and brutalisation!"[96]

A quarter of a century later, when Hitler's army was rampaging across Europe, Wilhelm II again declared Germany to be the land of monarchy and therefore of Christ; England the land of Liberalism and therefore of Satan and Antichrist, the land, that is, of "Juda," for in his mind England, the Jews, and liberal democracy were so intertwined that he now spoke of "Juda-England" as one hyphenated word. Germany's real enemy, the Kaiser explained in 1940, was not the British people as a whole but the English ruling classes, who were, he said, "Freemasons thoroughly infected by Juda." "The British people must be *liberated* from the *Antichrist Juda*," he wrote. "We must drive Juda out of England just as he has been chased out of the Continent." Echoing Hitler's notorious speech of January 1939, the Kaiser claimed that twice—in 1914 and again in 1939—the Jews and Freemasons had unleashed a war of "extermination" against Germany with the aim of establishing an international Jewish empire held together by British and American gold. But then "God [had] intervened and smashed their plan!" "Juda's plan has been *smashed* to pieces and they themselves swept out of the European Continent!" Now the Continent was "consolidating and closing itself off from British influences after the elimination of the British and the Jews!" The result would be a "U.S. of Europe!" the Kaiser cried in triumph.[97] In late 1940 he told his sister: "The hand of God is creating a new World & working miracles.... We are becoming the *U.S. of Europe* under German leadership, a united European Continent, nobody ever hoped to see."[98] One of Queen Victoria's German grandchildren writing to another, but the only sign in this letter of the Kaiser's English ancestry is the language in which it is written: As Britain stood alone against Hitler's might, the two surviving children of the "English" Crown Princess still corresponded with one another in their mother tongue.

Notes

1. Sir Edward Malet to Queen Victoria, 15 June 1889, George E. Buckle, ed., *The Letters of Queen Victoria,* third series, 3 vols. (London, 1930–32), I:503f. See also Royal

Archives (RA), Queen Victoria's Journal (QVJ), 23 July 1889; Sir Henry Ponsonby to Queen Victoria, 23 July 1889, RA A67/82; Queen Victoria to Viktoria Princess of Hessen, 7 August 1889, RA Add. U173/154. I am most grateful to H.M. Queen Elizabeth for permission to quote from documents in the Royal Archives.

2. Eulenburg to Herbert Graf von Bismarck, 17 July 1889, in John C. G. Röhl, ed., *Philipp Eulenburgs Politische Korrespondenz*, 3 vols. (Boppard-am-Rhein, 1976–83), I, no. 228.

3. Kaiser Wilhelm II to Sir Edward Malet, 14 June 1889, Buckle, *Letters of Queen Victoria*, I:504.

4. Herbert Bismarck, Aufzeichnung, 67f., Bundesarchiv (BA) Koblenz, Nachlaß Bismarck FC 3018 N.

5. Ibid., 70ff.

6. Ibid., 70.

7. Ibid., 72f.

8. Ibid., 75f.

9. Vice-Admiral Paul Hoffmann, diary, 26–28 October 1889, in the possession of Dr. Margot Leo-Hoffmann, St. Georgen/Schwarzwald, whom I thank for kindly making this document available to me.

10. Kaiser Wilhelm II to Queen Victoria, 17 August 1889, Buckle, *Letters of Queen Victoria*, I:526f.

11. Vice Admiral Albert Hopman, diary, 23 March 1912, Bundesarchiv-Militärarchiv (BA-MA) Freiburg, Nachlaß Hopman N326.

12. Count Philipp zu Eulenburg to his mother, 4 October 1888, in Röhl, ed., *Philipp Eulenburgs Politische Korrespondenz*, I, no. 197. See also Eulenburg to Kaiser Wilhelm II, 15 October 1888, ibid., no. 199.

13. Lord Salisbury to Queen Victoria, 31 October 1889; Monson to Salisbury, 31 October 1889, RA I57/69–70.

14. Crown Princess Victoria to Prince Wilhelm, 16 July 1878, quoted in John C. G. Röhl, *Wilhelm II. Die Jugend des Kaisers 1859–1888* (Munich, 1993), 282, 864. See also Röhl, *Young Wilhelm: The Kaiser's Early Life 1859–1888* (Cambridge, 1998), 267.

15. Crown Princess to Prince Wilhelm, 15 May 1878, quoted in Röhl, *Jugend des Kaisers,* 282f. and 864. See also Röhl, *Young Wilhelm,* 268.

16. Hinzpeter to Crown Princess, 8 February 1876, Röhl, *Jugend des Kaisers*, 282; *Young Wilhelm,* 267.

17. See Röhl, *Jugend des Kaisers,* 297–99.

18. Wilhelm's letters to Tsar Alexander III and to his grandfather Wilhelm I are quoted in Röhl, *Jugend des Kaisers,* 440ff. and 486; see *Young Wilhelm,* 430ff. and 481f.

19. Crown Prince Wilhelm to Eulenburg, April 1888, in Röhl, *Eulenburgs Korrespondenz,* I, no. 169.

20. *Eulenburgs Korrespondenz,* I, 225 and nos. 111 and 153. See also Brigitte Hamann, *Rudolf, Kronprinz und Rebell* (Vienna-Munich, 1978), 328ff.

21. Waldersee, diary entry for 15 July 1891, Waldersee Papers, GStA Berlin.

22. Malet to Salisbury, 14 July 1888, RA I56/86.

23. Colonel Leopold Swaine to Ponsonby, 4 July 1888, in Sir Frederick Ponsonby, ed., *Briefe der Kaiserin Friedrich* (Berlin, 1929), 344.

24. Wilhelm's speech of 16 August 1888 is printed in Johannes Penzler, ed., *Die Reden Kaiser Wilhelms II. in den Jahren 1888–1895* (Leipzig, 1896), 19–21.

25. Queen Victoria to her son Arthur Duke of Connaught, 27 September 1888, RA Vic Addl Mss A15/5166. See also Queen Victoria to Princess Victoria of Battenberg, 2 October 1888, RA Add U173/145.

26. Queen Victoria to Lord Salisbury, 15 October 1888, Buckle, *Letters of Queen Victoria*, I:440f. See also Queen Victoria to Salisbury, 13 November 1888, RA Z280/67.

27. Alexandra Princess of Wales to Prince George, 17 October 1888, RA Geo V, AA31/1.

28. Kaiser Wilhelm II, marginal comment on Bismarck, *Gedanken und Erinnerungen*, III:143, Geheimes Staatsarchiv (GStA) Berlin, BPH 53/170; W. H. H. Waters, *Potsdam and Doorn*, (London, 1935), 7. See also Kaiser Wilhelm II to Waters, 24 April 1928, cited ibid., 95–97.

29. Holstein to Hatzfeldt, 25 April 1896, in Gerhard Ebel, ed., *Botschafter Paul Graf von Hatzfeldt, Nachgelassene Papiere*, 2 vols. (Boppard-am-Rhein, 1977), II, no. 680.

30. Kaiser Wilhelm II to Queen Victoria, 2 February 1899, Buckle, *Letters of Queen Victoria*, III:337.

31. Eulenburg to Kaiser Wilhelm II, 26 January 1901, in Röhl, *Eulenburgs Korrespondenz*, III, no. 1443.

32. Kaiser Wilhelm II to Eulenburg, 5 February 1901, ibid., III, no. 1444.

33. Eulenburg to Bülow, 6 February 1901, ibid., III, no. 1445.

34. Adolf Freiherr Marschall von Bieberstein, diary, 3 January 1896, in Friedrich Thimme, "Die Krüger-Depesche," *Europäische Gespräche*, May–June 1924, 201–244, here 212ff. See also Holstein to Bülow, 2 April 1897, BA Koblenz, Nachlaß Bülow.

35. See Lothar Reinermann, *Der Kaiser in England. Wilhelm II. und sein Bild in der britischen Öffentlichkeit* (Paderborn, Munich, Vienna, Zürich, 2001), 145–79; Norman Rich, *Friedrich von Holstein. Politics and Diplomacy in the Era of Bismarck and Wilhelm II,* 2 vols, (Cambridge, 1965), II:469.

36. Queen Victoria, diary, 5 January 1896, RA QVJ. Queen Victoria to Kaiser Wilhelm II, 5 January 1896, Buckle, *Letters of Queen Victoria*, III:7ff.

37. Kaiser Wilhelm II to Queen Victoria, 8 January 1896, RA Z500/5. See Karl Alexander von Müller, ed., *Fürst Chlodwig zu Hohenlohe-Schillingsfürst, Denkwürdigkeiten der Reichskanzlerzeit* (Stuttgart-Berlin, 1931), 154f.

38. Eugen von Jagemann, report of 9 January 1895, in Walter Peter Fuchs, ed., *Großherzog Friedrich I. von Baden und die Reichspolitik,* 4 vols. (Stuttgart, 1969–80), III, no. 1407. On the origins of the German battleship program, see Jonathan Steinberg, *Yesterday's Deterrent: Tirpitz and the Birth of the German Battle Fleet* (London, 1966), and in particular Volker R. Berghahn, *Der Tirpitz-Plan. Genesis und Verfall einer innenpolitischen Krisenstrategie* (Düsseldorf, 1971). For further evidence of the Kaiser's growing naval enthusiasm, see Röhl, *Personal Monarchy*, 999–1039.

39. The Empress Frederick to Queen Victoria, 24 October 1896, Archiv der Hessischen Hausstiftung (AdHH), Schloß Fasanerie.

40. The Empress Frederick to Kaiser Wilhelm II, 29 May 1898, GStA Berlin, BPHA Rep. 52T no. 13.

41. Kaiser Wilhelm II to his mother, 1 June 1898, draft, not sent, Politisches Archiv des Auswärtigen Amtes (PA AA) Bonn, Preußen 1 no. 1d, Bd. 1. Printed in Norman Rich and M. H. Fisher, eds., *The Holstein Papers*, 4 vols. (Cambridge, 1956–63), IV, no. 657.

42. Kaiser Wilhelm II to Tsar Nicholas II, 30 May 1898, in Walter Goetz, ed., *Briefe Wilhelms II. an den Zaren* (Berlin, 1920), 309ff. Copy in PA AA Bonn, Preußen 1 Nr. 1d Bd. 1. See also Kaiser Wilhelm II to Tsar Nicholas II, 18 August 1898, ibid. Also Hatzfeldt to Holstein, 31 May 1898, *Holstein Papers,* IV, no. 655; Holstein to Hatzfeldt, 11 June 1898, Hatzfeldt, *Nachgelassene Papiere,* II, no. 728.

43. Lord Salisbury to Queen Victoria, 3 June 1899, RA I62/15.

44. Kaiser Wilhelm II to his mother, 20 November 1898, AdHH Schloß Fasanerie.

45. Lord Salisbury to Queen Victoria, 26 November 1898, RA I61/77; Sir Frank Lascelles to Queen Victoria, 9 December 1898, RA I61/78.

46. Holstein to Hatzfeldt, Hatzfeldt, Nachgelassene Papiere, II, no. 757.

47. Kaiser Wilhelm II to Queen Victoria, 27 May 1899, RA I62/14.

48. RA QVJ, 5 June 1899.

49. Queen Victoria to Kaiser Wilhelm II, 12 June 1899, RA I62/19.

50. Eulenburg to Bülow, 10–11 July 1899, Röhl, *Eulenburgs Korrespondenz,* III, no. 1396.

51. The Empress Frederick to Kaiser Wilhelm II, 19 March 1900, GStA Berlin, BPHA Rep. 52T Nr. 13.

52. Kaiser Wilhelm II to Albert Edward Prince of Wales, 21 December 1899 and 4 February 1900, RA W60/26–28 and W60/66–67.

53. Hermann von Eckardstein, *Ten Years at the Court of St. James* (London, 1921), 196ff.

54. Albert Edward Prince of Wales to Kaiser Wilhelm II, 7 March 1900, printed in *Die Große Politik der europaischen kabinette,* XV, no. 4480.

55. Kaiser Wilhelm II to Eulenburg, 5 February 1901, Röhl, *Eulenburgs Korrespondenz,* III, no. 1444.

56. King Edward VII to Lascelles, 25 December 1901, RA X37/49.

57. Kaiser Wilhelm II to King Edward VII, 30 December 1901, RA X37/51.

58. King Edward VII to Kaiser Wilhelm II, 15 January 1902, RA W42/58.

59. Lascelles to Sir Francis Knollys, 17 January 1902, RA W42/61; Lascelles to Lord Lansdowne, 22 and 24 January 1902, RA W42/64, Public Record Office (PRO) London, FO 800/129.

60. Kaiser Wilhelm II, marginal note on Coerper to Tirpitz, 27 December 1902, quoted in Roderick R. McLean, *Royalty and Diplomacy in Europe, 1890–1914* (Cambridge, 2001), 32.

61. Ibid., 50f.

62. Heinrich von Tschirschky to Bülow, 22 August 1905, Bernhard Fürst von Bülow, *Denkwürdigkeiten,* 4 vols. (Berlin, 1930), II:152f.

63. McLean, *Royalty and Diplomacy,* 61f. See Sir Sidney Lee, *King Edward VII: A Biography,* 2 vols. (London, 1925–27), II:355.

64. Ladislaus Graf von Szögyény to Vienna, 14 June 1905, quoted in Fritz Fellner, "Die Verstimmung zwischen Wilhelm II. und Eduard VII. im Sommer 1905," *Mitteilungen des österreichischen Staatsarchivs,* Vol. 11 (1958), 504.

65. Paul Graf von Wolff-Metternich to Bülow, 14 August 1905, *Große Politik,* XXII, no. 6870.

66. Lansdowne to Lascelles, 25 September 1905, McLean, "Monarchy and Diplomacy," 70.

67. Metternich to Bülow, 21 February 1902, *Holstein Papers,* IV, no. 799.

68. Eulenburgs memorandum of 11 July 1892 is printed in Röhl, *Eulenburgs Korrespondenz*, II, no. 688.

69. Quoted in Arthur Gould Lee, *The Empress Frederick Writes to Sophie, Letters 1889–1901*, 2 vols. (London, 1955), II:11.

70. Bülow to Kaiser Wilhelm II, 6 August 1900, GStA Berlin, BPHA Rep. 53J, Lit. B no. 16a.

71. See Rudolf Vierhaus, ed., *Das Tagebuch der Baronin Spitzemberg* (Göttingen, 1960), 428.

72. H. H. Asquith, *The Genesis of the War* (London, 1923), 19f.

73. Kaiser Wilhelm II to Bülow, 29 January 1901, *Große Politik*, XVII, no. 4987, 28f.

74. Eckardstein, *Ten Years,* 194.

75. Sir Francis Knollys to Sir Charles Hardinge 13 November 1909, McLean, *Royalty and Diplomacy,* 87.

76. Philipp Fürst zu Eulenburg, "Psyche und Politik," manuscript.

77. Zedlitz-Trützschler, *Twelve Years,* 112. Knollys to Lansdowne, 27 December 1904, PRO FO 800/12, quoted in McLean, "Monarchy and Diplomacy," 57. See also Spitzemberg, *Tagebuch,* 12 February 1905, 445.

78. King Edward VII to Prince Louis of Battenberg, 15 July 1905, quoted in McLean, *Royalty and Diplomacy,* 66.

79. King Edward VII to Prince Louis of Battenberg, 15 April 1905, quoted ibid., 60.

80. Ibid., p. 82. See also Paul Kennedy, *The Rise of the Anglo-German Antagonism, 1860–1914* (London, 1980), 444.

81. Kaiser Wilhelm II to Lady Mary Montagu, 17 October 1905.

82. Kaiser Wilhelm II to Lady Mary Montagu, 8 January 1910.

83. Kaiser Wilhelm II, marginal note, 31 March 1912, *Große Politik*, XXXI, no. 11422.

84. Kaiser Wilhelm II to Theobald von Bethmann Hollweg, 26 February 1912; Bethmann Hollweg to Admiral Georg Alexander von Müller, 26 February 1912, BA-MA Freiburg, RM3/v9.

85. Diary of Lord Haldane's visit to Berlin, 8–9 February 1912, RA Geo.V.M450/15a and b.

86. Tirpitz to Kaiser Wilhelm II, 9 October 1917, BA Berlin, Nachlaß Nowak 24.

87. Kaiser Wilhelm II, marginal comments on Lichnowsky's report of 3 December 1912, *Große Politik*, XXXIX, no. 15612.

88. Kaiser Wilhelm II to Afred von Kiderlen-Wächter, 8 December 1912, *Große Politik*, XXXIX, no. 15613

89. Kaiser Wilhelm II to Archduke Franz Ferdinand, 9 December 1912, printed in John C. G. Röhl, "An der Schwelle zum Weltkrieg. Eine Dokumentation über den 'Kriegsrat' vom 8. Dezember 1912," *Militärgeschichtliche Mitteilungen* (1977), doc. no. 8. See R. A. Kann, "Emperor William II and Archuke Francis Ferdinand in their Correspondence," *American Historical Review* 57 (1952), 344f. Also R. A. Kann, *Erzherzog Franz Ferdinand. Studien* (Munich, 1967), 74f.

90. Kaiser Wilhelm II to Karl von Eisendecher, 12 December, Röhl, "An der Schwelle," doc. no. 13. See also Fritz Fischer, *Krieg der Illusionen* (Düsseldorf, 1969), 236f.

91. Hugo Graf von Lerchenfeld-Koefering to Georg Graf von Hertling, 14 December 1912, in Ernst Deuerlein, ed., *Briefwechsel Hertling-Lerchenfeld* (Boppard-am-Rhein, 1973), Part I, 189ff. See also Karl Alexander von Müller in *Süddeutsche Monatshefte,* July 1921, 294f.

92. Bernhard Huldermann, *Albert Ballin* (Oldenburg 1922), 273f.

93. Alfred de Claparède, report of 10 December 1912, printed in Terence F. Cole, "German Decision-Making on the Eve of the First World War. The Records of the Swiss Embassy in Berlin," in John C. G. Röhl, ed., *Der Ort Kaiser Wilhelms II. in der deutschen Geschichte* (Munich, 1991), 62f.

94. See the four documents on the "war council" of 8 December 1912 quoted in Röhl, *The Kaiser and his Court,* 162–65.

95. Kaiser Wilhelm II, marginal comment on Pourtalès to Jagow, 30 July 1914, Imanuel Geiss, ed., *July 1914: The Outbreak of the First World War: Selected Documents* (London, 1967), no. 135.

96. Kaiser Wilhelm II to Houston Stewart Chamberlain, 15 January 1917, quoted in Röhl, *The Kaiser and his Court,* paperback edition (Cambridge, 1996), 208.

97. Kaiser Wilhelm II to Alwina Gräfin von der Goltz, 28 July and 7 August 1940, quoted ibid., 211.

98. Kaiser Wilhelm II to his sister Margarethe Landgräfin von Hessen, 3 November 1940, quoted in John C. G. Röhl, *Kaiser Wilhelm II. 'Eine Studie über Cäsarenwahnsinn'* (Munich, 1989), 7.

CHAPTER 8

Appeasement and Counter-Appeasement
Nazi-Soviet Collaboration 1939–1941[1]

Hartmut Pogge von Strandmann

> Of all the countries which have diplomatic relations with us, the strongest economic links have existed and continue to exist with Germany. They are necessitated by the interests of both countries.
>
> Molotov, 27 January 1933

Throughout the twentieth century Germany's relationship with Soviet Russia was strongly influenced by economic considerations, perhaps more so than with any other state. The German and Russian economies complemented each other since Germany was able to sell increasingly industrialized goods to Russia while that country, rich in natural resources, found its western neighbor a keen customer for its commodities. Neither the First World War nor the revolutions of 1917 and the peace treaty of Brest-Litovsk changed this trading pattern for any length of time. Although the Second World War and its aftermath severely hampered any normalization of trade relations and transfers of technology, trade was resumed during the 1950s and the economic factor again played a crucial role, this time in the bilateral relationship between West Germany and the Soviet Union.

Whereas in the 1920s and early 1930s the Weimar Republic wanted to buy good relations and foreign political support from the first socialist state, in the 1960s and 1970s West Germany returned to this aim, but this time with the specific purpose of buying peace. Ironically this had also been the purpose of the Nazi-Soviet Pact, even if other more sinister goals lay behind it. The Third Reich had increased its trade with Stalinist Russia first to prevent any intervention in Germany's war with Poland and the West and secondly to buy essential raw materials for a German economy that was ultimately gearing up for war against the Soviet Union itself. It is clear that the twenty-two months of the Pact must be seen in a very different light from the peaceful continuities that dominated Germany's foreign policy toward Russia in preceding and later eras. Those peaceful intentions were supplanted by the negative aims of conquest, exploitation, domination, and even complete suppression of a Russian state. Yet, it will be argued here that even in this period economic interests continued to play an intriguing and complex role in shaping the German-Soviet relationship.

Historians have often tried to single out the most important factor in German-Soviet relations between 1917 and 1941, be it foreign political, ideological, military or economic. However, the complexity of the relationship between the two countries has made this difficult. This problem is further exacerbated by the varying significance of different phases in the interwar years. Thus the so-called "community of fate" of the early 1920s was replaced in the second half of the Weimar Republic by the "community of interests" based on large-scale Russian orders of investment goods from Germany, placed so that the industrial targets of the first Five Year Plan should be attained. For example, in 1932, Germany sold a record 11 percent of its exports to Russia. This figure appears even more significant if one bears in mind that the German exports to the Soviet Union may have helped to prevent a total collapse of the Weimar Republic.[2] On the political side exports to Russia were regarded as of such importance that in 1933 Hans von Seeckt recommended a strategy that would not only restore Germany to the status of a Great Power but also would "make German industry indispensable and appreciated in Russia."[3] Russian orders were so important that the new chancellor, Adolf Hitler, despite being well-known in Russia for his anti-communist and anti-Russian attitudes, found himself having to reschedule the repayment of the Russian debts, standing at about 1.2 billion marks, since the Russians were finding it difficult to repay their debts on time.[4] This deferment was to some extent welcomed by German economic circles since the delayed payments would provide a reviving German economy with staggered injections of foreign currency with which raw materials could be bought on the world market. However, this early indication that Hitler would be prepared to work within the framework of the "community of interests" did not last. The government became less willing to trade with the Soviet Union for ideological reasons. This unwillingness was matched by the Soviet inability to pay for massive new orders.[5] All that was possible was a relatively low credit arrangement in 1935 worth 200 million marks spread over a period of five years which was not to satisfy either the Russians or the Germans.

In his new book on Hitler and Stalin, Richard Overy has underlined the role of ideological contradictions in causing the unsatisfactory relationship. From August 1939 to June 1941, he argues, "politics succeeded in masking how wide the ideological chasm was that separated the two dictatorships." Accordingly, Overy has played down the economic continuities in German-Russian relations as well as the aspect of collaboration during the "pact-period."[6] But it must be emphasized that the two dictators were not constantly colliding with each other. There was an economic rationale behind their short-lived collaboration that was based on the positive experience of trade and technological transfer during the Weimar Republican period. Without this factor the chasm would not have been bridged and an agreement would not have been possible. By emphasizing the political side of the agreements, Overy underrates the complexity of German-Soviet relations and does not demonstrate why the Russian side regarded trade with Germany as a positive phenomenon which might reduce the ideological confrontation to less dangerous levels.

By contrast Lew Besymenski's latest book does highlight the economic relations between the two countries and is able to demonstrate that it was Stalin himself who in a cautious way was prepared to do business with the Third Reich.[7] Besymenski points to a Politburo decision on 21 January 1939, responding to German overtures for trade talks, that led to the preparation of a wish list of German goods, including armaments. Important People's Commissars wanted to buy them under a hoped-for new credit arrangement. On 11 February 1939 Politburo member Anastas Mikoyan handed over two lists to the German ambassador. What followed according to Besymenski was "a complicated political and diplomatic procedure which came to its conclusion at the end of August 1939."[8] Stalin regarded the German acceptance of the two lists of goods as a test of the sincerity of the German commitment to improving German-Russian relations.[9] But as the diaries of Georgi Astakhov, the Soviet chargé d'affaires in Berlin, reveal, the road to the pact would not be a straight one.[10] Thus Russia's negotiations with the Western powers forced the German side to increase its efforts to reach a satisfactory economic deal with Moscow. Ribbentrop, for one, hoped this would become "the beginning of a political rapprochement."[11]

What the new unused documents in Besymenski's book reveal is that historians will need even more knowledge of the Russian sources in order fully to understand this period. We have yet to piece together how Russian decisions were reached in preparing for the Nazi-Soviet Pact and the period of economic collaboration, nor do we fully understand how Soviet leaders responded to German developments in the subsequent months up to 22 June 1941. A case in point is Besymenski's intriguing indication that the Politburo apparently never discussed the Pact or the new international constellations which emerged as a consequence of the conclusion of the Russo-German agreement![12]

Even so, in recent years a number of historians have ventured important new interpretations of Russian policy. Albert Weeks includes in his *Stalin's Other War* a speech to the Politburo from 19 August 1939 in which Stalin argued that "it was in the interests of the USSR ... that war breaks out between the Reich and the capitalist Anglo-French bloc.... We must agree to the Pact proposed by Germany and use it so that once this war is declared, it will last for a maximum amount of time."[13] Weeks argues from this that the Russian General Staff attempted to prepare for an offensive strategy against the potential German enemy, a strategy that culminated in the Zhukov Plan of 15 May 1941. To Weeks the Soviet army was "designed more for waging offensive rather than defensive war."[14] Although this may have been true, in general the available evidence in May and June 1941 speaks against offensive preparations and instead points to improving defensive measures.[15] Weeks neglects the economic side of Russian politics while concentrating on the military side. Russian exports to Germany are mentioned in only a few lines of his book and German deliveries to Russia do not figure at all except for the cruiser Lützow. Generally speaking, the role of German-Russian trade is not discussed in the book and its importance not understood.

For the period before the outbreak of the Second World War, Silvio Pons has recently provided a more complex interpretation of the Soviet leadership's response to the unfolding international crisis in the summer of 1939.[16] To Pons, the "concept of security assumed a specific meaning under Stalin." It meant appeasing Germany and extending a territorial "security system" into Eastern Europe. Thus the "old Bolshevik survival strategy" was replaced by an "antagonistic strategy" based on the conviction of the inevitability of war and the "inter-imperialist rivalry." Again the economic side of Russia's foreign policy and the role this played in Stalin's strategies is not adequately dealt with. Pons regards the economic aspects as a mere technicality which as far as the Pact is concerned led to the Soviet request in the middle of August 1939 for all economic negotiations to be concluded before final political dealings could begin in Moscow.[17]

While they may underplay the economics, what these new studies have in common is that they make use of new Russian sources that have become available since the 1990s. The use of new documentation has led to new interpretations especially in the field of Soviet foreign policy. While older accounts tended to concentrate on Stalin, for example, it is now clear that Molotov's role was much more important than previously thought. Not only has the role of particular leaders come under greater scrutiny, but the aims and strategies of Soviet policy have also been assessed anew. A case in point is Gabriel Gorodetsky's recent attempt to widen the historical debate on Soviet foreign policy and geostrategic aims in the year "preceding" the German attack on Russia.[18] Using new Russian archival material, Gorodetsky demonstrates convincingly that apart from the Hitler-Stalin Pact of 1939 and the ensuing Russo-German economic collaboration, Soviet foreign policy also pursued far-reaching aims in the Balkan states and in Turkey. These findings throw new light on Soviet foreign policy in general and Stalin's thinking in particular, not least as regards the Non-Aggression Pact of 1939. Within the context of Stalin's *realpolitik* and the lack of Soviet alternatives after British guarantees to Poland and Rumania in March 1939, Gorodetsky believes that, by sorting out the spheres of influence in northeastern Europe and Poland, the pact offered the Soviet Union the opportunity to concentrate its efforts on Yugoslavia, Bulgaria, Rumania, and Turkey. The aim was to prevent a British as well as a German predominance in these countries and to establish the Soviet Union as the foremost power in South Eastern Europe. After Germany's victory over France, Stalin aimed at gaining "full control of the Black Sea littoral and the mouth of the Danube."[19] In Stalin's eyes, the achievement of this aim would complete the security arrangements he had tried to establish through different means with the Germans and the Finns. In line with this thinking, Stalin and Molotov hoped to bring the Germans back to the negotiating table in 1941 by concluding neutrality and friendship pacts with Japan and Yugoslavia. The German occupation of Yugoslavia in that year may have shattered the Soviet leadership's aspiration to establish Russian predominance in the Balkans, but it did not end Stalin's belief in a division of the German side between Hitler and Ribbentrop on the one hand and the military leadership on the other.

According to Gorodetsky, Stalin received various reports that suggested the two German leaders, in cahoots with leading German industrialists, "supported the unanimous recommendations of the four-year planning committee that German stood to 'gain much more' by pursuing trade with Russia than through" military conquest.[20] The fact that it was Hitler, and most generals, who pressed for an invasion of the USSR, was either unknown to Stalin or not believed. Stalin even dismissed diplomatic rumors circulating in Moscow that Germany was poised to grab the southern areas of Russia in a military campaign in order to gain access to oil, grain, and coal. Instead he preferred to accept a report by Vselov Merkulov, the head of the Foreign Intelligence of the NKVD. It was a survey of German economic resources put together in Walther Funk's Ministry of Economics. According to that report, Germany had economically only one alternative: peace with England or improved ties with Japan and the Soviet Union. And cooperation with the S.U. depended on Russia's ability to increase deliveries of raw materials.[21] All this was grist to Stalin's mill. He was keen to come to a new diplomatic understanding in May and June 1941 with Hitler, mistakenly as it turned out. Rather than face the imminent prospect of a German attack, the Soviet leadership, in following Stalin, clung to every bit of information that suggested the Germans were divided and hoped to achieve other goals such as making Turkey into a German satellite state rather than attacking the S.U. By analyzing the multitude of intelligence reports in the Russian archives and drawing on hitherto unavailable military sources, Gorodestky is able to show that, although the expectation of an imminent German attack grew steadily during the spring of 1941, Stalin and most members of his entourage still believed in the delivery of a German ultimatum and subsequent negotiations. Despite Stalin's fear of provoking the German forces into an attack, Zhukov, the Russian Chief of Staff, began to plan for a state of war preparedness by 1 July.

Gorodetsky's narrative is persuasive when laying open Stalin's blunders and miscalculations, but he fails to emphasize the significance—within the scenario he has set—of the economic collaboration between Russia and Germany following the Non-Agression Pact of August 1939. By paying little attention to what the German side gained from the collaboration with the Soviet Union, he has overlooked the benefits Russia also drew from this deal. This is surprising, as the economic give and take between the two states may have provided Stalin with some rationale for his belief that Hitler would propose a new round of negotiations in late spring of 1941.

Whatever the reasons for Gorodetsky's interpretation, the economic cooperation has attracted a number of recent studies that are based mainly on German archival material. Apart from Heinrich Schwendemann's comprehensive and detailed work, which has nevertheless been criticized for its analysis of policy-making in Berlin and Moscow and for its interpretation of the economic collaboration between Russia and Germany as a possible German alternative to the war with the Soviet Union, two new books have appeared. One is by Edward Ericson III and titled *Feeding the German Eagle,* and the other is by Robert Mark Spaulding and titled *Osthandel and Ostpolitik.*[22]

Whereas Spaulding, in his wide-ranging study, considers trade as a foreign political instrument based on a consensus between the government and the private sector, Ericson tries to refute the argument that Stalin used trade with Germany as the main plank of a supposed appeasement policy. To Ericson there are two schools of thought: the appeasers and the expansionists. The former argue that Stalin was forced by the Western dilatory attitude toward the Soviet Union into a last-minute agreement with Germany and, when German power began to grow, into the role of an appeaser to avoid Nazi aggression or an Anglo-German encirclement. The latter, on the other hand, have tried to prove that Stalin ultimately preferred an economic alliance with Hitler because "it offered him security, territory, technology," and the possibility of being an arbiter over European affairs.[23] Ericson was unable to detect much of a sense of appeasement in the tough negotiating stance of Russia toward Germany. According to him, the Soviet side defended its interests well and used its collaboration with Germany to increase its own influence in foreign politics. Perhaps toward the end of the pact, just before the German attack, it is possible contrary to Ericson to find elements of appeasement, namely, Stalin's effort to avoid provoking Germany and to more than fulfil his economic treaty obligations.[24]

Spaulding has used quite a different approach when discussing trade developments in Eastern Europe. To him trade policy is "foreign policy and domestic policy simultaneously."[25] His main concern is Germany's trade with the East in its political and economic context, not only before the First and Second world wars but also in the 1950s and 1960s. After having analyzed the difficult path of German-Soviet economic relations in the 1930s, especially after 1932, Spaulding has deemed the purchases and deliveries between the S.U. and the Third Reich between August 1939 and July 1940 "as [possibly] the most important trade [deal] in the first half of this century [i.e., the twentieth]."[26] For the Nazi leadership in summer 1939, political rapprochement with the Soviet Union may well have been of greater importance than any economic dealings. However, German industry and some ministries clamored for raw materials from Russia in order to construct the armaments wanted by the armed forces. This need coincided with the Soviet preference for an economic deal. But the Soviets had an additional motive. They insisted on the renewal of credit arrangements and more economic trade to test the Nazis' sincerity. Thus the economic agreement of 19 August 1939 had to be signed before the Non-Aggression Pact. Moreover, one of the stumbling blocks to earlier trade agreements between the Soviet Union and the Third Reich, namely, Hitler's veto of any armaments sales, had been overcome. But what was the significance of the newly emerging economic relations between Germany and Russia? Did they help the German armed forces in their invasion of Poland or in the German conquest of Denmark and Norway in spring 1940? The answer is "No." Were early Russian deliveries vital for the German campaigns against the Benelux countries and France, as was maintained by Hillgruber and Weinberg?[27] This is more difficult to establish, but it looks likely that the answer is again "No." As Germany had by May 1940 stockpiled sufficient economic resources for a campaign of up to four months, Russian deliveries came too late to be decisive. By the end of May the Soviets had shipped only 155,000 tons of oil to Germany, an insignificant figure compared with German reserves of over 1.1 million tons. The SU had also delivered 8,600 tons of manganese ore and 128,100 tons of grain—again, tiny amounts, when set against German stockpiles of 230,000 tons of manganese and 4.7 million tons of grain.[28] Yet the arrival of Russian oil did at least help to replenish rapidly diminishing German reserves and to reduce German fears about not having enough for future military campaigns. Thus the quick victories in the West reduced the immediate need for Russian deliveries. But this was to change once preparations were under way for the invasion of Soviet Russia itself.

According to older accounts, by the summer of 1940 Germany had barely mobilized its economic resources and yet was still easily winning the war.[29] So the newly established political and economic relations with Russia would have meant relatively little to the Nazi economy. More recent research by Overy, Herbst, Volkmann, and Harris has shown, however, that Germany was pursuing total mobilization much earlier and that after the outbreak of war it was forced into a "total war of improvisation."[30] Any additional imports of scarce raw materials would have been greeted with great relief within a German economy so dependent on them. But in securing deliveries from the Soviet Union, the business community faced a major obstacle, namely, how to generate the production capacity for forthcoming Russian orders. Industry's commitment to the German war effort made it very difficult to fulfill Soviet wishes for arms and the latest armament technology from Germany. In this situation, the economic agreements were not the only testing ground for general cooperation. So, political arrangements were utilized to overcome German industry's lack of capacity and meet the level of Soviet demands. Only a political pact would provide the framework for an exchange of goods vital to both countries and would give the German government some leverage to put pressure on industrial suppliers to comply with Soviet orders.

The twenty-two months between the conclusion of the Nazi-Soviet Pact and the German attack of 22 June 1941 were characterized by an increasingly paradoxical economic cooperation that was to result in an actual exchange of goods worth nearly 1.2 billion marks and a total of placed orders of over three billion marks.[31] Percentage-wise, imports from Russia amounted to 7.6% of German imports in 1940 and 6.3% in the first six months of 1941. According to German statistics, the SU took in 4.5% of German exports in 1940 and 6.6% in the first half of 1941. These did not match trade figures from the early 1930s or those before the First World War, but proved to be essential for strategic reasons. The paradoxical difference in 1940/41 was that both sides equipped each other in order to fight each other.

The pact may have given some leading industrialists the impression of improved relations with the S.U. and of a return to the Rapallo era. However, the political parameters had completely changed in Berlin and the industrialists' own influence had declined. In the preparation for war, industry had been subjected to heavy state interference prioritizing arms for Germany. One of Germany's leading corporations put it in a nutshell: "The transition to the war economy in 1939 had run smoothly ... [as] all essential elements of a war economy had been in place [for some time]."[32] Although German-Russian trade had reached its nadir in the years before 1939, arms had been sold to Russia despite Hitler's categorical ban. Thus Krupp had sold, with Goering's approval, a small amount of arms worth just over 5 million marks between 1936 and 1938, but had also turned down a larger Russian order because it lacked sufficient production capacity and did not expect approval from Berlin.[33] Germany's limited exports to Russia must have been discouraging to those Soviets keen on transfer of German technology. In 1938 and 1939 German exports to the S.U. amounted to 34 and 31 million marks or no more than 0.6% of German exports. Russia had fallen from second position among Germany's customers in 1932 to thirty-fifth in 1938.

While the desire for an economic agreement grew in German industrial circles, it was the events of the summer of 1939 that made it possible to combine an economic with a political agreement. The real breakthrough in the run-up to the economic agreements came when the German side—and this time it included Hitler—accepted the Russian demands for German armaments in return for a sale of strategic raw materials. Once this hurdle had been cleared, Moscow accepted the economic agreements as the first step to a political understanding in the form of the Pact. Thus it is quite clear that the original initiative for improved economic relations with Russia came from Germany, although Hitler was not made aware of this move until later. The German Foreign Office had been engaged in overtures toward the Soviet Union for some time in its so-called *Nebenaußenpolitik,* something that Hitler, however, had stopped in January 1939. During the first half of 1939 the Soviet Union had continued to be interested in better relations without achieving any tangible results. Only the changing German assessment of the international situation brought the two sides closer together, and on 7 July 1939 Berlin finally decided to renew economic negotiations with Russia. Alongside these negotiations other talks developed that would result in a political rapprochement. Welcomed by the Russians, the rapprochement had been Ribbentrop's initiative. The German foreign minister's aim was to avoid war against Russia while Germany was attacking Poland and at a time when it might become involved in a war with the Western powers. So Karl Schnurre was able to emphasize subsequently to his Soviet counterparts the common interests both sides had in improving economic relations as well as in settling territorial questions in Eastern Europe.[34] This paved the way for the eventual pact. The credit agreement was regarded in Moscow as a first step toward a political "understanding" that was to consist of a nonagression pact or the confirmation of the Berlin Treaty of 1926. Moscow had proven to be very flexible in that it had abandoned its previous stance, namely, to have political agreements first. The economic agreement was finally signed on the 19th and 20th of August, only three days before the pact was signed.[35]

Nothing could demonstrate more clearly how closely the economic and political rapprochement was interlinked than the proximity of the dates of the economic and political agreements. But the sequence of agreements had not been planned well in advance. In fact, it emerged during August 1939.[36] And it was the entire package of agreements and secret protocols that had enormous repercussions on Eastern Europe, on international politics, on the German plans for attacking Poland, and the beginning of the Second World War as well as the economies of Germany and the Soviet Union. The latter point especially has led to controversies among historians; but apart from the economic effects the agreement had—and they were not insubstantial—there were also psychological benefits for the German side.[37] Although the economic negotiations had been vital, the novum was, however, the non-aggression pact which among other points signaled a return from emphasizing multilateral security pacts to bilateral agreements. The credit agreement, on the other hand, followed a pattern that had been worked out throughout the 1920s and early 1930s.[38]

The second pact, the so-called Pact of Friendship on 29 September 1939, was concluded in the spirit of the previous non-aggression pact. Again a secret protocol was attached as well as further economic particulars. The two pacts provided the political framework for the later two economic agreements on 11 February 1940 and 10 January 1941. Especially these last two agreements were not easily reached. Disputes over price levels, quantities, delivery schedules, and qualities made it very hard for the negotiators to come to agreements. The bargaining process was fraught with difficulties and was often on the brink of collapse. The relationship between the two countries might not have worked out and obstacles might not have been overcome had it not been for the previous experience of industrial cooperation over several years in the 1920s and early 1930s, and had it not been for the two pacts that had helped to introduce a better atmosphere between the two states. In terms of German-Russian relations, the period from August/September 1939 until February 1940 had in effect concertinaed the achievements of Rapallo, the Berlin Treaty of 1926, and the increased trade of the early 1930s into one concentrated phase, the difference being that military considerations had become paramount.

Individual firms welcomed the new political climate and the economic agreements. Russian orders had been in the past highly profitable but many firms lacked the capacity to take on Russian orders. Only the pressure from Berlin and the prospects of supplies of scarce raw materials made them more amenable to producing for the S.U. There was also a lot of competition between German firms, and Krupp even went so far as to denounce its old rival Rheinmetall when that firm was alleged to have made a profit of 70% on a Russian arms' order of 40 million marks in the early 1930s.[39] Krupp found such practices "scandalous." It is not clear whether this intervention helped Krupp to new orders. In any case, as it will be shown later, Krupp was heavily involved in supplying arms and machines to Russia. When some firms made it public that they were working as suppliers for the S.U. the Ministry of Economics advised them to refrain from phrases such as "trade with Russia had a great future."[40] Instead the need for foreign currencies ought to be mentioned.

During the first round of political agreements the Russians seemed to have fared better than the Germans. They had made potential territorial gains in the Baltic, in Eastern Poland, and in Bessarabia, and it looked as if Hitler had been the "appeaser" attempting to maintain Russian neutrality in the forth-coming war against Poland. Gradually over the next few months, the relation-ship changed in accordance with the international situation. As far as trade was concerned it took some time to work out the details, as the credit agree-ment of August 1939 had been very general. The basis of the Soviet wish-lists that had been circulated among German firms went back to Stalin's orders of January 1939.[41] Russia's demands created from the outset problems that had to be overcome. Ribbentrop's second visit to Moscow at the end of September was also to clarify "commercial relations."[42] For instance, the Russian demand for "industrial goods" had to be interpreted. The Soviet insistence that "indus-trial goods" include arms was initially contested in October 1939 by the Ger-man negotiators Karl Schnurre and Karl Ritter.[43] However, it had been clear from the beginning and from the draft lists handed to Krupp that Russian ar-maments purchases were part of the whole deal. In fact Schnurre had raised these objections for tactical reasons. His aim was to achieve a better bargain as he hoped to buy raw materials worth 1.5 billion marks in return for "indus-trial goods" of up to 1.0 billion marks. The German delegation wanted to bal-ance the remaining difference of 500 million marks by selling investment goods to Russia over a longer time span.

Further difficulties arose because of delaying tactics employed by Russian negotiators. German keenness for early Russian deliveries was matched on the Soviet side by caution and circumspection. Thus, when a Soviet delegation arrived in Berlin under the leadership of Ivan Tevosyan, the Commissar for Shipbuilding, it wanted to inspect German armament plants and see demon-strations of German weapons. When Hitler-inspired objections to Tevosyan's tour became known, the Russian appealed to Göring directly. He counteracted Hitler by asking German firms to satisfy Russian demands as soon as possi-ble.[44] Thus Tevosyan managed to visit the Krupp plants in Essen twice in No-vember in 1939.[45] These initial difficulties were eventually overcome but showed the mutual suspicion of both sides. It took until 11 February 1940 for the com-mercial deal to be signed and the goods to begin to flow. Even then the ex-change was not an easy one and was dependent on the international situation. The goods flowed more freely from the Russian side when either Russia's inter-national position improved or when it suited the Soviet side to transfer goods. Typical for this attitude was the reluctance of the Russians to start deliveries at a time when they faced the prospect of Allied intervention during the Russo-Finnish war. The pressure was finally removed when Germany started its campaign against Norway and Denmark and in the West, which meant for instance that Russia was able to increase its oil exports to Germany. The Ger-man side matched the Soviet deliveries with the sale of armaments. The Soviet negotiators had pitched their demands very high. They initially targeted two and later three main areas. The first was the extension of their battle fleet. So the Russian side had put on their list the nearly completed cruisers *Seydlitz*, *Prince Eugen*, and *Lützow*, the blue prints of the battleship *Bismarck*, 31,000 tons of armor plate along with torpedoes, ammunition, and other items. The second target was to buy models of all the German planes currently in production and serving in the Luftwaffe. Further items mentioned were artillery pieces, dehydration equipment for making synthetic fuel, Widia technology (the steel-hardening process), and synthetic rubber plants. All this proved to be too much for the German industry. It was due to Stalin's intervention that the "friendship" was saved by Russian demands being substantially reduced. Nevertheless, Molotov and Mikoyan insisted that as a sign of German goodwill the cruiser *Lützow* should be handed over. This was done at a price of 100 million marks, and the unfinished ship was then towed to Leningrad. What these difficulties reveal is that the Russo-German economic relationship was fraught with difficulties and vacillating attitudes. So after a relatively easy period in the summer of 1940, a shift in the relationship began to be felt after the autumn of 1940 when Hitler decided that the Soviet Union would be the next target of German expansion and the Russians cut their exports to Germany in order to exert pressure for further deals. This changed again when the negotiations began for the economic agreement covering the years 1941/42, which was finally signed on 10 January 1941. The German army was increasingly reluctant to transfer sensitive technology to the S.U. but Moscow seems not to have realized this. Instead, the Soviet leadership interpreted Germany's continuing willingness to sell arms and modern technology as a sign that the Nazi-leadership was keen to put cooperation on a long-term footing. Even a number of German negotiators began to believe that a war with Soviet Russia would be delayed for a considerable time.

What proved to be crucial for the Russians in this respect was the deal with Krupp over six battleship turrets armed with 38-cm guns. In the complicated negotiations between the Soviet customers, the German naval authorities, and the firm of Krupp it was agreed on the German side that if the guns were ready earlier than the turrets, they would be used for coastal defences on the island of Sylt and delivered to Russia as second-hand equipment once the turrets had been completed.[46] Originally the turrets had been destined for the German battleships "S" and "G," but after Britain declared war on Germany the work on these systems was halted and only recommenced when it emerged that the turrets could be sold to the S.U.[47]

While the negotiations about the deal with Krupp continued, and while Hitler's plans of attack on Russia were beginning to take shape, Goering intervened and ordered that Krupp accelerate a deal with the Soviets.[48] So the impression the Soviets must have received was that Germany was keen on a good economic relationship with the S.U. Given the positive political atmosphere, it was not surprising that in the late autumn of 1940, Stalin still believed he could expect German acceptance of his plans to complete Russian security on its western borders.[49] However, on the day of his arrival in Berlin on 12 November 1940, Molotov found an obdurate German dictator who, unbeknownst to his visitor, issued an order on the same day that preparations for an attack on Russia in spring 1941 should continue irrespective of the outcome of Molotov's visit. It was therefore not surprising that despite two long talks, Hitler and Molotov failed to come to an agreement. They clashed openly over Finland and Bulgaria.[50] Molotov, however, did not give up hope and handed a modified plan to German Ambassador Schulenburg a few days later. This might have led the Soviet Union to joining Ribbentrop's project of a four-power Euro-Asiatic alliance, but Hitler would have no truck with this project and instead used Molotov's visit to Berlin to declare that he had finished with the Soviet Union.

Molotov's visit was also linked to the outstanding sale of Krupp arms to Russia, which was finally agreed on 30 November 1940. At this point in time the German plans for an attack on the S.U. in May 1941 were finalized, but the Soviet side seemed unaware of the deterioration in the political climate. The Krupp deal gave the impression that favorable conditions prevailed. According to this deal, Krupp would receive the first instalment of the payment for the contract worth 25 million marks. Originally Krupp had asked for 144 million marks for the whole order but had yielded to Soviet bargaining and had gradually reduced the price to 85 million marks.[51] By the time Germany attacked the SU neither guns nor turrets had been delivered. All the Russians had received were the construction plans of the turrets.[52] In addition to this deal Molotov had assured the German ambassador in Moscow, Count Schulenburg, that Russia would step up its delivery of strategic goods to Germany. Over the next few months this was achieved. Molotov himself hoped for increased trade volumes and may possibly have played into Stalin's thinking that increased trade would ultimately prevent or at least delay a German attack on Russia.[53] So the auspices for the second trade treaty to be signed on 10 January 1941 were good. The fact that Germany was still regarded as a favored partner, despite Molotov's failure in Berlin, is further supported by the performance in Moscow of Wagner's opera "Walküre" under the direction of Sergej Eisenstein![54]

German industrialists were initially unaware of Hitler's changed program. They interpreted Göring's instruction to treat Russian contracts on a par with orders from the German armed forces as a sign that they should put German-Russian cooperation on a long-term footing. A number of German negotiators had become convinced that a war with the Soviet Union would be delayed for a considerable time. In the trade agreement of 10 January 1941, Russia agreed to mobilize its own strategic reserves and to export 2.5 million tons of grain and nearly one million tons of oil by the end of August. In return, it expected machine tools and armament manufacturing equipment and 30,000 tons of aluminium. Apart from the naval orders and the acquisition of aircraft, the purchase of machines helping to make arms and machine tools was the third major sector in the technological transfer to the Soviet Union. Industry was well informed about the economic negotiations and was fully in support of the final agreement of 10 January 1941. After the defeat of France, Russian orders had become increasingly attractive as they guaranteed a supply of raw materials and also labor. The S.U. gained a special place on the German export table while other customers lost their prominent positions on it. By 22 June industry had taken additional orders worth 600 million marks despite the hefty price increases on both sides. German deliveries to Russia grew steadily, and, indeed, there is virtually no evidence to support the view that Germany withheld deliveries after January 1941. In fact, in May, a record high was reached of goods crossing the borders in both directions.

During the spring of 1941, the paradoxes between the two countries esca-lated further. The good trade relations did not hinder Germany's political offensive in the Balkans, which clashed with the declared intentions of the S.U. Yet even the German Foreign Office continued to be keen on an increase in Russian exports. Other members of the German leadership tried to argue against the forthcoming war with Russia because Germany would benefit less from a war-torn and partially destroyed Soviet Union than from a trading one. These arguments did not change the mind of the army leaders or of Hitler.[55] Even the particularly high level of grain deliveries in the spring of 1941 and the Russian shipment of 5,000 tons of cautchuk (natural rubber), which the S.U. had bought on Germany's behalf and had transferred on the Trans-Siberian Railway did not have much of an impact. Yet Germany continued to comply with the economic agreement. German payments were not withheld and de-liveries were not halted. In February, Germany even provided the USSR with 22 million marks in gold to pay for special cereal exports from Bessarabia. In these months Krupp, for example, continued to work on the large Russian order and to keep the Russian side informed of the firm's progress. At the end of May, Russia was on course to fulfil its contractual obligations with 90.3% of its agreed exports. Bearing in mind that the launch of the German invasion was then only three weeks away, German deliveries grew steadily to reach 81.5% of the agreed quota of 80%. Only in the last few days before the 22nd of June did German military authorities stop some military shipments across the Russian border. All of this must have been puzzling to the Russian side at a time when the German expansion in the Balkans in spring 1941 overrode Soviet interests, when Hitler did not react to any Russian overtures for further negotiations, and when, most importantly, the German military deployment on Russia's western borders continued unabated. Did the Soviets believe that Germany would ultimately not attack because it was desperate for the supplies from the East? Did the Soviets not know—despite all the intelligence they had received—what kind of war the Nazis were going to fight and what was going to happen to the territories Germany might manage to occupy? Or did they believe that ultimately Hitler would need active Russian participation in the war with the West ? With regard to the first question it was obvious that Germany had a need for Russian supplies, although it could just about manage without them. Imports of oil are a case in point. In 1940, imports from the Soviet Union amounted to about a third of all German oil imports, a figure that was to drop to 10% in 1941. The oil from Rumania was much more important in those years and the Russians were aware of that.

Perhaps the massive order the Soviets placed with Krupp might give us some clues about the German thinking behind this major deal. Whether Krupp had been reluctant to agree to the deal because of rumors about a possible war with Russia is unclear, but it was Goering's intervention in October that forced Krupp to settle the deal and speed up the construction of the turrets and guns. The navy was also involved in the negotiations but for different motives. Krupp was to produce these guns but then turn them over to the navy, which wanted to use them itself. Meanwhile, the Ministry of Economics was to pay the contract penalty for nondelivery. In any case, Krupp received from Russia the first instalment of the payment of the contract worth 25 million marks.

After war broke out in June 1941, military authorities argued that Krupp was not entitled to the advance payment. It was argued by Krupp-representatives that the potential Russian claims would need renegotiation once hostilities were over, but this argument was rejected on the grounds that the S.U. would cease to exist and therefore there would be no Russian government with which to negotiate.[56] This attitude was symptomatic for the military authorities, but the matter of the advanced payment did not rest there. In fact, the army claimed successfully the 38-cm guns for its own usage and paid to Krupp only the reduced inland prices. This was not the end of the story, either. After the war, in June 1945, Tevosyan returned to the Krupp factories in Essen, which he had last visited in the autumn of 1939, and discovered that some of the turrets destined for the S.U. had been completed and survived the bombing. It is not quite clear what happened to these turrets, but it looks as if they were finally shipped to the Soviet Union.[57]

What was the point of this special and complicated deal when the German military knew that an attack on Russia was imminent? The intention was to keep the Soviet Union peaceful. As Krupp representatives were told: "The purpose of the deal is to cast 'sand into her [Russia's] eyes."[58] The earlier sale of the cruiser *Lützow* had also been an act of "political bluff."[59] The main purpose of the economic relations was an "act of deception and disguise."[60] As long as Stalin did not order a preventive strike—something Hitler feared—it was considered that the deception would work. The risk involved in the Russian acquisition of modern German arms technology was brushed aside by the military conviction that Russia would not have been able to make full use of German technology by the time the German forces had launched their offensive.

So far it is not known whether the German deception was properly understood in Moscow or whether the Soviet side became a victim of the German tactics. As far as we know, Stalin was not able to imagine that a regime that supplied him with armaments, high technology, and blueprints of weapon developments would launch a military invasion. This was not part of the business rationale, which had dominated the various phases of the Russo-German economic relationship from 1921 onward. Trade created an atmosphere of "normalcy" that could not be easily turned into military confrontation. It would have been difficult, especially for Marxist-Leninist thinking, to separate politics from economics completely. Stalin has been pictured as a realist and as someone who was not much influenced by ideological thinking, but the determining force of economic factors on politics may have been part of his basic mindset. However, the calculation that a steady supply of Russian raw materials would prevent Hitler from attacking the S.U. proved to be false. Another rationale behind the Soviet strategy was that Germany would hope to benefit more from Russian exports than from a war of plunder in which high levels of destruction would reduce Russia's capacity to continue supplying Germany with oil, grain, and special ores. The German minister of finance, Schwerin-Krosig, did think along those lines, but nothing could change Hitler's determination in this respect.[61]

However, it remains difficult to accept that Stalin fell victim to the German tactics of deception since the uneasy interrelationship was characterized by mutual distrust, deceit, and miscalculation. Of course there were moments of cooperation when everything went smoothly, but the real test of the relationship came in June 1941 when it appeared that the Soviet leadership had fallen victim to the Nazi tactics of deceit. Had the political leaders of the Soviet Union been sleepwalking? The negotiations between the two countries since 1939 had been very tough, and several times on the point of breaking down. There was no question of mutual aid or, indeed, easy appeasement, although the latter may have been intended on occasions. And it was expected in the Kremlin that some time in the near future Germany might become Russia's foremost enemy when the "Russian-German conspiracy" would turn into a life and death struggle. It remains therefore remarkable that these strange bedfellows should make so many efforts to fulfil each others' demands. Even the massive intelligence information about the thinking of the Nazi leadership and the armed forces did not prevent Stalin from making vital mistakes that nearly lost the Soviet Union the war. As has been pointed out above, Stalin seems to have started from different assumptions about the interplay of economic and political considerations. For Hitler, the economic side was a means to an end to his ultimate ideological war against the S.U., whereas Stalin valued the economic side of the German-Russian relationship much more highly. He must have seen in the trade a basis for cooperation that was also directed against Britain, a trade that was of mutual benefit and a potential stop to plans of German aggression. In this way the massive growth of the Soviet army when completed was to act as a deterrent. To this end, the transfer of German technology must have been as important as was later the crucial transfer on a much more massive scale of the Lend-Lease agreements with the Western powers.[62] So it does not come as a surprise that Stalin took a great interest in the economic details of the Nazi-Soviet relations, as they probably provided him with the rationale for his belief that the economy was the main factor in shaping bilateral relations.

Although Hitler was in the long run committed to his war with the S.U., the pact exerted a certain fascination on him and influenced his political thinking. His letter to Mussolini written a day before the German attack showed that for a while his "conspiracy with Stalin" may have weakened his determination to attack Russia. As the day of S.U. invasion approached, he began to feel liberated from previous restraints. He told Mussolini that he now felt "spiritually free. The partnership with the Soviet Union, in spite of the complete sincerity of the efforts to bring about a final conciliation was nevertheless often very irksome to me, for in some way or other it seemed to me to be a break with my whole origin, my concepts, and my former obligations. I am happy now to be relieved from these mental agonies."[63]

Notes

1. This article is a revised version of H. Pogge von Strandmann, "Escalating Paradoxes. Hitler, Stalin and the German-Soviet Economic Relations 1939–1941," in A. O. Chuberian and G. Gorodetsky, eds., *War and Politics 1939–1941* (Moscow, 1999 [in Russian]). More generally, see for a bibliographical survey and a guide to various debates about the period of the Nazi-Soviet Pact and Hiler's subsequent war in the East, R. D. Müller and G. R. Ueberschär, *Hitler's War in the East 1941–1945: A Critical Assessment* (Providence and Oxford, 1997), 3–53.

2. H. Pogge von Strandmann, "Industrial Primacy in German Foreign Policy? Myths and Realities in German-Russian Relations at the End of the Weimar Republic," in *Social Change and Political Development in Weimar Germany*, ed., R. Bessel and E. J. Feuchtwanger (London, 1981), 240–67.

3. R. D. Müller, *Das Tor zur Weltmacht. Die Bedeutung der Sowjetunion für die deutsche Wirtschafts- und Rüstungspolitik zwischen den Weltkriegen* (Boppard, 1984), 232–3.

4. D. Doering, *Deutsche Außenwirtschaftspolitik 1933–5. Die Gleichschaltung der Außenwirtschaft in der Frühphase des nationalsozialistischen Regimes* (Diss. Berlin,

1969), 169–75. See, for trade statistics, H. Pogge von Strandmann, "Grossindustrie und Rapallopolitik. Deutsch-sowjetische Handelsbeziehungen in der Weimarer Republik," *Historische Zeitschrift* 222 (1976): 337.

5. With regard to trade, H. E. Volkmann has rightly criticized W. Birkenfeld's tendency to overemphasize the ideological differences between Nazi-Germany and the USSR. H. E. Volkmann, "Die Sowjetunion im ökonomischen Kalkül des Dritten Reiches 1933–1941," in R. G. Foerster, ed., *Unternehmen Barbarossa. Zum historischen Ort der deutsch-sowjetischen Beziehungen von 1933 bis Herbst 1941* (München, 1993).

6. R. Overy, *The Dictators: Hitler's Germany and Stalin's Russia* (London, 2004), 484.

7. L. Besymenski, *Stalin und Hitler. Das Pokerspiel der Diktatoren* (Berlin, 2002), 183–206.

8. Ibid., 186.

9. Ibid., 187.

10. Ibid., 193–209.

11. Ibid., 206, Astakhov's talks with Ribbentrop and Weizsäcker, 2.8.1939.

12. Ibid., 228–33.

13. A. L. Weeks, *Stalin's Other War: Soviet Grand Strategy, 1939–1941* (Lanham Boulder, New York, Oxford, 2002), 171–73. It is expected that this document is authentic.

14. Ibid., 161 and 169–70 for the Zhukov Plan of 15 May 1941.

15. Gorodestky, *Grand Delusion: Stalin and the German Invasion of Russia* (New Haven and London, 1999), 275–81. Besymenski, *Stalin und Hitler,* 435–53.

16. S. Pons, *Stalin and the Inevitable War 1936–1941* (London, 2002), xiii–xv and 168–81.

17. Ibid., 173.

18. G. Gorodetsky, *Grand Delusion,* xii.

19. Ibid., 318.

20. Ibid,181 and 183.

21. Ibid., 189.

22. E. E. Ericson III, *Feeding the German Eagle: Soviet Economic Aid to Nazi Germany, 1933–1941* (Westport and London, 1999). R. M. Spaulding, *Osthandel and Ostpolitik: German Foreign Trade Policies in Eastern Europe from Bismarck to Adenauer* (Westport, 1999).

23. Ibid., 61–72.

24. Ibid., 170–73.

25. Spaulding, *Osthandel and Ostpolitik,* 6.

26. Ibid., 278.

27. A. Hillgruber, *Hitlers Strategie, Politik und Kriegsführung 1940–1941* (Frankfurt, 1965), 105. G. L. Weinberg, *Germany and the Soviet Union* (repr., Leiden 1972), 75. Idem, *A World at War: A Global History of World War II* (New York, 1994), 63–4.

28. Ericson, *Feeding the German Eagle,* 116

29. It may suffice here to point to Alan Milward's study, *The German Economy at War* (London, 1965), 1–27.

30. R. Overy, "Mobilization for Total War in Germany, 1939–41," *English Historical Review* (1988): 613–39. L. Herbst, *Der totale Krieg und die Ordnung der Wirtschaft im Spannungsfeld von Politik, Ideologie und Propaganda 1939–1945* (Stuttgart, 1982). H. E.Volkmann, "Die Sowjetunion im ökonomischen Kalkül des Dritten Reiches

1933–1941," in *Unternehmen Barbarossa*, ed., R. G. Foerster (München, 1993) 89–107. J. P. Harris, "The Myth of Blitzkrieg," *War in History* 2, no. 3 (1995): 335–52.

31. H. Schwendemann, *Die wirtschaftliche Zusammenarbeit zwischen dem Deutschen Reich und der Sowjetunion von 1939 bis 1941. Alternative zu Hitler's Ostprogramm* (Berlin, 1993), 367–8.

32. Historisches Archiv Krupp Essen, WA 070/030–03, Report of the Executive Board of the Friedrich Alfred Hütte, 30.11. 1940.

33. HA Krupp Essen, WA 4, 2926.

34. Schwendemann, *Wirtschaftliche Zusammenarbeit*, 50–5. See Astakhov's talk with Schnurre on 26 July and Astakhov's discussion with Weizsäcker and Ribbentrop on 2 August 1939 in Besymenski, 203–9.

35. K. H. Blumenhagen, "Die deutsch-sowjetischen Handelsbeziehungen unter besonderer Berücksichtigung der Kredit- und Wirtschaftsabkommen von 1939 bis 1941" (unpubl. Hamburg, M.A.thesis 1988) 76–8.

36. Besyminski, *Stalin und Hitler*, 213–21.

37. Ericson, *Feeding the German Eagle*, 57–8.

38. M. Zeidler, "Deutsch-sowjetische Wirtschaftsbeziehungen im Zeichen des Hitler-Stalin-Paktes," in *Zwei Wege nach Moskau. Vom Hitler-Stalin-Pakt bis zum Unternehmen Barbarossa*, ed., B. Wegner (Munich; Zürich, 1991): 9, 95–6. Russia gained a credit worth 200 million marks which was to run for seven years with an interest rate of 4.5%. Russia also agreed to deliver raw materials worth 180 million marks within the next two years for which the German side offered in return investment goods of 120 million marks. According to Schnurre the whole package would come close to nearly one billion marks. See also Ericson, *Feeding the German Eagle*, 57.

39. HA Krupp, WA 200, 51b, OKW-decree, 25.8.1941.

40. HA/GHH (Gutehoffnungshütte) 40810/12, Reusch on 27.3.1939.

41. Besymenski, *Stalin und Hitler*, 183–92. HA Krupp, WA 200, 14, Krupp's representative in Berlin to Krupp in Essen, 23.8.1939. In his list Schwendemann produces other figures. Idem., *Wirtschaftliche Zusammenarbeit*, 62.

42. National Archives Washington, 761, 621/220, Steinhardt to Secretary of State, 29.9.1939.

43. Schwendemann, *Wirtschaftliche Zusammenarbeit*, pp. 90–7.

44. Ibid., 102–12.

45. HA Krupp, WA 7, F 1044, 7.–9. and 14.–15.11.1939.

46. HA Krupp, WA 40 B, 38, Krupp to OKM, 12.6.1940.

47. Ibid., WA 7 FR 1577, Internal report for 1939/40.

48. Ibid., WA 40 B, 381, 4.10.40.

49. Gorodetsky, *Grand Delusion*, 73–5. Besymenski, *Stalin und Hitler*, 299, 314–29.

50. Gorodetsky, *Grand Delusion*, 67–86. Besymenski, *Stalin und Hitler*, 314–29.

51. See for the double dealings, HA Krupp, WA 4, 2925, Krupp to Min. of Econ., 8.10.1940 and *ibid.*, Discussion at the OKM, 31.11.1940.

52. Schwendemann, *Wirtschaftliche Zusammenarbeit*, 241.

53. Ibid., 241–2.

54. Besymenski, *Stalin und Hitler*, 333.

55. Schwendemann, *Wirtschftliche Zusammenarbeit*, 296–99.

56. HA Krupp, WA 4, 2925, 23.9.1941. See also Schwendemann, *Wirtschaftliche Zusammenarbeit*, p. 215.

57. HA Krupp, WA 4B/136, Tevosjan's visit to Essen, 2.6.45.

58. HA Krupp, WA 40 B, C. 381, 30.9.41.

59. Ibid., 27.9.41.

60. Schwendemann, *Wirtschaftliche Zusammenarbeit,* 265–79.

61. Ibid., 296–99.

62. B. Sokolov, "The Role of Lend-Lease in Soviet Military Efforts 1941–1945," *Journal of Slavic Military Studies* 7 (1994): 569–86.

63. Gorodetsky, *Grand Delusion,* 88.

CHAPTER 9

Imperialism as a Paradigm for Modern German History[1]

Uta G. Poiger

In the election campaign of summer 2005, opposition candidate and soon-to-be German chancellor Angela Merkel insisted repeatedly that "Germany and its citizens could become winners of globalization." Commentators criticized the vagueness of this and other statements during Merkel's campaign, but Merkel gave some hints at what she meant. In a July interview in *Der Spiegel*, she explained that "Germany could decide to be again among the winners of globalization, or be content with losing a thousand jobs a day." While Merkel's new coalition government of Social and Christian Democrats has continued much of the foreign policy its predecessor geared toward multinational cooperation and selective German military deployments in peace missions, her rhetoric raises some interesting issues. At least for the German electorate, she imagines Germany as an agent in world politics, and the citizens of the nation-state Germany—rather than, for example, blue-collar workers, or the citizens of the European Union, or all human beings—as a unit of solidarity in a system where some nations are winners and others are losers of globalization. The gaining of jobs in this logic is the key both to German might and to achieving satisfying lives for German citizens that include work, the maintainance of living standards, and access to consumer goods. In policy terms, "winning globalization" in 2005 remained unclear. Most certainly, it is a far cry from the "place in the sun" that German Chancellor Bernhard von Bülow demanded for Germany in 1897 at a time when German leaders hoped to use military and economic might as part of their "Weltpolitik" for German dominance during a period of imperial ambitions in Europe and overseas. However, like Bülow's "place in the sun," Merkel's call for a German victory in globalization rhetorically pits Germans against others.[2]

I begin this essay with Merkel's and Bülow's statements to point to two questions. First: How have the terms changed in which Germans have imagined Germany's international position and their own international links since the nineteenth century? And second: Are empire and imperialism useful categories for thinking about these developments? Whereas scholars use imperialism, linked to authoritarianism, to characterize both the Imperial and the Nazi periods, imperialism and empire have thus far not been categories for most historians of the years after 1945, when neither East nor West Germany ruled over formal colonies. If imperialism has any potential as a broad paradigm in German history, it needs to encompass periods of informal as well as formal German empires. I broadly define formal empire as the effort to build structures of governmental and military control beyond German borders; by informal empire I mean efforts to control areas and peoples outside of Germany through economic and political means.

In its first two sections, this article provides an admittedly cursory discussion of historiography with a few specific issues in mind. How might we adapt questions asked of the Imperial period to design fruitful studies about more recent German history? What do we have to gain by thinking about questions of imperialism and empire for the years after 1945? Are imperialism and empire categories that help us think about German history before and after 1945 together? And what are some of the dangers of such an approach?

In the third section, I apply some of the insights gained from the historiographical discussion to explore new research agendas. In particular, I investigate one possible avenue: I ask how inquiries into commodity culture and international relations can lead to new insights. While histories of consumption have fruitfully explored the relationship between modes of self-articulation for different groups (for example, workers or youth) and changing national politics,[3] we need to add another dimension—how consumption relates to the understanding and obscuring of international relations and inequalities. The reception of American imports has received considerable attention, but most histories of European consumption in the twentieth century, in contrast to those pioneered by early modern scholars, have thus far failed to take other international dimensions into account.[4]

Imperialism and empire have the advantage of locating Germany in complex international webs.[5] (The Americanization paradigm has clear limits: it tells all too often either a story of positioning Germany as a subject of U.S. power or even U.S. imperialism or a story of successful modernization. In any case, it puts little emphasis on German power abroad.)[6] Since the late nineteenth century, Germany has had one of the most powerful economies in the world, and German consumption has to be located in power relations that have extended well beyond the United States. The effort to think about empire and consumption together also opens methodological ruminations on the changing ways in which cultural representations relate to mentalities, to formations of racism and hybridity, to visions of social change as well as to projections of economic, political, and military power.

Such work has the potential to throw new light on the international engagements of Germans in the Weimar Republic, after the forced end of formal German colonialism in 1919, and to investigate the continuities and ruptures between Weimar and Nazi Germany from a new angle. For the period after 1945, such an exploration modifies the stories of democracy, Americanization, Westernization, and consumer culture, and of coming or not coming to terms with the Nazi past that currently dominate historians' accounts of West German history. It might also alter the stories of dictatorship, Stalinization, and lack of access to consumer culture, and of coming or not coming to terms with the Nazi past that currently dominate historians' accounts of East German history. Finally, inquiry into German actions geared toward informal empire can be relevant also for understanding unified Germany, which has raised some anxieties about German political and economic might, and where a politician like Merkel perceives a need for new German victories.

Historiography of German Imperialism

"Imperialism" has had an uneven career in German historiography. In the 1960s and 1970s, scholars scrutinized the development of a German overseas empire during the Bismarckian and Wilhelmine periods. Responding to the Fischer controversy about German culpability for the outbreak of World War I, several historians contributed analyses that linked domestic politics to German expansionism before and during the war.[7] While the rise of National Socialism was always the implicit or explicit backdrop for this scholarship, others pursued Hannah Arendt's and Aimé Césaire's idea that imperialism was a laboratory for the later policies of the Nazis.[8] After something of a lull in studies of imperialism in the 1980s, we have recently seen a revived interest in the history of German colonialism and what some scholars have termed "colonialist discourse" and "imperialist imagination."[9] Some of this scholarship has asked questions about longer continuities from the eighteenth to the twentieth century, and thus has considered periods of formal German empire during the Kaiserreich and World War II together with periods when Germany did not formally rule over territories outside of Europe. However, this has not led to a new consensus on the significance of imperialism beyond the fairly short history of a formal German overseas empire from 1884 to 1919. Thus imperialism receives scant attention in German history surveys.[10]

Scholarship written in the wake of the Fischer controversy about the origins of World War I attributed great significance to the economic and domestic political motivations behind Bismarck's decision to begin building a formal overseas empire in 1884 and the subsequent expansion of that empire in the context of *Weltpolitik.* Numerous soon-to-be-prominent historians addressed colonialism and imperialism in the 1960s and 1970s.[11] This scholarship built on earlier accounts of imperialism that saw the search for colonies in the late nineteenth century not primarily as a result of the competition among major European powers but as a result of capitalist development, industrialization, and domestic strife.[12] Hartmut Pogge von Strandmann, for example, showed in 1969 that the pursuit of colonial policy allowed Bismarck to rally right-wing forces in the Reichstag, unleashing a dynamic that Bismarck ultimately could not control and that contributed to his downfall.[13] Around the same time, Hans-Ulrich Wehler argued that an alliance of agrarians and big industry was designed to combat the growing threat of Social Democracy through a politics of "social imperialism" that diverted discontent about domestic German conditions into expansionist policies and dreams.[14]

Vigorous debate ensued. For example, Wehler's critics pointed out that he at times exaggerated the significance of domestic factors at the expense of power politics among competing empires and also overstated continuities between Bismarck and his successors.[15] While Bismarck was a somewhat reluctant colonialist, Wilhelmine Germany saw the flowering of ideas and policies designed to achieve world power status. In spite of some disagreements, left-liberal scholars developed a consensus about the significance of economic and social dislocation for the development of the rush to formal colonies in the late nineteenth century. The industrial revolutions in Europe and the United States, appeared, in Paul Kennedy's words, as "the basic underlying cause of the 'New Imperialism.'"[16] Relying on research in the papers of German business and political elites, this scholarship also showed however, that imperialism could not be reduced to economics, and that various colonial players had different motivations.

From today's perspective, it is striking that these histories of German colonialism rarely talked about race and that they were largely histories of colonialism without the colonized.[17] By contrast, scholarship on German colonialism that has appeared over the last few years has made race central in identifying links between colonialism, German society and what Pascal Grosse has termed a new *Herrschaftsform,* a new form of governing. This scholarship is influenced by the rise of racist violence in Germany since the 1980s, greater attention to the Third Reich as a racial state, and the rise of postcolonial scholarship in the academy. Grosse has argued that in the context of colonialism a new bourgeois social order arose in Germany (as elsewhere) based on anthropological categories, specifically race. The rise of eugenics and a politics of dissimilation between Germans and those not considered Germans went hand in hand with increasing interconnections of metropole and colony. Germans linked belonging to the German nation to whiteness, but race and nation were never equivalent, a fact that led to continuous debate and tension. Lora Wildenthal has traced the complex investments that German women had in these developments, and Andrew Zimmerman has studied the interconnections between anthropology and imperialism in Imperial Germany. What unites this recent scholarship is an effort to show that colonialism had an impact well beyond the 20,000 or so German overseas colonists, and beyond political and business leaders. In that sense German historians of colonialism have produced works that answer a call made by Ann Stoler and Frederick Cooper in 1996—to think carefully about the interconnections between metropole and colony and trace how what happened in the periphery changed societies of the metropole. In an effort to fulfill Stoler and Cooper's injunction to put metropole and colony into a "single analytical field," Andrew Zimmerman is also one of the few to address the albeit limited agency of the colonized in these processes. This newer scholarship about cultural and political manifestations of German colonialism pays considerably less attention to the economic factors raised by the previous generation.[18]

How have historians tackled the question of continuity beyond the period of a formal German overseas empire in Africa, China, and the South Pacific from 1884 to 1919? Approaches have differed. Marxist-Leninist scholars including historians in the GDR made links between German colonialism, National Socialism, and the so-called "neocolonialism" of the Federal Republic, referring to all as "imperialist." As Woodruff Smith has pointed out, their conceptualization was at once "too broad and too narrow": the range of phenomena they sought to subsume under imperialism was far too broad, while their reduction of imperialism's causes to capitalism and its contradictions was too narrow.[19] West German and U.S. historians have been more comfortable employing the category of imperialism to trace concrete links between Imperial Germany and the Third Reich. Smith, for example, has examined "the ideological roots of Nazi imperialism" in the Imperial period and Weimar. From the perspective of foreign policy, Klaus Hildebrand has analyzed continuities in German expansionist agendas from Imperial Germany to World War II. Mark Mazower has suggested what was new about Nazi rule in eastern Europe was that it applied methods of imperialist domination to white Europeans.[20]

Formal German imperialism had changing, and always debated, targets. After 1884 Germany acquired colonies in Africa, China, and the South Pacific, where Germans ruled over nonwhite populations. In the decades before World War I, German influence in Central and Eastern Europe was the subject of much disagreement, as politicians and business leaders debated whether German economic dominance should be bolstered by formal political rule. What united various factions was an unquestioned belief in German cultural superiority over East Europeans, including Slavs and Jews. World War I radicalized

German positions. Chancellor Bethmann Hollweg's infamous "September Memorandum" in 1914 contained a call for formal annexations in Western and Eastern Europe as well as additional colonies in Africa, and the treaty of Brest-Litovsk was a German effort to colonize in Eastern Europe. The Versailles Treaty of 1919 put an end to formal colonial rule and charged Germany with having been an overly brutal colonizer who had to be excluded from the community of civilized nations. However, the proposed reacquisition of colonies remained a burning issue in the Weimar Republic. For the Nazis the acquisition of colonies outside of Europe took a back seat to expansion and the displacement and murder of populations in Europe, including the Jewish Holocaust.

Historians now seem to agree that German colonial practice, including the colonial wars in Africa and the increased organizing of German society by racial categories, prefigured National Socialism in complex ways: as Isabell Hull has shown, the genocidal wars against the Herero and Nama in German Southwest Africa, enabled by an insufficiently critical German political culture, fostered "final solutions" as a legitimate goal for the German military. Even so, colonial rule during Imperial times was not the same as the Nazi racial state or the Nazi occupation of Europe; nor were the rise of National Socialism and the Nazi genocide of European Jews the logical or inevitable consequence of colonialism. Moreover, while many colonists and colonialists were particularly prone to joining the Nazi movement, the obsession with the recapture of colonies during the Weimar years was not restricted to the right wing. For example, Foreign Minister Gustav Stresemann, a "republican by reason," used the lament of Germans as a "people without space" at the 1925 colonial exhibition in Berlin.[21]

More bold than most historians in thinking about continuities in Germans' investment in imperialism have been literary scholars. They have pointed to the significance of "mentalities and imaginary configurations" often outside of institutional structures of formal rule.[22] Susanne Zantop has identified "colonial fantasies" before the building of a formal German empire, fantasies that, while centered on South America, were, in her interpretation, a precondition for the German colonial enterprise.[23] By contrast, Russell Berman has argued that German colonial discourse, and by that he means representations and beliefs associated with colonialism, was at times on a positive *Sonderweg* and less racist than that of other colonial powers.[24] In their anthology *The Imperialist Imagination,* Zantop, Sara Friedrichsmeyer, and Sara Lennox have pursued the question of continuities beyond 1919 and beyond 1945 and have found that colonial fantasies persisted after the relinquishing of formal colonies and even after the Holocaust.[25] What these works reveal is the multiplicity of imaginary colonial investments. These have ranged from fantasies of marriage with the "natives," by which Germans would civilize nonwhites, to expressions of deep fears over contact with the colonized.

Marcia Klotz has formulated a related project in a special issue on German colonialism that she edited in 1999 for the *European Studies Journal*. She shows that the globe has been an important reference point for constructions of the German nation since the nineteenth century. Thus she points to German (including Nazi) participation in a worldview that divided the globe into "colonial powers on the one side" and "regions destined for colonization on the other." Through readings of films, fiction, political tracts, and historical scholarship, she traces the roots of the Holocaust in ideological formations that created hierarchies between colonizers and those to be colonized, ideological formations that were not restricted to Germany.[26] Klotz proposes two key concepts for understanding these ideological formations: the Foucauldian concept of "biopower" stresses the propagation of the colonizer's "racial bloodline" and "monetary power," and frequently justifies violence against the colonized. The overlapping concept of "civilizationism" sees the globe as populated "by unequally developed cultures that made the civilizing mission into an imperative for European nations."[27] Klotz's account follows the suggestion made by Arendt and Césaire, namely, that the roots of the Holocaust have to be traced to European, not just German, imperialism and to the Enlightenment. The article is suggestive in a couple of other ways. It reminds readers of the intermingling of economic power and racism. It also points to the various ways in which Germans and others have turned an imperial logic against perceived internal threats. One staple of modern anti-Semitism was to imagine the Jewish diaspora as a form of colonization, in which Germans saw themselves as victims of Jews. Finally, like the volume edited by Friedrichsmeyer, Lennox, and Zantop, Klotz emphasizes the continued yet changing relevance of race and racism outside of German colonial rule, and outside of Nazi anti-Semitism and the Holocaust, that is, beyond 1919 and 1945.

Empire and Imperialism after 1945?

Thinking about German imperialism and empire for the period after World War II has to be done with great caution. After 1945, in the aftermath of the defeat of the Nazi state and in the context of increasing pressure on the other European colonial powers to decolonize, there was no more public discourse about a German state establishing formal colonies overseas or deploying military might abroad. In that sense, the issue of formal political imperialism disappeared. As several commentators have concluded, the years after 1945 were characterized by a general amnesia about the German history of colonialism or a selective reinterpretation of that history. Images of Germans as benevolent colonizers had become prevalent already during the interwar years. Perhaps because Germany lost its colonies at the hands of other Western powers and the United States and had never faced a successful colonial revolt, Germans also had developed a particularly sentimental attitude toward former colonial subjects.[28] The idea that Germans and their colonial subjects had had amicable relations survived, and the notion that anti-black racism was not a particularly German problem persisted—in spite of the genocide of the Herero and Nama committed by German troops 1904 and 1907, the brutal suppression of the Maji Maji rebellion in East Africa during those same years, Germans' racist outcry over the presence of Senegalese soldiers in the French occupation of the Rhineland in the 1920s, and the sterilizations of Afro-Germans under National Socialism.[29] As Uwe Timm put it in 1986: "[A]fter the horrors of German fascism—Germans thought that in this area at least [that is in the area of colonialism and its racist aftermath] they had an edge on other peoples."[30] As recently as 2001, some German and African politicians have claimed a special role for Germany in mediating international conflict because of its shorter history of colonialism.[31] Many recent studies have of course shown that racism persisted in Germany after 1945, even if in different form. For example, studies of German reactions to American blacks, or the children of black GIs and German women in the post–World War II period have concluded that Germans continued to equate Germanness with whiteness.[32]

Amnesia about colonialism or the persistence of racism do not automatically mean that imperialism or empire are relevant categories when thinking about Germany after 1945. However it is clear that even in the absence of desires for formal empire, cultural, economic, and political investments in establishing German spheres of influence abroad did not disappear. In other words, we need more research on German actions geared toward informal empire.

Volker Berghahn's conceptualization of Germany's "quest for economic empire" is useful in this context: Berghahn has suggested the relevance of the concept empire in looking at the actions of German businesses abroad throughout the twentieth century. He has reminded us of the plurality of visions that existed before 1914, a plurality that already contained "in embryo all the arguments that remained on the agenda between 1914 and 1945."[33] One extreme position, not held by many members of the business community, was that of the Pan-Germans who envisioned an authoritarian German empire stretching far into Eastern Europe. At a time when markets remained relatively open, other industrialists debated the economic desirability of formal colonies in Africa, of a closed economic bloc in *Mitteleuropa,* or of German participation in a world economy. What united diverse factions was the conviction that Germany would largely be able to control business relations and economic development in Eastern and Central Europe. Berghahn traces the short-lived ascendancy of formal imperialists during World War I and the narrowing of the spectrum of economic visions with the Depression and the rise of National Socialism. International cooperation seemed less and less feasible, as industrialists and politicians discussed how open or autarkic a German economic bloc should be. During World War II, German industry pursued Germanization and exploitation policies as part of an increasingly formal German empire.

For the period after 1945, Berghahn identifies both continuities and ruptures: in spite of difficulties in adjusting, West Germany reentered a world market. German industries worked hard to regain a stake in pre-1930 markets, especially in Europe, including Eastern Europe, and again became major exporters, while being cautious about direct foreign investment. If there is agreement that unified Germany is Europe's dominant economic power, there is, as Berghahn concluded in 1995, much disagreement about how to assess this dominance and how to label it. This still seems to be true today, even as German businesses (for example Daimler-Chrysler) are participating more forcefully in the transnationalization of the world economy, a globalization that does not dissolve power differentials within and between nations. Berghahn's work is an important reminder that any effort to see German history in international or transnational frameworks has to take the actions of business elites seriously. Further, it shows that we need much more research on changing German economic interests and foreign relations after 1945, beyond the focus on relations with the superpowers and *Ostpolitik* that structured thinking during the Cold War. To direct such attention at Germany and Europe seems particularly important in a post-9/11 world, where a focus on U.S. efforts at empire and French and German dissent on the invasion of Iraq in 2003 threaten to obscure Germany's exertion of power abroad.

Scholars might pursue several routes of inquiry. Thus one might ask how the ideological formations of biopower and civilizationism that Klotz has outlined were transformed at a time when politicians and business leaders publicly disavowed a German *Reich* or empire. Scholars have just begun to examine the history of East and West German involvement in "development." Both Germanies engaged in a variety of projects in the Third World, including in former German colonies.[34] Frequently, these projects were covered in the mainstream German press and also in textbooks for grade and high school students. The Cold War shaped German relations to Third World countries in important ways: thus the two Germanies declared allegiances to different governments: during the conflicts over the decolonization of the Congo in the early 1960s, for example, East German leaders voiced support for Patrice Lumumba, while the West German government, like the U.S., declared its allegiance to Moise Tshombe, who was linked to the murder of Lumumba. We need to know more about the assessments of economic and political interests and of "difference" that emerged in these varying venues.[35] Following the lead of scholarship on formal German colonialism it remains important to explore the relationship between economic relations and racial hierarchies, without assuming that one preceded the other.

Second, historical scholarship has thus far often ignored the complicated position of each Germany in Europe after 1945.[36] Although the East German economy ultimately failed to satisfy the consumer desires of East German citizens, it was generally the envy of members of the Soviet bloc before 1989. We need to know more about the relations East Germans forged with neighbors through trade and travel. Moreover, both the East and West German economies depended increasingly on foreign contract laborers. As Dennis Kuck has shown, bilateral agreements between the GDR and the "home countries," including Poland and Vietnam, routinely ignored the individual needs of such laborers, who had to live in segregated quarters in East Germany under careful surveillance.[37] Even before unification in 1990, West Germany had the most populous and largest economy in Europe, an economy that has relied heavily since the late 1950s on the importation of laborers from southern Europe and Turkey. Many of these migrants have since settled permanently in Germany, and their presence has been a crucial factor in debates about citizenship and Germany as a multicultural, multi-ethnic society. In fact Merkel's reference to German citizens rather than Germans as the potential winners of globalization appears to be a recognition of the increasingly multi-ethnic character of the German electorate in the aftermath of citizenship reform. How the presence of migrants affects the formulation of German interests in and outside of Europe remains an issue for further research.

In contrast to earlier German business and political elites that sought to achieve political hegemony or even formal empire in Europe, the Bonn and Berlin Republics have been integrated into multilateral institutional frameworks, such as the European Union, and thus in Konrad Jarausch's words, successfully "tamed." Jarausch has conjured up the image of "East Elbian Junkers, paternalistic industrial tycoons, and militarist generals or chauvinist professors" as well as "merciless SS henchmen" and "greedy war profiteers" who have all "been replaced by cosmopolitan managers who have studied abroad, speak English with ease, frequently meet with European partners, and own vacation houses at the Costa Brava in Spain."[38] As Jarausch would agree, the forces that have made "cosmopolitanism" a desirable attribute for many Germans, the developments that have made speaking English a necessity for German elites, or the factors that have shaped the presence of German tourists and property owners in southern Spain all deserve further investigation. All are part of more recent German efforts to wield power at home and abroad, in Europe and beyond. Additional research on how inner-European dynamics bear on German and European relations to non-Europeans, to the United States on the one hand, and to the Third World on the other, is sorely needed.[39]

Such work would also shed further light on the varied contexts, in which some Germans have employed charges of imperialism and colonization to express dissatisfaction with their own social and political systems. Rarely have the authors of such charges looked back at the history of Germany as a colonial power. Rather, West German radicals in the late 1960s, for example, saw themselves as part of an international struggle against imperialism, in particular U.S. military and economic power, and against societies in the metropole allegedly dulled by commodity culture.[40] More recently critics of German unification have attacked its mechanisms as a form of colonization by West Germans of their East German countrymen.

If the category of empire can be of any use for understanding Germany's changing international position in the twentieth century and its interrelations with German society, it needs to take the nation-state seriously as an analytical unit—Merkel's rhetoric with which we began the essay provides but one reminder for this imperative. Therefore, Michael Hardt and Antonio Negri's account of empire as a global postmodern order—one that has made territorial borders, center–periphery divisions of labor and wealth, and even traditional imperialism, largely irrelevant—seems of little use for historical analysis. Published with its untranslated title in Germany, *Empire* has been much discussed for its diagnosis of the contemporary world and its utopian imagining of a "mulitude" that would create a counter-empire. However, the book has also been roundly criticized for, in Lisa Rofel's words, not being "troubled by the problem of universality and specifically the imposition of universal definitions of human needs and desires." Equally important is Rofel's concern that *Empire* does not account for the culturally specific workings of capitalism.[41]

Some of the work in American Studies that has tried to connect the cultural and political manifestations of an often informal American empire since World War II may be of more help to Germanists. Revising Edward Said's "Orientalism" paradigm, scholars such as Amy Kaplan or Melani McAlister have traced the complex links between U.S. foreign policy and cultural production. McAlister has examined the cultural, economic and political "logics that helped to make [U.S.] expansion [in the Middle East] seem meaningful and even necessary to many Americans." In particular, she has analyzed U.S. representations of the Middle East in movies, newscasts, and novels in relation to both the domestic politics of race and contests over U.S. foreign policy in the Middle East. As her work shows, empire does not require a metropole characterized by uniformity in order to function. Indeed, social stratification within the United States, for example along ethnic and gender lines, is very much linked to the politics of expansion abroad. Even though the positions of the two Germanies after 1945 and of unified Germany after 1990 differ significantly from that of the United States in military and political might, McAlister's conceptualization of links between domestic inequalities, foreign relations and cultural representations could prove useful for understanding Germany in the twentieth century.[42]

Commodities, Race, and German Power Abroad

Investigations into the dynamics of commodity culture can help in the project of tracing the changing politics of German involvement abroad before and after 1945 and in testing whether "empire" can be a useful category for historical analysis. A few examples from advertising and press reporting will have to suffice here. In Germany, as in other European metropoles, the rise of advertising in the late nineteenth century was very much intertwined with the quest for empire and the attending ideologies.[43] Visions of empire were used to sell not just imports but European-produced products as well. For example, German ads in the Wilhelmine period, like British ads, tried to sell soap at home by alluding to its alleged civilizing role abroad. One Wilhelmine ad for "Lilienmilchseife"—Lily Milk Soap—showed childlike and sparsely clad black men throwing away their spears and shields, running toward an oversized bar of the soap, and staring at it in wonder. The ad announced that Lily Milk Soap was "for soft, white skin" and could be had everywhere for fifty pfennig.[44] Such ads created and appealed to a European sense of superiority, which was very much racialized through depictions of sparsely clad African men as uncivilized. This sense of superiority was of course also fostered in other venues, in the Social Darwinist thought of the period, or in ethnographic shows that brought Africans, Asians, and Native Americans to Europe.

But there were also less racist Wilhelmine ads, like one that made reference to the Tropical World and West Africa (which was a French, not a German, colony). In this ad, an inventor, Dr. Hey, described the success of his "cosmetics" product, AMOL, in West Africa. The ad figured both blacks and whites, men and women, as knowledgeable customers who made AMOL their choice against rheumatism, fatigue, and all sorts of pains. Like many colonialists, the ad saw the colonized as consumers.[45] The varying images in these ads reveal the ambiguous relationships to the colonized that advertisers portrayed for their audiences. Like other representations they were characterized by a tension of contempt and desire, distance and appropriation.[46]

Wilhelmine consumers were linked to colonialism not just through advertising strategies, but also through the consumption of so-called colonial goods, including for example coffee or tea. Advertising for these goods in Wilhelmine Germany as elsewhere frequently relied on exotic imagery while making no reference to the conditions of production for colonial goods such as coffee. In Germany's African colonies such conditions included forced labor systems. At least some colonial goods stores in Wilhelmine Germany tried to appeal to the patriotic duties of German women as consumers. One retailer urged, "German women! Help your colonies by buying their products: colonial cocoa, colonial chocolate, colonial coffee, colonial oil."[47] Such pronouncements were designed to foster support for German colonists, but generally,

German investments in and imports from South America, which was under Anglo-American hegemony, and from the colonies of other nations outstripped investments in and imports from formal German colonies.[48]

The brief discussion above shows that gender is an important category when understanding the relations between Germans and "others." The racism of the soap ad, for example, relied on gender norms, to which Africans allegedly did not conform, to construct the hierarchy of colonizer and colonized. And the ad for German colonial imports reveals that advertisers addressed German consumers in gender-specific ways.

Several related questions deserve further investigation: Was the obscuring of the conditions of production abroad challenged at all by opponents of imperialism, or by consumer cooperatives in the Wilhelmine era? In other words, did alternative visions of international relations and consumption exist? We know that consumption and luxury were attacked as decadent, for example by the conservative *Heimatschutz* movement. It would be important to know whether consumption in its international dimensions could be a topic in other ways.

References to colonial relations remained a staple of German cosmetics advertising in the early 1920s. An ad for Kaloderma shaving cream from 1924, for example, relied on a racism based on colonial relations in advertising the product. A white man is looking into a mirror, which is held by a smaller black adolescent. At a time when Germany had lost formal control of its colonies with the Versailles Treaty of 1919, the image appears to make reference to the history of German settler colonialism in Africa, where Germans employed black Africans in their households. Before World War I, Ludwig Hohlwein, the designer of the ad, had also drawn advertisements for other products, for example Riquet Pralines, that focused on diminutive nonwhite figures, including Chinese, as servants with childlike proportions. As David M. Ciarlo has pointed out, such imagery coalesced into much-repeated stereotypical representations in the years before World War I. In his 1924 Kaloderma shaving cream ad, Hohlwein drew on such imagery, but also transformed it by depicting both the white man and the African servant in a realist fashion with fairly realistic proportions. The image thus both relied on and transformed racist conventions of German pre–World War I advertising. Other cosmetics advertisements of the period harked back more explicitly to the imagery of diminutive Chinese or "Oriental" servants, by portraying white women as served by such subservient figures. This imagery fostered racist fantasies of German control over nonwhite bodies at a time when Germany had lost its formal overseas colonies and claimed to be humiliated by the presence of Senegalese French colonial troops in the Rhineland and relations between these men and German women.[49]

Such ads disappeared in the second half of the 1920s when cosmetics advertisers followed visions of universal modernity that professional journals and international exhibitions promoted in Germany. For example, one of the journals dedicated to advertising announced in 1927 that "the size of today's commerce transcends all national boundaries and is assuming the character of world economics. This requires an international understanding of advertising, its most valuable expression." Konrad Adenauer called the 1928 Cologne Pressa exhibition that featured the international press and international advertising "an international pageant of civilization." In 1929 the former German chancellor Hans Luther used the occasion of a World Advertising Convention in Berlin to speak of advertising "as a language of the new world." He urged Germans to "learn from other countries who had more experience in this language" but also to "create a German dialect of this language in the German spirit and with German aesthetic feeling."[50] Such appeals to universality (and a special German role in this universal vision) coincided with a new style in German cosmetics advertising that drew on modernist angular lines and followed Japanese and American examples in creating ethnically ambiguous, "cosmopolitan" types. An example of such an ad was a drawing by Jupp Wiertz for Vogue perfume by the F. Wolff and Sohn company, which featured a recognizably modern woman in tight cap, short hair, bathing-suit-like gown, and exposed arms adorned with jewelry. Her most outstanding feature was her East Asian eyes. Such a fantasy of universality was probably a result of rearranged visions of civilization: by the late 1920s, Japan was increasingly considered an industrialized, urbanized, civilized, and modern nation in the West. In this period some German companies also followed the example of ads for American cosmetics products in Germany and stressed the world reach of their products, a strategy that was likely particularly attractive for an industry with a history of strong exports. Like all conceptions of universality these were implicitly or explicitly exclusionary: advertising and commentary on it continued to rely on distinctions between "primitive" and "civilized" people, and the World Advertising Convention in Berlin included only Europeans and North Americans.[51]

The increase in racist policies and rhetoric, and the greater significance given to plans for formal imperialism during the Third Reich, did not lead to a resurgence of overtly racist imagery from the first quarter of the twentieth century in cosmetics advertising after 1933. In line with pronouncements for autarky by regime leaders, and also following a decline of their exports in the Great Depression, German cosmetics advertisers dropped references to the world reach of their products and used photographic portrayals of white women of a variety of types, ranging from the "vamps" to sporty blondes tanning in the sun.

In spite of this "narrowed" vision in cosmetics ads, commodities continued to be part of how Germans conceived their relations with non-Germans. An article in the *Berliner Illustrirte Zeitung* from 1939, for example, expressed explicit support for the Indian National Congress and Indian independence from British colonialism. It juxtaposed an India "that forgets itself" with one that "remembers itself and comes back to reason." The first India featured "Europeanized Indians in a night club in Bombay" and Indians who were "admiring U.S. revue girls." As captions under the images reported, the Indian National Congress was fighting a bitter fight against "unhealthy influences of Western culture." The India that "remembers itself" was represented by a woman pictured at "the symbol of the Indian liberation movement, the spinning wheel" and by a poster that contrasted the beauty of inexpensive Indian-made cloth and fashions shown on a woman with sari and long hair with the ugliness of much more expensive clothing from the West that was worn by a woman with a bob.[52]

A few weeks later another article in the same magazine made it clear that Germans were helping in India's effort to "find itself"; the piece stressed the participation of a German director and manager in the Malad film industry, which "selects its material out of the life of the people and thus helps to liberate the country from the import of kitschy films about India." Perhaps this German aid was particularly welcome to German readers, since Indians could in some racist ideologies lay claim to "Aryanness." However, the tensions in this vision of German aid for an Indian return to folk tradition were revealed when the article labeled the main star of the Malad film company, Devika Rani, "the Garbo of the miracle country." Hollywood icon Greta Garbo (who had begun her world career in Germany in the 1920s) remained a yardstick under the Nazis for measuring Rani's beauty and significance.[53]

A German civilizing mission, and the commodities that connoted it, were also bound up with German actions in World War II, which scholars rightly refer to as "the racist war." In 1943, when Germans and their helpers were perpetrating the "final solution" against European Jews, Roma and Sinti, and also killing millions of Slavs, an article on a young woman in Mostar claimed that the German occupation of Yugoslavia meant new opportunities, and indeed an unveiling, for Muslim women. The article, "The Change of the Girl Nera," contrasted the traditional dark dress that covered her body, including a large hood over her head, with her "new fashion." Nera was working as a stenographer in an office for the Germans, and a picture of her in a short dress and with uncovered hair walking next to German men in uniform was described as follows: "In an airy dress ending above the knee, Nera marches with her girlfriend next to a unit of men from the OT *[Operation Todt]*." Nera's display of her "new fashion" was a sign of both her modern transformation and her allegiance to Germany. The article suggests that strategies of civilizationism, dissimilation, and genocide could exist side by side in Nazi ideology, as they did in practice under the German occupation of Yugoslavia.[54]

Consumption and images of commodities became ever more significant after 1945, in both Cold War Germanies. The import of foreign commodities and the export of German-produced commodities were crucial for maintaining German prosperity. This happened at a time when "modernization" and "development" discourses replaced biologically based racism and formal empires, anticolonial movements rose up against European colonizers, and each Germany was itself drawn into the informal empire of a superpower, the United States or the Soviet Union. As we have seen, by the 1970s both Germanies were engaged in development efforts in the Third World, and West German tourism abroad became a major factor by which Germans related to others.[55] For the years since World War II, it is worth examining how these developments have affected the marketing of foreign goods in Germany, especially from the "Third World" and also the marketing of German products at home and abroad. For example, it would be important to know whether East Germans developed distinct marketing strategies and attitudes toward the consumption of goods from the Third World, given their state's history of aligning itself rhetorically with movements for liberation.

In West Germany, by the 1960s, in the context of widespread European decolonization, certain references to colonialism were no longer acceptable. Thus the term *Kolonialwaren,* "colonial goods," disappeared. But in 1970 the German company Beiersdorf advertised its global face cream NIVEA in West Germany in a way that hearkened back to the idea of Western civilizing missions. The ad showed a hut in Guatemala, and was titled in big letters "NIVEA: The German Message."[56] And by the 1980s Beiersdorf was advertising its cream by means of a blue globe bearing the NIVEA logo and the slogan: "75 years of care without limits or borders."[57] Such imagery confirms Marcia Klotz's point that Germans have located themselves in global contexts, in spite of German claims to provincialism after 1945.

By the 1980s the politics of consumption had undergone some dramatic changes in West Germany. Along with radical criticism of Western political and social systems, the demand emerged for consumer knowledge not just of the locations but also of the conditions of production for various imports. These demands went hand in hand with the founding of so-called Third World stores, which imported "artisan" work from different parts of the world. We need to know more about the debates over the political meanings of fashion and consumption among various groups of radicals, including leftists, feminists, and environmentalists, and the responses of the West German "mainstream." Such an investigation may also reveal problematic ways of identifying with the Third World.

These developments had an impact on larger companies. Coffee companies for example began to show happy, independent Colombian coffee growers in their advertisements. And by the late 1980s, this had a definite effect on the marketing strategies of big multinational companies. For example, the British-based chain Body Shop, present in Germany and many other countries, has used references to the conditions of production for the ingredients of it beauty products in its marketing strategies and stresses that the all-natural ingredients are produced under ecologically sound conditions and that its consumers are a multiracial crowd committed to human rights. The company also responds to global feminist concerns by emphasizing that female producers in the Third World receive crucial resources through Body Shop's responsible purchases of raw materials. All this has not happened without some scandals, and one can certainly wonder about new forms of exoticization in Body Shop's marketing strategies. Nonetheless Body Shop seems part of important changes in the politics of consumption over the last thirty or so years. Its presence in Germany (and elsewhere) needs to be analyzed in the context of the history of development and of tourism.[58]

New Questions for Scholars of Germany?

In conclusion, what kind of questions does an inquiry into empire and commodity culture raise? Neither empire nor consumption has stable meanings. One of the dangers of empire and imperialism studies is that these categories can obscure the great variety of power relations within and between nations. We need to take seriously the insights of scholars who have identified "Orientalism" and "development" as Western forms of domination beyond formal imperialism, but at the same time it is important to try and draw a complex picture. This means accounting for differences within the West and within Germany itself; we need to examine how various groups of Germans—among them policymakers, business leaders, producers of mass culture, intellectuals, and consumers—constructed, analyzed and contested the links that the flow of images, goods, and people forged between Germany and the world. Further, we need to explore how ideologies of consumerism have been transformed in interaction with changing foreign relations and economic interests and changing relations within the nation—between women and men, between different classes and generations, and among different ethnic groups. And, finally, representations need to be analyzed in relation to the complicated encounters between Germans and non-Germans. What makes the concept of empire potentially compelling is that it focuses attention on the uneven power relations between Germany and other areas of the world. Yet empire does not and should not provide us with a new master narrative: it can only be useful as a category of analysis if it encompasses the dramatic changes in ideology, economic organization, and international power that Germany underwent in the twentieth century. Thus it remains to be seen what policies Angela Merkel's government will associate with her calls for German citizens as winners of globalization.

In order to give a full picture of the dynamics of empire, representations need to be analyzed in the context of the actions of decision makers in business and politics. Decisions about just what was to be exported or imported were important in shaping encounters between Germany and other nations. In this context, it is important to identify examples of commodities that were foreign-produced but were not marketed as such. Another question is how selective knowledge about the conditions in which they were produced added value to commodities and was used to sell them. In the end, however, processes of empire building have not been controlled exclusively by small elites, and an important task is to ask how different groups of consumers affirmed, challenged, or reshaped the meanings offered by businesses or politicians.

An inquiry that tries to address the issue of imperialism by looking at the changing politics of empire and consumption in twentieth-century Germany can then ask the following questions: What political relations, including for example formal colonialism, occupation, or development efforts, have enabled the flow of commodities in and out of Germany at different moments? How did the terms in which Germans express their attraction to the foreign and the exotic change in the course of the twentieth century? How do changing patterns of consumption relate to German foreign policies? How were visions of empire contested at different moments of German history?

Notes

Research for this article has been supported by grants from the Keller Fund of the History Department, the Simpson Center for the Humanities, and the Institute for Transnational Studies at the University of Washington, Seattle. For research assistance, I would like to thank Katrina Hagen, Kristy Leissle, John Foster, and Teresa Mares; for their helpful comments on earlier versions of the article, Frank Biess, Jane Brown, Alon Confino, Paul Kennedy, Robert Moeller, Mark Roseman, Lynn Thomas and the members of the History Research Group and the Simpson Humanities Center Society of Scholars at the University of Washington. My thinking on the issues discussed has been influenced by my involvement in a research collaboration with five colleagues at the University of Washington. See in particular The Modern Girl Around the World Research Group (Tani E. Barlow, Madeleine Yue Dong, Uta G. Poiger, Priti Ramamurthy, Lynn M. Thomas and Alys Eve Weinbaum), "The Modern Girl around the World: A Research Agenda and Preliminary Findings," *Gender and History* 17 (August 2005), and idem, ed. *The Modern Girl Around the World*, anthology under review.

1. This is a revised version of Uta G. Poiger, "Empire and Imperialism in 20th-Century Germany," *History and Memory* 17 (Fall 2005): 117–43.

2. http://www.angela-merkel.de/pdf/2005_07_25_interview_pv_spiegel.pdf, accessed November 22, 2005; Jane Kramer, "The Rise of Angela Merkel," *New Yorker*, 19 September 2005. On *Weltpolitik* see references in note 5.

3. See Victoria de Grazia, ed., *The Sex of Things: Gender and Consumption in Historical Perspective* (Berkeley, 1996); Alon Confino and Rudy Koshar, "Regimes of Consumer Culture: New Narratives in Twentieth-Century German History," *German History* 19 (June 2001):135–61; Konrad H. Jarausch and Michael Geyer, *Shattered Past: Reconstructing German Histories* (Princeton, 2003), chap. 10, 269–314.

4. See Craig Clunas, "Modernity Global and Local: Consumption and the Rise of the West," *American Historical Review* 104 (Dec. 1999): 1497–511; Volker Wünderich, "Zum globalen Kontext von Konsumgesellschaft und Konsumgeschichte: Kritische und weiterführende Überlegungen," in Hannes Siegrist, Hartmut Kaelble and Jürgen Kocka, eds., *Europäische Konsumgeschichte: Zur Gesellschafts- und Kulturgeschichte des Konsums, 18. bis 20. Jahrhundert* (Frankfurt/Main, 1997), 793–810.

5. Sebastian Conrad and Jürgen Osterhammel have forcefully argued for locating German history in transnational frameworks: see Sebastian Conrad, "Doppelte Marginalisierung," *Geschichte und Gesellschaft* 28 (2002): 145–169; Sebastian Conrad and Jürgen Osterhammel, eds., *Das Kaiserreich transnational: Deutschland in der Welt, 1871–1914* (Göttingen, 2004).

6. On the possibilities and limits of Americanization, see for example Heide Fehrenbach and Uta G. Poiger, "Americanization Reconsidered," in idem, eds., *Transactions, Transgressions, Transformations: American Culture in Western Europe and Japan* (New York, 2000), xiii–xl.

7. See John A. Moses, *Politics of Illusion: The Fischer Controversy in German Historiography* (New York: Barnes and Noble, 1975). For example of scholarship generated in the wake of the Fischer controversy, see, Hartmut Pogge von Strandmann, "Domestic Origins of Germany's Colonial Expansion under Bismarck," *Past and Present*, no. 42 (1969): 140–59; Hans-Ulrich Wehler, *Bismarck und der Imperialismus*, 4th ed. (Munich, 1976); Karin Hausen, *Deutsche Kolonialherrschaft in Afrika: Wirtschaftsinteressen und Kolonialverwaltung in Kamerun vor 1914* (Zurich, 1970); Volker Berghahn, *Der Tirpitz-Plan: Genesis und Verfall einer innenpolitischen Strategie unter Wilhelm II* (Düsseldorf, 1971); Paul M. Kennedy, *The Samoan Tangle: A Study in Anglo-German-American Relations, 1878–1900* (New York, 1974).

8. Hannah Arendt, *The Origins of Totalitarianism*, new ed. (New York, 1973); Aimé Césaire, *Discourse on Colonialism* (New York, 1972).

9. See Russell A. Berman, "German Colonialism: Another *Sonderweg?*" in Marcia Klotz, ed., *German Colonialism*, special issue of *European Studies Journal* 16 (Fall 1999): 25–36; Sara Friedrichsmeyer, Sara Lennox, and Susanne Zantop, eds., *The Imperialist Imagination: German Colonialism and Its Legacy* (Ann Arbor, 1998).

10. On this point, see Lora Wildenthal, "The Places of Colonialism in the Writing and Teaching of Modern German History," *European Studies Journal* 16 (Fall 1999): 9–24.

11. See n. 1 above.

12. Especially influential was Eckart Kehr, *Schlachtflottenbau und Parteipolitik 1894–1901: Versuch eines Querschnitts durch die innenpolitischen, sozialen und ideologischen Voraussetzungen des deutschen Imperialismus* (Berlin, 1930). See also Wolfgang Mommsen, *Theories of Imperialism* (New York, 1980).

13. Pogge von Strandmann, "Domestic Origins."

14. Wehler, *Bismarck und der Imperialismus.*

15. See for example, Paul M. Kennedy, *The Rise of the Anglo-German Antagonism, 1860–1914* (Boston, 1980).

16. P. M. Kennedy, "German Colonial Expansion: Has the 'Manipulated Social Imperialism' Been Antedated?" *Past and Present,* no. 54 (1972), 134–41.

17. See Wildenthal, "The Places of Colonialism," 13.

18. Pascal Grosse, *Kolonialismus, Eugenik und bürgerliche Gesellschaft in Deutschland, 1850–1914* (Frankfurt/Main, 2000); Lora Wildenthal, *German Women for Empire, 1884–1945* (Durham, N.C., 2002); Andrew Zimmerman, *Anthropology and Anti-Humanism in Imperial Germany* (Chicago, 2001); Frederick Cooper and Ann Laura Stoler, eds., *Tensions of Empire: Colonial Cultures in a Bourgeois World* (Berkeley, 1996).

19. Woodruff D. Smith, *The Ideological Origins of Nazi Imperialism* (New York, 1986), 4. For an example of this scholarship, see Heinz Tillmann and Werner Kowalski, eds., *Westdeutscher Neokolonialismus: Untersuchungen über die wirtschaftliche und politische Expansion des westdeutschen Imperialismus in Afrika und Asien* (Berlin, 1963).

20. Klaus Hildebrand, *Vom Reich zum Weltreich: Hitler, NSDAP und koloniale Frage 1919–1945* (Munich, 1969); Mark Mazower, *Dark Continent: Europe's Twentieth Century* (New York, 1998).

21. See for example, Wildenthal, *German Women for Empire;* Grosse, *Kolonialismus;* Smith, *Ideological Origins;* and Wolfe W. Schmokel, *Dream of Empire: German Colonialism, 1919–1945* (New Haven, 1964); Isabel Hull, "Military Culture and the Production of 'Final Solutions' in the Colonies: The Example of Wilhelmian Germany," in Robert Gellately and Ben Kiernan, eds., *The Specter of Genocide: Mass Murder in Historical Perspective* (Cambridge, 2003), 141–62; and idem, *Absolute Destruction: Military Culture and the Practices of War in Imperial Germany* (Ithaca, 2004). Stresemann on "Volk ohne Raum" quoted in Sara Friedrichsmeyer, Sara Lennox and Susanne Zantop, "Introduction," in idem, eds., *The Imperialist Imagination,* 1–29, 16.

22. Friedrichsmeyer, Lennox, and Zantop, "Introduction," 18.

23. Susanne Zantop, *Colonial Fantasies: Conquest, Family, and Nation in Precolonial Germany, 1770–1870* (Durham, N.C., 1997).

24. Russell A. Berman, "German Colonialism: Another *Sonderweg?*" *European Studies Journal* 16 (Fall 1999): 25–36; and idem, *Enlightenment or Empire: Colonial Discourse in German Culture* (Lincoln, Neb., 1998).

25. Friedrichsmayer, Lennox, and Zantop, "Introduction," 21–25.

26. Marcia Klotz, "Introduction," and "Global Visions: From the Colonial to the National Socialist World," *European Studies Journal* 16 (Fall 1999): 1–8, 37–68, 5.

27. Klotz, "Global Visions," 50.

28. Wildenthal, *German Women for Empire,* 174.

29. Besides the extensive literature on the Holocaust of European Jewry, see for example Reiner Pommerin, *Sterilisierung der Rheinlandbastarde: Das Schicksal einer farbigen deutschen Minderheit 1918–1927* (Düsseldorf, 1979); Annegret Ehmann, "From Colonial Racism to Nazi Population Policy: The Role of the So-Called Mischlinge," in Michael Berenbaum and Abraham J. Peck, eds., *The Holocaust and History* (Bloomington, 1998), 115–33; Pascal Grosse, Tina Campt and Yara-Colette Lemke-Muniz de Faria, "Blacks, Germans and the Politics of Imperial Imagination," in Friedrichsmeyer, Lennox, and Zantop, eds., *The Imperialist Imagination,* 205–29; Clarence Lusane, *Hitler's Black Victims: The Historical Experiences of Afro-Germans, European Blacks,*

Africans, and African Americans in the Nazi Era (New York, 2003); Tina M. Campt, *Other Germans: Black Germans and the Politics of Race, Gender, and Memory in the Third Reich* (Ann Arbor, 2004).

30. Uwe Timm quoted in Friedrichsmeyer, Lennox, and Zantop, "Introduction," 24.

31. Henning Melber, "'... dass die Kultur der Neger gehoben werde!' Kolonialdebatten im deutschen Reichstag," in Ulrich van der Heyden und Joachim Zeller, eds., *Kolonialmetropole Berlin: Eine Spurensuche* (Berlin, 2002), 67–72, 67.

32. See Heide Fehrenbach, *Race after Hitler: Black Occupation Children in Germany and America* (Princeton, 2005), and idem, "Of German Mothers and *Negermischlingskinder*: Race, Sex, and the Postwar Nation," in Hanna Schissler, ed., *The Miracle Years: A Cultural History of West Germany, 1945–1968* (Princeton, 2001), 164–86; Grosse, Campt and Lemke-Muniz de Faria, "Blacks;" Maria Höhn, *GIs and Fräuleins: The German-American Encounter in 1950s West Germany* (Chapel Hill, N.C., 2002); Uta G. Poiger, *Jazz, Rock, and Rebels: Cold War Politics and American Culture in a Divided Germany* (Berkeley, 2000).

33. Volker R. Berghahn, "Introduction: German Big Business and the Quest for a European Economic Empire in the Twentieth Century," in Berghahn, ed., *The Quest for Economic Empire: European Strategies of German Big Business in the Twentieth Century* (Providence, R.I., 1995), 1–33, 10. For his conceptualization Berghahn draws on J. A. Gallagher and R. E. Robinson, "The Imperialism of Free Trade," *Economic History Review*, 2d ser., 6, no. 1 (1953): 1–15; and Michael W. Doyle, *Empires* (Ithaca, 1986).

34. See William Gray, *Germany's Cold War: The Global Campaign to Isolate East Germany, 1949–1969* (Chapel Hill, N.C., 2003); Brigitte H. Schulz, *Development Policy in the Cold War Era: The Two Germanies and Sub-Saharan Africa, 1960–1985* (Münster, 1995); Hans-Joachim Döring, *"Es geht um unsere Existenz: Die Politik der DDR gegenüber der Dritten Welt am Beispiel von Mosambik und Äthiopien* (Berlin, 1999).

35. Katrina Hagen is currently working on a project that explores some of these questions: "German Internationalism in the Cold War," dissertation in progress, University of Washington, Seattle.

36. For a call to put German history into contexts of inner-European encounters during war and postwar periods, see Ute Frevert, "Europeanizing German History," *GHI Bulletin* no. 36 (Spring 2005), 9–24, and the comment by David Blackbourn in the same issue.

37. Dennis Kuck, "'Für den sozialistischen Aufbau ihrer Heimat?' Ausländische Arbeitskräfte in der DDR," in Jan C. Behrends, Thomas Lindenberger, and Patrice G. Poutrus, eds., *Fremde und Fremdsein in der DDR: Zu historischen Ursachen der Fremdenfeindlichkeit in Ostdeutschland* (Berlin, 2003), 271–82.

38. See Jarausch and Geyer, *Shattered Past*, chap. 6, "From Empire to Europe: The Taming of German Power," quotes from 193–94.

39. In addition to the texts cited above, see Katrin Sieg, *Ethnic Drag: Performing Race, Nation, and Sexuality in West Germany* (Ann Arbor, 2002).

40. See Uta G. Poiger, "Imperialism and Consumption: Two Tropes in West German Radicalism of the 1960s and 1970s," in Axel Schildt und Detlef Siegfried, eds., *Between Marx and Coca-Cola: Youth Cultures in Changing European Societies, 1960–1980* (New York, 2006), 161–172.

41. Michael Hardt and Antonio Negri, *Empire* (Cambridge, Mass., 2000), German edition (Frankfurt/Main, 2002); Lisa Rofel, "Modernity's Masculine Fantasies," in

Bruce M. Knauft, ed., *Critically Modern: Alternatives, Alterities, Anthropologies* (Bloomington, 2002), 175–93.

42. Amy Kaplan and Donald Pease, eds., *Cultures of United States Imperialism* (Durham, N.C., 1991); Melani McAlister, *Epic Encounters: Culture, Media, and U.S. Interests in the Middle East, 1945–2000* (Berkeley, 2001).

43. See, for example, Thomas Richards, *The Commodity Culture of Victorian England: Advertising and Spectacle, 1851–1914* (Stanford, 1990); Anne McClintock, *Imperial Leather: Race, Gender, and Sexuality in the Colonial Conquest* (New York, 1995); David M. Ciarlo, "Rasse konsumieren: Von der exotischen zur kolonialen Imagination in der Bildreklame des Wilhelminischen Kaiserreichs," in Birthe Kundrus, ed., *Phantasiereiche: Zur Kulturgeschichte des deutschen Kolonialismus* (Frankfurt/Main, 2003), 135–79.

44. Ad reprinted in Manfred O. Hinz, Helgard Patemann and Arnim Meier, eds., *Weiss auf Schwarz: 100 Jahre Einmischung in Afrika: Deutscher Kolonialismus und afrikanischer Widerstand* (Berlin, 1984), 57.

45. Ad in *Beiblatt der Fliegenden Blätter* 135, no. 3441 (ca. 1908).

46. On these complexities, and the danger of flattening them out, see Birthe Kundrus, "Die Kolonien—'Kinder des Gefühls und der Phantasie,'" in *Phantasiereiche*, 7–15, 12; and Eric Ames, "From the Exotic to the Everyday: The Ethnographic Exhibition in Germany," in Vanessa R. Schwartz and Jeannene M. Przyblys, eds., *Modernity and the Nineteenth Century: A Visual Culture Reader* (New York: Routledge, 2004), 313–27; Eric Ames, Marcia Klotz, and Lora Wildenthal, *Germany's Colonial Pasts* (Lincoln, Neb., 2005).

47. Ad reprinted in Hinz, Patemann and Meier, eds., *Weiss auf Schwarz*, 57.

48. See David Blackbourn, *The Long Nineteenth Century: A History of Germany, 1780 to 1918* (New York, 1998).

49. See David M. Ciarlo, "Rasse konsumieren," esp. 147–48. Ad for Kaloderma, *Leipziger Illustrirte Zeitung*, 28 August 1929; Khasana, *Leipziger Illustrirte Zeitung*, April 9, 1925.

50. *Gebrauchsgraphik* 4, no. 1 (1927), quoted in Jeremy Aynsley, *Graphic Design in Germany 1890–1945* (Berkeley, 2000), 129; Adenauer quoted in ibid, 141; Hans Luther, "Geleitwort," in Alfred Knapp, *Reklame, Propaganda, Werbung: Ihre Weltorganisation* (Berlin, 1929), 3–4.

51. For a more extensive discussion of these themes, see my manuscript "Fantasies of Universality? Neue Frauen and 'Others' in Weimar and Nazi Germany," in Tani E. Barlow et al., eds., *The Modern Girl around the World* (forthcoming). For an appeal to cosmopolitan types, see H. K. Frenzel in a conversation with Frederic Suhr, *Gebrauchsgraphik* 3, no. 10 (Oct. 1928), quoted in Aynsley, *Graphic Design in Germany*, 134–35; Vogue ad in Arnold Friedrich, *Anschläge: Deutsche Plakate als Dokumente der Zeit, 1900–1960* (Eberhausen, 1963), 64.

52. "Wolfgang Weber besuchte den Kongress eines Erdteils," *Berliner Illustrirte Zeitung*, 5 April 1939, 532.

53. "Indien filmt selbst," *Berliner Illustrirte Zeitung*, 29 June 1939, 1126–27.

54. "Die Wandlung des Mädchen Nera," *Berliner Illustrirte Zeitung*, 30 Dec. 1943, 616.

55. Research on German tourism abroad is only beginning. See Hermann Bausinger, Klaus Beyrer und Gottfried Kroff, *Reisekultur: Von der Pilgerfahrt zum moder-*

nen Tourismus (Munich, 1999); Rudy Koshar, *German Travel Cultures* (New York, 2000); Shelley Baranowski, *Strength through Joy: Consumerism and Mass Tourism in the Third Reich* (Cambridge, 2004). On problems associated with foreign travel and the tourism industry, see Martina Backes, Tina Goethe, Stephan Günther, Rosaly Magg, eds., *Im Handgepäck Rassismus: Beiträge zu Tourismus und Kultur* (Freiburg, 2002).

56. Cited in Harm G. Schroeter, "Marketing als angewandte Sozialtechnik und Veränderungen im Konsumverhalten: Nivea als internationale Dachmarke, 1960–1994," in Siegrist, Kaelble and Kocka, eds., *Europäische Konsumgeschichte*, 615–47, 641.

57. See Rainer Gries, *Produkte als Medien: Kulturgeschichte der Produktkommunikation in der Bundesrepublik und der DDR* (Leipzig, 2003), 529.

58. See the Body Shop company website at http://www.thebodyshop.com/web/tbsgl/about.jsp. See also Caren Kaplan, "'A World Without Boundaries': The Body Shop's Trans/National Geographics," *Social Text* (Fall 1995): 45–66.

CHAPTER 10

Americanization as a Paradigm of German History

Mary Nolan

Throughout the 1990s Americanism and Americanization seemed a useful paradigm for understanding twentieth-century German history, or at least a paradigm whose strengths and defects had to be seriously debated. Indeed, Americanization seemed to be a useful paradigm for the post–World War II history of much of Western Europe and, in the recent decades of U.S.-dominated globalization, for the economic and cultural development of much of the rest of the world as well. Think of such best-selling works as Ben Barber's *Jihad vs. McWorld,* with its insistence that the quintessentially American infotainment-telesector was reshaping the world in its image.[1] Or Thomas Friedman's *The Lexus and the Olive Tree,* which outlined the new system of economics, culture, and international relations that Americanized globalization had created— no countries with McDonalds ever fought a war against each other—and warned of the catastrophically high costs for countries that failed to knuckle under and join in.[2] Even those scholars of the postcolonial world who argued that American goods and forms were appropriated, reinterpreted, hybridized, and localized in diverse modern economies, social practices, value systems, and identities acknowledged that American goods, cultural products, and economic and political practices were crucial foundational elements in these complex processes of constructing alternative modernities.[3]

To be sure, the imitation of American democracy has proceeded much more slowly outside of Europe and in the formerly Communist states of Central and Eastern Europe than various American administrations claim to have wished, and the political goals and power relations of the new world order were unclear through much of the 1990s. The U.S. economic, social, and cultural vision of neoliberal economies, modern individualized societies, and Americanized mass culture and consumption was, however, clear. And Germany, or the formerly western part thereof, seemed a model of economic, social, and cultural Americanization and of how such transformation might promote political democratization and close cooperation with the American global hegemon.

Fast forward to the last few years and we find anti-Americanism—or what is labeled as such by the government and media of the U.S.—not just in the Middle East or across the global south but in Europe. And, within Europe, not just in France, long noted for its cultural anti-Americanism,[4] but in Britain, despite or because of Tony Blair's abject loyalty to Bush, and even more so in Germany. What kind of anti-Americanism has emerged in Germany, that seemingly most Americanized of European countries, and why has it emerged only recently? Has Germany turned out to be less Americanized than we thought, even those who have argued for negotiated and hybridized adaptations of American ideas, goods, structures, and practices? What has the paradigm of Americanization in which discussions of anti-Americanism have played a key role allowed us to see, and to what has it blinded us?

To begin to answer these admittedly ambitious questions, I want to situate Americanization within the interpretative debates in which it is most often deployed—Americanization-modernization-westernization. After a regrettably brief review of the contributions of the rich literature on Americanization in twentieth century Germany, a literature to which Volker Berghahn has made significant contributions, I want to suggest some of the conceptual and methodological shortcomings of the Americanization paradigm. The concluding section will explore whether we need to abandon or modify the analytical strategies and research foci of the last decades in order to understand the current resurgence of anti-Americanism.

∼

Americanization is a very elusive term, for it alternately describes an object of study, functions as an analytical category, and serves as shorthand for an overarching interpretation of the history of twentieth century Germany, especially of the Federal Republic. Americanization as a topic of research looks at the adoption of American forms of production and consumption, technology and techniques of management, cultural goods and institutions of mass culture, gender roles and leisure practices. It analyzes not only what was and was not adopted, but also how such borrowings were selectively appropriated and how they functioned and acquired particular meanings. Americanization was and is shaped by Americanism, that is, by the images and discourses that imagined or constructed America as a model of economic, social, and cultural development—as one possible, extremely powerful, and appealing model of modernity. Americanization is shaped as well by anti-Americanism, a set of anxieties and criticism about Americanization and Americanism that reflects—depending on which interpretation one accepts—a resentment and fear of modernity that is informed by anti-capitalism and anti-Semitism or, by contrast, a jealousy of American life, prosperity, freedom, and power or, finally, a justified criticism of both the actions of America and the cost of modernity American style.[5]

As an analytical concept Americanization has been defined by historians, such as Anselm Doering-Manteuffel, as the one-way cultural transfer of norms, practices, goods, and icons, with the American state and business being the active exporters to passive recipients abroad.[6] Such a simplistic definition of Americanization ignores the movement of goods, practices, and ideas back and forth across the Atlantic and the intense debates, negotiations, and adaptations entailed in the appropriation of things American. It both ignores the agency of recipients and then condemns the concept for giving Germans no agency.[7] Preferable are the definitions of such scholars as Berghahn and Kaspar Maase, which insist in different ways that Americanization as an analytical concept must capture how Germans made their own history but under conditions not of their own choosing. Both acceptance of and resistance to things American should be subsumed under the category of Americanization, Berghahn argues, because mass culture and consumption, Taylorism and Fordism, were coded as American—not abstractly modern or Western—and after 1945 American hegemonic pressure planned and deliberately tried to import significant elements of the American model.[8] Taking an individual view rather than a macro-structural one, Maase, who defines Americanization as appropriation and focuses on the postwar era, argues that "Americanizing oneself was not a purely willful act. It was the utilization of an objectively given constellation and in this respect it depended on the dynamics of Cold War politics and the world economy." He goes on to argue that "'Americanness' was established in Western Europe in qualitatively new ways as a primary reference system. 'America' provided physical, ideational and symbolic materials, arguments, and examples which were being utilized (and increasingly had to be utilized) in the old world in order to articulate and strengthen different interests."[9] Maria Höhn's study, *GIs and Fräuleins,* persuasively argues that Germans in the 1950s understood what was happening to them and their society as Americanization; they responded, positively and negatively, to goods and styles and values that were labeled American as well as to actual Americans.[10]

As an overarching interpretation of twentieth-century German history, Americanization argues that America and American goods, practices, norms, cultural forms, military personnel, and civilians played a significant role in the transformations of German economic, social, cultural, and political life. These transformations began and were first debated in the Weimar Republic, with its love-hate relationship with mass culture and modernity; they continued in muted and less explicitly American forms in the Third Reich; took on vastly accelerated and qualitatively new forms in the Federal Republic from the1950s on—with much debate about exactly which aspects of Americanization were most important when—and they culminated in the transformations occurring in the former GDR after 1989. This Americanization was either accompanied by continued anti-Americanism of the old form, which rose and fell in waves—Dan Diner's view—or by a steady diminution of anti-Americanism, defined as a rejection of Americanization, over the last five decades—Berghahn's argument.[11]

Those who reject the Americanization interpretation do not deny that the Germany of 2006 bears little resemblance to that of 1906 or even 1956. Rather they dispute the analytic rubric under which these changes should be subsumed. Proponents of the theory of westernization emphasize that cultural flows went in two ways, that Germans played a key role in shaping the new political institutions and values that emerged after 1945 in the West, and that they drew on a "Western" tradition of political values and forms. Rock-'n'-roll and Coca-Cola—and even new gender roles—might have come to Germany by processes of Americanization, aided by occupying GIs, but democracy and the abandonment of the ideas of 1914 and aspirations for a middle position between east and west were the accomplishment of German, male elites.[12]

The westernization paradigm, which privileges political and intellectual exchanges over mass cultural and material ones, is most unclear about which ideas and institutions qualify as Western and why. Liberalism, democracy, intellectual freedom certainly, but in which national ideological and institutional variant? And what about nationalism, racism, colonialism, and sexism? The raced and gendered character of liberal thought, which feminist and postcolonial scholarship has uncovered, is nowhere present in the westernization model.[13] To become Western is unambiguously positive, for "the West"—a term whose post–World War II discursive deployment cries out for analysis—is seen as uniformly beneficent and uncontradictory. The westernization model leaves unexplored who was hegemonic after 1945, how ideas were coded American, whatever their provenance, and to whom precisely Germans were talking and paying attention in the first postwar decades. Finally, the westernization model ignores the structuring Cold War context and the complex ways in which, since 1917, Americanism and anti-communism, anti-Americanism and communism were mutually constitutive of one another.

Others prefer to talk about modernization. Axel Schildt and Arnold Sywottek argue for modernization in—or really after—reconstruction, a two-phase model, as the appropriate interpretation of the 1950s and 1960s. Ulrich Beck speaks of the structural breakthrough of the modern, while Christoph Klessmann argues for modernization under conservative guardianship.[14] Many of the critiques made of westernization apply to modernization as well. Modernity was not and is not imaged in abstract Weberian categories of disenchantment, rationalization, and secularization but rather in terms of concrete images of technology and productivity, consumption and leisure, movies and mobility, gender and sexuality that were and are drawn overwhelming from America. Modernity, like tradition, is a construct; yet the modernization interpretation fails to explore how modernization theory, which drew on evolutionary thought and functionalism, was above all an American idea, developed by American social scientists, based on American patterns of consumption and production, civil society, and politics. Modernization was presented as the future toward which other countries in Europe as well as the Third World could, indeed must, move. (Such an analysis displays a determinism comparable to Marxism's prediction about the socialist future toward which all countries were inevitably moving.) And countries would head in the prescribed direction within the relatively sealed container of the nation-state, for modernization gives primacy to indigenous developments rather than to transnational flows and forces. Contrary to what its proponents assert, modernization, like westernization, is normative rather than empirical, a means of sorting the good/progressive/modern from the bad/regressive/traditional according to criteria shaped by the American experience and Cold War anti-communism.[15]

The rich scholarship on Americanism, Americanization, and anti-Americanism has focused thematically on culture and the economy, chronologically on Weimar[16] and the long 1950s,[17] and analytically on German borrowings and resistance rather than on transnational interactions or American intentions and actions.[18] While attention is increasing being paid to the visible and hidden elements of Americanization in Nazi Germany,[19] few historians venture into the treacherous waters of 1960s, and none go beyond.[20] Work on Americanization has contributed greatly to our understanding of how Germany was transformed in the twentieth century not as part of some ill-defined processes of modernization or westernization but rather in specifiable ways that built on German structures, institutions, values, and practices but borrowed from American models in many fields and resulted from American active interventions.[21] Studies of Americanization have shed significant light on the development of German capitalism and the particular variant of Fordism and, now, post-Fordism that emerged from the rationalization of the 1920s and 1930s, from the postwar adaptation of American management practices, and from Modell Deutschland and its current crises.[22] Americanization has been formative for analyses of mass culture and consumer society in Germany, just as anti-Americanism has been central to our understanding of criticism of them.[23] Finally, Americanization as subject of study and category of analysis has highlighted the gendered character of discourses about modernity, mass culture, and democracy and revealed much about the actual experiences of women embracing, resisting, or redefining Americanism (but much less has been said about the "Americanized" man outside of work and politics).[24] Like all ambitious and provocative paradigms, however, Americanization has limitations and distortions, three of which I want to discuss.

Americanization as overarching interpretation intersects problematically with narratives of modernity, a central category deployed by historians of twentieth-century Germany. In one variant, the first half of the century is a story of thwarted infatuation with Fordism, rejection of cultural Americanization, and failed economic and political modernization, while the second half is a tale of Americanized modernization in the west and the foolish and doomed pursuit of alternatives to it in the east. In another variant, the first half of the century is the story of the crisis of classical modernity in Weimar, the distinctly modern aspects of Nazi economy, society, and culture, and the contribution of modern science, planning, population politics, medicine, the state, and economic organizations to the Holocaust, while the second narrates the triumph of good modernity.[25] Let's leave aside the question of how problematic grand narratives are and instead focus on how each variant of the Americanization grand narrative disassociates Americanization from the bad first half of the century. Simultaneously, each links Americanization to the politically and economically good and the culturally positive or at least ambivalent second half.

Such approaches hardly do justice to the complexities of Americanism and Americanization. If Nazi Germany was modern and modernizing in the multiple ways that recent scholarship has suggested,[26] what role did Americanization play? Christian Kleinschmidt has reconstructed how German businessmen tried to maintain ties to their American business partners and colleagues and even sought to visit the United States until the late 1930s.[27] Historians of economic rationalization have traced how the German adaptations of Taylorism and Fordism, stripped of their references to America, were implemented in Nazi Germany.[28] The close ties between the Nazi and American eugenics movements and the links between IBM and the anti-Semitic and genocidal practices of the Nazi state have been exposed.[29] The general works of Philipp Gassert and Hans Dieter Schäfer—as well as more specific studies of jazz and film— suggest not only the ongoing infatuation with American mass culture but also the ability of Nazis to rework and deploy elements of it, to create what Michael Geyer has called the nationalist variant of modern mass culture.[30] We need to examine further how American goods, practices, values, and cultural products were appropriated and deployed in the Nazi model of modernity and how some elements of this may have carried over into both the FRG and GDR in order to grasp the full and often contradictory impact of Americanization.

Assessments of the negative values and practices imported along with the American model in the post World War II decades have been very one-dimensional. Mass culture and consumption have been singled out, for they featured so prominently in the anti-Americanism of the late 1940s and 1950s, but analysis must not stop there. After 1945, American liberalism and cultural practices were posited as an antidote to German racism and anti-Semitism, but both those prejudices persisted in the American occupation army and in American society. Maria Höhn, Heidi Fehrenbach, and Uta Poiger have done pioneering work on the impact of American racial categories and practices in postwar Germany, showing how new racial others, above all African-Americans, emerged even as anti-Semitism persisted beneath the officially sanctioned philo-Semitism. Historians of Americanization have not examined how this partial Americanization of racial thinking influenced Germany's relations with its "guest workers" and asylum seekers and shaped its painful discussions about multiculturalism and immigration. And we know virtually nothing about how or whether America shaped German attitudes toward decolonization, neo-colonialism, and development. (A transnational study of development ideologies and policies would be especially revealing here.)

America was the dominant language through which modernity was debated in the twentieth century, but it was not the only one. Until 1989 there was a socialist language and model of modernity, which sought consciously to construct an alternative to capitalist modernity American style, even as it did, in fact, borrow from and share elements with the American model.[31] The ultimate failure of the socialist model should not blind us to its early appeals, complex developmental history, and multiple meanings. The GDR, Ina Merkel argues, tried to construct a *Gegenmoderne*, a guided or directed modernity with its own kind of consumer culture, property structure, values about necessity, luxury, and practices of distribution and use. This developed not only under pressure from the Soviet Union but in dialogue with other Communist countries and with west European models of consumer modernity, such as France and Sweden, which differed significantly from the more Americanized Federal Republic.[32] The Americanization paradigm, which posits America as the only model of modernity and views other societies as incomplete versions of it, cannot readily accommodate alternative models of modernity, be they fascist, socialist, or capitalist. In positing America's exceptionalism, even as it insists others can and should emulate America, the Americanization paradigm rejects the idea of what Harry Harootunian calls co-eval modernity, with its suggestion of contemporaneity yet the possibility of difference.[33]

A second limitation of the Americanization paradigm is the flip side of its strength. The very recognition of the hegemonic position of America and the activist strategies deployed by its businessmen, government officials, and intellectuals has led to a productive but restricted focus on the German-American relationship. (The westernization and modernization approaches focus even more narrowly on West Germany.) Even as the power of the American economy, the appeals of American mass culture, and the interventionist practices of the American state are acknowledged, it is necessary to reconstruct the complex borrowings, multiple exchanges, and transnational flows that were occurring simultaneously with Americanization and that profoundly shaped the kind of economy, culture, and values that resulted. An example from Kleinschmidt's *Der produktive Blick* is revealing here. German industrialists and managers, who had borrowed so heavily from America in the 1950s and 1960s, turned to Japan from the 1970s on. The ideas of quality management they adopted had, in fact, originated in America—where they initially found scant resonance—been taken up and developed by the Japanese, and then migrated to Germany from both Japan and the U.S.[34]

My current project on Cold War domesticity, which explores links between American policies, commodities, and images on the one hand and European experiences of domesticity, mass consumption, and conceptions of femininity and masculinity on the other hand, also seeks to capture multidirectional flows and exchanges and varied models of modernity. This project traces the European sources of efforts to create modern individuals, with modern subjectivities and modern ways of living at home and outside that have been ignored in an exclusive focus on Americanization or its Cold War counterpart, Sovietization. It examines how these European projects of becoming modern, which originated in the interwar years, negotiated with hegemonic American goods, forms, and values. It pays particular attention to the varied post–World War II national efforts to protect, stabilize, and reform the family by transforming domesticity. At first glance, the retreat into the home in the 1950s and 1960s in Eastern and Western Europe looked similar to that undertaken in the early Cold War America, even if it occurred later and more slowly; but everywhere the retreat was from nationally and culturally specific problematic pasts and threatening presents. In the U.S., Elaine Tyler May has argued, home and family were both a refuge from the Cold War and the home front of that multifaceted struggle.[35] In Europe, the Cold War was only one source of anxiety, containment only one political project among many. In West Germany, for example, the retreat into the home and the restoration of sharply demarcated definitions of femininity and masculinity offered a means to restore the material and emotional damage of fascism and war and to live in the present and for the future without confronting the past.[36] The 1951 Festival of Britain, with its celebration of and plea for modern products and model homes, offered a diversion from both austerity and the loss of Empire by seeking to direct attention away from the anxiety and drabness of the war and postwar years onto the promise of a bright new future.[37] In Eastern Europe, the popular retreat into the home—usually one with inadequate household technology and consumer goods—represented an escape from the claims of the regime. The home was a refuge, just as it was in Cold War America, but from a different set of political forces and fears that led to a different valuation of public and private.[38]

To understand Cold War domesticity, one needs to trace the flow of ideas, goods, and people from America to a receptive or resisting Europe. But one must be equally attentive to the movement of ideas, cultural products, and consumer goods from Europe to America, in the pre–World War I and inter-war periods and especially from the 1960s on, and to the flows of ideas, goods, gender ideologies, and people among European countries themselves. European nations engaged with the ways in which other European societies, and not just the United States, developed and interpreted an international modernism. Modern furniture, for example, was adopted from and coded as Scandinavian or Italian as readily as American; appliances were adapted to European specifications and tastes. The West German *Rationalisierungskuratorium für Wirtschaftlichkeit* and popular magazines studied and wrote on Sweden, as did the East Germans.[39] American domestic architecture was built on prewar borrowings from Germany, France, and the Netherlands, but post 1945 it was coded and promoted in Europe as quintessentially American.[40] The postwar housing booms across Europe shared a commitment to a modernized infrastructure, basic household technology, and an aesthetic of functionalism and simplicity; but in each country the new apartment complexes and single-family suburban homes took on distinctively national forms and served distinctive domestic political visions. "During the 1950s and 1960s Sweden was labeled the most Americanized nation in Europe," according to Orvar Löfgren, "but visiting Americans found that the American styles, goods and rituals mostly had been Swedified beyond recognition." The use of appliances, the preferred color schemes of homes and offices, the shape of brooms, even the smell of multinational disinfectant—in short, everyday modernity—was at once American, international, and profoundly if often elusively national.[41] In order to understand these transformations, it is necessary to recapture the multidirectional exchanges of products, people, cultural values, and gender regimes. A more transatlantic and less Americacentric approach to the American century, and a less bipolar view of Cold War culture, are needed.

Americanization as cultural transfer, category of analysis, and master narrative existed before 1945, but it was profoundly shaped in all its aspects by Cold War anti-communism and the control, real and imagined, of the superpowers over their clients. A richer history of Americanization requires both an analysis of Americanization in that structuring Cold War context and a critical questioning of assumptions about that context. This entails looking not only at the complex relationship among Western European states and the ambivalent as well as envious attitudes of the East to the West. It also involves investigating how the Communist countries of Central and Eastern Europe exchanged goods, cultural products, and visions of modernity. East Germany, for example, seen as a failed modernizer in the Americanization paradigm, was an exporter of modern technology, furniture, and plastic goods to the

Soviet Union, while Poland pioneered in bringing modern art to other social-ist countries.[42] Much more work needs to be done on Sovietization in East Germany, building on the pioneer collection by Konrad Jarausch and Hannes Siegrist.[43] Such comparative work should look not only at the many, readily apparent differences but also at underlying similarities in the organization of production—for capitalist and communist models alike drew on Taylorism and Fordism.[44] Or, following the provocative suggestion of Kate Brown that "Kazakhstan and Montana Are Nearly the Same Place," one might explore the creation of postwar housing and uses of space.[45]

A third limitation of the Americanization paradigm involves its treatment of the state. Proponents and opponents of Americanization have hotly debated whether American models and Americans themselves promoted or retarded democratization in the immediate postwar period. They have analyzed the in-fluence of American models and direct recommendations on institutions and laws, argued over how allegiance to the *christliche Abendland* did or did not re-semble allegiance to the liberal democratic West of Anglo-American discourse, and traced the emergence of less ideological catch-all political parties and dis-tinctly American styles of political campaigning.[46] But little attention has been paid to social policy and labor law, initially because they were among the least Americanized aspects of West Germany[47] and, more recently, because with the abandonment of Keynesianism and the neoliberal attack on the Social Demo-cratic model, the welfare state and German labor law have been dismissed as anachronistic if not objectionable, as unaffordable luxuries of a bygone era.

West Germany's innovations in the field of co-determination and social policy fall far short of the more socialist and reformist aspirations of Social Democrats in both Weimar and the early post-1945 years, but they did set a much more empowering and protective framework for workers, the elderly (the 1957 pension reform), and those of all ages needing health care than what the American model prescribed. Why did Americanization make so few in-roads here? How do the German welfare state and labor laws shape experiences of consumer culture and Americanized capitalism? What expectations about security and risk, about work and leisure, about entitlement and inequality do they promote? Claus Leggewie argues, for example, that the Rhenish model of capitalism aims at social integration and the minimization of poverty, while the Anglo-Saxon model fears unemployment but tolerates insecurity and high levels of inequality.[48] Despite the pressure of globalization and European inte-gration, Germany has not converged with the American neoliberal economic model, insists Vivien Schmidt. Rather it represents a form of managed capital-ism that is distinct from the American model in the role of the state, in busi-ness networks and relations with the state and labor, and in social policy.[49] It is imperative to examine whether German and European welfare states, labor laws, and varieties of capitalism have created not only a different material context in which Americanized mass production and mass culture are consumed but also a different vision of the good life and the just society.

∿

If we attended to all the complexities of Americanization that I have suggested, would we be better able to explain the current situation of growing German and European anti-Americanism and, of equal importance, growing anti-Europeanism in America? This is a question to which no simple Yes or No answer suffices and on which scholars are bitterly divided. Diner insists that America is resented now, as in the past, for what it is and not for what it does.[50] Stanley Hoffmann, Tony Judt, and Claus Leggewie, among others, view German and European anti-Americanism as a new response to the altered post–Cold War world and America's claimed place in it.[51] The current escalation of anti-Americanism is not déjà vu all over again, as Diner insists, but rather a new product of how Germany has changed and what America is now doing.

Germany has become American, or, more precisely, through negotiated Americanization it has developed a model of capitalist and democratic modernity that is similar to that in the U.S. in many aspects of culture, consumption, economic organization, and practices. The issues that were so central to anti-Americanism in the interwar years and the first postwar decades—mass culture, mass consumption, mobility, and Americanized gender relations with their purportedly liberated women and narrowly materialistic men—have receded. *Kultur, Bildung,* and patriarchy have all been transformed, at least partially Americanized. The ambivalence about, if not hostility to, modernity and capitalism that pervaded much earlier anti-Americanism is gone, unless one equates criticisms of unregulated capitalism and minimalist social policies with a rejection of capitalism and modernity *tout court.* Only in the former GDR are there still echoes of the earlier unease about the effects of consumption on identity and culture. *"Ostalgie,"* the nostalgia for consumer goods specific to the GDR, has swelled after the first years of frantic consumption of the once longed-for West German/Americanized goods.[52]

What is at issue now, to quote the realist IR expert Charles Kupchan from his book bearing the counterintuitive title *The End of the American Era,* is no longer "America's culture, but its power"—and what it should do with that power. "At issue are competing values, not just competing interests."[53] America once had, to borrow Geir Lundestad's phrase, an "empire by invitation." It was a self-consciously liberal hegemon, operated through multilateral institutions that disguised, legitimized, and moderated its dominance and provided a narrative (or rationale) of common values shared by the 'free world,' which were declared to be universal in their application."[54] After 1945, Germany was assigned a subordinate role and was viewed, as Petra Goedde has shown, as a feminized, passive nation, victimized by the misbehavior of a few, dependent and in need of help and guidance.[55] Now the Cold War is over, the Soviet Union is gone, and America is dedicated to unilateralism, preemptive/preventative war, an extreme variant of neoliberal capitalism, and a Pax Americana to which the rest of the world is told to accommodate itself or suffer irrelevance if not worse.[56] There is an increasingly explicit advocacy of empire, coming not only from such right-wing groups as the Project for the New American Century but also from such liberal human rights advocates as Michael Ignatieff.[57]

Germany, along with the government and peoples of many other European countries, remains committed to multilateralism, international institutions, international law, and social welfare at home. These commitments, which America sometimes shared and sometimes subverted but now has abandoned, have often been overlooked in the literature on Americanization. So too has the German, and to a lesser extent the European, concern with environmental issues, a concern that has led not only to mass social movements against nuclear power and nuclear weapons and strong governmental commitment to international environmental protocols, but also to the formation of the Green Party and its participation in coalition governments.

America's reordered priorities, aggressive unilaterialism, and disdain for international law are couched in religious language and reflect the pervasive religiosity of American society. This linkage of religion and politics contrasts markedly to Germany, suggesting not only the limits of Americanization but also increasingly divergent paths of development. In constitutional theory, church and state are more separate in the U.S. than in Germany, where churches get federal funds and religion is taught in schools. The U.S. has no party comparable to the CDU/CSU, with its close ties to both the Protestant and Catholic churches. In the first postwar decades, Germany was as religious as America; both had large church memberships; religiosity and respectability were closely associated, and religious rhetoric was a key element in anti-Communism. (In West Germany religion also featured prominently in the attack on an excessively materialistic, morally lax Americanism.[58]) Since the 1970s, Germany has become more secular, even if official church membership has not declined significantly.[59] Religion does not permeate everyday life or pervade politicians' speeches; fundamentalism has not taken root. Whereas two-thirds of Americans go to church weekly, only 20 percent of West Germans and 14 percent of East Germans do.[60] And, as *Der Spiegel* wrote in early 2003, "Whenever an American president links his Christianity with a wish to reorder spheres of interest in the most harmonious way, Europeans react with deep skepticism."[61]

Accompanying European anti-Americanism is a vitriolic new American anti-Europeanism. According to Robert Kagan and participants in an *American Enterprise* symposium, Europeans have an aversion to power, reject healthy and necessary competition, and lack virility—literal and metaphorical.[62] France and Germany belong to the "Axis of Weasel," according to a *New York Post* headline.[63] Germany criticizes America in pursuit of crass material interests and, in a return to "the old Berlin imperiousness," as part of a Franco-German design to dominate the small democracies of the European Union.[64] The repeated references to Euroweenies, wimps, and EU-nuchs suggest that Americans are no longer feminizing and paternalistically supervising Germans as they did in the first post–World War II decades. Rather, they are homosexualizing and marginalizing them.[65] In the 1950s, Americans presented themselves as pragmatic, optimistic, rational, and possessing technological cures for every imaginable problem, while Europeans were pessimistic, suspicious, and preferred philosophy to social science.[66] Now, it is the Americans who claim to be pessimistic realists, aware that reason will likely not prevail and prescribing military might, not nonmilitary technology, as the principal solution. Europe, foolish old Europe, opined Kagan, thinks it can live in "a self-contained world of laws and rules and transnational negotiation and cooperation … a post-historical paradise of peace and relative prosperity."[67]

The anger driving American anti-Europeanism has several roots. There is fear about the state of the global economy and America's place in it; for whatever Europe's economic problems, and they are many, the 1990s American boom, based on stock-market speculation and the high-tech sector, is over and, with it, the hope or fear that that would indeed be the model of the future.[68] There is, further, the American fear about what power the EU and the Euro will develop. The U.S. is confused about what it wants militarily from Europe—or rather angry that it cannot square the circle of wanting Europe to do more in terms of spending and deployment while having the U.S. make all the key decisions about goals and strategy.[69] There is frustration at possessing so much military might—the American defense budget is bigger than that of the next twenty biggest spenders and almost as much as the rest of the world combined[70]—and not being able to get everyone to defer and cooperate.

American anti-Europeanism also comes from the fact that in profound ways Kagan is correct: "America is from Mars and Europe is from Venus." Europeans learned different political lessons from the first half of the century. For America, World War II was the good war, a just war, the war it hopes to fight again instead of another Vietnam.[71] For Germany, World War II was a nightmare of destruction and guilt by which it is still haunted. Colin Powell could glibly have Picasso's *Guernica* covered over at the United Nations in early 2003 so as better to make his pitch for war against Iraq. Germany, which perpetrated Guernica and much worse and paid the price, cannot so easily mask the costs of war. Germany and much of Europe have built a different model of modernity, have a different sense about social justice, and are moving toward a post-national identity. More importantly, they no longer harbor imperial dreams—except perhaps in the case of Blair—even if they have not come to terms with their colonial pasts or their neocolonial presents. They seek a different kind of order, not one imposed by a single imperial capital and purchased at the price of perpetual warfare.

The Cold War and American economic, military, and political dominance in Germany led West Germany to stress America's commitment to international organizations and international law in the 1950s and 1960s and to ignore such interventions as Guatemala and Iran. Vietnam aroused anger on the part of the West German younger generation but did not generate a fundamental critique of the U.S. What's different now? Iraq was not just one more intervention, but rather the proclaimed opening of a war against "evildoers," against the barbarians, who are potentially everywhere. It was—and still is—a crusade, undertaken with messianic zeal and religious rhetoric. The war against Iraq (and then whom?) has been promoted by a state that insists no other state will be allowed to contest its military might or challenge its dominance in international politics; by a state that shuns international treaties and institutions—the ICC, the ABM treaty, the Kyoto Protocol, and CEDAW (the Convention to End All Forms of Discrimination Against Women), to name but a few—and sees international law as applying only to other, weaker states. Some claim America will create a different kind of empire, imposing a beneficent order on those it controls and occupies even as it rejects formal colonization. In any case, others maintain, like it or not there is no alternative to a Pax Americana.

Germany was not persuaded before the Iraq War, nor has it been convinced to commit military forces or substantial funds during the American occupation or after the nominal transfer of sovereignty. The "new" Europe of Britain, Poland, Italy, and Spain was eager to join the imperial adventure, despite widespread popular opposition, while the "old" Europe of Germany, France, and Holland refused.[72] Whether Germany, France, and other European states can develop a viable alternative to the American imperial dream remains to be seen. Whatever the final outcome, the reluctance of Germany to accept its assigned place in the new American world order, clearly shows the limits of its Americanization. It suggests the need to explore more fully the complex relationship of cultural Americanization and political anti-Americanism, and to understand more fully the German and European models of capitalist modernity, that both are and in profound ways are not like that of America.

Notes

1. Benjamin R. Barber, *Jihad vs. McWorld* (New York, 1995).

2. Thomas Friedman, *The Lexus and the Olive Tree* (New York, 1999).

3. James L. Watson, ed., *Golden Arches East: McDonald's in East Asia* (Stanford, 1997). Arjun Appadurai, *Modernity At Large: Cultural Dimensions of Globalization* (Minneapolis, 1996).

4. Henri Astier, "La maladie francaise," *TLS*, January 10, 2003.

5. For a longer discussion see Mary Nolan, *Visions of Modernity: American Business and the Modernization of Germany* (New York, 1994); and Nolan, "America in the German Imagination," in *Transactions, Transgressions, Transformations: American Culture in Western Europe and Japan,* eds. Heide Fehrenbach and Uta G. Poiger (New York, 2000), 5–10.

6. Anselm Doering-Manteuffel, *Wie westlich sind die Deutschen? Amerikanisierung und Westernisierung im 20. Jahrhundert* (Göttingen, 1999), 10–11, 23–36.

7. Ibid.

8. Volker Berghahn, "Conceptualizing the American Impact on Germany: West German Society and the Problem of Americanization," conference paper from "The American Impact on Western Europe: Americanization and Westernization in Transatlantic Perspective." GHI March 17–19, 1999 www.ghi-dc.org/conpotweb/westernpapers/berghahn.pdf

9. Kaspar Maase, "'Americanization,' 'Americanness' and 'Americanisms': Time for a Change in Perspective?," conference paper from "The American Impact on Western Europe: Americanization and Westernization in Transatlantic Perspective." GHI March 17–19, 1999 www.ghi-dc.org/conpotweb/westernpapers/maase.pdf

10. Maria Höhn, *GIs and Fräuleins: The German-American Encounter in 1950s West Germany* (Chapel Hill, 2002).

11. Dan Diner, *Feindbild Amerika: Über die Beständigkeit eines Ressentiments* (Munich, 2002). Berghahn, "Conceptualizing the American Impact," 9. Berghahn's recent book *America and the Intellectual Cold Wars in Europe* (Princeton, 2001) tells a more complex story of the decline of anti-Americanism in the older generation and the resurgence of new forms in the 1968ers.

12. Doering-Manteuffel and the Tübingen school of which he is the head. See conference paper from "The American Impact on Western Europe: Americanization and Westernization in Transatlantic Perspective." GHI March 17–19, 1999 www.ghi-dc.org/conpotweb/westernpapers for a sampling of this work.

13. Ann Laura Stoler, *Race and the Education of Desire: Foucault's History of Sexuality and the Colonial Order of Things* (Durham, 1995) and Frederick Cooper and Ann Stoler, eds., *Tensions of Empire: Colonial Cultures in a Bourgeois World* (Berkeley, 1997).

14. Axel Schildt and Arnold Sywottek, "'Reconstruction' and 'Modernization': West German Social History during the 1950s," in *West Germany under Construction: Politics, Society and Culture in the Adenauer Era,* ed. Robert G. Moeller (Ann Arbor, 1997), 413–43. Axel Schildt and Arnold Sywottek, eds., *Modernisierung im Wiederaufbau. Die Westdeutsche Gesellschaft der 50er Jahre* (Bonn, 1993).

15. Dean C. Tipps, "Modernization Theory and the Comparative Study of Societies: A Critical Perspective," *Comparative Studies in Society and History* 15 (June 1973):199–226.

16. Nolan, *Visions of Modernity* and *Amerikanisierung. Traum und Alptraum im Deutschland des 20. Jahrhunderts,* eds. Alf Lüdtke, Inge Marßolek, Adelheid von Saldern (Stuttgart, 1996).

17. Volker Berghahn, *The Americanisation of West German Industry, 1945–1973* (Cambridge, 1983). Heide Fehrenbach, *Cinema in Democratizing Germany: Reconstructing National Identity After Hitler* (Chapel Hill, 1995). Kaspar Maase, *BRAVO Amerika: Erkundungen zur Jugendkultur der Bundesrepublik in den fünfziger Jahren* (Hamburg,

1992). Uta Poiger, *Jazz, Rock, and Rebels: Cold War Politics and American Culture in a Divided Germany* (Berkeley, 2000). Heide Fehrenbach and Uta G. Poiger, eds., *Transactions, Transgressions, Transformations: American Culture in Western Europe and Japan* (New York, 2000).

18. Berghahn, *America and the Intellectual Cold Wars in Europe.* Petra Goedde, *GIs and Germans: Culture, Gender and Foreign Relations, 1945–1949* (New Haven, 2003).

19. Philipp Gassert, *Amerika im Dritten Reich: Ideologie, Propaganda und Volksmeinung, 1933–1945* (Stuttgart, 1997) and Hans Dieter Schäfer, *Über deutsche Kultur und Lebenswirklichkeit, 1933–1945* (Munich, 1982).

20. Dagmar Herzog is currently working on the 1968 generation, but historians have largely left it to political scientists and sociologists.

21. Höhn, *GIs and Fräuleins.* Maase, *BRAVO Amerika.* Poiger, *Transactions.*

22. Nolan, *Visions of Modernity.* Tilla Siegel and Thomas von Freyberg, *Industrielle Rationalisierung unter dem Nationalsozialismus* (Frankfurt, 1991). On the 1950s, see S. Jonathan Wiesen *West German Industry and the Challenge of the Nazi Past, 1945–1955* (Chapel Hill, 2001) and Christian Kleinschmidt, *Der produktive Blick: Wahrnehmung amerikanischer und japanischer Management-und Produktionsmethoden durch deutsche Unternehmer 1950–1985* (Berlin, 2002) as well as Berghahn, *The Americanization.*

23. Erica Carter, *How German Is She? Postwar West German Reconstruction and the Consuming Woman* (Ann Arbor, 1997).

24. Carter, *How German?* Höhn, *GIs and Fräuleins.* Poiger, *Transactions.*

25. Detlev Peukert, *The Weimar Republic: The Crisis of Classical Modernity* (London, 1991). Frank Bajohr, Werner Johe and Uwe Lohalm, eds., *Zivilisation und Barbarei: Die Widersprüchlichen Potentiale der Moderne* (Hamburg, 1991).

26. Michael Prinz and Rainer Zitelmann, eds., *Nationalsozialismus und Modernisierung* (Darmstadt, 1991).

27. Kleinschmidt, *Der produktive Blick,* 311–12.

28. Siegel and Freyburg, *Industrielle Rationalisierung.* Tilla Siegel, *Leistung und Lohn in der nationalsozialistischen "Ordnung der Arbeit"* (Opladen, 1989).

29. Stefan Kuhl, *The Nazi Connection: Eugenics, American Racism, and German National Socialism* (New York, 1994). Edwin Black, *IBM and the Holocaust: The Strategic Alliance between Nazi Germany and America's Most Powerful Corporation* (New York, 2001).

30. Gassert, *Amerika im Dritten Reich.* Schäfer, *Über deutsche Kultur und Lebenswirklichkeit.* Konrad H. Jarausch and Michael Geyer, *Shattered Past: Reconstructing German Histories* (Princeton, 2003), 289ff.

31. Susan Buck-Morss, *Dreamworld and Catastrophe: The Passing of Mass Utopia in East and West* (Cambridge, Mass., 2001).

32. Ina Merkel, *Utopie und Bedürfnis: Die Geschichte der Konsumkultur in der DDR* (Cologne, Weimar, Vienna, 1999).

33. Harry Harootunian, *Overcome by Modernity: History, Culture, and Community in Interwar Japan* (Princeton, 2000), xvi–xvii.

34. Kleinschmidt, *Der produktive Blick,* 24.

35. Elaine Tyler May, *Homeward Bound: American Families in the Cold War Era* (New York, 1988), 10–15.

36. Robert G. Moeller, *Protecting Motherhood: Women and Family in the Politics of Postwar West Germany* (Berkeley, 1993). Elizabeth Heineman, *What Difference Does A*

Husband Make? Women and Marital Status in Nazi and Power War Germany (Berkeley, 1999). Carter, *How German Is She?* 20–43, 109–13. Frank Biess "Survivors of Totalitarianism; Returning POWs and the Reconstruction of Masculine Citizenship in West Germany, 1945–1955," in *The Miracle Years,* 57–82.

37. Becky Conekin, "'Here is the Modern World Itself': The Festival of Britain's Representations of the Future," in *Moments of Modernity: Reconstructing Britain 1945–1964,* eds. by Becky Conekin, Frank Mort and Chris Waters (London, 1999), 228–33.

38. Barbara Einhorn, *Cinderella Goes to Market: Citizenship, Gender and Women's Movements in East Central Europe* (London, 1993). Susan Gal and Gail Kligman, *The Politics of Gender After Socialism* (Princeton, 2000).

39. Jennifer A. Loehlin, *From Rugs to Riches: Housework, Consumption and Modernity in Germany* (Oxford, 1999). RKW, *Rationalisierung in Schweden: Einflüsse und Stand der Anwendungen auf die Hauswirtschaft* (Berlin, 1956).

40. Gwendolyn Wright, "Good Design and 'The Good Life': Cultural Exchange in Post-World War II American Domestic Architecture," in *Across the Atlantic: Cultural Exchanges between Europe and the United States,* ed. Luisa Passerini (Brussels, 2000), 269–78.

41. Orvar Löfgren, "Materializing the Nation in Sweden and America," *Ethnos* 58, no. 3–4 (1993): 190.

42. Susan E. Reid and David Crowley, ed., *Style and Socialism: Modernity and Material Culture in Post-war Eastern Europe* (Oxford, 2000). Especially the essays by Crowley, Stokes, Gerchuk, and Reid.

43. Konrad Jarausch and Hannes Siegrist, eds., *Amerikanisierung und Sovietisierung in Deutschland 1945–1970* (Frankfurt/New York, 1997).

44. Several historians have noted that both East and West Germany in the late 1940s and 1950s recovered economically not through new technology but through more productive and extensive use of labor. Gerold Ambrosius, "Wirtschaftlicher Strukturwandel und Technikentwicklung," and Joachim Radkau, "'Wirtschaftswunder' ohne technologische Innovation? Technische Modernität in den 50er Jahrer," and Wolfgang Mühlfriedel, "Zur technischen Entwicklung in der Industrie der DDR in den 50er Jahren," all in *Modernisierung im Wiederaufbau,* 107–169. Less explored is that both economies inherited the same Nazi wage structures and rationalization that had begun in Weimar and were continued after 1933. In addition, some of what was imported into German industry in the 1950s as new Soviet methods was based on earlier Soviet appropriations of American methods.

45. Kate Brown, "Gridded Lives: Why Kazakhstan and Montana Are Nearly the Same Place," *American Historical Review* (February 2001):17–48.

46. Diethelm Prowe, "The 'Miracle' of the Political-Cultural Shift: Democratization Between Americanization and Conservative Reintegration," in *The Miracle Years,* 451–58 provides a useful introduction to these debates.

47. Wade Jacoby, "'Ization' by Negation? Occupation Forces, Codetermination, and Works Councils," http://www.ghi-dc.org/conpotweb/westernpapers/jacoby.pdf.

48. Claus Leggewie *Amerikas Welt: Die USA in unseren Köpfen* (Hamburg, 2000), 91–92, 109.

49. Vivien A. Schmidt, *The Futures of European Capitalism* (Oxford, 2002).

50. Diner, *Feindbild Amerika,* 8.

51. Stanley Hoffmann, "The High and the Mighty: Bush's National Security Strategy and the New American Hubris," *American Prospect,* January 13, 2003. Tony Judt, "Its Own Worst Enemy," *New York Review of Books,* August 15, 2002. Leggewie, *Amerikas Welt.* The Pew Global Attitudes Project's report *What the World Thinks in 2002* argues that "in general, antipathy toward the U.S. is shaped more by what it *does* in the international arena than by what it *stands for* politically and economically" (italics in original), 69. www.people-press.org.

52. Martin Blum, "Remaking the East German Post: *Ostalgie,* Identity, and Material Culture" *Journal of Popular Culture* 34, no. 3 (2001): 229–53.

53. Charles A. Kupchan, *The End of the American Era: U.S. Foreign Policy and the Geopolitics of the Twenty-First Century* (New York, 2002), 70, 156.

54. William Wallace, "Living with the Hegemon: European Dilemmas," in *Critical Views of September 11: Analyses from Around the World,* eds., Eric Hershberg and Kevin W. Moore (New York, 2002), 101.

55. Goedde. *GIs and Germans,* passim.

56. *The National Security Strategy of the United States of America,* September 2002. Anatol Levien, "The Push for War," *London Review of Books,* October 3, 2002. Hoffmann, "The High and the Mighty."

57. Michael Ignatieff, "The Burden," *New York Times Magazine,* January 5, 2003 www.newamericancentury.org. In light of the American occupation, Ignatieff has expressed more ambivalence about the American imperial project. "Mirage in the Desert," *New York Times Magazine,* June 27, 2004. Jay Tolson, "The American Empire: Is the U.S. Trying to Shape the World? Should It?" *U.S. News and World Report,* January 13, 2003.

58. Maria Mitchell, "Materialism and Secularism: CDU Politicians and National Socialism, 1945–1949," *Journal of Modern History* 67 (June 1995):255–77. Höhn, *GIs and Fräuleins.*

59. "Umfrage: Nur noch jeder dritte ein Christ," *Der Spiegel,* December 24, 1979, 70–78.

60. "Krieg aus Nächstenliebe," *Der Spiegel,* February 22, 2003, 95.

61. Ibid., 91.

62. Robert Kagan, "Power and Weakness," *Policy Review* 113 (June–July 2002). Karl Zinsmeister, "Old and in the Way," *The American Enterprise* 13 (December 2002).

63. *New York Post,* January 24, 2003.

64. William Safire, "'Bad Herr Dye,' *New York Times,* January 23, 2003.

65. Timothy Garton Ash, "Anti-Europeanism in America," *New York Review of Books,* February 13, 2003, for a review of the epithets and an assessment of the varied American forms of anti-Europeanism.

66. Berghahn, *America and the Intellectual Cold Wars.*

67. Kagan, "Power and Weakness."

68. Leggewie emphasizes how attractive elements of the 1990s American economy were to Germans, 87.

69. Kupchan, *The End of the American Era,* 119–59.

70. http://en.wikipedia.org/wiki/US_military_budget. http://www.globalissues .org/Geopolitics/ArmsTrade/Spending.asp

71. Marilyn Young, "Dreaming of World War II, Living with Vietnam," http:// www.nationinstitute.org/tomdispatch/index.mhtml?pid=354.

72. The sarcastic language of "old" and "new" is from Secretary of Defense Rumsfeld and provoked extremely hostile reactions in the German press and among German politicians. See, for example, *Frankfurter Rundschau*, January 23, 2003.

~

PART FOUR

SMOOTH SURFACES, MURKY DEPTHS

The Social and Cultural History of the Federal Republic

~

CHAPTER 11

The Radicalization that Never Was?

Refugees in the German Federal Republic

Ian Connor

Even before the end of the Second World War, German refugees began to flee from the eastern parts of the Reich as the Red Army moved westward, and by September 1950 over 7.8 million refugees and expellees had settled in the German Federal Republic. Some 4.4 million of these refugees were "National Germans" *(Reichsdeutsche)*—the former inhabitants of those areas east of the Oder-Neisse line that had belonged to Germany on 31 December 1937—while 3.4 million were "Ethnic Germans" *(Volksdeutsche)*—Germans who had lived as minority groups in foreign countries. Silesians (2,053,000) comprised the most numerous group of *Reichsdeutsche,* followed by East Prussians (1,347,000), Pomeranians (891,000) and East Brandenburgers (131,000). Sudeten Germans (1,912,000) were by far the largest group of *Volksdeutsche,* while smaller groups came from Austria, the Soviet Union, Poland, Yugoslavia, Rumania, Hungary, the former free city of Danzig, and the Baltic States of Latvia, Estonia, and Lithuania.[1] Some of these refugees had fled as Soviet troops advanced westward in the last few months of the war, but most had either been expelled after hostilities ended or compulsorily transferred as a result of the decisions taken at the Potsdam conference (17 July–2 August 1945).

The task of integrating more than 7.8 million refugees and expellees into German society was one of the most formidable facing Allied and German politicians and administrators after the Second World War. The newcomers were very unevenly distributed within the Western Zones of Germany, and, as Table 1 shows, three predominantly rural states—Bavaria, Lower Saxony, and Schleswig-Holstein—were most heavily overburdened by the refugee influx. In fact, between 1939 and 1950 Bavaria registered a population increase of 29.6 percent, Lower Saxony 49.7 percent, and Schleswig-Holstein no less than 63.3 percent.[2]

Table 1: Refugees in the West German States, September 1950

	Total Population	Total Refugees	% of Refugees in Population
Bavaria	9,184,466	1,937,297	21.1
Hesse	4,323,801	720,583	16.7
Württemberg-Baden	3,907,848	649,597	16.6
Bremen	558,619	48,183	8.6
Württemberg-Hohenzollern	1,183,748	113,554	9.6
Baden	1,338,629	98,375	7.3
Rhineland-Palatinate	3,004,752	152,267	5.0
North Rhine-Westphalia	13,196,176	1,331,959	10.1
Lower Saxony	6,797,379	1,851,472	27.2
Hamburg	1,605,606	115,981	7.2
Schleswig-Holstein	2,594,648	856,943	33.0
Totals	47,695,672	7,876,211	16.5

Source: Archiv für Christlich-Demokratische Politik (ACDP), Nachlass (NL) Nahm, 1-518-008/2, *10 Millionen Binnenwanderer in Westdeutschland;* Statistisches Landesamt Baden-Württemberg, ed., *Ergebnis der Volks- und Berufszählung vom 13. September 1950,* vol. 2 (Stuttgart, 1954), 2, 5, 40, 46, 52 and 58.

The economic prerequisites for integrating the refugees and expellees in postwar Germany could scarcely have been less auspicious. The food crisis prevailing in the Western Zones of Germany after the Second World War had a particularly serious impact on the newcomers, and, according to a public opinion poll conducted in the American Zone in the autumn of 1947, 80 percent of refugees as compared to 66 percent of the indigenous inhabitants believed that they were not getting enough to eat.[3] In the longer term, however, housing and unemployment proved to be more intractable problems. The overwhelming majority of the refugees had to be accommodated in the countryside, where employment opportunities were scarce, because the Allied bombing campaign had created grave housing shortages in the towns and cities where job prospects would have been more promising. This led to severe overcrowding in the countryside, and in Schleswig-Holstein 20,000 refugee families with at least three children had just one room at their disposal as late as March 1952.[4] Refugees located in isolated, outlying rural areas were most severely affected by the unemployment crisis following the Currency Reform of June 1948 and in Schleswig-Holstein more than a quarter of the working population was without a job in December 1949, more than four years after the end of the war.[5] It is clear, then, that the refugees and expellees represented a huge economic burden for the Western Zones of Germany in the early postwar years.

The integration of the refugees into postwar Germany has become a major area of historical research in the last fifteen years. During the 1950s a substantial number of studies of the refugee problem were undertaken, many by scholars who were themselves refugees or expellees.[6] These studies often reflected the political mood of the Cold War, focusing mainly on the expulsion of the refugees from their homelands[7] or the legislative measures introduced by the "political elites" to promote their integration into West German society. During the 1960s and 1970s historians paid little attention to the refugee problem since it was widely believed that the economic and social integration of the newcomers had been successfully achieved. In fact, in 1979 a West German government representative referred to the integration of the refugees in the German Federal Republic as "the true miracle of the post-war period."[8] However, research undertaken since the mid-1980s has indicated that the integration process was more problematic than previously assumed.[9] This research, which has focused on the refugees themselves and their interaction with the indigenous inhabitants, found expression in regional and, above all, local case studies.[10] Another characteristic of this work is its assessment of the refugees' impact on the areas where they had settled and their contribution to the modernization and industrialization of West German society.[11]

While these studies concentrated on the economic and social aspects of the refugee question, the *political* integration of the refugees and expellees has so far received surprisingly little attention from historians. In fact, Helga Grebing's book on Lower Saxony remains the only study which specifically addresses the relationship between the refugees and political parties.[12] The dearth of research on this aspect of the refugee problem may reflect the fact that the refugees and expellees from the East are regarded in Germany as firm supporters of the political system established after the Second World War. However, the situation looked very different to leading Allied and German politicians in the years directly after the war. Hans-Peter Schwarz argued on one occasion that German political attitudes in the early postwar period were characterized by deep fears that the new political state would collapse in the same way as the Weimar Republic had done and there is no doubt that the refugees and expellees were considered to be one of the most likely sources of political instability.[13] Confronted with the task of finding food, accommodation and employment for some 7.8 million newcomers at a time when the economy was still recovering from the war, the political elites viewed these new population groups not as likely upholders of the new democratic state but as an unpredictable, volatile force that represented a real threat to political stability in postwar Germany.

Set against this background, this chapter has three aims. First, to show that leading German and Allied politicians in the Western Zones of Germany regarded the refugees as a source of political radicalization and potential unrest in the early postwar years. Second, to assess, on the basis of the refugees' voting behavior, the extent to which the fears expressed by the political elites about the radicalization of the newcomers were justified. And third, to examine the factors that facilitated the integration of the refugees into one of the established political parties, the Christian Democratic Union (*Christlich-Demokratische Union,* CDU), in the 1950s.

In the early postwar years, then, the political elites in the Western Zones of Germany were deeply fearful about the political and ideological implications of the refugee problem. The assumption that economic distress would engender political radicalization was fundamental to the way in which leading Allied and German politicians perceived the refugee question. For example, a British Military Government official warned in September 1948 that, "unless action is taken to improve the condition of refugees … there will be a large body of discontented persons ... who will either rise in revolt or become facile tools in the hands of … political agitators."[14] Around the time the Federal Republic came into being, German politicians closely acquainted with the refugee problem voiced particular concern about the danger of unrest breaking out in refugee camps since these institutions were considered an ideal location for the growth of *organized* opposition to the new state.[15] They feared the emergence of irresponsible demagogues in the camps who would be able to exert control over the other occupants.

This latter fear, which presupposed the malleability of the camp population, sheds light on the attitude of the political elites to the so-called "masses." Implicit in the perception of the refugee problem by leading political figures was a deep mistrust of the political behavior of the ordinary population. They viewed the refugees not as rational, thinking human beings capable of making independent decisions but as "rootless," helpless individuals whose gullibility made them susceptible to the overtures of political agitators. Government ministers and officials responsible for integrating the refugees and expellees expounded frequently about the dangers of *Vermassung,*[16] a term that implied that, once the refugees had lost their individuality and identity, they would follow the majority view, irrespective of the merits of a particular issue. Politicians closely associated with the refugee problem also expressed concern about the newcomers' electoral behavior. It was feared that, unless the established parties such as the CDU and Social Democratic Party (*Sozialdemokratische Partei Deutschlands,* SPD) took measures to improve the refugees' economic predicament, the new population groups would become alienated from the established parties and driven into the arms of radical groups.[17]

A recurrent theme of the public statements and private correspondence of leading Allied and German political figures in the early postwar years was that the severe economic distress endured by the refugees and expellees would make them vulnerable to communism. They subscribed to the widely held view at that time that the decision of the Soviet Union and its allies to expel the refugees from their homelands was designed to create the economic chaos in the Western Zones of Germany on which communism was believed to thrive.[18] While the political elites acknowledged the absence of evidence indicating refugee support for the German Communist Party (*Kommunistische Partei Deutschlands,* KPD), they continued to express disquiet about the newcomers' susceptibility to left-wing radicalism even in the early 1950s. This preoccupation with the threat of communism reflected their view of the fickleness of the economically impoverished refugee masses who, it was argued, might give their support to any party, including the KPD, which promised to relieve their poverty.

At the same time, Allied and German officials believed that the refugees were also susceptible to the overtures of radical right-wing parties and fears of a nationalist revival increased steadily in 1948–49. For example, the refugee minister in Lower Saxony, Heinrich Albertz (SPD), a clergyman from Silesia, argued in 1949 that "the expellees from the East have reached the stage where they are receptive to fascist ideas."[19] Similarly, the British military governor, Brian Robertson, expressed the view in February 1949 that "the loss of self-respect which these people [the refugees] have undergone and the discontent which their mode of life engenders lays them open to the temptations of nationalist agitation and provides ready made material for the first unscrupulous leader that comes to power."[20] It is interesting to note that this statement does not imply any special ideological susceptibility to right-wing nationalist slogans on the part of the refugees and expellees even though some of the areas from which they originated ranked among the NSDAP's strongholds in the closing years of the Weimar Republic.[21] On the contrary, Robertson assumed that the refugees' severe economic deprivation and rootlessness made them likely to support any party which took up their cause, irrespective of the political views it represented.

In fact, in the early postwar years many leading political figures believed that the same groups of newcomers might defect to either the communist or nationalist camp. Guy Swope, the head of the Refugee Department of the United States High Commission for Germany, expressed the opinion at the beginning of 1950 that the new elements of population might unite behind "a militant, radical political leadership of the extreme right, or even the extreme left."[22] This remark, which suggests that he considered left- and right-wing radicalism to be essentially interchangeable, is consistent with the postwar interpretation about the rise of totalitarian movements in the 1930s. According to this view, the systems of Bolshevik Russia and Nazi Germany possessed many common features and were, in fact, variations of the same totalitarian model.

A brief analysis of the refugees' voting behavior in the early postwar years substantiates the fears of Allied and German politicians that the refugees would become alienated from the established political parties. The decision of the occupying authorities in 1946 to ban the formation of refugee organizations of a political nature compelled the refugees to channel their political energies into the mainstream parties and at the first state elections in Bavaria (December 1946), Schleswig-Holstein, and Lower Saxony (April 1947) the refugees voted in considerable numbers for the Social Democratic Party.[23] The newcomers' support for the SPD was based on the assumption that it would alleviate their suffering and poverty. However, these hopes did not materialize. In Schleswig-Holstein, for example, where the SPD took office in April 1947, the party was held responsible for the long delay in passing the Emergency Refugee Law and the failure to activate the resettlement program.[24] As a result, it lost the support of a significant number of refugees who switched their allegiance to their own independent candidates at the district elections held in October 1948.[25] This pattern was also discernible in other states, especially Bavaria, where independent refugee candidates polled 12.6 percent of the vote at the district elections held in the spring of 1948.[26] This illustrates that large numbers of newcomers were already alienated from the established political parties by the autumn of 1948.

However, while Allied and German politicians were undoubtedly justified in regarding the refugees as a source of political instability in the early postwar years, they misjudged the nature of the political threat posed by these new population elements. An assessment of the refugees' voting behavior between 1946 and 1950 revealed their immunity to the overtures of the KPD in spite of the severe economic deprivation they were suffering. In the Bundestag election of August 1949, the KPD polled well below the national average in the three main refugee states *(Flüchtlingsländer)*—4.1 percent in Bavaria and 3.1 percent in both Lower Saxony and Schleswig-Holstein. However, refugee support for the communists was even smaller than these figures would suggest, because the KPD invariably obtained its best results in constituencies where newcomers comprised a small proportion of the electorate and suffered its most ignominious defeats in constituencies heavily populated with refugees. This is nicely illustrated by the performance of the KPD in Bavaria at the first Bundestag election, where the party won 8.1 percent of the vote in constituencies where refugees comprised less than 14 percent of the population but just 1.9 percent in constituencies in which they made up more than 26 percent of the inhabitants.[27]

The hostility of the refugees and expellees to communism is confirmed by local examples. Although the KPD mounted a particularly vigorous propaganda campaign in refugee camps, the election results in municipalities *(Gemeinden)* dominated by such camps reaffirmed the newcomers' antipathy to left-wing radicalism. For example, the *Gemeinden* of Kaltenkirchen and Seedorf in the constituency of Segeberg-Neumünster (Schleswig-Holstein) returned votes of just 1.5 and 1.4 percent respectively for the KPD at the first

Bundestag election.[28] Similarly, support for the Communist Party in *Flücht-lingsgemeinden*—municipalities where refugees comprised at least 90 percent of the population—was negligible.[29] The newcomers also emphatically rejected the KPD in Lower Saxony even though the highly respected party leader, Kurt Müller, was himself a refugee who was appointed chairperson of the refugee committee of the Zonal Advisory Council in the British Occupation Zone.[30]

It is evident, then, that the refugees and expellees in the Western Zones of Germany roundly rejected communism in the early postwar period even though they were experiencing the severe economic distress on which left-wing radicalism was thought to thrive. Even before the Second World War, communism held little ideological attraction for the refugees from the eastern territories, and the KPD consistently polled below the national average in East Prussia, Pomerania, and Lower Silesia in the period 1924–33.[31] However, the refugees' antipathy toward the Communist Party can be attributed primarily to the events of 1944–45, when many fled or were expelled from their homes as Soviet troops advanced westward seeking to avenge the atrocities committed in the name of National Socialism. The refugees' hostility to left-wing radicalism was further reinforced by the outbreak of the Cold War and, in particular, the Berlin Blockade of 1948–49. In fact, there were reports during the Korean War of refugees who were living in remote border areas of Lower Saxony having their rucksacks packed in readiness to flee in the event of a communist invasion.

On the other hand, the refugees' voting behavior in 1949–50 does give some credence to the fears that they would be attracted to radical right-wing parties. This was particularly the case in Bavaria, where the Economic Reconstruction Union (*Wirtschaftliche Aufbau-Vereinigung*, WAV) attracted 14.4 percent of the vote at the first Bundestag election. It was led by Alfred Loritz, a highly controversial figure whose magnificent oratory prompted one political commentator to describe him as the "blond Hitler."[32] There is no doubt that the WAV's spectacular electoral success can be attributed mainly to the refugees, and, as Table 2 shows, the party's share of the vote generally increased in relation to the number of newcomers resident in a particular constituency. In the rural districts, where support for the WAV went up from 0.9 percent in the district elections of 1948 to 14.3 percent in August 1949, the refugee vote was undoubtedly the crucial factor.[33] The key to this support for the WAV was an electoral pact Loritz signed with the New Citizens' Alliance (*Neubürgerbund*), a refugee organization founded in Passau in 1948 by Günter Goetzendorff. According to this agreement, half of the WAV's candidates at the Bundestag election would be refugees.[34] Goetzendorff was a native of Silesia whose polemical speeches at election rallies rivalled those of Loritz himself, arguing on one occasion that he "would force the government to

Table 2: Refugee Composition and Support for the WAV in Bavaria
at the Bundestag Election of 1949

% of refugees in population	% voting WAV (all areas)	% voting WAV in rural districts
Under 14	14.1	12.1
14–18	12.2	11.0
18–22	13.3	13.1
22–26	15.4	15.3
Over 26	17.4	17.5
Bavaria	14.4	14.3

Source: Compiled from BSL, *Die erste Bundestagswahl*, 13.

introduce Equalization of Burdens legislation, even if it necessitated burning down houses in the process."[35] There is no doubt, then, that a vote for the WAV was not a vote for political moderation.

Further evidence of refugee support for the radical right came from Württemberg-Baden where Franz Ott, leader of the Emergency Association (*Notgemeinschaft*, NG), was directly elected to the Bundestag in 1949 by winning the constituency of Esslingen. Ott, a Catholic priest who had studied in Prague, was a gifted orator whose speeches fully justified the U.S. Military Government's concern about his "extreme nationalist" attitudes.[36] He had joined the NSDAP in 1940, and, significantly, some 80 percent of the NG's officials in Esslingen were also former Nazis.[37] It is clear, then, that some refugees did support nationalist demagogues such as Loritz, Goetzendorff, and Ott at the first Bundestag election.

The apprehension expressed by the political elites about the growth of organized opposition to the new state was justified by events following the relaxation of the ban on refugee political organizations. In January 1950, a refugee party, the Bloc of Expellees and Dispossessed Persons (*Block der Heimatvertriebenen und Entrechteten*, BHE), was founded, and, to the consternation of political observers inside and outside Germany, it won no less than 23.4 percent of the vote in a Landtag election in Schleswig-Holstein in July 1950. While the precise nature of the BHE varied from state to state,[38] it certainly bore some of the hallmarks of radical right-wing parties. Although its appeals were mainly directed at the refugees and expellees, it also curried favor with former Nazis, denigrating the denazification procedure as a communist-inspired plot to eliminate those elements most likely to resist a Soviet takeover of the German Federal Republic.[39] Its leaders included many prominent former Nazis such as Waldemar Kraft, who was arrested by the Aliies in 1945 in connection with his actions in Poland during the war,[40] and Theodor Oberländer, who retired from political life in 1960 following allegations that he had taken part in the massacre of Jews in the Ukraine in 1941.[41] By the end of 1951 the BHE was represented in as many as five of West Germany's state assemblies, often holding the balance of power between the established political parties. The frequently expressed fear by Allied and German politicians that the refugees would constitute an organized political force had become a reality.

There is also some evidence of unrest among the refugees in the early postwar years, occasionally accompanied by violence. The situation was particularly tense during the autumn of 1948 when the newcomers' economic plight deteriorated sharply as a result of the introduction of the *deutschmark*. Bavaria was the state most severely affected by the unrest which was instigated by Egon Herrmann, a notorious demagogue based in Dachau refugee camp who was regarded by Bavarian government ministers as a communist spy.[42] On 4 September 1948, the 1,117 occupants of Dachau refugee camp began a hunger strike in support of their demands for improved food rations, structural repairs to the camp, and an increase in pocket money.[43] The strike quickly spread to the mass camp at nearby Rosenheim, Munich-Allach transit camp, Winkl housing camp near Berchtesgaden and a camp in Augsburg.[44] Although the Bavarian government made concessions to the hunger strikers, the unrest continued and a protest meeting at Dachau camp on 2 October 1948, attended by the representatives of some thirty camps, made a series of radical demands, including the resignation of the Bavarian government and the dismissal of the state secretary for refugees, Wolfgang Jaenicke.[45] In November 1948, the tension at Dachau camp degenerated into violence when a car carrying government officials who had held negotiations with Herrmann was surrounded by a mob of refugees who threatened to lynch them.[46] Herrmann, who provoked this incident, was charged with a breach of the peace and sentenced to eleven months in prison.[47] Violent incidents involving refugees also took place in other states in the Western Zones of Germany. In September 1948, several thousand expellees broke up an SPD election meeting for refugees at Ludwigsburg. The speaker, Karl Gerbrich, was attacked and chased out of the hall by several hundred refugees before being rescued by the U.S. military police.[48] In an incident in North Rhine-Westphalia, also in September 1948, newcomers attacked and injured several policemen who attempted to arrest a leading refugee "for making a most outspoken speech against the Land authorities and Military Government."[49]

There is no doubt, then, that the refugees represented a source of political instability in the early postwar years. At the Bundestag election of 1949, a significant minority of the newcomers in the main *Flüchtlingsländer* snubbed the established political parties and voted instead for their own independent candidates or right-wing parties led by demagogues such as Loritz and Goetzendorff. The spectacular electoral successes gained by the BHE in the *Landtag* elections in Schleswig-Holstein, Bavaria, and Lower Saxony in 1950–51 reaffirmed the refugees' defection from the established parties. However, support for the BHE eroded steadily during the 1950s. At the Federal election in 1953, it polled just 5.9 percent and in 1957 failed to overcome the 5-percent hurdle. By this stage it was clear that many refugees had switched their allegiance to the Christian Democrats under Konrad Adenauer. But how can this development be explained? The last section of this chapter will seek to explore briefly the reasons for this development.

The growing identification of refugee voters with the CDU in the 1950s was partly due to ideological factors since refugees from the predominantly agricultural eastern territories were, generally speaking, conservative in outlook and therefore potential CDU/CSU voters. This was particularly true of the East Prussians and Pomeranians, the majority of whom settled in Lower Saxony and Schleswig-Holstein. Another positive feature of the CDU in the eyes of refugee voters was the party's reputation as a bulwark against communism. Christian democracy was considered to be synonymous with anti-communism and the flood of newcomers from the German Democratic Republic throughout the 1950s served as a constant reminder to the refugees of what they perceived as the evil of communism.

The Christian Democratic Union under the leadership of Konrad Adenauer adopted a number of strategies for attracting refugee voters. At the party's first national conference in Goslar in October 1950, it established an association for the refugees and expellees (Landesverband Oder-Neisse) and a separate association (Exil-CDU) for party members in the German Democratic Republic. The combined voting power of these two groups exceeded any of the other sixteen CDU Landesverbände.[50] Another important factor was the close relationship the CDU enjoyed with the compatriot societies (Landsmannschaften). In fact, the federal minister for expellees in Adenauer's first administration, Dr. Hans Lukaschek, also held the post of president of the Central Association of German Expellees (Zentralverband der vertriebenen Deutschen, ZvD).[51] Lukaschek's successor as ZvD President was Dr. Linus Kather, a lawyer from Königsberg (East Prussia) who campaigned tirelessly within the CDU on behalf of the refugees in the period 1946–54 and became known as the "father" of the Equalization of Burdens Law, passed in August 1952.[52] Adenauer's links with the Landsmannschaften were so close that he allowed them to determine Lukaschek's successor as expellee minister in 1953, even though he had personal misgivings about the National Socialist background of the candidate they proposed, Theodor Oberländer (BHE).[53]

Adenauer's decision to appoint Oberländer as expellee minister formed part of a wider strategy to cooperate closely with the BHE's leaders with the ultimate aim of integrating them and their supporters into the ranks of the CDU. In fact, from 1953 onward the CDU made regular payments to the BHE leadership in Bonn in order to retain its loyalty. Donations were also given to BHE politicians at Land level who were sympathetic to the CDU, and in December 1955 Hans-Adolf Asbach, the BHE's Chairperson in Schleswig-Holstein, was offered 60,000 deutschmarks a year on condition that his party continued its coalition with the CDU in Schleswig-Holstein.[54] Although these financial inducements to the BHE were obviously not made public, Adenauer's overtures to the BHE's leaders provoked deep indignation among CDU refugee politicians, and at a meeting of the party's Federal expellee committee shortly before the Bundestag election of September 1953, Hermann Eplee concluded that "we should have resigned from the CDU in 1947."[55] His colleague Linus Kather was equally bitter and left the party in June 1954. However, despite this dissent from within his own party, Adenauer's "integration policy" toward the BHE proved to be very successful. In fact, seven of the BHE's delegates in the Bundestag defected to the CDU in July 1955, including its two most prominent politicians, Oberländer and Kraft.[56] These developments undoubtedly contributed to the increasing support for the CDU among refugee voters during the second half of the 1950s.

There is no doubt, however, that the most important reason for the sharp increase in support for the CDU among refugee voters during the 1950s was that the Adenauer government gained the credit for the substantial improvement in the newcomers' economic and social position. Although the refugees' standard of living in 1960 was still lower than that of the indigenous inhabitants, it was significantly higher than when the first federal government took office in September 1949. In the period 1950–60, the proportion of refugees who were renting a property as tenants increased from 22.4 to 70.1 percent, while the number who were subtenants fell from 66.6 to 22.1 percent.[57] Similarly, the refugees' employment situation experienced a sharp improvement during the 1950s. While 546,000 expellees were out of work in December 1949, just 14,000 were registered as unemployed in 1961.[58]

The first Adenauer government took a number of measures to promote the economic integration of the refugees in the German Federal Republic. It introduced legislation to resettle newcomers from the main *Flüchtlingsländer* to states where overcrowding was a less serious problem or states such as North Rhine-Westphalia where the prospects for economic integration were more favorable. It initiated a major house building program and an average of 500,000 houses were constructed each year between 1955 and 1960.[59] However, the most important single piece of legislation was the Equalization of Burdens Law, not just because of its long-term material benefits for the refugees but also because of its psychological significance in convincing the newcomers that the government was taking their concerns seriously. This had important political effects and, as Ulrike Haerendel has argued, the introduction of the Equalization of Burdens Law "removed the expellees' main motivation to operate as an independent factor in West Germany's … parliamentary system."[60] It was therefore a major factor in the defection of refugee voters from the BHE to the CDU.

In conclusion, the German refugees and expellees from the East have long since been regarded as a source of political stability in the German Federal Republic. However, German politicians and Allied officials viewed them in a very different way in the early postwar years. They considered the newcomers to be a likely source of political radicalization and one prominent German politician predicted in 1947 that, if the refugees were not integrated into the Western Zones, they would become "a … potentially revolutionary element in our country."[61] An assessment of the refugees' voting behavior indicates that, while the political authorities were justified in regarding the newcomers as a source of political instability, they misperceived the nature of the threat posed by these new population elements. While successive elections refuted the authorities' fears that the refugees would be attracted to communism, the outcome of the first Bundestag election indicated the newcomers' susceptibility to the slogans of radical right-wing parties. The establishment of a refugee party in 1950 reaffirmed the authorities' apprehension that they would become an organized force in postwar German politics. In fact, it was not until the refugees started to enjoy the benefits of the "Economic Miracle" that they began to identify with the established political parties, especially the CDU. The British military governor, Brian Robertson, maintained in 1949 that "if the economic integration [of the refugees] can be solved, … political … considerations [will] lose much of their importance"[62] and developments during the 1950s confirmed the accuracy of this prognosis.

Notes

I would like to thank Professor Jonathan Wiesen for his invaluable comments on an earlier version of this chapter. I am also indebted to Professor Volker Berghahn for his support and encouragement over many years. In addition, I would like to acknowledge the generous financial support I received from the German Academic Exchange Service which enabled me to undertake the research on which this chapter is based.

1. Statistisches Bundesamt Wiesbaden, ed., *Statistisches Taschenbuch über die Heimatvertriebenen in der Bundesrepublik Deutschland und in West-Berlin* (Wiesbaden, 1953), 3.

2. Bayerisches Statistisches Landesamt, ed., *Volks- und Berufszählung am 13. September 1950 in Bayern. Volkszählung. Teil1: Gliederung der Wohnbevölkerung*, Beiträge zur Statistik Bayerns, no. 171, 25.

3. Quoted in R. Messerschmidt, *Aufnahme und Integration der Vertriebenen und Flüchtlinge in Hessen 1945–1950. Zur Geschichte der hessischen Flüchtlingsverwaltung* (Wiesbaden, 1994), 140–41.

4. *Die Neue Zeitung*, 6 March 1952, in Archiv für Christlich-Demokratische Politik (ACDP), Nachlaß (NL) Nahm, 1–518–008/2.

5. Bundesministerium für Arbeit, ed., *Entwicklung und Ursachen der Arbeitslosigkeit in der Bundesrepublik Deutschland 1946–1950* (Bonn, 1950), 6.

6. For example, most of the thirty-eight contributors to the massive three volume publication in 1959 entitled *Die Vertriebenen in Westdeutschland*, edited by Eugen Lemberg and Friedrich Edding, were themselves refugees or expellees. For further details, see Volker Ackermann, *Der "echte" Flüchtling. Deutsche Vertriebene und Flüchtlinge aus der DDR 1945–1961* (Osnabrück, 1995), 24.

7. See, for example, the voluminous study of the refugees' expulsion from their homelands: Theodor Schieder, ed., *Dokumentation der Vertreibung der Deutschen aus Ost-Mitteleuropa*, 8 vols. (Bonn, 1953–61).

8. Quoted in F.J. Bauer, "Zwischen 'Wunder' und Strukturzwang. Zur Integration der Flüchtlinge und Vertriebenen in der Bundesrepublik Deutschland," *Aus Politik und Zeitgeschichte* 32 (1987), 23.

9. The pioneering work was published by Paul Lüttinger in 1986. His empirical study of the economic and social position of the refugees and expellees in the early 1970s revealed that, in times of economic recession, older refugees, in particular, were more susceptible to unemployment than the native population, while the proportion of refugees working as unskilled labourers was higher than among the indigenous inhabitants. See, Paul Lüttinger, "Der Mythos der schnellen Integration. Eine empirische Untersuchung zur Integration der Vertriebenen und Flüchtlinge in der Bundesrepublik Deutschland bis 1971" *Zeitschrift für Soziologie* 15 (1986), 20–36.

10. See, for example, Andreas Lüttig, *Fremde im Dorf. Flüchtlingsintegration im westfälischen Wewelsburg 1945–1958* (Essen, 1993).

11. See, for instance, Paul Erker, "Revolution des Dorfes? Ländliche Bevölkerung zwischen Flüchtlingszustrom und landwirtschaftlichem Strukturwandel," in *Von Stalingrad zur Währungsreform. Zur Sozialgeschichte des Umbruchs in Deutschland*, eds. M. Broszat, K.-D. Henke and H. Woller (Munich, 1989).

12. Helga Grebing, *Flüchtlinge und Parteien in Niedersachsen. Eine Untersuchung der politischen Meinungs- und Willensbildungsprozesse während der ersten Nachkriegszeit 1945–1952/53* (Hanover, 1990).

13. H.-P. Schwarz, "Die ausgebliebene Katastrophe. Eine Problemskizze zur Geschichte der Bundesrepublik," in *Den Staat denken. Theodor Eschenburg zum Fünfundachtzigsten*, ed. Hermann Rudolph (Berlin, 1990), 151–74.

14. Public Record Office (PRO), FO1013/368, Matheson (Regional Governmental Office) to Chief Manpower Officer, 27 September 1948.

15. For example, in a letter to George Shuster, U.S. State Commissioner for Bavaria, Wolfgang Jaenicke, Bavarian State Secretary for Refugees, stated that it was "unnecessary to elaborate on the political dangers associated with people constantly living in a very confined space." See, Jaenicke to Shuster, 2 September 1950. Copy submitted to a meeting of the Bavarian government's committee for refugee questions, 15 September 1950.

16. For instance, an official in the refugee administration in Hesse asserted in October 1948 that, among the refugees, " the danger of *Vermassung*, as well as moral and political anarchy is acute." Quoted in York Winkler, *Flüchtlingsorganisationen in Hessen 1945–1954. BHE—Flüchtlingsverbände—Landsmannschaften* (Wiesbaden, 1998), 22.

17. For example Willibald Mücke, co-chairperson of the main committee of refugees and expellees in Bavaria, commented in March 1948 that "the overwhelming majority of the expellees reject the existing political parties." See, W. Mücke, *Drei Jahre deutsches Flüchtlingsproblem* (unpubl. ms., 1948), 5, in, Bayerisches Hauptstaatsarchiv (BHStA), MArb 8005a 1752.

18. For instance, Bavaria's Minister-President Hans Ehard argued at a CSU election meeting in October 1948 that "the expulsion had been planned in Moscow in the expectation that the Germans would tear themselves apart in their ... overcrowded rump state." *Fränkischer Tag*, 19 October 1948, in Kriegsarchiv Munich (KA), Bayerische Innenpolitik, 1948/22.

19. J. Mosler, "Zwischen den Parteien. Um die politische Eingliederung der Ostvertriebenen" *Christ Unterwegs* (November 1949): 12.

20. Quoted in Rainer Schulze, "Growing Discontent: Relations between the Native and Refugee Populations in a Rural District in Western Germany after the Second World War," *German History* 7, no. 3 (1989), 347.

21. This was particularly true of East Prussia and Pomerania. See, Walter Ziegler, ed., *Die Vertriebenen vor der Vertreibung. Die Heimatländer der deutschen Vertriebenen im 19. und 20. Jahrhundert: Strukturen, Entwicklungen, Erfahrung*, 2 vols. (Munich, 1999), vol. 1, 166 and 278.

22. *Die Neue Zeitung*, 15 March 1950, in Bundesarchiv (BA), NL Jaenicke, 30.

23. See H. Grebing, "Politischer Radikalismus und Parteiensystem. Die Flüchtlinge in der niedersächsischen Nachkriegspolitik," in *Rechtsradikalismus in der politischen Kultur der Nachkriegszeit. Die verzögerte Modernisierung in Niedersachsen*, ed. Bernd Weisbrod (Hannover, 1995), 261–63; Ian Connor, "Flüchtlinge und die politischen Parteien in Bayern 1945–50" *Jahrbuch für deutsche und osteuropäische Volkskunde* 38 (1995), 146–47. The SPD leadership in Schleswig-Holstein believed that its victory at the *Landtag* election on 20 April 1947 "was to a large extent due to the refugees." See, Archiv der sozialen Demokratie (AdsD), Landesverband (LV) Schleswig-Holstein (S-H), 1139, Report on a Meeting of the SPD Party Executive, 10 September 1947, 4.

24. See, for instance, AdsD, LV S-H, 1139. Minutes of the meeting of the SPD party executive in Schleswig-Holstein, 1 April 1948. Paul Dölz reported that "there was a lot of dissatisfaction with the Emergency Refugee Law and the fact that its supplementary provisions have still not appeared."

25. In Plön, for example, where refugee candidates won 19.7 percent of the vote, the SPD's share of the vote was 12.1 percent lower than at the Landtag election of 1947. See AdsD, LV S-H, 129, *Schleswig-Holsteinische Zeitung*, 26 October 1948.

26. Compiled from Bayerisches Statistisches Landesamt (BSL), ed., *Die erste Bundestagswahl in Bayern am 14. August 1949*, Beiträge zur Statistik Bayerns, no. 150, 36–43.

27. Ibid., 13

28. AdsD, LV S-H, 79, *Statistische Untersuchungen über die Bundestagswahl in Schleswig-Holstein (Flüchtlinge)*, 3 and *Schleswig-Holsteinische Volkszeitung*, 16 August 1949.

29. At the Bavarian Landtag election of November 1950, the KPD won 0.7 percent of the vote in Bubenreuth (Rural District of Erlangen), 0.8 percent in Geretsried (Rural District of Wolfratshausen), 1.1 percent in Traunreuth (Rural District of Traunstein) and 1.4 percent in Waldkraiburg (Rural District of Mühldorf am Inn). See, BSL, *Wahl zum Bayerischen Landtag am 26. November 1950*, 17, 24, 27, 100.

30. Grebing, "Politischer Radikalismus und Parteiensystem," 261.

31. Alfred Milatz, "Das Ende der Parteien im Spiegel der Wahlen 1930 bis 1933," in *Das Ende der Parteien 1933. Darstellungen und Dokumente,* eds. Erich Matthias and Rudolph Morsey (Düsseldorf, 1979), 778.

32. *Die Zeit,* 4 August 1949.

33. In fact, the WAV captured over 20 percent of the vote in sixteen districts it had not even contested in 1948 and, significantly, each one had an above-average refugee population. See BSL, *Die erste Bundestagswahl,* 13, and BHStA, MArb 27, *Statistischer Informationsdienst,* No. 101.

34. Franz Neumann, *Der Block der Heimatvertriebenen und Entrechteten 1950–1960. Ein Beitrag zur Geschichte und Struktur einer politischen Interessenpartei* (Meisenheim, 1968), 17.

35. BA, Z18,119, *Radikalisierung der Vertriebenen. Kirchliche Hilfsstelle stellt beunruhigende Syptome fest,* 8 February 1950.

36. Sylvia Schraut, *Flüchtlingsaufnahme in Württemberg-Baden 1945–1949. Amerikanische Besatzungsziele und demokratischer Wiederaufbau im Konflikt* (Munich, 1995), 440.

37. Ibid., 439.

38. Helga Grebing concludes that, while the BHE in Bavaria and Lower Saxony had "nationalist" leaders, the party in Lower Saxony pursued "national but not nationalist policies." See, Grebing, "Politischer Radikalismus und Parteiensystem," 266.

39. *Sonderrundschreiben Nr. 1 des Landesverbandes Bayern des BHE,* 14 November 1950. Quoted in Neumann, *Der Block der Heimatvertriebenen und Entrechteten,* 327–28.

40. Michael L. Hughes, *Shouldering the Burdens of Defeat: West Germany and the Reconstruction of Social Justice* (Chapel Hill and London, 1999), 136.

41. Pol O'Dochartaigh, *Germany since 1945* (Basingstoke and New York, 2004), 53.

42. Bavarian Minister-President, Hans Ehard, noted in September 1948 that he had received reports of refugee camp occupants being threatened with violence if they refused to join communist-backed "campaign committees." *Süddeutsche Zeitung,* 30 September 1948 in KA, Bayerische Innenpolitik, 1948/22a.

43. Institut für Zeitgeschichte (IfZ), RG 260 OMGUS, 1948/145/5, Van Wagoner (Head of the Office of Military Government for Bavaria, OMGB) to General Lucius Clay, 7 September 1948.

44. *Süddeutsche Zeitung,* 7 September 1948, in KA, Bayerische Innenpolitik, 1948/22a.

45. IfZ, RG 260 OMGUS, 1948/146/1, George Jacobsen (U.S. Army Dachau) to OMGB, 5 October 1948.

46. E. Pscheidt, "Die Flüchtlingslager," in *Integration und Neubeginn. Dokumentation über die Leistung des Freistaats Bayern und des Bundes zur Eingliederung der Wirschaftsbetriebe der Vertriebenen und Flüchtlinge und deren Beitrag zur wirtschaftlichen Entwicklung des Landes,* 2 vols., ed. Friedrich Prinz (Munich, 1984), I:267–68.

47. *Der Neue Tag,* 31 March 1949, in, KA, Bayerische Innenpolitik, 1949/50.

48. Archiv des Deutschen Liberalismus der Friedrich-Naumann Stiftung, Gummersbach (ADL), FDP Britische Zone, 8, Dr. Fritz Oellers to Franz Blücher, 13 September 1948.

49. PRO, FO 1013/368, Matheson (Regional Governmental Office) to Chief Manpower Officer, 27 September 1948.

50. Frank Bösch, "Die politische Integration der Flüchtlinge und Vertriebenen und ihre Einbindung in die CDU," in *Zwischen Heimat und Zuhause. Deutsche Flüchtlinge und Vertriebene in (West-) Deutschland 1945–2000*, eds. Rainer Schulze, Reinhard Rohde and Rainer Voss (Osnabrück, 2001), 116.

51. Marion Frantzioch, *Die Vertriebenen. Hemmnisse, Antriebskräfte und Wege ihrer Integration in der Bundesrepublik Deutschland. Mit einer kommentierten Bibliographie* (Berlin, 1987), 145

52. Sabine Lee, "CDU Refugee Policies and the Landesverband Oder/Neiße: Electoral Tool or Instrument of Integration?" *German Politics* 8, no. 1 (April 1999), 145.

53. Bösch, "Die politische Integration der Flüchtlinge," 121–22.

54. Ibid., 119.

55. ACDP, 1–377–6/1, Linus Kather and Hermann Eplee to Konrad Adenauer, 22 August 1953.

56. Bösch, "Die politische Integration der Flüchtlinge," 117.

57. Frantzioch, *Die Vertriebenen*, 204.

58. Statistisches Amt des Vereinigten Wirtschaftsgebietes, ed. *Statistische Unterlagen zum Flüchtlingsproblem* 5, (28 April 1950), and Bauer, "Zwischen 'Wunder' und Strukturzwang," 23.

59. Karl Führer, *Mieter, Hausbesitzer, Staat und Wohnungsmarkt. Wohnungsmangel und Wohnungszwangswirtschaft in Deutschland 1914–1960* (Stuttgart, 1995), 44.

60. Ulrike Haerendel, "Die Politik der 'Eingliederung' in den Westzonen und der Bundesrepublik Deutschland. Das Flüchtlingsproblem zwischen Grundsatzentscheidungen und Verwaltungspraxis," in *Vertriebene in Deutschland. Interdisziplinäre Ergebnisse und Forschungsperspektiven*, eds. Dirk Hoffmann, Marita Krauss and Michael Schwartz (Munich, 2000), 118.

61. Quoted in Bundesarchiv and Institut für Zeitgeschichte, ed., *Akten zur Vorgeschichte der Bundesrepublik Deutschland 1945–1949*, 5 vols. (Munich and Vienna, 1979), II:557.

62. Quoted in Rainer Schulze, "The Struggle of Past and Present in Individual Identities: The Case of German Refugees and Expellees from the East," in *Coming Home to Germany? The Integration of Ethnic Germans from Central and Eastern Europe in the Federal Republic*, eds. David Rock and Stefan Wolff (New York and Oxford, 2002), 40.

CHAPTER 12

Germany's Special Path?

Economic Sciences and Politics in the Federal Republic, 1945–1970

Alexander Nützenadel

The postwar economic development of West Germany has often been described as a "special" or even as an "aberrant case" among Western industrial nations.[1] Compared to other countries, the Federal Republic was long characterized not only by extremely stable social and political conditions, but also by particularly high and sustained economic growth. As a result, since the 1950s West Germany's "economic miracle" has received considerable attention.[2] In search of an explanation for the exceptional growth, many studies have stressed the emergence of economic liberalism after 1945. Unlike the French system of *planification economique,* based on public investment steering or the Keynesian concepts of full employment adopted by Great Britain or the United States, German postwar governments reduced the role of the state as an economic agent.[3] This is often attributed to the influence of the neoliberal school around Walter Eucken and Franz Böhm that dominated economic thinking in West Germany after 1945 and reestablished the free-trade and non-interventionist ideals of the nineteenth century. According to the neoliberals, the state should guarantee competitive markets through free trade and anti-cartel legislation, while abstaining from intervention in the economic process. Social stability was supposed to be achieved through limited redistribution of income by progressive taxation and some basic welfare provisions. In the framework of the "social market economy," Keynesian and other regulatory ideas could hardly gain ground.[4]

Yet the picture of German economic "exceptionalism"[5] after 1945 has been thrown into question by recent literature. On the one hand, explanations for Germany's growth now place less emphasis on neoliberalism's contribution than on the favorable international context. Christoph Buchheim and Rheinhard Neebe have demonstrated how quickly West Germany was integrated into world markets after 1945 and how important this was for its economic recovery. Barry Eichengreen has pointed out that the outstanding growth of the "Golden Age" was determined not by domestic factors alone and depended largely on a favorable international framework provided by the Marshall Plan, the European Payments Union, the GATT, and the monetary system of Bretton Woods. This interpretation is indirectly confirmed by Ludgar Lindlar's comparative analysis of postwar economic growth. According to Lindlar, Germany's growth performance was part of a general process of economic and technological catching-up with the United States that also affected other European countries after 1945.[6]

On the other hand, historians are also increasingly aware of the degree to which West German elites looked abroad for inspiration on economic matters. Volker Berghahn has shown that in postwar decades West Germany became more open to American economic and industrial culture.[7] While Berghahn's concept of "Americanization" has inspired a series of studies on the postwar development of West German industry,[8] we know very little about the transformations of national economic policy in this period. Most studies have concentrated on the immediate postwar years,[9] whereas the 1950s and 1960s have received scant attention from historians.

This article explores the changing relationship between state and economy, arguing that German reception of international—and especially Anglo-American—economic thought has played a crucial role in this process. The traditional "Nationalökonomie," itself strongly influenced by the German "Historical School," disappeared, while modern macroeconomics based on mathematical and statistical instruments rapidly gained ground. This had a strong impact on economic policy, especially on the role of the state in securing economic growth and stability.

German *Nationalökonomie* and the Challenges of American *New Economics*

It is usually argued that West German economic sciences were almost entirely dominated by the neoliberal Freiburg School around Walter Eucken, Alexander Rüstow, Wilhelm Röpke, and Franz Böhm.[10] This is accurate insofar as this group had a deep impact in the 1945–49 period, when the Federal Republic's basic economic order was being designed. Ludwig Erhard and Alfred Müller-Armack, the most prominent figures in economic policy during the postwar years, were both impressed by Eucken's and Böhm's ideas. Moreover, the Freiburg School's combination of economic liberalism and anti-communism was also supported by the American authorities in West Germany.

From the middle of the 1950s, however, the Freiburg School's influence began to fade, especially in the field of economic sciences. One reason was that the first generation of this group was no longer alive or had retired from their academic position. Indeed, three of the most prominent neoliberals—Walter Eucken, Alfred Lampe, and Leonhard Miksch—died during or shortly after the war. For the rest, Alexander Rüstow was until the mid-1950s an influential professor at Heidelberg, but considered himself primarily a sociologist, while Franz Böhm taught at the law faculty in Frankfurt. Others, such as Friedrich A. Lutz and Wilhelm Röpke, refused to return to Germany after the war.

A second reason for the Freiburg School's fading influence was that institution building was almost complete by the middle of the 1950s. According to the neoliberal theories, the role of the state was mainly to set the legal framework for efficient markets. The market process itself should not be influenced by state activity. This position became less and less tenable, since moderate signs of monetary instability became visible in West Germany around 1955/56. Even though these symptoms were not really disturbing, they led to a fierce debate about the future course of economic policy.[11] These debates were stimulated by several publications on the Great Depression in Germany. In most cases, these publications were not merely of historical interest, but had also a political background as the Depression was interpreted as an obvious example of government failure.[12] It was widely accepted that the devastating consequences of the Depression could have been prevented, or at least mitigated, by enacting a consistent set of counter-cyclical measures. Chancellor Heinrich Brüning's refusal to adopt such measures was not only considered a fatal error in economic policy, but was also held responsible for the internal disintegration of the Weimar Republic and, ultimately, the rise of Hitler. The historical experience of the crisis was not the main reason for the reorientation in economic policy, but it had an important argumentative function in discrediting the idea of the self-healing power of a free market order.

Thirdly, the concepts of the Freiburg School seemed increasingly old-fashioned in the light of the Anglo-American "New Economics," which spread rapidly in the Western world after 1945.[13] Keynesian ideas influenced not only economic policy, but also dominated theoretical debates in most countries. Apart from their political implications, Keynesian macroeconomics with their strong inclination toward formal model-building and quantitative analysis were hardly compatible with the more traditional methodology of the Freiburg School, which considered econometric analysis and forecasts as an instrument of socialist planning.

From the early 1950s onward, interest in Anglo-American economics grew rapidly at German universities and research institutes.[14] A general orientation toward Western—especially American—cultural and scientific trends, combined with the fear that German universities could fall behind international standards, explains much of this development. As early as 1950, an introduction to Keynes theory was available, written by Andreas Paulsen, professor of economics at the Free University of Berlin.[15] Moreover, American textbooks such as Paul Samuelson's *Economics* were translated into German and helped to disseminate the ideas and methods of American economic thought among students and scholars in the Federal Republic.[16] Keynesianism was not adopted in the pure and original form expounded in the *General Theory* and other publications of John Maynard Keynes, but rather in the form of the "Neoclassical synthesis," integrating Keynesian and neoclassical instruments, developed by scholars such as Paul Samuelson and John Hicks.[17] Thus it was the more moderate, American version of Keynesianism that spread in West Germany.

This is manifest in the most authoritative economic textbook of the postwar years, a three-volume work written by Erich Schneider that became the "bible" of economics for a whole generation of German students.[18] As a former student of Joseph Schumpeter and professor at the University of Aarhus in Denmark between 1936 and 1945, Schneider was deeply influenced by Anglo-American approaches. As a professor at the University of Kiel and, since 1961, director of the Institute of World Economics, Schneider had a great impact on the reorientation of economic theory in West Germany during the postwar era.

Indeed, a small group of economists who had emigrated during the Third Reich played an important role in connecting West German economics to the international mainstream after 1945. This was the case for Fritz Baade, who had been teaching for many years first in Turkey and then in the United States before becoming director of the Kiel Institute of World Economics. Other economists did not return permanently to Germany but reestablished their previous connections with the German scientific community. For example, Carl Landauer, professor of economics in Berkeley, acted as visiting professor at the newly founded Free University of Berlin in 1949/50. Fritz Karl Mann, professor at the American University in Washington, taught regularly at Cologne University where he had been a professor prior to 1933. Gerhard Colm came to Germany in 1946 as an advisor of the American Military Administration. During the 1950s, he regularly published in West German academic journals, gave dozens of talks, and deeply influenced reforms of budget policy in the Federal Republic. This goes also for Richard A. Musgrave. His publications, some translated into German, had a strong impact on the theory of public finance and on the implementation of new budget planning policies.[19]

But there was another crucial ingredient to the rapid spread of Anglo-American economic theory. An increasing number of German economists participated in academic exchange programs with North American universities after 1945. In most cases, these were researchers early in their careers, often more open to new approaches than their established older colleagues. Many of them—including Walther G. Hoffmann, Herbert Giersch, Heinz Sauermann, Wilhelm Krelle, and Carl Christian von Weizsäcker—were impressed by what they had learned on the other side of the Atlantic, and they often became advocates of new economic ideas within the German economic establishment.

The Rise of Economic Experts

The postwar era was characterized not only by a rapid growth of economic sciences at universities and research institutes, but also by the new role of the economist in politics and public life. In the United States, the New Deal years are usually regarded as the beginning of a new relationship between politics and economic expertise.[20] The "Washington economics industry" expanded rapidly as the demand of both state and military agencies for economic and statistical information grew.[21] During and after World War II, new economic advisory councils and think tanks emerged. With the creation of the "Council of Economic Advisors to the President" in 1946, economists were officially involved in the policy process.

This new relationship between economic knowledge and politics was not limited to the United States.[22] In West Germany too, the postwar period saw economists enjoying growing influence in public policy-making. Already in January 1948, an Economic Council was established on the advice of the bi-zonal economic authority. The deliberations and statements of this body exerted a strong influence on the economic and political discussions of the Federal Republic's early years.[23]

Moreover, semipublic research institutes and think tanks such as the Kiel Institute for World Economy, the *Institut für Wirtschaftsforschung* in Berlin (the former *Institut für Konjunkturforschung*), and the *Ifo-Institut* in Munich expanded considerably and began to engage in market research, economic statistics, and forecasts. The new role of these research and advisory institutions was emphasized by the rising importance of econometric studies, while at most German universities a theoretical approach to economics still prevailed.[24] The *Ifo-Institut* produced a monthly economic report and forecast, based on newly developed methods of business surveys, while the *Institut für Wirtschaftsforschung* focused primarily on the development of a national accounting system.[25] The growing importance of applied economics corresponded with an increasing political demand for economic expertise and statistical forecasting. In 1950, the Advisory Council of the Ministry of Economics decided to transfer the task of reporting on the economic situation to research institutes.[26] Subsequently, the six largest of these institutes produced half-yearly joint reports on the economic situation that became an authoritative source of information for politicians and private enterprises alike.[27]

The enlargement of economic policy counseling, national accounting and statistical forecasting in the postwar period was due to both domestic and international factors. One the one hand, there was increasing demand for economic data coming from both the private and the public sectors. Corporations were highly interested in market research and forecasting in order to calculate prices and sales potential, while ministries and other state agencies required macroeconomic data for public income calculation, social policy, or infrastructure planning. On the other hand, statistical conventions of international institutions such as the OEEC/OECD forced Germany to adopt the modern national accounting and income analysis that had been developed primarily by American and British statistical agencies during the war.[28]

Even more important was the establishment of the "Council of Economic Experts" *(Sachverständigenrat zur Begutachtung der gesamtwirtschaftlichen Entwicklung)* in 1963. The idea of a centrally organized advisory committee had been in discussion since 1956. The strong opposition of Chancellor Adenauer, who was suspicious about giving too much power to the "professors" and who preferred a more political organ such as the "Reichswirtschaftsrat" of the Weimar Republic, obstructed the establishment of the *Sachverständigenrat* for several years.[29] The council owed much to the American model of policy consultancy, while being politically more independent than the U.S. Council of Economic Advisors founded after World War II.[30] The *Sachverständigenrat* was assigned the task of periodically evaluating the situation with regard to the four goals of macroeconomic stability (full employment, low inflation, external balance and steady growth). The council had to draw up an annual report, including a forecast of the following year's likely economic trends, and to compile special reports whenever the economic situation called for a thorough analysis of an important policy issue. Maladjustments and tensions between aggregate demand and supply had to be pointed out together with the means of avoiding or correcting them. The "five wise men," as they were popularly called, became an extremely authoritative voice and exerted a strong influence on economic debates and political decision-making.[31]

The institutional enlargement of professional macroeconomic counseling was associated with changing concepts of policy-making. Boundaries between economic sciences and economic policy became more permeable. Prominent researchers supported not only a "scientifically based policy," but also a "complete de-ideologization, de-politicization, objectification" of economic policy.[32] The notion that the economic process could be rationally planned and scientifically projected gained tremendous ground in this period. It was part of a widespread optimism associated with planning and progress, culminating in the assumption that political decision-making could be entirely rationalized and supplanted by scientific methods.

The Politics of Economic *Growthmanship*

While economic theory converged in the Western world after 1945—and convergence was almost identical with Americanization—there was a similar development discernible in the field of economic policy. The idea that the state had to guarantee economic growth and stability by fiscal and monetary interventions became ubiquitous. This was the Keynesian consensus of the "Golden Age," even though in West Germany these principles were adopted a few years later than in Great Britain or the United States.

The "Law for the Promotion of Economic Stability and Growth," which was implemented in June 1967 with the support of a broad majority of Social Democrats and Conservatives, has often been characterized as the "Magna Carta" of Keynesianism and as a watershed between a neoliberal and a Keynesian orientation in economic policy.[33] But it is important to note that the law was the result of a change of direction in economic policy that had begun many years before. The SPD had presented a "Bill for the Promotion of a Stable Economic Growth" to the Federal Parliament as early as June 1956.[34] It was designed to set a legal framework for achieving the three macroeconomic goals of full employment, price stability, and a steady economic growth. Even though the bill was rejected, it had a strong impact on macroeconomic policy discussions in the following years.[35] A joint report drafted by the Scientific Councils of the Ministries of Economics and Finance in July 1956 recommended a comprehensive reorientation of economic policy based on fiscal and monetary demand management. Furthermore, it called for the introduction of modern national accounting to enable the government to draw up a yearly "economic program" and to implement medium-term financial planning.[36] Since 1960, a working group of both ministries discussed details and legislative prerequisites of such a policy. An expert report produced in December 1961 served as the basis for the first draft of the Stability Law presented to the Federal cabinet in January 1962.[37]

The draft was remarkable for two reasons. First, though it defined a wide range of macroeconomic instruments, there was a strong emphasis on fiscal policies. The scope for monetary intervention was seen as limited in view of increasing international integration, the system of fixed exchange rates and the high mobility of capital.[38] Secondly, unlike earlier recommendations and reports produced by the Ministries of Economics and Finance,[39] the focus was no longer on contractive measures. Instead, particular attention was given to reflationary policies, including the possibility of deficit spending. Even though the German economy was soaring in the years between 1960 and 1962, with real GDP growth rates between 4.4 percent and 9 percent,[40] the authors of the bill were concerned with the danger of future economic crises. Historical arguments played a prominent part in justifying state intervention. The bill was prefaced with a long historical digression on the 1929 slump and the lessons to be drawn from it.[41]

The law was approved not only by the major political parties but also by the trade unions and, with some reservations, the employer's federations. However, the implementation turned out to be more difficult than anticipated. While the broad outline of the bill was undisputed, deliberations focused on minor problems, reflecting internal conflicts within the government.[42] A more serious problem was that the law affected the financial autonomy of the Federal states and therefore required a constitutional amendment. It is no accident that the bill passed only in June 1967, after Christian Democrats and Social Democrats had formed a "grand coalition," which made constitutional amendments more feasible.[43]

The Stability Law has rightly been characterized as the "most Keynesian legislation of the postwar era."[44] The state was now committed to far-reaching demand management in order to achieve the macroeconomic goals of the "magic polygon" (price stability, full employment, and external balance at "stable and adequate" growth).[45] In the general public, the law was widely praised as a modern and efficient instrument of economic policy. This appraisal was largely related to the speed with which the recession affecting West Germany in 1966/67 was overcome. Even though the real impact of the slowdown had been anything but dramatic—in 1967, GNP growth stagnated, while unemployment rose only to a moderate 2.1 percent—many were alarmed.[46] Accustomed to the extraordinary rates of postwar growth, contemporaries worried that the downturn of 1966/67 portended a longer period of stagnation and severe economic problems.

The vigor demonstrated by the new coalition in the management of the recession was therefore generally approved and accompanied by supporting measures of the Federal Bank. Between the fall of 1966 and May 1967, the Federal Bank reduced the discount rate from 5 to 3 percent, which was followed by massive expansionary open-market operations in fall 1967. Reflationary fiscal measures were drawn up in January 1967. The government put up a public investment program that amounted to 2.5 billion deutschmarks, but with limited effects. As signs of a more severe recession emerged, the Council of Economic Experts recommended a second and more decisive spending program. In accordance with this advice, the government announced a new program of over 5 billion deutschmarks in July 1967. It is disputed to what extent the fast recovery—in 1968, growth peaked at 6.5 percent, while unemployment dropped to 1.5 percent[47]—can really be attributed to the expansive effect of fiscal and monetary stimulation. At least part of the upswing was due to a sharp increase of exports in 1968 because of the undervalued mark and the moderate wage contracts in the wake of the recession.[48]

Among the public it was generally accepted that the crisis management of Minister of Economics Karl Schiller was the main force in putting the economy back on the growth track. The notion of a "tailor-made upswing" turned up repeatedly in public reporting.[49] Schiller's competence in economic matters made many believe that the magic tools of "global guidance" *(Globalsteuerung)* could prevent future cyclical movements and economic stagnation alike. The successful implementation of demand steering appeared to be a striking verification of Keynesian theories and their political implications.[50] A series of new economic advisory bodies like the Business Cycle Council and the Financial Planning Council were established, giving further evidence to the idea that the "right" policy was only a matter of scientifically based fine-tuning of macroeconomic parameters. In this context, much attention was dedicated to Schiller's "Concerted Action," a regular meeting of high representatives of the Federal Bank, Trade Unions, employer's federations, and economic experts in order to coordinate various aspects of economic policy. In this matter, Schiller had followed a recommendation that the Council of Economic Experts had already made in its annual report of 1965/66.[51] Though the body abstained from fixing mandatory rules for wage increases, the consultations helped to moderate wage increases and price inflation in the first years.

After 1969, as a first wave of wildcat strikes swept over West Germany, the "Concerted Action" proved more and more vulnerable. In the light of surging business profits, the unions were increasingly reluctant to accept further wage moderation.[52] For both employer and union representatives, cooperative arrangements lost their appeal. Also, the dream of a crisis-proof economic development without stagnation and cyclical movements soon came to an end. Keynesian prescriptions turned out to be ineffective against the economic problems that Germany and most other industrialized nations had to face after the oil price-shock of 1973/74. By the end of 1974, the Federal Bank had announced a target for the growth of money supply and hence passed to an explicitly monetarist course. The Council of Economic Advisors strenuously supported this paradigmatic change of direction.[53] Increasing budgetary deficits and a combination of high inflation rates and unemployment ("stagflation") not only discredited Keynesianism, but also shattered the general confidence in the capability of economic crisis management and state intervention.[54]

Conclusions

The findings of this paper confirm the doubts of recent studies about a "German Sonderweg"[55] in international economic development after 1945. Not only West Germany's postwar growth, but also the pattern of its economic policy was closely related to the experience of most other industrialized countries of the

Western hemisphere. American economic ideas, in particular, spread rapidly in West Germany: the principles of open markets and competition combined with the commitment of the state to foster economic growth and stability.

It is an intriguing paradox that Keynesianism became most influential during the era of the "Great Boom," in a period when Keynesians' policy prescriptions seemed less necessary. Indeed, the emergence of Keynesianism can hardly be explained on economic grounds alone. Rather, it was the result of a complex interaction of cultural factors, scientific developments, and political arrangements at the national and international level.[56]

Four aspects have been explored in this paper. The first concerns the role of economic knowledge. West Germany was strongly affected by the postwar internationalization of economic sciences, mainly due to the increasing dominance of American economics. Though the theoretical traditions of the Freiburg School did not completely disappear, they rapidly lost ground. The reception of Keynesian theories was closely linked to the professionalization of the economic sciences. There was a considerable growth in the number, scale, and importance of economists and economic research institutes during the 1950s and 1960s. Many academically trained economists found a new role as experts strongly committed to applied economics. The increasing importance of private research institutes involved in business cycle studies, market research and political advising was a decisive factor in this development.

The second aspect discussed in this paper was international influence. Beyond the direct impact of Allied occupation policy, West Germany's integration into a net of international economic and monetary relations removed any notion of national autonomy. The Federal Republic had to adopt international statistical standards and was continually confronted with the experiences of other Western countries. Moreover, the ideological background of the Cold War changed attitudes toward managed growth and stability. Indeed, the shift from a liberal economic policy toward managed growth came in a period when the economic reforms under Walter Ulbricht gained momentum, and the GDR growth rates seemed to be rising considerably.

Third, the adoption of Keynesianism in West Germany was influenced by historical and political debates over the rise of National Socialism. Since the early 1950s, a wealth of historical and economic publications appeared, dealing with the Great Depression and the destruction of the Weimar Republic. Most Germans were convinced that the economic slump—and the failure of the political establishment to take countermeasures—was one of the main reasons for Hitler's seizure of power. The "economic" interpretation of the "German catastrophe" became popular because it seemed to ease the burden of individual responsibility.[57]

Fourth, it can be argued that a moderate Keynesianism became a component of the political compromises that structured social and economic policy in the Western world during the postwar period.[58] This is especially the case in West Germany, where "national" identity was closely linked to economic prosperity and social security. Not only in economic theory, but also in political discourse, "growth" and "stability" became the key concepts of West Germany's political economy. From about 1955 onward, there was an increasing convergence of economic ideas, as the Social Democrats definitively moved away from Marxist positions and neoliberal positions were marginalized among the Christian Democrats. Thereafter, almost all important decisions in the field of social and economic policy, starting with the anti-cartel legislation and the social security reforms of 1957 up to the Stability Law of 1967, were based on a broad consensus of all major political forces. The technocratic character of these reforms and the growing impact of economic experts helped to externalize political conflicts and opened the way to the informal centrist coalition of West Germany's postwar era.

Notes

1. See e.g. Kenneth H. F. Dyson, "German Economic Policy after Fifty Years," in *The Federal Republic of Germany at Fifty: At the End of a Century of Turmoil*, ed. Peter H. Merkl (London, 1999), 219.

2. Cf. Henry C. Wallich, *Mainsprings of the German Revival* (New Haven, 1955); Norman J. G. Pounds, *The Economic Pattern of Modern Germany* (London, 1963); Andrei S. Markovits, *The Political Economy of West Germany: Model Deutschland* (New York, 1982); Alan Peacock and Hans Willgerodt, eds., *Germany's Social Market Economy: Origins and Evolution* (London, 1989); Alan Kramer, *The West German Economy, 1945–1955* (New York, 1990).

3. For a comparative framework, see Geoffrey Denton, Murray Forsyth, and Malcolm MacLennan, *Economic Planning and Policies in Britain, France and Germany* (London, 1968); Peter A. Hall, ed., *The Political Power of Economic Ideas: Keynesianism Across Nations* (Princeton, 1989); Martin Chick, *Governments, Industries, and Markets: Aspects of Government-Industry Relations in Great Britain, Japan, West Germany, and the United States of America since 1945* (Aldershot, 1990).

4. Wendy Carlin, "West German Growth and Institutions," in *Economic Growth in Europe since 1945*, eds. Nicholas F. R. Crafts and Gianni Toniolo (Cambridge, New York, 1996), 470; Harald Hagemann, "The Post-1945 Development of Economics in Germany," in *The Development of Economics in Western Europe since 1945*, ed. A. W. Bob Coats (London, New York, 2000), 117; Christopher S. Allen, "The Underdevelopment of Keynesianism in the Federal Republic of Germany," in *Political Power*, ed. Hall, 288.

5. Dyson, "German Economic Policy," 221.

6. Christoph Buchheim, *Die Wiedereingliederung Westdeutschlands in die Weltwirtschaft 1945–1958* (Munich, 1990); Reinhard Neebe, *Weichenstellung für die Globalisierung. Deutsche Weltmarktpolitik, Europa und Amerika in der Ära Ludwig Erhard* (Cologne, Weimar, Vienna, 2004); Barry J. Eichengreen, "Mainsprings of Economic

Recovery in Post-war Europe," in *Europe's Post-War Recovery,* ed. idem, (Cambridge, New York, 1995), 3–35; Ludgar Lindlar, *Das mißverstandene Wirtschaftswunder. Westdeutschland und die westdeutsche Nachkriegsprosperität* (Tübingen, 1997).

7. Volker R. Berghahn, *The Americanization of German Business* (Lemington Spa, 1986).

8. See Christian Kleinschmidt, *Der produktive Blick. Wahrnehmung amerikanischer und japanischer Management- und Produktionsmethoden durch deutsche Unternehmer 1950–1985* (Berlin, 2002); Susanne Hilger, *"Amerikanisierung" deutscher Unternehmen. Wettbewerbsstrategien und Unternehmenspolitik bei Henkel, Siemens und Daimler-Benz (1945/49–1975)* (Stuttgart, 2004).

9. See, for example: James C. van Hook, *Rebuilding Germany: The Creation of the Social Market Economy, 1945–1957* (Cambridge, New York, 2004).

10. Cf. Anthony J. Nicholls, *Freedom with Responsibility: The Social Market Economy in Germany 1918–1963,* 2nd ed. (Oxford, New York, 2000).

11. Daniel Koerfer, *Kampf ums Kanzleramt: Erhard und Adenauer* (Stuttgart, 1987), 88–111; Volker Hentschel, *Ludwig Erhard: ein Politikerleben* (Munich, 1996), 245–57.

12. Werner Ehrlicher, *Die deutsche Finanzpolitik seit 1924* (Bonn, 1961); Wilhelm Grotkopp, *Die große Krise. Lehren aus der Überwindung der Wirtschaftskrise 1929* (Düsseldorf, 1964); Gerhard Kroll, *Von der Weltwirtschaftskrise zur Staatskonjunktur* (Berlin, 1958).

13. Hall, ed., *Political Power.*

14. Dudley Dillard, "The Influence of Keynesian Thought on German Economic Policy," in *The Policy Consequences of John Maynard Keynes,* ed. Harold L. Wattel (Armonk, 1985), 116–27.

15. Andreas Paulsen, *Neue Wirtschaftslehre. Einführung in die Wirtschaftstheorie von John Maynard Keynes und die Wirtschaftspolitik der Vollbeschäftigung* (Frankfurt am Main, 1950).

16. Paul A. Samuelson, *Economics: an Introductory Analysis* (New York, 1948); German translation: idem, *Volkswirtschaftslehre: eine Einführung* (Cologne, 1955).

17. See Albert O. Hirschman, "How the Keynesian Revolution was Exported from the United States, and other Comments," in *Political Power,* ed. Hall, 347–59.

18. Erich Schneider, *Einführung in die Wirtschaftstheorie,* 3 vols. (Tübingen, 1949–1952).

19. Alexander Nützenadel, *Stunde der Ökonomen. Wissenschaft, Expertenkultur und Politik in der Bundesrepublik 1949–74* (Göttingen, 2005), chaps. I and II.

20. William J. Barber, "Government as a Laboratory for Economic Learning in the Years of the Democratic Roosevelt," in *The State and Economic Knowledge: The American and British Experiences,* eds. Mary O. Furner and Barry Supple (Cambridge, 1990), 103–37; Alice M. Rivelin, "Economics and the Political Process," *American Economic Review* 77 (1987): 1–10.

21. Herbert Stein, "The Washington Economics Industry," *The American Economic Review* 76: (1986), 1–17.

22. Joseph A. Pechmann, ed., *The Role of the Economist in Government: An International Perspective* (New York, 1989); Ernst Mohr, ed., *The Transfer of Economic Knowledge* (Cheltenham, Northampton, 1998); Robert H. Nelson, "The Economic Profession and the Making of Public Policy," *Journal of Economic Literature* 25 (1987): 49–91; A. W. Bob Coats, ed., *Economists in Government: An International Comparative Study*

(Durham, 1981); David C. Colander and A. W. Bob Coats, eds., *The Spread of Economic Ideas* (Cambridge, 1989).

23. See Norbert Kloten, "Wissenschaftlicher Beirat beim Bundesministerium für Wirtschaft" in *30 Jahre Sachverständigenrat zur Begutachtung der gesamtwirtschaftlichen Entwicklung*, eds. Otto Schlecht and Ulrich van Suntum (Krefeld, 1995), 60–62.

24. Hagemann, "Post-1945 Development," 121.

25. Hans Langelütke and Wilhelm Marquardt, "Das Konjunkturtestverfahren. Aufgabe, Methode und Erkenntniswert," *Allgemeines Statistisches Archiv* 35 (1951): 34–67; see also Ifo-Institut für Wirtschaftsforschung, *Aufbau und Aufgaben* (München, 1961); Ralf Marquardt, ed., *Dreißig Jahre Wirtschaftsforschung im Ifo-Institut: 1949–1979* (Munich, 1979); R. Krengel, *Das deutsche Institut für Wirtschaftsforschung (IfK), 1925 bis 1979* (Berlin, 1985).

26. Heinz König, "Economic Knowledge Transfer by Research Institutes in Germany: Some reflections," in *The Transfer of Economic Knowledge*, ed. Ernst Mohr (Cheltenham, Northampton, 1998), 94.

27. See Arbeitsgemeinschaft wirtschaftswissenschaftlicher Forschungsinstitute, *Die Lage der Weltwirtschaft und der westdeutschen Wirtschaft* (Bonn, 1950 ff.). In 1950, 19 research institutes formed a working group for cooperative econometric and applied business studies *(Arbeitsgemeinschaft wirtschaftswissenschaftlicher Forschungsinstitute)*.

28. Donald Patinkin, "Keynes and Econometrics: On the Interaction between the Macroeconomic Revolutions of the Interwar Period," *Econometrica* 44 (1976): 1091–1123; for a general account, see A. W. Bob Coats, ed., *Economists in International Agencies: An Exploratory Study* (New York, Westport, London, 1986).

29. See documents in Bundesarchiv Koblenz (BAK), B 136 (Bundeskanzleramt), No. 7452.

30. Henry C. Wallich, "The American Council of Economic Advisors and the German Sachverständigenrat: A Study in the Economics of Advice," *Quarterly Journals of Economics* 82 (1968): 349–79; Silvio Borner, *Die amerikanische Stabilitätspolitik seit 1946: Strategien und Erfahrungen des Council of Economic Advisors* (Bern, Stuttgart, 1977).

31. Otto Schlecht and Ulrich van Suntum, eds., *30 Jahre Sachverständigenrat zur Begutachtung der gesamtwirtschaftlichen Entwicklung* (Krefeld, 1995); Hans G. Fabritius, *Konjunkturtheoretische Vorstellungen des Sachverständigenrates zur Begutachtung der gesamtwirtschaftlichen Entwicklung. Eine Analyse der bis einschließlich 1972 veröffentlichten Gutachten* (Berlin, 1975).

32. Albert Wissler, "Wissenschaft und Politik nach der Erfahrungen der modernen empirischen Konjunkturforschung," in *Wirtschaftsfragen der freien Welt*, eds. Erwin von Beckerath, Fritz W. Meyer, and Alfred Müller-Armack (Frankfurt am Main, 1957), 305; see also Albert Wissler, ed., *Die wissenschaftliche Fundierung der Konjunkturpolitik. Bericht über die 18. Mitgliederversammlung der AG Wirtschaftswissenschaftlicher Forschungsinstitute* (Berlin, 1956); Erich Schneider, *Money, Income, and Employment* (New York, 1962).

33. Egon Tuchtfeldt, "Social Market Economy and Demand Management: Two Experiments in Social Policy," *German Economic Review* 12 (1974): 111–33.

34. BAK, B 126 (Bundesfinanzministerium), No. 2076.

35. A striking piece of evidence to support this interpretation is a long letter by Minister of Finance Franz Etzel to Chancellor Konrad Adenauer, 4 June 1956; BAK, N 1254 (Etzel papers), No. 167.

36. "Gutachten über Instrumente der Konjunkturpolitik und ihre rechtliche Institutionalisierung," 3 June and 8 July 1956; in Wissenschaftlicher Beirat beim Bundesministerium für Finanzen, *Entschließungen, Stellungnahmen und Gutachten 1949–1973* (Tübingen, 1974), 103–30.

37. BAK, B 126, No. 22312: Report, 8 February 1961, and "Kabinettvorlage" 11 January 1962.

38. The lack of attention to monetary policies was also due to the autonomy of the Bundesbank. For the problems of monetary stabilization policies under fixed exchange rates, see Carl-Ludwig Holtfrerich, "Geldpolitik bei festen Wechselkursen (1948–1970)," in *Fünfzig Jahre Deutsche Mark. Notenbank und Währung in Deutschland seit 1948*, Deutsche Bundesbank, ed. (Munich, 1998), 347–438.

39. See, for example, the joint recommendations of Ludwig Erhard and Fritz Schäffer of 3 October 1955, BAK, B 136, No. 652.

40. See Herbert Giersch, Karl-Heinz Paqué and Holger Schmieding, *The Fading Miracle: Four Decades of Market Economy in Germany* (Cambridge, New York, 1992), 2–3.

41. BAK, B 126, No. 22312: "Kabinettvorlage" 11 January 1962: "Die große Wirtschaftskrise in den dreißiger Jahren hat die überragende Bedeutung konjunkturgerechter Wirtschafts- und Finanzpolitik bewußt werden lassen. Das deutsche Schicksal seit 1933 ist ursächlich mit dem Unvermögen der Weimarer Republik verknüpft, der großen Arbeitslosigkeit Herr zu werden."

42. Conflicts arose especially between the Ministries of Economics and Finance; see, for example, BAK, B 126, No. 22312: Report Dr. Bonus, 2 February 1962.

43. For the deliberations of the law, see BAK, B 102, No. 59384, 59385, 93258, 93259: "Gesetz zur Förderung der witschaftlichen Stabilität," vol. 1–4; see also Egbert Osterwald, *Die Entstehung des Stabilitätsgesetzes: eine Studie über Entscheidungsprozesse des politischen Systems* (Frankfurt am Main, 1982).

44. Dillard, "Influence of Keynesian Thought," 124–25.

45. Alex Möller and Christoph Böckenförde, *Gesetz zur Förderung der Stabilität und des Wachstums der Wirtschaft und Art. 109 Grundgesetz; Kommentar unter besonderer Berücksichtigung der Entstehungsgeschichte* (Hannover, 1968).

46. Joachim Fels, "1966/67—Anatomie einer Rezession," Institut für Weltwirtschaft, Kiel, Working Paper, No. 320 (1988).

47. Ibid.

48. Giersch, Paqué, and Schmieding, *Fading Miracle*, 147.

49. Klaus Hildebrand, *Von Erhard zur Grossen Koalition 1963–1969* (Stuttgart, Wiesbaden, 1984).

50. For Schiller's notion of "Globalsteuerung," see Karl Schiller, *Preisstabilität durch globale Steuerung der Marktwirtschaft* (Tübingen, 1966).

51. Sachverständigenrat zur Begutachtung der Gesamtwirtschaftlichen Entwicklung, *Jahresgutachten 1965/66* (Stuttgart, Mainz, 1966), paras. 187–208; see also BAK, B 102, Report Dr. Tietmeyer, "Konzertierte Aktion und Lohnpolitik," 8 February 1967.

52. For detailed information on the "Concerted Action," see BAK, B 136, No. 7046 and 7047; see also Manfred Kern, *Konzertierte Aktion als Versuch einer Verhaltensabstimmung zwischen Regierung und Wirtschaftsverbänden* (Köln, 1973).

53. Jürgen von Hagen, "Geldpolitik auf neuen Wegen," in *Fünfzig Jahre Deutsche Mark. Notenbank und Währung in Deutschland seit 1948*, Deutsche Bundesbank, ed.

(Munich, 1998), 439–73; Sachverständigenrat zur Begutachtung der Gesamtwirtschaft-lichen Entwicklung, *Jahresgutachten 1974/75* (Stuttgart, Mainz, 1975), paras. 131, 139 f. and 310.

54. Giersch, Paqué, and Schmieding, *Fading Miracle*, 185 ff.; Alexandra Ehrlicher, *Die Finanzpolitik 1967–1976 im Spannungsfeld zwischen konjunkturpolitischen Erfordernissen und Haushaltskonsolidierung* (Berlin, 1991); for a more general account, see Robert J. A. Skidelsky, ed., *The End of the Keynesian Era: Essays on the Disintegration of the Keynesian Political Economy* (New York, 1977).

55. Hagemann, "Post-1945 Development," 113–28; see also the comparative study of Jytte Klausen, *War and Welfare: Europe and the United States, 1945 to the Present* (New York, 1998), 165–201.

56. For a theoretical discussion of this problem, see Hall, ed., *Political Power*.

57. See Nützenadel, *Stunde*, chap. II.1

58. For a more general account of this interpretation, see John H. Goldthorpe, "Problems of Political Economy after the Postwar Period," in *Changing Boundaries of the Political: Essays on the Evolving Balance between the State and Society, Public and Private in Europe*, ed. Charles S. Maier (Cambridge, 1987), 363–407.

CHAPTER 13

Catholic Elites, Gender, and Unintended Consequences in the 1950s

Toward a Reinterpretation of the Role of Conservatives in the Federal Republic

Mark Edward Ruff

When compared to earlier epochs in German history, the first twenty years of the Federal Republic have generated relatively few historical controversies.[1] This lack of acrimonious exchange stems, at least in part, from the simple reality that explaining catastrophes is inherently more controversial than accounting for success. To be sure, the 1950s and early 1960s were years of remarkable achievements, economically, socially, and politically. Economic prosperity helped integrate once marginalized groups such as Roman Catholics and socialist workers into the mainstream. Adenauer's foreign policy during the Cold War placed the Federal Republic firmly into the camp of the liberal West.[2] To repeat the cliché, Bonn was not Weimar.

Historians of postwar Germany instead have disagreed over whether the early years of the Federal Republic, an interlude between the National Socialist dictatorship and the emancipatory movements of the second half of the 1960s, were an era of "restoration or of a new beginning."[3] Many concluded that the 1950s were, indeed, an era of patriarchal quasi-authoritarianism, one characterized by a noteworthy continuity in personnel, administration, and institutions. Not surprisingly, the images that surface in these works are those of a reconstituted repressive bourgeois normality—of the nuclear family; of a morality of hard work and virtue; of *Heimatfilme* that emphasized "traditional" gender roles, and of protests against films like *Die Sünderin* that were deemed subversive; and, in the popular imagination, of Sunday afternoon walks followed by Kaffee and Kuchen.

As a result, many interpretations of the Federal Republic now center on paradox, in which a quasi-authoritarian restoration appears to have been the engine of unprecedented economic and social dynamism, a "modernization under conservative auspices."[4] In the words of Mark Roseman, this becomes a "story where remarkably limited innovation seems nevertheless to have generated an entirely different outcome."[5] Yet explaining this paradox is far from simple. Many histories of this era now emphasize the impact of economic and cultural modernization and, in particular, the tremendous growth of consumerism and the blossoming of a more individualistic culture of consumption, especially by the late 1950s and early 1960s.[6] Some argue that the foundations for economic growth and, in turn, stability were laid already during the pre-1945 era.[7] Other accounts correctly point to the central role played by youth and the new youth culture of the 1950s in accelerating these cultural shifts.[8]

But these interpretations do not directly resolve this paradox: how did conservative Catholic elites become the agents of cultural transformation in Germany? Did these cultural transformations take place because of or in spite of this conservative restoration? Did the actions (or lack thereof) of these conservative elites provide the preconditions for the social stability and cultural dynamism that came to characterize the Federal Republic, especially by the 1960s? How extensive and deeply rooted, in fact, was this restoration?[9]

Explaining this paradox ultimately requires examining the policies and visions of the conservative elites at the helm of the Federal Republic, and, most critically, assessing the often unintended consequences of these initiatives. It is clear that the Roman Catholic Church, perhaps more than any other institution, was an indispensable pillar of this restoration. While the church had suffered grievous damage especially during the war, its institutional structures remained largely intact. Roman Catholics, equally importantly, were no longer a beleaguered minority in the new West German state. The creation of the German Democratic Republic severed 15 million mostly Protestant voters from the West German state while the expulsion of mostly Protestants from East Prussia, Pomerania, and Lower Silesia destroyed the traditional conservative-Protestant stronghold. The result was a new relative parity between Catholics and Protestants in the West.[10] Many Catholics perceived themselves to be the decisive victors in the elections of 1949, 1953, and 1957, although the CDU owed its victories also to a substantial Protestant vote.[11] German Catholics in the West and South retained their own unique subculture—the so-called "Catholic milieu"—through the early 1960s.[12] This was a world of countless *Vereine* and *Verbände* (ancillary organizations), of pilgrimages and festivals, of Marian piety, of rituals and organizations that helped integrate daily life from the cradle to the grave.[13]

Yet most histories of the Federal Republic pay little more than lip service to Catholicism during this era.[14] Scholars of German Catholicism have produced an extensive and growing literature, but their works have yet to be integrated into the larger, secular narratives in both Germany and the United States: it is fair to say that many of these newer accounts have remained confined to a Catholic ghetto.[15] Some scholars underscore the creation of a modern conservatism during the 1950s, one that had finally shed the *Kulturpessimismus* and the fears of mass society and culture that had dominated German conservatism in the first half of the twentieth century—but Catholic conservatives are absent from this picture.[16] While existing secular histories of the Federal Republic continuously refer to the enormous power of social conservatives in shaping a national discourse on power, gender, politics and sexuality, these works rarely examine more than fleetingly the many nuances and, above all, significant changes within the religious world of West German social conservatives of the 1950s.[17]

It was precisely these changes and nuances within the world of German Catholics that mirrored larger social and cultural transformations within the Federal Republic in its first twenty years. German conservatism accommodated itself to postwar liberal democracy, albeit to a somewhat authoritarian version.[18] But more importantly, the internal changes in German Catholicism were also partially responsible for the larger revolution in values, culture, and social norms that took place nationally during this period, especially by the second half of the 1950s. Catholic religious and political leaders often pursued policies with unforeseen consequences: their policies often inadvertently diluted ideas, ideologies, and traditions they were intended to uphold. Even the stellar political successes Catholics achieved through the CDU-CSU were accompanied by—and helped bring about—an irreversible erosion of the social base of the Catholic milieu, first among many young men and women, and, by the late 1960s, among many adults.[19] The Catholic world of the Federal Republic might rightly be described as one of paradox, in which a thin veneer of conformity and diluted authoritarianism masked a much deeper underlying ferment.

This chapter will examine, first, the incomplete nature of the Catholic restoration after 1945 and argue that this Catholic world was never as monolithic as some accounts would have it. It will subsequently analyze why the Catholic milieu disintegrated from the 1950s onward, an era that has often been seen (not entirely correctly) as a high-water mark of religious authority and influence.[20] It will focus, in particular, on the attempts already in the 1950s to reform positions of gender norms and moral theology. It will focus on how these efforts at reform inadvertently contributed to the erosion of the Catholic milieu by the 1960s. Finally, it will attempt to explain the deeper underlying paradox: how could apparent forces of conservative continuity produce such dynamic change?

~

Many recent writings argue that the West German political culture of the immediate postwar era was shaped by a restorationist conservative discourse on gender and sexuality.[21] Not surprisingly, these works emphasize the role of religious leaders and Roman Catholic politicians in creating what is often depicted as a fairly uniform political discourse. As Robert Moeller succinctly put it, "when it came to the political discussion of women's status and the structure of families, the Adenauer era created little political space for experimentation of any kind."[22]

Bolstering this interpretation is the fact that Roman Catholic leaders pulled off what to outsiders appeared to be a picture-perfect restoration in the midst of unprecedented upheaval. Many churches had been reduced to piles of stone, thousands of priests been killed in concentration camps or on the front, and millions of Protestant refugees from the East fundamentally altered the confessional landscape in many once Catholic regions. In spite of such convulsions, the church maintained a remarkable continuity in its personnel. Most of the leaders of the restoration, especially in the Verbände, were the same leaders who had been active in the church prior to 1933, a situation that gave rise to a saying, "The men of the first hour were the men of the last hour."[23] Of the twenty bishops from the dioceses which were to become part of the Federal Republic, fourteen remained on their thrones between 1939 and 1945.[24] In addition, Catholic leaders restored or attempted to resurrect nearly all of the organizations destroyed in the preceding twelve years, many of which had dated back to the second half of the nineteenth century. They reconstituted the Catholic Center party, more than one dozen youth organizations, sporting leagues, workers' clubs, and library associations, among many others.[25]

These leaders from the past resurrected not just personnel and organizations but also mentalities that had been a mainstay of church teachings prior to 1933. For more than a century, church teachings had been implacably hostile to materialism, communism, emancipatory gender norms, mass culture, and, to a lesser extent, liberalism.[26] Many Catholic leaders, as did some non-Catholic conservatives, now linked these forces to ongoing processes of secularization and, in turn, ascribed to them the blame for the debacles of 1933.[27] The moral impotence, spiritual flabbiness, and political strife that were the hallmark of Weimar had driven many Catholics from the church and left a collapse of some sort inevitable. The twelve years of National Socialism, some leaders even argued, were divine retribution for secularization, just as the children of Israel were repeatedly punished for having turned their backs on the Lord.[28] Not surprisingly, many Catholic leaders insisted that the reconstruction of German society after the 12 years of secularization under National Socialism had to begin with reconstruction of the German nuclear family, the cornerstone of society. These impulses were strengthened by the reality that under the years of Nazi persecution of the churches, the family—and not the outlawed *Verbände*—served as the institution that transmitted religious values to children.[29] That the Nazis themselves in their organizations such as the BDM (League of German Girls) turned a blind eye toward sexual indiscretions between Aryan girls and boys in order to pursue their racial agenda, strengthened Catholics in their belief that traditional sexual and gender norms needed to be restored.[30]

It was not just the apparent success of this Catholic restoration that may have led to the conclusion that the church's positions on questions of the family, sexuality, and gender were uniform. Adenauer's successes in marginalizing his political opposition on the Catholic left may have contributed to this picture of a uniform Catholicism after 1949. More importantly, Catholic leaders themselves for tactical reasons strove to depict German Catholicism as unified, hierarchical, and strong. The church itself succeeded in cultivating an image of strength and might in the midst of the rubble and ashes in order to intimidate ideological rivals and gain additional political and social influence. In addition, many church leaders saw internal disunity as the factor that had led to the ignominious defeats of 1933 and, not surprisingly, strove to paper over and minimize disagreements.[31]

The rhetoric of unity, however, masked underlying disagreements on fundamental questions of family values and gender roles. In fact, numerous voices within the church vied for the chance to shape church doctrines on questions of sexuality, marriage, and gender. Behind the scenes, many theologians and even lower-ranking youth leaders drafted their own counterpoints to official church encyclicals. Even when the church appeared to be speaking with one voice, the "official position" after 1945 was often derived from contrasting traditions, including neo-scholasticism from the late nineteenth century and the youth and liturgical movements of the 1920s and 1930s. By the 1950s, some church workers were deriving their ideas from the writings of sociologists while some younger youth leaders based their ideas, in part, on the emerging youth culture imported from America.[32]

Some of the disagreements within German Catholicism stemmed from the manner in which the twelve years of National Socialist rule had transformed the Catholic milieu. While this subculture bore deep scars not just from years of state persecution but, more importantly, from the devastation of six years of war, it had not been destroyed.[33] To be sure, religious organizations lost a sizeable number of members who had participated with a lower level of engagement; yet other organizations retained an elite cadre of dedicated volunteers who had been inspired by the movements for revival—the Catholic youth movement, the Bible movement, and the liturgical movement—from the 1920s and 1930s. As most Catholic ancillary organizations were dissolved, in which the laity often had leadership roles, this elite had been drawn more tightly to the church in what many historians have described as a process of *Verkirchlichung.*[34] Some members of this group argued that Catholic organizations should retain the elite organizations that had developed after 1933, while other Catholic leaders insisted that they should try to recreate the mass organizations that had existed prior to 1933. Making the task of reconstruction more complicated was the reality that some organizations had been completely destroyed by the Nazis, while others, such as the Kolping organization for artisans, had been only partially dissolved.

As a result, some Catholics often broadly disagreed over how to rebuild the Catholic milieu after 1945. They were often at odds over whether they should merely replicate what had existed prior to 1933 or instead seek new models. In the realm of politics, most Catholic leaders ultimately accepted the need to abandon the sectarianism of the pre-Nazi era and as a result, the CDU, unlike the old Center party (which was also reconstituted) became officially interconfessional.[35]

Other religious leaders disagreed over the role of gender in this reconstruction. In Catholic youth work, the individual in charge of the female youth work, Hermann Klens, whose pronouncements on sexuality and gender would seem to indicate the strength of this conservative restoration, found his work and efforts marginalized by the overall leader of the youth work, Ludwig Wolker.[36] Wolker, a Bavarian monsignor, had created a new organization for Catholic youth, the League of German Catholic Youth *(Bund der deutschen katholischen Jugend),* in which the male and female youth "columns" stood side by side. The two approaches stood in sharp contrast to one another. Klens sought to instill values of sacrifice, chastity, service to others, humility, piety, and reverence *(Ehrfurcht)* in his young women and insisted that young women needed a safe space in which to live and work, free of the domination of men. Wolker, in contrast, rarely emphasized these supposedly "female" virtues and even called for the relaxation of prohibitions against masturbation. He was more concerned instead with creating the public appearance of action, militancy, and unity. On at least one occasion, he accused Klens of beating to death his message of self-sacrifice, humility, and motherliness. Klens was a product of a rural nineteenth century agrarian world, Wolker a child of the militant Catholic youth movement of the 1910s and 1920s. Wolker and those who were like-minded represented in the 1920s and 1930s a new militant right that sought to replace what they regarded as weak, feminine forms of piety from the nineteenth century, the product of an era of "feminization," with more dynamic models. Another dynamic leader of the Youth Movement from the group, Bund Neudeutschland, Ludwig Esch, sought to transform the image of Mary from that of a sweeping and weeping woman to a strong matriarch: "The picture of Mary had been misrepresented through softness, sweetness and pious blathering. As a result, I, as a boy who made a point of not showing any weakness (at least publicly), did not want to have anything to do with it. So I turned away, until Mary was portrayed as the strong woman. Then I gladly served."[37]

In the ensuing struggles, Klens and his supporters in the female youth work routinely complained that they received less money and had even been "steam-rolled" by Wolker in his efforts to create "unity" in youth work.[38] Throughout the early 1950s, they lamented that Wolker refused to support their efforts to resuscitate the moribund Marian Congregations for young maidens, a form of organization that dated back to the Counter-Reformation and had grown dramatically in the nineteenth century.[39] At the top levels of youth work, masculinizing Catholic identity was necessarily accompanied by starkly reducing or even eliminating the female sphere altogether. This was an outright rejection of models of "feminization" that had been characteristic of Catholic forms of piety in the second half of the nineteenth century.[40]

Similar ambiguities can be seen in Catholic attempts to define the proper roles within the family after 1945. Traditions of natural law from earlier centuries emphasized patriarchal authority. Such proponents of neo-scholasticism insisted that God himself decreed that women were to be subordinated to men within the family and that the proper function of sexuality was procreation.[41] While these traditions were certainly cultivated further after 1945, other Catholic thinkers were now applying new doctrines from the Liturgical Movement, a renewal movement from the 1920s and 1930s, to marriage and the family. Traditionally, such questions were the domain of moral theologians, not Catholic social thinkers.[42] The family was to be a smaller representation of the church *(die Kirche im Kleinen);* the church, inversely, was a large family. According to the Paderbornian theologian Josef Höser, who strove to apply the thought of Pius XII to this domain, the family was to serve as the "original fount of life for the church" and was the "actual or even most important place for lay priestdom."[43] By citing Pius' "Rundschreiben" from 1943, "Mystici corporis," the idea that marriage was the sacrament with which Christ envisioned providing the "social needs of the church," Catholic social theorists effectively placed the family on the same level sacramentally as the priesthood. Giving birth to children could almost be seen as a rite of consecration.[44] The organic language of a mystical body also bore the classic hallmarks of the Catholic Liturgical Movement of the 1920s and 1930s, a movement that had been embraced by many young men and women during this time often to the dismay of more elder and traditional clerics.

These theological developments reflected the reality that many laity had been drawn closer to the church during the 1930s and 1940s during the years of Nazi persecution, as part of the *Verkirchlichungsprozess.*[45] They were sometimes accompanied by a renewal program of Catholic Action, a movement that had first taken shape in Italy.[46] Catholic Action sought to keep the power of the laity somewhat curtailed and subordinated to the church hierarchy, a reaction to power struggles that had broken out in previous decades between members of the hierarchy and the leaders of ancillary organizations. Catholic Action, however, also strove to send laity into regions traditional Catholic organization had not been able to reach. An emphasis on the family was, therefore, a recognition that the traditional *Vereinswesen* had not been power-ful enough to strengthen the family in its hour of need.[47] This slightly altered understanding of the family represented, more fundamentally, the hopes to maintain the insularity of the Catholic milieu. On a certain level, it served as a plea for new priests, whose numbers had dropped off precipitously in the 1940s after reaching relative highs in the 1930s, when many young men were inspired to enter seminaries after their experiences in the Catholic Youth and Liturgical Movements.[48] Church leaders believed that close-knit, religious families were a more fertile soil from which new priests could emerge; on the shoulders of these new priests rested the fate of this insular subculture.

Perhaps more than any bishop, Bishop Michael Keller promoted in his Münster diocese both Catholic Action and this new understanding of the fam-ily.[49] As late as 1959, Keller attempted to place the date for the first commun-ion preferably before the start of school, but at the very latest at the age of seven. This reform was part of an effort to strengthen the "eucharistically living fam-ily," which he declared to be part of the "salvation of our time." Like other Catholic theorists, he explicitly urged families to become a "church in minia-ture" *(Kirche im kleinen)*, believing that it might become well nigh impossible for children to receive religious education in the schools.[50] Writing at the apex of the Cold War in the 1950s, Keller argued that such a deepening of the faith for individual Christians went hand in hand with "christianizing the sur-rounding world."[51]

But this new theology also represented yet another attempt to distance one-self from the "feminized" church from the nineteenth century and early twen-tieth centuries. While it reaffirmed the position of the man in the family as the true "teacher, priest and shepherd of the family ... a second Christ," it explic-itly began to redefine the relationship between man and woman within the marriage by calling on men to play a much greater role in instilling religious values in children, an area which traditionally had been the domain of women.[52] At the Katholikentag in Berlin in 1952, Elisabeth Burger argued, "The most important question is the question of the father. It depends on him, first and foremost, that the family finds a new form."[53] The ideal father was to be the understanding comrade and companion of the children. A number of Catho-lic theorists began to call for a truer partnership in the family. The father was to help with the housework and assist more actively in raising the children. In-stead of advocating separate spheres for men and women, educational tracts, lectures, and even seminars for young farmers urged cooperation between men and women, insisting on equal worth for men and women. One brochure from 1964 observed, "All areas in which men and women stand together in a healthy and moral relationship take on a family-like atmosphere and form the nucleus of a larger whole."[54] Another booklet explained: "The goal of being a good and virtuous housewife is insufficient for today. On the other hand, women must help men to win back an interest in the domains of life: familial and social questions."[55] By the early 1960s, some Catholic leaders presented love, and not authority, as the mainstay of their moral theology of the family. They were more likely to speak of the authority of love than the authority of the parents.

Klens's conception, in contrast, involved sharply delineated separate spheres for men and women. Echoing past theologies, he argued that men were to be "knightly" and were to show reverence for their women. Even so, Klens's highly romantic writings were disproportionately directed toward women and their responsibilities for their families. He spoke, for instance, of the "frailty" *(Labilität)* of women in the immediate postwar era, a condition that required chivalrous conduct by men: "The general destruction and lack of order is borne least well by women. In their weaknesses, they are particularly vulnerable to these conditions. As a result, women become most easily unrestrained and disordered."[56]

Quite obviously, one can explain this new emphasis on the duties of the father by pointing to the immediate circumstances of postwar Germany, factors that included the absence of fathers as a result of the war and POW camps, rising employment for women, the growing strength of women, and ultimately increased divorce rates.[57] But these observations go only so far. First, the emphasis on the father stemmed from a larger theological imperative—the necessity of combating secularization. The experience of the father by the child was seen as "determining the fate of the religious existence of the human being."[58] Others likened the absence of God in society to the absence of the father in the family and sought to restore patriarchal authority in both instances.[59] Even at the time, it was a truism that women attended church far more regularly than did men.

Second, this discourse of the father actually increased in importance later in the 1950s, if anything, at a time when fathers and men had been largely reintegrated into society. While some of this can be attributed to a decision by federal courts in 1959 to uphold a parliamentary measure giving wives and mothers a legal basis for claims to equal rights, the emphasis on the family can also be interpreted as a response to economic prosperity.[60] Catholic social theorists had long noted that industrialization had torn apart the traditional agrarian model of the family.[61] It had separated living quarters from the workplace, and ultimately led to increases in female employment (it appears that many church leaders believed that the 1950s witnessed a significant rise in women's employment, although this growth was actually quite modest) and, in turn, led to movements for female employment.[62] In religious newspapers, many young women were writing letters to the editor and participating in open forums on questions of employment and marriage. Already in the early 1950s, many had registered their disgust with "traditional" forms of employment such as working as a maid in other households, citing poor working conditions and equally abymssal wages. "It is quite understandable that young women say that only idiots go to work as a maid."[63] This dissatisfaction had led many young women by the late 1950s to vote with their feet and seek employment in white-collar professions, disregarding religious directives and pleas to work in more "motherly" professions.

By the late 1950s, the economical miracle had proceeded at such a pace that its effects were being felt not just in the industrial agglomerations of the Ruhr and Rhine but even in the most rural corners of Western Germany, in the enclaves that had comprised the Catholic heartland. The lives of many young men and women were being altered by the spread of prosperity and a culture of consumption, both of which began to change relations between men and women. In light of this transformation, it is not surprising that Catholic social theorists would pay increased attention to changes within the family. Internal considerations—power struggles, concern over the health of this Catholic subculture—thus played as powerful a role in the reformulation of the Catholic understanding of the family as the by now familiar social changes in postwar society such as the "oversupply of women," the problems of prostitution, or the presence of libidinous American GIs.[64]

Still, one should not overestimate the extent and influence of this new theological development. While some moral theologians, priests, and Jesuit fathers began to teach this new theology, in many other regions, priests continued to expound the old neo-scholastic understanding of the family and its roles. They continued to extol the "hierarchical structure of marriage and family" and emphasized the fundamental differences between men and women.[65] These different currents existed side by side for much of the later 1950s and early 1960s, until the full impact of the Second Vatican Council (from 1962 to 1965) could be felt.[66] Proponents of the newer emphases could find themselves on the defensive, subject to reproaches from more conservative voices in the senior hierarchy. One young youth leader, Heidi Carl, who called for moderate reforms in women's youth work and urged Catholic teenagers to be both "Catholic and modern," found herself the target of criticism and reproach from a number of church leaders.[67]

These discrepancies between the different currents of moral theology on the family and between the idealized rhetoric of the family and the often harsh reality, not only led to a certain schizophrenia in the late 1950s and especially by the 1960s but accelerated the disintegration of the Catholic milieu.[68] The promise of reform actually led to religious revivals in many regions, particularly in the more conservative rural strongholds of Bavaria, the Western Münsterland and the rural Rhineland. The Rural Catholic youth movement attained explosive rates of growth in rural parts of the Münsterland and Lower Franconia, so that religious leaders could boast of a revival and significant "movement" among young persons.[69] In these regions, these newer approaches led to a new optimism, especially among young persons, and allowed for greater questioning of traditional church teachings. But the failure to deliver on these promises led to an exodus of young people, especially young women, from religious organizations and institutions in other, often more urban regions. Youth organizations, for instance, mustered a mere million young men and women, a noticeable decline from the nearly 1.5 million members from the mid-1930s, the high-water mark of the Catholic youth movement.[70] Between 1953 and 1959, moreover, Catholic youth organizations for women lost more than 40 percent of their members in North-Rhine Westphalia. By contrast, youth organizations for men lost only 15.8 percent of their members in the same region.[71]

To a certain extent, the departure of many young Catholics was the result of expectations for reform that went unmet in a climate of otherwise tremendous optimism, economic dynamism and new opportunities. In some regions, the possibility of reform whetted the appetites of eager young men and women; six years later, the movement faltered, as the realities failed to change apace. The simple reiteration of traditional gender roles and the family set the stage for a backlash by the 1960s. (A similar trajectory can be seen in the American civil rights movements, in which the violent explosions of the mid to late 1960s were a result of hopes for more dramatic changes that had gone unmet.) After the 1960s, church attendance fell off dramatically, a plunge that, with some fits and starts, has continued unabated until the present.[72]

What had fundamentally changed was the understanding of authority, the ingredient which more than any other factor led to the disintegration of the Catholic milieu. Religious leaders themselves helped undermine the very foundation of their authority by providing open forums for young persons to question traditional doctrine and then, in turn, failing to deliver the goods. Ultimately, many religious leaders began to emphasize the role of the individual conscience in making fundamental decisions about marriage, family, and sexuality.

It was on the question of sexuality within marriage that religious authority was most powerfully questioned, auguring a crisis within Catholicism later in the 1960s. According to neo-scholastic teachings, the purpose of sexuality lay in procreation. Catholic literature dutifully put forward shibboleths such as "Children: The crown of marriage," and "The more children, the more blessings."[73] Already at the turn of the century, Catholic women were giving birth to fewer children, a trend that accelerated in the 1950s; Catholic women with many children were often regarded as dim-witted. Faced with a growing problem, no less a figure than Pope Pius XII attempted to soften the blow:

"Service to motherhood ... not in the sense of a blind subservience to the force of nature, but in the sense of a regulated operation of the marital rights and privileges in accordance with the principles of reasons and faith."[74] In other words, Catholic women were no longer required to produce an "unreasonable number of children"; rather, they were to have only as many children as they could reasonably care for and rear.[75] Ultimately, it was the individual conscience that was to determine how many children were "reasonable."

While this subtle change of emphasis did not fundamentally alter Catholic teachings on sexuality—Catholic theorists continued to insist that the world was large enough to accommodate even billions more human beings—it clearly raised expectations of more substantial changes, particularly with the onset of the Second Vatican Council in 1962 and the introduction of the birth-control pill in the early 1960s.[76] During the Council, even Cardinal Frings of Cologne, not known for his theological radicalism in the 1940s, described marriage as the "most inward community of life and love that exists on Earth. Men and women are to become happy in their love and create life for new persons through God's creative power."[77] Bit by bit, the foundation for the traditional prohibitions against birth control were being called into question, as theologians, priests, and lay Catholics awaited what they believed would be a final verdict by Pope Paul VI. When he reaffirmed the church's traditional position on this issue, the response was frequently one of disillusionment and embitterment. As figures on fertility rates made clear, most German Catholics simply disregarded this pronouncement—just as many Catholic teenagers had ignored dictates against wearing makeup, against revealing clothing, and against popular music in the 1950s.[78] Already in the 1950s, authority had been demystified; by the late 1960s, it was openly flouted and mocked. Many religious organizations by the 1970s adopted more extreme emancipatory positions, the inverse of the positions adopted in the 1950s.[79] Religious leaders, including social conservatives, thus unwittingly helped foster a new climate of individualism, which proved exceptionally corrosive of the hierarchical structure of authority on which the power of the church rested.

The story of the church's position on sexuality in the 1950s and 1960s gives credence to those who argue that religious institutions were, to a certain degree, victims of self-secularization.[80] Religious leaders offered a greater openness but ultimately reaffirmed traditional positions, the equivalent of letting the genie out of the bottle. The acrid controversies that subsequently emerged between reformers and conservatives only accelerated the erosion of a traditional Catholic identity and, in turn, the Catholic subculture in Germany. Conservatives, in reiterating traditional positions that no longer corresponded to the needs of a new era, drove many young men and women away from religious institutions and suffered a fatal loss of authority in the process. Reformers diluted traditional religious identities and failed to provide convincing alternatives: a fairly vague theology of love was ultimately not substantial enough to meet spiritual needs. In addition, the battles that ensued wasted much time and energy that might have been used to carry out the apostolic mission of the church itself.

The reality of power also further eviscerated the Catholic milieu. By holding political power for so long in the 1950s and 1960s, representatives of political Catholicism made it nearly impossible for German Catholics to rely on a traditional array of enemies—liberals, socialists, Communists, materialists—that had helped hold together the Catholic milieu. Alliances with liberals and socialists certainly helped undermine the efficacy of the images that religious leaders had used for decades. Political power also meant that Catholics, once a whipping boy of the German political culture, had entered the mainstream, and as a result, lost the outsider status that had kept the Catholic subculture tightly unified. In addition, legislation that had passed undermined the rationale behind a tightly unified, insular subculture. The effects of the social-market economy, which Catholic leaders played an instrumental role in drafting and passing, helped spread a culture of consumption, further undermining the Catholic subculture. The aging Adenauer ironically became an agent of consumerism. Even the legislation on the family often diverged from the ideals of Catholic leaders.

The Catholic story of the 1950s and 1960s tells how success, in turn, bred failure. Or perhaps inversely, it is the account of how certain perceived failures in German Catholicism paved the way for the success of the larger society. As Catholics (and Socialists as well) lost—or gave up—their own subculture, the fissures of denomination and class that had defined the German political culture for nearly a century were finally overcome. Conservative religious leaders ironically played a significant role in bringing about this remarkable transformation, for the restoration that they helped engineer inadvertently proved to be a source of their own demise. In its wake stood a pluralized and increasingly fractious German Catholicism, in which Catholic organizations routinely put forward positions on questions of morals and values that openly diverged from those of the hierarchy. German Catholicism came to resemble the culturally more pluralized but socially more homogeneous society of the Federal Republic.[81]

Notes

1. This is a point also made by Mark Roseman. See Mark Roseman, "Division and Stability: The Federal Republic of Germany, 1949–1989," in *20th Century Germany: Politics, Culture and Society 1918–1990,* ed. Mary Fullbrook (New York, 2001): 177–203.

2. Ronald J. Granieri points out, however, that the integration of West Germany into the West was much more complicated and contested than has often been realized,

citing divisions, for instance, between Atlanticists and Gaullists. See Ronald Granieri, *The Ambivalent Alliance: Konrad Adenauer, the CDU/CSU and the West, 1949–1966* (New York, 2003).

3. For a summary of the debates over restoration or new beginnings, see Jürgen Kocka, "1945: Restauration oder Neubeginn?," in *Wendepunkte deutscher Geschichte, 1848–1945,* eds., Carola Stern and Heinrich August Winkler (Frankfurt am Mein, 1979), 141–68. For accounts that analyze the conservative restoration, see Eberhard Schmidt, *Die verhinderte Neuordnung 1945–1952* (Frankfurt, 1970), Theo Pirker, *Die verordnete Demokratie: Grundlagen und Erscheinungen der Restauration 1945–1949* (Frankfurt, 1972), Ute Schmidt and Tilman Fichter, *Der erzwungene Kapitalismus: Klassenkämpfe in den Westzonen 1945–1948* (Berlin, 1971).

4. On "modernization under conservative auspices," see Christoph Kleßmann, *Die doppelte Staatsgründung: Deutsche Geschichte 1945–1955* (Göttingen, 1982).

5. Roseman, "Division and Stability," 178.

6. The pioneering works here are Axel Schildt, *Moderne Zeiten: Freizeit, Massenmedien und "Zeitgeist" in der Bundesrepublik der 50er Jahre* (Hamburg, 1995) and the massive collection of essays in Axel Schildt and Arnold Sywottek, ed., *Modernisierung im Wiederaufbau: Die westdeutsche Gesellschaft der 50er Jahre* (Bonn, 1993). For an excellent summary of recent accounts of consumption, see the chapter "In Pursuit of Happiness: Consumption, Mass Culture and Consumerism," in *Shattered Past,* Konrad Jarausch and Michael Geyer (Princeton, 2003), 269–316. For a long-term perspective on the development of mass culture and entertainment, see Kaspar Maase, *Grenzenloses Vergnügen: Der Aufstieg der Massenkultur, 1850–1970* (Frankfurt, 1997).

7. Werner Abelshauser has argued that the 1920s were characterized by severe disruptions in Germany's normal patterns of economic growth. The postwar economic miracle featured a catch-up that was more rapid than it otherwise would have been. See Werner Abelshauser, *Wirtschaftsgeschichte der Bundesrepublik Deutschland, 1945–1980* (Frankfurt, 1983) and Werner Abelshauser, *Die langen fünfziger Jahre: Wirtschaft und Gesellschaft der Bundesrepublik Deutschland, 1949–1966* (Düsseldorf, 1987).

8. See Uta Poiger, *Jazz, Rock and Rebels: Cold War Politics and American Culture in a Divided Germany* (Berkeley, 2000). For a more comprehensive analysis of her arguments, see Chapter 2. See also Erica Carter, *How German is She? Postwar West German Reconstruction and the Consuming Woman* (Ann Arbor, 1996). For another work that fits into this newer literature, see Maria Höhn, *GIs and Fräuleins: The German-American Encounter in 1950s West Germany* (Chapel Hill, 2002).

9. In response to the argument that the conservative discourse carried the day in the 1950s, one must ask why church attendance plummeted by the 1960s and membership in youth organizations fell in the 1950s, if these conservatives were indeed so powerful.

10. As late as 1970, by which point the refugees had been long resettled in the Federal Republic, Roman Catholics comprised 44.6 percent of the population, and Protestants made up 47.0 percent. Roman Catholics, however, were much more likely to attend church regularly than Protestants. See Günter Hollenstein, "Die Katholische Kirche," in *Die Geschichte der Bundesrepublik Deutschland: Gesellschaft,* ed., Wolfgang Benz (Frankfurt, 1989), 124–61.

11. On the tensions between Catholics and Protestants in the CDU, see Martin Greschat, "Konfessionelle Spannungen in der Ära Adenauer," in *Katholiken und Protes-*

tanten in den Aufbaujahren der Bundesrepublik, ed., Thomas Sauer (Stuttgart, 2000), 19–34. See, in particular, his analysis on page 23 of the election results and ensuing confessional tensions over questions of school reform.

12. For an excellent compilation of the recent controversies that have arisen over the use of the "milieu" vocabulary, see Christoph Kösters and Antonius Liedhegener, "Historische Milieus als Forschungsaufgabe: Zwischenbilanz und Perspektiven," in *Konfession, Milieu, Moderne: Konzeptionelle Positionen und Kontroversen zur Geschichte von Katholizismus und Kirche im 19. und 20.* Jahrhunder, ed., Johannes Horstmann and Antonius Liedhegenert (Katholische Akademie Schwerte, 2001). For another excellent summary of the literature on "milieus," see Klaus Tenfelde, "Historische Milieus— Erblichkeit und Konkurrenz," in *Nation und Gesellschaft in Deutschland,* ed., M. Hettling und P. Nolte (München, 1996), 247–68. For the most convicing analysis of the term, "Catholic milieu," see Arbeitskreis für kirchliche Zeitgeschichte, Münster, "Katholiken zwischen Tradition und Moderne: Das katholische Milieu als Forschungsuafgabe," *Westfälische Forschung* 43 (1993): 588–654. For works which criticize the use of the phrase, "milieu," see Wilfried Loth, "Milieus oder Milieu? Konzeptionelle Überlegungen zur Katholizismusforschung," in *Politische Deutungskulturen: Festschrift für Karl Rohe,* ed., Othmar Haberl and Tobias Korenke (Baden Baden, 1999), 123–36, and Wilfried Loth, *Katholiken im Kaiserreich: Der politische Katholizismus in der Krise des wilhelminischen Deutschlands* (Düsseldorf, 1984). In light of the controversies that have arisen, this essay will use the term "Catholic milieu" descriptively, not prescriptively.

13. On the Catholic milieu in the 1950s and its political bases, see Franz Walter, "Milieus und Parteien in der deutschen Gesellschaft," in *Geschichte in Wissenschaft und Unterricht* (1995): 479–93, Karl Gabriel, *Christentum zwischen Tradition und Postmoderne* (Freiburg, 1992), Herbert Kühr, "Katholische und evangelische Milieus: Vermittlungsinstanzen und Wirkungsmuster," in *Wirtschaftlicher Wandel, religiöser Wandel und Wertwandel,* ed., Dieter Oberndörfer (Berlin, 1985), 245–61, Cornelia Quink, "Milieubedingungen des politischen Katholizismus in der Bundesrepublik," in *Politische Kultur in Deutschland,* ed., Dirk Berg-Schlosser und Jakob Schissler.

14. See, for instance, Hanna Schissler, ed., *Miracle Years: A Cultural History of West Germany, 1949–1968,* (Princeton, 2001). Of the 22 separate chapters (including the introduction and conclusion), none examines religion in the West German state. Michael Geyer and Konrad Jarausch, *Shattered Past: Reconstruction German Histories* (Princeton, 2003), likewise does not examine religion in any detail for the period of the Federal Republic. The same is true of the collection of essays in Robert Moeller, ed., *West Germany under Construction: Politics, Society and Culture in the Adenauer Era* (Ann Arbor, 1997). See also Elizabeth Heinemann, *What Difference Does a Husband Make? Women and Marital Status in Nazi and Postwar Germany* (Berkeley, 1999),

15. The recent works on German Catholicism in the post-1945 era can, by and large, be divided into several distinct groups. "Die blaue Reihe" of the Kommission für Zeitgeschichte contains numerous works by mostly younger historians. Of these, the most important remains Wilhelm Damberg's excellent work, *Abschied vom Milieu? Katholizismus im Bistum Münster und in den Niederlanden 1945–1980* (Paderborn, 1997). On the Familienpolitik of German Catholics, see Lukas Rölli-Alkemper's excellent work, *Familie im Wiederaufbau: Katholizismus und bürgerliches Familienideal in der Bundesrepublik Deutschland, 1945–1965* (Paderborn, 2000). See also Thomas Groß-

mann, *Zwischen Kirche und Gesellschaft: Das Zentralkomitee der deutschen Katholiken 1945–1970* (Mainz, 1991), Petra von der Osten, *Jugend- und Gefährdetenfürsorge im Sozialstaat: Auf dem Weg zum Sozialdienst katholischer Frauen, 1945–1968* (Paderborn, 2003), Dietmar Grypa, *Die Katholische Arbeiterbewegung in Bayern nach dem zweiten Weltkrieg 1945–1963,* (Paderborn, 2000). Another series, the Konfession-und Gesellschaftreihe, includes Joachim Köhler and Damian van Melis, eds., *Siegerin in Trümmern: Die Rolle der katholischen Kirche in der deutschen Nachkriegsgesellschaft* (Stuttgart, 1998), Thomas Sauer, ed., *Katholiken und Protestanten in den Aufbaujahren der Bundesrepublik* (Stuttgart, 2000), Anselm Doering-Manteuffel und Kurt Nowak, ed., *Kirchliche Zeitgeschichte: Urteilsbildung und Methoden* (Stuttgart, 1996), and Joachim-Christian Kaiser und Anselm-Doering Manteuffel, ed., *Christentum und politische Verantwortung: Kirchen im Nachkriegsdeutschland* (Stuttgart, 1990). One must also note the collection of works by an older generation of Catholic scholars associated with the Kommission für Zeitgeschichte in Bonn. See also Detlaf Pollack, "Funktionen von Religion und Kirche in den politischen Umbrüchen des 20. Jahrhunderts. Untersucht anhand der politischen Zäsuren von 1945 und 1989 in Deutschland" *Kirchliche Zeitgeschichte* Heft I (1999): 64–105.

16. Axel Schildt, "Modernisierung im Wiederaufbau: Die Westdeutsche Gesellschaft der fünfziger Jahre," in *Die Kultur der 50er Jahre,* ed., Werner Faulstich (Munich, 2002), 20.

17. The German social historian, Michael Klöcker, likewise depicts the 1950s as a period where the traditional Catholic education (he provides "ideal types" of Catholic values and education) exerted a nearly unrestricted hold over faithful and fearful Catholics throughout Germany. His account, though well-written and thorough, remains all too static and does not account for the changes in Catholic doctrine that were beginning at this time. Michael Klöcker, *Katholisch von der Wiege bis zur Bahre: Eine Lebensmacht im Zerfall?* (München, 1991). For an exception to this pattern, see Wilhelm Damberg, "Kritiker Adenauers aus dem Katholizismus," in *Adenauer und die Kirchen,* ed., Ulrich von Hehl (Bonn, 1999), 149–63.

18. On how postwar conservatives reconciled themselves to liberal democracy, see Jean Solchany, "Vom Antimodernismus zum Antitotalitarismus: Konservative Interpretationen des Nationalsozialismus in Deutschland, 1945–1949," *Vierteljahrshefte für Zeitgeschichte,* no. 3 (1996): 373–94, and Frank Bösch, *Das konservative Milieu: Vereinskultur und lokale Sammlungspolitik in ost- und westdeutschen Regionen, 1900–1960* (Göttingen, 2002).

19. On Catholic youth and the erosion of the Catholic milieu in the 1950s and 1960s, see Mark Edward Ruff, *The Wayward Flock: Catholic Youth in Postwar West Germany, 1945–1965* (Chapel Hill, 2005).

20. This position has been taken by both those on the left (see footnote no. 18) and from the right. For a perspective from the right, see Hans-Peter Schwarz, *Die Ära Adenauer* (Stuttgart, 1991).

21. See for instance, Heide Fehrenbach, *Cinema in Democratizing Germany: Reconstucting National Identity after Hitler* (Chapel Hill, 1995), and Heide Fehrenbach, "The Fight for the 'Christian West:' German Film Control, the Churches and the Reconstruction of Civil Society in the Early Bonn Republic," *German Studies Review* 14 (1991): 39–63. She concludes her article by pointing to the success of this conservative restoration in the early years of the Federal Republic: "*Heimatfilm,* the reigning film

genre of the 1950s, reinforced the conservative agenda for the social reconstruction of the postwar Germany. Indeed, there would be no more *Sünderins* in store for German audiences in the 1950s; rather, the traditional escapist and politically insidious *Heimatfilm*, first popularized under the Nazis, would become the national product of Bonn." (p. 56). See also the essay by Dagmar Herzog in this volume.

22. Robert Moeller, *Protecting Motherhood: Women and the Family in the Politics of Postwar West Germany* (Berkeley, 1993), 212.

23. See Ruff, *The Wayward Flock*, 74.

24. I have compiled these statistics from information provided in Erwin Gatz, ed., *Die Bischöfe der deutschsprachigen Länder, 1945–2001: Ein biographisches Lexikon* (Berlin, 2002). Quite obviously, the situation in the dioceses in the parts of Germany that were turned over to Poland and the Soviet Union was quite different.

25. For two accounts of this process for the diocese of Münster and the archdiocese of Paderborn, see, respectively, Wilhelm Damberg, *Abschied vom Milieu?* See also Matthias Schulze, *Bund oder Schar: Verband oder Pfarrjugend? Katholische Jugendarbeit im Erzbistum Paderborn nach 1945* (Paderborn, 2001).

26. See Maria Mitchell, "Materialism and Secularism: CDU Politicians and National Socialism, 1945–1949," *Journal of Modern History* 67 (1995): 278–308.

27. On how German conservatives attributed National Socialism to secularization and "Vermassung," see Jean Solchany, *Compendre le nazisme dans l'Allemagne des années zéro (1945–1949)* (Paris, 1997), 178–255, and especially, 236–55.

28. See quotes by Joseph Godehard Machens, bishop of Hildesheim, in Wolfgang Löhr, *Hirtenbriefe und Ansprachen zu Gesellschaft und Politik* (Würzburg, 1985), 137–38. On reading such quotes, one wonders whether Catholic leaders unintentionally drew parallels between the recent Jewish experience in the Holocaust and the recent upheavals and destruction in Germany. For an account of how religious leaders' understanding of secularization shaped their postwar Weltanschauung, see Konrad Repgen. "Die Erfahrung des Dritten Reiches und das Selbstverständnis der deutschen Katholiken nach 1945," in *Die Zeit nach 1945 als Thema kirchlicher Zeitgeschichte: Referate der internationalen Tagung in Hüningen/Bern (Schweiz) 1985*, ed., Victor Conzemius, Martin Greschat and Hermann Kocher, 127–79, and in particular, 138–40.

29. On these points, see Rölli-Alkemper, *Familie im Wiederaufbau*, 83–84.

30. See also Dagmar Herzog's essay in this volume.

31. See Ruff, *The Wayward Flock*, 36–38.

32. This is my conclusion after having examined hundreds of files from Catholic Youth workers in the 1950s. By the late 1950s, many youth leaders and even diocesan officials were discussing the ideas of the sociologist, Helmut Schelsky, for instance, whose groundbreaking work, *Die Skeptische Generation*, seemed to sum up the contradictions in that generation of "teenagers."

33. See Werner Blessing's convincing analysis of the diocese of Bamberg, "'Deutschland in Not, Wir im Glauben…' Kirche und Kirchenvolk in einer katholischen Region 1933–1949," in *Von Stalingrad zur Währungsreform: Zur Soziologie des Umbruchs in Deutschland*, Martin Broszat (München, 1989), 3–111.

34. Christoph Kösters underscores the extent to which the Catholic milieu in Munster was able to resist the encroachments of the NS state and analyzes the process of Verkirchlichung in his work, *Katholische Verbände und Moderne Gesellschaft: Organisationsgeschichte und Vereinskultur im Bistum Münster, 1918 bis 1945* (Paderborn,

1995). For an analysis of the milieux in the Saarland, see Gerhard Paul and Klaus-Michael Mallmann, *Milieus und Widerstand: Eine Verhaltensgeschichte der Gesellschaft im Nationalsozialismus* (Bonn, 1995).

35. See Ute Schmidt, *Zentrum oder CDU: Politischer Katholizismus zwischen Tradition und Anpassung* (Opladen, 1987), and Noel Cary, *The Path to Christian Democracy: German Catholics and the Party System from Windhorst to Adenauer* (Cambridge, 1996). See also Ronald Granieri, *The Ambivalent Alliance.*

36. On Klens, see Ingeborg Rocholl-Gärtner, *Anwalt der Frauen: Hermann Klens: Leben und Werk* (Düsseldorf, 1978). On Wolker, see Barbara Schellenberger, "Ludwig Wolker, 1887–1955" in *Zeitgeschichte in Lebensbildern: Aus dem deutschen Katholizismus des 19. und 20. Jahrhunderts,* ed., Jürgen Aretz (Mainz, 1982), 134–46. See Mark Edward Ruff, "Katholische Jugendarbeit und junge Frauen in Nordrhein-Westfalen, 1945–1962: Ein Beitrag zur Diskussion über die Auflösung des katholischen Milieus," *Archiv für Sozialgeschichte,* 38 Band (1998): 263–84.

37. Irmtraud Götz von Olenhusen, *Gottesreich, Jugendreich, Deutsches Reich: Junge Generation, Religion und Politik, 1928–1933* (Cologne, 1997), 82.

38. See Jugendhaus Hardehausen (JHH), 1.2201.3, München-Fürstenriedkonferenz, 26 April 1947.

39. Katholische Frauengemeinschaft (KFG), NL Klens, #570, Schneider an das Kongregationssekretariat Zürich, 28 February 1948. Wolker himself was personally devoted to Marian traditions but separated his own spirituality from his own work.

40. On feminization, see Irmtraud Götz von Olenhusen, ed., *Wunderbare Erscheinungen: Frauen und katholische Frömmigkeit im 19. und 20. Jahrhundert* (Paderborn, 1995) and Irmtraud Götz von Olenhusen, ed., *Frauen unter dem Patriarchat der Kirchen: Katholikinnen und Protestantinnen im 19. und 20. Jahrhundert* (Stuttgart, 1995). See also David Blackbourn, *Marpingen: Apparitions of the Virgin Mary in Nineteenth-Century Germany* (New York, 1994). See also the essay by Michael Gross in this volume. The concept of "feminization" has remained, however, somewhat vague, usually referring to the fact that women were attending mass in much larger numbers and rates than men and to the maudlin forms of piety of the late nineteenth century. It may be time for historians to delve beneath the surface of "feminization" and subject this concept to more rigorous analysis.

41. Rölli-Alkempter, *Familie im Wiederaufbau,* 48.

42. Ibid., 73.

43. Ibid, 79.

44. Ibid.

45. See Christoph Kösters, *Katholische Verbände und moderne Gesellschaft: Organisationsgeschichte und Vereinskultur im Bistum Münster 1918 bis 1945* (Paderborn, 1995) for a thorough discussion of this argument.

46. The literature on Catholic Action is fairly extensive. For an overview, see Wilhelm Damberg, "'Radikale katholische Laien an die Front!'—Beobachtungen zur Idee und Wirkungsgeschichte der 'Katholischen Aktion,'" in *Siegerin in Trümmern: Die Rolle der katholischen Kirche in der deutschen Nachkriegsgesellschaft,* ed., Joachim Köhler and Damian van Melis (Stuttgart, 1998), 142–60. See also Wilhelm Damberg, *Abschied vom Milieu?* 85–92, 128–30, and Angelika Steinmaus-Pollak, *Das als Katholische Aktion organisierte Laienapostolat: Geschichte seiner Theorie und seiner kirchenrechtlichen Praxis in Deutschland* (Würzburg, 1988).

47. Rölli-Alkemper, *Familie im Wiederaufbau*, 79.

48. Wilfried Evertz, "Im Spannungsfeld zwischen Staat und Kirche," in *Studien zur Kölner Kirchengeschichte*, ed., Historisches Archiv des Erzbistums Köln (Siegburg, 1992), 336–37.

49. For the most comprehensive portrait of Keller, see Wilhelm Damberg, *Abschied vom Milieu?*, 73–106.

50. Wilhelm Damberg, *Moderne und Milieu, 1802–1998, Band V, Geschichte des Bistums Münster* (Münster, 1998), 326–28.

51. Ibid. The rhetoric of rechristianization is ubiquitous in the Catholic literature in the late 1940s and early 1950s, less so by the late 1950s. In spite of the widespread use of this rhetoric, the allocation of resources and the creation of new programs were not usually derived from this topos. In fact, many of the few efforts at rechristianization, such as the Christliche Arbeiter-Jugend, failed, in part, from lack of funds. See Mark Edward Ruff, "Die christiche Arbeiterjugend in Deutschland, 1945–1965." in *Christliche Arbeiterbewegung in Europa, 1850–1950*, ed., Claudia Hiepel and Mark Ruff (Stuttgart, 2003).

52. Rölli-Alkemper, *Familie im Wiederaufbau*, 80.

53. Ibid., 100.

54. Diözesanarchiv Würzburg (DAW), Kasten, BDKJ, Jubiläumsausstellung (1987), Burg Rothenfels, 1954, 1964.

55. BDKJ-Würzburg, Folder 5, Autorität der Liebe erforderlich," Allgemeines Volksblatt, 8 May 1962, and DAW, LV/LB, LVHS, K3, "Themenvorschläge für die Familienarbeit—Diözese Würzburg."

56. Kommission für Zeitgeschichte, Bonn, NL Willy Bokler, D II 1, Referat Msgr. Klens zur Lage der Frauenjugendseelsorge, die Erste Hauptkonferenz der Katholischen Jugendseelsorge und Jugendorganisationen in den deutschen Diözesen, Bericht an die Diözesen, 29 April–3 May 1946.

57. See, for instance, Frank Biess, "Survivors of Totalitarianism: Returning POWs and the Reconstruction of Masculine Citizenship in West Germany, 1945–1955," in *The Miracle Years*, ed., Schissler, 57–82.

58. Rölli-Alkemper, *Familie im Wiederaufbau*, 104, see footnote 327.

59. Rölli-Alkemper, *Familie im Wiederaufbau*, 104, see footnote 322. 'As long as God is absent in public opinion—similar to the father in the family—so long with the man not be able to serve as a convincing authority for the young human being."

60. On the passing of this legislation in 1957 and the court decision of 1959, see Moeller, *Protecting Motherhood*, 180–209.

61. For a discussion of the impact of industrialization on the Catholic milieu in Bochum, see Antonius Liedhegener's magisterial work, *Christentum und Urbanisierung: Katholiken und Protestanten in Münster und Bochum, 1830–1933* (Paderborn, 1997).

62. On trends in female employment, see Eva Kolinsky, *Women in West Germany: Life, Work and Politics* (Oxford, 1989), Annette Kuhn, ed., *Frauen in der deutschen Nachkriegszeit* (Düsseldorf, 1984) and a controversial work, Klaus-Jörg Ruhl, *Verordnete Unterordnung: Berufstätige Frauen zwischen Wirtschaftswachstum und konservativer Ideologie in der Nachkriegszeit, 1945–1963* (München, 1994). Between 1952 and 1959, working women as a percentage of the total labor force rose from 30.9 to 33.9 percent, hardly a dramatic increase.

63. KZK, 1951, 47. These debates flourished already in the early 1950s.

64. See footnote no. 13 for literature that discusses such problems.

65. Rölli-Alkemper, *Familie im Wiederaufbau*, 102.

66. On the impact of the Second Vatican Council, see Franz-Xaver Kaufmann and Arnold Zingerle, ed., *Vatikanum II und Modernisierung: Historische, theologische und soziologische Perspektiven* (Paderborn, 1996).

67. See the reprint of this speech in "Jahresthema: Das christliche Menschenbild," Der junge Katholik: Die Jugendbeilage des "Christlichen Beobachter," January 1955.

68. On the larger erosion of the Catholic milieu during this time, see Ruff, *The Wayward Flock*, and Damberg, *Abschied vom Milieu?* 505–19.

69. On these processes, see Ruff, *The Wayward Flock*, 163–65, and Damberg, *Abschied vom Milieu?* 384–421.

70. See Jugendhaus Düsseldorf, A 526, Hauptversammlung 1953, Drucksache 21, and Statistische Sammlung, Jahresstatistik der Gliedgeminschaften 1964, Stichtag 31. 12. 1964. For another set of statistics, see Martin Schwab, *Kirche Leben und Gesellschaft Gestalten: Der Bund der Deutschen Katholischen Jugend (BDKJ) in der Bundesrepublik Deutschland und der Diözese Würzburg* (Würzburg, 1997), 45.

71. These were figures used to determine the level of state funding. See Konrad Adenauer Stiftung, NL Josef Rommerskirchen, I 234 024, Milteilungsblatt Landesjugendring Nordrhein-Westfalen, no 18, February-March 1960, 18–19.

72. On this plunge, see Michael Ebertz, *Erosion der Gnadenanstalt? Zum Wandel der Sozialgestalt der Kirche* (Frankfurt, 1999), 114. For a more popular and sensationalized account of the recent changes in the major religious bodies in Germany, see "Liebster Jesu, Wir sind Vier …" in *Der Spiegel*, 52, 1997, 58–73.

73. Rölli-Alkemper, *Familie im Wiederaufbau*, 118.

74. Ibid., 127.

75. Ibid.

76. For an example of this schizophrenia—the appeal to conscience, while insisting that the world could accommodate more humans—see Ottilie Mosshammer, *Werkbuch der katholischen Mädchenerziehung* (Freiburg, 1951), and especially, the chapter on "Mutterschaft," 266–79.

77. Cited in Rölli-Alkemper, 164–65. For a biography of Frings, see Norbert Trippen, *Josef Kardinal Frings (1887–1978), Band I* (Paderborn, 2003).

78. See Ruff, *The Wayward Flock*, 86–120.

79. On the Marxist currents in the BDKJ, see Martin Schwab, *Kirchlich, Kritisch, Kämpferisch: Der Bund der Deutschen Katholischen Jugend (BDKJ), 1949–1989* (Würzburg, 1994), 81–87.

80. In the last fifteen years, a number of sociologists of religion have debated theories of secularization which dated back to the 1960s. Some of the critics of these theories have argued that religious institutions sometimes secularized themselves by diluting doctrine and offering unpalatable products. For the most vocal of these criticisms, see Rodney Stark and Roger Finke, *Acts of Faith: Explaining the Human Side of Religion* (California, 2000).

81. Of course, German Catholicism had been pluralized since the nineteenth century, when dozens of Verbände, representing the diverse constituencies within the Catholic milieu—farmers, artisans, blue-collar workers—frequently quarreled with each other and with the church hierarchy. I would argue, however, that the challenge

to the authority of the church hierarchy was much greater in the years after 1965, the close of the Second Vatican Council, than before. On the other hand, German society became noticeably more diverse with the arrival of *Gastarbeiter* from Southern European nations and Turkey by the 1960s.

CHAPTER 14

Memory, Morality, and the Sexual Liberalization of West Germany

Dagmar Herzog[1]

> One's own offspring did penance for Auschwitz with ethics and
> morality forcefully jammed into them, with notions of cleanliness
> that constantly broke against reality and had to break.

—Olav Münzberg[2]

Why would the Federal Republic of Germany so soon after the end of Nazism, world war, and Holocaust, direct so much moral energy into the reorganization of sexual relations? As sociologist Martin Dannecker summarized the situation cuttingly in 2001, "When one looks at the early Federal Republic one gets the very real impression that it had no other concern than to put sexual matters in order."[3] Many who came of age in this climate subsequently recalled their childhoods as suffocating and claustrophobic, and the 1950s as a time when external adherence to propriety was vigilantly enforced by neighbors and parents. The pedagogy professor Ulf Preuss-Lausitz, for example, retrospectively described a 1950s adolescence this way: "The postwar child was *surrounded*, under the motto 'that just isn't done,' *with prohibitions and injunctions, with the compulsion to a fictive normality....* The postwar German family (or what was left of it) was fixated on conformity, on not standing out."[4] Yet as scholars have begun to seek explanations for (what is summarily called) the "yearning for normalization" or "search for 'moral' restabilization" that so clearly characterized the 1950s, they have identified these primarily as responses to the intensely disruptive experiences of war and its immediate chaotic aftermath.[5] What remains unaddressed is how sexual conservatism also served as a crucial site for managing the memory of mass murder.

While the half-dozen immediate postwar years were a time of remarkable "erotic liberality" or even "erotic overstimulation," and an era of avid and open public discussion of a broad range of sexual issues, the early to mid-1950s saw an unexpected shift toward far greater sexual conservatism.[6] Within a short time, liberal commentators on sexual matters were on the defensive, while conservatives took an aggressive lead and quickly won a series of significant victories. An unusual convergence of efforts between more right-wing Christian Democrats in the Bundestag and otherwise more left-leaning Christian intellectuals successfully defeated attempts to liberalize abortion laws. Concerted church and political campaigns at the municipal and state level to shield adolescents from any exposure to naked images led in 1952 to the passage of a national law against "youth-endangering publications" that censored the display and sale of nude pictures and sexually explicit texts; nudity in films was also strictly censored. (Under Nazism, by contrast, nudity in publicly displayed art had been routine, and nudity in film was considered fully permissible.) In other cases, developments in the 1950s unabashedly reconnected to the Nazi era. For example, after a brief postwar period of relative tolerance and uncertainty in legal decisions regarding men accused of homosexual acts, the 1950s witnessed an escalation of police persecution and punitive sentencing. In several states, the Himmler order of 1941 (banning the advertisement and sale of all birth-control products except condoms) remained in effect, and efforts to decriminalize the marketing of birth-control products failed. From the mid-1950s on, court decisions made access even to condoms more rather than less difficult in some regions. The difficulty of accessing contraception made sexual encounters more risky, and contributed to the high rate of illegal and often dangerous abortions.

And it was not only in the realm of law that conservatism was ascendant. The popular media, especially illustrated magazines, and marriage and sex advice books, were enormously influential in elaborating conservative ideas about gender roles, familial relations, and sexual mores. Politicians' and church leaders' rhetoric in favor of reestablishing female submission to male authority and popular magazines' idealization of a wife's selfless delight in pleasing and nurturing her husband, worked in conjunction. With the censoring of sex-liberal publications, there was no counterbalance to the unapologetically regressive advice-literature soon flooding the market in millions of copies; this literature emphasized the values of chastity and self-restraint, taught that both masturbation and premarital heterosexual sex would result in miserable marriages, and treated homosexuality as a pathological condition. In sharp contrast to the late 1940s and early 1950s, frank and detailed discussion in print of sexual practices—including sex within marriage—was heavily censored.

Some conservative laws and attitudes that had been promulgated during the Third Reich were experienced as being even more directly oppressive by the majority of young people in the 1950s than they had been before 1945. Key among these was the Nazi ruling prohibiting pimping *(Kuppeleiparagraph)*, which—although only infrequently formally enforced—still served in the 1950s as the backdrop against which parents, landlords, and hotel managers had reason to fear that neighbors might have them arrested if their children, renters, or guests received overnight visitors of the opposite sex. Strikingly, by contrast, during the Third Reich parents had been exempted from this "pimping paragraph."

Sexual relations became premier sites for memory management for multiple reasons, and the result was ultimately overdetermined. Although this is poorly understood now—precisely because we still today labor under many misconceptions with regard to the Third Reich's sexual politics—one powerful impetus for sexual conservatism in postwar Germany lay in the fact that encouragement to sexual activity and pleasure had been a major feature of National Socialism. Restoring conservative sexual mores was thus important to Christians not least because sex had been a main element in Christians' specific conflicts with Nazis *during* the Third Reich.

At first, the Nazis' vociferous early attacks on pornography, the regime's closure of gay and lesbian bars, and assurances that conservative sexual mores would be restored had been crucial factors in facilitating Protestant and Catholic leaders' effusively enthusiastic endorsement of Hitler's rise to power in 1933. But within two to three years, Christian clergymen and lay activists were appalled to find Nazi leaders actively encouraging pre- and extramarital heterosexuality as long as both partners were deemed "racially" appropriate. Widely read Nazi newspapers and sex advice literature missed few opportunities to attack Christians as sexually uptight and to mock the churches for their restrictive sexual mores. (Christian spokespeople, for their part, articulated more frequent distress over the regime's incitements to nudity and nonmarital sex than over its anti-Semitism; Protestant and Catholic church leaders not only did not protest anti-Semitic invective but also directly expressed it and thereby lent to it their own moral authority.) The massively disruptive impact of World War II exacerbated trends toward liberalization of heterosexual mores that had been gradually underway since the beginning of the twentieth century and that had also been decisively encouraged by the National Socialist regime. In this context, turning against nudity and licentiousness in the early 1950s, especially in the name of Christianity, could quite legitimately be represented and understood as a turn against Nazism. This was not merely a matter of political expediency but also one of profoundly held belief.

In general, of course, the emphasis on the need to re-Christianize German society was understood as a logical countermove to the secularization so manifestly furthered by Nazism. Insisting that there was a God in heaven who not only gave people strength in conditions of adversity but also made demands on human beings to be concerned with peace, justice, and care for the weak and vulnerable, was a powerful moral claim to make in the wake of an era in which human beings had set *themselves* up as the lords of life and death, in which the so-called German race had treated itself as divine and the Führer had acted as though he were God, and in which every moral value had been perverted into its opposite. Furthermore, the move to re-Christianize postwar German culture also provided an unexpectedly effective way of adapting to the expectations of the American occupiers. The pressure from the rest of the West (not least American and British church leaders) to come to some kind of terms particularly with the Judeocide cannot be underestimated as a key cause for the renegotiation of moral concerns that occurred in early 1950s West Germany.

Unaware of the churches' entanglement with Nazism, the Western military authorities permitted the churches to run their own denazification procedures, and encouraged them in their newfound roles as arbiters of post-fascist morality. Interestingly, moreover, and however incongruously, West German conservatives were able to fool the American occupiers with a hyperbolic rhetoric of moral cleanliness while simultaneously—since blaming Jews for sexual immorality among Germans had abruptly become taboo—blaming American culture for any licentiousness which Germans evinced.[7] At the same time, it became commonplace in the postwar years to blame the Nazis for pervasive popular secularization. This was yet another telling substitution, since during the Third Reich Catholic and Protestant spokespeople had been all too eager to please their new Nazi masters by blaming popular secularization on Jews (and their supposedly deleterious and disproportionate influence on Weimar culture).

Certainly, the dynamic whereby the moral crisis engendered by Nazism was resolved via enforcement of sexual conservatism also had to do with strongly felt needs to repair individual partnerships and reconstruct families to the extent that either was possible after the disruptions of total war and mass death. "Nesting" and reprivatization were utterly reasonable responses both to years of wartime and postwar deprivation, separation, stress, and loss, and to the Nazi state's aggressive invasion of the private realm alike. And yet, the official re-Christianization of West German culture as it concretely ensued—as sociologist Y. Michal Bodemann especially has pointed out—itself needs to be seen as a way to manage the metaphysical catastrophe engendered by mass murder by casting questions of concrete German complicity in cruelty, expropriation, and genocide in deliberately universalizing (and hence no longer specifically German) existential categories of suffering, guilt, and redemption.[8]

Re-Christianization too, then (however superficial it might have been), became a way of avoiding responsibility. In fact, many clergymen made this connection explicit when they angrily challenged the Allies' war crimes trials and denazification efforts with the argument that only God could judge human transgressions.[9] In addition, by a perhaps unintended though thereby no less crucial turn, postwar Christians' emphasis on cleaning up sexual mores also provided a remarkably convenient way to erase from view and from popular memory both Christian churches' own complicity *with* Nazism—not only with its anti-Bolshevism but also explicitly its anti-Semitism.

The postwar decade—and this is crucial to register—also saw the articulation of a progressive version of Christianity, one that drew different lessons from the Nazi past than Christian conservatives did. This strand of Christianity combined hope for a renewal of serious spirituality with openness to some aspects of socialism and with a profound opposition to remilitarization. But these more progressive views were minority ones; they also typically did not extend to matters of sexuality and reproduction. Even the most politically leftist of Christian antifascists tended to share assumptions about sexuality with their more conservative counterparts. In a post-fascist climate in which even Social Democrats scrambled to disassociate themselves from any taint of Weimar-era sexual radicalism, committed Christians were unlikely to be vigorous defenders of sexual freedom or reproductive choice.

Perhaps, however, the single most powerful basis for the postwar Christian consensus that sexual freedom was not a moral value worth defending was precisely the deep perception that there had been some kind of (difficult-to-articulate but nonetheless intimate) link between Nazi inducements to sexual licentiousness and genocide. The Catholic physician Anton Hofmann struggled to express this perspective in 1951. "NS-schools and the like," Hofmann uncontroversially observed, had forced "premature sexual contact" on young people under the guise of "a natural and free experience of the erotic event." But in his view, this Nazi encouragement of nonmarital sexual activity was inseparable from Nazism's larger criminality. For Hofmann, the disrespect for the spiritual dimension of life evident among people overly obsessed with erotic pleasure was inextricably connected with disrespect for the bodies of others and therefore facilitated brutality and mass murder. Or, as he put it, linking "overvaluation of the body" with "godlessness and cruelty," what needed to be understood was "the paradoxical fact that the same person who raises the body to dizzying heights, can in an instant sacrifice the bodies of a hundred thousand others."[10]

Yet not least because of the connections Hofmann was identifying, frank discussion of Nazism's sexual stimuli subsided during the 1950s. The fact that the regime that had been sexually inciting had also been responsible for continent-wide carnage and the systematic torture and murder of its own citi-

zens and millions of citizens of other nations now rendered it particularly unwelcome to recall popular receptivity to Nazism's pleasure-enjoining aspects.
Specifically the fact that taboo-breaking with regard to sexual mores had been
accompanied by such massive rupture of the taboo against killing the weak
made it both psychologically and politically congenial to excise certain elements from the retrospective portrait of Nazism while highlighting others.[11]
This, then, was yet another reason for the postwar shift in moral focus from
murder to sex.

Significantly, moreover, a main effect of (what Hanna Schissler has succinctly named) "the normalization project of the 1950s" was precisely that the
sexually inciting aspects of Nazism were—over the course of the 1950s—assiduously forgotten.[12] Admitting to their children or to the rest of the world
that they had had any particular pleasures during the Third Reich increasingly
did not fit with one of postwar Germans' most successful strategies for dealing with guilt (whether internally felt or externally imposed) about the Third
Reich: the tendency to present themselves as victims of Nazism rather than its
supporters and beneficiaries. Stressing that familial and sexual conservatism
were timeless German values that transcended political regime changes offered a way of hiding from view, and subsequently also from memory, one's
own youthful departures from traditional norms, as these had been facilitated
by Nazism, and one's own enthusiasm for Nazism more generally. In other
words, although the populace in many parts of Germany, both in Catholic and
Protestant regions, was at a minimum strongly anticlerical, if not more thoroughly secularized, even those who were not particularly involved with the
churches had their own reasons for not challenging the ascendancy of sexually conservative rhetoric and laws.

Meanwhile, the relentless emphasis placed by postwar Christian spokespeople on the moral requirement of premarital heterosexual chastity functioned successfully to distract attention from what were also some notable
continuities between Nazis and postwar Christians. Stressing the importance
of premarital chastity, for example, allowed postwar Christian commentators
to delineate their difference from Nazism in especially stark terms, since Nazis
had been so particularly eager to celebrate premarital sex and challenge the
churches for their "prudery" on this matter. Yet the manifest postwar departure
from Nazi values with respect to premarital heterosexual sex was often accompanied by unapologetic perpetuation of Nazi-era laws and attitudes. Homophobia and eugenics were both refurbished and given renewed legitimacy
under Christian auspices.

Precisely this convoluted conjunction of rupture and continuity between
Nazism and postwar conservative politics, together with the sense that the hyper-
preoccupation with sexual morality only thinly veiled some deeper entanglement in national guilt—as well as ongoing anger and resentment at the fact of

that guilt—was unnervingly palpable to more critical young people coming of age in this climate. That the atmosphere was "stuffy" *(muffig)* and "philistine" *(spiessig)* was powerfully felt by many in 1950s West Germany. What was perplexing was the disconnect young people experienced between official Christianization and popular disaffection, even disdain, for the churches. The fact that the apparent transition to a more Christianized culture was often rather superficial in what was an already considerably secularized society was not lost on many postwar observers. (Only one in four West Germans attended church regularly in the late 1940s, and although the rate rose again to one in three in the early 1960s, this percentage disguised the fact that substantially more Catholics than Protestants were regular churchgoers. Expert analysts in the early 1960s were also in agreement that church attendance was often a sign more of superstition or of public respectability than vibrant faith.) As novelist Hermann Peter Piwitt (born 1935) would sardonically write many years later:

> After all, the churches were that which offered postwar Germans the most convenient solution for that which had happened. What had led to fascism? "Dearth of faith." "A turning-away from God." "After the collapse of the state to be embraced by the church" ([a comment from Protestant politician] Eugen Gerstenmaier), that was the yearning of many. And the business of selling indulgences went correspondingly well. Churches sprung up, as though there was nothing else to build, and every village architect developed the sweeping fantasy of a Corbusier.... But then it turned out that these churches did not function at all. They stood around like freshly dedicated train stations at tracks that have just been shut down. And the people made their jokes: "Soul-rocketing ramps." "Christ's power plant." Here too one had only "kept up appearances."[13]

Equally unnerving was the lingering sense that many older Germans were not remorseful. Privately, vicious anti-Semitism was still routinely expressed. And an only barely contained aggressive sense of national pride and feeling of superiority toward the military occupiers was part of public discussion in the media and politics as well. As Günter Grass, during World War II a soldier in the Wehrmacht, remarked critically about the 1950s from the perspective of 1980s hindsight: While some West Germans might subsequently have felt nostalgia for this decade of apparently successful democratization, integration into the West, and the "economic miracle," "how much Christian hypocrisy lay like mildew on the society," "how corrupt and full of lies it was," "how sassily the murderers stood among us," and "how it stank so badly in the fifties, it took one's breath away."[14]

The point, then, is not only to call attention to the complex and ever-shifting mixture between eras of continuity and rupture, retrieval and reconstruction and new departure. Rather, what we need to become attuned to above all are the subtler dynamics of *redefinition* and *reinterpretation,* the development of new legitimations for old practices (in other words, continuity presented as change), as well as the opposite (something new introduced in the name of tradition). And what finally also demands investigation is the confluence of factors and strategies by which the conservative culture that gained hold in the 1950s was eventually liberalized. For central to the transformation of West Germany's sexual culture in the early 1960s was the formulation of a wholly new interpretation of the Third Reich, one on which parents and children, leftists, liberals, and conservatives, could all agree—although for completely different reasons and with utterly divergent investments.

~

Especially worth attending to are the meaning-making processes engaged in by postwar commentators and the changing *interpretations* of Nazism proffered in the context of evolving battles over sexual politics. In the fight to maintain the criminalization of abortion in the Western zones and then the Federal Republic, for instance, it is noteworthy that even in the first years after the war we find such terms as concentration camps, gas chambers, and Auschwitz regularly being invoked, specifically by Catholic physicians, journalists, and politicians. It was apparent that abortion—not least due to its prevalence in the first few postwar years—served to condense a whole bundle of negative feelings about Nazism and to fuse distress over its genocidal policies with opposition to its libertinism. But this involved a distinctly one-sided reading of Nazism's abortion politics. After all, under Nazism, the enforcement of involuntary abortion on tens of thousands of so-called "unworthy" German and foreign forced laborer women had been only one side of the coin; the other had been the denial of abortion rights to so-called "superior" women and the intensified prosecution and punishment of voluntary abortion (including the death penalty for abortion providers after 1943).

Yet one would not know much at all about the Nazis' intensified prosecution of abortion-seekers or abortion providers from reading the first decade of postwar commentary.[15] Walter Dirks, for example, one of the leading Catholic progressives in Weimar and in the post–World War II years the coeditor of the prestigious intellectual journal *Frankfurter Hefte,* declared bluntly in 1946 that abortion was "the path of least resistance, the easy solution, … the perfect solution, if one has managed to shut one's eyes before the single uncomfortable fact that the killing of human life is murder—all one has to do is walk in the footsteps of the SS-doctors."[16] Similarly, the Catholic physician Hermann Frühauf suggested that a comprehensive antiabortion stance was the only way to be truly anti-Nazi. According to Frühauf, whoever favored abortion rights, "whether he intends this or not, whether he understands this or not, serves those forces and powers that trespass against humanity; he finds himself at a particularly dangerous point on that precipitous slope that in its last consequences leads to the gas chambers of an Auschwitz."[17] Maria Probst, representative to the Bundestag of the Bavarian CSU, declared for her part that any modification of Paragraph 218, the law prohibiting abortion, would be disastrous:

> This is not about the woman's so-called democratic right of self-determination with respect to her own body. This is a matter of the existence or nonexistence of another life.... I can only indicate the moral consequences here. Naked materialism, uninhibited sexuality, dying eros, growing neglect of youth, declining respect for the woman are results that must be taken very seriously.... It is a fact that childlessness frequently reduces the impulse to hard work and to thriftiness.... Even to relax Paragraph 218 partially would mean the state was permitting murder. Here the course would be set whose final step must lead to a new Auschwitz.[18]

In similar fashion, Probst's CSU colleague Franziska Gröber imaginatively merged abortion and Nazi crimes—even as, simultaneously, she unapologetically repeated Nazis' (rather Lamarckian and scientifically insupportable) ideas about genetics: "Women who manage to kill the life they carry under their heart will also manage to kill any life. Then in addition to that comes genetic inheritance *[die Erbfolge]*; about that no one has today yet spoken.... If ... a mother has already herself murdered two children, do you think that has no consequences for genetic inheritance? Will you be surprised if we then once again have concentration camps here or if more murderers are born out of such families? You will not have to be surprised about this!"[19] That Probst unselfconsciously expressed punitive affect about "work-shy" tendencies, or that Gröber's arguments lacked even the semblance of logical coherence, was not the point. What was above all significant was the accumulation of intense emotion that linked sexual freedom with death.

In a fundamentally different but complementary manner, the antipornography campaigns of the early 1950s provided numerous occasions for merging negative feeling about Nazism with negative feeling about sexual explicitness while simultaneously redirecting the focus of moral concern from Nazism to sex. To the stunned dismay of liberal anticensorship activists, a bill concerning the "Dissemination of Youth-Endangering Publications" passed the Bundestag in 1952 by 165 votes to 133 with seven abstentions. While a mere handful of journalists suggested that the renewed postwar rise of right-wing elements "may contribute far more to the moral degradation of youth than nudities have ever been able to do," or that "the orgies of smut and trash" that had as their subject "the stupidest gossip about former Hitler-cronies" was more wor-

risome and deleterious to a young person's psychological health than naked-
ness could ever be, the majority even of anticensorship commentators believed that kiosk porn was "real poison," that there was necessarily damage to
young people's "character development" resulting from "strong sexual stimuli," or that porn in picture and print could stimulate "the erotic fantasy of our
youth ... into the pathological."[20] Conservatives, for their part, were unambiguous in their assessment that the prevalence of pornography in postwar
Germany was an indication of the "lost state of human existence."[21] As one
paper editorialized after the vote, "No one can deny that youth today, in the
aftermath of National Socialism and the Second World War, is in greater moral
danger than ever before and thus needs to be protected more than ever before."[22] The slippage from a morality concerned with the aftereffects of fascism
to a morality concerned above all with the restriction of talk about and representations of sex was well underway here.[23]

   While contemporaries remember how abruptly (and thoroughly) all nude
images disappeared from public display after the law went into effect, the most
significant result of the law involved the censorship of liberal sex-advice materials, with the consequence that conservative literature came to dominate
the sex-advice market. Through their considerable influence on government
policies and school curricula, conservative publicists would be able to set the
terms of public debate about sex in West Germany until well into the 1960s.
Whether they themselves or their families were believers or unbelievers, young
people could hardly avoid a climate where it was routine to hear that homosexuality and premarital intercourse were sins, or that masturbation had the
most severely deleterious psychological consequences.

   Advice writers brought maximum moral intensity to the task of convincing young people that "every premarital sexual experience imperils the lasting
bond of a future marriage and inhibits a proper stance towards sexuality in
general." "Through strict moral guidance and influence youth should deny
themselves sexual activities, so that they do not damage their future capacity
for marriage."[24] Marital sex would be enhanced by premarital abstinence.[25]
Premarital intercourse could lead to erectile dysfunction, according to a Catholic expert, and "the full blissful richness of sexual love can only remain pre-
served undiminished for that person who has not violated it with untamed
greed."[26] Or as an influential Protestant writer put it: "Only those who do not
have an inkling of or do not respect mature love-lust can allow themselves the
attempt to preempt it prematurely.... It is as impossible as harvesting grapes
in the snows of March."[27] In the meantime, although a range of experts in the
Weimar and Nazi and early postwar years had emphasized not only the harm-
lessness of youth masturbation, but even its value as a preparatory experience
for later sexual relationships, the majority of 1950s experts with forcefulness

and unanimity insisted on the opposite. Masturbation was a "reprehensible practice" that could lead to the incapacity ever to love another human being.[28] Homosexuality was anathema. Protestant physician Erich Schroeder advised boys to turn suspected homosexuals in to the police.[29] Most Christian commentators on male homosexuality in the 1950s opposed decriminalization. As one Protestant pastor concluded in 1953, "what remains is the necessity ... to protect developing youth during the time of their bisexual lability and homosexual receptiveness."[30] The archconservative Catholic moral purity organization, the *Volkswartbund,* actually went so far as to ask that lesbianism be criminalized as well on the grounds of consistency. Homosexuality simply was a "moral perversion and thereby a crime against nature" and "those who disdained marriage must be punished."[31] The journal *Christ und Welt* (The Christian and the World) expressed repugnance at the idea advanced by campaigners against paragraph 175 of the criminal code (which criminalized homosexuality) that sexual self-determination could be seen as part of the constitutionally guaranteed "free development of the personality." "Divine law" opposed this. Homosexuality could not be legalized, even if psychiatric care might be better than prison terms. The rise in incidence of homosexuality, especially among youth, was "frighteningly high" and "unmistakably spreading." Clergymen needed to exploit the "depression" that often befell incarcerated homosexuals and to help lead these people "back to the center of existence and to an inner renewal."[32]

The churches' opposition to decriminalization efforts had a decisive impact.[33] Although courts in the late 1940s and early 1950s had come to widely varying and often liberal decisions, by 1954, a judge at the Federal Constitutional Court could summarily observe that "case law nearly unanimously takes the view that Paragraph 175 is compatible with the Basic Law."[34] Recurrent efforts to challenge Paragraph 175—either on grounds of unconstitutionality, or on grounds that it represented an inheritance of Nazi *racial* law and hence should be considered invalid due to the occupiers' revocation of all laws related to Nazi racism—were all defeated.[35] The law was not modified until 1969. During the 1950s and 1960s, close to 100,000 men suspected of homosexual acts were registered in police files; every year brought between 2,500 and 3,500 convictions. As the historian of religion and anti-175 activist Hans Joachim Schoeps once remarked in retrospect, "for homosexuals, the Third Reich actually only ended in 1969."[36]

Postwar Christian writers on sex also often picked right up where Nazi sex commentators had left off in their discussion of eugenics. The prominent postwar Catholic commentator Werner Schöllgen not only described contraception as "biological suicide" but also contended expressly that "the eugenic idea" had not lost its value despite "the abuse in the Third Reich."[37] Catholic eugenics expert Hermann Muckermann expressed his vociferous concern that the disabled cost society more than the healthy ("the thought is unbearable that hopeless progeny from mentally debilitated hereditary lines would be cared for with greater devotion than the progeny of healthy parents").[38] And the highly regarded Protestant sex advice expert Theodor Bovet in 1955 was similarly concerned "with the healthy inheritance of our *Volk*." Bovet bemoaned the fact that "the less valuable elements, especially the mentally deficient, reproduce approximately twice as much as healthy families. It is therefore absolutely necessary, if we want to avoid being completely flooded by those [elements], that everyone who deems himself to be healthy ... give life to as many children as possible."[39]

Meanwhile, postwar West German culture was peculiarly inhospitable to open discussion of birth-control products or practices. In comparison with the U.S. in the 1950s, for instance, there were in West Germany fewer family planning clinics; there was also less medical literature on the subject available to specialists and of what literature there was, much expressed strong criticism of birth control. And yet the resistance to fertility control among physicians, judges, and politicians should not be seen solely as an inheritance of Nazism, for just as crucial was the indirect but no less powerful impact of the conservative Christian backlash *against* Nazism's sexual incitements. Symptomatically, for instance, while condom vending machines had been fairly familiar aspects of the streetscape, of public toilets and the backs of bars or barbershops, in many German towns throughout the Third Reich and in many places—as soon as rubber was available again—also into the mid-fifties, the years from the mid-1950s to the early 1960s saw heated discussion among jurists and journalists over the desirability of these machines and their potential for corrupting the morals of youth. Even the neutral display of condoms in vending machines could be interpreted—as some courts did—as an offense to "morals and decency [*Sitte und Anstand*]," a vague but for that reason all the more effective traditional legal category employed by conservative jurists in their efforts to deter youth (and inevitably also adult) access to fertility control.[40] Again, Catholic activists set the terms of the conversation. While in 1951–52 conservative Catholic youth organizations had demonstratively burned down kiosks which marketed pornography, in 1953 they initiated "actions" against condom vending machines. And once again, far from being legally censured, this activism itself inspired conservative jurisdiction.[41] Crucially, moreover, throughout this time, the major opposition party of Social Democrats did not provide much of an alternative to the Christian Democrats on sex-related issues, but instead remained wary of challenging the churches well into the 1960s.

A main theme in Christian advice literature involved the absolute link between reproduction and marital happiness. And as they made their case for procreation, postwar Christian commentators struggled particularly over how best to specify the differences between Nazi and Christian values. Thus as early as 1946 the *Frankfurter Hefte* had argued that, in contradistinction to Christian attitudes, the Nazi-encouraged "joy in children" was actually "the opposite of the true order of life that is realized in humble acceptance and not in the goal-orientation of a state's hubris."[42] The prominent Protestant bishop Hanns Lilje ran into similar conundrums in 1954 as he attempted to articulate the distinctions between Nazi and Christian ideals. On the one hand, he pointed out that Nazism was ultimately about a "fundamental denial of the family ... despite all wordy pro-family declarations." And he insisted that it must be self-evident that "it is the end of all ethics in this matter, when one wants to make a biological breeding institute out of marriage and family." On the other hand, however, he urgently wished his readers to understand that having the "will to the child" (*Wille zum Kind*—a term frequently used in Weimar and even more in the Third Reich and which Lilje employed unselfconsciously) was a powerful act of Christian faith.[43] And also in 1954, a Catholic commentator in a "sexual-pedagogical lecture series" sponsored by the city of Bad Godesberg near Bonn, made arguments for reproductive rather than "egotistical" marriage. While Nazis had seen in sex only "the biological function ... the breeding purpose," and while this was indeed offensive, reproduction *was* central to marital life; spouses fundamentally violated their bond "if they say no to the child."[44]

Experts on sexuality in 1950s West Germany thus continually worked to suture aspirations for lasting happiness, passion, and love to anxieties about non-normative sexual practices and pregnancy-prevention strategies. Anything directed solely at (what commentators regularly referred to as) "egotistic drive-satisfaction [*egotistische Triebbefriedigung*]" was deemed unacceptable, both from the moral point of view and—significantly—also from the point of view of pleasure. Indeed, couples were informed that even intercourse in the missionary position, if one's thoughts were not completely focused on the spiritual bond with the partner, was little more than "reciprocal masturbation [*gegenseitige Onanie*]."[45] But more than that: any emptiness a couple might feel, any vague sense of incomplete satisfaction or ambivalence about one another had its source in an inability fully to focus on the other person, and pregnancy prevention tactics constituted such an inability. Christian advice-givers styled themselves (in a manner that could be construed as proto-feminist) as dedicated to women in their forceful insistence that men should never treat women like objects. But they also and repeatedly emphasized that women needed to give themselves fully, both in the sense of being selfless, and in the sense of being receptive and open to the man. This openness (and hence real pleasure) was not possible if fear of pregnancy dominated sexual encounters. The solution, however, was seen not in effective contraception, but rather joyful receptivity to the possibility of procreation.

It was small wonder that young people coming of age in this climate would have trouble understanding the distinctions between Nazi and postwar pronatalism. Even as a postwar court, for example, rejecting in 1955 one company's efforts to market pessaries and contraceptive powders and gels, argued that "not every legal measure that serves population growth has a National Socialist tendency.... For every healthy state ... a growth in population is absolutely desirable," the defensiveness evident in this remark suggested the acute awareness that the populace was not quite clear on how postwar conservatism differed from its fascist predecessor.[46] Moreover, perhaps the most devastating consequence of all the high-minded injunctions offered by conservative advice literature coupled with inadequate access to contraception and derogatory attitudes or ignorance about noncoital practices was that by the early 1960s an estimated one million illegal abortions occurred in West Germany each year (approximately one abortion for every birth). For what bears emphasis is that the claustrophobic and conservative climate of shaming did not so much lower the rates of premarital coitus in West Germany (these remained remarkably high in comparison with France, Britain, and the U.S., by some estimates between 80 and 90 percent of the populace), nor did it stop married women from seeking abortions as a way to manage their fertility; what conservatism did—and powerfully—was to shape *how* people experienced the sex that they had.

～

The eventual sexual liberalization of West Germany in the course of the 1960s would depend on four crucial dynamics: One was the medical-technological invention of the birth-control pill; indeed, arguably the pill's single most important effect was to bring down the rate of abortion.[47] A second important dynamic was the ever-intensifying use of sexual stimuli (that is, nude and semi-nude images and titillating narratives) in advertising and journalism— in other words a dynamic largely intrinsic to economic processes. The third dynamic—in complex interaction with the first two—was a process of direct political mobilization against the official culture of sexual conservatism. This political mobilization, beginning tentatively in the late 1950s, and escalating in ardor and strategic effectiveness in the first three or four years of the 1960s, involved both prominent liberal public intellectuals and younger, often left-leaning student activists. And there is no question that liberals and leftists, while on the one hand exceedingly critical of the commodification of sex and its role in consumer capitalism, also used the space opened by the manifest contradictions between conservative norms and sexualized marketing to press their own claims.

Yet nothing was more important in helping liberals and leftists redirect the *moral* terms of conversation about sex in West Germany than a fourth dynamic: the return with full force to public discussion of the Holocaust as its details were made public in the postwar trials of perpetrators. Preeminent among these was the trial of Adolf Eichmann in Jerusalem in 1961 and the trial, held in Frankfurt am Main from 1963–65, of twenty-two SS men and one prisoner Kapo—all perpetrators in Auschwitz. The Auschwitz trial in particular provided a focal point for rewriting the memory and lessons of the Third Reich for liberal-left purposes. Yet, even before the Auschwitz trial began, the political mobilization against the culture of sexual conservatism had already gained considerable momentum.

A proposed reform of the Federal Republic's criminal code with respect to sexual matters served as an early occasion for the coordinated emergence of critical liberal voices. The development of a new criminal code had been underway since 1954, when a commission comprised of jurists and politicians had been established for this purpose. Medical and legal experts were consulted at various stages, and in 1960 a first draft was published, with a revised version of the draft appearing in 1962. This revised draft rapidly won approval from the cabinet of the Christian Democratic government and thereafter the Federal Council. By 1963, discussion of the draft was imminent also in the Bundestag.

The 1962 draft *("Entwurf 1962")* was profoundly conservative. It maintained the criminalization of adultery, and of pornography and mechanical sex aids. It constrained the advertising and marketing of contraceptives and maintained the criminalization of abortion. Throughout, the draft was suffused with the notion that the purpose of the law was to guard morality, and it frequently invoked the idea of "the healthy sensibility of the people *[das gesunde Volksempfinden]*" as a legitimate reference point for legal rulings. On abortion, moreover, the commission notably passed over in silence the scandalous state of affairs in West Germany. The 1962 draft also maintained the criminalization of male homosexuality. The draft averred that homosexuals did *not* act from an "inborn disposition," but rather were "overwhelmingly persons who ... through seduction, habituation or sexual supersatiation have become addicted to vice or who have turned to same-sex intercourse for purely profit-seeking motives."[48] And the commission expressed the view that homosexuals should in most instances be capable, if they made enough of an effort, of suppressing their desires and hence living lives in accordance with the law. The commission reiterated key notions about youthful fluidity in sexual orientation and about homosexuality as a deficit of heterosexuality that had been developed under Nazism. But unlike in the climate of the 1950s, by the early 1960s critics of such notions were less easily cowed. The commission's recommendation that male homosexuality continue to be criminalized was both found to be the single most offensive aspect of the draft *and* was seen as symptomatic of the commission's broader antisexual attitude.

One book, a pathbreaking interdisciplinary anthology entitled *Sexualität und Verbrechen* (Sexuality and Crime, 1963), contributed more than any other text to reframing the terms of debate about sexuality in postwar West Germany and thereby helped set in motion the official (and not just popular) liberalization of postwar sexual culture. In retrospect, it remains shocking how impoverished public discussion of sexual matters was by the early 1960s, and how urgently new perspectives were needed. The anthology brought together Jewish reemigrés like Frankfurt School philosopher Theodor Adorno and the jurist Fritz Bauer (soon to be the main prosecutor at the Frankfurt Auschwitz trial) with ex-Nazis like the head of the family planning association ProFamilia, Hans Harmsen, and the sexologists Hans Giese and Hans Bürger-Prinz, together with gentile non-Nazis like the liberal jurist Herbert Jäger. In so doing, the book itself—with its more than twenty contributors—provided a key instantiation of the intense cultural energy produced in postwar West Germany precisely by the mix of Jewish, ex-Nazi and non-Jewish liberal intellectuals.[49] It also demonstrated by example how *all three* of these constituencies were essential to the democratization of West Germany. (Moreover, the enthusiasm with which young activists received this book opens an important window onto the intimate interrelationship between liberalism and New Leftism and the transgenerational affiliations we often neglect in our overemphasis on intergenerational conflict in the 1960s.)

Sexualität und Verbrechen vigorously challenged the 1962 conservative draft of the criminal code. Overall, the book strongly advanced the legal ideals of consent and privacy and called for separating the realm of morality (the business of religion) from the realm of crime (the business of the law). What is most notable, however, both in this book and in its reception, is how extraordinarily important the invocation of the Holocaust was for pushing the case for sexual tolerance. Far from blocking homosexual suffering from view, for instance, the recovery of the details of the mass murder of European Jewry in the context of the Auschwitz trial of 1963–65—through a complicated conjunction of circumstances—ultimately did a great deal to make ongoing criminalization of male homosexuality (as of adultery, pornography, the advertisement and marketing of contraceptives, and eventually also of abortion) morally insupportable in West Germany.

Two essays from the collection would be cited more than any others: one by the liberal Berlin education professor and psychotherapist Wolfgang Hochheimer, the other by Theodor Adorno. Hochheimer offered the most outraged condemnation of the commission's draft. He pointed out that empirical reality in no way lined up with the commission's conservative ideals. The vast majority of West Germans—perhaps 90 percent—were not virgins when they married; 40 percent of sexually mature individuals were not married at all; nor did sexual behavior within marriage match normative expectations. Hochheimer forcefully contended that homosexuality was simply a natural variant of human sexuality; he also did not hesitate to ascribe twisted impulses to the homophobic members of the commission. But his punch line invoked the Third

Reich. Hochheimer above all made plain how offensive it was for the commission to justify its conservative opinions with repeated references to such concepts as "the moral sensibility of the people [*sittliches Volksempfinden*]," and he observed acerbically that "just yesterday" (i.e. during the Third Reich), "the 'sensibility of the people' was addressed and unleashed quite differently ... in order cruelly to annihilate 'those of a different nature' as though they were 'insects,' 'lice,' 'devils,' 'animals,' 'subhumans.' Also the sexually 'abnormal' were expressly included here."[50]

Adorno too invoked Nazism and its legacies to promote the liberalization of 1960s West German sexual mores. Interestingly, Adorno did remind readers of Nazism's sexually inciting aspects, as he noted the "breeding farms of the SS" and "the injunctions to girls to have temporary relationships with those who had declared themselves ... as the elite." Yet he made clear as well that the Third Reich was no "kingdom of erotic freedom." Disgusted by the lack of courage evinced by so many otherwise progressive postwar German intellectuals whenever the subject turned to sex, Adorno decisively defended sexual freedom. "Precisely when it is not warped or repressed, sex harms no one," he wrote. But Adorno also pointed out how, specifically in the midst of both the growing commodification of sex and the increasingly popular attitude that coitus was natural and healthy, taboos against perversion were nonetheless intensified. In a brilliant turn of argument, Adorno opined that "indeed, genitality itself, if completely purified of all those accompanying impulses that are so decried as perverse, is an impoverished thing, dull, and shriveled up, as it were." And (without heroizing them) he described prostitutes and homosexuals in particular as the representatives and, in a sense, the guardians, of all the enriching forms of "perversion" *(Perversität)* and "sophistication" *(Raffinement)* that made sex beautiful. Adorno found it especially disturbing—but indicative—that even as taboos against premarital heterosexuality had become obviously outdated, sexually conservative, even aggressively punitive, messages against sexual minorities still reached a wide audience. All the more reason to be suspicious, he thought, that the one kind of nongenital sexuality that was not just permitted but actively cultivated in the society was voyeurism. And, like Hochheimer, Adorno concluded caustically that the sexual taboos still prevailing in his contemporary moment were a piece of the very same "ideological and psychological syndrome of prejudice that helped to create the mass basis for National Socialism and whose manifest content lives on in a depoliticized form."[51]

Sexualität und Verbrechen did not single-handedly defeat the commission's proposal for a revised criminal code. But it did provide opponents of the commission with new ways of thinking that would substantially alter how both sexuality *and* the memory of the Third Reich would be read and interpreted by a new generation of young West Germans. Rather than placing their emphasis on Nazism's sexual excess and inducements, as for example Christians had done in the more immediate aftermath of the war, liberals and leftists began ever more frequently to stress Nazism's conservative and sexually repressive aspects. This collective move would deal a staggering blow to the commission's draft for the new criminal code, and would finally cause the Bundestag first to set the matter aside—and then fail eventually ever to return to it.

Among the groundswell of criticism that accrued around the commission's draft proposal, there is another contribution that deserves mention. In December 1962, writing in the journal *Der Monat,* the historian of religion Hans Joachim Schoeps, like Adorno a Jewish reemigré, stressed how repulsed he was by the widespread cowardice among postwar German intellectuals when it came to taking a stand for homosexual rights. Schoeps called for the abolition of Paragraph 175 and demanded that the members of the Bundestag closely examine their own conscience if they intended to continue to criminalize homosexuality:

> Since the persecution of the Jews during the Third Reich, in the eyes of the world the German people stands under the suspicion that it has a tendency to torment, persecute and terrorize its minorities. Of course homosexuals are not an ethnic-religious minority, but certainly they are a biological-anthropological minority within the *Volk* as a whole. After the gas ovens of Auschwitz and Maidanek ... one should think twice, or three times, whether in the new criminal code one still wants to continue to treat the minority of homosexuals as people for whom there must be separate laws.[52]

Here then were new ways to theorize the relationship between sexuality and crime: In a reversal of the earlier postwar formula that had linked sexual *ex*pression with cruelty and murder, now cruelty and murder were linked with sexual *re*pression. Over and over, West Germans now began to argue that sexual repression was the root of all evil.

Youth magazines frequently cited Schoeps, Hochheimer, and Adorno in their own attacks on the commission's draft. Progressive youth magazines not only documented the concrete damage done by laws which criminalized consensual sexual activity and its consequences, but also, and with increasing fervor, challenged what they saw as the hypocrisy of sexual conservatives and religious leaders the moment moral discussion turned to questions of racism and murder. They noted with outrage the way conservatives apparently found nudity more offensive than antisemitism. Liberals and leftists began to contend that the right to sexual activity was a fundamental human right, and that the desire for sex was something for which no one needed ever again to apologize. Sick of a decade of talk when "pleasure-craving" *(Genusssucht)* had been routinely treated as self-evidently morally repugnant, even when pursued within marriage, enraged at also the Social Democrats' "servile currying of the churches' favor," particularly left-leaning students increasingly declared that there was nothing wrong or sinful or indecent about pleasure, indeed that the pursuit of pleasure was a genuinely just pursuit.[53] They started to assert forcefully that sexual pleasure was itself a moral good.

In this context, the lesson that linked Nazism to sexual repression provided an especially important resource for turning the moral tables on conservatives. Already in 1962, for instance, the Frankfurt student newspaper *Diskus* had criticized the persistence of sexual taboos in postwar West Germany, noting that "without taboos there is no drive-denial, and without this there are no accumulated aggressions, which can, at the appointed moment, be directed against minorities or external enemies—Jews, capitalists, communists."[54] The new reading of the Third Reich as above all marked by sexual repression proved unstoppable. Leftists and liberals alike began to press the case that in German fascism there had been a "connection between the suppression of sexual drives on the one hand and the antisemitic persecution mania and its raging in manifest cruelty on the other."[55] By 1966, the liberal news magazine *Der Spiegel* firmly aligned itself with the side of sexual liberation and for this cause, crucially, it not only attacked the churches (the church fathers' hostility to sex became, according to *Der Spiegel,* "the trauma of a whole culture") but also invoked Adolf Hitler as a negative counter-example of sexual self-repression and repressiveness. Offering a one-sided reading of *Mein Kampf*—which quoted Hitler's disgust with the "suffocating perfume of our modern eroticism" but did not mention that in the same sentence he had criticized "unmanly" prudery—*Der Spiegel* printed a photograph of Hitler demonstratively captioned "Sex-Critic Hitler."[56] By 1967, in an authoritative book on "society and evil," the young philosopher Arno Plack was arguing that "It would be wrong to hold the view that all of what happened in Auschwitz was typically German. It was typical for a society that suppresses sexuality."[57]

In sum: it was the project of struggling to liberalize sexual mores in West Germany in the 1960s that brought a new and different version of the Third Reich into public discussion. While in the early 1950s, Christians had been able to present themselves and their sexually conservative agenda as the antithesis of Nazism and its licentious sexual politics, by the mid-1960s Christians and Nazis were increasingly presented as comparable in their visceral hostility to sexual freedom. So, for instance, by 1969 the journalist Hannes Schwenger, in an influential book criticizing the "antisexual" politics of the Christian churches, could specifically identify the postwar churches' attacks on "free love, premarital intercourse, adultery and divorce" as speaking "the language of fascism."[58] That the Nazis had themselves once vigorously encouraged premarital intercourse, adultery and divorce had become simply unimaginable.

This rewriting of the past would prove remarkably durable. That Nazis had been uptight and anti-sex rapidly became *the* cultural common sense, and this conviction lent an air of tremendous moral righteousness to the sexual revolution that would sweep Germany in the later 1960s, wiping away almost overnight the postwar culture of sexual conservatism. In the reconfigured social and political climate of the later 1960s, under the quadruple impact of the "sex wave," the Social Democrats' ascension to power in the Grand Coalition, the rise of the student movement and the growing popular conviction that the morality of the Christian churches was hypocritical, there was far greater openness across the political spectrum to liberalizing sex-related law. The CDU too went through an unprecedented process of internal liberalization. On May 1969, the Bundestag voted to decriminalize not only adultery but also homosexual acts for men age 21 or older; by 1973, consensual homosexual acts were legalized for men age 18 or older. And by 1974, the Bundestag had passed a law permitting first-trimester abortions. Although this law was quickly nullified and deemed unconstitutional by the Federal Constitutional Court, by 1976 abortion became legally available in West Germany in cases when a woman could persuade physicians of the existence of a "social indication" (the difficulty of raising a child under her current circumstances).

In conclusion, the debates over paragraphs relating to sexual matters in West Germany's criminal code foregrounded yet again Nazism's lasting yet complex impact on postwar culture. On the one hand, the conservative commission draft of 1962 itself offered a key example of postwar Christian-inflected sexual conservatism in its double nature as both a backlash against some elements of Nazism and a continuity with other elements. On the other hand, the energetic liberal and New Left reaction against the conservative draft marked the moment that an utterly new (and ultimately enormously consequential) interpretation of Nazism as thoroughly sexually repressive entered public discussion, an interpretation that drew its overwhelming moral force not least from the return to public attention of the details of the Holocaust as these were made public in the Frankfurt Auschwitz trial. By the 1970s, it was practically impossible to find anyone who disagreed with the new consensus that sexual repression was not merely a characteristic of fascism, but its very cause. As one author put it, gesturing to lessons learned from the Frankfurt trial: "Brutality and the lust for destruction become substitutes for bodily pleasure.... This is how the seemingly incredible contradiction that the butchers of Auschwitz were—and would become again—respectable, harmless citizens is resolved."[59] Or as yet another phrased the point even more succinctly: "In the fascist rebellion, the energies of inhibited sexuality formed into genocide."[60] That it was ultimately a false version of history—a fictive memory—that produced conditions for progressive social change, is a fact that historians might do well to meditate on.

Notes

1. This is a revised version of Dagmar Herzog, "Sexuality, Memory, Morality," *History and Memory* 17, (Spring/Summer 2005), 238–88.

2. Olav Münzberg, "Wovon berührt? Vom jüdischen Trauma? Von den Traumata der Eltern?" *Ästhetik und Kommunikation* 51 (June 1983): 25.

3. Martin Dannecker, "Die verspätete Empirie: Anmerkungen zu den Anfängen der Deutschen Gesellschaft für Sexualforschung," *Zeitschrift für Sexualforschung* 14 (June 2001), 173.

4. Ulf Preuss-Lausitz, "Vom gepanzerten zum sinnstiftenden Körper," in Preuss-Lausitz et al., eds., *Kriegskinder, Konsumkinder, Krisenkinder: Zur Sozialisationsgeschichte seit dem Zweiten Weltkrieg* (Weinheim, 1989), 90, 92. Emphasis in the original.

5. See Hans-Peter Schwarz, *Die Ära Adenauer: Gründerjahre der Republik 1949–1957* (Stuttgart, 1981), 382; and Ulrich Herbert, "Legt die Plakate nieder, ihr Streiter für die Gerechtigkeit," *Frankfurter Allgemeine Zeitung* (29 Jan. 2001), 48.

6. Walter Dittmann, "Die Krisis der Ehe—Die Ansicht des Geistlichen," *Nordwestdeutsche Hefte* 2, no. 10 (1947), p. 34; Johannes Leppich, "Thema 1," in Günther Mees und Günter Graf, eds., *Pater Leppich Spricht: Journalisten hören den "roten" Pater* (Düsseldorf, 1952), 44.

7. I thank Werner Kremp and Mark Roseman for calling my attention to this phenomenon.

8. Y. Michal Bodemann, "Eclipse of Memory: German Representations of Auschwitz in the Early Postwar Period," *New German Critique* 75 (Fall 1998): 61–72 and 88–89.

9. See Frank Stern, *The Whitewashing of the Yellow Badge: Antisemitism and Philosemitism in Postwar Germany* (Oxford, 1992), 302–10; and Micha Brumlik, "Post-Holocaust Theology: German Theological Responses since 1945," in *Betrayal: German Churches and the Holocaust,* eds. Robert Ericksen and Susannah Heschel (Minneapolis, 1999).

10. Anton Christian Hofmann, *Die Natürlichkeit der christlichen Ehe* (Munich, 1951), 5, 9–10, 38–39.

11. On these two kinds of taboo-breaking, see also Sophinette Becker, "Zur Funktion der Sexualität im Nationalsozialismus," *Zeitschrift für Sexualforschung* 14 (June 2001).

12. Hanna Schissler, "'Normalization' as Project: Some Thoughts on Gender Relations in West Germany during the 1950s," in *The Miracle Years: A Cultural History of West Germany, 1949–1968,* ed. Schissler (Princeton, 2001), 366.

13. Hermann Peter Piwitt, "autoritär, betulich, neckish und devot," *Konkret,* May 1979, 34.

14. Günter Grass, "Geschenkte Freiheit: Versagen, Schuld, vertane Chancen," *Die Zeit,* 10 May 1985, 21.

15. One of the first instances of a reversed reading of the lessons of Nazism for abortion policy (i.e., that to be in favor of abortion rights was to be appropriately anti-Nazi) can be found in a court decision reported on by *Der Spiegel,* 6 Aug. 1958, 23–24.

16. Walter Dirks, "Ein Wort an die Arbeiterschaft in Sachen Paragraph 218," *Frankfurter Hefte,* (Dec. 1946): 794.

17. Hermann Frühauf, "Paragraph 218," *Frankfurter Hefte* (Oct. 1946): 590.

18. Probst quoted in Angela Delille and Andrea Grohn, "Es ist verboten … Empfängnisverhütung und Abtreibung," in *Perlonzeit,* eds. Angela Delille and Andrea Grohn (Berlin, 1985), 124.

19. Gröber quoted in ibid.

20. F. M. Reifferscheidt, "Was steckt hinter 'Schmutz und Schund?,'" *Frankfurter Rundschau* 10 (Jan. 1950); "Schund und Schmutz," *Rhein-Echo*, 2 March 1950; "Was ist 'jugendgefährdend'?," *Frankfurter Neue Presse*, 6 May 1950; Heinz Neudeck, "Pressefreiheit und Jugendschutz," *Die neue Zeitung*, 18 March 1950; Helmut Thielicke, "Schmutz und Schund: Massnahmen von unten her," *Stuttgarter Zeitung*, 4 May 1950.

21. "Das Wichtige und die halbe Wahrheit," *Münchner Allgemeine*, 15 Jan. 1950.

22. "Mit Unbehagen," *Die Welt*, 19 Sep. 1952.

23. A 1952 brochure for the censorship law, *Jugend in Gefahr* (Youth in Danger), exemplified the rewriting of the memory and meaning of fascism: "We turn to all those who care about the future of the German *Volk* and who are prepared to help German youth in their search for new life-forms. Every German is convinced of the necessity of clean spiritual guidance for our youth so that the unhappy inheritance of our past may be overcome. We thus may not make ourselves guilty once more by being silent in the face of the attempt being carried out by profit-hungry smut-publishers, and escalating constantly in extent and intensity, once again to assassinate the souls of our youth." In this interpretation, the assault on youthful minds represented by pornography was no different from the "assassination" of souls undertaken by Nazism. See *Jugend in Gefahr* (1952), brochure of the Vereinigte Jugendschriftenausschüsse, quoted in Petra Jäschke, "Produktionsbedingungen und gesellschaftliche Einschätzungen" in *Zwischen Trümmern und Wohlstand: Literatur der Jugend 1945–1960*, ed. Klaus Doderer (Weinheim and Basel, 1988), 394; see also 324.

24. Toska Hesekiel, *Eltern antworten: Eine Hilfe zur Aufklärung unserer Kinder* (Berlin, 1955), 27; Heinrich Oesterreich (1954) quoted in Peter Kuhnert and Ute Ackermann, "Jenseits von Lust und Liebe? Jugendsexualität in den 50er Jahren," in *"Die Elvis-Tolle, die hatte ich mir unauffällig wachsen lassen": Lebensgeschichte und jugendliche Alltagskultur in den fünfziger Jahren*, ed. Heinz-Hermann Krüger (Opladen, 1985), 48.

25. See, for example, Hans Wollasch, "Der menschliche Sinn des Geschlechtslebens," in *Familie in Not: Sexualpädagogische Vortragsreihe*, ed. Stadtverwaltung Bad Godesberg (Bad Godesberg, 1954), 16.

26. Hofmann, *Die Natürlichkeit*, 50, 83.

27. Theodor Bovet, *Die werdende Frau* (Bern, 1962), 20–21; the book previously appeared in Switzerland in 1944, and was first published in Germany in 1950. Bovet was Swiss, but was one of the most influential and esteemed advice writers in West Germany.

28. Wolfgang Fischer, "Selbstbefriedigung und geschlechtliche Erziehung" *Der evangelische Erzieher* 6 (May-June 1954): 74–75.

29. Erich Schröder, *Reif Werden und Rein Bleiben: Briefe eines Arztes an seinen Patensohn* (Konstanz, 1956).

30. A. Ohm, "Homosexualität als Neurose," *Der Weg zur Seele* 5 (1953), 56.

31. See "Literatur-Umschau," *Kriminalistik* 6, nos. 13–14 (1952): 67–68.

32. "Not um den Paragraphen 175," *Christ und Welt* 4, no. 20 (1951): 4–5.

33. Mario Kramp and Martin Sölle, "Paragraph 175—Restauration und Reform in der Bundesrepublik," in *"Himmel und Hölle": Das Leben der Kölner Homosexuellen 1945–1969*, eds. Kristof Balser, et al. (Cologne, 1994), 132, 139–41.

34. Wilhelm Ellinghaus, "Verfassungsmässigkeit des Paragraphen 175 RstGB," *Kriminalistik* 8, no. 3 (1954): 63.

35. See Robert G. Moeller, "The Homosexual Man is a 'Man,' the Homosexual Woman is a 'Woman,': Sex, Society and the Law in Postwar West Germany," *Journal of the History of Sexuality* 4, no. 3 (1994).

36. Statistics on registrations and arrests and Schoeps summarized in Kramp and Sölle, "Paragraph 175," 133, 142.

37. Schöllgen in *Die Kirche in der Welt* 1, no. 35 (1947–8): 160.

38. Muckermann's post-1945 comments quoted in Ernst Klee, *Was sie taten—Was sie wurden: Ärzte, Juristen und andere Beteiligte am Kranken- oder Judenmord* (Frankfurt/Main: Fischer, 1986), 148–49.

39. Theodor Bovet, *Von Mann zu Mann: Eine Einführung ins Reifealter für junge Männer* (Tübingen, 1955), 47.

40. See Clemens Bewer, "Verkauf von Gummischutzmitteln durch Aussenautomaten" *Zeitschrift für ärztliche Fortbildung* 50, no. 6 (1961): 460–62.

41. See Hans Harmsen, "Mittel zur Geburtenregelung in der Gesetzgebung des Staates," in *Sexualität und Verbrechen,* eds. Fritz Bauer et al. (Frankfurt/ Main, 1963), 185.

42. Maria Jochum, "Frauenfrage 1946" *Frankfurter Hefte* 1 (June 1946): 24–25.

43. Hanns Lilje, "Zerfall der Familie?," *Sonntagsblatt,* 7 Feb. 1954, 24.

44. Wollasch, "Der menschliche Sinn," 7 and 17.

45. See in this context Theodor Bovet, "Sexualethik oder eheliche Partnerschaft" *Radius* 4 (1963): 28; Siegfried Keil, "'Zur Jugendliebe gehört die Empfängnisverhütung'" *Der Spiegel* 35 (1966): 55; and *Denkschrift zu Fragen der Sexualethik: Erarbeitet von einer Kommission der Evangelischen Kirche in Deutschland* (Gütersloh, 1971), 28.

46. Court decision quoted in Harmsen, "Mittel": 183; see also the 1959 Hamburg case, 186.

47. On the complex effects of the pill in West Germany—on the one hand its contribution to reducing abortion rates, on the other hand its contribution to refiguring sexual practices and the ambivalent consequences of this in view of the simultaneously emerging market-driven commodification of sex and women's bodies—see Dagmar Herzog, "Between Coitus and Commodification: Young West German Women and the Impact of the Pill," in *Between Marx and Coca Cola: Youth Cultures in Changing European Societies, 1960–1980,* eds. Axel Schildt and Detlef Siegfried (New York, 2005).

48. See "Anhang: Auszüge aus der Bundestagsdrucksache IV/ 650 vom 4. Oktober 1962 (Regierungsentwurf eines Strafgesetzbuches—E 1962)," in *Sexualität und Verbrechen,* pp. 406–7, 409–11.

49. See on this point about Jews and ex-Nazis also Wolf Lepenies, "Exile and Emigration: The Survival of 'German Culture.'" *Occasional Paper,* no. 7 (March 2000), School of Social Science, Institute for Advanced Study: 11, 14.

50. Wolfgang Hochheimer, "Das Sexualstrafrecht in psychologisch-anthropologischer Sicht," in *Sexualität und Verbrechen,* 90, 97–98.

51. Theodor W. Adorno, "Sexualtabus und Recht heute," in *Sexualität und Verbrechen,* 301–3, 305, 310.

52. Hans-Joachim Schoeps, "Soll Homosexualität strafbar bleiben?," *Der Monat* 15, no. 171 (Dec. 1962): 26–26.

53. Heribert Adam, "Spiesser Moral," *Diskus* 15 (June 1965): 1.

54. Christian Crull and Hans Hagedorn, "Sex und Profit," *Diskus* 12 (Aug. 1962): 1.

55. Wolfgang Fritz Haug, "Vorbemerkung," *Das Argument* 32 (1965): 30–31.

56. *Der Spiegel*, "Die gefallene Natur," 2 May 1966, 57–58.

57. Arno Plack, *Die Gesellschaft und das Böse* (Munich, 1967), 309.

58. Hannes Schwenger, *Antisexuelle Propaganda: Sexualpolitik in der Kirche* (Reinbek, 1969), 34–36.

59. Anton-Andreas Guha, *Sexualität und Pornographie: Die organisierte Entmündigung* (Frankfurt/Main, 1971), 126–27.

60. Michael Rohrwasser, *Saubere Mädel, Starke Genossen: Proletarische Massenkultur?* (Frankfurt/Main, 1975), 9.

CHAPTER 15

The Modern Guild

Rotary Clubs and Bourgeois Renewal in the Aftermath of National Socialism

S. Jonathan Wiesen

On 11 March 1957, a prominent judge in Ulm, West Germany, presented his life story to fellow members of his local Rotary Club. Acknowledging that the typical résumé consisted of a string of facts and dates, he wanted to offer a more "human" picture of himself. He spoke about his fighting as a bewildered Wehrmacht soldier on the Eastern front, his capture by the Soviets in June 1944, and the poor nutrition and brutality of his two-year camp experience. The judge went on to discuss the existential crisis engendered by captivity, his return to a bombed-out home, and the rebuilding of his career in a new democracy. Even with such rebounding fortunes, however, the life of a judge could be very lonely. The Ulm Rotary club, the speaker concluded, provided him with the opportunity to break out of this solitude—to interact with members of other professions and to forge new social relations.[1]

On the surface, these self-disclosures might have seemed unbecoming of an upstanding public figure. Yet the Ulm judge was not alone in his desire to discuss his personal traumas and career successes with a gathering of professional men. Throughout the 1950s and 1960s, thousands of other West Germans met on a weekly basis to share their private stories and aspirations as members of an international service organization. With the founding of the Federal Republic in 1949, Rotary clubs sprang up in almost every city in West Germany. Inspired by the motto "Service above Self," their members raised money for charities, supported international student exchanges, and gave speeches on culture and current events. But who were these *Rotarier*? Why did they find such a welcome home in postwar Germany? How did this American-born association of professionals reflect the social and cultural priorities of the new West German democracy?

This essay takes up these questions by focusing on Rotarians as self-avowed "elites" who saw as their calling the infusion of universal ethical norms into West German society. In meeting regularly with their fellow members, or "Friends" *(Freunde),* Rotarians took the cultural and political issues of their time—the nature of democracy, the Cold War, the fate of the country's youth, transatlantic relations—and employed them to build a collective self-image of the international bourgeois citizen, committed to an ethos of philanthropy and responsibility. Creating (or reviving) this new elite, however, was not a care-free enterprise. The traumatic legacy of National Socialism and war, and the Rotarians' own complicated trajectories through the Third Reich, made this task of bourgeois renewal all the more urgent and complicated.[2]

In its use of the terms *Bürgertum* and "elite," this essay offers a new perspective on a long-standing sociological and historical debate about whether a middle-class had survived the scourges of depression and war. Scholars have disagreed about the extent to which the class divisions of the Wilhelmine period disappeared amid the upheavals of inflation, depression, and two world wars. Only recently has the discourse widened to include what Volker Berghahn has referred to as the "norms, values, and social conventions" of the West German *Bürgertum.* How did professionals, regardless of their relative economic position, *perceive* themselves as elites in a new democracy?[3] In answering this question, historians have all but overlooked West German Rotary Clubs as sites of bourgeois self-fashioning.[4] Yet at their weekly meetings, Rotarians wrestled with some of the central issues facing all West German professionals: How could one balance professional and community service with an enjoyment of prosperity and mass leisure? How could one assert oneself as an individual while adhering to a collective morality? How could one adhere to the ideals of truth and integrity while also avoiding a confrontation with the Nazi past? Looking at how Rotarians responded to these questions provides a glimpse into the mental world of West German elites after 1945.

Rotary Germany: From Weimar to the Federal Republic

Rotary first came to Germany in 1927. At the time German leaders, notably industrialists, were looking to America for models of modern business practices—whether in Fordist assembly-line production, mass consumption, or human relations.[5] It is perhaps not surprising that Wilhelm Cuno, the general director of the Hamburg-American Steamship lines, was Germany's first Rotarian. The industrialist and former German chancellor brought the American service organization to a city, Hamburg, known for its openness to outside cultural influences, especially from the Anglo-American world. At the time of its German debut, Rotary was the oldest and the largest of what would eventually be the "big three" service organizations, namely, Rotary, Kiwanis, and Lions. It was founded in 1905 in Chicago and instantly spread, with every major American city having a Rotary club by 1911 and many European countries founding clubs in the 1920s and 1930s.[6] Of the major organizations, Rotary carried the most prestige, celebrated for its merging of business, culture, and social activism. It was based on an ethos of fraternity, philanthropy, and social networking. To this day, Rotary clubs around the world attempt to realize "the advancement of international understanding, good will and peace through a world fellowship of business and professional men united in the ideal of service."[7]

The centrality of these social and ethical goals was apparent from Rotary's initial arrival in Germany. Victoria de Grazia has written splendidly on the first decade of Rotary in Germany, when Rotary Club Munich drew the likes of Thomas Mann into the world of "clubby fraternizing."[8] In Club Dresden, free professionals ranging from the Lord High Mayor of the city to the chief of police, from bankers to theater directors, met weekly over lunch and at formal celebrations to discuss the social and intellectual issues of the day. Whether at the Rotary Club Berlin or the Rotary Club Cologne, the educated bourgeoisie and the economic bourgeoisie *(Bildungsbürgertum* and *Wirtschaftsbürgertum)* came together for a dialogue about the meaning and practice of "world citizenship."[9] German Rotarians were "practical idealists,"[10] whose commitment to bourgeois humanism *(Bürgerlichkeit)* entailed a greater turn to philosophy and the arts than their more commerce-minded counterparts in the United States. By 1937, when Rotary Germany dissolved itself under pressure from the Nazi government, there were forty-two clubs with approximately 1,200 members.[11]

There is not the space in this essay to elaborate on the early history of Rotary Germany, first in the waning years of the Weimar Republic and then during the Third Reich. It is important, nonetheless, to note the untimely proximity of Rotary's arrival in Germany to its demise. Six clubs in Germany were founded after Hitler's coming to power, only to face almost immediate pressure to remove their Jewish members and adhere to the tenets of National Socialism.[12] The tension between Rotary's internationalism, which the Nazis lumped together with Free Masonry, and the pressure to put nation above all else, ultimately forced the Rotary clubs to disband. Even after their official disbanding, former club members continued to meet informally and at some risk, occasionally giving their groups new names. The Berlin Rotary Club renamed itself the "Beuth-Tisch," after Prussian Finance Minister Peter Beuth, who founded a men's professional discussion group in 1821,[13] and members of the Frankfurt am Main Rotary Club met regularly in private homes until 1943, under the name "The Wednesday-Society" *(Mittwochs-Gesellschaft).*[14]

After 1945, West Germans rebuilt their professional associations under the watchful eye of Allied occupation officials. In the case of Rotarians, former members faced the assumption among military authorities that too many of them had accommodated, if not embraced, National Socialism. Indeed the assumptions were not unfounded: a fair number of Rotarians had attempted to reconcile the Rotary service ideal with the promise of a vibrant *Volksgemeinschaft*.[15] After the war, this reality would hamper initial attempts to reconstitute the Rotary clubs of Germany. Even as former Rotarians began meeting again, the Rotary International (RI) headquarters in Chicago surveyed the newly constituted associations with suspicion and prevented them from using the word "Rotary." Rotarians met under a variety of names, with the umbrella title of "Clubs der Freunde von 1927." The fact that these men regrouped despite Allied scrutiny is a testament to the power of their identities as Rotarians. Yet when the Allies eventually conceded that former Rotary clubs might reform, RI initially held fast to the view that Germans could not reenter the international organization until there was a general peace treaty and Germany was reunited. With the founding of the Federal Republic in 1949, however, RI welcomed German Rotary clubs back into its ranks. This reconstitution of the Rotary movement mirrored the gradual reintegration of the country into a community of Western democracies.

Like in the 1920s and 1930s, a substantial percentage of Rotary members after 1945 represented the world of business and finance. According to Rotary's rules, only one member of a given profession could be represented in a local club. But Rotary's classification system allowed a number of executives and managers to represent industry as specialists in a particular industrial branch or trade. Some familiar names in German industry and politics counted among the ranks of these early postwar Rotarians. Ernst von Siemens of the Siemens electrotechnical concern joined the Munich Rotary Club in the 1950s, as did Franz Josef Schöningh, the publisher of the *Süddeutsche Zeitung*.[16] Robert Pferdmenges and Baron Waldemar von Oppenheim of the banking firm Oppenheim entered the reconstituted Cologne club.[17] Joining the Essen Rotary Club was Baron Tilo von Wilmowsky, former deputy chairman of the Krupp concern's supervisory board and the uncle of firm owner Alfried Krupp von Bohlen und Halbach.[18] Alfried Krupp's brother Berthold von Bohlen und Halbach also joined his uncle as a member, along with a large number of individuals tied to Ruhr industry. Entering the Wuppertal club was Ludwig Vaubel, the future director-general of the chemical firm Vereinigte Glanzstoff and organizer of the "Wuppertal Circle" of seminars for entrepreneurs.[19] Newly appointed Chancellor Konrad Adenauer, himself a member of 1927's Cologne Rotary Club, was considered an honorary member of the Bonn club, although he did not officially join.[20]

Surveying these names might suggest that the Rotary clubs were dominated by wealthy and politically powerful leaders who played visible roles in the rebuilding of a postwar democracy. Indeed a rumor existed that one had to be rich to become a Rotarian, prompting would-be candidates to make special appeals for admittance, attributing the loss of their personal wealth to the war or their flight from the East.[21] While many of the well-to-do, especially from the business world, were indeed drawn to the Rotary clubs, one must avoid the assumption that these clubs were merely pragmatic assemblies of political and economic power. The founding of the Federal Republic saw a number of other organizations that catered more specifically to the business world and its immediate partisan interests. In the early 1950s, the Federation of German Industry (BDI) and the public relations organization German Industry Institute (Deutsches Industrie-Institut) became sites of more practical discussions about local and national economic developments. While these associations were ostensibly devoted to lobbying and "interest politics," they drew into their orbit a number of cultural leaders as well. In 1951, the BDI established a Cultural Circle, or *Kulturkreis,* that was devoted to the patronage of art and architecture and to a broader cultivation of creative endeavor.[22] Likewise in 1951, the BDI established study groups *(Arbeitsgemeinschaften),* that brought business leaders into contact with the likes of historian Hans Rothfels and playwright Carl Zuckmayer to discuss the interrelationships among business, politics, religion, and culture.[23] But Rotary differed from these other associations by representing a wider cross-section of the educated and economic elite. At any given meeting, a businessman might find himself face-to-face with a lawyer, doctor, musician, or an esteemed professor, like historian Werner Conze of Rotary Club Münster.[24]

There were multiple motivations for accepting an invitation to join this elite circle of friends. Some members recognized the potential for professional networking and intellectual stimulation, in keeping with Germany's longer associational tradition. Others saw themselves as explicitly following in the footsteps of historic male organizations *(Männerbünde),* from the Hanseatic merchant guilds to Benjamin Franklin's Junto Society of men devoted to mutual improvement and the public good.[25] While different in multiple respects, the Rotary movement, according to one German member, shared with these predecessors the ideals of "selectivity, proving one's worth, mutual help, expressed utilitarianism, regular meetings, and multiple forms of conviviality."[26] But this self-proclaimed "modern guild"[27] differed from other associations in its rejection of any professional or religious particularism and in its emphasis on the idea of service on a global level. Noting with frustration Hitler's perversion of the concepts "service" and "sacrifice" (to a racially homogenous national community), Rotarians were careful to recast these ideals in strictly international terms. "Humanism," "understanding," "friendship," "responsibility," and "self-sacrifice" were the watchwords of the movement, all of which were meant to unite members from Latin America to Asia.

International Service, Mass Consumption, and Bourgeois Individuality

How did Rotarians enact these virtues in the 1950s, when West Germans were attempting to carve out a post-Nazi identity? They did so in three discernible ways: through community and international service, through an accommodation to the worlds of leisure and mass consumption, and through the promotion of bourgeois elitism.[28] First, on the most visible level, Rotarians were community activists. Guided by their motto "Service above Self," they sponsored clothing and food drives and hosted charity fund-raisers. They also promoted art exhibitions and awarded scholarships to financially disadvantaged students.[29] While Rotarians eagerly engaged in these local activities, such gestures were merely one dimension of larger national and international exercises in altruism. They sent Christmas care-packages to families behind the Iron Curtain, sponsored international exchange programs, and, in the aftermath of the Hungarian uprising in 1956, provided food, shelter, and clothes for exiles. The same year, they supplied aid to survivors of a mining disaster in Belgium and flood relief in India.[30] These forms of international benevolence had defined the Rotary movement since its inception in the United States, but in the setting of postwar West Germany, such humanitarian gestures were part of larger project of "moral rearmament."[31]

Rotarians were not the only men's clubs engaging in these activities. In the course of the 1950s, Lions International, by mid-decade the largest service organization in the world,[32] had set up dozens of clubs throughout Germany, inevitably challenging the sense of exclusivity that German Rotarians enjoyed. With the message "We serve" (Wir dienen) and their devotion to friendship and international goodwill, there was much overlap in the missions of both organizations, and a sense of competition and cooperation marked the relationship between the two. By 1955, the Lions Clubs in the Federal Republic could boast the membership of prize-winning Hamburg scientist Pascual Jordan[33] and, within Konrad Adenauer's cabinet, transportation minister Hans-Christoph Seebohm and justice minister Wolfgang Hauβman.[34]

The idea of international service took on special meaning in postwar Germany, as Lions and Rotarians tried to provide German professionals with an ethical sensibility and civic-mindedness in the aftermath of National Socialism. At their weekly meetings in the 1950s, Rotarians regularly implored each other to look beyond Germany—to engage in Europa-Arbeit ("work on behalf of European Unity")[35] and to follow wider developments in global politics and economics. Global humanism depended on an intimate knowledge of the world, and Rotarians shared stories of their trips to Japan, India, Cuba, the United States, and the Soviet Union. They led international visitors on tours of factories and other local sites of interest, and they met foreign Rotarians at trade fairs like the Leipzig Messe and at international expositions, where West Germans were finding new business opportunities.

This spirit of internationalism entailed a certain amount of pageantry. In 1955, to mark the Golden Anniversary of the Rotary movement, Rotary Club Hamburg engaged in a "flag exchange," sending its club banner to counterparts in Egypt, Chile, Argentina, and to the Rotary Club of Hamburg, Pennsylvania.[36] Celebrations of new club charters could be lavish affairs, with foreign visitors and new Rotarians enjoying sumptuous meals, a round of speeches, and classical music.[37] But amid the celebrations of communal and international fraternity, Rotarians did not shy away from controversial themes. Some Rotarians' speeches were charged with historical and political content, as they reflected on the dangers of communism, British colonial policy in India, the legacy of the Dreyfus Affair in France, the sad fate of the American Indian, the psychology of Hitler, and racial tensions in the United States.[38] By educating each other in history and politics, Rotarians hoped to position themselves as well-rounded world citizens, whose professional lives would be infused with an intellectual and global sensibility.

Rotarians in the 1950s were intent on promoting a distinct ethical worldview, and they did so both in their philanthropic activities and in their discussions about themes of international significance. Yet they also hoped to understand the changing nature of their own society. In the years of the "Economic Miracle," this meant acculturating themselves to the expanding worlds of leisure and consumption while still maintaining, to invoke Hans-Peter Schwarz's formulation, "bourgeois thought patterns and lifestyles."[39] The weekly club reports from 1957 reveal a host of themes relating to the increased opportunities for leisure that attended the recovering West German economy. Discussions of vacation travel, electronic music, and German literature were followed by reflections on the importance of self-irony, thoughts about Walt Disney, and discussions of astrology.[40] Rotarians listened to lunchtime lectures about the lifestyles and philosophies of effective and humane managers. They cautioned each other about diseases related to overwork—so-called *Managerkrankheiten* ("manager-illnesses")—and emphasized the importance of cultivating a relaxing hobby like stamp collecting.[41]

Taken together, there was a larger message in these discussions: after many years of war and hardship, it was important to safeguard one's bourgeois comforts. But, importantly, Rotarians had to be wary of letting material pleasures distract them from their true calling of service. Club members admonished their colleagues to avoid complacency in their newfound prosperity. Such "comfortism," argued one member, could lead to apathy—to an *ohne mich* ("without me") attitude that ran counter to Rotary ideals of civic engagement. Elites should undoubtedly enjoy their free time and family life and, ideally, cultivate an appreciation for art and music. But these pleasures were not ends in themselves. They allowed the Rotarian to discover his humanity amid the rapid pace of modern existence.[42] They served the higher purpose of creating a generation of men committed to public service.

Merging leisure and responsibility was by no means an effortless process in the midst of rapid socioeconomic change, and Rotarians spent much time trying to diagnose the problems facing modern society. They drew inspiration from European and American scholars and cultural critics. Most notably in Germany, sociologist Helmut Schelsky introduced the concept of the *nivellierte Mittelstandsgesellschaft* (literally, "leveled-out middle class society"), in which the distinctions between the proletariat, the middle classes, and the wealthy were being erased, as the social mobility of the working class converged with the downward mobility of the bourgeoisie.[43] If Economics Minister Ludwig Erhard's goal of "prosperity for all" *(Wohlstand für Alle)* was approaching reality by the end of the 1950s, not every German was comfortable with this widespread abundance. While liberals like Erhard and Schelsky took heart in the softening of rigid class structures, social conservatives revived longstanding fears of a "revolt of the masses." Would mass democracy and mass consumption lead to the elimination of socioeconomic distinctions and a lowering of cultural standards? In asking this question, West Germans echoed the worries of American Dwight Macdonald, the widely read critic of mass culture, who saw everything from comic books to Hollywood films as dangerous challenges to high-brow culture. This tyrannical reign of *Kitsch* could be attributed in part to the increasing sway of "the public" or "the masses" over cultural and social life.[44]

Within the German Rotary Clubs, one can observe a marked ambivalence toward this expanding world of mass consumption.[45] On the one hand, Rotarians, through their major ties to business, had a stake in seeing the expansion of the global economy and the increased purchasing power of domestic and foreign consumers. On the other hand, their self-understanding as elites was potentially threatened by the increasing "massification" of society.[46] While Rotarians represented the spectrum of neoliberal to conservative ideologies (and less commonly social-democratic), one can nonetheless find in their many speeches in the mid to late 1950s consistent reflections on the meaning of these changes for their own calling as Rotarians. In a lecture entitled the "Middle-Class Problem," a Rotarian from Club Recklinghausen bemoaned the passing of an "upright and estimable *Bürgertum* in Germany." Where once the spirit of the "dependable German handworker" symbolized the self-reliant free professional, there was now a smugness attending increased prosperity and economic growth. The greatest threat to the middle class was not government policies that favored widespread social and economic opportunity. Rather, the problem lay in the realm of the *Geist*. Increased prosperity was leading to a collective lack of responsibility and an erosion of personal relationships amid a faceless modern bureaucracy. The challenge for Germans was to tap into the high moral character embodied in the rapidly disappearing figure of the independent businessman.[47] The importance of this goal was summed up by another Rotarian in a talk entitled "Reflections on the Journey of an *unbürgerlich* Generation." "The proletarian of yesterday," he argued to his Friends in Rotary Club Wuppertal, is the "credit-worthy citizen of today." While this was a positive historical development, this economic leveling and consumerism also risked bringing about a "spiritual anarchy," which could be averted only though elitist displays of moral responsibility, most notably in cultural patronage and philanthropy.[48]

Such expressions of ambivalence about mass consumption, prosperity, and technology were familiar tropes of the 1950s. To a large degree, they emanated from the United States, where cultural commentators observed a society comprised of lonely and lackluster "organization men"—a crowd of corporate drones who lacked the self-initiative and individuality of an earlier era.[49] This diagnosis appeared in the writings of Cold War liberals and cultural conservatives on both sides of the Atlantic.[50] What made them so resonant for professional elites, however, was the extent to which these men considered themselves, in many respects, the antidote to the problems of social and moral decline. This is where the German Rotary movement came in. In imbuing their wealth and status with an ethical content, Rotarians saw themselves in a unique position to heal the problems of the modern world. The multiple manifestations of "civilization-sickness" (*Zivilisationskrankheit*)—apathy, egotism, ennui, as well as a host of physical ailments—could be addressed only in reinstating some measure of social and cultural stratification.[51] This project of *Elitebildung* ("elite formation") was by no means exclusive to the Rotary movement. Indeed the concept was omnipresent in the new German democracy, as politicians and businessmen discussed ways of fostering post-fascist leadership ideals in the country's youth.[52] But Rotarians were among the most vocal in this call for a new sociocultural elite, whose moral example would supplant the discredited ideologies of the past.[53]

But what actually characterized an "elite"? Rotarians spent much time trying to answer this question at their weekly meetings. Was elitism based on class, education, or more abstract ethical values and behaviors? Echoing Spanish philosopher José Ortega y Gasset, most Rotarians argued that "in the age of the masses" the elite could belong to any class.[54] An elite individual was defined not by his wealth but by his ethic of personal responsibility and his striving to exceed beyond what was merely expected of him. Embracing the human being with all of his creative potential would stave off the process of social leveling that had enabled both the rise of popular fascist movements and the embrace of vulgar, "Americanized" culture. As embodied by Rotarians, the new elites were above all individualists, men who would display the force of their personal character and thereby challenge the cultural power of the "mass man."[55]

The values of the individual—as entrepreneur, artist, or writer—defined the self-understanding of many elites during this period. Yet this celebration of individuality presented a potential dilemma for Rotarians, as it could appear at odds with the organization's motto "Service above Self." Did not this ideal entail the de-prioritizing of the self in the name of a universalist ethic? As Rotarians explained to each other, self-sacrifice did not mean self-abnegation.[56] Only by thriving in their professions—and perhaps in the process attaining wealth and status—could one serve as models of diligence and moral integrity. Individual achievement was the foundation of collective morality, allowing Rotarians to use their professional connections and social influence in the service of humankind. They would, by extension, give moral content to the materialism that attended West Germany's rapid economic recovery.

Rotarians and the Legacy of National Socialism

In the 1950s, debates about mass society, elitism, and leadership ethics were not unique to the Federal Republic. They accompanied wider discussions throughout the West about the meanings of freedom and conformity in an age of totalitarianism and mass democracy, and they could be heard in universities, political circles, and private clubs from Berlin to Berkeley. But these debates carried an extra weight for postwar West Germans. As Rotarians discussed contemporary social issues, the traumas of the recent past—Hitler, war, and defeat—were very much present. Recasting *Rotarier* as international elites entailed a series of uneasy confrontations with the discredited legacy of National Socialism. These moments of historical memory could hinge on the complicity of an individual Rotarian in Nazi crimes, or on the organization's own history during the early years of the Third Reich.

Recent historiography has revealed how widespread discussions of National Socialism were during the seemingly "silent years" of the 1950s. While it was not until the 1960s that the Holocaust as such began to pervade public discourses in West Germany, the experience and legacy of National Socialism nonetheless defined the terms of political and social debates during the first decade of the Federal Republic.[57] To a great extent, the history of Rotary Germany mirrors this general trajectory. In the early postwar years, moving beyond National Socialism meant proving to the world that their new clubs were not populated by former Nazis. Not surprisingly, members felt compelled to assert their non-Nazi or anti-Nazi credentials, especially when dealing with American Rotarians. Thus we have the case of the director of a city library asking Rotary International to consider his position as a representative of UNESCO as proof of his commitment to international understanding and "so that you are assured that you don't have an old Nazi before you."[58]

The sociological make-up of Rotary of Germany was indeed a source of some concern to RI officers, and at the direction of the Chicago headquarters, the new clubs were to make every effort to keep their memberships "young." Members had to be active in their professions and could not in any way be politically compromised.[59] But to what degree was the presence of potential ex-Nazis an issue? The membership list of Rotary Club Mönchengladbach, a typical, mid-sized club, offers but one example of Rotary's potentially nettlesome demographics in the early 1950s. When the club was established in 1953, it had 22 members, with a median age of 48 years. The oldest member was a 65-year old physician, and the youngest was a 40-year old art historian. The majority of members were born between 1905 and 1913,[60] representing a generation that Harold Marcuse has referred to as "1933ers." As a rule, this generation had "formed no strong relationship to the Weimar Republic," and had "experienced Nazism as a positive turning point."[61] A large number of postwar Rotarians had indeed established themselves professionally shortly before or during the Third Reich, and many had established comfortable working relations with the state and party apparatuses. These facts alone indicate little about true attitudes and behaviors of individual members during the Nazi years, whether in this particular club or more widely; indeed, some Rotarians went on an "internal emigration" from 1933 to 1945.[62] But they do reveal the extent to which Rotarians had accommodated themselves professionally to the Nazi regime.

Thus founding members in the early 1950s were naturally wary when a controversial name appeared in their ranks. Such was the case of Adenauer's chief of staff Hans Globke, who had co-written one of the official commentaries on the Nuremberg Racial Laws of 1935. When the newly constituted Rotary Club Bonn put forward its list of officers in 1950, Globke's name was second from the top, as vice president. Robert Haussmann, governor of Rotary's Germany district, had initially recommended Globke for the position, but when he learned of Globke's past, he registered his immediate disapproval. Now thrust into a negative spotlight, Globke, argued Haussmann, would lead to damaging publicity at a defining moment in the organization's history. "It would be very unfortunate for Dr. Globke, for the Club and, not least, for me, if this led to difficulties."[63] Haussmann's retroactive withdrawal of support was answered with defiance on the part of other Rotarians, who defended their nominee at the risk of public criticism.[64]

The Globke case was one of several examples of Rotarians having to decide between loyalty to a fellow member or shielding their clubs from unflattering attention. Which was a true demonstration of Rotarian values—fraternal fidelity or confronting, however pragmatically, the Nazi past? This was not always easy to answer. Rotarians in West Germany faced a similar choice in the 1960s, when Friedrich von Wilpert, a founding member of the Bonn club and Germany district governor from 1957–59, wrote a book length history of Rotary in Germany.[65] His 1962 study followed the organization from its arrival in Hamburg in 1927 through the readmission of Germany's clubs into Rotary International in 1949. Given Rotary Germany's short and tumultuous history, a large portion of the book concerned the fate of the clubs during the Nazi years. Wilpert offered a careful and unadorned portrayal of the organization during the years after Hitler's ascension to power. Rather than drifting into apologetics about the outright persecution of Rotarians, Wilpert instead painted a more nuanced picture of a movement struggling to reconcile its own internationalist aims with the hyper-nationalism of the Nazi period. During the early Nazi years, argued Wilpert, Rotarians did not distance themselves en masse from Nazism so much as try to put the best face on the political developments when non-Germans expressed concern over Hitler. Some Rotarians had been "careerists" during the 1930s and early 1940s, but the majority had been genuinely torn between duty to the Fatherland and commitment to the Rotary movement. Eventually, the Nazis forbade Rotarians from joining the NSDAP, and vice versa, before direct pressure from Goebbels spelled the end of the movement.

Forty years after its composition, Wilpert's portrayal of Germans' complicated choices under Nazism may seem uncontroversial. But in the early 1960s, it was bold in its unvarnished confrontation with the past, coming from the pen of a leading Rotarian.[66] Many individual Rotary clubs during the 1950s and 1960s published their own histories, which were less open about the internal struggles Rotarians faced.[67] They rarely mentioned the sad departure of Jewish Rotarians, as Wilpert had in his manuscript, nor the early hopes harbored by some Rotarians that they could steer Hitler along a more reasonable course.

To his consternation, Wilpert faced widespread criticism when he circulated his unpublished manuscript among fellow Rotarians. Some critics argued that too little time had passed for such an open rendering of the past. Other feared that young club members, who had not experienced the political pressures of the time, would not understand why their predecessors had placed their guarded faith in Hitler in 1933; with such knowledge, they might grow disillusioned with the organization. Still others expressed concern that the book, at its worst, could be misused by international critics of Germany. "What you have written," conceded one anonymous assessment, "is unfortunately too true." But, the statement concluded, as Rotarians, one was obliged to question whether the book passed the organization's "Four-Way Test": Is it the truth? Is it fair to all concerned? Will it build goodwill and better friendships? Will it be beneficial to all concerned? To most Rotarians the answer was No.[68]

Wilpert himself was not prepared to withdraw his manuscript, insisting that his work was written entirely in the spirit of Rotary, to provide a useful and truthful history to future Club Friends and historians. He initially rejected suggestions that he hand over the work to the Federal Archives, to be accessed only after the year 2000. For the next six years, Rotarians debated the fate of the manuscript. By 1964, Wilpert had agreed that publishing the book would "wake a sleeping dog," and he agreed to remove the developments from 1933 to 1937 from his work. Finally, in 1968, the Rotary Governor Council in Germany voted against publication altogether, and Wilpert conceded defeat, but not without a parting plea that Rotarians eventually face up to the truth of the Nazi years, when Rotarians had tried to save their movement by "making a pact with the powers in the Reich."[69] After sitting untouched for twenty years, the original manuscript was eventually made accessible in 1987, fifty years after the dissolution of Rotary Germany under National Socialism.[70]

At first glance Friedrich von Wilpert seemed an unlikely proponent of this "coming to terms with the past." A German nationalist and staunch anti-communist, he had been forced to leave his home in Danzig, where he had been the first secretary of the city's Rotary club in 1931. He eventually became a press officer in the West German Ministry for Expellees, Refugees, and the War-Damaged during the 1950s. His belief that his native Danzig was never a nazified city (despite the Nazis' dominance of the Danzig Senate since 1933) indicates how much Wilpert's views were in keeping with other, predominantly conservative German expellees.[71] Yet as district governor, Wilpert saw a faithful rendering of the Nazi years to be a fundamental expression of Rotary's commitment to honesty and to the country's reintegration into a community of democracies.

By the time Wilpert wrote his manuscript, the Holocaust was front-page news in West Germany. During the last year of Wilpert's tenure as district governor, West Germany had begun to witness a wave of anti-Semitic incidents, including the scrawling of swastikas on the Cologne synagogue and the defacement of Jewish cemeteries.[72] With the 1961 trial of Adolf Eichmann, Germans were beginning to reflect more openly on their own relationship to Nazi crimes. While it is unclear whether Wilpert was influenced by these events, his book reflected the expanding public discourse on Nazi crimes in the 1960s.

But the manuscript's controversial reception among his fellow Rotarians also reveals how reliving the past was still a fraught and painful exercise for West German elites. For, if some Rotarians had quietly disapproved of Hitler in the 1930s, others had put their faith in the regime and had tried to reconcile Rotary's aims with the racist and nationalist tenets of National Socialism. For them, and for the German bourgeoisie more broadly, the defeat in 1945 was not an unambiguous moment of celebration. As one Rotarian put it, "For us Germans, the military capitulation meant the simultaneous destruction of a vast number of ethical, material, and moral values."[73] Responding to this moral collapse took many forms in West German society, from abstract discussions of totalitarianism to reflections on one's own victimization by the Nazis and the Soviets.[74] Mirroring the tentative nature of memory in the 1950s and early 1960s, Rotarians were uneasy about the public nature of Wilpert's revelations. Rather than engaging in a public discussion about the different forms of behavior in the Third Reich, Rotarians chose to present their postwar commitment to service as a deeply ethical act that united all members, regardless of their or their predecessors' political choices in the past. Even if they did not declare it as such, for most Rotarians rebuilding their clubs in West Germany was itself an exercise in "coming to terms." Memory was selective and pragmatic, as organization leaders constantly weighed a historical reckoning against its public relations implications. But Rotarians did hope that a revival of bourgeois elitism—based on the ethos of service—would supplant the bankrupt Nazi Weltanschauung.

Taken together, these moments of controversy reflected the larger challenges facing West German society in its first decades, as debates over the role of former Nazis, and the political and moral legacy of the past, accompanied the building of democratic structures and discourses. How could Germany assert itself and move beyond its recent past without breeding international ill-will? This was a challenge for all Germans, but it resonated more loudly for an organization that saw itself as grounded in international ethical norms. For Rotarians, the answer to this question lay less in a dialogue with the Nazi past than in the values of their own organization. By explicitly espousing an ethos of global understanding and service, West German Rotarians hoped to offer models of ethical behavior to their fellow citizens. Reviving the values of the nineteenth century *Bürgertum*—reasoned debate, public service, male association, individuality—would not shield Germany from its compromised past. But it would ease the transition from authoritarianism to democracy. This had been the goal of the early Rotarians in the aftermath of World War I, and it again became the *raison d'être* of this new generation of elites, now faced with even greater practical and psychological hurdles.

～

Like any cultural and social movement, Rotary embodied a number of contradictions. On the one hand, German *Rotarier* echoed the ideals of groups like the *Wirtschaftspolitische Gesellschaft 1947* that envisioned a "free society without privileges, the conceits of family origin, higher social positions, or greater possessions."[75] On the other hand, the practice of philanthropy and social responsibility depended to some degree on real wealth and status. Likewise, the very concept of "elite," Rotarians conceded, aroused suspicion. It seemed to imply a reactionary challenge to the democratization of society, or could be misunderstood as a call for a plutocracy. But, agreed most Rotarians, "Even a democracy needs an elite," a group whose behavior stood as a model of moral rectitude.[76]

One must not downplay the pragmatic dimension of this ethical elitism. As one of the group's mottos "He Profits Most Who Serves Best" indicates, there was a measure of professional self-interest in Rotarian altruism. Certainly, Rotarians saw themselves not merely as cultural and social ambassadors but also as powerful leaders in a postwar world order. This view emerges not only in Rotary lectures but also in the advertisements that adorned the pages of the organization's magazines. A particularly revealing advertisement in 1957 depicts a man in the middle of negotiations at a setting resembling the United Nations. The placard in front of him bears the words, "Etats-Unis," and his expensive timepiece is very visible against the ad copy: "Men who guide the destinies of the world wear Rolex watches."[77]

These narratives of prestige and power were widespread throughout the West in the 1950s, and despite Rotary's commitment to international understanding, they often had an ideological component. Rotarians drew widely from prevailing Cold War discourses, wherein communism was seen as a dangerous "collectivist" challenge to Western individuality and capitalist freedom. Professional elites, whether in North America or Europe, could do their part in preventing the ultimate triumph of totalitarianism. Even if they were self-avowed internationalists, Rotarians saw European and Atlantic unity as the foundation of a stable and peaceful world order. This does not mean that the German Rotary movement merely echoed the ideological concerns of American elites. In the 1950s and 1960s, Rotary Germany remained a hybrid of national traditions and external influences. The organization borrowed its very language and structure from the original Rotarians in the United States. But Germans took an American organization and infused it with German priorities and concerns. Their goal of "recasting bourgeois Germany"[78] was necessarily a national project born of the country's recent history, when war and economic upheaval had weakened older social and cultural hierarchies. Ironically, it took an institution from America, the land of mass culture and democracy, to provide a model of elitism in postwar West Germany.

Ultimately, the true uniqueness of the West German Rotary movement lay in the proximity of a National Socialist past. In the early Federal Republic, the international ideals of the Rotary movement—service, friendship, loyalty, responsibility—had deep resonance in the aftermath of World War II. The moral failures of the Nazi years needed to be redressed through the promotion of democracy and peace, and West German Rotarians selectively drew lessons from the past—the meaning of mass movements, the nature of Hitler's rule, the fate of Rotary under National Socialism—to guide them in this process. Theirs was, to borrow Jürgen Kocka's words, "a project of civil society."[79]

In attempting to reconstitute a bourgeois public sphere, Rotary expressed the ethos of voluntary cooperation and association that had been inherited from the Enlightenment. The combination of elitism and democracy, individuality and collective morality manifested a much older bourgeois ideal—now revived in service of a postwar democracy. If Helmut Schelsky and other writers in the 1950s were "skeptics" who believed that a German *Bürgertum* had essentially disappeared, Rotarians can be seen as "cautious optimists" who at the very least endeavored to be the driving force behind its renewal.[80]

Notes

1. Lebenslauf von Rotarier S., 11 March 1957, RC Ulm/Donau, German Rotary Clubs Collection, B111 ("Deutsche Rotary Clubs"), Packet no. 38, (hereafter B111/38), Bundesarchiv Koblenz (hereafter BAK). Note that, as of the summer of 2000, this collection was only partially indexed. The number following "B111" corresponds to the number written on a specific box or packet. For another Rotarian reflection on captivity, see Vortrag des Rotariers G. in RC Hamburg, 30 November 1955, B111/9, BAK. On the postwar reflections of POWs and returnees more generally, see Frank Biess, "The Protracted War: Returning POWs and the Making of East and West German Citizens, 1945–1955," Ph.D. diss., Brown University, 2000; and Robert G. Moeller, *War Stories: The Search for a Usable Past in the Federal Republic of Germany* (Berkeley and Los Angeles, 2001).

2. I will be using the concept of *Bürgertum* interchangeably with "bourgeoisie," although the German term has deeper cultural connotations. From the massive literature on this theme, see as an introduction Hannes Siegrist, "Ende der Bürgerlichkeit? Die Kategorien 'Bürgertum' und 'Bürgerlichkeit' in der westdeutschen Gesellschaft und Geschichtswissenschaft der Nachkriegsperiode," *Geschichte und Gesellschaft* 20 (1994): 548–83.

3. Volker R. Berghahn, "Recasting Bourgeois Germany," in *The Miracle Years: A Cultural History of West Germany, 1949–1968*, ed. Hanna Schissler (Princeton/Oxford, 2001), 326–40; and Volker R. Berghahn, Stefan Unger, and Dieter Ziegler, eds., *Die deutsche Wirtschaftselite im 20. Jahrhundert. Kontinuität und Mentalität* (Essen, 2003). For a case study on postwar elites, see Michael R. Hayse, *Recasting West German Elites: Higher Civil Servants, Business Leaders, and Physicians in Hesse between Nazism and Democracy, 1945–1955* (New York/Oxford, 2003). On the history of German professions, see Geoffrey Cocks and Konrad H. Jarausch, *German Professions, 1800–1950* (New York/Oxford, 1990).

4. Rotary Germany, however, has recently published its history. See Manfred Wedemeyer, *Den Menschen verpflichtet. 75 Jahre Rotary in Deutschland, 1927–2002* (Hamburg, 2002). For an exhaustive history through 1949, also from the perspective of a Rotarian, see Friedrich von Wilpert, *Rotary in Deutschland. Ein Ausschnitt aus deutschem Schicksal* (Bonn, 1991). See also the sardonic and critical rendering in "Rotary: Filz in Nadelstreifen," *Der Spiegel* 21 (1983): 56–74. On the controversial inception of this book, see below. Many Clubs have short histories posted on their official websites.

5. See Mary Nolan, *Visions of Modernity: American Business and the Modernization of Germany* (Oxford, 1994).

6. Jeffrey A. Charles, *Service Clubs in American Society: Rotary, Kiwanis, and Lions* (Urbana/Chicago, 1993), 9 and Chap. 6.

7. Ibid., 128.

8. See Victoria de Grazia, *Irresistible Empire: America's Advance through Twentieth Century Europe* (Cambridge, 2005), msp. 26. I thank Professor de Grazia for providing me a draft copy of her chapter on interwar European Rotarians.

9. Ibid., 61.

10. Ibid., 49.

11. Ibid., 33.

12. These were Freiburg, Garmisch-Partenkirchen, Wuppertal, Friedrichshafen, Bielefeld, and Krefeld. The Krefeld club established its charter in April 1937, a mere six months before Rotary Germany's dissolution in October. See Wilpert, *Rotary in Deutschland,* 156, and 300–01.

13. The group was the *Verein zur Beförderung des Gewerbefleisses.* See ibid., 232. On this organization, and for an introduction to Rotary under Nazism, see also Manfred Wedemeyer, "Rotary in the Third Reich: Survival or Internal Emigration," in *Rotary's Global History Fellowship (An Internet Project) (http://rotaryhistoryfellowship.org/global/conflict/germany)* [Accessed 3 June 2004].

14. Wilpert, *Rotary in Deutschland,* 242.

15. At least 21 former Rotarians were decorated with the title of *Wehrdienstführer.* See the (sensationalist) discussion in Peter Wendling, *Die Unfehlbaren: Die Geheimnisse exklusiver Clubs, Logen und Zirkel* (Zürich, 1991), 154.

16. See Ottmar Katz, "Beziehungen muss man haben," *Abendzeitung* [Munich] (2 January 1957), in B111/20, BAK.

17. See files on the founding of RC Köln, in B111/4, BAK. Pferdmenges had also been the president of the Cologne Club before its dissolution in 1937. See De Grazia, 43.

18. On Wilmowsky's membership, see RC Essen, #41 1955/56, Bericht über die Zusammenkunft am 3. April 1956, B111/2, BAK. On Berthold von Bohlen, see files on the founding of RC Essen, B111/6, BAK. In the 1930s, Wilmowsky had been a member of RC Halle.

19. On Vaubel, see Bericht #40 (13 April 1956), in Wuppertal files, B111/1, BAK. On the "Wuppertal Circle," see Volker R. Berghahn, *The Americanisation of West German Industry* (Cambridge, 1986), 254.

20. On Adenauer, see file on the founding of RC Bonn in 1949, B111/5, BAK.

21. See e.g. Herr G. to Rotary International in Chicago, 8 September 1950, B111/1, BAK.

22. On the Kulturkreis, see Werner Bührer, "Der Kulturkreis im Bundesverband der Deutschen Industrie und die kulturelle Modernisierung der Bundesrepublik in den 50er Jahren," in *Modernisierung im Wiederaufbau: Die westdeutsche Gesellschaft der 50er Jahre,* eds. Axel Schildt and Arnold Sywottek (Bonn,1993), 583–96; and S. Jonathan Wiesen, *West German Industry and the Challenge of the Nazi Past* (Chapel Hill/London, 2001), 167–70.

23. On these *Arbeitsgemeinschaften,* see Wiesen, *West German Industry,* 177.

24. On Conze, see files on RC Münster/Westf., B111/26, BAK. For a brief introduction to Conze's postwar career, see Moeller, *War Stories,* 58. For a longer discussion

of Conze's controversial research during the Third Reich, see Ingo Haar, *Historiker im Nationalsozialismus, Deutsche Geschichtswissenschaft und der "Volkstumskampf" im Osten* (Göttingen, 2000).

25. "Der Historische Standort von Rotary International oder Männerbünde in der Geschichte," lecture (name and date unavailable) delivered at RC Neuss am Rhein, B111/14, BAK.

26. Ibid.

27. This reference to Rotary as a "modern guild" comes from the Rotary publication *Service is my Business* (Chicago, 1948).

28. Rotarians also explicitly emphasized the importance of service to their professions and to their own and other Rotary clubs. See Bericht über die Distriktskonferenz des 98. Distrikts am 3 November 1956 in Bad Kreuznach, B111/20, BAK.

29. For a list of typical Rotarian acts of philanthropy, see Clubtätigkeitenbericht, RC Bielefeld, January 1957, B111/17, BAK.

30. On these humanitarian activities, see *Reporting on Rotary, 1956–1957,* B111/21, BAK and ibid.

31. Originating in Oxford, England in the 1920s and later based in Caux, Switzerland, the Moral Rearmament movement brought together leaders from around Europe to discuss the reinfusion of ethics into European life and, more specifically, to foster a reconciliation between former enemies. Many German leaders, including Rotarians, took part in the meetings. See Referat über die 'Moralische Aufrüstung,' gehalten von Rotarier D., Anlage zum Bericht Nr. 32/55–56, 13 February 1956, RC Bentheim," B111/9, BAK.

32. By the end of 1955, there were 16,700 Lions clubs in 69 countries, as opposed to 8,400 Rotary clubs. See Dr. Jur. Heinz M. Wittenberg, District Governor of Germany, Lions International, to Herr K. 19 November 1955, B111/25, BAK.

33. Jordan appears to have been a member of, or an active participant in, RC Hamburg as well, despite the general Rotarian rule precluding membership in two service clubs, scattered files in B111/25, BAK.

34. Ibid.

35. Herr R. of the Geschäftsstelle der Europa-Union Wuppertal speaking on the European Union, 22 July 1956, RC Wuppertal files, B111/1, BAK.

36. On this "Flaggenaustausch," see reports from RC Hamburg in B111/9, BAK.

37. See e.g. the charter celebrations of RC Bad Homburg, RC Lündeberg, and RC Flensburg, B111/25, BAK.

38. On the Dreyfus Affair, see lecture by Rotarier H., 3 April 1957, RC Krefeld, B111/27, BAK. Likewise see "Probleme Indiens," RC Wuppertal, Bericht #5/1955/56, B111/1; "Adolf Hitler, ein neurotisches Problem," RC Hildesheim zum Bericht Nr. 52/57, 29 January 1957, B111/39, BAK; "Das Rassenproblem in den USA," Vortrag von Rot. M., RC Mülheim a.d. Ruhr, Anlage zum Wochenbericht, 19 March 1956, B111/6, BAK.

39. Hanz-Peter Schwarz, *Die Ära Adenauer,* 2 vols. (Wiesbaden, 1961–64), quoted in Berghahn, "Recasting Bourgeois Germany," in Schissler, ed., *The Miracle Years,* 328.

40. See the series of weekly reports from 1957 in B111/17, BAK., including "Die wundersame Geschichte von Walt Disney," von Rot. S., RC Mönchen-Gladbach, 27 February 1957, B111/6, BAK.

41. On "Managerkrankheiten," see RC Trier, #14–1955/56, meeting on 7 October 1955, B111/1. BAK.

42. "Komfortismus als Lebensstil," Kurze Inhaltsangabe des Vortrages von Rot. S., 7 October 1955, RC Wuppertal," B111/1, BAK.

43. On the influence of Schelsky in the 1950s, see Uta G. Poiger, *Jazz, Rock, and Rebels: Cold War Politics and American Culture in a Divided Germany* (Berkeley/Los Angeles, 2000), Chap. 3. See also Josef Mooser, "Arbeiter, Angestellte und Frauen in der 'nivellierten Mittelstandsgesellschaft.' Thesen," in Schildt and Sywottek, eds., *Modernisierung im Wiederaufbau*, 362–76.

44. Dwight Macdonald, "A Theory of Mass Culture," in *Mass Culture: The Popular Arts in America,* eds. Bernard Rosenberg and David Manning White (Glencoe, Ill., 1957), 59–73. For more on Macdonald, see Volker R. Berghahn, *America and the Intellectual Cold Wars of Europe* (Princeton, 2001), 98–103.

45. On consumerism in West Germany, see Michael Wildt, "Changes in Consumption as Social Practice in West Germany During the 1950s," in *Getting and Spending: European and American Consumer Societies in the Twentieth Century,* eds. Susan Strasser, Charles McGovern, and Matthias Judt (Washington D.C, 1998).

46. The concept of *Vermassung* pervaded the speeches and writings of Rotarians during the 1950s. On conservative elites and perceptions of "the masses" in the 1950s, see Axel Schildt, *Konservatismus in Deutschland. Von den Anfängen im 18. Jahrhundert bis zur Gegenwart* (Munich, 1998), 211–52. For a discussion of the economic and social realities of the 1950s, see Axel Schildt and Arnold Sywottek, "'Reconstruction' and 'Modernization': West German Social History during the 1950s," in *West Germany under Construction: Politics, Society, and Culture in the Adenauer Era,* ed. Robert G. Moeller (Ann Arbor, 1997), 413–43. On the cultural mood of the period, see Axel Schildt, *Moderne Zeiten: Freizeit, Massenmedien und "Zeitgeist" in der Bundesrepublik der 50er Jahre* (Hamburg, 1995).

47. "Das Mittelstandsproblem." Vortrag von Rot. W., 7 March 1957, RC Recklinghausen, B111/14, BAK.

48. "Gedanken zum Weg einer unbürgerlichen Generation." Vortrag von Rot. S, 19 October 1956, RC Wuppertal, B111/15, BAK.

49. William H. Whyte, Jr., *The Organization Man* (Garden City, 1957).

50. See Berghahn, *America and the Intellectual Cold Wars in Europe.*

51. For Rotarians' views on this theme, see "Zivilisationskrankheiten." Vortrag von Rot. K. am 13 February 1957, Anlage 2 zum Wochenbericht Berlin Nr. 31/1956/57, B111/40. Rotarians spoke often about the manifestation of sickness in society, e.g. "Ist die moderne Kunst krank?" Vortrag von Rot. F., 1 July 1957, RC Oldenburg, B111/39, BAK.

52. See e.g. "Führungsaufgaben des Unternehmers," Vortrag des Herrn R. vor Mitgliedern des Lions- und Rotary-Clubs, 6 June 1957, B111/39, BAK.

53. On the importance of authority and leadership, see "Vom Geheimnis der Autorität," Vortrag von Rot. Dr. E., 2. July 1956, RC Ulm, B111/38, BAK. On *Elitebildung* and leadership ideas among West German businessmen, see Morten Reitmayer, "'Unternehmer zur Führung berufen'—durch wen?," in *Die deutsche Wirtschaftselite im 20. Jahrhundert: Kontinuität und Mentalität* [Bochumer Schriften zur Unternehmens- und Industriegeschichte, Bd. 11], eds. Volker R. Berghahn, Stefan Unger, and Dieter Ziegler (Essen, 2003), 317–36.

54. See e.g. "Elite—im Zeitalter der Masse." Vortrag von Rot. P., 15 October 1956, RC Ulm/Donau, Bericht 15–56/57, B111/38, BAK.

55. On early postwar concepts of the "mass man," see e.g. Mark Roseman, "The Organic Society and the 'Massenmenschen': Integrating Young Labour in the Ruhr Mines, 1945–58," in *West Germany Under Construction,* ed. Moeller, 287–320.

56. On the importance of the "self" to Rotarians, see Gustav Hillard-Steinbömer, RC Lübeck, "Über das Wesen der Selbstbiographie." Reprinted in *Der Rotarier* (1955), B111/21, BAK.

57. On West German memory in the 1950s, see, as introductions, Norbert Frei, *Adenauer's Germany and the Nazi Past: The Politics of Amnesty and Integration* (New York, 2002), and Jeffrey Herf, *Divided Memory: The Nazi Past in the Two Germanys* (Cambridge, 1997).

58. Herr G. to Rotary International in Chicago, 8. September 1950, B111/1, BAK.

59. On some of these qualifications, see Bernhard Goldschmidt, Governor of the 74th District (West Germany) to Professor A., 14 November 1952, B111/1, BAK.

60. RC Mönchen-Gladbach, "Gründer-Mitglieder-Liste," 1953, B111/11, BAK. I have chosen this club based on the availability of membership data.

61. Harold Marcuse, *Legacies of Dachau: The Uses and Abuses of a Concentration Camp, 1933–2001* (Cambridge, 2001), 292.

62. Wedemeyer, "Rotary in the Third Reich."

63. Robert Haussmann, Governor des 74. Distrikts to Rot. S., 31 October 1950, B111/5, BAK.

64. When the correspondence ends, Bonn Rotarians are resisting Haussmann's pleas. I have not been able to determine whether Globke remained in the position of Vice President.

65. "Rotary in Deutschland. Ein Ausschnitt aus deutschem Schicksal. Von Friedrich von Wilpert (als Manuskript gedruckt, umfassend die Zeit, 1927–ca 1950)." Kl. Erw. (Kleine Erwerbungen): Nr. 474–1 (fol. 1), BAK.

66. Wilpert's manuscript is not without its biases. He refers, for example, to a Jewish and communist defamation campaign against Germany in the early 1930s. Wilpert, *Rotary in Deutschland,* 67.

67. See e.g. *Fünfundzwanzig Jahre Rotary Club Hannover: Festschrift, 1932–1957,* in B111/21, BAK.

68. "Urteile über das Manuskript 'Rotary in Deutschland.'" Kl. Erw. 474–2, folder 1, BAK. See the following series of correspondences about the manuscript, which span the years 1962 to 1968, in the same files.

69. Wilpert, "Schlussbemerkung zur bisherigen Behandlung meines Manuskriptes 'Rotary in Deutschland,'" 10 June 1968, Kl. Erw. 474–2, BAK.

70. The manuscript was eventually published in book form. See Wilpert, *Rotary in Deutschland.* For Wilpert's own description of this controversy, see ibid., 321. See also Wedemeyer, *75 Jahre Rotary,* 122–27.

71. On expellee organizations in West Germany, see Pertti Ahonen, "Domestic Constraints on West German Ostpolitik: The Role of the Expellee Organizations in the Adenauer Era" *Central European History* 31 (1998): 31–63.

72. On this wave of Antisemitism in 1959–60, see Detlef Siegfried, "Zwischen Aufarbeitung und Schlußstrich. Der Umgang mit der NS-Vergangenheit in den beiden deutschen Staaten, 1958 bis 1969," in *Dynamische Zeiten: Die 60er Jahre in den beiden deutschen Gesellschaften,* eds. Axel Schildt, Detlef Siegfried, and Karl Christian Lammers (Hamburg, 2000), 77–113.

73. "Wo stehen wir heute?" Redner: Rot. M., RC Siegen, Anlage zum Wochenbericht, 12 December 1955, B111/1, BAK.

74. This view came through in some Rotarians' autobiographical presentations. See Lebenslauf von Rotarier S., 11 March 1957, RC Ulm/Donau," B111/38, BAK. On the sense of victimization after World War II, see Moeller, *War Stories.*

75. See "Wirtschaftspolitische Gesellschaft Tagung in Frankfurt." Referat gehalten von Rot. H. beim RC Trier, am 27.1.56, B111/1, BAK.

76. "Problem der Elitebildung." Vortrag von Rot. H., 2 November 1955, Anlage 2 zum Wochenbericht Berlin Nr. 18/1955/56. B111/9 (Aktenordner #1), BAK.

77. *The Rotarian: An International Magazine* 90:5 (May 1957):1 in B111/18, BAK. There is an important gender component to this elitist message that demands further exploration. Rotarians—whether in Germany or abroad—saw their clubs as bastions of distinctly male economic and social power. Rotary International did not accept women as members until a 1987 U.S. Supreme Court decision mandated that they do so. On Rotary Germany as a "men's only" club, see De Grazia, *Irresistible Empire*, 44.

78. Berghahn, "Recasting Bourgeois Germany," [Title derived from Charles S. Maier, *Recasting Bourgeois Europe: Stabilization in France, Germany, and Italy in the Decade after World War I* (Princeton, 1975)].

79. See Jürgen Kocka, *Industrial Culture and Bourgeois Society: Business, Labor, and Bureaucracy in Modern Germany* (New York/Oxford, 1999), 284.

80. On this characterization of Schelsky, see Siegrist, "Ende der Bürgerlichkeit?"

CHAPTER 16

Fighting to Win the Peace

08/15 *and West German Memories of the Second World War*

Robert G. Moeller

West Germans who switched on their radios in early October 1954 could hear that "they are marching again."[1] "They" were men wearing the uniform of Hitler's army. "Eighteen kilometers from Munich," reported the *Frankfurter Rundschau*, passersby strolling through the Waldham forest were shocked when they heard the thud of army boots and saw men armed with rifles and singing the same songs sung by 14 million German soldiers between 1939 and 1945.[2] Germans were going to war again, but this time, commentators quickly added, the fighting would take place only at the movies. Carrying weapons scavenged in Italy and Czechoslovakia and wearing old uniforms from Austria, an army of actors was hard at work under the direction of Paul May, translating onto celluloid Hans Hellmut Kirst's novel *08/15*, an account of military training on the eve of the Second World that had been serialized, then published in book form.[3] Ernst von Salomon was the screenplay writer. His checkered past included participation in the plot to assassinate Foreign Minister Walter Rathenau and support for right-wing political movements that battled the Weimar Republic. Also opposed to the Nazis—because he did not share their racism and because they maintained ties to old elites and did not seek the complete "national revolution" he advocated—he was nonetheless arrested by the Americans in 1945 and held for a year as a "security threat." Once released, he continued to work as a writer, and he was May's pick to adapt Kirst's novel for the screen.[4]

08/15 was the name of a standard-issue pistol, and the designation came to symbolize all that could go wrong with the military. In Kirst's version, behind visions of a well-oiled Wehrmacht fighting machine was the reality of a bungling, barbaric, quotidian in which endless drills led nowhere but humiliation. Kirst told this story from the perspective of the common soldier, Herbert Asch, claiming to break a "taboo" that prohibited tarnishing military tradition and depicting soldiers as anything but storybook heroes.[5] The result was a smash hit in bookstores and movies theaters alike.

Actors in Wehrmacht uniforms did not first appear in West German movies in the mid-1950s. In *Die Mörder sind unter uns* (*The Murderers are Among Us;* Wolfgang Staudte, 1946), the earliest postwar German movie to address the end of the Second World War, Dr. Hans Mertens, an ex-officer, is haunted by his failure to stop the murder of innocent women and children in Poland in 1942. And in other "movies of the rubble" *(Trümmerfilme)* of the late 1940s, flashbacks recalled the shooting war, and returning veterans figured prominently, broken and disoriented in a postwar world. Even as cheerier filmic images of an imagined German *Heimat* began to displace the rubble in the early 1950s, the manly forester often let it be known that he too had "served," wearing the field grey of the Wehrmacht before he had donned the field green of the eternal forest.[6]

Beginning in the mid-1950s, however, the shooting war was not just a bad dream or an allusion. Wehrmacht uniforms abounded, and iron crosses and other medals attesting to soldierly accomplishments were seen in scene after scene. Movies, as one critic wrote of *08/15*, were finally ready to present the war in ways that "approached reality" and were "believable."[7] In part, the war conquered West German film production because American imports proved that Germans wanted to see men in uniform not as flashback but as the main event. The Field Marshal Erwin Rommel who entertained West German audiences in the early 1950s spoke dubbed German and was played by James Mason (*The Desert Fox;* Henry Hathaway, 1951). *Damned in All Eternity (Verdammt in alle Ewigkeit)* was known first to American audiences as *From Here to Eternity* (Fred Zinnemann, 1953), and the German version of *The Caine was Their Fate (Die Caine war ihr Schicksal;* Edward Dmytryk, 1954) replaced mutiny with destiny but still featured Humphrey Bogart.

Eager to make money where money was to be made, West German movie producers and directors began to churn out war films in which the actors spoke German. In 1954 and 1955, West Germans could see a World War I hero, now charged with developing Germany's air power, go head to head with the Nazi hierarchy in *Des Teufels General* ("The Devil's General"; Helmut Käutner, 1955). They could applaud Admiral Wilhelm Canaris, the head of military intelligence, who maintained his honor even as he served the Third Reich.[8] And they could reflect on those military men who attempted to bring an end to the war by assassinating Hitler in *Es geschah am 20. Juli* ("It Happened on July 20"; Georg Wilhelm Pabst, 1955). Mass-mediated war stories were extremely popular. By the end of a decade in which Germans went to the movies more than ever before, over ten percent of the films on offer were about the Second World War.[9]

In war movies, memories, not just markets, were at stake. Commenting on *08/15*, the critic Erwin Goelz noted that movies "do not *create* opinions, rather, they *follow* them and bring them to consciousness, and in the process, they reinforce them."[10] The opinions that *08/15* articulated were seen by millions. Scholars who write about film in the 1950s have no good answer to the question of audience reception, and gauging what impact movies had on viewers is impossible. However, at least in the case of *08/15*, we know that many people saw it. No war movie did better. When it opened, according to one press report, the number of tickets sold hit 5 million within a month. A movie that cost only about $200,000 to make had grossed $4 million in little over four weeks.[11] The success of the first installment generated two sequels. Life in the barracks was followed in Part II by the war in Russia. And in Part III, the war ended in the west. The movies' popularity also registered clearly in a wealth of film reviews in the popular press. Although critics are no stand in for the "public," their responses to May's movies suggest the range of opinion about this portrayal of the past.[12]

An article about *08/15* seemed appropriate for a collection of essays intended to honor Volker Berghahn. Among many other things, Berghahn's work has focused on the history of militarism and the significance of culture as a measure of popular attitudes. *08/15*, a cultural product, immediately became a part of intense West German discussions of plans to put Germans into uniform in the early 1950s. Thus, I hope my discussion can resonate with at least two of Berghahn's scholarly interests.

∽

"The right theme at the right moment, presented in the right fashion, therein lies the secret of the success of such books," remarked the journalist Thilo Koch about the publication of *08/15*, and his comments also applied to the movies that emerged from Kirst's trilogy.[13] Consider the bigger picture of which May's movie was a part. On 30 August 1954, the French parliament rejected a treaty that would have established a transnational European Defense Community (the EDC) that included West German soldiers. Since the late 1940s—and with growing intensity since the outbreak of the war in Korea— the victorious western Allies had reconsidered their judgment that Germans should permanently disarm. The realization that West Germany was on the front line of the European East-West divide brought a change of heart. In Paris, anxiety over whether a militarized Germany could be contained even within a pan-European structure combined with French ambitions to establish an independent military profile brought about the collapse of nearly four years of diplomatic wrangling intended to define a context in which West Germany could rearm.

Many West Germans opposed rearmament, but not all for the same reasons. Some advocated a thoroughgoing pacifism. Others chafed at the notion of German soldiers as part of a transnational, not a national, military structure. Others feared that West German entry into a western, anti-Soviet alliance would dash any hopes for German reunification. And still others resented Allied insistence that Germans put on the uniform while some former German officers were still jailed as "war criminals." But by the summer of 1954, even most opponents accepted that the question was not whether but in what form West Germany would rearm. French rejection of the EDC was a setback that left political leaders in Bonn, London, and Washington scrambling to come up with an alternative; but they rapidly crafted a plan to make German troops part of a military force controlled by the North Atlantic Treaty Organization. By late October 1954 the details were hammered out, and four months later, by a margin of more than two to one, the West German parliament approved this solution.

On 5 May 1955, the Allies lifted the postwar statute of occupation, leaving it largely to West Germans to run West Germany, the reward for West German agreement to rearm. In the months that followed, the parliament and Chancellor Konrad Adenauer's government moved swiftly to define the terms under which the Federal Republic would deliver the *quid* for this *quo*. Theodor Blank, a leader of the postwar Christian trade union movement, commander of an antitank company in the war, who had run Adenauer's military planning office, became the first Minister of Defense, and recruitment of the first soldiers soon followed. In mid-January 1956, 1,500 troops stood for the first time for a public military review.[14]

Even as West Germans put on uniforms to join ranks in an anti-Communist alliance, other Germans soldiers returned from a long, involuntary stay in the Soviet Union. In September 1955 Adenauer traveled to Moscow, trading the promise of diplomatic recognition and an exchange of ambassadors for the release of the last German POWs held by the Soviets. For four months, beginning in October 1955, the "last soldiers of the great war"[15] marched across the headlines of West Germans newspapers, on to TV screens, and into newsreels, providing other reminders of the past that Kirst's novels and May's movies addressed.

Against the background of this political drama, May's three-part movie drama played to huge audiences. A month after the French vote against the EDC, the first part of *08/15* opened, and as diplomats scurried from London to Paris to bring West Germany into NATO, West Germans scurried into movie theaters to see celluloid soldiers. Part II followed, opening in early August 1955, against the background of parliamentary negotiations over the design of the new military. And the trilogy ended just as the very last POWs came home and the first new recruits appeared in American-style uniforms.[16] The timing could not have been better, and contemporary events convinced the films' producers that there would be an audience ready to recall a time when German soldiers wore the *Stahlhelm,* not the American-style helmets issued to the soldiers of a West German army.

The action of *08/15* begins after German troops had marched into Austria in March 1938, annexing that German-speaking nation without opposition—implied in the film by the presence of an amiably incompetent Austrian officer—and ends in May 1945. The war story that the trilogy told thus goes from training in the barracks—in the town of Holzhausen, a real place on the West German map but also a generic small-town Germany—on the eve of the invasion of Poland and ends as Americans overrun Germany. Reviewers made much of the fact that May had recruited "anonymous actors to portray the anonymous millions, the 08/15 foot soldiers,"[17] everyman to depict everyman. However, if they were new to movies, they were not new to war, and many were now reprising parts they had played between 1939 and 1945. Art, reporters noted, was now imitating life.

The players included Herbert Asch (Joachim Fuchsberger), who is paired in Parts I and II with his mate Johannes Vierbein (Paul Bösiger). They are plagued by two noncommissioned officers, Schulz (Emmerich Schrenk) and Platzek (Hans-Christian Blech), who survive both sequels. Lieutenant Wedelmann (Rainer Penkert), an idealistic young officer, believes National Socialism's promises but his fantasy will not survive Part II, and Major Luschke (Wilfried Seyferth) is a wise commanding officer who embodies what's best about a military tradition that has not turned brown. Good for comic relief is another of Asch's buddies, Kowalski (Peter Carsten). Not entirely a world without women, the film also features Lore (Helen Vita), Schulz's wife, whose décolleté frequently precedes her when she comes onto the screen and whose insatiable search for sex is really a longing for understanding. She is the earth mother of the regiment. Asch also has a love interest, Elisabeth Freitag (Eva Ingeborg Scholz), a daughter of the working-class. And Vierbein's heart belongs to Ingrid (Gundula Korte), Asch's sister, who enthusiastically parrots slogans of the League of German Girls, suggesting that she needs someone older and wiser, telling her what to do. In a cameo role is Asch's father (Walter Klock), a café owner who is a Nazi party member but who is far more interested in his daily cash receipts than ideology. The paintings on his living room walls are not of Hitler but of himself in the uniform of World War I, a flower peeking out the muzzle of his rifle, and of his father, astride a canon from the Franco-Prussian War. The gun's muzzle sticks out from between his legs in a manner that suggests a time when masculinity and the military were a powerful match. The untimely death in a traffic accident of Wilfried Seyferth (Major Luschke), the only well-known actor in the original crew, led to his replacement in Part

II with O.E. Hasse, who was already well known to German audiences from his portrayal of Canaris.

In Part I, the story is told from the perspective of Asch and Vierbein, and from them we learn much about the senselessness of military training. Of the NCOs, Schulz is at the drunken buffoonish end of the spectrum, while Platzek tends toward the sadistic. Asch always knows what he's up against, but Vierbein is less well equipped to survive this irrational world. He is sustained by his love for Ingrid and his love of music. He aspired to be a pianist before Hitler changed his plans and occasionally his graceful hands can fill the barracks with strains of Beethoven.

The first half of Part I establishes that enlisted men are smarter than the martinets who bark out commands, and when they pull together, they can accomplish a lot, frequently with much hilarity. But in the second half of the movie, things get serious. Platzek submits his charges to minute after grueling minute of drills in a muddy field, where recruits respond to his whistle, hitting the ground, then getting up and running. His exploding face fills the screen as he screams commands, and the camera moves from him to a broken Vierbein. This kind of brutal behavior pushes both Asch and Vierbein over the top—but in different directions. Vierbein contemplates suicide, which he plans to accomplish with ammunition purloined from the shooting range, but Asch cunningly saves his comrade and outsmarts his superiors. Their paths converge. Asch incriminates the NCOs, charging them with responsibility for the missing ammunition, while convincing Vierbein that he should not take his life. Major Luschke, called upon to weigh charges of insubordination brought against Asch, finds in his favor, and Kowalski and Asch are rewarded, not punished. "I hear that recently you have had thoughts about how to improve the ranks of the junior officers, great, good, terrific," Luschke enthuses, promoting them so that "now you can translate your theories into practice."[18]

Music is important in all three movies, and the war's progression eastward in Part II is announced not only by the snowy landscape against which the credits roll but also by the strains of the "Song of the Volga Boatman," intertwined with the *08/15* theme of fife and drum, ubiquitous in Part I. In the movie, it is never clear where Asch is in the Soviet motherland, but there is no doubt why he is there: Hitler and his henchmen in the high command of the Wehrmacht are to blame. At the front, National Socialism is embodied in Captain Witterer (Rolf Kutschera), who has left a desk job to win a medal—something Asch and Vierbein have already earned. Who could doubt that this opportunistic Nazi will be Asch's new nemesis?

Platzek, the sadist of Part I, has rounded off his rough edges, and when training has moved from theory to practice, he has found meaningful employment as the company's "organizer." He rules over a storeroom filled with French cognac and Russian champagne, and the troops he now commands are Russians, freed from the Soviet yoke, apparently happy to serve another master in this misbegotten village. Not all Russians, however, so willingly accept these uninvited guests, and Natasha—a beauty who speaks some German—wants the Germans to leave. A Soviet spy, she finds, however, that her loyalties to Russia compete with a different sort of passion, awakened by Lieutenant Wedelmann. Still an idealistic Nazi, Wedelmann sees no inconsistency in also pursuing the study of Russian; an occupying force should learn as well as teach. For Natasha's Russian lessons he pays with his heart. Natasha, robbed by the Germans of both parents and an heirloom samovar, loves Wedelmann too but realizes that war makes such emotions *verboten*. She also remains a loyal comrade, using a hidden transmitter to broadcast the information about troop movements that Wedelmann innocently lets slip.

In the noncommissioned officers' barracks, other forms of love are in bloom, and a group of shapely "strength through joy" performers has arrived, evoking reactions from the men that put to rest any concern that in the homosocial world of the military there is any shortage of heterosexual desire. Asch, meanwhile married to Elisabeth and the father of a child he barely knows, not only constantly demonstrates Witterer's incompetence as a military leader, he also foils Witterer's attempts as a lover, spiriting away Lisa, the performer on whom Witterer's sights are fixed.

Vierbein, whose Iron Cross testifies to the seven Russian tanks he destroyed, has been dispatched home by the commanding officer to get needed equipment and troops by whatever means necessary. Luschke is gone, but the new Captain von Plönies (Hasse) is of the same ilk, a "continuation of the Canaris role" that Hasse had already occupied as one reviewer suggested.[19] Back at home, Vierbein is lost in a civilian society unaffected by the war and completely alienated from the barracks where Schulz remains in charge. Ingrid, still in a brown haze, offers him no solace. His vision of marriage as a union of soul mates collides head-on with her desexualized Nazi rhetoric of health and hygiene. He ultimately turns to Lore Schulz. Will he ever play the piano again? On her baby grand, he haltingly picks out Beethoven, but the fade out and crashing chords suggest that he has sought a different kind of comfort in Lore's embrace. Vierbein also secures the men and supplies Plönies needs but only by invoking a network to which Plönies has given him access with the secret code, "the chimneys are still smoking." With these magic words, Vierbein wins support from another commander who shares Plönies' antipathy for Hitler. This time, on Vierbein's flight back to the front, the music is Wagner.

At the front, Germans and Soviets save their artillery shells, knowing that neither side has anything to gain by rupturing the unspoken cease-fire in this wintry war of waiting. But Witterer disrupts the peace, firing on the Soviets, provoking a response, and demonstrating terrible military judgment. Unable to advance, the Germans are soon in retreat. "General Winter" has given way to "General Muck and Slime," and the trucks hauling soldiers, performers, and Platzek's treasures are slip-sliding through the mud. Visited by a military intelligence officer, Plönies learns that the Soviets had advance knowledge of the retreat and signs point to Natasha. The officer who tips off Plönies also knows that the "chimneys are still smoking," and they agree to keep the knowledge of Wedelmann's loose lips from the Sicherheitsdienst (SD) and the Gestapo, the *real* Nazis who would show the lieutenant no mercy. Wedelmann has also added up the evidence. He confronts Natasha, and she is ready to die. Wedelmann is unable to use his drawn pistol to mete out the justice due a partisan, however, and she escapes. Instead, he offers Plönies his own life, but the wise captain refuses, reminding Wedelmann that if he takes this way out, he will be replaced by someone in an SS or SD uniform. Together they join the retreat—and tacitly a war in which good Germans are fighting not only Russians but Nazis.

Vierbein returns to a ghost town, populated only by Asch, Witterer, and a few others. As Russian tanks approach, Witterer orders a suicide mission, an artillery barrage despite the fact that they are outgunned. When the going gets tough, Witterer gets going—in hasty retreat—and Vierbein is left to face an oncoming tank, crushed as he attempts to take cover. His legacy is a letter to Ingrid in which he dreams of a peaceful future and a houseful of children— all girls who will not be soldiers. Music again plays its part, this time, strains of "I had a comrade" *("Ich hatt'n Kamerad"),* with words penned by Ludwig Uhland for a past in which Germany was occupied by the forces of Napoleon, not one in which Germans occupied the Soviet Union.

By the spring of 1945—and Part III—the opening musical background of "Yankee Doodle" and the "Star Spangled Banner" leaves no doubt that the Americans are coming. When some of them arrive, a jazzed-up version of the *08/15* theme will blare from their transistor radios; it's already possible to hear an Americanized future. Nazi war crimes have been invisible so far, but in Part III, they loom large. The crimes Nazis commit, however, are not against Jews or other civilians; rather, the victims are German soldiers and the notions of honor that Asch and Plönies embody. The worst offenders are Greifer, an officer in the Secret Service (SD)—masquerading in the uniform of the regular military—and Hauk, an SS officer, who is similarly disguised. They seek to escape in front of the advancing American troops with a few truckloads of ill-gotten goods—French cognac, fine cigars, and a treasure in platinum bars. In a war that has provided chances for rapid advancement, Asch and Kowalski are now lieutenants, and Plönies is a general. Although Wedelmann lives on in Kirst's Part III, he has fallen in battle before the movie version begins, though Lieutenant Brack, clearly coded as a German, not a Nazi, now ably assists Plönies.

Greifer and Hauk—more film noir crooks than ideologically charged fanatics—who, Asch pronounces, "murder without pause," begin their killing

spree with a man sent on a reconnaissance mission to the front. The intelligence he's gathered includes Greifer and Hauk's misdeeds, and the bad guys
string him from a tree to make it appear as if he were a deserter. When Asch
first meets Greifer, he quickly puzzles out who has committed the murder, but
it will take him the rest of the film to assemble the evidence necessary to bring
this evildoer to justice. Meanwhile, Greifer and Hauk kill more innocents.
There is no doubt that these are really evil Nazis.

Asch and his men have come home just as the Americans arrive. The rav-
ages of war were little in evidence when Vierbein visited Holzhausen in Part
II. Three years later, a wall lies in ruins here and there, and in the background,
those bombed out or driven from their homes in eastern Europe occasionally
appear in the background. But the home front is remarkably well-preserved.
Father Asch's business has suffered some damage, but his café still stands and
quickly becomes a safe haven where Asch and his compatriots can plot to nail
Hauk and Greifer. Schulz, still turning civilians into soldiers, now commands
only over the unwilling elderly and overenthusiastic members of the Hitler
Youth. The latter, deployed at one point to defend a bridge against advancing
U.S. army tanks, play out as farce the tragedy that will be at the core of *Die
Brücke* ("The bridge"), an antiwar movie that appeared in 1959.

Greifer, who is so evil that he even attempts to deceive Hauk, taking off
with the booty but not his partner, is caught by Asch, and Plönies demonstrates that military justice can be swift. The "flying court martial," deployed
ruthlessly by the Nazis against alleged deserters and saboteurs in the last months
of the war, is used here to give Greifer his due. Plönies sentences him to death
by hanging. When the Americans arrive, however, they get it all wrong, mistaking Greifer for a resistance fighter and Plönies for a "war criminal." With
hordes of other prisoners-of-war, Plönies is shuffled off behind barbed wire.
The parade grounds and the barracks have been quickly converted into an
American detention facility; one sort of wall replaces another.

Relieved that the Americans are about to liberate them from the "spirit of
08/15," other Germans are rapidly reinventing themselves. Father Asch plants
his Party pin in a flower pot; Lore, Schulz's wife, uses her feminine wiles on
officers of the U.S. Civilian Intelligence Corps (CIC) hoping to advance Schulz
from *Lagerleiter*—head of the POW camp—a position he has gladly assumed,
to mayor; and Platzek, who has slipped into civilian clothing is already translating his talents as an "organizer" into success on a burgeoning black market.
The postwar period has begun.

Though the future looks rosy, Asch despairs that the Americans inaccu-
rately understand the past. He seeks to spring Plönies from behind barbed
wire, lest he fall victim to the Americans' inability to distinguish between perpetrators and victims. Though not guilty as the Americans have charged, this
"representation of the better Germany," as one reviewer remarked,[20] announces

that he is "in the same boat" with his men. For Hauk, a rougher justice will prevail. Rounded up by the Americans, he confronts a Wehrmacht lieutenant whom he once sent on an impossible mission, resulting in the deaths of many soldiers. No "flying court martial" or American military justice is needed: the lieutenant settles the score and kills Hauk. The movie ends with Kowlaksi and Asch patiently awaiting their fate behind barbed wire—smiling wryly with the assurance that things will turn out all right in the end—as they watch Barbara, a beautiful blonde who once had hooked up with Hauk, stroll by on the arm of a GI.

~

A number of historians have argued that *08/15* was part of a critical attack on rearmament. From within the military planning office in Adenauer's government came claims that it could sully the army's reputation and "contribute to undermining military strength." And Franz Josef Strauss, head of the Christian Social Union and a security expert in the CDU/CSU coalition, himself a veteran who would take over as minister of defense in October 1956, charged that Kirst's past as an enthusiastic National Socialist Leadership Officer disqualified him from judging how to run an army.[21]

Most contemporary critics did not share these views, endorsing instead Kirst's claims that *08/15* was a critique not of soldiers but rather "the fundamental evil of power in the wrong hands," hands that he insisted were not his, and May's testimony that he wanted to provide "optical evidence" that would show how bad things really were but would also honor "our best in uniform," because "a people who does not respect its past has no future."[22] Critics celebrated Part I as "daring and powerful,"[23] a giant step toward addressing pressing issues of the day. The *Frankfurter Rundschau* judged Part II "bold and unconventional," a "very good movie" that drew on humor but also "clearly illuminated the 'other side' in a realistic fashion," and writing in the *Frankfurter Allgemeine Zeitung*, Friedrich A. Wagner praised May for "responsibly facing … what happened back then a dozen years ago."[24] *08/15*'s popular "resonance" suggested that "buried in this piece of film [Part II]" was an "exemplary piece of existentialism," comparable to the work of Jean Paul Sartre.[25] And Part III was described as a "necessity" that presented the "conflict of good and evil and the shades of gray in between," a "contemporary document of absolute validity" that powerfully presented the "meaningless of war."[26]

For many critics the movies delivered an answer to the "question of what face a future German military should have."[27] In Part I, Major Luschke solemnly pronounces: "The transformation of a man into a soldier is a difficult process. I am actually happy when it does not run smoothly. That reveals what men are made of." Those in the office charged with designing the new West German military would hardly disagree, and as critics noted, Blank and his compatriots should welcome May's contribution to their efforts. Blank's response to the abuses of the past was to insist that a future German military would be guided by *"innere Führung,"* translated, as historian David Large explains, "as 'internal guidance,' 'inner leadership,' 'moral leadership,' 'independent leadership,' and 'moral education.'"[28] These values were on display in ample measure in *08/15;* they did not have to be created but rather had survived National Socialism.

In debates over the law defining the terms on which the first volunteers would enter the Bundeswehr, the CSU military expert Richard Jaeger insisted that the ideal trainer would see in the "recruit a human being, who is a son and a citizen of the people, the most valuable thing that a people can entrust to another."[29] *08/15* offered the reassurance that such ersatz fathers had existed in the depths of the Third Reich. When Blank and some of his staff went to see the film, one press account recorded, they left promising that the "new army will be different,"[30] though reform need not mean jettisoning the entire past. "Tradition," opined Wolf Graf von Baudissin, one of Blank's chief advisors, "provides no recipe for the future," but the Nazis had not successfully perverted all that was good about Germany.[31] Asch, Luschke, and Plönies provided the "optical evidence" that the core values that should define that new army existed in the old, an invitation to overcome what one reviewer called the "neurosis" that prevented some Germans from seeing anything positive in military tradition.[32]

As the first installment of *08/15* opens, the camera pans along a wall topped with barbed wire, and a voice-over comments: "Everywhere and in all times, the wall is a symbol of seclusion. Where there are walls, they surround a world within a world. They surround a state within a state." Again, Kirst and May seemed to second the public pronouncements of those charged with ensuring that the German military would not repeat the mistakes of the past. The way to tie the military to the society it sought to defend was to acknowledge that soldiers were rooted in their families and communities. Scaling walls at will, as comfortable in civilian clothing as in uniform, happier in his father's café than in the barracks, Asch embodied precisely the values of the "citizen in uniform" *(Staatsbürger in Uniform),* the model soldier proposed by Baudissin and Blank. He is closely tied to civilian society, letting neither real nor metaphoric walls block his vision. His commanding officers recognize those qualities and allow him to lead. The call for a commitment to defend "freedom, civilization, democracy and human rights that had its origins in civilian life" came not only from Blank and Baudissin, but also, according to reviewers, from May and Kirst. Asch walked off the pages of reformers' attempts to describe a soldier who would be a representative of the "triumph of healthy, human understanding,"[33] not the "military pathos" that had gotten Germany into trouble. Redeeming the army also represented the redemption of Germany. As reviewers noted, the wall surrounding the barracks could easily be understood as the wall that had surrounded Germany under the Nazis, a "Reich circumscribed by its own laws." The state was "one big barracks," and the "troops" were a stand-in for the nation.[34] Asch, the good soldier, is also the good German.

In *08/15*, a real Nazi is hard to find. By the middle of the 1950s, most West Germans accepted the movies' clear distinction between Hitler and a handful of his followers and the overwhelming majority of Germans in uniform who fought a war not of their choosing. Although at Nuremberg in 1945, the Allies charged the German military with war crimes, most Germans came to see this as a reflection of the myopia of the victors. In Part III, an American soldier admiring Lore's legs, quips, "You look like a Walkyrie from *Tannhäuser*." That's how little Americans understand about the country they are occupying, mistaking Venus for a dame on horseback with horns on her helmet. No wonder they were unable to identify the real criminals and instead made blanket accusations based on a misunderstanding of the facts. Popular memories of this postwar confusion are reflected in the movie by the arrival at the U.S. headquarters of a few crates of the "Questionnaire" *(Fragebogen)*, developed by the Americans to determine who the real Nazis were. As one delighted American officer announces, "now we can finally establish the truth." How little he knows. In the movie, the scene is a none too subtle reference to the book of the same name, written by Salomon, the screenplay writer. A best seller published in 1951, *Der Fragebogen* drew on Salomon's own life to demonstrate the occupation forces' confused understanding of National Socialism.[35]

The buffoonery of the Americans in *08/15*, however, conveyed little of the bitterness of Salomon's book. By 1956, West Germans and Americans were allies and Americans had demonstrated their ability to know a Nazi from a German. The movie evoked a past of misunderstanding that no longer characterized the present. By the early 1950s, not only Germans but their Cold War Allies were ready to cease the search for Nazis, forgive "fellow travelers" and amnesty those sentenced as war criminals. In 1945, Dwight D. Eisenhower, the supreme Allied commander in Europe, publicly maintained that "the Wehrmacht, and especially the German officer corps, had been identical with Hitler and his exponents of the rule of force," perpetrators of the same crimes, subject to the same penalties. But only six years later—under pressure from West Germans who insisted that they should not endorse rearmament until the good name of soldiers from the last war had been cleared—Eisenhower distinguished sharply between "the regular German soldier and Hitler and his criminal group."[36] The U.S. decision to pardon many Germans sentenced for war crimes translated words into deeds and indicated that the past that the movies presented—in which bungling occupiers had mistaken resisters for war criminals—was long since laid to rest. In May 1955, as the Allied statute of occupation was lifted, the metaphor of the wall appeared again in a column by the journalist Erich Dombrowski. Writing in the *Frankfurter Allgemeine*

Zeitung, he proclaimed that Germany was finally liberated from the "huge barracks and parade grounds of the forces of occupation" in which we were "commanded back and forth. Our will to live asserted itself, never driven astray by any external adverse circumstances."[37] That outcome was visible from the beginning, the movie announced, and from the vantage point of 1955, Americans and Germans could let bygones be bygones, making it possible for Germans to laugh with, not at, their enemies turned allies over the confusion of the immediate postwar period.

If criminals still lurked in a democratic Germany, Germans would know how to bring them to justice—as they had in Part III. Even as the final installment opened, in late 1955 and early 1956, the last POWs from the Soviet Union arrived in West Germany, among them, the Auschwitz doctor Karl Clauberg, renowned for sterilization experiments, and "Iron" Gustav Sorge, an infamous SS officer who had served at Sachsenhausen. *08/15* echoed the headlines of the same dailies in which the movie was reviewed. The insistence of press accounts that West German courts would go after the truly guilty left no doubt that by 1955 Germans were ready to judge their own, something, the movie suggested, they had been able to do all along.[38]

If *08/15* is largely free of Nazis, it is also largely free of Jews, and again, the movies revealingly suggest what parts of National Socialism had been cut out in the editing room of the Federal Republic's early history. By the mid-1950s, acknowledgment of the "unspeakable crimes" committed against Jews "in the name of the German people" had been relegated to the agreement to provide restitution for victims of National Socialist persecution who could present evidence of their claims and reparations for the state of Israel.[39] Walls as metaphor figured here too. In the final debate over the reparations treaty with Israel, CDU spokesman Eugen Gerstenmaier described how Germany had received just retribution for the crimes Germans had committed as "all of Germany was transformed into a huge ghetto. For us Germans, less easily surmounted than the walls of an oriental ghetto were the walls of hate, scorn, and rejection that had already been built around us during the war and that still held us captive after the war." Reparations were "documentation of a new spirit" that allowed Germany to get "out of the ghetto once and for all."[40]

With this act, many Germans hoped they had closed the moral ledger on the crimes of National Socialism, and *08/15* was not about to open it explicitly. As one commentator noted, in Part I of *08/15,* the walls prevent the new recruits from seeing the smoke rising from synagogues in flame in November 1938,[41] and in Part II, Natasha may be a spy but she is not a representative of "Judeo-Bolshevism." The one Jew who appears is in Part III, and he wears the uniform of an American CIC officer. The returning immigrant, he wants to bring Germans to justice, but he also exhibits compassion toward an elderly couple whose house the Americans occupy, innocent Germans who have committed no crimes.[42] The analogy Gerstenmaier suggests between the victims of Germans and Germany as victim is not entirely absent from the film. The trilogy's opening reminder that all sorts of walls create states within states implies the equivalence of many types of prisons. When the movie ends, Asch and his mates are once again captives in the same parade grounds where the story began, held this time by Americans. And in the closing scenes, the barbed wire surrounding German POWs evokes the barbed wire surrounding concentration camps, holding Jews and others deemed outside the "community of the people." Such visual clues drew on a discourse, well-established by the mid-1950s, in which Nazi tyranny and the war had claimed many victims, some German, some Jewish, all of whom suffered similar fates. And the code—"the chimneys are still smoking"—of the military resisters in Part II suggests opposition to Nazi crimes of which some military men know too much. In the movie version of *08/15*, however, the presence of Jews is at most implied, and the reasons for their absence are never addressed.[43]

The war of *08/15* has been cleansed of other unpleasant memories. The "optical evidence" that *08/15* delivered was as much of how postwar memory had evolved as it was of the war itself. Praised by one reviewer as the "surgeon of German consciousness,"[44] Kirst's scalpel did not cut into certain bits of gray matter, and there is remarkably little evidence of the death and destruction that dominated the visual landscape of the immediate postwar years. Writing of "rubble films" in the late 1940s, one reviewer remarked that movies that dwelled on devastation were ceasing to be big draws. Audiences were sated with stories that focused only on the "hopelessness of the first postwar years," and it was "time for spiritual restoration. We have had enough of violent emotions."[45] When the violence of war returned to the screen, it was in an expurgated version in which little blood flowed, few scars were visible, and hopefulness abounded. Within the midst of "the darkest chapter of German history"— how *08/15* characterized the Nazi era as the last reel of the trilogy rolled to an end— "spiritual restoration" reigned.

Given how far West Germans were from confronting the enormity of the Holocaust ten years after the end of the war, it is perhaps not surprising that there are no Jewish victims in the film, but more remarkable is that the movies depict little German death. When soldiers die, it is off screen, and the only casualty of war the camera captures is largely symbolic—Vierbein ground to a pulp by a Soviet tank. In an interview, May explained that "anyone who has experienced something really horrifying doesn't want to be reminded of it,"[46] but the consequence was a movie in which Asch's battery loses almost no men. They remain a tight-knit group, a reflection of the imagined war of postwar veterans who focused more on myths of comradeship than on the massive death rates that had ensured that few "primary groups" made it through the war unscathed. One reviewer of Part II admitted to a nostalgia prompted by the film's "realistic presentation of the front" that awakened memories of "comradeship that is hammered out in adversity." But as the work of historian Thomas Kühne has amply demonstrated, such visions drew on myths that were fostered by the Wehrmacht and embellished in organized veterans' groups after the war. They highlighted memories of the bonds that made survival possible, not mass death, and they cordoned off a war in which Germans had killed millions and in which millions of Germans were killed.[47] When Vierbein returns to the *Heimat* in Part II, he watches recruits marching up and down, and May suddenly morphs their faces into death masks. But this is as close as *08/15* gets to the more than 5 million Germans in uniform who were dead by 1945, 1.4 million in the last four months of the war, 10,000 daily, as spring busts out all over in Part III of *08/15*.[48]

08/15 also reinstated a division between front and home front that had dissolved by 1945 as the Red Army pushed westward, Allied bombers leveled German cities, and British and American troops stormed into Germany. By the early 1950s, the proliferation of veterans' groups and their increasing control of the public commemoration of the war meant that the war that was most often publicly remembered was the one fought by men in uniform. With the rubble largely cleared away, so too were public memories—or film representations—of the war women experienced. In *08/15,* the best of what German womanhood has to offer, Elisabeth, Asch's wife, flirts chastely through Part I, gets married off-screen and gives him a son in Part II, but once she's fulfilled this duty, she is completely absent in Part III. Other images of women played on familiar stereotypes. Ingrid Asch is the clueless blonde who mouths Nazi platitudes. Lore, Schulz's wife, and Barbara, Nazi Hauk's erstwhile paramour, trade on sex as "fraternizers," evoking in farcical form an unflattering representation of women that had emerged immediately after the war.[49]

In the "rubble films" of the postwar years, returning veterans recovered only because of heterosexual unions orchestrated by women who had survived more successfully than men. Ten years later, men are in charge. The intact town to which Asch's men return testifies to their success at defending the Fatherland. Even at the front, in Part II Asch protects a woman from the advances of Witterer, and Wedelmann cannot bring himself to kill a woman, even a Soviet spy. Chivalry trumps Nazi orders to kill all partisans. The newsreels that preceded showings of Parts II and III of *08/15* might well have featured other black-and-white images of the return of the last POWs from the Soviet Union, men who were also represented as embodying a self-assured masculinity, survivors of a second war behind barbed wire. Gone from the visual landscape were the beaten, bedraggled men who had returned in 1945, and in their place was a revived masculinity that could contribute to postwar West German recovery.[50]

The rehabilitated masculinity on display in *08/15* was, however, a far cry from the militarized manhood promoted by the Nazis. When Vierbein visits the *Heimat* in Part II, he meets Elisabeth, Asch's wife, in a park. As he gently reaches to pick up Asch's baby, May positions him against a background of sculptures of muscle-bound nudes, the type of masculinity mass-produced by Hitler's favorite sculptor, Josef Thorak. In an ironic twist, featured in prepro-duction stories about the movie, Thorak's studio outside Munich had been transformed into the film's barracks, and in a nod to this past, sculptures like those Thorak produced become part of the home front in which Vierbein feels so confused. His pianist's hands that long to embrace a baby present a very dif-ferent masculinity than the one Thorak—and the Nazis—had to offer.[51]

The western Germany of the war's end as it appears in Part III seems al-ready well on its way to recovery. The Germans who welcome their liberators are well-dressed, well-fed, well-housed, and well-bred, sharing little in com-mon with the Germans in the rubble—or the "rubble films"—of the immedi-ate postwar years. By 1955, West Germans had some reason to claim that the postwar years were over and indications abounded that they had rapidly moved beyond the devastation of 1945. A thriving economy, the integration of millions of Germans driven out of eastern Europe by the Red Army, accept-ance as a sovereign partner in the western alliance, and a spate of rebuilding were all markers of the "German miracle."[52] The movie depicts a past bursting with signs of renewal—from the spring flowers that explode to fill the screen to the ease with which former soldiers slip into civilian uniforms to start new lives. In debates over the shape of a future West German military, Hasso von Manteuffel, a former general who represented the Free Democratic party, re-minded his colleagues of the "thousands upon thousands of former career sol-diers who have been integrated into the daily life of democracy where they fulfill their obligations in a trustworthy, decent, and orderly fashion."[53] In *08/15* they filled the screen. One reviewer described Kirst as a "historian who was looking ahead,"[54] and his books and the movie that emerged from them fore-shadowed what West Germans had achieved by the mid-1950s as much as they analyzed the painful past Germans had left behind. Germans may have lost the war, but *08/15* suggests how hard they had fought to win the peace.

~

Praise for *08/15* was not universal, and what some critics found lacking suggests that not all West Germans agreed on how National Socialism fit into their history. In an open forum in the pages of a Berlin daily, a reader rejected those who counseled Kirst and May to "leave the past alone," instead insisting that only by "remaining aware of the mistakes of the past and understanding the consequences" would it be possible to "pursue a reconstruction in a fash-ion that would promote the desired ideal of a humane, peaceful prosperity."[55] As one reviewer commented, had a film like *08/15* opened in 1930, it would have been met not by lively debate but by the scare tactics of Geobbels and

SA-Stormtroopers or the white mice deployed in Berlin to disrupt the premier of *All Quiet on the Western Front*.[56] However, other critics demanded more, interpreting the film's silences as an indication of the limits of the past West Germans wanted to face. As one commentator put it, writing in the Social Democratic party's periodical, *Die neue Gesellschaft*, the trilogy "attacked the dictator and his helpers," but was silent about the fact that "a significant part of those who were depicted as victims were actually guilty and had believed in the dictator right up to the last moment." Viewers could go home "relieved, because [the movies] confirmed the lie that they bore no responsibility for what happened." Another reviewer remarked, by starting the story in 1939, *08/15* failed to ask when the "darkest chapter in German history" had actually begun.[57] The attempt at sobriety at the end of Part I—the bombers on their way to level Poland—failed to show the innocent women and children on whom the bombs would fall.[58] Even in answering the question it most directly posed—how should the military be reformed—Kirst and May trivialized a vitally important subject, presenting the Wehrmacht as an "amusing bunch of complete idiots," not the "horrifying machine" that it had been until May 1945.[59] When *08/15* moved to the eastern front, it left behind "what was typical of war—namely death, death without honor or meaning,"[60] offering instead a new "legend of a stab in the back," according to which it was the corrupt officer who lost the war.[61] And Part III could leave audiences with the feeling that "World War II [was] mostly merry." "We really had a nice little defeat," quipped one critic. "In any case, there's never been so much laughter about the catastrophe of 1945."[62]

Read together, the critical assessments of *08/15* do not offer a uniform political perspective or a coherent alternative to the story of the war the movies told, but they do suggest a public that sought to understand a past that included not only the Second World War but the path Germans had followed to arrive at 1939. Rudy Koshar writes that "if a nation were to remember, if a nation were to take responsibility for its deeds, it had to be reconstructed as a nation first."[63] In *08/15,* there were many indications of how that process of reconstruction had taken place—the symbolic reintegration of millions of men in uniform who had fought a war of enormous barbarity, the creation of an alliance with former enemies, the compartmentalization of blame in ways that made only a few responsible for National Socialism, and a selective memory that included some victims and not others. And perhaps because that process was so advanced, it was possible for others to demand more, signaling the end of the postwar years in ways that opened a space in which a more critical examination of the *pre*-postwar years was possible.

At least some war movies from the late fifties would contribute to this project. For example, in Falk Harnack's *Unruhige Nacht* ("Troubled Night," 1958), a military pastor provides comfort to a deserter, sentenced to death for fleeing the madness of war to live with a Soviet war widow. And Bernhard Wicki's *Die Brücke* ("The Bridge") (1959) depicts battle scenes of enormous ferocity in a story of youth recruited to hold off American tanks in the spring of 1945, boys who die terrifying deaths that Wicki's direction graphically captures and whose war has little in common with the comic romp of the Hitler Youth in *08/15*. But by the 1960s, Germans in uniform had more or less vanished from West German movies made for a mass public, and when they returned—in Wolfgang Petersen's *Das Boot* (1981) and Josef Vilsmaier's *Stalingrad* (1993)— crazed Nazis were pitted against innocent Germans in color movies that still depicted a moral world of black and white. When other pictures—this time photographs—went on tour nationally in the mid-1990s in the exhibition of the crimes of the Wehrmacht, providing staggering evidence of the army's participation in the murder of Jews and other civilians on the eastern front, they triggered a massive negative response that suggested how difficult it was to revise the vision of the "clean" Wehrmacht to which movies like *08/15* contributed and how trapped war stories—particularly those that are produced for mass consumption—remain in melodramatic narratives that divide the world neatly into good and bad, guilt and innocence, with most Germans landing on the side of the angels.[64]

∿

Writing in the *Münchner Merkur* in 1956, Herbert Hohenemser remarked that "one day it will be possible to use the three parts of *08/15* as a lens through which to view the political history of the three years in which they were created and circulated."[65] Few historians of postwar West Germany have taken seriously this suggestion that mass-mediated fiction can provide insights into the history of politics and society. Many films from the 1950s belonged to a popular culture that offered intriguing commentaries on the Nazi past and suggested how this past could be selectively incorporated into the West German present. The historian Thomas Lindenberger has presented the case for the importance of visual and oral sources for understanding contemporary history (*Zeitgeschichte*), inviting us to "hear and see the past."[66] At the movies, we can do both.

In the case of *08/15*, seeing and hearing the past is easy. Viewing the movies requires no trip to the screening room of the Bundesarchiv in Berlin; in subtitled versions, they are a mouse click away at "the American video store for German movies," www.germanvideo.com. This article is about culture and militarism, and in closing, I want to touch upon another abiding interest that defines Berghahn's career—a commitment to teaching and finding new and better ways to engage students. Thus, I also offer these thoughts on *08/15* as an invitation to others who teach the history of post-1945 Germany to take their students to the movies, introducing them to a key source for social and political historians and a medium through which memories of the Second World War were mediated for millions of postwar Germans.

Notes

This is a significantly shortened and revised version of an article that originally appeared as "Kämpfen für den Frieden: *08/15* und westdeutsche Erinnerungen an den Zweiten Weltkrieg," *Militärgeschichtliche Zeitschrift* 64, 2 (2005): 359–389. It appears here with permission of the publishers of that journal.

1. Erwin Goelz, "Anti-Kommißfilm mit Einschränkungen" (Sendereihe: Film unter der Lupe), typescript of radio broadcast, Süddeutscher Rundfunk, 4 October 1954, Historisches Archiv des Südwestrundfunks (SWR), Stuttgart, Reg.-Nr. 19/1635 Goelz, Film unter der Lupe. Thanks to Rolf Aurich of the Filmmuseum Berlin, who provided me with Goelz's commentary, and Jörg Hucklenbroich of the Historical Archive of SWR who made it available to him. Kirst's work is available in translation: Hans Hellmut Kirst, *Zero Eight Fifteen: The Strange Mutiny of Gunner Asch*, trans. Robert Kee (London, 1955); idem, *Gunner Asch Goes to War: Zero Eight Fifteen II*, trans. Robert Kee (London, 1956); and idem, *The Return of Gunner Asch: Zero Eight Fifteen III*, trans. Robert Kee (London, 1957). In German, the trilogy is still in print in a cheap paperback edition.

2. Richard Ray, "Kommiss—Auch in der Drehpause," *Frankfurter Rundschau*, 14 August 1954.

3. As many as 1.8 million copies of Kirst's book were in print, more than any other war novel. See Walter Nutz, "Der Krieg als Abenteuer und Idylle: Landser-Hefte und triviale Kriegsromane," in *Gegenwartsliteratur und Drittes Reich: Deutsche Autoren in der Auseinandersetzung mit der Vergangenheit,* ed. Hans Wagener (Stuttgart, 1977), 265; also Michael Kumpfmüller, "Ein Krieg für alle und keinen: Hans Hellmut Kirst: *08/15* (1954/55)," in *Von Böll bis Buchheim: Deutsche Kriegsprosa nach 1945,* ed. Hans Wagener (Amsterdam, 1997), 249–64.

4. Jost Hermand, *Ernst von Salomon: Wandlungen eines Nationalrevolutionärs* (Stuttgart, 2002).

5. "Achtung, Herr Major von links…,"*Münchener Merkur,* 3 October 1954.

6. Heide Fehrenbach, *Cinema in Democratizing Germany: Reconstructing National Identity After Hitler* (Chapel Hill, 1995), 148–68.

7. Friedrich A. Wagner, "Null-acht-fuffzehn im russischen Winter: Der zweite Teil des Films nach dem Roman von Kirst," *Frankfurter Allgemeine Zeitung,* 20 August 1955. See Ulrike Weckel, "The *Mitläufer* in Two German Postwar Films: Representation and Critical Reception," *History & Memory* 15, no. 2 (2003): 64–93.

8. Peter Reichel, "Der Widerstand im Film der 50er Jahre: Citizen Canaris," *Süddeutsche Zeitung,* 19 July 2004.

9. Richard C. Helt and Marie E. Helt, *West German Cinema Since 1945: A Reference Handbook* (Metuchen, N.J, 1987), 8; Eric Rentschler, "Germany: The Past that Would Not Go Away," in *World Cinema Since 1945,* ed. William Luhr (New York, 1987), 217; and Knut Hickethier, "Der Zweite Weltkrieg und der Holocaust im Fernsehen der Bundesrepublik der fünfziger und frühen sechziger Jahre," in *Der Krieg in der*

Nachkriegszeit: Der Zweite Weltkrieg in Politik und Gesellschaft der Bundesrepublik, ed. Michael T. Greven and Oliver von Wrochem (Opladen, 2000), 93–112; also Bärbel Westermann, *Nationale Identität im Spielfilm der fünfziger Jahre* (Frankfurt am Main, 1990), 30–95.

10. Goelz, "Anti-Kommiss Film."

11. "Hundertausend Düsseldorfer sahen '08/15,'" *Düsseldorfer Nachrichten*, 25 October 1954; and "Germany's 'Eternity'" *Newsweek*, 10 January 1955. In 1955, Part I was seen by more West Germans than any other film. Part II—which opened only in August—was in tenth place. See Klaus Sigl, Werner Schneider, Ingo Tornow, *Jede Menge Kohle? Kunst und Kommerz auf dem deutschen Filmmarkt der Nachkriegszeit* (Munich, 1986), 129.

12. Weckel, *"Mitläufer."* My thanks to Rüdiger Koschnitzki of the Deutsches Filminstitut (Frankfurt/Main), who facilitated my access to reviews of the film.

13. "Des Teufels Hauptwachtmeister: Eine Debatte rund um 'Null-acht Fünfzehn,'" *Der Monat* 6, no. 69 (1954): 248.

14. David Clay Large, *Germans to the Front: West German Rearmament in the Adenauer Era* (Chapel Hill, 1996).

15. Jan Molitor, "Die letzten Soldaten des grossen Krieges," *Die Zeit*, 13 October 1955; and in general, Robert G. Moeller, "Heimkehr ins Vaterland: Die Remaskulinisierung Westdeutschlands in den fünfziger Jahren," *Militärgeschichtliche Zeitschrift* 60 (2001): 403–36.

16. Large, *Germans to the Front*, 244.

17. "Karabiner 98k: Geheimsache bei '08/15,'" *Der neue Film*, 5 August 1954; also Karena Niehoff, "Zivilisten hatten es schwer," *Der Tagesspiegel*, 11 November 1954.

18. I am responsible for all translations from the films' dialogue.

19. Wagner, "Null-acht-fuffzehn."

20. Ludwig Gatter, "Appassionata in Panje-Moll," *Kölnische Rundschau*, 27 August 1955.

21. Alaric Searle, *Wehrmacht Generals, West German Society, and the Debate on Rearmament, 1949–1959* (Westport, CT, 2003), 194–95; Hans Ehlert, "Innenpolitische Auseinandersetzungen um die Pariser Verträge und die Wehrverfassung 1954 bis 1956," in *Anfänge Westdeutscher Sicherheitspolitik 1945–1966*, Vol. 3, *Die NATO-Option*, ed. Militärgeschichtliches Forschungsamt (Munich, 1993), 311; and Large, *Germans to the Front*, 45. On opposition to rearmament, see Michael Geyer, "Cold War Angst: The Case of West-German Opposition to Rearmament and Nuclear Weapons," in *The Miracle Years: A Cultural History of West Germany, 1949–1968*, ed. Hanna Schissler (Princeton, 2001), 376–408. And on critical responses from the military, see "Des Teufels Hauptwachtmeiser," 245–63.

22. "'Gegen das Übel der Macht in unrechten Händen': Paul Mays Verfilmung von Hans Hellmuth Kirsts Roman '08/15,'" *Süddeutsche Zeitung*, 7 April 1992; "'08/15': Ein unerfreulicher Film," *Neue Presse*, 6 November 1954; and Hans Hellmut Kirst, *Das Schaf im Wolfspelz: Ein deutsches Leben* (Herford, 1985), 327–55.

23. Will Fischer, "'08/15,'" *Rhein-Neckar-Zeitung*, 4 October 1954; Gunter Groll, "Barsch, aber mit Bravour: 'Null-Acht Fünfzehn,'" *Süddeutsche Zeitung*, 2 October 1954.

24. "Neuer Film in Frankfurt," *Frankfurter Rundschau*, 18 August 1955; "Null-acht-fuffzehn im russischen Winter."

25. "Da wiehert der alte Schlachtengaul," *Mindener Tageblatt*, 14 January 1956.

26. "Spiess Schulz wurde Hauptman," *8 Uhr Blatt,* 21 January 1956; "Erinnern wir uns noch? Was war fünf Minuten vor Zwölf," *Bergdorfer Zeitung,* 9 June 1956.

27. Heinz Ohff, "Wie macht man aus Menschen Soldaten?" *Heidelberger Tageblatt,* 2 October 1954; also "Glücklich ist, wer vergisst…?" *Bergische Wochenpost,* 2 October 1954.

28. Large, *Germans to the Front,* 177.

29. *Verhandlungen des Bundestags* (hereafter *VDB*), 2. Wahlperiode, 93. Sitzung, 28 June 1955, 5230.

30. "Germans Laugh at Wehrmacht Film," *Dundee Evening Telegraph,* 21 October 1954.

31. Peter v. Schubert, *Wolf Graf von Baudissin: Soldat für den Frieden* (Munich, 1969), 85, 210.

32. Konrad Kraske, "Ein Buch und eine Neurose," in "Des Teufels Hauptwacht-meister," 258.

33. Ohff, "Wie macht man aus Menschen Soldaten?"; also "Glücklich ist, wer ver-gisst…?"; "Der Kasernenhof-Film '08/15'," *Badisches Tageblatt,* 26 November 1954.

34. "Was an dem Film '08/15' nachdenklich macht: Die Gefahr hinter den Mauern," *Wiesbadener Kurier,* 7 October 1954; Carl Andriessen, "In der Kaserne 1939," *Weltbühne,* 17 November 1954; Richard Adelt, "Null-acht-fünfzehn," *Main Post,* 4 May 1954; and Adelbert Weinstein, *Armee ohne Pathos: Die deutsche Wiederbewaffnung im Urteil ehemaliger Soldaten* (Bonn, 1951).

35. Ernst von Salomon, *Der Fragebogen* (Hamburg, 1951). By March 1953, over 200,000 copies had been published. See Richard Herzinger, "Ein extremistischer Zuschauer: Ernst von Salomon: Konservativ-revolutionäre Literatur zwischen Tatrhe-torik und Resignation," *Zeitschrift für Germanistik* 8, no. 1 (1998): 83–96; also Her-mand, *Ernst von Salomon.*

36. Quoted in Donald Abenheim, *Reforging the Iron Cross: The Search for Tradi-tion in the West German Armed Forces* (Princeton, 1988), 70.

37. Erich Dombrowski, "8. Mai 1945," *Frankfurter Allgemeine Zeitung,* 7 May 1955.

38. See Robert G. Moeller, *War Stories: The Search for a Usable Past in the Federal Republic of Germany* (Berkeley, 2001), 112–13; also Searle, *Wehrmacht Generals,* 286. Searle concludes that the trials in West German courts of generals reflected the will-ingness of some West Germans to engage in a more thoroughgoing analysis of the Nazi past.

39. Quotations are from Adenauer's 1951 speech, announcing his intention to pursue reparations for Israel. See Moeller, *War Stories,* 26–27.

40. Eugen Gerstenmaier, *VDB,* 1. Wahlperiode, 254. Sitzung, 18 March 1953, 12276.

41. Curt Riess, *Das Gibts nur einmal: Das Buch des deutschen Films nach 1945* (Hamburg, 1958), 347–48.

42. In the novel, there are two Jewish officers, both more developed as characters. See Kirst, *The Return of Gunner Asch,* 41.

43. Moeller, *War Stories.*

44. Walter Bittermann, "Salomonischer Kirst," *Rheinischer Merkur,* 22 October 1954.

45. "Überholte Filme," *Wirtschaftszeitung,* 16 July 1949.

46. "An der Ostfront: 'II. Teil 08/15,'" *Nürnberger Nachrichten,* 17 August 1955; and the critical response in "08/15," *Die Rheinpfalz,* 11 December 1954.

47. "Da wiehert der alte Schlachtengaul." And on the myth of comradeship, Thomas Kühne, "Zwischen Männerbund und Volksgemeinschaft: Hitlers Soldaten und der Mythos der Kameradschaft," *Archiv für Sozialgeschichte* 38 (1998): 165–89.

48. Rüdiger Overmans, *Deutsche militärische Verluste im Zweiten Weltkrieg* (Munich, 1999), 265, 267, 279.

49. Elizabeth Heineman, "The Hour of the Woman: Memories of Germany's 'Crisis Years' and West German National Identity," in Schissler, *Miracle Years*, 21–56.

50. See the pathbreaking work of Frank Biess, *Homecomings: Returning POWs and the legacies of defeat in Postwar Germany* (Princeton, 2006).

51. Hansjakob Stehle, "Gefreiter Asch steht nicht still…: Ein Bericht über die Dreharbeiten an einem heiklen Filmthema," *Main Post*, 7 August 1954.

52. See Klaus Naumann, "Die Frage nach dem Ende: Von der unbestimmten Dauer der Nachkriegszeit," *Mittelweg 36* 8, No. 1 (1999): 21–32.

53. *VDB*, 2. Wahlperiode, 93. Sitzung, 28 June 1955, 5243.

54. Bittermann, "Salomonischer Kirst."

55. "Diskussion um den Film '08/15,'" *Spandauer Volksblatt*, 23 January 1955; also "HN-Leser zu dem Film 08/15," *Hessische Nachrichten*, 26 October 1954.

56. Theodor Reichert, "Nicht in alle Ewigkeit," *Hamburger Fremdenblatt*, 16 October 1954.

57. Georg Michael Kahn-Ackermann, "Der deutsche Film ist 'Zeitgerecht,'" *Die neue Gesellschaft* 3, Nr. 31 (1956): 190–93.

58. "Ein Buch und ein Film: Zweimal 08/15," *Hamburger Volkszeitung*, 9 October 1954.

59. Karl Korn, "Ordnung? Gehorchen? Ein Nachwort zu 08/15," *Frankfurter Allgemeine Zeitung*, 3 November 1954.

60. "'08/15' (Zweiter Teil)," *Rheinische Post*, 20 August 1955; also "II. Teil 08/15," *Hamburger Anzeiger*, 4 August 1955.

61. "Kleiner Dolchstoss—noch nicht 'gemischt,'" *Freie Presse*, 30 July 1955; and "Neu in Deutschland," *Der Spiegel*, 7 September 1955.

62. Herbert Hohenemser, "…übrig bleibt brüllendes Vergnügen," *Münchner Merkur*, 28 May 1955; and Fred Hepp, "Das dicke Ende kommt nicht nach," *Süddeutsche Zeitung*, 8 March 1956.

63. Rudy Koshar, *From Monuments to Traces: Artifacts of German Memory, 1870– 1990* (Berkeley, 2000), 153

64. Hamburger Institut für Sozialforschung, ed., *Verbrechen der Wehrmacht: Dimensionen des Vernichtungskrieges 1941–1944* (Hamburg, 2002). This was a revised version of the exhibition that originally appeared in the mid-1990s. And on the continued discussion of the exhibition, http://www.verbrechen-der-wehrmacht.de/ (accessed on 18 August 2004).

65. Herbert Hohenemser, "Wer steckt schon in der richtigen Uniform?" *Münchener Merkur*, 3 March 1956.

66. Thomas Lindenberger, "Vergangenes Hören und Sehen: Zeitgeschichte und ihre Herausforderung durch die audiovisuellen Medien," *Zeithistorische Forschungen* 1 (2004) Url http://www.zeithistorische-forschungen.de/portal/alias__zeithistorische-forschungen/lang__de/tabID__40208148/DesktopDefault.aspx (last accessed on 14 July 2004).

CHAPTER 17

Rehabilitating Father*land*
Race and German Remasculinization

Heide Fehrenbach

At the opening of a 1952 conference in Wiesbaden on "The Fate of Mixed-Blood Children in Germany," Erich Lißner, editor of the *Frankfurter Rundschau,* was declared a "hero of humanity." Lißner was fêted not for his journalistic achievement but for becoming an adoptive father to Donatus, an interracial child born to a German refugee allegedly raped by an African-American GI shortly after German defeat. Lißner's heroization underlined his exceptionality as a rare role model for socially responsible paternalism. Indeed, his anecdotes chronicling Doni's integration into Lißner's white family emphasized less the personal relationship between adoptive father and son than the social implications and social utility of interracial fathering after National Socialism. Lißner's experience, that is, was packaged as a pedagogical example for the moral rehabilitation of German masculinity and the West German nation.[1]

The self-congratulatory atmosphere of these proceedings contrasted sharply with the negative, emotionally charged reception accorded the tens of thousands of "occupation children" born to German mothers and fathered by Allied personnel during the four years of military occupation.[2] Immediately and irresistibly following the first births in 1946, public attention focused on a small but visible racial subcategory of these children, the so-called *Mischlinge* ("mixed-bloods"), distinguished from the others by their black paternity.[3] Although they constituted only a tiny minority of postwar German births (under 2 percent of all out-of-wedlock births in 1947, for a total of 3,000 by 1950), contemporary estimates inflated their numbers to between 10,000 and 950,000, indicating the disproportionately great symbolic significance accorded these children in post-Hitler Germany.[4] In a period of military occupation and enforced political democratization, their very existence challenged historical definitions of national identity by invoking issues of race, transgressive female sexuality, and reproduction, and by linking these with German military defeat, the loss of national sovereignty, and debilitated native masculinity.

Postwar Germany, in fact, was said to be suffering from a serious *Männermangel*, or shortage of men. Indeed, the "crisis years" of the early occupation have been referred to as the "hour of women" because of both the inordinate amount of productive and reproductive work assumed by women in the wake of defeat and the absence or low public profile of German men, who were either killed or missing in the war, held in prisoner-of-war camps, physically or mentally disabled, emotionally exhausted, or unemployed due to reasons of health or their former political loyalties.[5] In public and private parlance, moreover, German defeat was widely identified with demasculinization, as countless contemporary stories thematizing humiliated husbands unable to work, earn, or function—whether socially or sexually—suggest.[6]

Despite the prevalence of such accounts, this characterization was not quite accurate. Public life in postwar Germany did retain a masculine profile, as the ubiquitous uniformed men of the occupation forces attested; all Germans, male and female alike, were subject to the "masculine" military governments of the victorious Allies. And that was precisely the problem. The issue was not the putative wholesale "demasculinization" or even "feminization" of daily life, but the absence of adequate *German* male authority and a corresponding increase in displays of female social and sexual autonomy. This lack of German male authority was sorely felt both in the overtly political public sphere and, in an era of severe housing shortages, the less-than-private domestic sphere, where there could be, at least initially, no ready reversion to normative social and sexual relations between the sexes. In the wake of defeat and occupation, German men lost their status as protectors, providers, and even (or so it seemed for a short time) as procreators: the three "P"s that had traditionally defined and justified their masculinity.

In this essay I investigate just one aspect of the postwar project to reassert native male authority in postwar West Germany by focusing on social policy and cultural representation concerning the relationships and offspring of white German women and African-American GIs. My interest is two-fold: first, to illuminate the particular ways that discourses of race figured in the "remasculinization" of postwar West Germany (to borrow from Susan Jeffords)[7]; and second, to sketch briefly the prescriptive nature and political function of this "new German man."

≈

Into the 1950s, official and public discourses regarding "occupation children" were conditioned by two distinct tales of origin that focused obsessively on the mother and the moral circumstances of conception.[8] The first was one of *victimization*, in the form of German women's brutal rape by victorious enemy soldiers. Here Soviet soldiers played a prominent, but not exclusive, role. In southern Germany, terrifying stories circulated about the violence done to German women by French Moroccan troops and, to a lesser extent, African-American GIs. By the early 1950s, moreover, stories involving the brutal rape of German women by Allied troops came to serve a double duty as a trope for the national defilement and victimization of Germany in the local vernacular of *Heimat* histories, where the suffering of a small German community came to represent the experience of the nation as a whole.[9] In Rudolf Albart's description of the "last and first days" in Bamberg (those, that is, leading up to and following defeat and occupation by American troops), he tells the story of a rape that reportedly took place the day the Americans entered the town:

> That evening the engineer's wife, Betty K., was disturbed by a loud banging on the door while sitting in her kitchen. As she opened the door with her one-and-a-half year old in her arms, two tree-tall negro soldiers stood before her and immediately pushed past into her apartment.... According to her account, they jumped on her and raped her three times. During the crime, her father was forcibly restrained and finally gunned down. He died instantly. Only after completing their gruesome deed did the negroes depart the scene of their outrage, leaving behind a dead man and a degraded woman.[10]

What is striking and, as it turns out, paradigmatic about this account is the representation of rape by soldiers of color as a victimization of both the German woman, who is depicted as maternal rather than sexual, and the German man (or more precisely, the German father), an insubstantial image of ineffectuality. This double victimization narratively linked female defilement with the displacement and, ultimately, the death of native masculinity.[11]

A second trope, which appeared in such diverse sources as church sermons, feature films, and intelligence, police, and social welfare reports, focused on German women's willing (some would say willful) fraternization with occupying soldiers. Like the first, this too was a national narrative of social and sexual disorder, but one that distinctly shifted the attribution of guilt from vengeful masculine invaders to disloyal domestic partners. In 1946, to cite just one example, the Protestant High Consistory in Stuttgart denounced German women and girls who "degrade themselves through licentious behavior.... They forget the thousands of graves that surround them.... They forget their husbands, brothers, sons, boyfriends, who are still imprisoned or missing. They forget the many thousands of war-wounded. They forget the entire plight and affliction of the Fatherland. Their conduct is an affront to the returning men and a vexation for the entire public."[12] German women's fraternization with occupation soldiers was widely characterized as dishonoring the memory and martial sacrifices of German men, and desacralizing—and in some cases, literally denigrating—the German fatherland. The German mothers of postwar *Mischlinge* became particular targets of public condemnation.[13] In a period of debilitated German patriarchy and pride, native officials stepped in to fill the void with a particular brand of state paternalism.

Within a month of defeat, German state officials sought to nullify the reproductive consequences of conquest by relaxing, temporarily, Paragraph 218, which outlawed abortion. Indeed in spring 1945, before war's end, the Bavarian *Landesregierung* issued a secret memo (later burned) that expressly encouraged abortions in rape cases involving "colored" troops. Abortions were readily granted to women who provided a sworn written statement detailing "forceful" rape by enemy soldiers.[14] Evidence from Augsburg indicates, moreover, that state and municipal authorities continued to refer to the memo when authorizing abortions during the months following defeat.[15]

By early 1946, however, there was a swift tightening around the issue of the woman's innocence. If either her reputation or the details of her story seemed suspect, abortions were denied. Applications were increasingly rejected if the putative perpetrator was white, unless a commission of three doctors certified the existence of "severe medical indications." Medical review boards, local and state officials, and Christian clergymen rapidly began to suspect that women were relying on officially sanctioned abortion to rid themselves of the unwanted consequences of casual consensual sex with occupying soldiers. They feared that the availability of abortion was encouraging wily German women to surrender to their promiscuous proclivities and afterward misuse abortion as a form of state-sponsored birth control.[16]

Strikingly, however, women's motives were suspected exclusively when the putative perpetrator's race was white. In cases involving soldiers of color, applications continued to be approved on the basis of applicants' uncontested claims that bringing the pregnancy to term would result in unbearable "psychological or emotional suffering" for the woman and, not incidentally, for her husband or fiancé, who could not be expected to bear with equanimity such an unbearable sexual and social affront. In the early days of occupation, then, racial stereotypes of sexually predatory black males tipped the balance in favor of women's applications; only somewhat later would the image of the pathologically promiscuous and materialist *Negerliebchen,* or "negro-lover," be propagated and popularized.[17]

By spring 1946, as the incidence of rape and legal abortions declined, the first "occupation children" were born. The high number of births in Bavaria rankled state officials there, who sought in vain to negotiate with the American military government regarding the status of the children. Ultimately, all occupation children—including those of color—were grudgingly extended German citizenship, but only after Allied military government officials made it clear that they would neither entertain paternity suits nor readily grant citizenship to their troops' illegitimate offspring abroad. Despite this resolution, between 1946–48, state officials attempted to deny public support to the mothers of interracial children in Bavaria, where the greatest percentage resided.[18]

By the end of the occupation, women's real or putative victimization played an ever-diminishing role in the formation of social policy regarding occupation children and their mothers. With the gradual return of German husbands from the war and POW camps, in fact, there was a marked increase in divorce and paternity suits, particularly if a new child had appeared during a husband's long absence. In many such cases, the husband contested paternity and petitioned to be absolved of his legal and financial responsibilities; under German law, all children lacking a male guardian became wards of the local or state youth office and hence eligible for public support.[19]

German state officials and social workers gradually retreated from their hostile attitude toward women's fraternization with white soldiers, particularly by 1948, when marriage was permitted between occupation soldiers and German women in the Western zones, and currency reform promised an end to the "hunger prostitution" thought to motivate much of the sexual promiscuity of the immediate postwar period. Interracial relations, however, continued to be considered transgressive of racial and national boundaries and subject to general condemnation, in part (ironically) *because* interracial marriages remained rare.[20] In a period of enforced social and sexual normalization, when the commitment to renew the German family transcended partisan politics,[21] women who gave birth to the interracial children of African-American GIs were held up to public scrutiny as a morally unacceptable anti-norm. Most were assumed (incorrectly) to be prostitutes or of the most lowly social rank, motivated by materialism rather than love, and thus by definition outside the bounds of respectable German femininity. The continued emphasis on these women's sexuality and materialism meant that well into the 1950s many observers, including social workers, had a hard time seeing them as properly maternal. Press reports early in the decade depicted them as uncaring or unwilling mothers, who opted to institutionalize their children rather than nurture them (when in fact over 70 percent of the children remained with their mothers), or who raised their children outside a proper family environment.[22] Emigration to the United States would likely have satisfied such critics. But the paucity of transnational interracial marriages meant that the offspring of such relationships were overwhelmingly "illegitimate" and that the interracial child and its offending mother would remain German citizens on German soil.

~

For the balance of this essay, I discuss a remarkable transformation: how and why public and official discourse moved from a passionate renunciation of paternal responsibility and support for Afro-German children to, by the mid-1950s, an equally passionate public commitment to their protection and nurture.

Shortly after the 1949 foundation of the Federal Republic, and again in 1952 as the first postwar interracial German children were entering German schools, West German federal and state officials, educators, sociologists, and psychologists began to collect statistical data and undertake scientific studies on German *Mischlinge*. The first in this series was an informal census ordered in 1950 by the federal Ministry of the Interior to establish the overall number of interracial occupation children in the former French and U.S. zones of occupation (the American military government had forbidden such a survey throughout the occupation) and to determine the number maintained by public funds in orphanages, private or public homes, or foster care. Since the first births in late 1945, German state officials had lobbied Allied and particularly American officials to facilitate the recognition of paternity by occupation personnel, and into the 1950s continued to seek ways to mandate the payment of child support by the fathers. After 1949, the new federal government took up the cause, exhibiting a marked reluctance to assume the reproductive costs of occupation.[23]

In 1955, as the Federal Republic regained full national sovereignty, the newly established Foreign Ministry attempted to include the issue of child support in negotiations regarding West Germany's entry into NATO (North Atlantic Treaty Organization). These efforts met with very limited success. While an agreement was reached on the procedures by which German authorities could establish American paternity and determine child support payments in German courts, attempts at implementation collapsed due to a distinct lack of cooperation from American military officers. Until the early 1960s, in fact, German youth offices found it extremely difficult to summon an American soldier to a paternity hearing, and German courts found it legally impossible to enforce payment of child support.[24]

By 1955, West Germany was both remilitarizing and remasculinizing— and the two were not, of course, unconnected. Yet the revitalized *Vaterland* that was emerging by mid-decade was not the militarist one of yore. Military service had lost its allure, and the martial ideal never again presented itself as either a viable or particularly attractive model for masculinity in postwar West Germany.[25] Rather, in the decade following the end of the occupation, the West German *Vaterland* was discursively refashioned as a *land of fathers* for reasons I hope to make clear.

∾

After 1950, there were increasing cultural signs of an ideological reassertion and reformulation of German patriarchy. Articles in the West German popular and scholarly press continued to bemoan persistent problems stemming from the social dislocations of the war and its immediate aftermath. Particular attention was devoted to the proper socialization of youth, especially given alarming indications of endemic youthful criminality, sexual precociousness, moral confusion, and deficiencies in school performance and the ability to concentrate—a litany of ongoing concerns for public commentators, educators, and social welfare workers since the occupation years. What was new, however, was a small but steadily increasing sociological and psychological literature focusing on the role and responsibilities of fathers for reversing this trend.[26]

This wake-up call to German fathers took on a much more public and popular dimension that same year when the theme of paternal responsibility became a favorite among moviemakers and their state and federal sponsors. In 1951, the first Federal Film Prize was awarded by the West German Ministry of the Interior to *Das doppelte Lottchen,* the story of identical twin sisters of divorced parents who meet by chance at a girls' camp in the Bavarian Alps and hatch a plan to switch identities so they can each meet the unknown half of their former parental pair. Rapidly, the film focuses on the transformative effect that the overresponsible little Lotty has on her self-absorbed composer-father, so prone to self-indulgent self-expression (both artistic and sexual). At the end of the film, he reunites with his former wife, not out of any apparent rekindled attraction to the struggling working mother, but because of a deep if unanticipated devotion to his daughter, who had been reduced to a state of physical and emotional collapse by her strenuous efforts to restore their ruptured family. Ultimately, the German family is healed by the father's belated recognition of his paternal devotion and duties—a melodramatic finale that scored big at the box office and with critics, and received official sanction as the year's best feature film.[27]

The cultural rehabilitation of German fathers was implicated in, and indeed helped to construct a newly liberalized discourse of race in early 1950s West Germany. This symbiotic relationship was hardly fortuitous, but served to revamp both postwar German masculinity and national identity in particular, highly political ways.

In the popular 1952 West German feature film *Toxi,* released the year that the first interracial occupation children were entering German schools, the "problem" of the postwar *Mischlingskind* arrives quite literally and unexpectedly on the doorstep of a German *bürgerliche* family.[28] Toxi's biological father is absent, having abandoned his child to return to the United States, and her mother is inexplicably dead, which leaves only her gravely ill maternal grandmother, who out of desperation sends the child to seek succor at the door of the middle-class home.

Notably, this film severed the fate of the child from the "fall" of the mother, shifting the focus away from the latter's sexual and racial transgressions. Thus Toxi is unburdened from the taint of the past national traumas, both military and moral. References to defeat and occupation are elided, since the sexually transgressive mother has mercifully disappeared. The racial problem was construed less as persistent than presentist, and purged of reference to the double pasts of National Socialism and the (later) loss of national sovereignty. Thus viewers were firmly encouraged to focus on the plight of the child, rather than the circumstances of conception.

In the film, Toxi (played by an Afro-German girl, Elfie Fiegert) arrives in the middle of a birthday party, causing consternation and disrupting the familial celebration.[29] The nature of her reception, however, fractures along generational lines. She is treated sympathetically by those characters whose formative generational experience pre- or postdated National Socialism, thus she is warmly received by the family's young children and by the aged grandfather, who cannot bring himself to fulfill his assigned task of putting her in an orphanage, insisting instead that she make her home with their extended family. Theodor, Grandpa's middle-aged son-in-law and the indifferent father of two young daughters, resents Toxi's presence and, when he is not busily pursuing business investments, strategizes to have the child removed from the house. The dramatic culmination comes when Grandpa suffers a heart attack, which prompts Theodor to take action. Early the next morning before anyone is up, Theodor awakens Toxi and readies her for the drive to the orphanage. On the way, however, his car breaks down, which allows Theodor and Toxi to get acquainted. Through a series of false moves, Toxi gets lost. Theodor gets worried, acquires a sense of social responsibility, and ultimately repents his prejudiced ways.

Thus, the film is explicitly about the need to strengthen the German family by weaning the German father from his unexamined racial prejudices. The implications are that eager and myopic pursuit of profit resulted in an insufficient liberalization of the *pater familias* and that the budding economic miracle led to a serious neglect of the social responsibilities of father and citizen, which demanded attention and address for the sake of the future of the West German family and nation. The film suggested that the German family and German identity would be healed only after their patriarchs confronted and conquered their residual racial prejudices. That having been done, (amid the self-congratulatory tears of white German moviegoers) the *functional* public purpose of the social problem of race was exhausted. Thus, the problem could disappear—or rather be transported "back" to the United States—the imaginary origin of its source.

At the end of the film, Toxi is accepted into the family, and the effacement of race is symbolically acted out in the family Christmas pageant, in which Theodor's white birth child plays King of the Magi in blackface, while Toxi performs in whiteface. The blurring of the color line, however, turns out to be no more than playacting. Indeed, the painted faces initiate a scene that reasserts racial boundaries (a point reinforced by the fact that the filmmakers felt the need to darken Elfie's light brown skin with make-up during the filming of the movie so it would not "appear too light").[30] For at that very moment the narrative takes a dramatic turn, as Toxi's fashionable African-American father arrives unexpectedly at the family's door to collect his child and take her "home" to the United States. In the film's last shot, the camera lingers on the emotional reunion of father and daughter, pulling in for a medium close-up that visually severs the pair from the German domestic scene, in effect initiating the unseen fantastic voyage that promises to restore the postwar German family and nation to whiteness. Thus, the normalization of postwar domestic life was scripted in a way that managed to bypass ideological associations with the Nazi past while nonetheless reaffirming race-based definitions of German identity.

Promotional literature for the film speculated that its tug on the audience's heartstrings would result in a sizable increase in adoptions of Afro-German children, who were otherwise markedly shunned by most prospective adoptive parents in West Germany. Such adoptions did not, in fact, increase. Rather, the film had the opposite effect: of facilely encouraging among its German viewers fantasies of *repatriation* as a solution to the "problem" of what to do with the living "legacies of the occupation." Into the late 1950s, moreover, educators, social workers, and West German officials argued for the need to give Afro-German children good educations and solid job training so they would have the option, upon attaining majority, of emigrating to the land of their fathers.[31]

Despite the persistence of such racialist thinking in Germany after 1945, it would not best serve one's understanding to conclude too facilely that it was a direct extension of the Nazi variety of racism. For what Barbara Fields said of the United States during Reconstruction also holds for reconstructing Germany: "It is easy enough to demonstrate a substantial continuity in 'racial attitudes.' But doing so does not demonstrate a continuity of racial ideology.... Although there was no appreciable decline or mitigation of *racialist* thinking, there was a decisive shift in its character."[32] And, I would add, in its function.

A survey of official discourse and social policy toward Afro-German children reveals a parallel instrumentalization in discussions of race in Bonn. If the problem of race was used in the film to assist in reforming and reformulating German masculinity at the domestic level (and in the domestic arena), it was used by federal officials in the Interior, Family, and even Foreign Ministries to rehabilitate the (West) German nation at the international level.[33]

Since 1949, German federal and state officials consistently pointed out that, under the law, interracial children enjoyed the same rights and were treated in ways equal to their white counterparts; that there were no separate state-funded homes for black *Mischlinge* (although some privately operated ones did exist);

and that they were educated in integrated, rather than segregated, school class-rooms. The latter point was somewhat disingenuous for a number of reasons: first, because the small number and geographical dispersion of interracial children made segregated schools unlikely; and second, because despite the obvious difficulties, the option had been discussed by religious leaders, educators, and likely some state officials. To cite one of the more outrageous suggestions, the Protestant Inner Mission proposed to the Hessian *Landrat* that *Mischlinge* be educated in special segregated schools and afterward shipped to Africa to serve as Christian missionaries.[34] Nonetheless, in 1952 there was a significant amount of self-celebration and backslapping among West German federal, state, and school officials for rejecting the socially divisive "American solution" of Jim Crow. In this case, the greatest public relations payoff was not so much on the domestic, but on the international level. At a time when the National Guard was needed to compel integration in the American South, the "frictionless" integration of West German schools was reported in white and black newspapers in places like New York, Chicago, and Philadelphia, and in a feature article in *Ebony*.[35]

Yet public pronouncements of the children's equality coexisted quite comfortably with racialist attitudes and the determination to scrutinize the *social implications* of the children's difference both for the West German present and—more alarmingly as the children approached puberty—for the West German future.[36] Despite the liberal public rhetoric, officials in the federal Interior and Family Ministries could not quite shake the conviction that the children were "foreign" and, what is more, that military occupation had *introduced* into Germany a race problem of a type that had never before existed there.[37] As a result, they actively encouraged having the "problem solved" by means of international adoptions, particularly to the United States where the children could be adopted by "their own kind." This was facilitated by a relaxing of the German adoption law in 1950. Within a few years, American demand for white German children of Allied paternity was extremely high, and German social workers, church, and government officials were heartened as queries from African-American families trickled in expressing interest in black German children.

By 1955, however, as West Germany attained full sovereignty, the federal Interior and Family Ministries ordered the wholesale export of children to the United States stopped. This reversal had partly to do with negative press coverage, which alleged that state youth offices were "selling" *German* children to the highest bidder—usually to well-off American couples who "ordered" children via expensive proxy adoptions rather than make the trip to select the son or daughter they were to nurture to adulthood. Grave concerns about the market mentality of Americans extending into the intimate sphere of the family were expressed by national leaders in German youth matters such as Heinrich Webler, director of the German Institute for Youth Guardianship. In May

1955, Webler published an article urging native youth officials to clamp down on transatlantic adoptions. While he conceded in passing that some American adoptive parents acted out of a desire to help the children, he listed other "frequent" and much less admirable motives for adoptions, such as unwillingness to bear one's own children (a swipe at the putatively independent yet indolent modern American woman); desire for a tax break; and, more sinister yet, adoption with the intention of selling the child to a third party or even into indentured servitude. Webler, among others, argued that with the rapid improvement of the postwar German economy, the pressing material crisis that originally motivated foreign adoptions had disappeared, thus transforming "illegitimate occupation children" into a domestic problem requiring domestic solutions. As a result, "occupation children" previously considered foreign became recharacterized as "our German children."[38]

Many fewer Afro-German children than white German children were adopted to the United States, in part, as German youth and state officials complained, both because "white American families would not adopt them" and "American officials made it clear that they didn't want them sent to their country" (an interesting story that cannot be told here).[39] But some were adopted, and German social workers did not find the results encouraging. One child, who was referred to repeatedly in state, youth office, and federal memos, was said to have suffered severe psychological and emotional stress after being placed with an African-American family. The problem was analyzed as twofold: first, the child's shock at, and inability to adjust to, the move from a white environment in West Germany to an all-black family and neighborhood; and second, the child's subjection to racial segregation and Jim Crow laws. As a result, the federal Interior, Family, and Foreign Ministries issued memos discouraging adoptions of *Mischlinge* to the United States.[40] And while they never convinced themselves that the children were unproblematically *German,* they at least decided that they were more *European* than *American.* As a result, the preferred destination for adoption of *Mischlingskinder* (since few German families were taking them) was Denmark, where, many German commentators assured the public and each other, "racial prejudice does not exist."[41]

By 1955, then, the West German state assumed the role of protector and beneficent guardian to the postwar *Mischlinge.* The negative experiences that German youth offices collected and recorded regarding the adoption of Afro-German children to the United States were circulated and recirculated in federal and state ministry memos, German press reports, and to Christian welfare associations and international youth welfare organizations.[42] While federal and state officials stopped short of engaging in explicit social criticism, they more than suggested that the United States had been tested—and found wanting—on the very principles with which it had come armed to reeducate and democratize Germany. As one sociologist publicly noted: "One shouldn't overlook the fact that even in the U.S.A. the professed ideal and the practiced reality are not always identical. The illusion that America is, among other things, also a paradise for colored people should not be nourished." In other words, as a local German newspaper more pithily and provocatively put it, "The *USA* prefers blondes."[43] In one short decade after Hitler's defeat, a chastened nation seemed to have surpassed its tutor in the lessons of democracy; the West German government could claim moral victory on the issue of race and race relations.

If that message was circulated quietly in West German sociological literature and local press reports, it was nevertheless loud enough to carry across the Atlantic and appear periodically in the African-American press. Given Cold War conditions, however, West German federal officials understood that it would serve neither German nor Western interests to expose and irritate the Achilles heel of American race relations. Yet West German officials were not nearly as reticent when it came to attacking the failings of the American legal system, which, by appealing to the time-honored principles of personal liberty and privacy, allowed American men stationed in Germany to shirk their social responsibilities as *fathers*. In criticizing the situation, federal officials pointed out that while maintenance claims of German children against American fathers were nearly impossible to enforce, "such claims of [foreign-born] non-German children against fathers living in Germany may be enforced without difficulty ... including as an attachment of a [West German] soldier's pay." If a *German* man did not voluntarily perform his social duty, they argued during negotiations, he would be compelled to do so by the West German state.[44]

It is no coincidence that German soldiers got refashioned as responsible fathers at a 1956 conference on the status of military forces in postwar Germany. The rhetoric at the conference suggested that West Germany had become (and urged its new Allies to be) a new-style *Vaterland* where "might" would be tempered by "moral accountability"—due to both its wartime *and* postwar experience.[45] But there was also a second subtext, which had to do with German sovereignty. For as long as the Federal Republic lacked the authority to command such accountability among foreign troops on its own territory, postwar conditions persisted, and German patriarchy still could not establish itself as domestic master.

Notes

1. The research for this essay, and for the larger project from which it derives, was made possible by the generous support of the German Academic Exchange Service, the National Endowment for the Humanities, the Colgate University Research Council, and the Rutgers Center for Historical Analysis. The essay first appeared with same

title in: *Signs: Journal of Women and Culture* 24, no. 1 (1998): 107–27, and reappears here by courtesy of the University of Chicago Press. ©University of Chicago. All rights reserved.

"Protokoll der Arbeitstagung über das Schicksal der farbigen Mischlingskinder in Deutschland am 15. und 16. August 1952 im Amerika-Haus zu Wiesbaden" (Wiesbaden, 1952), 4. The conference was sponsored by the Society for Christian and Jewish Cooperation [SCJC]. Founded in 1948 with much encouragement from the Office of Religious Affairs of the American Military Government in Germany, the society's goal was to "analyze and eliminate existing prejudices ... and promote justice, understanding and cooperation between Protestants, Catholics, and Jews." The society's work was in line with the American reeducation program and devoted particular attention to problems of youth, education, teacher training, and curriculum reform for German schools. In 1952, the society became active in addressing "the race problem" in relation to interracial children. For a general discussion of the SCJC's activities in the early postwar period, see Frank Stern, *The Whitewashing of the Yellow Badge: Antisemitism and Philosemitism in Postwar Germany* (New York, 1992), 310–11 and more generally, 310–34. The same year, a widely disseminated pamphlet titled *Maxi, unser Negerbub* thematized German men's social responsibility in a story of a male teacher's concern for the successful social and educational integration of "his" Afro-German pupil. This pamphlet became recommended reading for all primary school teachers in West Germany at the advice of state youth and welfare offices and ministries of education. Alfons Simon, *Maxi, unser Negerbub* (Bremen, 1952).

2. A 1951 estimate of the total number of "occupation children" born to German mothers since 1945 was 94,000. By 1955, a federal survey concluded that births of Allied paternity for the decade 1945–55 numbered 68,000. Bundesarchiv Koblenz (BAK), B153: Bundesministerium für Familien- und Jugendfragen, File 342, "Uneheliche Kinder von Besatzungsangehörigen." Also BAK, B189: Bundesministerium für Jugend und Familie, 6858, Files: "Besatzungs- u. Flüchtlingskinder" and "Besatzungs-, einschliesslich Mischlingskinderstatistik."

3. After 1945, the use of the term *Mischlinge* underwent a transformation. Earlier a designation for the children of so-called mixed unions between German Christians and Jews, or Africans, African-Americans, Roma or Sinti, it was now employed solely in reference to children of German women and African or African-American men, and to a much lesser extent to those of Puerto Rican or Indonesian paternity. Nonetheless, by the 1950s such fine distinctions of paternity tended to be elided in official and public discourse. By 1952, when the first interracial children were entering German schools, *Mischlingskinder* were widely perceived as an unwelcome U.S. import.

4. The absurdly exaggerated second figure was uttered by Pater Leppich, as reported in Hermann Ebeling, "Berichte: Zum Problem der deutschen Mischlingskinder," *Bildung und Erziehung* 7, no. 10 (1954): 612–30. See also Office of the Military Government for Germany, U.S. (hereafter OMGUS), Land and Sector Offices, OMG-Bavaria, Civil Administrative Division, Public Welfare and DP Branch (CAD, PWDP), General Records, Box 37: "Children of American Fathers" file. Also Luise Frankenstein, *Soldatenkinder. Die unehelichen Kinder ausländischer Soldaten mit besonderer Berücksichtigung der Mischlinge* (Munich, 1954), 5.

5. Robert G. Moeller, *Protecting Motherhood: Women and the Family in the Politics of Postwar West Germany* (Berkeley, 1993). Elizabeth Heinemann has explored the re-

lationship between collective memory of women's experiences and the articulation of national identity in "The Hour of the Woman: Memories of Germany's 'Crisis Years' and West German National Identity," *American Historical Review* 101, no. 2 (April 1996): 354–95.

6. See, e.g., Annamarie Tröger, "Between Rape and Prostitution: Survival Strategies and Chances of Emancipation for Berlin Women after World War II," trans. Joan Reutershan, in *Women in Culture and Politics,* ed. J. Friedlander et al. (Bloomington, 1986), 97–117; and Barbara Willenbacher, "Zerrüttung und Bewährung der Nachkriegs-Familie" in *Von Stalingrad zur Währungsreform,* ed. M. Broszat, et al. (Munich, 1990), 595–618. See also my discussion in *Cinema in Democratizing Germany: Reconstructing National Identity after Hitler* (Chapel Hill, 1995), 92–117.

7. Susan Jeffords, *The Remasculinization of America* (Bloomington, 1989).

8. For a companion piece to this essay which focuses on postwar public and official responses to German mothers and their interracial children, see Heide Fehrenbach, "Of German Mothers and '*Negermischlinge*': Race, Sex, and the Postwar Nation," in *Revisiting the Miracle Years: West German Society from 1949 to 1968,* ed. Hanna Schissler (Princeton, forthcoming).

9. For a discussion of the historical development and meanings of *Heimat* in modern German history, see Celia Applegate, *A Nation of Provincials* (Berkeley, 1990); Alon Confino, "The Nation as Local Metaphor," *History and Memory* 5, no. 1 (1993): 42–86; and Alon Confino, *The Nation as Local Metaphor: Württemberg, Imperial Germany, and National Memory, 1871–1918* (Chapel Hill, 1997). On the role of *Heimatfilm* in the creation of postwar German identities, see Fehrenbach, *Cinema in Democratizing Germany,* 148–68; and Johannes von Moltke, "Trapped in America: The Americanization of the Trapp-Family, or 'Papas Kino' Revisited," *German Studies Review* 19 (October 1996): 455–78.

10. Rudolf Albart, *Die letzten und die ersten Tage. Bamberger Kriegstagesbuch 1944/ 46* (Bamberg, 1953), 116–17, boldface in the original. See also the notorious local history of Freudenstadt, which depicts the day of defeat as a second visitation (likened to that after World War I) of marauding and murdering French Moroccan troops. The booklet ends with a list of Germans slain in the process, including brief details of German women abducted and killed by the troops, as well as German men done in trying to protect them. Hans Rommel, *Vor zehn Jahren. 16.–17. April 1945. Wie es zur Zerstörung von Freudenstadt gekommen ist.* (Freudenstadt: Freudenstädter Heimatblätter Beiheft I, 1955). On the "black horror" stories of World War I: Sally Marks, "Black Watch on the Rhine: A Study in Propaganda, Prejudice, and Prurience," *European Studies Review* 13 (1983): 297–334; and Keith L. Nelson, "The 'Black Horror on the Rhine': Race as a Factor in Post-World War I Diplomacy," *Journal of Modern History* 42, no. 4 (December 1970): 606–27, among others.

11. This is also evident in archival sources. See, e.g., the statements of witnesses (as well as the women themselves) accompanying German women's application for abortion following alleged rape by an Allied soldier in Staatsarchiv Augsburg, Nr. 30: Gesundheitsamt Sonthofen.

12. "Rundschreiben" des Stuttgarter Oberkirchenrats, 20 March 1946. Quoted in Clemens Vollnhals, "Die Evangelische Kirche zwischen Traditionswahrung und Neuorientierung," in *Von Stalingrad zur Währungsreform: Zur Sozialgeschichte des Umbruchs in Deutschland,* ed. M. Broszat, et al. (Munich, 1990), 151–52. This concern

outlived the occupation. See my discussion of the furor provoked in state and church offices by the 1951 film, *Die Sünderin,* which thematized the failure of masculine will. Fehrenbach, *Cinema in Democratizing Germany,* 92–117.

13. These women were characterized in the press and by social workers and sociologists as asocials, mentally impaired, or as professional or informal prostitutes. This characterization persisted into the 1950s, although nearly one-third of German mothers of interracial children questioned in a survey at the beginning of the decade offered that their involvement with African-American soldiers was motivated by love, and one-fifth of those questioned said they hoped to marry their partner. These percentages are likely low since it required substantial courage on a woman's part to make such admissions, given the unambiguously critical public assessment of interracial fraternization in postwar Germany at the time. See Herbert Hurka, "Die Mischlingskinder in Deutschland, Teil I: Ein Situationsbericht auf Grund bisheriger Veröffentlichungen," *Jugendwohl* 37, no. 6 (1956): 213–21.

14. Applications for abortion followed a particular pattern; women's statements consistently described the use of overpowering force (through focus on the attacker's considerable size, weight, and strength, or the presence of a weapon) as well as the woman's frantic but failed attempts at physical resistance. Staatsarchiv Augsburg, Nr. 30: Gesundheitsamt Sonthofen, Memo from the *Bürgermeister des Marktes Sonthofen,* regarding "Schwangerschaftsunterbrechung" dated 7 June 1945. Atina Grossmann has noted that the relaxation of the abortion law in the case of rape after German defeat was anticipated by a similar relaxation announced by the Reich Ministry of the Interior in March 1945 in the case of rape of German women by advancing Soviet troops, see her "A Question of Silence: The Rape of German Women by Occupation Soldiers," *October* (Spring 1995): 56. Also Staatsarchiv Augsburg, Nr. 30: Gesundheitsamt Sonthofen, Memo of *Reichsministerium des Innern,* "Unterbrechung von Schwangerschaften" dated 14 March 1945. For historical background, including interwar attempts to repeal Paragraph 218: Atina Grossmann, *Reforming Sex* (New York, 1995).

15. StA Augsburg, Nr. 30: Gesundheitsamt Sonthofen, Memo from the Bürgermeister des Marktes Sonthofen, regarding "Schwangerschaftsunterbrechung" dated 7 June 1945. Also StA Augsburg, Nr. 30: Gesundheitsamt Sonthofen, Memo of Reichsministerium des Innern, "Unterbrechung von Schwangerschaften" dated 14 March 1945.

16. These fears were expressed with force and frequency in Bavaria, and in 1947 the leadership of the Evangelical Church in Bavaria issued a position paper, arguing against abortion in the case of either "miscegenation" or rape, in part *because* it could not be proved with certainty that the sexual relations were not consensual. Interestingly, then, concerns about national and racial sexual "transgressions" took a back seat to concerns about policing women's behavior. By 1950/51, Bavarian doctors were ordered to report all miscarriages so that officials could investigate whether the affected women were attempting to pass off an intentional abortion as an "act of God." Staatsarchiv Augsburg, Gesundheitsamt, File 19: Neuberg; and File 91: Nördlingen. For a discussion of abortion policy in East Germany see Donna Harsch, "Society, the State, and Abortion in East Germany, 1950–1972," *American Historical Review* 102 (February 1997): 53–84.

17. Staatsarchiv Augsburg, Nr. 30: Gesundheitsamt Sonthofen, applications for abortions, 1945–46; and Gesundheitsamt (GA), Nr. 19: Neuburg. By mid-1946, German and American officials were constructing images of criminality linking African-

American troops and their white German mistresses. OMGUS, Executive Office, Office of the Adjutant General, General Correspondence, Box 43, File: Incidents-American. For a more general discussion of *"Amiliebchen"* and *"Negerliebchen"* see Elizabeth Heinemann, *"Standing Alone"*: *Single Women from Nazi Germany to the Federal Republic* (Ph.D. diss., University of North Carolina, 1994), and "The Hour of the Woman"; also Maria Höhn, *GIs, Veronikas and Lucky Strikes: German Reactions to the American Military Presence in the Rhineland-Palatinate during the 1950s* (Ph.D. diss., University of Pennsylvania, 1996).

18. RG260: OMGUS/Bavaria-CAD, PWDP, General Records, Box 25 and 37.

19. For example, Staatsarchiv Augsburg, VA Lindau, 1948. Also Siegfried Boschan, *Die Vormundschaft* (Cologne, 1956); Deutsches Institut für Vormundschaftswesen, *Neues Unehelichenrecht in Sicht* (Heidelberg, 1961); Franziska Has, *Das Verhältnis der unehelichen Eltern zu ihrem Kinde* (Berlin, 1962); and Barbara Schadendorf, *Uneheliche Kinder* (Munich, 1964). For a historical survey of legal guardianship of children in Germany since the nineteenth century, see Edward Ross Dickinson, *The Politics of German Child Welfare from the Empire to the Federal Republic* (Cambridge, Mass., 1996); for the post-1945 period, Elizabeth Heineman, "Complete Families, Half Families, No Families at All: Female-Headed Households and the Reconstruction of the Family in the Early Federal Republic," *Central European History* 29, no. 1 (1996): 19–60.

20. In the American zone, this was due in large measure to American officers' reluctance or refusal to give their necessary permission to interracial marriage applications. Marriage between American soldiers and German women was officially permitted in 1947, but nevertheless continued to be officially discouraged and subject to the rigorous review and approval of one's superior officer and military chaplain. Marriage applications were further subject to the "six months and three" rule, which allowed a GI only a narrow temporal window of opportunity to petition to marry his German girlfriend. He had to have no more than six months and no fewer than three remaining in his tour-of-duty; after petitioning he had to wait three months for approval, and then another five months (unofficially dubbed the "cooling off period," by which time he would have returned home) before he would be permitted to import his fiancee for the nuptials. OMGUS, Circular 181.

21. For a comprehensive discussion of social policy toward women and the family in the Adenauer era, see Moeller, *Protecting Motherhood*.

22. For a corrective to these misconceptions see: Vernon W. Stone, "German Baby Crop Left by Negro Gis," *The Survey* 85 (Nov. 1949): 579–83. Also Frankenstein, *Soldatenkinder.*

23. The informal survey of interracial occupation children, ordered in late 1950, of "those states where *Mischlingskinder* were present," was confined to Baden, Bayern, Hesse, Rheinland-Pfalz, Würrtemberg-Baden, and Württemberg-Hohenzollern. In 1954, the federal Ministry for Youth and Family undertook a nation-wide survey of all occupation children; statistics on children of color were kept separate. BAK, Bundesministerium für Familien- und Jugendfragen, B153/342; and BAK, Bundesministerium für Jugend und Familien, B189/6858. Also Bayerisches Hauptstaatsarchiv (BayHStA), Ministerium des Innerns (MInn) 81089, "Uneheliche Kinder von Besatzungsangehörigen—Berichte der Jugendämter"; and BayHStA, MInn 81083, 81085, 81086, 81088, 81090, 81094.

24. Only a reported 6.7 percent of all Allied birth fathers legally recognized paternity of their out-of-wedlock child. Nonetheless, German officials came to consider the child support problem a particularly American one. Statistics showed that of all occupation children born between 1945–1955, 55 percent were of American paternity; moreover, among so-called occupation children born in 1954, this percentage had increased to 80 percent. BAK, B189: Akten des Bundesministeriums für Jugend und Familie, 6858, 6859, 6861. Also Hauptstaatsarchiv Stuttgart (HStAStg), EA2/007, Akten des Innenministeriums Baden-Württemberg, Nr. 1177: "Jugendwohlfahrt: Statistik und Unterhalt der unehelich geborenen Kinder..., 1951–55." And especially, HStAStg, EA2/008, Akten des Innenministeriums, Nr. 1176, "Jugendwohlfahrt: Unterhalt für uneheliche Kinder—Unterhaltsverpflichtung von Mitgliedern ausländischer Streitkräfte (1955–70)." Complaints were also prevalent in Bavaria, see BayHStA, MInn 81087, "Verfolgung von Unterhaltsansprüchen gegen Angehörige von ausländischen Streitkräften—Pariser Verträge, 1955–57." See also Becker, "Die unter Vormundschaft stehenden unehelichen Kinder von Besatzungsangehörigen," Jugendwohl 37, no. 12 (1956): 438–40.

25. As David Clay Large put it: "With its admission to NATO, Bonn was formally empowered.... But Germany's first soldiers, all volunteers, did not make their appearance for several more months, and then with such modesty that it seemed as if they hoped to slink unnoticed onto the historical stage. This was indeed a low-profile army, one that appeared to be embarrassed by its very existence." Germans to the Front: West German Rearmament in the Adenauer Era (Chapel Hill, 1996), 234. For a discussion of German masculinity in the 1950s, and especially the influence of American models of identification, see Kasper Maase, Bravo Amerika: Erkundungen zur Jugendkultur der Bundesrepublik in den fünfziger Jahren (Hamburg, 1992); also the important work by Uta Poiger, "Rebels with a Cause? American Popular Culture, the 1956 Youth Riots, and New Conceptions of Masculinity in East and West Germany," in The American Impact on Postwar Germany, ed. R. Pommerin (Providence, 1995); and Uta Poiger, Jazz, Rock, and Rebels: Cold War Politics and American Culture in a Divided Germany (Berkeley, 2000).

26. See the Internationale Bibliographie der Zeitschriften Literatur for 1947 through 1959. While there are extensive entries for "Mutter" and "Mutterschaft" from the first postwar volume in 1947, entries for "Vater" and "Vaterschaft" appear and expand only with the 1951 volume. Some samples from youth welfare and Christian publications are: "Kinder ohne Väter," Jugendwohl 30 (1949); Hanns R. Müller-Schwefe, "Die Welt ohne Väter," Evangelische Welt VII, no. 17 (1 September 1953): 497–500; and Joachim Bodamer, "Die Frage nach dem Vater," Christ und Welt VIII, no. 34 (25 August 1955).

27. Das doppelte Lottchen (1950) was directed by Josef von Baky; the script was written by Erich Kästner, based upon his book of the same name. For an analysis of the girlish femininity represented in this film, and its broader implications for West German cinema, spectatorship, and identity, see Fehrenbach, Cinema in Democratizing Germany, 148–68. This was one of many West German films to appear throughout the decade dramatizing the need for new, more responsible and responsive German fathers. Other titles include Suchkind 312 (1955), Gefangene der Liebe (1955), Anders als du und ich (1957), Heimat deine Lieder (1959).

28. *Toxi* (1952) was directed by R.A. Stemmle. Unlike *Das doppelte Lottchen*, this film received no state or federal film credits, although over 75 percent of all domestic feature films of the period did.

29. Elfie Fiegert won the part in a mass audition of 400 children in Munich. In the marketing of the film, much was made of the parallel's between Elfie's background and that of her character. In fact, in the film credits the historical Elfie is literally rein-scribed as her fictional counterpart: the character "Toxi," that is, is listed as played by the actor "Toxi." As a result, the story of Toxi became the story of all West German *"Mischlinge."* Elfie's father was an African-American soldier who was ordered to Korea; her mother was not dead, but placed the child in a home where she was later adopted by the Fiegerts, *Flüchtlinge* and former cinema-owners from Schlesien, whose two-year-old daughter died upon their arrival West after fleeing from Soviet troops and tanks. Thus this well-publicized story connected the integration of refugees and ex-pellees to the integration of Afro-Germans in the Federal Republic. A more detailed and nuanced reading of the film will appear in my book, *"Race in German Reconstruction: African American Occupation Children and Postwar Discourses of Democracy, 1945–1965* (Chapel Hill, forthcoming).

30. Günter Herbst, "Fünfjähriges Negerkind spielt sein Schicksal" in *Bonner Rundschau*, 20 May 1952.

31. BAK, B149: Bundesministerium für Arbeit und Sozialordnung, #8679. Also BayHStA, Papers of the Bavarian *Innenministerium*, MInn 81084 "Fürsorge für Kinder ausländischer Väter 1954–60," Letter from Dr. Rothe of the *Bundesministerium des Innerns*, dated 9 Sept. 1955. For a discussion of the mutating West German policies on international adoptions of "occupation children," see Fehrenbach, "Of German Mothers and *'Negermischlinge.'"*

32. Barbara Fields, "Race and Ideology in American History," in *Region, Race and Reconstruction* (1983), 154.

33. By the mid-1950s, the nature of the children's significance had shifted and a number of German commentators began stressing the children's important social and pedagogical function in postwar Germany. They invested the *children* with the respon-sibility to reeducate Germans from notions of racial superiority, something they ex-pected would both "unburden Germans from the guilt of the past and redeem the German name worldwide." In 1961, a West German lawyer made the outrageous com-ment that the "non-white" children should be cultivated in the Federal Republic as "a living warning *(Mahnmal)* of what the hubris of the Nazi state directly led to." *Münchner Merkur*, Letter to the editor in response to an article published on "the problem of colored occupation children," dated 22/23 April 1961. Also Hurka, "Die Mischlings-kinder in Deutschland, Teil I"; and Gustav von Mann, "Zum Problem der farbigen Mischlingskinder in Deutschland," *Jugendwohl* 36, no. 1 (1955), 50–53.

34. This proposal was rejected by American officials. OMGUS, OMG-Hesse, CAD, Public Welfare Branch, Box 1069, File: "Correspondence: Child and Youth Wel-fare," Memo of Conference with *Regierungsrat* Crueger on 17 July 1947.

35. The response of Bavarian state officials to inquiries by white American and African-American journalists and academics can be found in BayHStA, Akten des Bayerischen Staatsministerium für Unterricht und Kultus, MK62245: "Volksschulwe-sen Negerkinder."

36. This extended to the federal level. See BAK, B149: Bundesministerium für Arbeit und Sozialordnung, File 8679: Berufsberatung u. Vermittlung von Ausbildungsstellen für uneheliche farbige Besatzungskinder deutscher Staatsangehörigkeit. For an expanded discussion of this issue, see Fehrenbach, "Of German Mothers and 'Negermischlinge'."

37. They were not explicitly denying the racialist basis of the state-sponsored murders of millions during the Third Reich; they simply skirted that issue and suggested that this was the first time that Germany had to come to terms with the existence of a colored minority among its citizenship. This too was nonsense. See May Opitz, Katharina Oguntoye, and Dagmar Schultz, *Showing our Colors: Afro-German Women Speak Out,* trans. Anne V. Adams (Amherst, Mass., 1992); and Lora Wildenthal, "Race, Gender and Citizenship in the German Colonial Empire," in *Tensions of Empire: Colonial Cultures in a Bourgeois World,* ed. Frederick Cooper and Ann Stoler (Berkeley, 1997). Also Reiner Pommerin, *"Sterilisierung der Rheinlandbastarde": Das Schicksal einer farbigen deutschen Minderheit, 1918–1937* (Düsseldorf, 1979); and Tina Campt, Pascal Grosse, and Yara-Colette Lemke-Muniz de Faria, "Blacks, Germans, and the Politics of Imperial Imagination, 1920–1960," in *The Imperialist Imagination: German Colonialism and Its Legacy,* ed. Sara Friedrichsmeyer, Sara Lennox, and Susanne Zantop (Ann Arbor, 1998).

38. According to Webler, a domestic solution would also ensure the fiscal and physical health of the new West German state by helping to reverse the historical trend toward an increasingly aging population: "Our entire social welfare system is built upon the requirement that the young generation does not disappear." It is striking, then, that as the number of adoptions increased over the first half of the decade, suspicions regarding the reasons for—and national implications of—this upswing also flourished. Nonetheless, it is notable that the children's race was rarely mentioned in these accounts, which indicates that authors were concerned primarily with the overseas adoption of *white* German children. Heinrich Webler, "Adoptions-Markt" *Zentralblatt für Jugendrecht und Jugendwohl* 42 (May 1955): 123–24. See also BAK, B153: Bundesministerium für Familien- und Jugendfragen, File 1335, I–II: "Material über Probleme des Internationalen Adoptionsrechts. Also HStAStg, Akten des Innenministeriums, EA2/007: Vermittlung der Annahme an Kindesstatt, Band II, 1955–66: especially the copy of the memo from the Internationaler Sozialdienst to the Bundesministerium für Familien- und Jugendfragen dated 27 January 1958. Also Franz Klein, "Kinderhandel als strafbare Handlung," *Jugendwohl* Heft 3 (1956): 95.

39. For a detailed discussion of the adoption of Afro-German children to the United States, see Heide Fehrenbach, *Race after Hitler: Black Occupation Children in Postwar Germany and America* (Princeton, 2005).

40. BAK, B153:Bundesministerium für Familien- und Jugendfragen, File 1335. Also HStAStg, EA2/007, Nr. 1750: "Vermittlung der Annahme an Kindesstatt—Allgemeines." Band II: 1955–66.

41. BAK, B189: Bundesministerium für Jugend und Familie, no. 6862. Also Franz Klein, "Zur gegenwärtigen Situation der Auslandsadoption" *Unsere Jugend* Heft 9 (1955): 401–408.

42. For example, HStAStg EA2/007, Nr. 1750, "Vermittlung der Annahme an Kindesstatt," Bd. II, 1955–66: "Abschrift of Internationaler Sozialdienst, Bericht über Adoption deutscher Kinder durch fremde Staatsangehörige" dated 27 January 1958.

43. This incipient *double entendre* was an ironic allusion to the recent German past, rather than American popular culture, since Marilyn's movie wouldn't be released until the following year. The first quote is from Herbert Hurka, "Die Mischlingskinder in Deutschland, Teil II," *Jugendwohl* 37, nos. 7/8 (1956): 275. The second is from an article on U.S. immigration and the new McCarran bill to ensure the "purity of the American race," "Die USA bevorzugen 'Blonde,'" in *Rheinische Post* (24 July 1952), press clipping in BAK, B-106 Bundesministerium des Innern, File 20620.

44. HStAStg, EA2/008 Akten des Innenministeriums, Nr. 1176, Jugendwohlfahrt: Unterhalt für uneheliche Kinder—Unterhaltsverpflichtung von Mitgliedern ausländischer Streitkräfte 1955–70: German Delegation to the Status of Forces Conference, Bonn 18 April 1956, "Memorandum submitted by the German Delegation." While negotiations applied to all troops stationed on West German territory, it was clear that federal officials were aiming at the Americans. In a statistical survey, they determined that American troops were responsible for over half of all "soldiers' children"; moreover, when they solicited information from state offices on success rates for establishing paternity and securing maintenance claims, reports on experiences with American troops were specifically requested. Also in the same file, "Amerikanische Väter zahlen nicht gern," an undated press clipping from an unnamed Mannheim newspaper, presumably from June or July 1957, judging from the context. And for Bavaria, BayHStA, MInn 81094, "Statistische Erfassung der Besatzungskinder, 1952–61." For a discussion of the very low percentage of German fathers willing to provide child support for their wartime non-German offspring, see Frankenstein, *Soldatenkinder*.

45. The tendency to focus on postwar suffering rather than wartime aggressions was widespread. See Robert G. Moeller, "War Stories: The Search for a Usable Past in the Federal Republic of Germany," *American Historical Review* 101 (October 1996): 1008–48. For a critical analysis of filmmaker Helke Sander's recent "feminist" cinematic depiction of the period, see Gertrud Koch, "Blood, Sperm, and Tears," *October* 72 (Spring 1995): 27–41.b

Epilogue

CHAPTER 18

Zeitgenossenschaft
Some Reflections on Doing
Contemporary German History

Hanna Schissler

The Framing of Contemporary History

The capacity for self-reflection is what constitutes us as human beings. The will-ingness actually to engage in self-reflection, however, is very unevenly distrib-uted. Some cultures or subcultures promote this basic human ability and even indulge in it, others tend to ignore it or even fend it off. Thus, psychoanalysts are usually more self-reflective than politicians or technocrats. Historians might be expected to be somewhere in between. Yet historians, and especially the practitioners of contemporary history, have long established a culture of disconnectedness and "objectivity." This has changed to a certain degree now that History (with a capital H) has diversified into all kinds of hyphenated his-tories, and especially since the emergence of oral history in the 1980s. Yet, as I will argue in this chapter, an externalizing and disconnected mode of doing history continues to have detrimental consequences, particularly when it comes to contemporary history, and this needs to be overcome.

It remains the case that the frames or scripts of historical writings are mostly "just there" and not sufficiently reflected upon. Contemporary his-tory—and all historical research, for that matter—depends to a greater or lesser degree on the ways in which we try to make sense of the present. Sometimes social movements like the student movement of the 1960s or the feminist movements since the 1970s, trigger a change of reference for thinking about history. Sometimes it is dramatic events, like the implosion of the Soviet bloc in 1989/1990, or the September 11 attack on the World Trade Center and the

Pentagon in 2001 that force us—or provide us with the chance—to reconceptualize how we think about history, and about contemporary history in particular.

When historians write contemporary history, they confront all kinds of challenges. For example, when it comes to writing about the Nazi period, German and Austrian historians of the old generation (those born in the 1920s) speak and write about a time in which they either actively participated or that they endured in one way or another. The next generation of historians (in Germany this would be the *Flakhelfer* generation) spent its formative years of childhood and youth in the Third Reich. The sixty-eighters, those born into what Ralph Giordano has called a "second-hand guilt," had to deal with the fact that their parents or grandparents were "perpetrators, victims, or bystanders," as Raul Hilberg put it. For that generation of West Germans (West Germany having grown over the decades into a culture of high self-reflectivity), the psychological load of "delineated" guilt was frequently particularly difficult to deal with. It brought about a much greater willingness to deal with the frames of reference of German history itself.[1] In the United States, things have played out in different ways. The motives for becoming a historian of modern Germany varied widely. Frequently, however, after the generation of refugees from Nazi Germany died, their children or grandchildren turned to German history, with their own stake in trying to make sense of their parents' or grandparents' fate.

For historians of contemporary history, of one stripe or another, there is thus usually a strong personal or even autobiographical element in contemporary history, an enormous entanglement, which is rarely reflected upon.[2] Not only the darkest or most dramatic chapters of German history, but also more peaceful times cannot be analyzed without some personal memory and thus a fair degree of personal involvement—an involvement that can and should be put to productive use in writing those histories.[3] If historians grew up in the 1950s, for example, personal memory cannot but influence what they have to say about that decade, about its consumer culture, the gender system, the division of Germany, the presence of Allied occupation troops, the return of the last POWs, the jokes that children heard in school and that alluded in strange and painful ways to Jews, the fear of nuclear war, and the *Heimatfilme* portraying an idyllic world that contrasted dramatically with the bombed-out cities still quite visible in 1950s Germany.[4] "1989" has forced Germans yet again to reflect on their place as scholars and contemporaries. Not only did post-nationality, which was the political as well as the intellectual credo of the generation of 1968 in West Germany, look somewhat different from before, but now East Germans too had their own dealings with the German nation, past and present, to rethink.[5] Nor were they alone in having to rewrite history after 1989. The nation, memory, "coming to terms with the

past" (West Germany), anti-fascism (in the GDR), the welfare state—of eastern as well as of western provenance—civil society, right-wing radicalism, and
multiculturalism all became topics of thorough rethinking after 1990 in a unified Germany.[6] But instead of opening up and broadening their questions,
German historians after 1989 were, at least for a while, busy discussing the national question yet again, in whatever shape it came: the end of the German
Sonderweg or the challenge of growing together as one nation.[7] While this is
understandable to a degree, it meant that historians in Germany were focusing on the national question at a time when historians in other countries were
trying to overcome the national focus and embrace transnational and even
global perspectives.

Personal involvement, and in some cases personal entanglement, thus play
a role, even if it is not the highly loaded issue of Germans' guilt that is investigated, although in most cases National Socialism and the Holocaust proves
to be a "black box" that has the tendency to swallow all of German history before and after the Holocaust.[8] The consequences of this atrocious and most
painful period of German history continue to have a long reach into the present—sometimes even in unexpected locations. Adelheid von Saldern has, for
example, attributed the fierceness of West German historiographic debates
even in the 1990s to the knock-out impact that National Socialism had on the
historical profession. According to von Saldern, much of the sharpness and
unusual aggression of recent debates (e.g. about gender history or the history
of daily life) can be attributed to the struggle that the current "guardians of
the profession" themselves experienced when as social historians in the 1960s
they sought to distance themselves from overly nationalistic and apologetic
approaches in German history and found themselves embroiled in ferocious
generational battles.

Historians of contemporary history engage in different language games
and conceptual frameworks, according to different rules in different academic
cultures. Ludwik Fleck in 1935 developed the idea of *Denkstile* and *Denkkol-
lektive*, by which he meant communities of scholars who conceptualize along
common lines and develop a common intellectual style, which leads them to
view the world along similar organizing principles or paradigms. Johan Galtung has argued that the academic cultures in which these styles are anchored
in common assumptions encompass not only "style" and academic demeanor
but also influence the organization of research. Thus, they create specific social hierarchies and, most interestingly, directly influence the content of scholarship itself.[9] All of the approaches and language games that historians engage
in have unquestionable strengths, but they also come with a price tag. Scholars play their various language games with a certain exclusionary obsession, as
if their own game were the only one worth playing. While the rewards of these
games might be obvious within a specific academic, social, and national set-

ting, the costs frequently are not and only reveal themselves to a "second-degree observation"—in other words, an observation and analysis of the ways in which scholars frame their questions and their research and the contexts in which they unfold.[10] As scholars, we are deeply implicated in our academic cultures with their specific language games. Each of these games tends to become recursive and self-reinforcing and might reach a point of stasis. This point (or the "Nash equilibrium," as mathematicians call it) is reached when players no longer have an incentive to deviate from their strategy, even if the strategy is undesirable. Our preference for the ways in which we organize our research and pose our questions has little to do with "truth" and everything to do with who we are and how we want to position ourselves in the present. Only by standing back and observing historical practice itself can we disturb the pattern and bring about change.

Contemporary German history is looked upon differently in the United States and in Germany (or in Austria, for that matter). It is interesting to explore some of the organizing principles, the advantages as well as the costs that influence the ways in which questions have been posed and issues raised. In view of the intense transatlantic exchanges and connections, such an endeavor can only be tentative, point to some trends, and convey personal impressions. Scholars immersed in particular cultural and academic environments can rarely distance themselves from those environments' cultural codes and mental blind spots. However, there are differences in the ways in which issues of contemporary history have been framed and taught that are particularly obvious for transatlantic travelers and for those who have learned to operate in more than one academic culture and no longer take the academic culture in which they initially were socialized to be an unchangeable given.

Approaches to Contemporary History in (West) Germany

In West Germany, the writing of *Zeitgeschichte* has been powerfully informed by two impulses, namely, the idea of "coming to terms with the past," on the one hand, and the aspiration to be good democrats and, indeed, to demonstrate what good democrats Germans have become, on the other.

The price of the "coming to terms with the past" approach seems to be the continued self-absorption of many German historians. Their ongoing focus on national frames goes hand in hand with a certain distancing from or even outright rejection of more varied and innovative historiographic approaches.[11] A striking and somewhat odd example of German self-absorption is a recent issue of *Vierteljahrshefte für Zeitgeschichte*, celebrating fifty years of contemporary history in Germany and featuring some of the most senior and respected scholars of German *Zeitgeschichte*. Karl Dietrich Bracher could offer no more pressing agenda for contemporary history than that it must not neglect the Weimar Republic. Hans-Peter Schwarz discusses at some length whether it seems justified now, after all, to speak of *"neueste Zeitgeschichte"* and not just *"Zeitgeschichte."* The notorious fixation of Germans on the nation also shows when Schwarz goes so far as to propose a new paradigm, one that allows us to understand in "which ways the nation-state is willfully as much as hastily abandoned and dissolved." It is willfully abandoned because of the political elites' obsession with the deepening and the broadening of the European Union. It is thoughtlessly dissolved because "the self-determination of the German people and thus the precondition of the democratic fashioning of its own fate are being relinquished."[12] At a time when transnational histories offer the main incentives for a renewal of historical questions, this digging in of one's heels in national self-limitation seems out of step with the times. Not all German historiography is self-absorbed to the same degree,[13] but it does seem that German unification itself has encouraged further turning inward.

The mainstream of contemporary history writing in Germany continues to be methodologically surprisingly conservative, as Lutz Niethammer already noted in the mid-1980s.[14] This methodological orthodoxy emerged from archival research on National Socialism and extended itself to postwar historiography; or, as Michael Geyer and Konrad Jarausch put it: "German historians … tended to think of themselves primarily as caretakers of facts, viewing 'history' as a set of physical remains, archival traces, or collective memories to be measured, weighed, and assembled—with or without a framing theory."[15] "Contemporary history evolved as a predominantly investigative history that hooked up with the 19th-century master narrative by default." The methodological conservatism of German historiography has also been held accountable for the reluctance to embrace the innovative research approaches that have transformed American historiography over the last decades. As Karin Hausen has observed, only minimal deviations, hardly recognizable as such, will be tolerated in German academic historiography. The fate of new historiographical approaches in Germany has thus been difficult: "Defamation, misinterpretation *(Unterstellungen)* and 'cheap' criticism, followed by marginalization and simultaneous attempts to coopt (and neutralize) the new research into mainstream history, finally a partial acknowledgment and readiness for dialogue" were the mechanisms with which historians in Germany adopted new approaches and paradigms.[16] Frequently it was colleagues' influence from abroad and transnational travelers who generated or eased some change, which was then more or less reluctantly also acknowledged by historians in Germany.

In any case, contemporary history in Germany tends to ask "the big questions" of perpetrators (sometimes, but not often, also of the victims) of National Socialism and the events and structures that made National Socialism possible. That gives *Zeitgeschichte* in Germany a weight and seriousness that can hardly be found in other countries. "German historians had no room for play since there were lies to be revealed and traditions to be salvaged. The impulse of German historians was to recover a lost past and to hold a disastrous one at bay."[17] Contemporary history in Germany rarely ever allows being "side-tracked" by cultural history or feminist approaches.[18] In fact, one gets the impression that contemporary history in Germany has hardly even taken notice of the major feminist challenge to doing history, which has subsequently broadened into any number of deconstructionist endeavors. Instead, the newcomers are put under the load of justification *ad eternum:* "The absent reception of gender-related questions continues to be framed as a problem of gender history, not as a deficit of the patterns of argumentation in the historical sciences as a whole," observe Martina Kessel and Gabriela Signori.[19] Germans were far too busy reconstructing a national narrative they could live with and now are integrating the West and East German narratives into one.[20] As far as the West German narrative is concerned, Germans seem to have "made it" after much deviation and a "special path" of historical development. They have "arrived in the West."[21] Some, like Heinrich-August Winkler, believe that after unification Germans have become a "normal" nation again, whatever that might mean in view of the burdened German past. The concentration on National Socialism and the Holocaust as well as the serious attempt to establish a democratic self-image after the first (and now also after the second) German dictatorship is understandable, especially in the land of the perpetrators. However, after the world-historical events of 1989 and September 11, 2001, along with their various consequences, it seems again strangely out of step for Hans-Peter Schwarz to see the "macro-historical erosion of the nation state" as the only threat to Germans' democratic birthright.[22]

German provincialism and self-absorption is hard to match—with quite a number of notable exceptions, to be sure. The hotly debated question of the mid-1980s historians' debate about the uniqueness or comparability of the Holocaust, which at the time was associated with both left- and right-wing political attitudes, looks completely different when placed in a world-historical context.[23] Even at the time, Charles Maier pointed out that the apparent choice between the uniqueness or comparability of the Holocaust was a false polarization; yet leading historians in Germany dug in their heels to fight for the hegemonic power of definition within a hotly contested national framework.[24] Indeed, Zygmunt Bauman in his book *Modernity and the Holocaust* had argued specifically against an exclusive German appropriation of the Holocaust. His message has been much more disconcerting for everybody, and can hardly be read as the big exculpation of the Germans—a reading that some in Germany had feared at the time of Bauman's book's release. As Michael Geyer and Konrad Jarausch put it, "The history is intimately German, but the message is of universal appeal."[25]

The fear of relativizing the Holocaust is a specifically West German concern. However, as much as the Holocaust has its uniquely German traits and needs to be located in the specificities of German history, there was genocide before the Holocaust, and genocide and other state-organized crimes continue to be carried out well into the present.[26] The illusionary dream of a "pure" nation seems not yet to have run its course; instead, it has turned into a nightmare all over the globe. Comparative genocide studies, as disturbing as they are, are on the rise. "Ethnic cleansing" and genocide have been a major characteristic of the entire twentieth century. Even worse, they continue to be threats in the present, as much through the ways in which some modern nation building tries to create social cohesion through an illusionary ethnic purity as through the erosion of modern nation-states. Sometimes the creation of new nations, liberated from former hegemonic empires, sometimes the demise of previously cohesive state formations (like the former Yugoslavia), is at fault. The atrocities of our times seem to be triggered by the condition of modernity itself, a condition and its implications not easily understood in all their ramifications and sometimes disastrous manifestations and outcomes. These catastrophic events pose tremendous challenges to historians and social scientists alike. Only a few scholars have tackled them systematically and/or comparatively.[27] However, in Germany, the preoccupation with the Third Reich and the Holocaust continues to take place mainly in a strictly national framework. Until quite recently, it continued to feed into enduring hegemonic fights for the power of definition, which seem to be ineradicable in Germany and continuously produce "public intellectuals" who fight over the paradigms of the German past.[28]

The public significance of the Third Reich and the Holocaust for contemporary German self-understanding and political culture strangely collides with its objectivist stance. This objectivism goes back to the influence of the doyen of contemporary history in West Germany, Hans Rothfels, who though himself a Jewish refugee of Nazi Germany, pursued a thoroughly conservative and nationalistic approach to German history.[29] Rothfels demanded a special self-discipline for the field of contemporary history: the suppression of one's own personal involvement *(Betroffenheit)*. "Critical distance" and scrupulous methodology should inform research in contemporary history. Rothfels' approach to *Zeitgeschichte* was extremely influential in West Germany. He actually provided the blueprint for contemporary history in Germany, to which most scholars involved in this field continue to adhere. "Critical distance" continues to be the magic formula, and many contemporary historians stick to that well-known methodological convention to this day. In arguing for an "objectivist" approach in establishing contemporary history, Rothfels brought about a trade-off between methodological innovation and academic recognition for contemporary history, in which the latter won. To be sure, critical distance is indispensable for scholarly work. However, it is also true that "critical distance" has all too often translated into disconnectedness and pseudo-objectivism. Generations of historians were taught in such an objectivist manner. "Never say 'I'" was one of the messages instilled in generations of students during their graduate training. The assumption that such rather structuralist training conveyed, is quite clear: the historical world exists *out there* and needs to be conceptualized, systematized, and understood. The "I" is severed from the process as much as possible. It steps back and becomes invisible, its influences thus cannot be reflected upon, because their existence is overlooked. The circular character of all scholarship is thus not something that is much reflected upon in contemporary history.

Such an objectivist stance seems to be particularly problematic in view of the fact that people are confronted with their own life stories or with the life stories of their parents or grandparents. The *Wehrmacht* exhibition and the reactions to it were a striking example of this.[30] Sometimes recognition of the circular character of our scholarship comes as a personal surprise, a kind of revelation—and it does so at unexpected moments, as when Jürgen Reulecke recently wondered "whether historians might not in fact always or even exclusively be writing their own history in 'concentric circles.'"[31] For most historians, this insight comes rather late in life. Practitioners of contemporary history seem to have a particularly difficult time reflecting on their subject position and instead resort to an objectivist stance—all the while ignoring their own relevance to and existence in their narratives. Scholars write about issues that have touched them very personally, yet they tell the story as if it were something completely disconnected, something far removed. Eric Engstrom has suggested that *Zeitgeschichte* "takes greater account of professional identity and reflexive narratives." "Professional identity needs to be grounded in personal experience…. It therefore behooves practitioners of *Zeitgeschichte* to make more room for personal experience and memory in their narratives. And one place to start experimenting on how that could be done, is in the history of the profession and in one's own (auto) biography."[32] However, something nearly every branch of historical research has overcome by now, i.e., a mechanical subject-object-relation, seems for the most part alive and well in *Zeitgeschichte*. Neglecting the "I" in historical narratives comes at a price. As Engstrom points out: "Either practitioners of *Zeitgeschichte* will tackle the problem of memory and its implications for their work, or they may find that others have usurped their claims to professional jurisdiction over collective historical consciousness and perhaps even over the history of their own professional past."[33] The rise of memory as a subject of inquiry may in fact lead to a paradigmatic shift in historical research, as Dan Diner has claimed.[34]

Hitler's "First Victim"? Contemporary History in Austria

The notion that Austria was Hitler's "first victim" continues to inform scholarship on contemporary history to a considerable degree in Austria. As many deplore, it clogs more productive avenues of dealing with a troubled past, in which Austrians were by no means merely the victims of German aggression.[35]

Contemporary history in Austria, even more than in Germany, seems to be overdetermined by research on National Socialism and the Holocaust. However, more and more historians in Austria have started to challenge the deep-seated conviction that Austria had been Hitler's "first victim," pointing out that Austrians had been perpetrators too.[36] It took quite a while for historians in Austria to make Austrian involvement in National Socialism a topic of research. This, however, had a specific effect on contemporary society in Austria. The delayed dealing with National Socialism led to a split in society, such that "progressives" point to Austrians as perpetrators, enablers, or endorsers of National Socialism, while conservatives indulge in the pleasures of a dubious victimhood. These two sides tend to continuously reconfirm each other in a carefully crafted *pas de deux*. However, to quote Ludwig Wittgenstein: Proposition P and its negation talk about the same thing: P.[37] Heinz von Foerster, an emigrated Austrian, concerned about this mutual fixation on a locked world-view, reminded his leftist friends in Austria:

> If you scream: Down with the King, it looks like you were *paid* by the King, because repeatedly, you mention him. The main thing for the king is that he continues to be a presence, no matter how. If you really want to get rid of the King, then you need to stop talking about him. Only then will he disappear.[38]

Austrian progressives and conservatives continue to be stuck with each other and remain fixated on one another, much like the West Germans were in the late 1950s and 1960s. The world view thus remains remarkably stable. Such a scenario makes it hard to learn anything new or to change the reference frames. The "first victim game" produces predictable, trivial truths.

In Germany as well as in Austria, some developments throughout the last decades have helped to soften the boundaries of history writing that accompany "objectivist" approaches. Oral history is clearly the front-runner here. While the historians' debate of the mid 1980s in West Germany as well as the Waldheim controversy in Austria revealed the severe limitations of contemporary history as currently practiced and its overdetermination, the memory boom, the presence of new historical agents finding their voice, the generational approach, and in particular "1989" as a world-historical event have all contributed to an increase in methodological self-reflection among historians of contemporary issues.

Contemporary German History in the United States

In the United States the variety of approaches that have spilled over to Europe and that have influenced and enriched research on German history is immense. They defy easy classification. The reduction of German history to its catastrophic culmination, the period from 1933 to 1945, continues to feed interest in things German. American research on German history sometimes falls into a transference trap. It has been ever so convenient to keep the Germans in the role of the historical "bad guys," even if Daniel Goldhagen might have pushed it too far, as most scholars agree. For a long time the Germans-as-bad-guys approach strengthened a positive self-perception of Americans and their role in the world. September 11 might have displaced not only the former Cold War enemy but also the Germans in their well-established role, with yet unforeseeable consequences for the contextualization of German history in the United States. The "catastrophic" appeal of German history in the United States is not something that needs to be commented on at any length. What deserves a closer look, however, is on the one hand a particular sensitivity to difference that characterizes American research on German history, and on the other hand a bold model of contextualizing national history in a global framework. To take a closer look at the role that difference histories and global context play for doing German history in the United States means to touch upon approaches that circumvent and relativize the national focus that informs so much of historical research in contemporary history in Germany itself.

The role that the deconstructionist and identity-based categories of gender and "race" play for American research on German history is quite pronounced. It is anchored in specific debates on equality within American society itself. The civil rights and women's movements have had an impact on historical research that has thoroughly changed paradigms in American historiography.[39] The application of those analytical categories to German history has, in turn, much enriched the field. Frequently, gender and "race" have served as an eye-opener for a German readership. The work of Maria Höhn, Heide Fehrenbach, Elizabeth Heinemann, Robert Moeller, and Frank Biess might serve as examples.[40] Their work focuses on gender and, in the case of Höhn and Fehrenbach, on "race" as analytical categories to decipher major trends in postwar German history. To pull German history out of a stifling national straitjacket, or, as in the case of Elizabeth Heineman, to look at the gendered character of national self-imagery, means to throw a productive new light on the West German construction of identity and nation. The outcome of much of this innovative research is markedly different from conventional wisdom about the postwar period of German history.

However, the use of "race" follows a very different logic in the American and German contexts and points to major differences between these two different academic cultures. In Germany the term cannot be used naively for historical reasons. "Race" is associated with stigmatization, disenfranchisement, and ultimately annihilation. In the United States, however, the framing of "race" has evolved entirely differently. "Race" now legitimizes a political program of compensation for historical guilt and the deeply rooted racism in American society. It legitimizes affirmative action. In the German context, "race" itself thus has a racist connotation, while in the American context it has become associated with progressive and compensatory politics. Natural sciences for a long time have argued that the application of "race" to humans is inappropriate, since there is only one human race.[41] Among the scholars in the United States who are concerned with racism and new forms of social injustice, only a few are willing to do without the term "race." A notable exception is Gerda Lerner, who has acknowledged that the use of the term "race" itself springs from a racist background. While it seems to be difficult (also in Germany) to do without a term that has worldwide recognition as a marker of difference in contemporary societies, nevertheless an awareness of the problematic nature of the term "race" needs to be maintained.[42]

Besides the sensitive and sensible use of difference along the lines of gender and "race" in the writing of history, it is the global contextualization that opens new avenues of thinking about German history. In 2000, Charles Maier published his article "Consigning the Twentieth Century to History: Alternative Narratives for the Modern Era."[43] In this article, Maier suggested a framework for global history that, if taken seriously, will have a major impact on the ways in which we think about German history. Maier suggests nothing less than a paradigm shift of truly global proportions, and maps out ways in which global history can be reconciled with the usual national preoccupations. According to Maier, the historical epoch, which lasted from the second half of the nineteenth century until the late 1960s, was based on "an enhanced concept of territoriality." As 1989 and the following developments have shown, we continue according to Maier to be caught up in the logic of the territorial epoch, which has, on the one hand, produced imperial exploitation of whole continents, and on the other hand led to two distinct ways of containing or repudiating modern (capitalist) societies: fascism/Nazism and communism. This territorial logic has produced related narratives of human suffering: the postcolonial narrative, the Holocaust narrative, and the story of the Gulag. Maier argues that as important as the Holocaust and Gulag narratives are for people's lives and for the ways in which we think about the past, they nevertheless have run their course. They lie in the past and have become history. The postcolonial narrative, however, gains in importance and urgency on a worldwide level. Currently the world is experiencing an erosion of the territorial base of politics and economic development—conventionally framed as processes of globalization. These changes of unseen proportions are shaking the foundations of our societies and of our personal existence in a way comparable only to the Industrial Revolution's displacement and creation of new organizing principles of society and the world at large. As William McNeill has stated, "I suspect that human affairs are trembling on the verge of a far-reaching transformation."[44] Contemporary history has yet to find the intellectual framework in which to discuss these changes.[45]

If the Holocaust (and the Gulag) are being displaced as organizing principles for interpreting contemporary history and human suffering, a process which will take a while and will not make sense to everybody immediately, then German history will indeed have to do what Michael Geyer and Konrad Jarausch have suggested, namely, put together multiple interacting stories within a fractured history of Germans. German history inside as well as outside of Germany will have to develop a whole new mind-set—a postcolonial and a global mind-set—that is in tune with the empirical processes of a globalizing world. For the time being nothing but an "informed bewilderment," as Manuel Castells has noted, grabs us in the face of this new world.[46] To place German history into this internationalizing framework is a task that has yet to be tackled.

Attempts at Overcoming Objectivist Approaches in Contemporary History

The "cultural turn," gender studies, psychoanalysis, ethnology, and ultimately world history have changed our understanding of history in Germany, Austria, and, most notably, the United States. Many authors have described the role of transference in history writing and have repeatedly argued for reflecting on the subject position of the researcher.[47] *Zeitgeschichte's* objectivist stance explains why the methodological and epistemological challenges that have upset the historical profession for the last three decades left contemporary history mostly untouched.[48] However, to reflect upon one's own positionality should no longer be considered "unprofessional," as in Rothfels' time, and the "I" might have a legitimate place in history after all.[49] *Zeitgeschichte* no longer needs to demonstrate its high professional standards by splitting off the "personal" from the "scholarly." Instead of being all over the place anyhow, memories, imperfect as they may be, lived lives, the biographical aspect that is invested in our research and usually drives what we are doing, as well as our own transference should be reflected and used productively in our research.

However, when it comes to increasing the degree of self-reflectivity of contemporary history, at least three factors need to be considered. The first, as noted, is the dilemma of *Zeitgenossenschaft:* The recent past, or better, segments thereof, are still remembered by contemporaries who played some kind of role in it, or who through either their own involvement or through family ties have some stake in the ways in which the recent past is interpreted. Historians, who interpret the past and consider themselves to be the guardians of or at least experts on the past, also are contemporaries and have their own personal stake in recent history.

Second, memory selects or forgets according to its own rules. As research on historical memory has shown, the remembering of the past usually follows a personal logic and responds to the need to position oneself or to establish (moral or other) claims in the *present*.[50] The need to position oneself in the present, however, operates as a powerful selector of what is remembered and has little to do with any kind of "objectivity." This by no means should be taken as an argument for dismissing personal memory as irrelevant; but personal memory often tell us more about our relationship to the present than anything else.[51] Memory as historical source needs to be placed into a complex framework of forces that link together the remembered past and the acted-upon present—something that requires considerable methodological as well as psychological abilities from historians. However, if we open ourselves up to personal memory and other memory sources, like oral-history interviews, which have become the major challenge to an orthodox contemporary history, we also need to be careful. It is not sheer "historical truth" that comes out of interviewees' mouths. Neurobiology as well as psychology and psychoanalysis have taught us a few things about memory—as has Binjamin Wilkomirski, who wrote a false autobiography. To this day he claims that his memoir of surviving Auschwitz as a three- or four-year-old is true. His "memoir" was translated into numerous languages and received lots of praise.[52] His book raises any number of interesting issues about how memory works and what truth in history is. In all of our encounters with history, especially when it comes to memory sources, it is history's circular character that we must make work for our interpretation. This, however, directly involves the observer in the process.

The third factor that plays a role and is closely connected to the ways in which people think about their place in time and space is the issue of agency in the face of impersonal historical forces. Mostly, when people think about their past, they think that they were solely the objects of historical development, that history acted upon them without their doing and without giving them much leverage, which is fair enough in most cases. However, people walk a fine line between structure and agency, between forces that sweep over them with relentless force and personal decisions that are taken under favorable or adverse circumstances. As we know from history, individuals who believe that they do have agency make personal decisions even under the most difficult circumstances. People make history, but not under circumstances of their own choosing, as the famous quote by Karl Marx from the *Eighteenth Brumaire of*

Louis Bonaparte goes. This fact plays an important role in all of history. The dialectic of overpowering circumstances and personal agency operates in the usual uneventful stories of people's lives as much as it operates in "victim stories," and it surely also plays a role that needs to be carefully investigated in "perpetrator stories."

History is not a "trivial machine" with clear and mechanical subject-object relations; there is always an interaction between the researcher and his or her object.[53] The interaction includes us as observers, our audiences, and the past, present, and future that we explore. This interaction continuously changes the past through our interpretations. It influences the present in which we position ourselves, and it sets the stage for a yet unknown future. It also changes us. The process of knowing is necessarily circular and makes the world unpredictable. Scholars must take responsibility for what they say or write, but they have little control over what the listener hears or what the reader understands. As communication theory has it: The world emerges in the eye of the observer or, for that matter, in the ear of the listener.[54] What those to whom we convey our message do with it is beyond our control, since it is the listener, not the speaker or writer, who decides on the meaning of an interpretation.[55] However, that does not result in an "anything goes" philosophy, since it is our responsibility as scholars to bring across our message as clearly as possible. Nevertheless, we need to learn and to take into consideration that we cannot control the ways in which readers, students, and listeners understand it. This might make us less inclined to fight for the power of definition, and it might make us more aware of our personal involvement, thus helping us along to more differentiated and more insightful views of contemporary history.

Notes

1. Dan Bar-On, *Legacy of Silence. Encounters with Children of the Third Reich* (Cambridge, 1998). Heinz Bude, *Bilanz der Nachfolge. Die Bundesrepublik und der Nationalsozialismus* (Frankfurt, 1992). Heinz Bude, *Das Altern einer Generation. Die Jahrgänge 1938–1948* (Frankfurt, 1997).

2. See in this context, and as an exception, the interviews that H-Soz-u-Kult conducted with leading historians in Germany in 1999: http://hsozkult.geschichte.hu-berlin.de/beitrag/intervie/a_fragen.htm and the following interviews with Wolfram Fischer, Lothar Gall, Immanuel Geiss, Helga Grebing, Jürgen Kocka, Hartmut Lehmann, Hans Mommsen, Wolfgang Mommsen, Gerhard A. Ritter, Reinhard Rürup, Adelheid von Saldern, Wolfgang Schieder, Winfried Schulze, Michael Stürmer, Rudolf Vierhaus, Hans-Ulrich Wehler and Heinrich-August Winkler. A selection of these interviews has been published by Hohls and Jarausch.

3. Michael Geyer and Konrad Jarausch, *Shattered Past: Reconstructing German Histories* (Princeton, 2003). Hanna Schissler, "Writing about 1950s West Germany,"

in *The Miracle Years: West German Society from 1949 to 1968. A Cultural History,* ed., Hanna Schissler (Princeton, 2001), 3–15.

4. Schissler, *The Miracle Years.*

5. Hanna Schissler, "Postnationality—Luxury of the Priviledged? A West German Generational Perspective," *German Politics and Society* 15, no. 2 (1997): 8–27; Helga Schulz, "La nación tras el diluvio. Una perspectiva germano-oriental" ("German Nationalism in Historical Perspective"), *Cuadernos de Historia Contemporánea* 22 (2000): 303–24.

6. Michael Geyer, "The Long Good-Bye: German Culture Wars in the Nineties," in *The Power of Intellectuals in Contemporary Germany,* ed. Michael Geyer (Chicago, 2001).

7. Martin Sabrow, "Die Historikerdebatte über den Umbruch von 1989," in *Zeitgeschichte als Streitgeschichte. Große Kontroversen seit 1945,* eds., Martin Sabrow, Ralf Jessen and Klaus Große Kracht (München, 2003), 114–37.

8. Dan Diner, "Zwischen Aporie und Apologie. Über Grenzen der Historisierbarkeit des Nationalsozialismus," in *Ist der Nationalsozialismus Geschichte? Zu Historisierung und Historikerstreit,* ed., Dan Diner (Frankfurt, 1991), 62–73.

9. Johan Galtung, "Deductive Thinking and Political Practice. An Essay on Teutonic Intellectual Style," in *Papers on Methodology. Essays in Methodology,* vol. 2 (Copenhagen: 1979), 194–250. Johan Galtung, "Struktur, Kultur und intellektueller Stil. Ein vergleichender Essay über sachsonische, teutonische, gallische und nipponische Wissenschaft," *Leviathan. Zeitschrift für Sozialwissenschaft* 11 (1983): 303–38.

10. Dirk Baecker, "Kybernetik zweiter Ordnung," in *Wissen und Gewissen. Versuch einer Brücke* ed. Heinz von Foerster (Frankfurt, 1993), 17–23. Yehuda Elkana, "Problem Choice in Science. Reflections on the Structures of Research" http://www.mpiwg-berlin.mpg.de/ringberg/Talks/alkana/Elkana.html. Yehuda Elkana and Alessandro Maranta, "Verantwortungsvoller Umgang mit Wissenschaft als Aufgabe von Bildung," in *Beiträge zur Lehrerbildung* 16, issue 1 (1998): 78–85. Heinz von Foerster, "Kybernetik einer Erkenntnistheorie" and "Verstehen verstehen," in *Wissen und Gewissen. Versuch einer Brücke* (Frankfurt, 1993), 50–71 and 282–98. Heinz von Foerster "Abbau und Aufbau," in *Lebende Systeme. Wirklichkeitskonstruktionen in der systemischen Therapie,* ed., Fritz Simon (Frankfurt, 1998), 32–51.

11. Geyer, *Shattered Past.* Karin Hausen, "Die Nicht-Einheit der Geschichte als historiographische Herausforderung. Zur historischen Relevanz und Anstößigkeit der Geschlechtergeschichte," in *Geschlechtergeschichte und Allgemeine Geschichte. Herausforderungen und Perspektiven,* eds., Hans Medick and Anne-Charlott Trepp (Göttingen, 1998), 15–55. Konrad Jarausch, eds., *Die historische Meistererzählung. Deutungslinien der deutschen Nationalgeschichte nach 1945* (Göttingen, 2002). Thomas Lindenberger and Michael Wildt, "Radikale Pluralität. Geschichtswerkstätten als praktische Wissenschaftskritik," *Archiv für Sozialgeschichte* 29 (1989): 393–411. Thomas Lindenberger, "'Alltagsgeschichte' oder: Als um die zünftigen Grenzen der Geschichtswissenschaft noch gestritten wurde," in *Zeitgeschichte als Streitgeschichte. Große Kontroversen seit 1945,* eds. Martin Sabrow, Ralf Jessen, and Klaus Große Kracht (Munich, 2003), 74–91. Adelheid von Saldern, "'Schwere Geburten.' Neue Forschungsrichtungen in der bundesrepublikanischen Geschichtswissenschaft (1960–2000)," *Werkstatt Geschichte* (40, 2005): 5–30.

12. Hans-Peter Schwarz, "Die Neueste Zeitgeschichte," *Vierteljahrshefte für Zeitgeschichte* 51, no. 1 (2003): 5–29. My translation. The German reads: "... weil damit

die Selbstbestimmung des deutschen Volkes und somit die Voraussetzung zur demokratischen Gestaltung der eigenen Geschicke preisgegeben wird," 26.

13. Such as Christoph Conrad and Sebastian Conrad, *Die Nation schreiben. Geschichtswissenschaft im internationalen Vergleich* (Göttingen, 2002). Gangolf Hübinger, Jürgen Osterhammel, and Erich Pelzer, eds., *Universalgeschichte und Nationalgeschichten* (Freiburg, 1994). Wilfried Loth and Jürgen Osterhammel, eds., *Internationale Geschichte. Themen, Ergebnisse, Aussichten* (München, 2000). Jürgen Osterhammel, *Geschichtswissenschaft jenseits des Nationalstaates* (Göttingen, 2001).

14. Lutz Niethammer, "Stufen der historischen Selbsterforschung der Bundesrepublik Deutschland. Ein Forschungsessay," in *Deutsche Geschichte nach 1945* (1986): 24. Deutsches Institut für Fernstudien, Tübingen.

15. Geyer and Jarausch, *Shattered Past,* ix.

16. Saldern, "Schwere Geburten" 28. My translation. The German reads: "Zuerst Diffamierungen, Unterstellungen sowie 'billige' Kritik, dann Marginalisierung und gleichzeitig Vereinnahmungsversuche, schließlich eine partielle Anerkennung und Dialogbereitschaft."

17. Geyer, *Shattered Past,* ix.

18. Saldern, "Schwere Geburten." Hausen, "Die Nicht-Einheit."

19. Martina Kessel and Gabriela Signori, "Geschichtwissenschaft," in *Genderstudien. Eine Einführung,* eds. Christina von Braun and Inge Stephan (Stuttgart, 2002), 124. My translation. The German reads: "Die mangelhafte Rezeption geschlechtergeschichtlicher Fragestellungen wird … nach wie vor als Problem der Geschlechtergeschichte formuliert, nicht als Defizit der Argumentationsmuster in der Geschichtswissenschaft insgesamt."

20. Konrad Jarausch, "'Die Teile als Ganzes erkennen'. Zur Integration der beiden deutschen Nachkriegsgeschichten," *Zeithistorische Forschungen. Studies in Contemporary German History* 1, issue 1 (2004): 10–30.

21. See Axel Schildt, *Ankunft im Westen. Ein Essay zur Erfolgsgeschichte der Bundesrepublik* (Frankfurt, 1999) and Heinrich-August Winkler, *Der lange Weg nach Westen,* 2 vols. (München, 2000). For works critical of arrival in the west, see Klaus Naumann, "Die Historisierung der Bonner Republik," *Mittelweg 36,* no. 3 (2000): 53–67. Klaus Naumann, "Reden wir endlich vom Ende! Das Ancien Régime der Zeitgeschichte bleibt von der Gegenwart ungerührt: Sie kennt nur den Erfolg der Bundesrepublik," *Frankfurter Allgemeine Zeitung* 44 (2001).

22. Schwarz, "Die Neueste Zeitgeschichte," 27.

23. James Knowlton and Truett Cates, translators, *Forever in the Shadow of Hitler? The Dispute about the Germans' Understanding of History* (Atlantic Highlands, N.J., 1993). Ulrich Herbert "Der Historikerstreit. Politische, wissenschaftliche, biographische Aspekte," in *Zeitgeschichte als Streitgeschichte. Große Kontroversen seit 1945,* eds. Martin Sabrow, Ralf Jessen and Klaus Große Kracht (München, 2003): 94–113.

24. Charles Maier, *The Unmasterable Past. History, Holocaust, and German National Identity* (Cambridge, 1988).

25. Geyer and Jarausch, *Shattered Past,* ix.

26. Robert Gellately and Ben Kiernan, eds., *The Specter of Genocide: Mass Murder in Historical Perspective* (Cambridge, 2003). Norman Naimark, *Fires of Hatred: Ethnic Cleansing in Twentieth-Century Europe* (Cambridge, 2001). Eric Weitz, *A Century of Genocide: Utopias of Race and Nation* (Princeton, 2003).

27. Zygmunt Baumann, *Modernity and the Holocaust* (Ithaca, 1989). Manuel Castells, *The Information Age: Economy, Society and Culture*. Vol 1: *The Rise of the Network Society*. Vol II: *The Power of Identity*. Vol. III: *End of Millenium* (New York, 1996–1998). Gellately, *Specter of Genocide*. Isabell Hull, *Absolute Destruction: Military Culture and the Practices of War in Imperial Germany* (Ithaca, 2004). Naimark, *Fires of Hatred*. Weitz, *Century of Genocide*.

28. Norbert Frei, "Goldhagen, die Deutschen und die Historiker. Über die Repräsentation des Holocaust im Zeitalter der Visualisierung," in *Zeitgeschichte als Streitgeschichte. Große Kontroversen seit 1945*, eds. Martin Sabrow, Ralf Jessen and Klaus Große Kracht (München, 2003), 138–51. Herbert, "Der Historikerstreit." Sabrow, "Die Historikerdebatte."

29. Berg, Nicolas, *Der Holocaust und die westdeutschen Historiker* (Göttingen, 2003).

30. Hans-Ulrich Thamer, "Vom Tabubruch zur Historisierung? Die Auseinandersetzung um die 'Wehrmachtsausstellung,'" in *Zeitgeschichte als Streitgeschichte. Große Kontroversen seit 1945*, eds. Martin Sabrow, Ralf Jessen and Klaus Große Kracht (München, 2003), 171–86.

31. My translation. The German reads: "ob man als Historiker nicht eigentlich immer auch—oder letzten Endes sogar immer nur—in 'wachsenden Ringen' seine eigene Geschichte schreibe." See Jürgen Reulecke, *"Ich möchte einer werden so wie die …" Männerbünde im 20 Jahrhundert* (Frankfurt, 2001), 9.

32. Eric J. Engstrom, *"Zeitgeschichte* as Disciplinary History—On Professional Identity, Self-Reflective Narratives, and Discipline-Building in Contemporary German History," *Tel Aviver Jahrbuch für deutsche Geschichte* 29 (2000), 403.

33. Ibid., 424.

34. Dan Diner, "Von 'Gesellschaft' zu 'Gedächtnis'—Über historische Paradigmenwechsel," in *Gedächtniszeiten. Über jüdische und andere Geschichten* (München, 2003), 7–15.

35. Gerhard Botz and Gerald Sprengnagel, eds., *Kontroversen um Österreichs Zeitgeschichte. Verdrängte Vergangenheit* (Frankfurt, 1994). Ernst Hanisch, "Die Dominanz des Staates. Österreichische Zeitgeschichte im Drehkreuz von Politik und Wissenschaft," in *Zeitgeschichte als Problem. Nationale Traditionen und Perspektiven der Forschung in Europa*, eds. Alexander Nützenadel and Wolfgang Schieder. Special issue 20 of *Geschichte und Gesellschaft* (Göttingen, 2004). Siegfried Mattl, "Nicht die Vergangenheit irrt, sondern die Gegenwart," in *Kontroversen um Österreichs Zeitgeschichte. Verdrängte Vergangenheit*, eds. Gerhard Botz and Gerald Sprengnagel (Frankfurt, 1994), 113–19. Alexander Pollak, "Vergangenheit und Reflexion. Konsens- und Streitlinien im Umgang mit der NS-Vergangenheit in Österreich," in *Zeitgeschichte als Streitgeschichte. Große Kontroversen seit 1945*, eds. Martin Sabrow, Ralf Jessen and Klaus Große Kracht (München, 2003), 326–46. Karl Stuhlpfarrer, "Über die Wandlungsfähigkeit des österreichischen Geschichtsbildes," in *Kontroversen um Österreichs Zeitgeschichte. Verdrängte Vergangenheit*, eds. Gerhard Botz and Gerald Sprengnagel (Frankfurt, 1994), 182–91.

36. Botz, *Kontroversen*. Hanisch, "Die Dominanz."

37. In his *Tractatus*, quoted in Heinz von Foerster, *Der Anfang von Himmel und Erde hat keinen Namen. Eine selbsterschaffung in sieben Tagen* (Berlin, 2002), 83.

38. My translation. "Wenn ihr schreit: 'Nieder mit dem König', dann sehr ihr so aus, als würdet ihr vom König bezahlt, denn er wird immer, immer wieder erwähnt. Die Hauptsache für einen König liegt darin, daß er erwähnt wird, im Spiel bleibt, auf

welche Weise ist ganz gleichgültig. Wenn ihr den König wirklich loswerden wollt, dann dürft ihr nicht mehr vom König sprechen, erst dann verschwindet er." Ibid., 83.

39. Peter Novick, *That Noble Dream: The "Objectivity Question" and the American Historical Profession* (Cambridge, 1988).

40. Schissler, *The Miracle Years*.

41. Marion Berghahn, *Continental Britons: German-Jewish Refugees from Nazi Germany* (Oxford, 1988).

42. Gerda Lerner, *Why History Matters: Life and Thought* (Oxford, 1997), viii, 184–97.

43. Maier, Charles S., "Consigning the Twentieth Century to History: Alternative Narratives for the Modern Era," *American Historical Review* 105 (June 2000): 807–31.

44. William McNeill, "The Changing Shape of World History," in *World History: Ideologies, Structures and Identities*, eds. Philip Pomper, Richard H. Elphick and Richard T. Vann (New York, 1998), 40.

45. Michael Geyer and Charles Bright, "World History in a Global Age," *American Historical Review* 100 (1995): 1034–60.

46. Castells, *End of Millenium*, 358.

47. Among them Pierre Bourdieu, "Understanding," in *The Weight of the World: Social Suffering in Contemporary Society*, ed. Pierre Bourdieu (Stanford, 1993), 607–26. Saul Friedlander, "Introduction," in *Probing the Limits of Representation: Nazism and the "Final Solution*," ed. Saul Friedlander (Cambridge, 1992), 1–21. Domink La Capra, "Representing the Holocaust: Reflections on the Historians' Debate," In *Probing the Limits of Representation: Nazism and the "Final Solution*," ed. Saul Friedlander (Cambridge, 1992), 108–27. Domink La Capra, *Representing the Holocaust. History, Theory, Trauma* (Ithaca, 1992), 46.

48. Christoph Conrad and Martina Kessel, "Geschichte ohne Zentrum," in *Geschichte schreiben in der Postmoderne* (Stuttgart, 1994), 9–36. Georg Iggers, *Historiography in the Twentieth Century: From Scientific Objectivity to the Postmodern Challenge* (Middletown, Conn., 1997). Peter Novick, *That Noble Dream: The "Objectivity Question" and the American Historical Profession* (Cambridge, 1988).

49. Irmgard Wagner, "Geschichtsschreibung und Psychoanalyse. Zur Frage der Positionalität in der Goldhaben-Debatte," in *Dimensionen der Historik. Geschichtstheorie, Wissenschaftsgeschichte und Geschichtskultur heute*, eds. Horst Walter Blanke, Friedrich Jaeger and Thomas Sandkühler (Wien, 1998), 415–25.

50. Pierre Bourdieu, "Understanding," in *The Weight of the World*, 607–26. Elena Esposito, *Soziales Vergessen. Formen und Medien des Gedächtnisses der Gesellschaft* (Frankfurt, 2002). Harald Welzer, *Das kommunikative Gedächtnis. Eine Theorie der Erinnerung* (München, 2002).

51. Welzer, *Das kommunikative Gedächtnis*.

52. See Jonathan Kozol, "Review of *Fragments* by Binjamin Wilkomirski," *The Nation*, October 28, 1996.

53. Heinz von Foerster, "Kybernetik einer Erkenntnistheorie" and "Verstehen verstehen," in *Wissen und Gewissen. Versuch einer Brücke* (Frankfurt, 1993) 50–71 and 282–98.

54. Humberto Maturana.

55. Heinz von Foerster, *Der Anfang von Himmel und Erde*. Niklas Luhmann, "Was ist Kommunikation?," in *Lebende Systeme. Wirklichkeitskonstruktionen in der systemischen Therapie*, ed. Fritz B. Simon (Frankfurt, 1998), 19–31.

Books by Volker Berghahn

Der Stahlhelm. Bund der Frontsoldaten 1918–1935 (Düsseldorf, 1966).
Der Tirpitz-Plan. Genesis und Verfall einer innenpolitischen Krisenstrategie (Düsseldorf, 1971).
Rüstung und Machtpolitik; zur Anatomie des "Kalten Krieges" vor 1914 (Düsseldorf, 1973).
Germany and the Approach of War in 1914 (Leamington Spa; New York, 1973).
Militarismus : Francis Carsten zum 65. Geburtstag (Cologne, 1975) (edited volume).
Germany in the Age of Total War (London, 1981) (edited with Martin Kitchen).
Militarism : The History of an International Debate, 1861–1979 (New York, 1982) (edited volume).
Modern Germany (Cambridge, 1982).
Unternehmer und Politik in der Bundesrepublik (Berlin, 1985).
The Americanization of West German Industry, 1945–1973 (Leamington Spa; New York, 1986).
Industrial Relations in West Germany (Leamington Spa; New York, 1987).
Perceptions of History : International Textbook Research on Britain, Germany, and the United States (Leamington Spa; New York, 1987) (with Hanna Schissler).
Rüstung im Zeichen der wilhelminischen Weltpolitik : grundlegende Dokumente 1890–1914 (Düsseldorf, 1988) (with Wilhelm Deist).
1993 Otto A. Friedrich, ein politischer Unternehmer : sein Leben und seine Zeit, 1902–1975 (Frankfurt/M, 1993) (with Paul J. Friedrich).
Imperial Germany (Providence; Oxford, 1994), (revised edition New York, 2005).
The Quest for Economic Empire: European Strategies of German Big Business in the Twentieth Century (Providence; Oxford, 1996) (edited volume).
Sarajewo, 28. Juni 1914 : der Untergang des alten Europa 1900–1929 (Munich, 1997).
America and the Intellectual Cold Wars in Europe: Shepard Stone Between Philanthropy, Academy and Diplomacy (Princeton, 2001).
Europa im Zeitalter der Weltkriege (Frankfurt/M, 2002).
Der erste Weltkrieg (Munich, 2003).
Die deutsche Wirtschaftselite im 20. Jahrhundert: Kontinuität und Mentalität (Essen, 2003) (edited with Stefan Unger and Dieter Ziegler).
Europe in the Era of Two World Wars: From Militarism and Genocide to Civil Society, 1900–1950 (Princeton, 2005).
Gibt es einen deutschen Kapitalismus? : Tradition und globale Perspektiven der sozialen Marktwirtschaft (Frankfurt/M, 2006) (edited with Sigurt Vitols).

Selected Readings

Abenheim, Donald. *Reforging the Iron Cross: The Search for Tradition in the West German Armed Forces* (Princeton, 1988).

Ackermann, Volker. *Der "echte" Flüchtling. Deutsche Vertriebene und Flüchtlinge aus der DDR 1945–1961* (Osnabrück, 1995).

Aly, Götz and Susanne Heim. *Vordenker der Vernichtung : Auschwitz und die deutschen Pläne für eine neue europäische Ordnung* (Hamburg, 1991).

Aly, Götz. *Hitlers Volksstaat. Raub, Rassenkrieg und nationaler Sozialismus* (Frankfurt am Main, 2005).

Anderson, Margaret Lavinia. *Practicing Democracy: Elections and Political Culture in Imperial Germany* (Princeton, 2000).

Anderson, Margaret Lavinia. *Windthorst: A Political Biography* (Oxford, 1981).

Arendt, Hannah. *Eichmann in Jerusalem. A Report on the Banality of Evil,* (Harmondsworth, revised and enlarged edition 1994).

Arendt, Hannah. *The Origins of Totalitarianism* (San Diego; New York; London, New Edition 1966).

Bankier, David. *The Germans and Final Solution. Public Opinion under Nazism* (Oxford, 1992).

Barber, Benjamin R. *Jihad vs. McWorld* (New York, 1995).

Bartov, Omer. *Hitler's Army. Soldiers, Nazis, and War in the Third Reich* (New York, 1990).

Berg, Nicolas. *Der Holocaust und die westdeutschen Historiker. Erforschung und Erinnerung* (Göttingen, 2003).

Berghahn, Marion. *Continental Britons. German-Jewish Refugees from Nazi Germany* (Oxford, 1988).

Berghahn, Volker. "NSDAP und „Geistige Führung" der Wehrmacht 1939–1945", *Vierteljahreshefte für Zeitgeschichte* 17 (1969): 7–71.

Berghahn, Volker R. *Der Tirpitz-Plan. Genesis und Verfall einer innenpolitischen Krisenstrategie* (Düsseldorf, 1971).

Berghahn, Volker R. *The Americanisation of West German Industry* (Cambridge, New York, 1986).

Berghahn, Volker R. (ed.). *The Quest for Economic Empire: European Strategies of German Big Business in the Twentieth Century* (Providence, RI, 1995).

Berghahn, Volker, *America and the Intellectual Cold Wars in Europe* (Princeton, 2001).

Berghahn, Volker R., Stefan Unger, and Dieter Ziegler, eds. *Die deutsche Wirtschaftselite im 20. Jahrhundert. Kontinuität und Mentalität* (Essen, 2003).

Bessel, Richard. *Germany after the First World War,* (Oxford, 1993).

Bessel, Richard. *Political Violence and the Rise of Nazism. The Storm Troopers in Eastern Germany, 1925–1934.* (New Haven, 1984).

Besymenski, Lew. *Stalin und Hitler. Das Pokerspiel der Diktatoren* (Berlin, 2002).

Biess, Frank. *Homecomings. Returning POWs and Legacies of Defeat in Postwar Germany* (Princeton, 2006).

Blackbourn, David. *The long 19th Century. A History of Germany, 1780–1918* (New York 1998).

Blackbourn, David. *Marpingen: Apparitions of the Virgin Mary in Nineteenth-Century Germany* (New York, 1994).

Bösch, Frank. *Das konservative Milieu: Vereinskultur und lokale Sammlungspolitik in ost- und westdeutschen Regionen, 1900–1960* (Göttingen, 2002).

Botz, Gerhard and Gerald Sprengnagel, eds. *Kontroversen um Österreichs Zeitgeschichte. Verdrängte Vergangenheit* (Frankfurt, 1994).

Broszat, Martin. Klaus Dietmar Henke, and Hans Woller, eds., *Von Stalingrad zur Währungsreform. Zur Sozialgeschichte des Umbruchs in Deutschland* (Munich: Oldenbourg, 1988).

Browning, Christopher. *Ordinary Men. Reserve Police Batallion 101 and the Final Solution in Poland* (New York, 1992).

Buchheim, Christoph. *Die Wiedereingliederung Westdeutschlands in die Weltwirtschaft 1945–1958* (Munich, 1990).

Bude, Heinz. *Bilanz der Nachfolge. Die Bundesrepublik und der Nationalsozialismus,* (Frankfurt, 1992).

Campt, Tina M. *Other Germans: Black Germans and the Politics of Race, Gender, and Memory in the Third Reich* (Ann Arbor, 2004).

Carter, Erica. *How German is She? Postwar West German Reconstruction and the Consuming Woman* (Ann Arbor, 1996).

Cary, Noel. *The Path to Christian Democracy: German Catholics and the Party System from Windhorst to Adenuaer* (Cambridge, 1996).

Cocks, Geoffrey and Konrad H. Jarausch. *German Professions, 1800–1950* (New York/ Oxford, 1990).

Connor, Ian. "Flüchtlinge und die politischen Parteien in Bayern 1945–50." *Jahrbuch für deutsche und osteuropäische Volkskunde,* vol. 38 (1995): 133–68.

Conrad, Christoph and Sebastian Conrad. *Die Nation schreiben. Geschichtswissenschaft im internationalen Vergleich* (Göttingen, 2002).

Conrad, Sebastian and Jürgen Osterhammel, eds. *Das Kaiserreich transnational: Deutschland in der Welt, 1871–1914* (Göttingen, 2004).

Crew, David F. *Germans on Welfare: From Weimar to Hitler,* (New York, 1998).

de Grazia, Victoria. *Irresistible Empire: America's Advance through Twentieth Century Europe* (Cambridge, 2005).

Dean, Carolyn. *The Fragility of Empathy after the Holocaust* (Ithaca, 2004).

Dickinson, Edward Ross. *The Politics of German Child Welfare from the Empire to the Federal Republic* (Cambridge, MA, 1996).

Diner, Dan. *Feindbild Amerika: über die Beständigkeit eines Ressentiments* (Munich, 2002).

Diner, Dan. *Ist der Nationalsozialismus Geschichte? Zu Historisierung und Historikerstreit,* (Frankfurt, 1991).

Doderer, Klaus, ed. *Zwischen Trümmern und Wohlstand: Literatur der Jugend 1945–1960,* (Weinheim and Basel, 1988).

Doering, D. *Deutsche Außenwirtschaftspolitik 1933–5. Die Gleichschaltung der Außen-wirtschaft in der Frühphase des nationalsozialistischen Regimes* (Diss. Berlin, 1969), 169–75.

Doering-Manteuffel Anselm, *Wie westlich sind die Deutschen? Amerikanisierung und Westernisierung im 20. Jahrhundert* (Göttingen, 1999).

Eichengreen, Barry J., ed. *Europe's Post-war Recovery*, (Cambridge, New York, 1995).

Eley, Geoff and James Retallack (eds.) *Wilhelminism and Its Legacies. German Moder-nities, Imperialism, and the Meanings of Reform, 1890–1930*, (New York, Oxford, 2003).

Engstrom, Eric J. "*Zeitgeschichte* as Disciplinary History—On Professional Identity, Self-Reflective Narratives, and Discipline-Building in Contemporary German History" *Tel Aviver Jahrbuch für deutsche Geschichte* XXIX (2000), 399–425.

Ericksen, Robert and Susannah Heschel eds. *Betrayal: German Churches and the Holo-caust* (Minneapolis, 1999).

Fehrenbach, Heide and Uta G. Poiger. eds., *Transactions, Transgressions, Transforma-tions: American Culture in Western Europe and Japan* (New York, 2000).

Fehrenbach, Heide. *Cinema in Democratizing Germany: Reconstructing National Iden-tity After Hitler* (Chapel Hill, 1995).

Fehrenbach, Heide. *Race after Hitler: Black Occupation Children in Germany and America* (Princeton, 2005).

Feldman, Gerald D. *The Great Disorder: Politics, Economics, and Society in the German Inflation, 1914–1924* (New York, 1997).

Fischer, Conan. *Stormtroopers: A Social, Economic and Ideological Analysis 1929–1935*, (London, 1983).

Fischer, Conan. *The German Communists and the Rise of Nazism* (Basingstoke, 1991).

Fischer, Conan. *The Ruhr Crisis, 1923–1924* (Oxford, 2003).

Fischer, Fritz. *War of Illusions* (New York, 1975).

Frei, Norbert, *Adenauer's Germany and the Nazi Past: The Politics of Amnesty and Inte-gration* (New York, 2002).

Frei, Norbert. *Vergangenheitspolitik. Die Anfänge der Bundesrepublik und die NS-Vergangenheit* (Munich, 1996).

Fröhlich, Elke. ed. *Die Tagebücher von Joseph Goebbels*, (Munich, 1993f.).

Gabriel, Karl. *Christentum zwischen Tradition und Postmoderne* (Freiburg, 1992).

Gassert, Philipp. *Amerika im Dritten Reich: Ideologie, Propaganda und Volksmeinung, 1933–1945* (Stuttgart, 1997).

Geiss, Imanuel. ed. *July 1914. The Outbreak of the First World War: Selected Documents* (London, 1967).

Geyer, Michael and Charles Bright. "World History in a Global Age" *American Histor-ical Review* 100 (1995): 1034–60.

Geyer, Michael and Konrad H. Jarausch. *Shattered Past: Reconstructing German Histo-ries* (Princeton, 2003).

Geyer, Michael. "The Long Good-Bye: German Culture Wars in the Nineties", in *The Power of Intellectuals in Contemporary Germany*, ed. Michael Geyer (Chicago, 2001).

Giersch, Herbert, Karl-Heinz Paqué and Holger Schmieding. *The Fading Miracle: Four Decades of Market Economy in Germany* (Cambridge, New York, 1992).

Gorodestky, Gabriel. *Grand Delusion. Stalin and the German Invasion of Russia* (New Haven and London, 1999), 275–81.

Götz von Olenhusen, Irmtraud, ed. *Frauen unter dem Patriarchat der Kirchen: Katholikinnen und Protestantinnen im 19. und 20. Jahrhundert* (Stuttgart, 1995).

Gross, Michael B. *The War against Catholicism: Liberalism and the Anti-Catholic Imagination in Nineteenth-Century Germany* (Ann Arbor, 2004).

Grosse, Pascal. *Kolonialismus, Eugenik und bürgerliche Gesellschaft in Deutschland, 1850–1914* (Frankfurt/Main, 2000).

Grossmann, Atina. *Reforming Sex* (New York, 1995).

Hall, Peter A. ed., *The Political Power of Economic Ideas: Keynesianism Across Nations* (Princeton, 1989).

Hamburger Institut für Sozialforschung, ed., *Verbrechen der Wehrmacht: Dimensionen des Vernichtungskrieges 1941–1944* (Hamburg, 2002).

Hannover, Heinrich and Elisabeth Hannover-Drück. *Politische Justiz, 1918–1933*, (Frankfurt a. M., 1966).

Hardt, Michael and Antonio Negri. *Empire* (Cambridge, MA, 2000), German edition (Frankfurt/Main, 2002).

Harvey, Elizabeth. *Women and the Nazi East. Agents and Witnesses of Germanization* (New Haven, 2003).

Harvey, Elizabeth. *Youth and the Welfare State in Weimar Germany*, (Oxford, 1993).

Hausen, Karin. *Deutsche Kolonialherrschaft in Afrika: Wirtschaftsinteressen und Kolonialverwaltung in Kamerun vor 1914* (Zurich, 1970).

Heineman, Elizabeth. *What Difference Does A Husband Make? Women and Marital Status in Nazi and Postwar Germany* (Berkeley, 1999).

Helt, Richard C. and Marie E. Helt. *West German Cinema Since 1945: A Reference Handbook* (Metuchen, N.J., 1987).

Henke, Klaus-Dietmar. *Die amerikanische Besetzung Deutschlands*, (Munich, 1995).

Hentschel, Volker. *Ludwig Erhard: ein Politikerleben* (Munich, 1996).

Herbert, Ulrich. *Best. Biographische Studien über Radikalismus, Weltanschauung und Vernunft 1903–1989* (Bonn, 1996).

Herbert, Ulrich. ed. *National-Socialist Extermination Policies: Contemporary German Perspectives and Controversies* (New York, 2000).

Herbst, Ludolf. *Der totale Krieg und die Ordnung der Wirtschaft im Spannungsfeld von Politik, Ideologie und Propaganda 1939–1945* (Stuttgart, 1982).

Hermand, Jost. *Ernst von Salomon: Wandlungen eines Nationalrevolutionärs* (Stuttgart, 2002).

Herzog, Dagmar. *Sex after Fascism: Memory and Morality in Twentieth-Century Germany* (Princeton, 2005).

Hilberg, Raul. *The Destruction of the European Jews* (New York, 1985).

Hilberg, Raul. *The Politics of Memory. The Journey of a Holocaust Historian* (Chicago, 1996).

Hilgruber, Andreas. *Zweierlei Untergang. Die Zerschlagung des Deutschen Reiches und das Ende des europäischen Judentums* (Berlin, 1986).

Hillgruber, Andreas. *Hitlers Strategie, Politik und Kriegführung 1940–1941* (Frankfurt 1965).

Hoffman, Eva. *After suchKknowledge. Memory, History and the Legacy of the Holocaust* (New York, 2004).

Höhn, Maria. *GIs and Fräuleins: The German-American Encounter in 1950s West Germany* (Chapel Hill, NC, 2002).

Hook, James C. van *Rebuilding Germany. The Creation of the Social Market Economy, 1945–1957* (Cambridge, New York, 2004).

Hübinger, Gangolf, Jürgen Osterhammel,and Erich Pelzer, eds. *Universalgeschichte und Nationalgeschichten* (Freiburg, 1994).

Hughes, Michael L. *Shouldering the Burdens of Defeat. West Germany and the Reconstruction of Social Justice.* (Chapel Hill and London, 1999).

Hull, Isabel. *Absolute Destruction: Military Culture and the Practices of War in Imperial Germany* (Ithaca, 2004).

Hüttenberger, Peter. *Die Gauleiter* (Stuttgart, 1969).

Iggers, Georg. *Historiography in the Twentieth Century. From Scientific Objectivity to the Postmodern Challenge* (Hannover, NH, 1997).

Kaiser, Joachim-Christian and Anselm Doering-Manteuffel, eds., *Christentum und politische Verantwortung: Kirchen im Nachkriegsdeutschland* (Stuttgart, 1990).

Kennedy, Paul M. *The Rise of the Anglo-German Antagonism, 1860–1914* (Boston, 1980).

Kershaw, Ian. *Hitler* (two vols.) (New York, 1999–2000).

Kleßmann, Christoph. *Die doppelte Staatsgründung: Deutsche Geschichte 1945–1955* (Göttingen, 1982).

Klöcker, Michael. *Katholisch von der Wiege bis zur Bahre: Eine Lebensmacht im Zerfall?* (Munich, 1991).

Kocka, Jürgen. *Industrial Culture and Bourgeois Society: Business, Labor, and Bureaucracy in Modern Germany* (New York/Oxford, 1999).

Koerfer, Daniel. *Kampf ums Kanzleramt: Erhard und Adenauer* (Stuttgart, 1987).

Köhler, Joachim and Damian van Melis, eds. *Siegerin in Trümmern: Die Rolle der katholischen Kirche in der deutschen Nachkriegsgesellschaft* (Stuttgart, 1998).

Konrad Jarausch and Martin Sabrow, eds., *Die historische Meistererzählung. Deutungslinien der deutschen Nationalgeschichte nach 1945* (Göttingen, 2002).

Koshar, Rudy. *German Travel Cultures* (New York, 2000).

Kramer, Alan. *The West German Economy, 1945–1955* (New York, 1990).

Kumpfmüller, Michael. *Die Schlacht von Stalingrad* (Munich, 1995).

Kundrus, Birthe. *Kriegerfrauen. Familienpolitik und Geschlechterverhältnisse im Ersten und Zweiten Weltkrieg* (Hamburg, 1996).

Kunz, Andreas. *Wehrmacht und Niederlage. Die bewaffnete Macht in der Endphase der nationalsozialistischen Herrschaft 1944 bis 1945* (Munich, 2005).

Langbein, Hermann. *People in Auschwitz* (Chapel Hill and London, 2004).

Langewiesche, Dieter. *Liberalismus in Deutschland* (Frankfurt am Main, 1988).

Large, David Clay. *Germans to the Front: West German Rearmament in the Adenauer Era* (Chapel Hill, 1996).

Latzel, Klaus. *Deutsche Soldaten-Nationalsozialistischer Krieg. Kriegserlebnis-Kriegserfahrung 1939–1945* (Paderborn, 1998).

Lerner, Gerda. *Why History Matters. Life and Thought* (Oxford, 1997).

Lindlar, Ludger. *Das mißverstandene Wirtschaftswunder. Westdeutschland und die westdeutsche Nachkriegsprosperität* (Tübingen, 1997).

Loth, Wilfried and Jürgen Osterhammel, eds. *Internationale Geschichte. Themen, Ergebnisse, Aussichten* (Munich, 2000).

Ludtke, Alf, Inge Marrsolek, Adelheid von Saldern eds. *Amerikanisierung. Traum und Alpentraum im Deutschland des 20. Jahrhunderts,* (Stuttgart, 1996).

Lusane, Clarence. *Hitler's Black Victims: The Historical Experiences of Afro-Germans, European Blacks, Africans, and African Americans in the Nazi Era* (New York, 2003).

Maase, Kasper. *Bravo Amerika: Erkundungen zur Jugendkultur der Bundesrepublik in den fünfziger Jahren* (Hamburg, 1992).

Maier, Charles S. "Consigning the Twentieth Century to History: Alternative Narratives for the Modern Era." *American Historical Review* 105 (June 2000): 807–831.

Maier, Charles. *The Unmasterable Past. History, Holocaust, and German National Identity* (Cambridge, 1988).

Mann, Michael. *The Dark Side of Democracy. Explaining Ethnic Cleansing* (Cambridge, 2005).

Markovits, Andrei S. *The Political Economy of West Germany: Modell Deutschland* (New York, 1982).

Merkel, Ina. *Utopie und Bedürfnis: Die Geschichte der Konsumkultur in der DDR* (Cologne, Weimar, Vienna, 1999).

Merkl, Peter. *The Making of a Stormtrooper,* (Princeton, 1980).

Messerschmidt, Rolf. *Aufnahme und Integration der Vertriebenen und Flüchtlinge in Hessen 1945–1950. Zur Geschichte der hessischen Flüchtlingsverwaltung.* (Wiesbaden, 1994).

Messerschmitt, Manfred and Fritz Wüllner. *Die Wehrmachtsjustiz im Dienste des Nationalsozialismus. Zerstörung einer Legende* (Baden-Baden, 1987).

Messerschmitt, Manfred. *Die Wehrmacht im NS-Staat. Zeit der Indoktrination* (Hamburg, 1969).

Milward, Alan. *The German Economy at War* (London 1965).

Moeller, Robert G. *Protecting Motherhood: Women and the Family in the Politics of Postwar West Germany* (Berkeley, 1993).

Moeller, Robert G. *War Stories: The Search for a Usable Past in the Federal Republic of Germany* (Berkeley and Los Angeles, 2001).

Mommsen, Hans. *Die verspielte Freiheit. Der Weg der Republik von Weimar in den Untergang 1918 bis 1933* (Frankfurt am Main, 1990).

Mommsen, Hans. *From Weimar to Auschwitz* (Princeton, N.J., 1992).

Mommsen, Hans. *The Rise and Fall of Weimar Democracy* (Chapel Hill, NC, 1996).

Mommsen, Hans. *The Third Reich between Vision and Reality: New Perspectives on German History, 1918–1945* (Oxford, 2001).

Mommsen, Wolfgang J. *Theories of Imperialism* (New York, 1980).

Mommsen, Wolfgang J., Hirschfeld, Gerhard. *Social Protest, Violence, and Terror in Nineteenth- and Twentieth-Century Europe* (New York, London, 1982).

Moses, John A. *Politics of Illusion: The Fischer Controversy in German Historiography* (New York, 1975).

Müller, Ingo. *Hitler's Justice: The Courts of the Third Reich* (Cambridge, MA, 1991).

Müller, Rolf-Dieter. *Das Tor zur Weltmacht. Die Bedeutung der Sowjetunion für die deutsche Wirtschafts- und Rüstungspolitik zwischen den Weltkriegen* (Boppard, 1984).

Müller, Rolf-Dieter. *Hitlers Ostkrieg und die deutsche Siedlungspolitik* (Frankfurt, 1991).

Müller, Rolf-Dieter and G.R. Ueberschär. *Hitler's War in the East 1941–1945. A Critical Assessment* (Providence; Oxford, 1997).

Neebe, Reinhard. *Weichenstellung für die Globalisierung. Deutsche Weltmarktpolitik, Europa und Amerika in der Ära Ludwig Erhard* (Cologne; Weimar; Vienna, 2004).

Neulen, Hans Werner. *Europa und das Dritte. Reich. Einigungsbestrebungen im deutschen Machtbereich 1939–1945* (Munich, 1987).

Neumann, Franz. *Der Block der Heimatvertriebenen und Entrechteten 1950–1960. Ein Beitrag zur Geschichte und Struktur einer politischen Interessenpartei.* (Meisenheim, 1968).

Nicholls, Anthony J. *Freedom with Responsibility. The Social Market Economy in Germany 1918–1963*, 2 ed. (Oxford; New York, 2000).

Nolan, Mary. *Visions of Modernity: American Business and the Modernization of Germany* (New York, 1994).

Nützenadel, Alexander. *Stunde der Ökonomen. Wissenschaft, Expertenkultur und Politik in der Bundesrepublik 1949–74* (Göttingen, 2005).

O'Dochartaigh, Pól. *Germany since 1945.* (Basingstoke and New York, 2004).

Osterhammel, Jürgen. *Geschichtswissenschaft jenseits des Nationalstaates* (Göttingen, 2001).

Overy, Richard J. *War and Economy in the Third Reich* (Oxford, 1994).

Overy, Richard. *The Dictators. Hitler's Germany and Stalin's Russia* (London, 2004).

Peacock, Alan and Hans Willgerodt, eds. *Germany's Social Market Economy: Origins and Evolution* (London, 1989).

Poiger, Uta G. *Jazz, Rock, and Rebels: Cold War Politics and American Culture in a Divided Germany* (Berkeley, 2000).

Pommerin, Reiner, *The American Impact on Postwar Germany,* (Providence, 1995).

Pons, S. *Stalin and the Inevitable War 1936–1941,* (London 2002).

Rebentisch, Dieter. *Führerstaat und Verwaltung im Zweiten Weltkrieg* (Stuttgart, 1989).

Reinermann, Lothar. *Der Kaiser in England. Wilhelm II. und sein Bild in der britischen Öffentlichkeit* (Paderborn, Munich, Vienna, Zürich, 2001).

Reuth, Ralph Georg. *Goebbels. Eine Biographie* (Munich, 1990).

Rich, Norman. *Friedrich von Holstein. Politics and Diplomacy in the Era of Bismarck and Wilhelm II*, 2 vols, (Cambridge, 1965).

Röhl, John C. G. *Kaiser Wilhelm II. 'Eine Studie über Cäsarenwahnsinn'* (Munich, 1989).

Röhl, John C. G. ed. *Der Ort Kaiser Wilhelms II. in der deutschen Geschichte* (Munich, 1991).

Röhl, John C. G. *Wilhelm II. Die Jugend des Kaisers 1859–1888* (Munich, 1993).

Röhl, John C. G. *Young Wilhelm. The Kaisers Early Life 1859–1888* (Cambridge, 1998).

Röhl, John C. G. *Wilhelm II. The Kaiser's Personal Monarchy, 1888–1900* (Cambridge, 2004).

Rosenhaft, Eve. *Beating the Fascists? The German Communists and Political Violence 1929–1933,* (New York, 1983).

Ross, Ronald J. *The Failure of Bismarck's Kulturkampf: Catholicism and State Power in Imperial Germany 1871–1887* (Washington, D.C, 1998).

Ruff, Mark Edward. *The Wayward Flock: Catholic Youth in Postwar West Germany, 1945–1965* (Chapel Hill, 2005).

Sabrow, Martin, Ralf Jessen, and Klaus Große Kracht eds. *Zeitgeschichte als Streitgeschichte. Große Kontroversen seit 1945,* (Munich, 2003).

Sauer, Thomas ed. *Katholiken und Protestanten in den Aufbaujahren der Bundesrepublik,* (Stuttgart, 2000).

Schäfer, Hans Dieter. *Über deutsche Kultur und Lebenswirklichkeit, 1933–1945* (Munich, 1982).

Schildt, Axel. *Moderne Zeiten: Freizeit, Massenmedien und "Zeitgeist" in der Bundesrepublik der 50er Jahre* (Hamburg, 1995).

Schildt, Axel. *Konservatismus in Deutschland. Von den Anfängen im 18. Jahrhundert bis zur Gegenwart* (Munich, 1998).

Schildt, Axel. *Ankunft im Westen. Ein Essay zur Erfolgsgeschichte der Bundesrepublik* (Frankfurt, 1999).

Schildt, Axel and Arnold Sywottek, eds. *Modernisierung im Wiederaufbau: Die westdeutsche Gesellschaft der 50er Jahre* (Bonn, 1993).

Schissler, Hanna. ed. *The Miracle Years: A Cultural History of West Germany, 1949–1968* (Princeton, 2001).

Schmidt, Ute. *Zentrum oder CDU: Politischer Katholizismus zwischen Tradition und Anpassung* (Opladen, 1987).

Schmokel, Wolfe W. *Dream of Empire: German Colonialism, 1919–1945* (New Haven, 1964).

Schuker, Stephen A. *The End of French Predominance in Europe: The Financial Crisis of 1924 and the Adoption of the Dawes Plan* (Chapel Hill, NC, 1976).

Schwarz, Hans-Peter. "Die ausgebliebene Katastrophe. Eine Problemskizze zur Geschichte der Bundesrepublik." In *Den Staat denken. Theodor Eschenburg zum Fünfundachtzigsten*, ed. Hermann Rudolph (Berlin, 1990): 11–74.

Schwarz, Hans-Peter. "Die Neueste Zeitgeschichte" *Vierteljahrshefte für Zeitgeschichte* 51, no. 1 (2003): 5–29.

Schwarz, Hans-Peter. *Die Ära Adenauer* (Stuttgart, 1991).

Siegel, Tilla and Thomas von Freyberg, *Industrielle Rationalisierung unter dem Nationalsozialismus* (Frankfurt, 1991).

Siegrist, Hannes, Hartmut Kaelble and Jürgen Kocka, eds. *Europäische Konsumgeschichte: Zur Gesellschafts- und Kulturgeschichte des Konsums, 18. bis 20. Jahrhundert* (Frankfurt/Main, 1997).

Smith, Helmut Walser. *German Nationalism and Religious Conflict in Germany: Culture, Ideology, Politics, 1870–1914* (Princeton, 1995).

Smith, Woodruff D. *The Ideological Origins of Nazi Imperialism* (New York, 1986).

Spaulding, R.M. *Osthandel and Ostpolitik. German Foreign Trade Policies in Eastern Europe from Bismarck to Adenauer* (Westport, 1999).

Speer, Albert. *Erinnerungen* (Frankfurt, 1969).

Sperber, Jonathan. *Popular Catholicism in Nineteenth-Century Germany* (Princeton, 1984).

Steinberg, Jonathan. *Yesterday's Deterrent. Tirpitz and the Birth of the German Battle Fleet* (London, 1966).

Stern, Frank. *The Whitewashing of the Yellow Badge: Antisemitism and Philosemitism in Postwar Germany* (Oxford, 1992).

Stern, Peter J. *The Fuehrer and the People* (London, 1975).

Swett, Pamela E. *Neighbors and Enemies: The Culture of Radicalism in Berlin, 1929–1933* (New York, 2004).

Traverso, Enzo. *The Origins of Nazi violence* (New York; London, 2003).

Wachsmann, Nikolaus. *Hitler's Prisons: Legal Terror in Nazi Germany*, (London, 2004).

Wagener, Hans, ed. *Gegenwartsliteratur und Drittes Reich: Deutsche Autoren in der Auseinandersetzung mit der Vergangenheit*, (Stuttgart, 1977).

Wagener, Hans. *Von Böll bis Buchheim: Deutsche Kriegsprosa nach 1945*, (Amsterdam, 1997).

Wallich, Henry C. *Mainsprings of the German Revival* (New Haven, 1955).

Wedemeyer, Manfred. *Den Menschen verpflichtet. 75 Jahre Rotary in Deutschland, 1927–2002* (Hamburg, 2002).

Weeks, A.L. *Stalin's Other War. Soviet Grand Strategy, 1939–1941* (Lanham Boulder, New York, Oxford, 2002).

Wegner, Bernd, ed. *Zwei Wege nach Moskau. Vom Hitler-Stalin-Pakt bis zum Unternehmen Barbarossa*, (München-Zürich, 1991).

Wehler, Hans-Ulrich. *Bismarck und der Imperialismus*, 4th ed. (Munich, 1976).

Wehler, Hans-Ulrich. *Deutsche Gesellschaftsgeschichte*, (Munich 1987).

Weinberg, Gerhard L. *A World at War. A Global History of World War II* (New York, 1994).

Weinberg, Gerhard L. *Germany and the Soviet Union*, (Leiden 1972).

Wiesen, S. Jonathan. *West German Industry and the Challenge of the Nazi Past, 1945–1955* (Chapel Hill, 2001).

Wildenthal, Lora. *German Women for Empire, 1884–1945* (Durham, NC, 2002).

Wildt, Michael. *Generation des Unbedingten. Das Führungskorps des Reichsicherheitshauptamtes* (Hamburg, 2002).

Wilpert, Friedrich von. *Rotary in Deutschland. Ein Ausschnitt aus deutschem Schicksal* (Bonn, 1991).

Winkler, Heinrich August. *Weimar 1918–1933. Die Geschichte der ersten deutschen Demokratie*, 2nd ed. (Munich, 1994).

Winkler, Heinrich-August. *Der lange Weg nach Westen*, 2 vols (Munich, 2000).

Zantop, Susanne. *Colonial Fantasies: Conquest, Family, and Nation in Precolonial Germany, 1770–1870* (Durham, NC, 1997).

Ziegler, Walter, ed. *Die Vertriebenen vor der Vertreibung. Die Heimatländer der deutschen Vertriebenen im 19. und 20. Jahrhundert: Strukturen, Entwicklungen, Erfahrung*. Vol. 1 and 2. (Munich, 1999).

Zimmerman, Andrew. *Anthropology and Anti-Humanism in Imperial Germany* (Chicago, 2001).

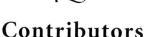

Contributors

Frank Biess

Frank Biess is Associate Professor of History at the University of California. He is the author of *Homecomings. Returning POWs and the Legacies of Defeat in Postwar Germany* (Princeton, 2006). He is currently working on an edited volume on the comparative history of the European "postwar" after 1945, and he has begun research on a new project tentatively entitled: "German *Angst*: Imagined Catastrophes and Security Concepts in 20th Century Germany."

Ian Connor

Ian Connor is Senior Lecturer in German at the University of Ulster at Coleraine (Northern Ireland). He has published a number of articles on German refugees and expellees from the East, the most recent of which is 'German Refugees and the SPD in Schleswig-Holstein, 1945–50' (*European History Quarterly*, 36, 2006). His book *Refugees and Expellees in post-war Germany* is to be published by Manchester University Press in 2007.

Heide Fehrenbach

Heide Fehrenbach is Professor of History at Northern Illinois University. She is author of *Race after Hitler: Black Occupation Children in Postwar Germany and America* (Princeton, 2005) and *Cinema in Democratizing Germany* (Chapel Hill, 1995), and co-author with Rita Chin, Geoff Eley, and Atina Grossman of *After the Racial State: Difference and Democracy in Postwar Germany* (forthcoming). Together with Uta Poiger, she edited *Transactions, Transgressions, Transformations: American Culture in Western Europe and Japan* (Berghahn Books, 2000). Currently, she is at work on an international study of the effects of World War II and military occupation on national practices and normative definitions of family constitution and citizenship in Europe and the United States.

Conan Fischer

Conan Fischer is Professor of European History at the University of Strathclyde in Glasgow. He is the author of *Stormtroopers. A Social, Economic and Ideological Analysis 1929–1935* (George, Allen and Unwin, 1983), *The German Communists and the Rise of Nazism* (Macmillan, 1991), *The Rise of the Nazis* (Manchester University Press, 1995, 2nd edition 2002), and *The Ruhr Crisis 1923–1924* (Oxford University Press, 2003). He is currently completing a history of Europe, 1900–1945 for Blackwell.

Michael B. Gross

Michael B. Gross is Associate Professor of History at East Carolina University in North Carolina. He is author of *The War against Catholicism: Liberalism and the Anti-Catholic Imagination in Nineteenth-Century Germany* (University of Michigan Press, hardback 2004/paperback 2005) which was awarded the 2004 John Gilmary Shea Book Prize of the American Catholic Historical Association. He is currently writing a book on images of hell, the Catholic revival, and peasant culture in nineteenth-century Germany.

Dagmar Herzog

Dagmar Herzog is Professor of History and Daniel Rose Faculty Scholar at the Graduate Center, City University of New York. She is the author of *Sex after Fascism: Memory and Morality in Twentieth-Century Germany* (Princeton, 2005) and *Intimacy and Exclusion: Religious Politics in Pre-Revolutionary Baden* (Princeton, 1996), as well as the editor of *Sexuality in Austria* (Transaction, 2007), *Lessons and Legacies VII: The Holocaust in International Perspective* (Northwestern, 2006), and *Sexuality and German Fascism* (Berghahn Books, 2004). She is currently writing a book on the rise of the religious right and the crisis over sex in the contemporary United States.

Robert G. Moeller

Robert G. Moeller teaches European history at the University of California, Irvine, where he is also faculty advisor for the UC Irvine History Project, a teacher professional development initiative. His research focuses on the political and social history of twentieth century Germany, and his publications include *Protecting Motherhood. Women and the Family in the Politics of Postwar West Germany* (University of California Press, 1993) and *War Stories: The Search for a Usable Past in the Federal Republic of Germany* (Berkeley, 2001).

Hans Mommsen

Hans Mommsen is Professor Emeritus of Modern History at the Ruhr-University Bochum. His numerous publications on the Weimar Republic, the Third Reich and democratic socialism include *The Rise and Fall of Weimar Democracy* (University of North Carolina Press, 1998), *Alternatives to Hitler. German Resistance under the Third Reich* (Princeton University Press, 2003) and (together with Manfred Grieger). *Das Volkswagenwerk und seine Arbeiter im Dritten Reich,* (Econ Verlag, 1996)

Mary Nolan

Mary Nolan is Professor of History at New York University. She is the author of *Visions of Modernity: American Business and the Modernization of Germany* (Oxford University Press, 1994) and co-editor of *Crimes of War: Guilt and Denial in the Twentieth Century.* Recent articles include "Anti-Americanism and Americanization in Germany," Politics & Society 33:1, 2005 and "Air Wars and Memory Wars," Central European History, 38:1, 2005.

Alexander Nützenadel

Alexander Nützenadel is Professor of European Economic and Social History at the University of Frankfurt (Oder). He is the author of *Landwirtschaft, Staat und Autarkie. Agrarpolitik im faschistischen Italien 1922–43* (Niemeyer, 1997) and *Stunde der Ökonomen. Wissenschaft, Expertenkultur und Politik in der Bundesrepublik 1949–74* (Vandenhoeck & Ruprecht, 2005). He has edited several collected volumes, including *Zeitgeschichte als Problem. Nationale Traditionen und Perspektiven der Forschung in Europa* (with Wolfgang Schieder, Vandenhoeck & Ruprecht, 2004) and *Food and Globalisation. Histories, Politics, Moralities* (with Frank Trentmann, Berg 2007).

Hartmut Pogge von Strandmann

Hartmut Pogge von Strandmann is Professor of Modern History at Oxford and Emeritus Fellow of University College, Oxford. He has published several books and articles on the topics of European Imperialism/German Colonialism, Revolutionary History (1848, 1918 and 1989), Wilhelmine Germany, Walther Rathenau and the Weimar Republic, Anglo/German Liberalism and the First World War. Most recently he has published *Ins tiefste Afrika. Paul Pogges präkolonialen Reisen ins südliche Kongobecken* (Trafo-Verlag, 2005).

Uta Poiger

Uta G. Poiger is Associate Professor of History at the University of Washington, Seattle, and Visiting Associate Professor of History at Harvard University. Her research focuses on the cultural history of German international relations. She is the author of *Jazz, Rock, and Rebels: Cold War Politics and American Culture in a Divided Germany* (California, 2000) and co-editor of the anthologies *Transactions, Transgressions, Transformations: American Culture in Western Europe and Japan* (Berghahn, 2000) and *The Modern Girl Around the World* (Duke, forthcoming). Among her current projects are a book titled *Beauty and Business in Germany: An International History* and *Documents in German History, Volume 9, 1945–1961*, an on-line collection coedited with Volker Berghahn for the GHI Washington.

John C. G. Röhl

John Röhl is Emeritus Professor of History at the University of Sussex in Brighton. He has edited the political correspondence of Prince Philipp zu Eulenburg-Hertefeld (Boldt-Verlag, Boppard-am-Rhein, 1976–83) and is the author of several books on the Kaiser and his court. The first two volumes of his biography of Kaiser Wilhelm II were published by the Beck-Verlag, Munich, in 1993 and 2001, and—in English translation—by Cambridge University Press in 1998 and 2004 respectively. He is currently writing the third volume, the central theme of which will be the approach of war in 1914.

Mark Roseman

Mark Roseman is Pat M. Glazer Chair of Jewish Studies at Indiana University. He is the author of *Recasting the Ruhr 1945–1957. Manpower, economic recovery and labour relations,* (Berg Publishers, 1992), *The past in hiding* (Penguin, 2000), *The villa, the lake, the meeting. The Wannsee Conference and the 'final solution'* (Penguin, 2002). He is the editor of *Generations in conflict. Youth rebellion and generation formation in modern Germany 1770–1968* (Cambridge University Press, 1995), and coeditor of *Three postwar eras in comparison. Western Europe*

1918–1945–1989 (Palgrave, 2002)(with Carl Levy) and of *German history from the margins* (Indiana University Press, 2006), (with Neil Gregor and Nils Roemer). He is currently writing a history of Nazi perpetrators.

Mark Edward Ruff

Mark Edward Ruff is Associate Professor of History at Saint Louis University. He is the author of *The Wayward Flock: Catholic Youth in Postwar West Germany* (Chapel Hill: University of North Carolina Press, 2005) and the co-editor of *Christliche Arbeiterbewegung in Europa, 1850–1950* (Stuttgart: Kohlhammer Verlag, 2003). He is currently working on a book, *German Catholics, Church Critics and the Nazi Past* and an edited volume, *The Churches and the Nazis.*

Hanna Schissler

Hanna Schissler is senior research fellow at the Georg Eckert Institute for International Textbook Research in Braunschweig, Germany and holds teaching positions at the University of Hannover and at Central European University in Budapest. Her publications include *The Miracle Years: A Cultural History of West Germany 1949 to 1968* (Princeton University Press 2001) and *The Nation, Europe, the World. Textbooks in Transition* (Berghahn Books 2005). Her current research project focuses on world history and the possibilities of developing a global consciousness.

Pamela E. Swett

Pamela E. Swett is Associate Professor of History at McMaster University in Ontario, Canada. She is author of *Neighbors and Enemies: The Culture of Radicalism in Berlin, 1929–1933* (Cambridge University Press, 2004) and co-editor of *Selling Modernity: Advertising in Twentieth Century Germany* (Duke University Press, forthcoming 2007). She is currently working on a study of advertising in Nazi Germany.

S. Jonathan Wiesen

S. Jonathan Wiesen is Associate Professor of History at Southern Illinois University Carbondale. He has published on historical memory, anti-Semitism, and transatlantic relations after World War II, including *West German Indus-*

try and the Challenge of the Nazi Past, 1945–1955 (University of North Carolina Press, 2001), which was a winner of the Hagley Museum book prize in 2002. He is coeditor of the forthcoming volume *Selling Modernity: German Advertising in the Twentieth Century* (Duke University Press, forthcoming 2007), and is currently writing a book about business leaders, consumer culture, and marketing in Nazi Germany.

Index